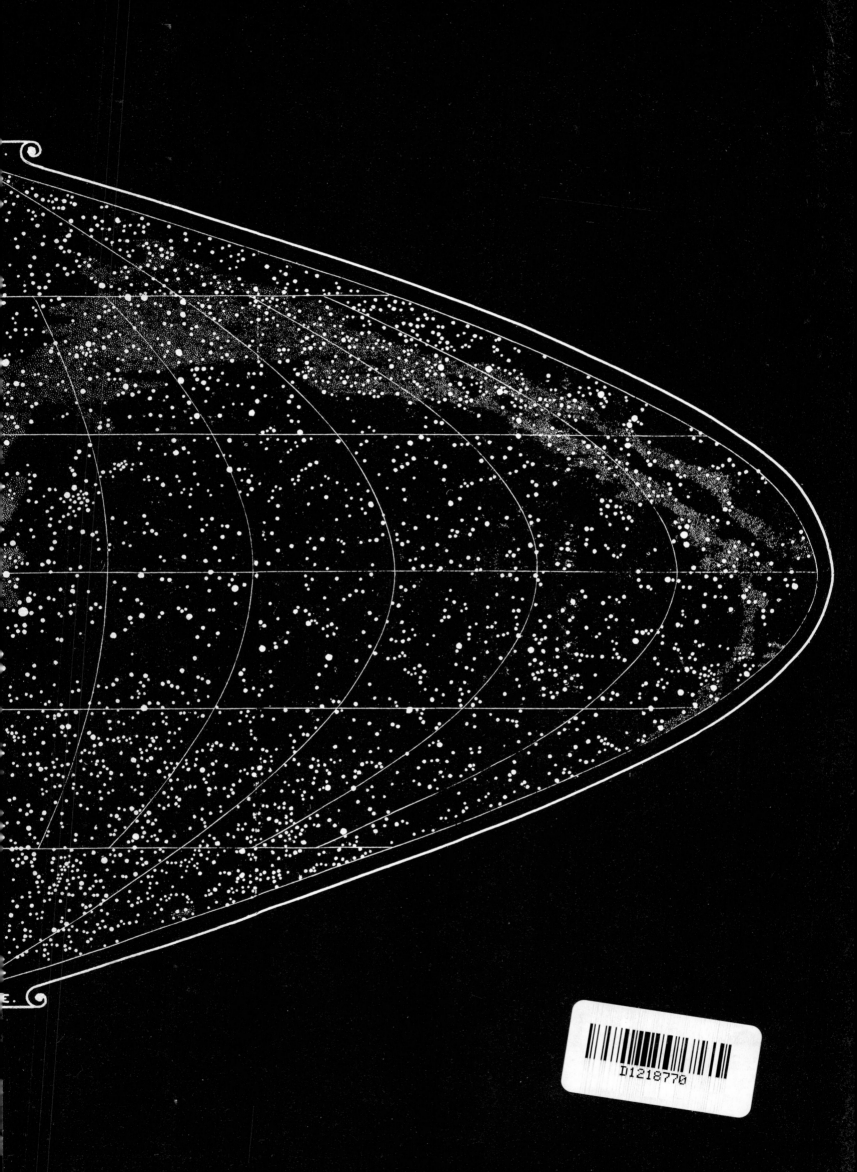

THE GLORIOUS CONSTELLATIONS

General Editor: Domitilla Alessi

GIUSEPPE MARIA SESTI

THE GLORIOUS CONSTELLATIONS
History and Mythology

Introduction by Elémire Zolla

Translated from the Italian by Karin H. Ford

HARRY N. ABRAMS, INC., PUBLISHERS, NEW YORK

Editor, English-language edition: Sharon AvRutick
Editorial Research, English-language edition: Alexandra Bonfante-Warren, Carey Lovelace
Designer: Giuseppe Maria Sesti

Grateful acknowledgment is made for permission to quote from the following works:

Apollonius of Rhodes: *The Argonautica*, translated by R. C. Seaton, Harvard University Press, 1961

The Epic of Gilgamesh, translated by N. K. Sandars, Penguin Books, 1977

Ezra Pound: *The Cantos of Ezra Pound*. Copyright 1940 by Ezra Pound. Reprinted by permission of New Directions Publishing Corporation. U.S. and Canadian rights. For British rights, refer to Faber & Faber

G. S. Kirk: *Myth: Its Meanings and Functions in Ancient and Other Cultures*, University of California Press, copyright © 1970 G. S. Kirk

Hyginus: *The Myths of Hyginus*, translated and edited by Mary Grant, University Press of Kansas, 1960

Pindar: *Victory Songs*, Johns Hopkins Press, 1980

The Rig-Veda: An Anthology, edited and translated by Wendy Doniger O'Flaherty, Penguin Books, 1981

The author wishes to express his gratitude to Mrs. Lake of the Royal Astronomical Society of London for her cooperation

Originally published in Italy as *Le Dimore del Cielo*, edited by Domitilla Alessi, Novecento Editrice, Palermo

LIBRARY OF CONGRESS CATALOGING-IN-PUBLICATION DATA

Sesti, Giuseppe Maria.
[Dimore del cielo. English]
The glorious constellations: history and mythology / Giuseppe
Maria Sesti; introduction by Elémire Zolla; translated from the
Italian by Karin H. Ford.
p.   cm.
Translation of: Le dimore del cielo.
Includes bibliographical references and index.
ISBN 0-8109-3355-1
1. Constellations.   I. Title.
QB802.S4713   1991
523.8—dc20   90-1141
                    CIP

Printed and bound at Istituto Grafico Basile, Genoa, Italy

FOR SARAH

FOR SARAH

Contents

THE GLORIOUS CONSTELLATIONS

Writings in the Sky

Introduction by Elémire Zolla

Three Examples of the Usefulness of the Zodiac in Nearby Areas

To understand a civilization, one should observe how it measures the year: one should study its zodiac. Time and again I have come into contact with unfamiliar, reticent, and secretive societies that have revealed themselves to me in all their glory the moment I have mastered their zodiac system.

For years I wandered around blind in the world of the Norse sagas, forever remaining an outsider. No matter how much I read, the archaic Icelandic and Anglo-Saxon prose remained inaccessible to me. These ancient tales seemed enigmatic and brutal. Speaking only of drunken warriors' grim songs echoing through desolate halls of stone and the howling of winds and wolves over gray, interminable expanses of ice, they related to me only sinister deeds and a stubborn, monotonous wrath. Full of dismal terrors, they seemed poor indeed. Then, one day, I began to consider the Norse runes—the letters of the ancient alphabet. They are not simply signs; in fact each one is a symbol of some aspect of life. I thought of arranging them on the zodiac circle, and suddenly Icelandic and Anglo-Saxon literature opened itself up to me, and the manifold souls of its characters unveiled their depths. I realized that each pair of runes exactly expressed the meaning of some zodiacal sign. I was now able to fit Norse myths and cosmogonies, their daily work, their inner experiences, and their gods into a familiar pattern.

The same thing happened to me with Celtic literature. These tales, far from dismal, were instead marvels of exultation. But this made them irretrievably distant, exotic. I read them with enjoyment, but I did not become involved. However, when I learned from reading Robert Graves to place the ogham, the Old Irish alphabetic system, on the zodiac these literatures too became comprehensible and familiar to me. The strangest and most garbled fables revealed themselves to be lucid, symbolic tales—transpositions of inner experiences into fantastic narrations.

I will only briefly mention here a third example of how the zodiac says, "Open Sesame!" to gates that history seems to have barred to us. As soon as certain Romanesque cloisters are placed within the framework of the zodiac, they become animated, tell their tales, and almost sing.[1]

Two Examples of How the Zodiac Can Help in the Remotest Places

The tilt of the earth's axis creates the zodiacal wave of time that envelops and shapes our lives. Every civilization divides this time with its own particular names and references, but the rhythmic structure of the wave with the twin breakers of the solstices and then the backwash of the equinoxes is uniform. All one has to do is superimpose this structure on the particular way in which each civilization lives its year, following the changing sky, and one will find the specific formula for that civilization.

This was proven to me again in Bali. It is the most charming of places, where India, China, and the South Seas meet and together form the perfect civilization. Its beauty is such that it practically paralyzes the mind; to compare, weigh, deduct, or compose seems almost impossible. However, when I identified the Balinese zodiacal progression, the overwhelming richness of this civilization began to take on order in clear and distinct ways, showing its manifest design. Its zodiac begins, or sprouts, from the spring equinox when all of life stops; the people even abstain from the use of fire. At this time the priests cast exorcisms to the four winds in order to create a new, sacred, and intact space from which the cycle may begin again and in so doing gradually build to the feast of the goddess who is the Word, Saraswati.

The zero, the nonbeing, has brought forth the Word out of which the cycle grows, renews itself, and finally reaches the summer solstice, the birthday of the cosmos. Then the waning phase of the manifestation begins, and as it progresses it diminishes until it arrives at the stopping point and then again absence, the zero, the initial equinox. Every spiritual experience of the Balinese, as well as every external work, is situated in some point on this circuit.

Once in the Korean countryside I was fortunate enough to attend a long ceremony during which a female shaman initiated a young female candidate. Once again the zodiac revealed to me the meaning of what I had seen. Shamanic sessions in Korea follow a structure (which they share with peoples as far north as Siberia), in which the shaman methodically identifies herself one by one with all of the sacred animals. She would transmute herself into each one and acquire its unique virtues and skills, becoming, by the end of the journey, a recapitulation of all life forms, a microcosm. The twelve phases of the Korean initiation ceremony derive from the major animals of the local fauna and their corresponding celestial forms—the constellations of the same name. The twelve phases of the ceremony correspond to the twelve animals of the Chinese zodiac, the same twelve animals whose forms parade through the streets during Chinese New Year celebrations. They are led by the figure of the Bear, the most sacred animal, loftier than all the zodiacal constellations. It is the bear with whom the shaman in essence identifies.

This role of the thirteenth and the primary is given to the bear throughout all of Eurasia's shamanism. Its memory is preserved in the English word "berserk." Originally the term referred to the person who actually wore a bearskin—bear (*björn*) and shirt (*serkr*) in Old Norse—as a means of entering into a trance and identifying himself with the sacred animal. Artemis (Diana) was a she-bear; medieval witches bowed to her in order to merge themselves with her.

We can understand why the shaman wanted to associate herself with a female bear since it is the Bear who reigns supreme over all the zodiacal constellations. It is she who marks the steady axis of the skies, the pole, the immobile vertex of the world.[2]

Devotees of the Zodiac.
Ezra Pound and the Imperial Chinese Zodiac

It is therefore no wonder that there exists a little-known society of devotees of the zodiac. They recognize each other with a password, "twenty-three and a half," the number of degrees of the angle of the earth's axis; it is the inclination of the zodiac over the equator. This same angle exists between the index and middle fingers of Christ in giving the blessing on Byzantine icons, as well as on the Buddha statues sculpted according to the canon.[3]

I have noticed a commendable use of the zodiac in modern poetry. As an introduction to the history of the Chinese dynasties, which is the center of his *Canto LII*, Ezra Pound allows us to spin the wheel of the imperial zodiac. He starts out with a dialogue between Taurus and Gemini or, as the Chinese would say, between the Dog and the Boar, and he establishes the structure upon which he builds the plot of dynastic succession, displaying the form that maintains the substance of Chinese history.

<blockquote>
Toward summer when the sun is in Hyades
Sovran is Lord of the Fire
  to this month are birds.
with bitter smell and with the odour of burning
To the hearth god, lungs of the victim
  The green frog lifts up his voice
   and the white latex is in flower
In red car with jewels incarnadine
  to welcome the summer
In this month no destruction
  no tree shall be cut at this time
Wild beasts are driven from field
  in this month are simples gathered.
The empress offers cocoons to the Son of Heaven
  Then goes the sun into Gemini
Virgo in mid heaven at sunset
  indigo must not be cut
No wood burnt into charcoal
  gates are all open, no tax on the booths.
Now mares go to grazing,
  tie up the stallions
Post up the horsebreeding notices
  Month of the longest days
Life and death are now equal
  Strife is between light and darkness
Wise man stays in his house
  Stag droppeth antlers
Grasshopper is loud . . . .
</blockquote>

It is one of the most graceful and ethereal passages of the Cantos. He makes the merry-go-round of the year turn until "Ice thickens. Earth cracks. And the tigers now move to mating. Cut trees at solstice and arrow shafts of bamboo..."

We Use Babylonia's Zodiac

The zodiac we use comes to us from Babylonia. (In the ancient world it superseded the Egyptian one, which began, not with Aries or the divine Lamb, but with the sacred Cat, and then went on to display a dozen animals of the Nile region—those best matched with the twelve constellations.) In the Middle Ages the Babylonian assemblage was faithfully conveyed, sculpted on the portals of Romanesque churches and painted on illuminated codices because shepherds and peasants continued impassively to recognize these zodiacal figures in their

Chinese astronomer Fuh-Hi

Christian skies. Until the beginning of the modern era, daily work was governed by the skies, starting out with the sun's rise during the windy dawns of spring from a ram made of stars. In the preceding month it had already spread its first radiance over the muddy fields as it emerged above the stars of Pisces. When the Sun rose from Gemini, it impelled the bringing of herds to new pastures. Conversely, when it entered into Scorpius, it commanded the securing of the sheep pens. There were those who ended up worshiping the all-knowing stars as in the days before the Christian dominance. Thus, "In 1272, Pasqueta of Villafranca was ordered to pay forty nickels because she had engaged in soothsaying using the stars."[4]

In the great oral culture of the Middle Ages, the twelve figures of the zodiac were like dancers in a pageant that told the tale of a grotesque and savage tragedy, a story of metamorphoses, crimes, and buffooneries. This story would be abundantly elaborated with fables and ballads and, above all, rustic pantomimes, country dances, sword dances, triumphal parades, and stately processions all telling the story of the Sun and the Moon.

The Zodiac as the Story of the Sun

The medieval zodiacal progression was presented as the tragedy of the Sun, a handsome gallant, who boldly impregnated the Moon during each of its twelve aspects, and arrived at Carnival exhausted and decrepit. In the Egyptian zodiac Carnival fell under the sign of the Monkey. In ours it falls under Pisces.

Carnival is the unprecedented month, the thirteenth. Its hero is a brazen Don Juan, a son of the Sun who tries to enter his mother's bed and is subsequently sacrificed to the father. He is impaled on the cross of the equinox as the Easter lamb or lamb of passage. Rejuvenated by the blood, the Sun, now under Aries, can take the leap beyond the thirteenth month, beyond the circle of death (actually shown as such in a Byzantine codex), and thus transforms himself into the first month of the new year.

The Zodiac as the Story of Mother Nature

Mother Nature of a thousand names is one and threefold. She is the crescent moon, the full moon, and the earth. She is Baby Girl, White Lady, and Dark Queen. Under Pisces she is a dirty little tomboy, a kitten who steals one's heart, a little carnival nymph with a following of salacious buffoons. On May Day, under Taurus, she is the voluptuous Maia, the fertile she-bear, lady of the rose, or, as depicted by Bosch, lady of the orchid. Under Virgo, toward Libra—the Scales whose trays were originally the mortal claws of Scorpius—she is Diana or Titania, the terrifying she-wolf who roams the mountains with her band of Maenads. As such she is served by a demon dressed in a suit decorated with diamond shapes, like the Etruscan Phersu, a sinister blacksmith with a black headband or with the brim of his floppy hat falling over his eye—the infernal Harlequin.

On St. John's night the zodiacal Virgo, who holds a harvested stalk of grain in her hand, may also appear as Herodias displaying the severed head of the prophet of the sun. The story is sometimes interchanged with other tales of men who have "lost their heads." In midsummer it was customary to make fun of old men who had lost their heads over some witch of a young girl, and virtuous women would gather herbs for potions and unguents that would have the same effect. With Diana-Herodias roaming around at night, it was imperative for men to be wary. In fact, in the provinces of Piedmont and Lombardy, it was the custom during this season for men to tie up their testicles with a little ribbon, just to be safe. (In a sonnet by nineteenth-century Italian author Carlo Porta, the testicles are still referred to as "the two of August.")

By All Saints' Day (November 1), however, the nimble she-wolf is a worn-out old dog, a bald Hecate, a gorgon howling under Scorpius. Love potions and shadowy incantations make her more frightful than ever. Under Capricornus and Aquarius she will be nothing more than a withered old woman. Under Pisces Perseus will sever the head of this Medusa who has turned the land to ice with one look. In this story hides the tale of the Sun, now resuscitated, whose head had been severed in midsummer. Pisces and Virgo tell the same tale, the tale of a head that falls: first she decapitates him in Virgo, then he, her, in Pisces. In fact, the two signs are located opposite each other on the zodiac, the zodiac being a game of mirrors and upside-down correspondences.

Thus the twelve aspects of femininity that are characteristics of the twelve signs of the zodiac are one single Sphinx in twelve permutations. From her— Moon and Earth, White Lady and Dark Queen—originate the terrifying gifts, bound together in a bundle, that men yearn for even at the risk of damnation: the slick licentiousness of Pisces, the hot voluptuousness of Gemini, the exhilaration and the power of Virgo, the cold knowledge of Scorpius.[5]

The Zodiac as the Great Landscape

In the Middle Ages the zodiac inherited from Babylonia was not only a ring circling the sky. It was actually perceived as the Great Landscape—full of visions, a synthesis of life. It consisted of three levels.

At the bottom: the nether regions—the night—the arch between Scorpius and Pisces. These regions were thought to be desolate and marshy wastelands, banks of reeds at the edge of the dark ocean.

In the middle: the sea of flames—purgatory—where the crowds of midsummer, frenzied Carnival, as well as vespers and matins, became, as if in a dream, as one with the merging flames of sunset and dawn.

At the top: the Cosmic Mountain, abode of the Celestial Lady, the arch from Aries to Libra—the day. The Cosmic Mountain has two peaks, that of the sun and that of the moon. This imagined shape was recognized with veneration in actual mountains whose names carry this reference—Rupescisse, Roquepertuse, Montserrat. The two towers of Notre-Dâme and other Gothic cathedrals seem to reproduce it.

In the landscape of visions, the three concentric spheres of the year, the month, and the day pervade each other, their parts interwoven. The three subdivisions of each of the three spheres pervade each other as well. They are: the winter solstice, the equinoctial time, and the summer solstice for the year; the new moon, the crescent moon, and the full moon for the month; and the daytime, the dusk, and the night in the arc of the day.

What Was Learned in Earliest Childhood

The mothers of old Europe taught their little ones in earliest childhood the precise art of surviving in that dreamlike landscape. Their lullabies gave lessons in the geography of the zodiac. These were sacred songs, exhortations against the evil dead wandering around in the darkness of the netherworld, solemn mythological compositions. Only with the coming of the modern age have mothers sunk to sentimental blatherings. For a period of time one scholar, Marius Schneider, dedicated himself entirely to the study of archaic Iberian lullabies. As literature they form a kind of anthology, or a repertory of haiku. They contain menacing couplets, such as this Galician vulgar, apocalyptic threat: "Executed by garrotes around their ass, the old men will kick the bucket/And we two, little one, will remain alone!" These lullabies also include merry little songs full of straightforward eroticism, like this one from Asturias: "I have my Johnny in my bed,/Today, handsome gallant, we can't do it./Sleep, little baby boy of my heart,/And you return tomorrow at three."

This literature itself, however, holds little interest anymore for either Schneider or us. What is of vital importance is the body of doctrines that it contains. The old lullabies describe with symbological precision the time and space of the Great Landscape and how they could be used to initiate children into the zodiac and the mysteries of the year.

The process of "becoming" in traditional civilizations is seen as circling back; it is a serpent that bites its tail—an eternal return—reflecting the nostalgia that precedes every becoming. It is, in fact, symbolized in the myth of the Great Landscape where the Dark Queen reigns, the She-Wolf of midsummer. The time and space of the Great Landscape are similar to a crystal—a plane rotated on itself—and, like a living animal, symmetrical.

While the baby is rocked, he is encouraged to identify himself with Lucifer:

> Lucifer of the dawn, sleep.
> . . .
> If the baby would sleep
> In his crib I would fling him
> With his little feet facing the Sun
> And his little face toward the Moon.
> . . .
> Little bird who sings in the olive tree
> Do not wake up, my little doll!
> . . .
> He is sleepy, the little baby.
> What shall we give him?
> Warmth of the little snail, make the horns sprout.[6]

The She-Wolf, the Dark Queen, Will Come

The lullabies also confronted this profound question: what happens when we sleep, the conscience extinguished? As celestial oracle, the zodiac replies: we become like the Sun between Scorpius and Pisces. The traditional lullaby above describes the voyage across the winter sky from one sign to the other, in the night, under the new moon, as follows:

♍ In the sky glitters Venus of the vespers. The lullaby makes her the zodiacal Virgo's double and tells the child that she wishes him good night from above, so that, with these wishes as provisions,

♎ the forces of the day and night will be balanced and he will slide into sleep.

♍ The child will now descend into the nether part of the Great Landscape, the dark, marshy wasteland, the reed banks along the sea of darkness.

On the sea he sails, runs, flies.

He makes the crossing in a crib that is a coffin, a boat, a fish. (From Babylonia to Egypt and farther to the Rhineland, sun boats are pulled along in the processions of Capricornus.)

The lullaby describes the navigation, offering the symbols of the vortex, the spiral, and the shell. The image of a small bird who sings in an olive or a flowering almond tree marks the end of the crossing.

We now enter into the purgatorial sea of fire, the raging sea of fever, just before dawn—the dreamlike time of Carnival. The lullaby speaks of a "warmth of the little snail" which will make horns grow.

Druid observatory near Keswick, Cumbria, England

Mother Nature makes her first Carnival appearance, in the form of the Little Snail. The song prepares the little "Lucifer of the dawn" for the subsequent frightening apparitions. If he doesn't go to sleep like a good boy, he will witness her fall on him as She-Wolf, or ferocious Dark Queen, accompanied by her devious accomplice. However, if he does go to sleep like a good boy he will sprout little horns and one fine day he will be up there on the Mountain of the Meridian and the Solstice—Mother Nature's darling.

Elémire Zolla

Notes and Bibliography

1. Zolla, E. "The Runes and the Zodiac," in *Sophiea Perennis*, Teheran, II, 2, 1976 (Kraus, Nendelm-Liechtenstein); Graves, R. *The White Goddess: A Historical Grammar of Poetic Myth*, London, 1948
2. *Conoscenza religiosa*, special issue on Bali, 2, 1978; on Eurasian shamanism (and Korean, in particular) 3/4, 1982
3. On the beliefs and rites that have migrated from Babylonia to Europe: Liungman, *Traditionswanderungen*, Euphart-Rhein, Helsinki, 1938; and the collection of *Mitteilungen der deutschen vorderasiatischen und aegyptischen Gesellschaft*, Leipzig, published in the first decade of this century. A great treasure kept hidden out of negligence or academic spite
4. Cantù, C. *Gli eretici d'Italia*, III, 349, Turin, 1868
5. The series of studies by M. Reimschneider on the Great Mother and the Babylonian zodiac and by M. Schneider on the myth of Lucifer–Don Juan in the last decade in *Conoscenza religiosa*
6. Schneider, M. *Tipologia literaria y musical de la canción de cuna en España*, Barcelona, 1948

THE PHENOMENON BOOK OF CALENDARS 1975·1976

Created by
Giuseppe Maria Sesti - A.T. Mann IV
Mary Flanagan - Painton Cowen
Sarah Sesti

PHENOMENON PUBLICATIONS

Preface

Since 1974, when the first volume of my book about calendars, *Phenomenon*, was published in London, the revolutions of the earth and the moon around the sun have been a fascinating bible for me to study.

The calendar systems in *Phenomenon* came from every part of the world and from every time period. They stretched from New Guinea to the island of Bali, from the Aztecs to the Maya, from the Hebrew to the Islamic, the Orthodox to the Christian, the Chinese to the ancient Roman, and so on.

Lunar calendars, solar calendars, lunar-solar calendars, Metonic cycles (periods of nineteen years), religious calendars, agricultural calendars, simple systems, and extremely complicated ones—all are evidence of how orienting ourselves in cyclical time is fundamental to the human being. These cycles invariably are indicated by the sky—the sky of the sun with the day, the night, the seasons, the solstices and the equinoxes, and the sky of the moon, primordial queen of time, mistress of seeds, of the tides and fertility cycles, protagonist in the calculation of time in the most ancient of civilizations.

My study of calendars gradually brought me to the point where I started observing the sky with new eyes. I realized how little I knew about the hundreds of stars that appear in the perplexing darkness every night. I recognized that the starry sky was an intellectual notion for me consisting of infinite galaxies, quasars, black holes, novas, and explosions so enormous as to create universes such as our own. Little by little I began observing the stars with the naked eye, contemplating them as humans have always done.

It's not easy to travel a distance of thousands of light-years in our dear old sky—with its summer scents and its clear winter nights—without the help of amplifying instruments. I tried to imagine how the observation and measurement of the stars could have been done from Sumerian ziggurats or from the circle of stones of Stonehenge in the Wiltshire countryside. I came to understand that our ancestors were scientists altogether worthy of the name and that they operated with the same limitations with respect to seeing the universe that modern scientists have with respect to tomorrow's.

The stars are marvelous objects; we succeed in perceiving them up to the fifth or sixth magnitude. We can observe the wonderful variety of colors, from blue to red, white to sapphire, orange to emerald, and yellow to aquamarine, but there are also pale-green ones and lilac and reddish yellow and azure green. There are so many colors that the nineteenth-century French astronomer Camille Flammarion was moved to exclaim, "The colors of the stars are not as coarse as those of our paintings; they are transparent and luminous; in order to reproduce them we would have to have as our palette the azure of the skies and be able to dip our brush in the rainbow."

In this "sphere" of suns that surrounds our world, ancient astronomers saw a series of lines represented by the circles of the zodiac belt and the meridians of the solstices and the equinoxes. The geometric model that was obtained from

Opposite: *Title page of* The Phenomenon Book of Calendars *(1975)*

21

this served to frame the apparent motion of the sun between constellations. The knowledge of the rules of this sphere followed, step by step, the evolution of agriculture and navigation, the first sciences.

Whoever invented the techniques of sowing, grafting, and harvesting had to explain when these operations were to be done. In order to do this, more precise data were needed than just the "Fifth Moon" or the "Middle of the Eighth." These data were furnished by the time that specific stars rose, and by the apparent location of the sun in a constellation at the moment it became invisible due to the sun's light. This gave rise to expressions like "the sun in Gemini" or "the sun in Sagittarius."

The ancient astronomers' great interest in the fixed stars resulted in their creation of globes on which the stars were grouped in constellations. The research I did on their origins brought me to the study of everything that had to do with this very ancient chapter of the human science. I began to examine which cultures had begun the systematic study of the sky and why certain constellations had been identified with one specific figure above all others. What I was looking for was a textbook that could explain to me what the starry sky seen by the naked eye had meant to ancient people.

I soon discovered that, with the exception of R. H. Allen's *Star Lore* (1899), and an infinite number of titles mainly on astrology, during the last century there have been practically no publications dedicated to the archaeology of the stars. In the various histories of astronomy, chapters on the "origins" far too often describe credulous primitives who, due to obvious technological limitations, were unable to understand the true essence of the surrounding universe. After a few acclamations for the most accomplished of Greek philosophers, these histories then move right on to the revolutions of Copernicus, Galileo, and Kepler.

The average modern scientist concentrates so on the specific battle against astrology that everything pertaining to stars and mythology necessarily is relegated to the Middle Ages of human culture. The result of all this is that a negative assessment has been extended, undeservedly, to the great scientific chapter of the protohistoric and historic period in which myths were the popularization of mathematical, astronomical, and technological attainments. Only those that pertain to the Bible have been admitted into the sphere of believability. Robert Graves has explained that since in English "mythical" means "incredible," this has caused biblical narratives to be omitted from European collections of mythology—even though they contain exact parallels to the myths of Persia, Babylonia, Egypt, and Greece.

So I decided that I would write the book that I wanted to read. I immersed myself for many months in the splendid seventeenth-century rooms of the Royal Astronomical Society Library in London and in that labyrinth of millions of volumes that is the British Museum Library. The task was overwhelming because, ideally, the author of this book should have been a mythologist with great astronomical knowledge or—vice versa—an astronomer steeped in mythology; I was neither. I therefore apologize from the outset to the specialists in these two fields of knowledge for any errors I may have made in the manipulation of their extremely sophisticated languages.

Except for remaining unrecognized, the worst thing that could happen to this book is that it be considered an astrology text, which it is not. What is fascinating is that in antiquity the true exchange occurred between astronomy and myth. (Chaldean astrology is a later phenomenon.) I would like to explain to the reader who is an astrologer that it is not true that in ancient times astronomy was strictly astrology. Even in Mesopotamia, fatherland of astrology, the horoscope was conceived only for use by the nation and the king. In order to write it, the motions of the planets in the zodiac belt and the entire sphere of the fixed stars was interpreted. Other than this, the great volume of astronomical knowledge was used for the tilling of the land (as in Virgil's *Bucolics* and *Georgics*), for the regulation of very sophisticated irrigation systems, for religious cults, and for a healthy contemplation of all creation.

The Glorious Constellations presents forty-eight ancient constellations and the Milky Way in alphabetical order; the reader can start with any section after having read the initial chapters. To allow each section to stand on its own, there is some necessary repetition.

Throughout the book there are frequent references to the precession of the equinoxes and the resulting shifts of the equinoctial and solstitial constellations occurring approximately every two thousand years. The dates have often been rounded off for simplicity's sake. For example, the Age of Taurus, which in reality lasted from 4380 to 2220 B.C., is in some cases listed as 4000 to 2000 B.C.

Giuseppe Maria Sesti
Argiano, Italy
January 15, 1987

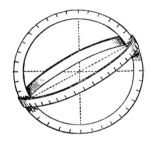

THE GLORIOUS
CONSTELLATIONS

I
Instinct and the Sky

Toward the end of the 1950s, German ornithologist E. G. F. Sauer of the University of Freiburg embarked on a long series of experiments on the orientation system of migratory birds. Observing the intense activity in the night sky that coincided with the migration period of many species held in captivity, Sauer was the first to develop the hypothesis that these birds determine the direction of their nighttime course from the disposition of the stars in the sky.

Since then, the study of the orientation system of birds has made great progress. It is now known that creatures weighing three-quarters of a pound, such as the bunting, are capable of safely flying more than two thousand miles over a variety of precise routes.

In a recent series of experiments, birds were placed inside cone-shaped cages constructed with an ink pad at the bottom and blotting-paper sides, and these special cages were placed inside a planetarium. When the starry sky was reproduced on the dome of the planetarium, it became obvious that the spring and autumn configurations, coinciding with the migratory periods of the birds being examined, provoked them to attempt to escape from the cage, always in the same direction. These data were gathered from the marks left by the animals who took off from the ink pad, staining the blotting paper with their claws ("The Stellar Orientation System of a Migratory Bird," *Scientific American*, August, 1975).

The implications of this discovery are significant because it removes us noticeably from the lunar-solar orientation suggested by two bodies with regular trajectories. The stars, on the other hand, rise and set while continuously changing configurations during the entire year. A hypothesis was made that birds have an innate, inherited star map, but this theory was quickly discarded because the stars are not fixed in the heavens—they move. The precession of the equinoxes—a slow westward shift of the equinoctial points—is caused by the anomalous oscillation of the rotation of the earth on itself, making the terrestrial axis describe a complete circle in the sky in a period of about 25,750 years. (In antiquity this period was called Platonic Year.) Thus, not only does the North Pole move one degree every seventy-two years on this circle, but all the constellations rise and set a bit further backward every year, with respect to the apparent motion of the sun. If birds had an inherited star navigation system these changes would cause noticeable route errors in a matter of only a few decades.

Experiments published by researcher Stephen Emlen in 1975 revealed that when a bunting in captivity from birth was shown an altered view of the stars in a planetarium, it migrated in the wrong direction; its calculations were based on the different polar star.

This and other studies have shown that the bunting and many other migra-

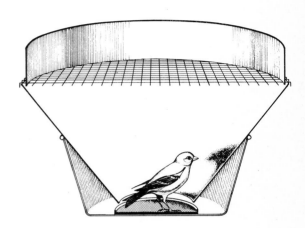

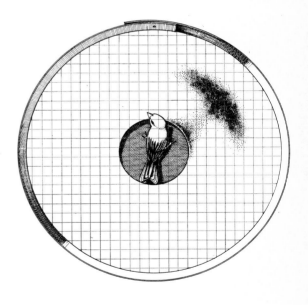

Two views of a cone-shaped cage used to study the influence of the stars' position on the flight direction of migratory birds.
Illustrations from Scientific American
(August, 1975)

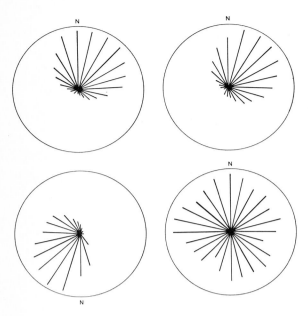

tory species study and acquire a feeling for the position of the stars in the sky as fledglings. In this way they can find a migration route without having to follow an older bird. Not only that, but the following year they are able to return to the same territory.

The study of the orientation system of migratory birds is in its infancy. Consistent experimentation has taken place only over the last thirty years. However, it is already possible to surmise from the results amassed thus far that many animals have an innate capacity for understanding the motion of the moon and the stars.

The question arises as to whether, at the beginning of our sojourn on earth, humans instinctively memorized the movement of the heavenly bodies, thus allowing them to subtly control the activities of hunting and fishing at first and the duties of the nomadic shepherds and mariners later. If a bird weighing less than a pound can use the motion of the stars as a precise compass, it would seem obvious that a mammal of about 150 pounds with almost three and a half pounds of brain tissue could do the same.

The diagram at top left shows the pattern of the marks made by a bird trying to escape from a cage under the spring sky. Those at top right were produced in a planetarium simulating the same stars. The diagram at bottom left, showing the opposite pattern, was obtained by moving the Polar Star toward the south in the planetarium. The last diagram reveals the marks made when the planetarium was lit diffusely with no stars
At right: *The predicted direction of a migratory bird's flight, based on the position of the circumpolar stars. Illustrations from* Scientific American *(August, 1975)*

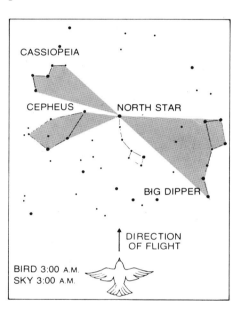

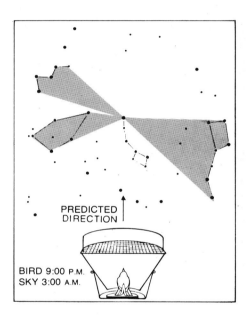

Some light may be shed on this question by anthropological studies done on some modern tribal societies (North American Indians, Eskimos, certain peoples of equatorial Africa, Australian aborigines, etc.). In many aspects some of these peoples are similar to those of the Paleolithic and Mesolithic periods. Knowledge of the motions of the sun, the moon, and the stars is widespread in these societies, as is the creative ability to weave legends, myths, fables, calendars, and personifications of the gods into these motions. In any latitude it is common for the most popular symbol of divinity to be a star.

Unfortunately, we can know only very little of the enormous bulk of the oral tradition of our prehistory. We can only imagine that ancient myths were gradually modified based on the increase in knowledge of the laws of nature and that, with the invention of writing, this knowledge began to be recorded.

Today we must necessarily start with these writings in tracing the history of human beings' relationship with the stars, remembering that the observations and discoveries they made were incorporated into legends and myths. It would be a mistake to try to read the myths using astronomy as the only key, but still, this key can open unexpected and fascinating stellar dimensions that are worthy of investigation.

II
The Empty Circle

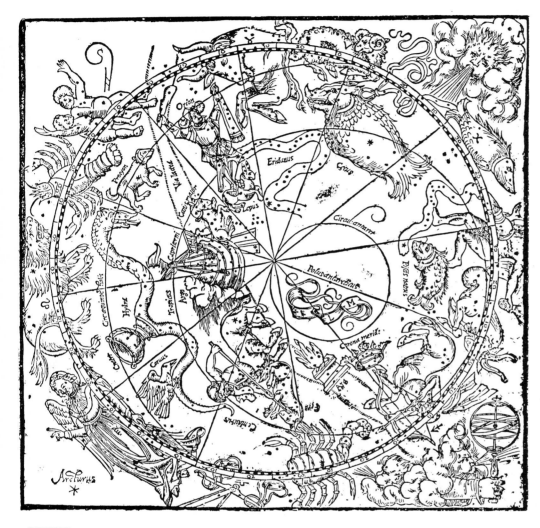

Celestial map showing the ancient gaps in the southern region (1559)

Representation of the sky, ancient Chinese jade

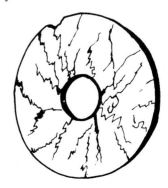

When one carefully observes star maps of the past, one notices that in the southern hemisphere there is a circular hole devoid of stars and constellations. The edge of this empty space must have corresponded to the visible horizon of the astronomers who designed those maps. The center of the circle represents the South Pole, which is invisible to an observer located in the northern hemisphere of the planet.

Based on an analysis of these descriptions, and taking into consideration the shifting due to the precession of the equinoxes, we have been able to determine that the people who designed the constellations could not have lived at a latitude below 33° N. or above 44° N.

Still keeping in mind the precessional changes, the position of this circle is useful for another very important calculation, that which determines when those constellations rose and set in the field of vision of these observers. This computation takes us more than five thousand years back in time to when the Polar Star was not the one it is today, but Thuban, in the tail of the constellation of Draco. This constellation was designed to bring together the North Pole of the equator and the North Pole of the ecliptic.

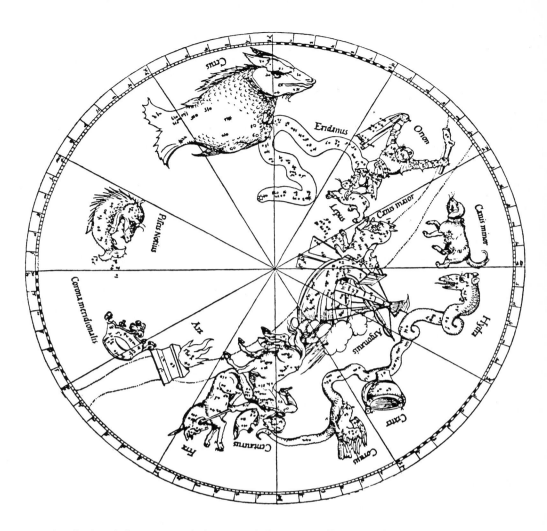

Albrecht Dürer's southern hemisphere

Position of the constellation of the Serpent (held by Ophiuchus) with respect to the equator, the meridian of the autumnal equinox, and the zenith in 2700 B.C.

Analysis of the original design of the constellations shows that it was drawn according to a preconceived plan. For example, the Serpent held by Ophiucus indicated the intersection of the celestial equator and the meridian of the equinox. The reptile followed the equator with its body, until suddenly, as soon as it encountered the meridian, it veered 90° away in order to follow that line. The Serpent finally ended with the star of its head exactly at the zenith. These early astronomers knew the zodiac belt, which they divided into twelve signs. (Four of these were cardinals—Taurus, Leo, Scorpius, and Aquarius.) The sun ascended the zodiac through the signs that looked toward the east and descended through those that looked toward the west, a logical and meaningful arrangement that could hardly have been dictated by coincidence.

Today these and other small harmonies of the initial design have been altered by precession and as a result the constellations appear to be the fruit of imaginative popular fantasies without any logical scientific meaning. The absence of such animals as the elephant, camel, hippopotamus, monkey, crocodile, and tiger from these maps would preclude countries such as India, China, and Egypt from having been instrumental in the conception of this sky.

The original number of these constellations was forty-eight, twenty-one to the north of the ecliptic (the apparent path of the sun among the stars), twelve in the zodiac, and fifteen to the south of the ecliptic. A large area in the southern part of the sky was called the Sea because it contained only aquatic constellations, such as Pisces, Aquarius, the marine monster Cetus, the rivers Eridanus and Aquarius, the aquatic serpent Hydra, and the ship *Argo*.

The fact that this Sea is placed to the south and that two rivers flow into it corroborates the thesis of those who identify Mesopotamia as the source of the constellations. If the original map had been conceived in Egypt, the Sea would have been to the north and there would have been only one river.

Historical studies indicate that civilization, in the modern sense of the word, as well as the beginning of the science of agriculture, occurred in the "Land between the Rivers," thanks to the Sumerians. Though these Mesopotamian people contributed much to the process of our civilization, their origins remain a mystery. Perhaps they came from the valley of the Black Sea at a time when it was flooded by the waters of the Mediterranean. (This may have happened when, at the end of the last ice age, the polar ice cap melted, bringing about a rise in sea level.) In fact, among the clay tablets of Sumer that were found in the royal palace of Assurbanipal in Nineveh, there is the most ancient written text on the universal flood. This was subsequently reported almost word for word in the Old Testament, probably contributed by Job, "the Sumerian who came from Ur." When the sea rose, salt water entered the Black Sea, killing the fresh-water life forms. Their decomposed remains poisoned the lower levels of this new sea, which is even today without life below a depth of about 250 feet (McEvedy, *Atlas of Ancient History*).

Sumerian culture revealed itself in Mesopotamia as far back as the fourth millennium B.C. The exquisite creativity of this people exhibited itself in almost all branches of knowledge, above all in their writings. Several millennia before Gutenberg invented the printing press, the Sumerians already had ready-made letters that, arranged in various ways, were used to transfer text onto fresh clay. They even anticipated the process of printing by cylinder when they invented the cylindrical seal that when rolled onto clay transferred a mark or a religious emblem.

Sumerian mathematical achievements were great. The system of counting was based on the number sixty, a combination of the terrestrial number ten and the celestial number six. The Sumerians divided the circle into 360 degrees and the week into seven days. They founded the first schools and the first legally regulated society, which, among other things, protected the blind, orphans, and widows. In their schools they taught subjects such as botany, zoology, geography, and theology. In 1974 a group of researchers at the University of California at Berkeley found a document of Sumerian origin with a musical score that was not only deciphered, but also performed. To everyone's surprise, it turned out to have been composed on the heptatonic-diatonic scale, characteristic of the music of the Greeks and of contemporary Western music as well.

As we become aware of the artistic and scientific accomplishments of the Sumerians, we experience a feeling of real familiarity with this people because, in them, we discover not only the roots of the arts and scientific thinking, but also the roots of our moral principles and sense of justice.

After the Assyrian conquest the Sumerian language continued to be spoken as a language of culture for more than a thousand years, exactly as occurred later with Latin.

Sumerian altar

Ziggurat

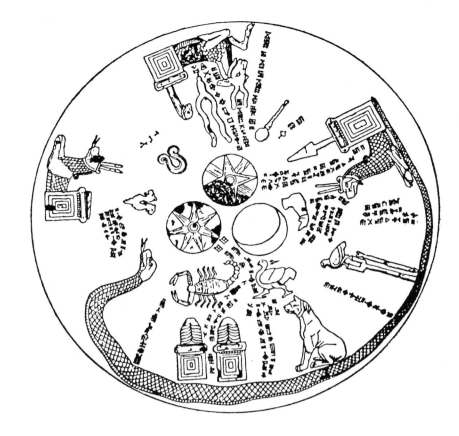

Kuruddu cup decorated with depictions of Sumerian star groups. In the middle are the sun, the moon, and Venus—respectively, Shamash, Sin, and Ishtar

The Fertile Crescent, where the human agricultural adventure began. From McEvedy, Atlas of Ancient History

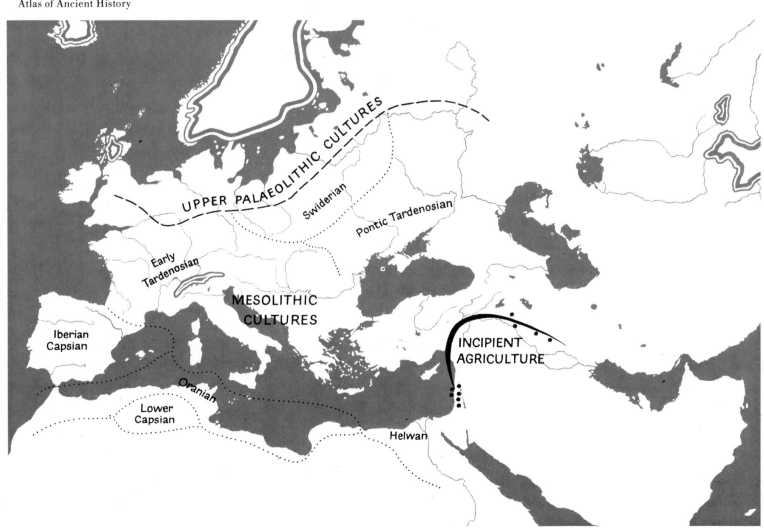

III
The Fertile Crescent

In atlases of ancient history, we can observe a type of arc drawn on the map of the Middle East. One of its two tips is pointed toward the estuary of the Tigris and the Euphrates; the other is in Palestine. The bend of the arc is in Turkey, near the sources of the two rivers. Scholars call this area the Fertile Crescent because it was here that the science most useful to human progress, agriculture, first developed.

At first (around 8000 B.C.), agricultural endeavors were limited to the harvesting of wild grains with flint sickles. The grains were pounded in a mortar with a pestle. In a few millennia agriculture developed enormously, along with the domestication of animals. Grains were selected for cultivation and the first irrigation was accomplished. Then the invention of grafting took place in the fourth millennium, which led to the cultivation of fruit trees and grapevines.

Agricultural work became specialized enough to demand the synchronization of particular operations with precise times of the year. In addition the primitive lunar calendar was no longer sufficient; it erred by several days after only two years. Agricultural and religious demands, as well as the great intellectual capacity of the Sumerian civilization, thus led to the creation of the first solar calendar of which we have any knowledge.

The study of the sky with its stars and its infinite variations was carefully recorded and interpreted. This eventually enabled these ancient astronomers to create a celestial sphere that contained the forty-eight original constellations, the band of the apparent motion of the sun, and the Tropics of Cancer and Capricorn. Thus it became possible to calculate the lunar points that allowed for forecasts of eclipses and the exact progression of the planetary motions.

It is almost always possible to trace the images of the constellations and their written descriptions, as well as the telling of the first myths about them, back to origins in Mesopotamia. Mesopotamian astronomers observed the sky from the tops of ziggurats and carefully recorded their data on small clay tablets.

The Assyrian conquest of Mesopotamia spelled the end of the royal Sumerian dynasties; it did not, however, obliterate their culture. On the contrary the new regime engaged scholars to perpetuate the ancient knowledge. However, with the passing of the centuries the original explosion of creativity grew increasingly rigid and began to emigrate, moving to Syria, Egypt, and Greece on the one side, and to Persia, all the way up to the Caspian Sea, and to the valley of the Indus on the other.

The sky of Mesopotamia was divided into three bands, or ways. The central one, which contained the zodiac, was called the Way of Anu, god of the sky corresponding to Uranus; it was flanked by the Tropics of Cancer and Capricorn. Above the Tropic of Cancer was the great region of the cold North, the Way of Enlil (or Bel), god of storms and wind. Below the Tropic of Capricorn sprawled the vast region of the celestial Sea called the Way of Ea, god of the water. The 360 degrees of the Way of Anu were divided into twelve zodiacal constellations in which the greatest gods of the Sumerian Olympus orbited. They included Shamash (the sun), Sin (the moon), Ishtar (Venus), Marduk

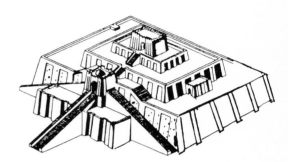

Reconstruction of the Ziggurat of Ur

A, the Way of Enlil—the northern sky; B, the Way of Anu—the celestial band of the sky, the moon, the planets, and the constellations of the zodiac; and C, the Way of Ea—the southern celestial Sea

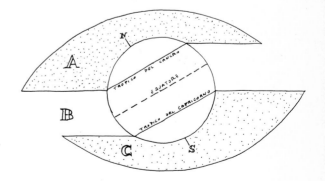

(Jupiter), Nergal (Mars), Ninurte (Saturn), and Nabu (Mercury). Stars, planets, and all the forms of animal and plant life had been brought forth by the primordial marriage between Anu and Ki, the earth. (We will encounter this cosmological concept again in the creation myths of Egypt and Greece.)

For the Sumerians there was an exact correspondence between the study of the celestial bodies and the direct observation of star gods, whose motion could inform humans about the wishes and the cycles of the gods. It was for this reason that they, more than any other people, exhibited patience, precision, and impartiality in measuring, cataloguing, and recording celestial phenomena. The astronomer-priest performed the highest rite of his religion in the scrutiny of the stars and the calculation of planetary orbits.

This worship of the stars was the true reason for their great astronomical successes. In this sense it is wrong to speak of the Sumerians as the fathers of astrology, which is a doctrine introduced later by the Chaldeans.

The Sumerian concept and description of the skies, with its geometry and its gods, became the cosmologic model for other Mediterranean and Middle Eastern mythologies. In the Egypt of the pharaohs, creation was said to have occurred according to the same model of Anu (sky) and Ki (earth), the sole modifications being that the sky was seen as the original female and the earth, as the original male. In fact, the Egyptians worshiped two goddesses of the sky, Nut and Hathor. Nut, the extremely ancient Lady of the Sky worshiped by the people of the Nile Delta, was the mother of many gods, including Isis, Osiris, Horus, and Set. She was always represented in the nude, with her body arched, touching the earth with the tips of her fingers and toes. This posture was meant to symbolize the celestial vault and, in fact, her body is strewn with stars. Stretched out on the soil underneath her is the god Keb, the earth, her lover and spouse. From their union, all things divine and terrestrial originated.

Despite Egypt's great political stability and the high standing of the priests who guaranteed the perpetuation of their research, Egypt was not very active in the area of astronomy. Many priests engaged in the interpretation, transcription, and prediction of celestial events in the crystal-clear Egyptian skies for forty centuries, but no science of the planetary motions evolved. Likewise, the surgeon-priests did not develop an original anatomic science, despite the fact that they had supervised the opening and dissection of hundreds of thousands of human bodies for embalming. (It must be pointed out that the astronomical developments that took place during the three centuries of the Ptolemaic dynasty in Alexandria were characterized by Hellenistic culture.)

During Napoleon's campaign in Egypt, a small army of archaeologists followed the troops in order to conduct excavations and studies of the ancient civilization. They discovered in the temple of Esneh at Dendera a sandstone ceiling with bas-reliefs that represented the vault of the sky, complete with constellations. At that time it was believed that this map of the skies was very ancient and confirmed the theories of those who maintained that Egypt was the fatherland of astronomy. However, recent studies have shown that this ceiling was not sculpted until 36 B.C., during the time that Egypt was a Roman province. All the classic constellations are present in this very beautiful representation of the sky, including the new sign of Libra cutting the claws of Scorpius, which had been introduced by Julius Caesar. Here the Big Dipper had become the thigh of an ox, the Dragon a hippopotamus, and in the place of Canis Major there was a cow with the star Sirius between her horns.

The twelve constellations of the zodiac were not particularly evident. Around the perimeter there were the thirty-six figures of the decans, stars representing ten-day intervals in the Egyptian months of thirty days. These decans were used as a type of calendar clock composed of stars, constellations, and parts of constellations, based on a yearly cycle of 360 days. A wide zone around the celestial equator was divided into thirty-six identical groups of stars. The idea was that, during the course of a lunar year, these stars rose in the east after sunset every ten days. The priests, who knew the length of the solar year, were able to prepare tables that anticipated the addition of five extra days for the realignment.

The Egyptian goddess of the starry vault, Nut, her body strewn with stars. Every evening Nut swallows the sun through the hole near her mouth; it is reborn every morning from the hole near her womb

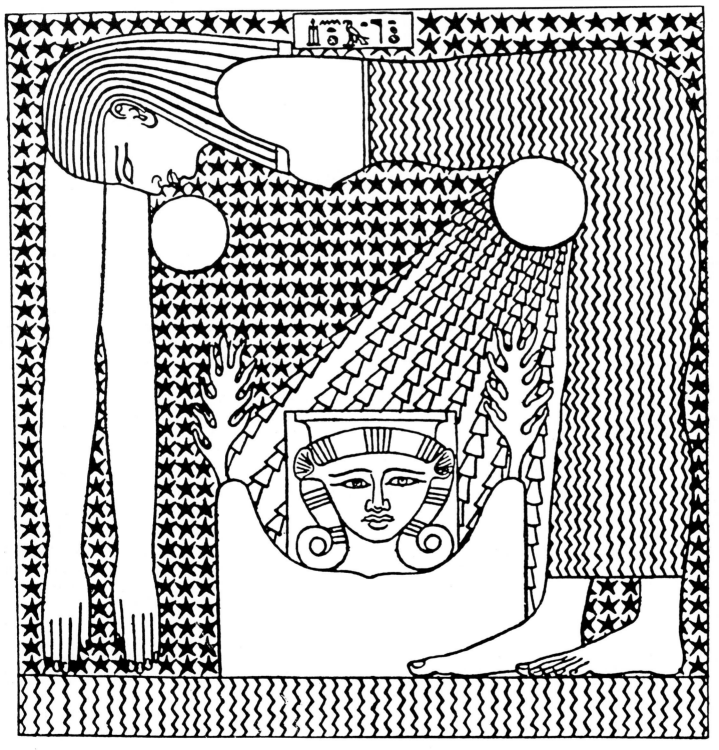

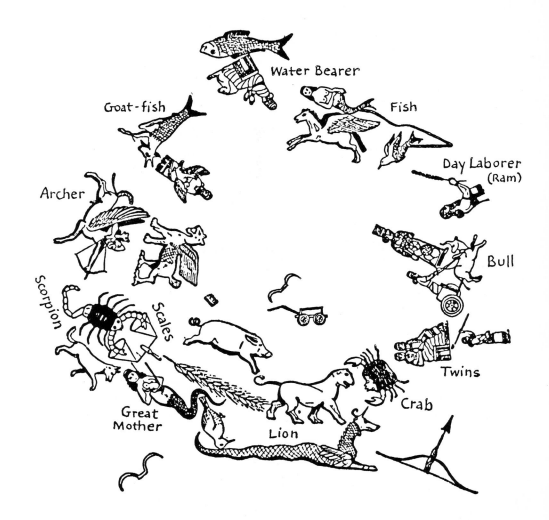

Late Babylonian zodiac

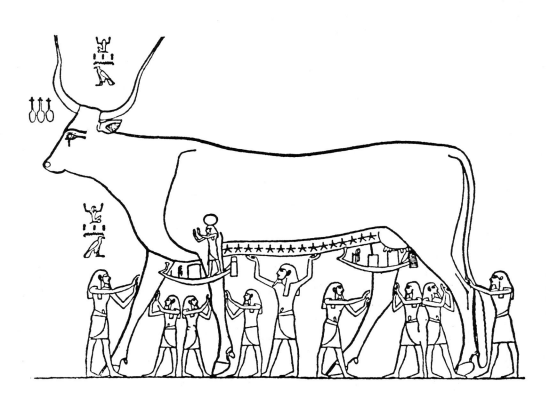

The celestial cow Nut-Hathor. The four
cardinal points correspond to the legs, while
the sun-udder makes its daily and nightly
voyage on the sacred boat

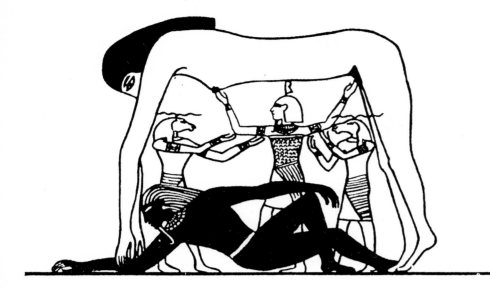

Three variations of the Egyptian celestial goddess Nut. Her husband, Keb, the earth, lies beneath her

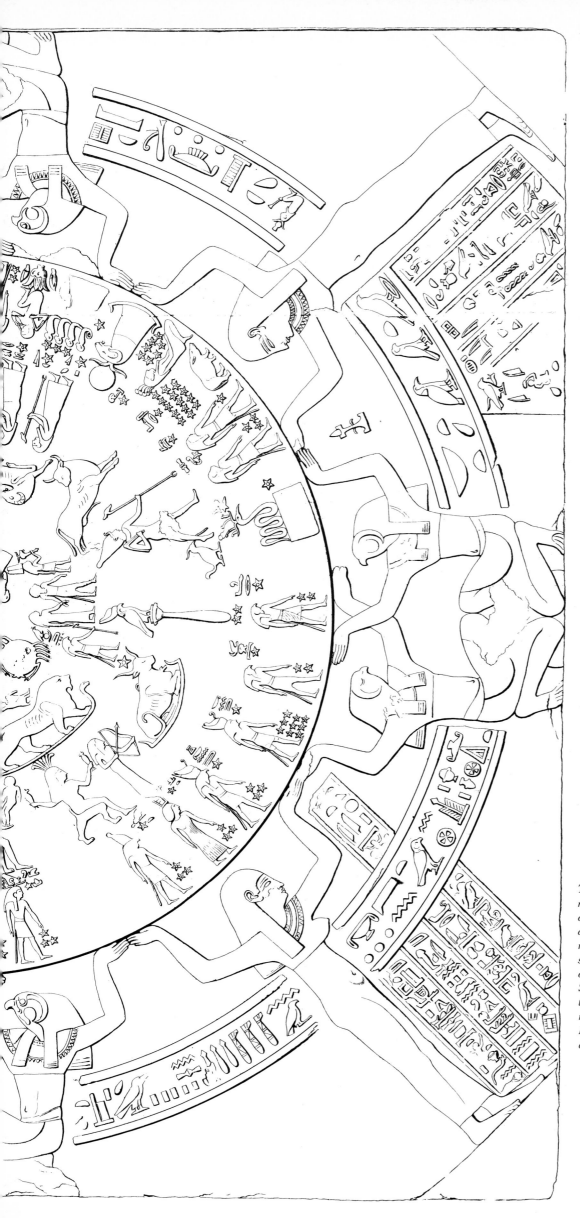

The celestial planisphere, a circular ceiling relief, at Dendera, Egypt. The four kneeling couples support the four cardinal points, while all twelve figures supporting the sphere itself represent the months of the year. Carved in sandstone during the Ptolemaic era, the design illustrates the Egyptian version of the Sumerian constellations, with the addition of the signs of Aries and Libra. Ursa Major is represented by the thigh of the celestial cow, Draco by a hippopotamus, and Ursa Minor by a jackal dedicated to the goddess Set

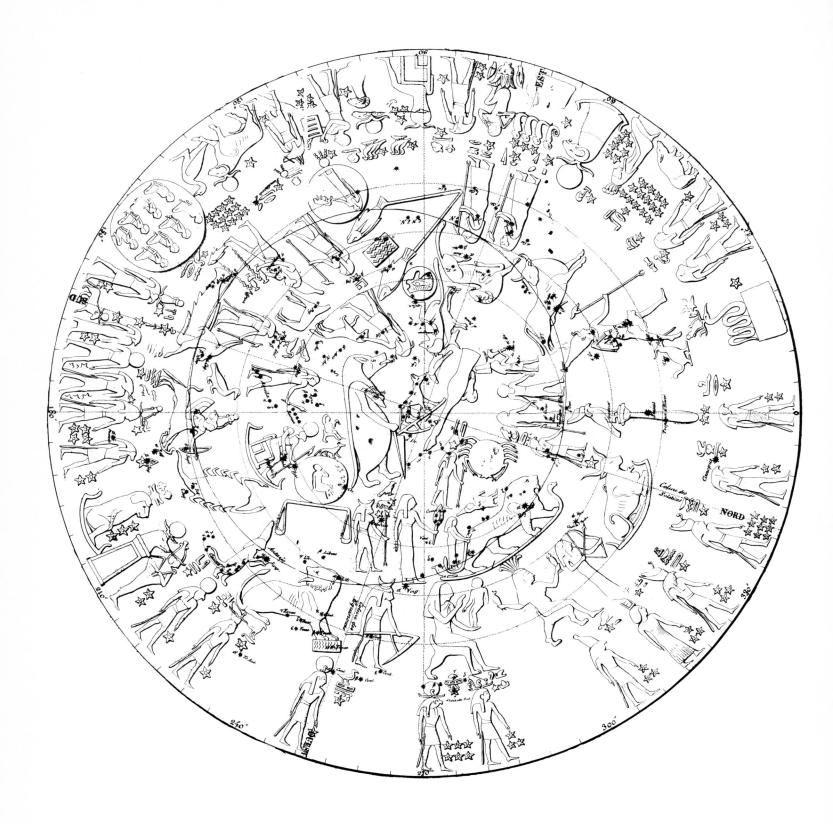

*The central section of the celestial map of
Dendera, with the main, fixed stars
superimposed on it. Along the outer circle
winds the procession of the thirty-six figures of
the decans, each representing the Egyptian
week of ten days*

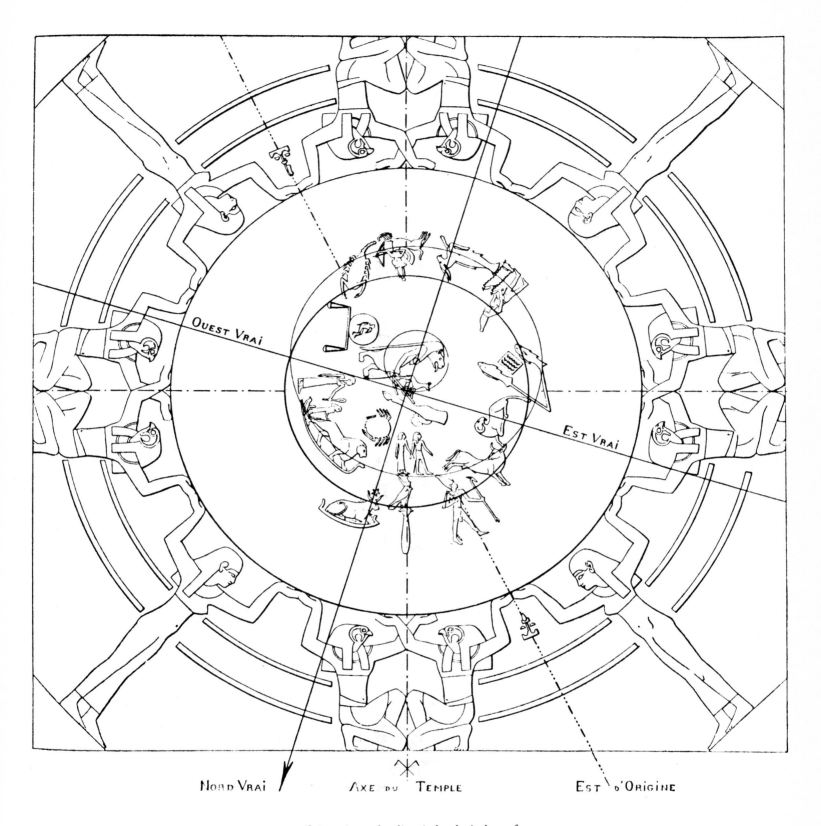

OUEST VRAI

EST VRAI

NORD VRAI AXE DU TEMPLE EST D'ORIGINE

*Orientation and zodiac circle, planisphere of
Dendera. Although carved in a later period,
this ceiling is oriented toward the equinoxes
and solstices of 4000 B.C.: Gemini (spring),
Sagittarius (autumn), Virgo (summer), Pisces
(winter). The lines of alignment in this
illustration are by Schwaller*

Egyptian sky maps of the paranatellonta, the
extrazodiacal constellations that were
transferred to the ecliptic for purely magical
and astrological calculations. A horoscope was
worthless if the paranatellonta were not also
interpreted. Illustrations from Kirker, Oedipus

ZODIAQUE CHRONOLOGIQUE ET MYTHOLOGIQUE.

Par Mr. Dupuis.

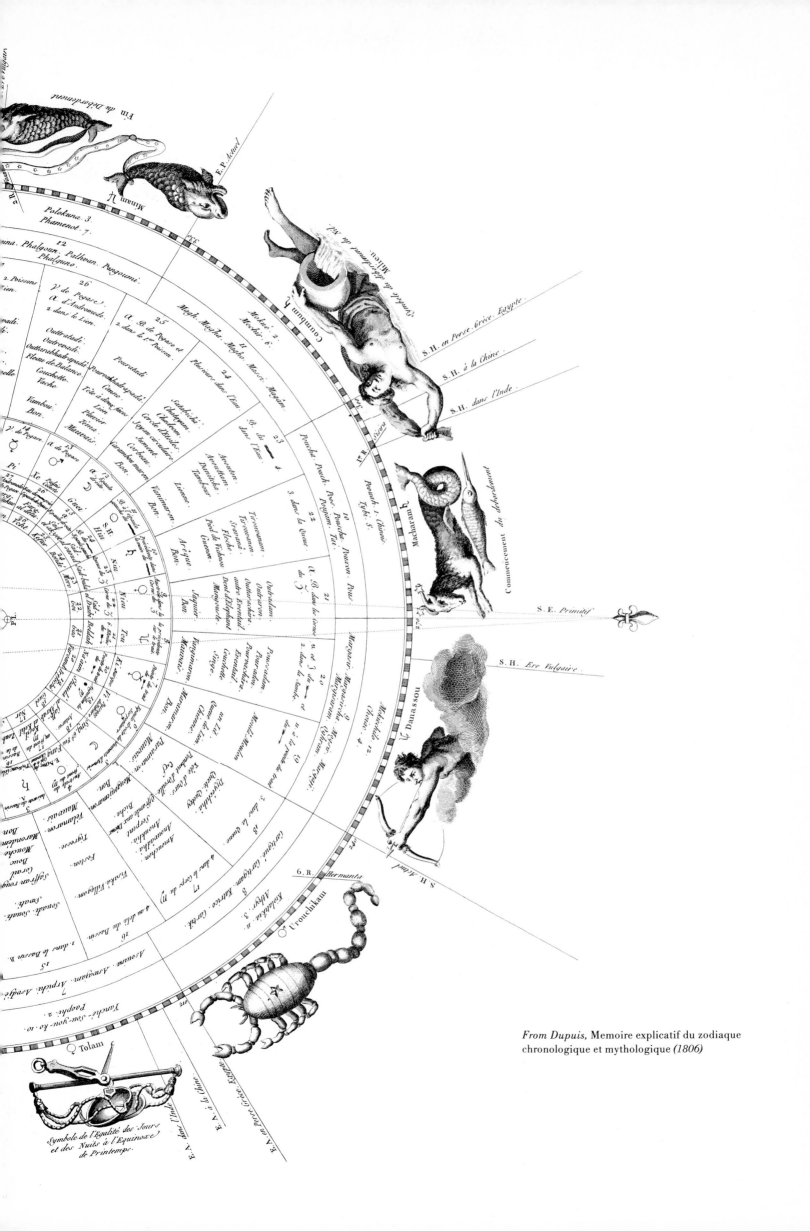

From Dupuis, Memoire explicatif du zodiaque
chronologique et mythologique *(1806)*

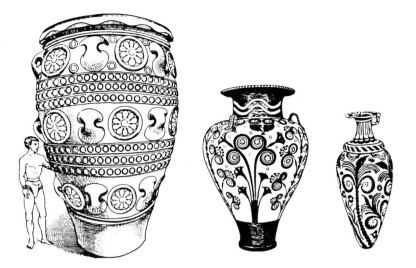

Three Greek vases with molded decorations
from the Palace of Knossos

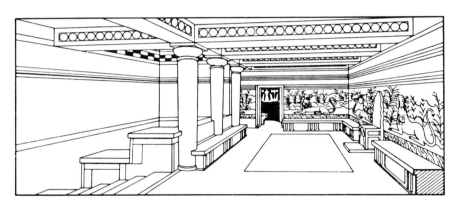

Reconstruction of the Throne Room, the
Room of the Double Axes, and the south
entrance of the Palace of Knossos on the island
of Crete

IV
The Mediterranean

Long before the people we know generically as the Greeks emerged, there already existed in the Aegean basin a Mediterranean civilization that had developed in the third millennium B.C., reaching its height in the sixteenth century B.C. Embracing the lands of the Lycians, Carians, Lydians, Phrygians, Minoans, and, later, the Mycenaeans, this civilization was centered on the island of Crete, and its branches reached all the way to Cyrenaica. It worshiped the Great Mother as the primary universal lunar principle, and it practiced cults of trees and animals. First among these was the cult of the Bull, which ultimately was replaced by Aries as the sign of the spring equinox.

Having come from Mesopotamia as the male solar symbol, the Bull became an amorous and passive partner for the great Cretan goddess Ariadne, Lady of the Labyrinth, custodian of the terrible Minotaur whom the hero Theseus was unable to defeat without her help. The Cretans cut off the arm of Atlas (Boötes) and transformed it into the Corona Borealis (Northern Crown), the golden crown the bull-god Dionysus gave her as a wedding present. Ariadne is Europa (the moon), the maiden who journeyed across the sea sitting on a bull. In an early version of the tale, she was married to Asterios (king of the stars), an ancient Cretan bull-god.

Even Pasiphae, wife of Minos and mother of Ariadne, succeeded in coupling with a bull, thus generating the Minotaur. The great Aegean mythical fantasies were fundamental in the introduction of famous figures to the star myths, such as the she-goat Amalthaea, Medusa, Cassiopeia, Andromeda, Pegasus, etc.

Cretan women engaged in acrobatics with a bull, and a frieze representing the horns of a bull

The decline of this civilization occurred around the twelfth century B.C. with the invasion of the Dorians, who conquered Crete, the Turkish coasts, and the Greek peninsula. After this time, we can speak of Greece as an entity distinct from the Aegean world. As often happens in these cases, a massive transfusion of ancient Mediterranean knowledge into Greek culture took place. Greek myth-writers called the Cretan legends "mythical."

The astronomical knowledge of the new conquerors was extremely poor. Homer cited only one planet, Venus, calling it Phosphorus (Lucifer), the morning star, and he called Hesperus (Vesper) the evening star. The other gods were not yet associated with the heavenly bodies. It was only when (in the fifth century B.C.) the Greeks learned from the Babylonians to distinguish the five "wandering stars"—planets—from the "fixed" stars, that they linked a Greek god to each planet. Still, at the time of Plato, there were no specific names for the planets themselves: to indicate Jupiter, they did not say Zeus, but "the Star of Zeus" (Diodoro Siculo, in J. Seznec, *La Sopravvivenza degli antichi Dei*).

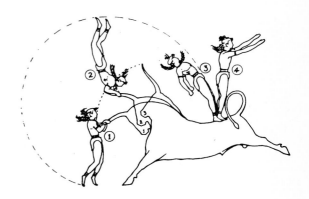

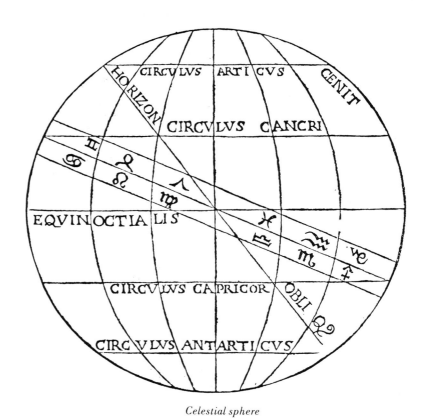

The zenith and the essential lines of the celestial sphere—meridians and parallels, Tropics of Cancer and Capricorn, polar circles, horizon, and zodiacal belt—without which it is impossible to draw a good celestial map

Celestial sphere

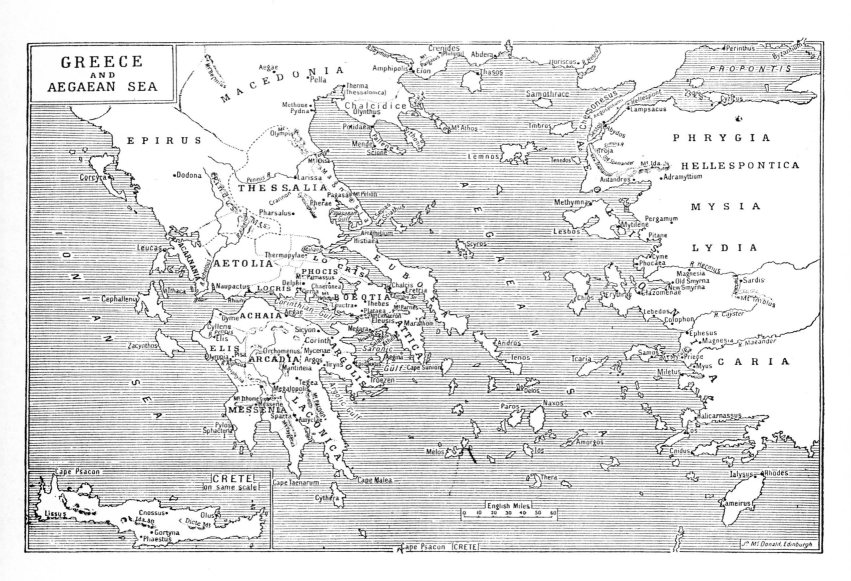

V
The Philosophers

Along the western coast of today's Turkey arose one of the numerous Hellenic states, formed by the coastal lands and a group of islands. This state, Ionia, numbered twelve cities; its capital was Miletus. It was here that during the seventh and sixth centuries B.C. the foundations of Greek philosophy and science were laid. The Ionians began to interpret nature in a completely new way, free from dogma and religious proscriptions. The theoreticians who created this course were called philosophers, which in Greek means lovers of knowledge.

The founder of the Ionian school was Thales of Miletus (624–546 B.C.), an ingenious, intense scholar who applied his research to all branches of knowledge, from hydraulics to mechanics, from geometry to astronomy. He was a tireless traveler, visiting Egypt and Mesopotamia, where he succeeded in learning so much about astronomy that he was able to predict the total eclipse of the sun that occurred punctually, as he said it would, on May 28, 585 B.C. According to Herodotus, it succeeded in interrupting the ongoing war between the Lydians and the Medes.

Thales' innovation was to propose a set of new universal principles that could facilitate the reading of the laws of nature. His theorems not only state the idea, demonstrated to be true, that a figure possesses certain characteristics, but they also state that thanks to these characteristics it is possible to verify the height of a temple or a mountain, or even calculate the distance that separates us from the sun. He studied the celestial sphere and the ancient constellations, and he introduced the constellation of Ursa Major, previously known as the Wagon.

A disciple of Thales was Anaximander (611–545 B.C.) who devised a bold idea—a theory of evolution based on life starting in the sea and evolving on land. His concept anticipated recent discoveries of modern science. Collecting information from navigators who sailed into the port of Miletus, he had them describe the routes they followed and the lands they encountered. Applying Thales' theorem of equilateral triangles, he succeeded in representing these large distances proportionally in a small space, thus inventing the geographic map. He was the first philosopher to conceive of the concept of the infinite as the universal principle of all things. He saw it as the origin and culmination of every evolution, including that of the celestial bodies. This is an eternal, incorruptible infinite from whose essence, at great intervals of time, immense whirlwinds are born that generate worlds such as ours. He wrote, "In that from which things take their beginning is likewise the cause of their ending."

Anaximander's infinite was quite close to the concept of the Tao, but it did not accept, as did Chinese thinkers, divine destiny. He was more interested in all the variations of both evolution and dynamics that pass from one infinite to another.

Solar eclipse

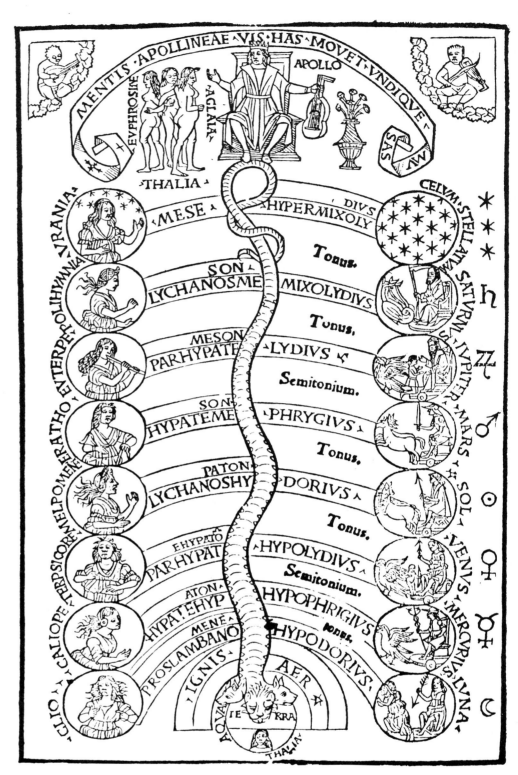

MUSIC OF THE SPHERES

Apollo, with the Graces at his side, conducts the music of the spheres emanating from the serpent of the Pythian oracle. The Muses are on the left, with Urania—the Muse of astronomy—at the top. On the right are the planets with the starry sky at the top. From Galfarius, Practica Musice *(1496)*

In the sixth century B.C. on the small island of Samos, Pythagoras, another great philosopher was born. A mathematician, he was persuaded by Thales to travel to Egypt and Babylonia to study. Later, he opened a school in the colony of Croton in Calabria where revolutionary work was done and significant discoveries—ranging from the general properties of numbers to fundamental numerical equations, from theorems on complex geometric figures to the codification of solid geometric figures, from the physics of vibrating strings to the music of the spheres—were made. Like Anaximander, Pythagoras believed the earth to be a free celestial body in space. He was the first, however, to state that the earth as well as the sun, the moon, and the planets were spherical.

Pythagoras succeeded in giving to the Greeks the model of all that was valued by the Hellenic spirit—beauty, order, moderation, imagination, and rationality. However, the contribution to philosophy of the Ionians certainly did not end with him. Leucippus of Miletus founded a school in Abdera in Thrace, in which, with the contributions of Democritus, he developed an atomic theory startlingly similar to some modern thinking.

Unfortunately, the political life of the Ionians was not always as free as the intellectual life of their philosophers. After having been conquered by Cyrus, they succeeded in liberating themselves from Persian dominion with the help of Athens. Then in 494 B.C. Miletus fell to Darius I and suffered the almost-complete extermination of its inhabitants. This notwithstanding, this admirable city succeeded in giving birth to its last great philosopher, Anaxagoras. Unable to tolerate living under foreign rule, he moved to Athens where he had as friends and disciples Pericles, Phidias, and Euripides. Through them, his ideas reached Socrates, Plato, and Aristotle.

Anaxagoras was the first philosopher to understand that the light of the moon is reflected sunlight, thus making it possible to understand the nature of eclipses. He was also the first to state that the sun is an incandescent physical mass.

Independent of its great many other merits, the dynasty of the Ionian thinkers created the basic principles for a renaissance of astronomy. It is symbolic that this science was reborn from the Middle East and that the cultural voyages of Thales and Anaximander took place in Mesopotamia and in Egypt.

Caria, a Greek-Phoenician state bordering on Ionia, gave birth to a philosopher, Eudoxus of Cnidus (408–355 B.C.), who was a determining factor in the study of the constellations. A superior geometrician and astronomer, he too traveled in order to learn the principles of the sciences. To him we owe the first systematic description of the constellations. His cosmologic system consisted of twenty-seven concentric spheres on which the sun, moon, planets, and stars revolved around the earth. This system explained the seasons and the motions of the planets, including retrograde, or backward, motion. Eudoxus built in Cnidus the first astronomical observatory in Greece of which historians have knowledge. Unfortunately, almost all his writings were lost, but his work has come down to us through the commentaries written about him by other philosophers.

The celestial sphere of Eudoxus contained forty-five constellations, twenty in the northern hemisphere, twelve in the southern, and thirteen in the zodiacal band (this last because the Pleiades were considered a separate group). Recent research has ascertained that this sphere represented the solstitial and equinoctial constellations of the year 2000 B.C. Eudoxus himself, in fact, admitted that they came "from remote antiquity."

The stars of Eudoxus have come down to us mainly because they were described in the famous astronomical poem *Phaenomena*, written by Aratus of Soli (the court poet of Antigonus Gonatas, king of Macedonia) about a century later.

The *Phaenomena* had an enormous success. About thirty-five Greek commentaries on this work are still extant. In the Roman era the poem was translated into Latin by Caesar Germanicus and Cicero, and we know that it continued to be used as a practical handbook of astronomy until the sixth century.

Astronomical observatory in Alexandria, Egypt. From Flammarion, Les Etoiles

52   *The Glorious Constellations*

VI
Alexandria

In the year 343 B.C. Philip of Macedonia called Aristotle to his court to take charge of the education of his son Alexander. The thirteen-year-old boy was thus initiated into the great humanistic and scientific world of Greek philosophy. His magnificent gift for the art of strategy and his great hunger for knowledge made him a sovereign unique both in his treatment of the vanquished and his protection of the temples and libraries of the conquered cities from looting.

Alexander invited sages and priests to his court to engage in learned conversations with him and translate local texts into Greek. In the brief years of his dazzling conquest he thus succeeded in collecting tens of thousands of poetic, scientific, and religious testimonies.

When death snatched him away in Babylonia in 323 B.C., at the age of thirty-three, the empire was divided among his generals. Egypt fell to Ptolemy Soter, Egyptian commander and close friend of Alexander, a convert to his humanistic ideals.

Ptolemy ordered all those texts that had been so avidly collected to be transported to Alexandria, the city Alexander had founded in the Nile Delta nine years earlier. With these he founded the library that was to become the largest and most important of the ancients.

Ptolemy began a dynasty of pharaohs that lasted more than three centuries, guaranteeing that political stability so necessary to great enterprises. The two cultures, Egyptian and Greek, merged and formed what is today called the Alexandrian culture—a body of poetic and scientific thought that reached its culmination under Ptolemy Philadelphus.

Men of letters and science were invited to Alexandria, showered with great honors and hospitality, and encouraged in their research. It is here that Euclid wrote his thirteen-volume *Elements* and Archimedes invented his famous screw. In Miletus the famous *History of Egypt* was commissioned, and the sacred books of the Jews, the Septuagint, were translated into Greek.

The first great Alexandrian astronomer was Aristarchus, supreme mathematician, who came from the island of Samos. Breaking with tradition, he openly proclaimed the sun to be an immobile sphere located at a practically infinite distance from the fixed stars. He organized the planets, which, he said, describe circular orbits around the sun, in this way: the internal planets (Mercury and Venus), Earth, around which the moon circles, and the external planets (Mars, Jupiter, and Saturn). Aristarchus believed the earth to be animated by two movements: its yearly revolution around the sun, and its daily rotation around its own axis.

Approximately seventeen centuries before Giordano Bruno's burning at the stake and the trial of Galileo, Aristarchus was left free to continue to proclaim his truths despite the criticisms of his colleagues.

His work stimulated new astronomical studies and great efforts were made to obtain more and more accurate maps of the sky. Timocharis and Aristyllus in-

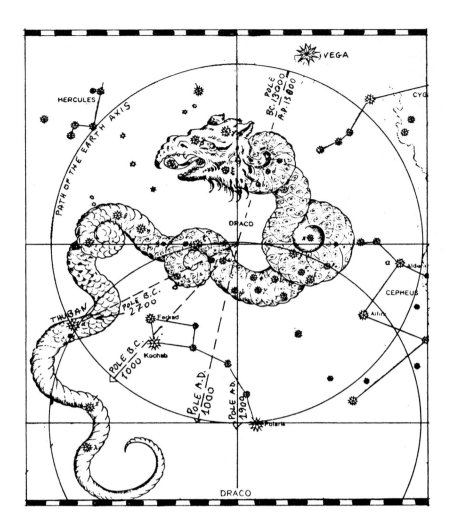

THE PRECESSION OF THE EQUINOXES

As the earth rotates on its axis, the gravitational forces of the sun and the moon pull it off center—just like a spinning top—so that over a period of 25,765 years the earth's axis describes a circle in the sky. As a consequence, approximately every two thousand years the sun enters the equinoxes and the solstices at a different sign of the zodiac. When Hipparchus discovered this long wave of sidereal time, he called it the Great Year of the Pleiades; later it became known as the Platonic Year.

In order to simplify references to the shifting of the equinoxes and the solstices, dates have been approximated throughout this book. So, for example, the Age of Taurus, which actually lasted from 4380 B.C. to 2220 B.C., is simplified to 4000 B.C. to 2000 B.C. Above: The Platonic Year, the circle that the earth's axis describes in 25,765 years, with Draco at the center

60 B.C. to A.D. 2100—Age of Pisces
2220 B.C. to   60 B.C.—Age of Aries
4380 B.C. to 2220 B.C.—Age of Taurus
6540 B.C. to 4380 B.C.—Age of Gemini
8700 B.C. to 6540 B.C.—Age of Cancer
10,860 B.C. to 8700 B.C.—Age of the Lion

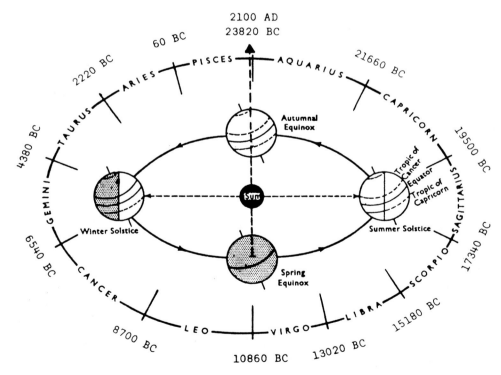

The precessional shift of the sun on March 21 (spring equinox) in the last Platonic year (23,820 B.C.–A.D. 2100)

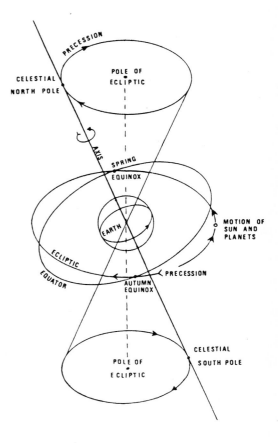

vented a system for positioning the fixed stars scientifically that was recognized by Arthur Berry as the first modern star catalogue.

The second great astronomer who worked in Alexandria came from Nicaea and was called Hipparchus (c. 190–120 B.C.). Although his observatory was located on the island of Rhodes, he had an enormous influence on Alexandrian astronomy. Hipparchus understood that in order to develop this science it was necessary to put aside theories and return to pure observation. Thus, he invented the diopter, an extremely accurate instrument used in locating the stars, considered the ancestor of the modern theodolite. With it he began the systematic exploration of the sky. He recalculated the position of all the stars and devised a famous star catalogue in which celestial coordinates were given for 850 stars. He also divided the stars into six categories representing their different magnitudes. Hipparchus' observations are known today because his work was preserved by the astronomer Ptolemy. It was used practically intact for sixteen centuries.

While he was at work Hipparchus made an interesting observation. Comparing his drawings with those of Timocharis and Aristyllus, compiled a century and a half earlier, he found that the equinoctial points had changed. It appeared that in the case of the star Spica, in Virgo, the distance from the equinoctial points (measured to the east) had increased by two degrees in 150 years, or at a speed of forty-eight seconds of arc per year. Continuing his observations, he came to the conclusion that the slow shifting only affected the stars' longitude, and not their latitude. The implications of this discovery were far-reaching: this was the scientific discovery of the precession of the equinoxes, the slow shifting of the celestial sphere due to the anomalous whirling of the

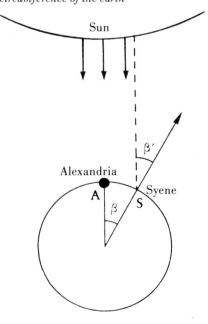

At the center of this diagram of an ancient carved agate, Pan sits with his flute, surrounded by the seven sorrows and the twelve signs of the zodiac. From Dupuis, L'Origine des tous les cultes

System used by Eratosthenes to calculate the circumference of the earth

terrestrial axis. Before Hipparchus, there existed only practical knowledge of this phenomenon, which embraces the long period of conical rotation of the axis of about 25,765 years.

The dating system of the star maps used in this book is based on precession because today observers at a given latitude will no longer see the constellations along the southern horizon that were familiar to their ancestors one or two thousand years ago.

In 244 B.C. the pharaoh Ptolemy Euergetes called Eratosthenes of Cyrene, a versatile genius, to Alexandria to direct the famous library there. Eratosthenes succeeded in perfecting Eudoxus' theories on the earth's circumference, calculating it to be 250,000 stades, slightly less than 24,800 miles, which is essentially correct. Eratosthenes conducted an in-depth study of the sky and its stars, analyzing it not only with the eyes of an astronomer but also with those of a writer of myths. To him we owe that panorama of myths and constellations described in the *Catasterismi,* often quoted in this book. Eratosthenes is said to have invented the armillary sphere composed of metal rings representing the celestial spheres; at least his is the first of which we have any knowledge.

Under Cleopatra Egypt became a Roman province. With both great respect and awe, the conquerors found themselves governing this extremely rich country overflowing with four thousand years of history. Its temples and pyramids were the largest ever seen. Its capital, Alexandria, was particularly impressive.

Built of white marble, it contained temples and palaces for which Greek building techniques had been added to the Egyptian. Its harbor was the most important commercial center on the Mediterranean.

The famous lighthouse rose on an island located in front of the harbor. It was an engineering work of such perfection and magnificence that it was considered one of the seven wonders of the world. Built in 285 B.C., it stood almost six hundred feet tall. Tons of wood were burned in its immense brazier, and the firelight was increased a hundredfold by a series of enormous convex mirrors.

In the city, which was organized as a kind of self-governing body, Greeks, Jews, and Egyptians—craftsmen, merchants, men of letters, and artists from all over the Macedonian empire—lived together. When Caesar came to Alexandria, he was enchanted, not only by the beautiful Cleopatra, but also, man of culture that he was, by the enormous cultural center of the Academy. It consisted of the museum and the library containing over 700,000 texts, which the philosopher Callimachus had listed in a catalogue of 120 volumes.

It was here that Caesar learned enough about astronomy to conceive the reform of the Roman calendar as well as the creation of the new constellation of Libra, drawn by cutting the claws off of the sign of Scorpius.

During the Roman dominion, various riots broke out between the ethnic

Armillary sphere

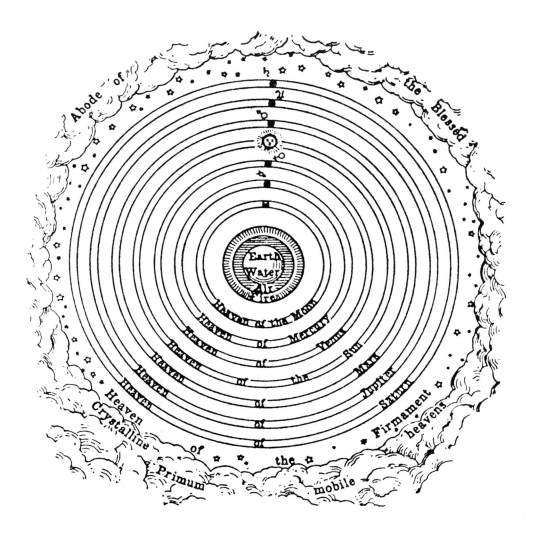

The Ptolemaic system, in which the earth is
immobile in the center of the universe

communities and the conquerors. During one of these (in 47 B.C.) the harbor
area went up in flames due to a tragic error and eventually the fire spread to the
Serapeum (Temple of Serapis), the library, and the museum. Maps, scientific
instruments, globes, engineering models, and, above all, books were burned in
this cultural catastrophe.

The shock was enormous. Cleopatra, Marc Antony, and others did everything
to try to save what they could and build a new library with what was left from
the old one. Marc Antony, then consul, ordered that Pergamum's library—the
second most important in the world, with 200,000 volumes—be transferred to
the Egyptian city. This new great library survived until A.D. 641, when the Arab
caliph Omar had it burned completely. This act was bemoaned by the Arabs
themselves when (as we will see later on) they set about building their store of
scientific knowledge in Baghdad and throughout the rest of the Islamic world.

Notwithstanding the changes resulting from the political shifts and the
subsequent disasters, Alexandria was still to produce her last great son, Ptolemy
(Claudius Ptolemaeus), just as Miletus, invaded by the Persians, had produced
Anaxagoras. There is very little information about the private life of Ptolemy. It
is not known when he was born or when he died, but it is sure that he worked
from A.D. 127 (the year in which he described a lunar eclipse) until 150.

Some cite his birth as having taken place in Pelusium in the Nile Delta
during the year 70, and his death is said to have occurred after that of Emperor
Antoninus Pius, who died in 161. Alexandria was in a period of great political,
religious, and economic turmoil. Emperor Hadrian visited the city in 130 and

found that the god of money had by then overtaken all others. He wrote, "There is no Hebrew leader of the synagogue nor a Samaritan or a Christian bishop who is not an astrologer, seer, and charlatan."

Fleeing from this world, Ptolemy took refuge in the museum and library of the Serapeum where he set up an observatory and began to study the celestial sphere of Hipparchus. He designed new measuring instruments and created an elaborate system of the planets' motions with the earth as the immobile center of the universe; Ptolemy also devised a mechanism of eighty spheres in which the firmament rotated. He had the genius of knowing how to take the best of the research done by his predecessors and with this build his geometric-mathematical masterpiece.

Although the dozens of books written by Hipparchus are lost, his knowledge has been transmitted to us through Ptolemy, who dependably attributed the origins of his thinking to the Nicaean scientist. His star atlas, based on the one designed in Rhodes by Hipparchus, included forty-eight constellations and a total of 1,028 stars, complete with longitude, latitude, and magnitude. It is significant that the catalogue did not contain any stars that were visible to Ptolemy at Alexandria's latitude but would have been invisible to Hipparchus in Rhodes.

Thus Greek astronomical knowledge was condensed into thirteen volumes which Ptolemy titled *Mathematical Syntax*, but are known to us as the *Almagest*. This work was extraordinarily important; it was used as the bible of astronomy until the revolution of Copernicus in 1500.

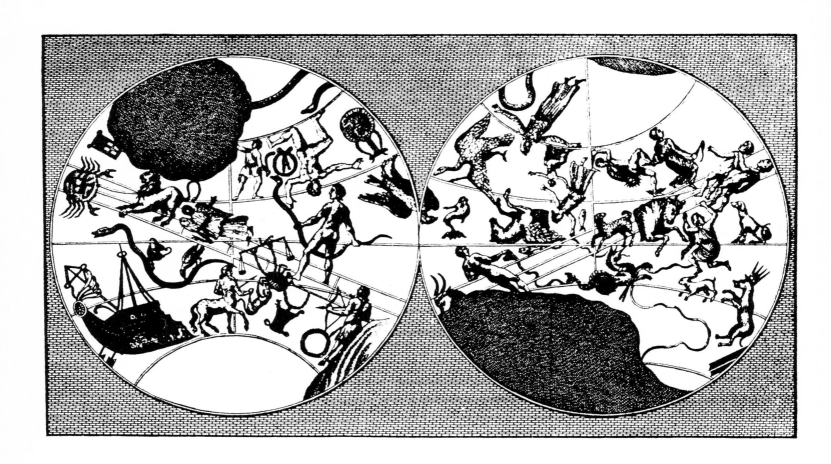

*The Farnese Atlas and a stereographic
projection of the celestial sphere that he
holds on his shoulders*

VII
Rome

Before the introduction of the Greek gods, the ancient Romans worshiped the spirits of the forests, fields, and houses, as well as the seas and the skies.

This Olympus of nature and animism included fauns, wood spirits, and spirits of wine and the beehive as well as the road crossings. Above all reigned Janus, who was identified with the sun, while Jana (Diana) was the moon. Since the sun opened and closed the day, Janus was considered the god of the beginning and the end; all that existed was begun and completed by him. His main temple in Rome had its east-west door open in time of war and closed in time of peace. The month of *Januarius* (January) was dedicated to him.

Janus

We do not have much information about the astronomical knowledge of the first Romans, but it was probably very primitive. Their calendar dates back to the time of Romulus. Numa Pompilius later replaced it—it was composed of only 304 days—with one of 354 days, also very imprecise. This testifies to the fact that the Romans were not interested in systematically observing the sky; they preferred to leave this task to Eastern astrologers, whose observations were only sporadically accurate.

Despite the fact that they had access to Greek knowledge, the Romans never acquired the instinct for pure research. They remained practical and attached to the land. Perhaps they were repelled by the sterile and ferocious battles of certain Greek philosophers that contributed so little to the idea of government and stability. Cicero stated, "The Greek mathematicians hold the field in pure geometry while we limit ourselves to the practice of calculations and measurements." The Roman genius turned to terrestrial mechanics based on the reasoning that the sky seemed to be immortal and sufficient unto itself, while the empire needed all possible attention.

Such poets as Ovid and Virgil made frequent mention of the stars and the constellations, but these were clearly borrowed from the Greek. Lucretius alluded to cosmological questions in *De rerum natura* (*On the Nature of Things*). Seneca studied the problem of comets carefully and concluded that they were celestial bodies endowed with periodic motion and therefore such that men of future generations would see them again. He also conducted a study on the antipodes, hypothesizing that the other side of the earth's sphere was inhabitable; this would later inspire Renaissance navigators. In his *Historia naturalis* (*Natural History*), Pliny the Elder also expounded upon his reasons for believing that the earth was a sphere. Columella researched questions of technical astronomy, but he committed the gross error of validating for Italy the coordinates of the rising and setting stars on a Middle Eastern latitude. Manilius' long poem *Astronomica* was of a purely astrological nature, presenting an overview of the influence of the zodiacal constellations and the fixed stars on men and nations.

The most outstanding personality of all was without a doubt Julius Caesar himself, who had studied Hipparchus' texts and written a work on astronomy entitled *De astris* (*On the Stars*), subsequently lost. It was he who instituted the sign Libra and, helped by Sosigenes, rearranged the calendar when he was

At right and opposite: *Mithras, surrounded by astronomical emblems, allegorically slays the celestial bull*

Roman calendar stone preserved in the Wurzburg Museum

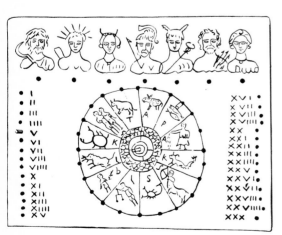

elected Pontifex Maximus. He decreed that the year 46 B.C., the famous "year of confusion," would have 445 days and, in so doing, he succeeded in reconnecting the months with the seasons. The new astronomical calendar, called the Julian calendar in his honor, was composed of 365¼ days and contained an error of only eleven minutes and eight seconds. Once every four years an additional day, February 29, was added to the year.

The rank and file of the Roman legionnaires practiced a solar cult, Mithraism, originating in the Middle East. The soldiers called the sun-god Mithras Sol Invictus (Invincible Sun). He came from the official religion of the Persians while under the reign of the Sassanian dynasty—Zoroastrianism. Their supreme god was Ahura-Mazda, god of the sky and conqueror of Angra-Mainyu or Ahriman, the prince of darkness worshiped by the Devas. Similar in many aspects to the new cult of Christ, Mithraism promised spiritual redemption through rituals that included voluntary castigation and strict self-discipline. For some time, it was a serious rival of Christianity. Inasmuch as he was associated with the sun, Mithras spent part of the year in the world of the living and part of the year in the dark world beyond the grave, just as the sun remains half of the year above the celestial equator and the other half below.

The astronomical orientation of Mithraism is evident from the principal representation of its cult—the sacrifice of a bull by Mithras, of which many versions have been found. In it Mithras, dressed in Phrygian clothes and hat, kneels next to a bull, representing the dying year, and, holding him tightly with one hand, plunges a sword into his neck with the other. Underneath the animal stretches a long serpent, a dog licks the blood that flows from the wound, a scorpion clasps onto the bull's genitals, and stalks of grain, the symbol of rebirth, sprout from the tip of its tail. The figures of the two divine torchbearers, Hesperus and Phosphorus, flank the bull; above is the sun with the raven, its messenger, and the moon. The entire scene contains the twelve signs of the zodiac or the twelve altars that represent them. This allegory is astronomically very interesting, especially since it reproduces the very ancient Sumerian myth of the slaying of the celestial Taurus (the equinox of spring) by

62   *The Glorious Constellations*

Gilgamesh (Orion), two constellations that set when the sign of Scorpius rises, thus giving the impression that it causes their disappearance. The sacrifice of the bull occurs over Hydra, the aquatic serpent, symbol of the celestial horizon. The dog is the star Sirius in the constellation Canis Major, and the raven is a star group situated above Hydra in the sky. Hesperus and Phosphorus represent the evening and morning aspects of the planet Venus. Finally, the stalks of grain are the Pleiades. We thus obtain a total of sixteen constellations, to which the sun, the moon, and Venus must be added.

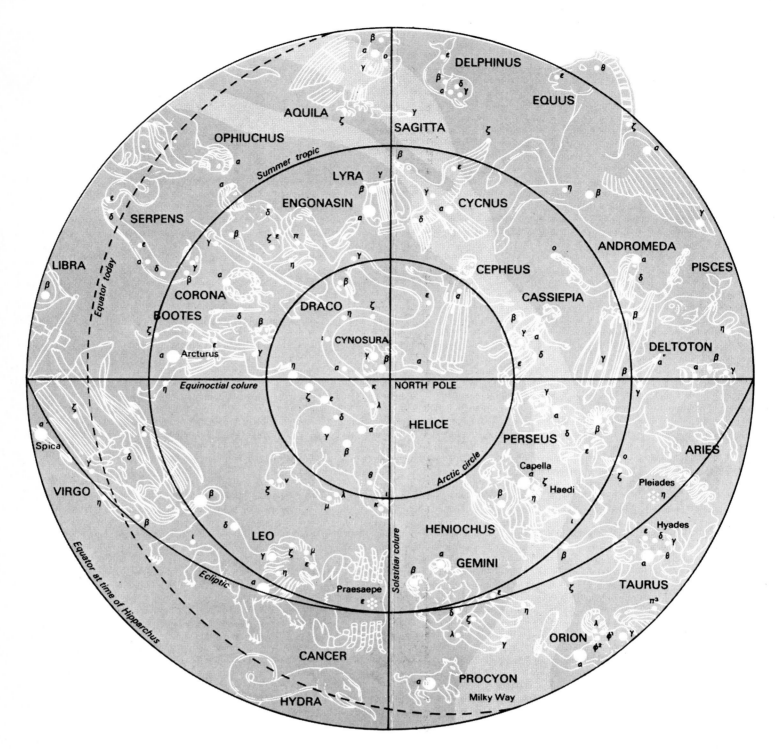

NORTHERN HEMISPHERE

On this and opposite page: *Representations of the constellations as described by Manilius in the* Astronomica, *taking the precessional shift into account. From the Loeb Classical Library*

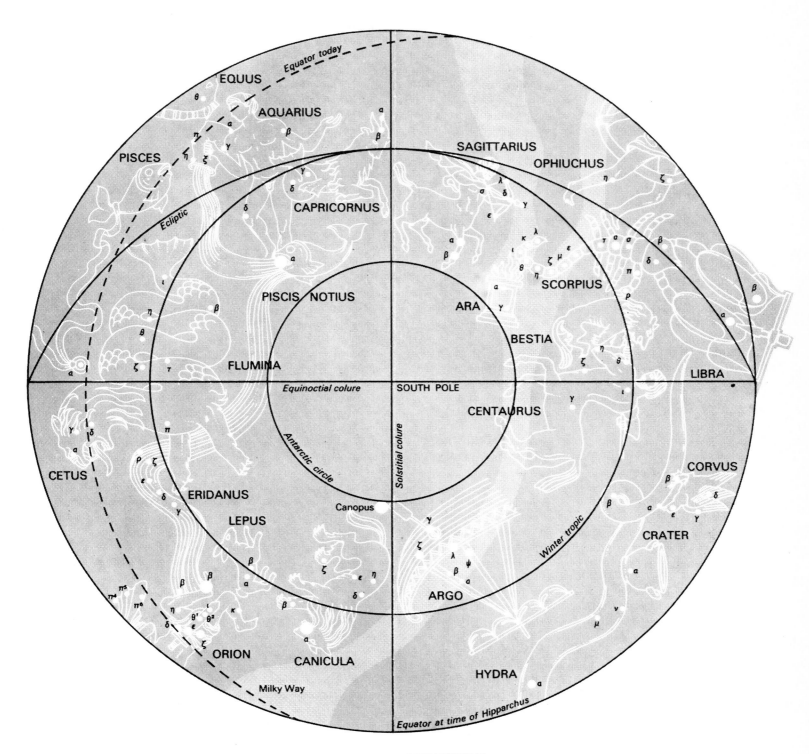

SOUTHERN HEMISPHERE

From the Koran:

قَالَ رَسُولُ اللَّهِ : طَلَبُ الْعِلْمِ فَرِيضَةٌ عَلَى كُلِّ مُسْلِمٍ .

The Holy Prophet has said, "To search for knowledge is the duty of every Moslem"

قَالَ رَسُولُ اللَّهِ : إِنَّ الْعُلَمَاءَ وَرَثَةُ الْاَنْبِيَاءِ

The Holy Prophet has said, "In truth, wise men are the heirs of the prophets"

قَالَ رَسُولُ اللَّهِ : اُطْلُبُوا الْعِلْمَ مِنَ الْمَهْدِ اِلَى اللَّحْدِ

The Holy Prophet has said, "Search for knowledge from the crib to the tomb"

VIII
Caliphs and Sultans

After the collapse of Rome, the empire was divided into two separate blocs. Italy and the rest of Europe, on the one hand, were directly exposed to barbarian invasions. The remainder of the Eastern empire, on the other hand, was more protected, so that a substantial number of scholars succeeded in surviving there even though the cultural structures had been largely destroyed. They continued the traditions of the philosophers, although without the flame of originality. For them too, however, the time came when new political and religious persecutions forced them into abandoning the traditional seats of knowledge in order to take refuge in Persia where they found monarchs inclined to give them the necessary protection.

Thus Gunde-Shapur was created to be a cultural center with ties to the Greek philosophical past. Somehow a library was installed with the summaries of and commentaries on the works of the past and with those original Greek texts that had escaped the great purges. To Gunde-Shapur came men of letters—Greek Christians, Hebrew Christians, Hebrews, Nestorian Christians, and Syrian Christians. They were entrusted with the translation of the Greek texts; this center remained in use until the ninth century.

While these scholars kept the torch of antiquity burning in Persia, the prophet Muhammad was born in Mecca between 570 and 580. It is said that the archangel Gabriel dictated six thousand sonnets to him, which were collected and popularized in 610 as the Koran, the spiritual guide of the new expansionist religious movement of Islam.

Stimulated by the new faith and facing an empire nearing its end, the Arabs did not take long to conquer Syria, Egypt (Alexandria fell in September, 642, after a year's siege), and Persia. By 670 they had invaded Asia Minor all the way to Constantinople. In 732 Islam extended from the Oxus River to north of the Pyrenees. If Charles Martel and his Christians had not stopped the conquests at Poitiers, it would have embraced the entire Mediterranean.

The new caliphs—rulers of Islam—soon understood the importance of Gunde-Shapur, and they encouraged the continuation of the translations of Greek texts into Syriac and Arabic. In the beginning they gave priority to the medical texts of Hippocrates and Galen; later, to the astronomical and mathematical texts.

The first capital of Islam was Damascus, Syria, the realm of the Umayyad caliphs who held power until the Abbasid caliphs founded the new capital, Baghdad, in Mesopotamia on the western banks of the Tigris. While Damascus had largely absorbed the Byzantine culture, Baghdad was more influenced by the Oriental cultures. Egypt, Greece, Persia, and even India had cultural representatives in Baghdad. The Abbasid caliphs were a dynasty that in certain ways can be compared to the Ptolemies of Alexandria. The first scholar of this dynasty about whom we have any knowledge relating to astronomy was al-Mansur. He ordered the translation of a text that was brought to him by an astronomer from India by the name of Sindhind. This work was interesting because it presented in Indian guise the ancient Ptolemaic theories that had traveled down the roads opened by Alexander's empire.

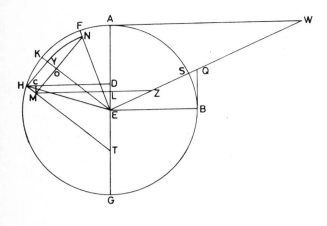

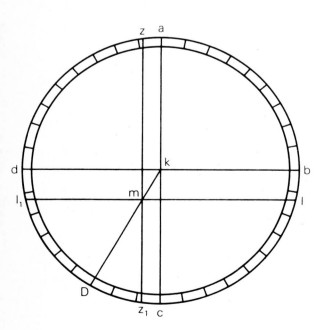

Two methods for finding the direction toward Mecca, the direction of prayer, according to al-Biruni (above) and Sardar Kabuli (below)

Al-Mansur had a famous son, Harun al-Rashid, who later became known as the model for the character of the despotic caliph to whom Scheherazade tells her tales in the *Thousand and One Nights*. In real life he was a learned man who founded various schools and also had the first Moslem paper mills built. Under his reign, the physicist and philologist Hunain ibn-Ishak was called to Baghdad from Gunde-Shapur. In addition to translating more works by Hippocrates and Galen, this scholar began the translation of Ptolemy's *Almagest*.

So it was that the Sumerian celestial sphere, which had started out in Mesopotamia and traveled through Egypt, Syria, India, and Greece, arrived triumphantly in its land of origin in a Hipparchan-Ptolemaic variant.

The greatest of the Abbasid caliphs was the son of al-Rashid, the enlightened al-Mamun, a true prince of the Arab Renaissance. He founded the grandiose House of Knowledge, with an immense library in which translators and scholars labored. The first coordinator of this complex was the Nestorian physicist Yahyah ibn-Masawaih, under whose guidance important works by Aristotle were translated. Subsequently the academy was directed by the astronomer al-Khwarizmi, author of important algebra texts. He also conducted many experiments in geography and calculations on the circumference of the earth that were executed with the sophisticated instruments constructed by al-Asturlabi, from whom the astrolabe takes its name. Orientation was an obsession for the Arabs who, in their daily routine, were required to face Mecca for their ritual prayers. Al-Khwarizmi also proposed changing the calendar from a lunar to a solar one, but his attempt failed because it went against the teachings of the Koran.

Another famous astronomer who worked in the House of Knowledge was Alfraganus (Ahmad ibn-Muhammad al-Fargani), whose *Elements of Astronomy* was translated into Latin in the twelfth century, making a great contribution to the rebirth of western astronomy.

Wise men of faiths that were in open contrast with the Moslem teachings found asylum and protection under al-Mamun; he even gained the nickname of "commander of the infidels." Two astronomers in particular belonged to a sect of mystical star worshipers. One was Albategnius (Muhammad ibn-Jazer ibn-Senau abu-Abdallah al-Harrani), who was nicknamed al-Battani because he was born at Battan in Mesopotamia. He authored the astronomical tables entitled *The Science of the Stars*. The other was Thabit ben-Qurra, a great scholar—a linguist and mathematician, theorist on the rituals for worshiping the celestial bodies, and author of a new and more precise translation of the *Almagest* and important mathematical works by Apollonius and Archimedes. This quote from one of his books plainly shows the great freedom of thought that existed at the court of Baghdad: "We are the heirs and progeny of paganism which has spread gloriously throughout the world. Blessed is he who out of love for polytheism tirelessly endures suffering."

As time went by, the power of the Abbasids waned and a new family, the Buwaihids, gradually installed itself in Baghdad. Then the caliphs were succeeded by the sultans, who became famous for their refinement and extravagance, as well as for the love they displayed for both earthly pleasures as well as for science and the arts. Under their reign, new observatories were built at Bukhara, Samarkand, and Khiva (in the delta of the Oxus). In 988 Sultan Sharaf al-Daula had an observatory erected in the garden of his palace in which many astronomers worked; among these was the eminent al-Buziani.

In Persia around the eleventh century, the Seljuk sultans rose to become patrons of the sciences in the city of Razi where, under the enlightened Jalal al-

Din, the poet-astronomer Omar Khayyám worked. He was a student of algebra and the author of the revision of the Persian calendar that was judged to be so perfect by the historian Gibbon as to exceed both the Julian and the Gregorian calendars. This calendar became .effective on March 16, 1079, but did not survive the subsequent political changes.

Persia was the country to give birth to the most interesting astronomer of this period, Abd al-Rahnan Bin Umar Bin Muhammad Bin Sahl Abul Usain al-Sufi al-Razi, known to us, for brevity's sake, as al-Sufi. We know very little about his life; from his name we know that he came from the Sufi sect (Dervishes) and that he was born in Razi. He lived at the courts of Shiraz and Baghdad under Adhat al-Davlat. Al-Sufi was rediscovered in Europe during the last century, when a Danish astronomer published a translation of one of his manuscripts. Forgotten for centuries and entitled *Description of the Fixed Stars*, it was a record of 1,018 stars. Al-Sufi did not limit himself, as his contemporaries did, to reporting the magnitudes Ptolemy had included in the *Almagest*; instead he carefully checked each one. In fact, he conducted an independent and original study of the constellations that surpassed even Ptolemy's work in terms of accuracy and remained without rival for more than eight centuries.

The star atlas of this master astronomer has been judged a model of precision by modern scientists. When research is done today on the variability of the light of the stars, al-Sufi's observations are always taken into consideration.

The Shiite dynasty of the Fatimids succeeded, almost contemporaneously with the events of the Seljuk sultans, in conquering Egypt, where they founded their capital, Cairo. They expanded into Syria and Palestine and, for a short time, even succeeded in conquering Baghdad.

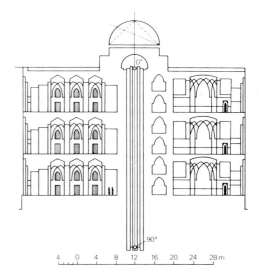

Reconstruction of the observatory at Samarkand. From S. H. Nasr, Islamic Science

Arab astronomers

TABVLÆ

LONG.AC LAT STELLARUM FIXARVM,
EX OBSERVATIONE

ULUGH BEIGHI,

TAMERLANIS Magni Nepo-

tis, Regionum ultra citràque *GJ 1 HVN*
(ı.*Oxum*) Principis potentiſſimi.

Ex tribus invicém collatis MSS. Perſicis jam primùm
Luce a Latio donavit, & Commentariis illuſtravit
THOMAS HYDE *A M. e Coll. Regina Oxon.*

In Calce Libri acceſſerunt *MOHAMMEDIS TIZINI*
Tabulæ Declinationum & Rectarum Aſcenſionum.
Additur demum, *Elenchus* Nominum Stellarum.

O X O N I J

Typis *Henrici Hall* Academiæ Typographi, Sumptibus Authoris. Venales
proſtant apud *Richardum Davis* Bibliopolam. CIƆIƆCLXV.

Venetian edition of the Zig Tables by Ulugh-Beg

Ulugh-Beg, grandson of Tamerlane. From Hevelius, Uranographia totum coelum stellatum *(1690)*

One of their caliphs, by the name of Hakim, had an observatory built on the Mokatim hill near Cairo where the astronomers ibn-Yunis and al-Hazen set about compiling celestial maps. Working as a team, they compiled the *Hakemite Tables*, the first astronomical tables published in Egypt since the golden age of Alexandria.

On the western front of the Islamic empire, on the Iberian peninsula, the caliphs had ordered the founding of libraries and observatories in such cities as Toledo and Seville. Here illustrious scientists worked. Azarchel (al-Zarkali) was born in Cordova and studied in Toledo where he published astronomical tables called *Toledan Tables* on the motion of the planets. Also in this city, astronomical research was conducted by two astronomers from Seville, namely, Geber (Jabir ibn-Aflah) and Alpetragius (Nur ed-Din al-Bitrugi).

In the thirteenth century the astronomy of Arab Spain produced its greatest genius, a Christian king, Alfonso X of Castile, nicknamed El Sabio (The Wise). He surrounded himself with a small army of researchers and with them he compiled the tables that became known as *Alfonsine Tables*. This is a large illustrated work on the sky and its stars that eventually became the spearhead for the beginning of the science of the constellations in medieval Europe.

During these centuries of Arab research on astronomy, the names of the stars were translated into Arabic from their descriptions in the *Almagest*, all based on their positions relative to the constellations. For example, a star in Leo was called in Greek Tail of Leo, which in Arabic became *al-Dhanab al-Asad*. When the *Alfonsine Tables* were translated, the long Arabic names were Europeanized. So *al-Dhanab al-Asad* became Deneb; Rigel was derived from *Ridjl al-Djanza*, the Leg of the Giant; and so on.

The adventures of Urania—the Muse of astronomy—did not end here, however. From the Far East came the powerful drumbeat of war. In Mongolia a great military leader had succeeded in gathering the nomadic tribes of horsemen into one army. Genghis Khan had started a great expansionist war that brought him as early as 1220 the conquest of Khorasan and the Trans-Caspian region, where he destroyed the city of Razi, the birthplace of al-Sufi. The following year he arrived in northern Persia. Under the leadership of Genghis Khan's nephew, Hulagu Khan, the Mongols occupied all of Persia in 1256, and then headed toward Mesopotamia. There they laid siege to Baghdad in 1258, taking the city by storm. For six days and six nights, the city was burned and robbed. The university was destroyed. However, the library of the House of Knowledge founded by al-Mamun was miraculously rescued by the intelligence and ingenuity of one man, Nasir ed-Din. He had been a member of a mysterious and notorious sect, called Assassins (from *hashashin*, consumer of hashish) and founded by one Hasan ibn al-Sabbah. Nasir ed-Din was an eccentric bandit and wise man who knew the secret books of astrology and alchemy. In addition he was the leader of a band of heretic Shiites who, while under the influence of hashish, became fearless avengers.

Nasir ed-Din succeeded in rescuing a library that, so it was said, at the time contained hundreds of thousands of texts. He thereby accomplished a heroic cultural feat worthy of praise even if for just the enormous physical task of the relocation, which required many caravans with hundreds of camels each.

Having massacred approximately 800,000 inhabitants of Baghdad, including the entire family of the caliphs, the great leaders of the Mongol tribes split up. Some continued the war of conquest toward Syria and Egypt while others turned back in order to consolidate the territories conquered in Persia. These last were joined by Nasir ed-Din, who soon became vizir and confidant of Hulagu Khan, convincing him to build a large observatory in Maragha. Here, surrounded by assistants, he prepared several treatises on mathematics and, for the first time, used trigonometry independently from astronomy. After twelve years of study he published an atlas of the stars and the planetary motions that became known as the *Il-Khanic Tables.*

After Maragha the last stronghold of astronomy was at Samarkand where another conqueror—Timur, or Tamerlane—governed the empire in the fourteenth century. His grandson Ulugh-Beg (born in 1394) built an observatory there that became one of the great wonders of its time. In 1437 Ulugh-Beg published the *Zig Tables,* extremely accurate astronomical tables used in Europe until the eighteenth century.

All the stars of the *Almagest* (except those that were invisible from Samarkand because they were too far to the south) were examined and positioned in the celestial sphere, with their latitudes and longitudes calculated up to a tenth of a degree. The *Zig Tables* were repeatedly translated in Europe in famous editions that could be found in the main libraries. With Ulugh-Beg's death in 1449, the last great Oriental astronomer was gone. However, just as Urania's star was setting in the Orient, it rose again in Europe.

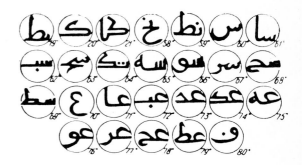

Astronomical writings from Ulugh-Beg's Zig *Tables*

Early Arab library

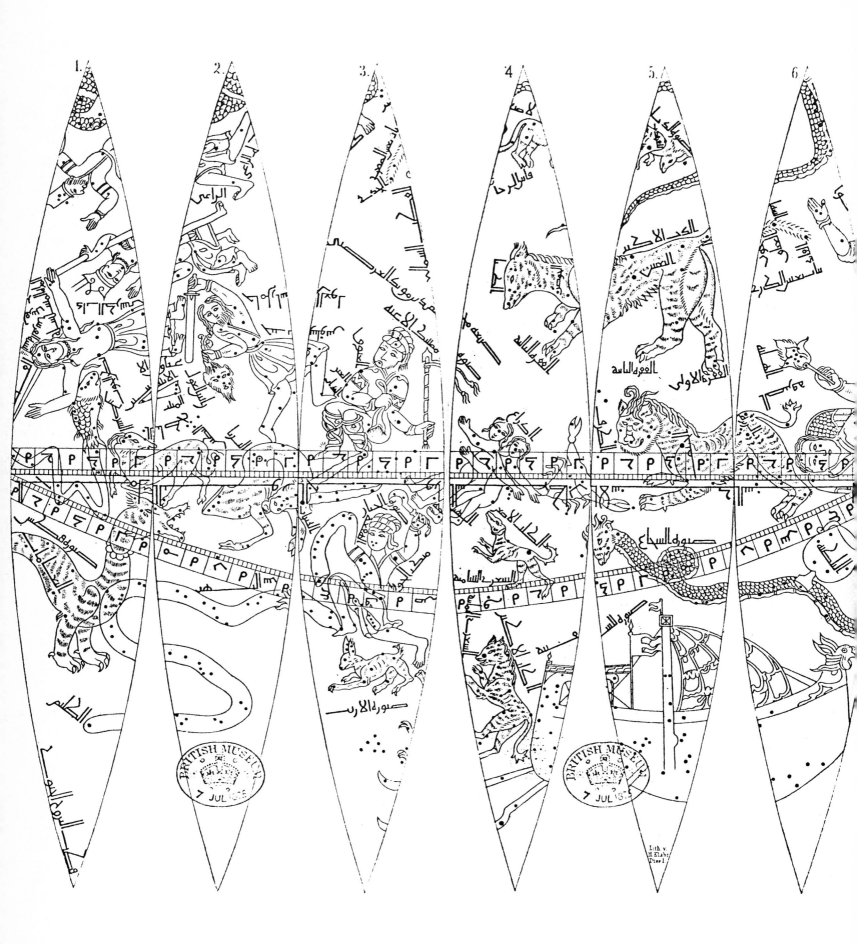

72   *The Glorious Constellations*

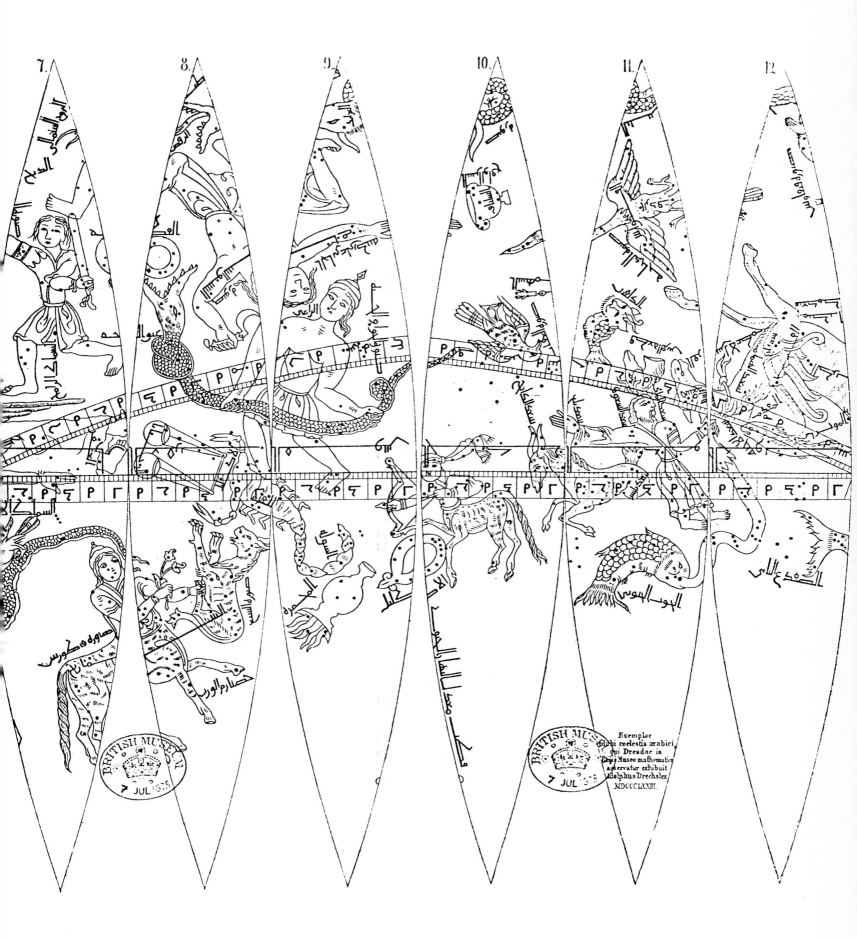

*Plan of the celestial globe of Muhammad
bin Muwajid Elardhi (1279)*

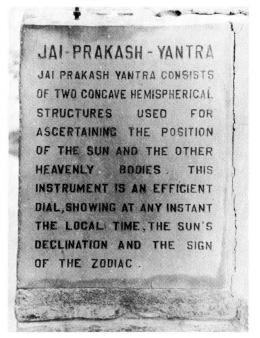

JAI-PRAKASH-YANTRA
JAI PRAKASH YANTRA CONSISTS
OF TWO CONCAVE HEMISPHERICAL
STRUCTURES USED FOR
ASCERTAINING THE POSITION
OF THE SUN AND THE OTHER
HEAVENLY BODIES. THIS
INSTRUMENT IS AN EFFICIENT
DIAL, SHOWING AT ANY INSTANT
THE LOCAL TIME, THE SUN'S
DECLINATION AND THE SIGN
OF THE ZODIAC.

JANTAR MANTAR

Jantar Mantar is an observatory composed of astronomical instruments constructed in masonry, built by Maharaja Jai Singh II of Jaipur (1699–1743). An enthusiastic astronomer, he studied all the systems that were known in both the East and West before embarking on this complex in Delhi. It was realized under the auspices of Emperor Muhammad Shah shortly before 1724. Subsequently, Jai Singh had similar observatories built at Jaipur, Ujjain, Varanasi, and Mathura, the last of which was destroyed. These instruments, plastered with lime, have graduated notches for celestial readings; many instruments have been restored. The best known of the observatory-buildings are Samrat-Yantra, Jai-Prakesh-Yantra, Ram-Yantra, and Misra-Yantra. Photographs by the author

MISRA – YANTRA

A COMPOSITE (MISRA) INSTRUMENT, IT COMPRISES: (i) NIYATA-CHAKRA, IN THE CENTRE INDICATING THE MERIDIAN (NOON) AT FOUR PLACES, TWO IN EUROPE AND ONE EACH IN JAPAN AND THE PACIFIC OCEAN; (ii) PARTS OF SAMRAT-YANTRA ON EITHER SIDE; (iii) DAKSHINOTTARA-BHITTI-YANTRA ON EAST WALL FOR OBTAINING MERIDIAN ALTITUDES; AND (iv) KARKA-RASI-VALAYA ON THE NORTH WALL INDICATING THE ENTRY OF THE SUN IN THE CANCER.

RAM-YANTRA

THE TWO CIRCULAR BUILDINGS WITH A PILLAR AT THE CENTRE OF EACH CONSTITUTE THE RAM-YANTRA, THE WALLS AND FLOORS OF WHICH ARE GRADUATED FOR READING HORIZONTAL (AZIMUTH) AND VERTICAL (ALTITUDE) ANGLES OF THE HEAVENLY BODIES.

Ancient constellations

The Arab mosque in Cordova, Spain,
now a Catholic cathedral

IX
The Sky and the Middle Ages

To the eyes of the sophisticated Arab rulers of Spain, the Europeans on the other side of the Pyrenees must have seemed an uneducated and backward lot. In the eleventh century a Moslem historian wrote, "These barbarians have fat bellies, pale bodies, and light-colored, straight hair. They are devoid of keenness, sensibility, and pure intelligence; they are overcome by ignorance, foolishness, blindness, and stupidity."

The great Islamic culture in Europe resided in Spain and Sicily, and it was through the cultural centers of Cordova, Toledo, Seville, and Siracusa that Latin scholars had their first contact with the Greek-Arabic tradition. In the tenth century, under the reign of the Umayyad caliphs, Cordova vied with Baghdad and Constantinople to be known as the biggest and most beautiful city in the world. Christian travelers who had dared to travel to it returned with stories about the marvelous mosques, the beautiful buildings, one library of 400,000 volumes and another seventy libraries distributed throughout the city, as well as the numerous public baths and hospitals. If the interest of these travelers had been more profound, they would have discovered a vast body of scientific knowledge that was completely unknown to the Latin scholars of the day.

The study of astronomy in Europe before the year 1000 was sparse and fragmentary. The English friar Bede the Venerable (673–735) carried out valuable observations on the equinoxes. The ninth-century scholastic philosopher Johannes Scotus (Erigena) conducted various studies on the planets. The pious Gerbert d'Aurillac (who died in 1003 after serving almost four years as Pope Sylvester II) dedicated himself to the construction of precision instruments for observation of the stars and wrote a book on astrolabes.

Following the civil wars and the resulting abolition of the caliphate in the Iberian peninsula, the Christian kings of Spain armed themselves for the reconquest of Islamic Spain. During the same period the Normans conquered Sicily and so the two European strongholds of Arab culture fell into Christian hands. As European scholars entered, the gates to a deluge of Arab knowledge were opened. French, Italian, German, and English scholars lost no time in consulting the texts in the libraries and translating them from the Arabic. Many Greek texts were translated from the Arabic versions. This was the beginning of that slow process that would later result in the Renaissance and a new world of theology, law, medicine, alchemy, mathematics, astrology, and astronomy. The basic text was Ptolemy's *Almagest,* which contained the work of Hipparchus, Eudoxus, Thales, and the ancient Sumerians.

Many Arab librarians had remained in Toledo, along with a large community of Jewish scholars fleeing religious intolerance. It was with their help that the European researchers faced the tens of thousands of texts as they began their study, classification, and translation.

The impact on European society was enormous. The new knowledge spread and could not be halted. It created a strong and independent lay culture. Universities were set up in Salerno, Bologna, Paris, and Oxford.

Since its foundation the Church had had the task of safeguarding the only acceptable truth—the solidity of the theologic edifice against heathenism and

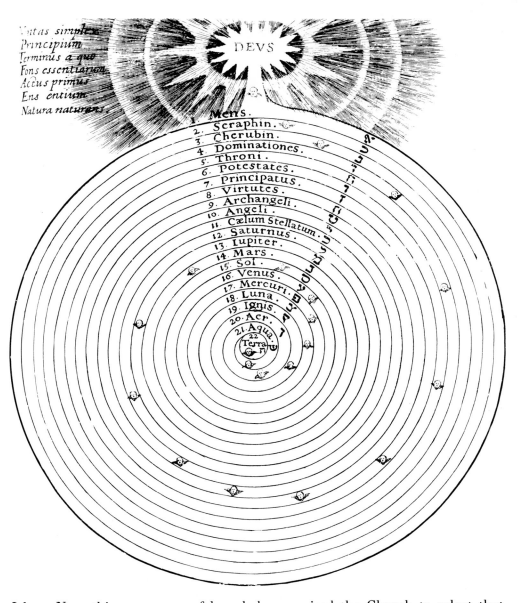

Unitas simplex
Principium
Terminus a quo
Fons essentiarum
Actus primus
Ens entium
Natura naturans

DEVS

Mens.
1. Seraphin.
2. Cherubin.
3. Dominationes.
4. Throni.
5. Potestates.
6. Principatus.
7. Virtutes.
8. Archangeli.
9. Angeli.
10. Cælum Stellatum.
11. Saturnus.
12. Iupiter.
13. Mars.
14. Sol.
15. Venus.
16. Mercuri.
17. Luna.
18. Ignis.
19. Aer.
20. Aer.
21. Aqua
22. Terra

This diagram represents the grafting of Aristotelian theory onto the Christian version of the cosmos

Islam. Now, this new surge of knowledge required the Church to select that which most probably could be adapted to its dogmas. The Dominicans led the way. In the thirteenth century Albertus Magnus Christianized the philosophical concepts of Aristotle so as to present the Greek philosopher as a kind of saint *honoris causa*. Albertus' student St. Thomas Aquinas followed in his master's footsteps and, though he did note the astronomical impracticability of the crystal spheres of Aristotle, he still accepted them as necessary because they supported the faith and the authority of the Church.

Thanks to these two Dominicans, Aristotle's cosmology became an integral part of the Catholic faith second only to the Scriptures. His primum mobile— the prime mover, the outermost concentric sphere in a many-sphere geocentric universe—was identified with God himself and, in this way, in the thirteenth century the cosmos lost its astronomical reality in favor of the moral and religious.

The sky became peopled with a new hierarchy of celestial figures who interceded between God and humans, but who also had godlike motory functions. Thus the seraphim were responsible for moving the sphere of the primum mobile, while the cherubim moved the spheres of the stars. This went on through the celestial hierarchy—from thrones, dominations, virtues, powers, principalities, and archangels all the way down to the angels, who were the protectors of the sphere of the moon. Humans were seen as the final motive of the creation inasmuch as they were the contemplators of God's order. Below were the animals, the plants, the elements, the demons, and the nether regions governed by Lucifer, the fallen angel, and populated by the damned. This was the point farthest away from God, the antithesis of the primum mobile.

This picture was meant to serve a practical and educational purpose, not only in explaining the heavens, but also for all of creation. Apart from some differences in details, it was to be reproduced on large frescoes, mosaics, and cupolas in churches all across Europe.

Dante Alighieri—who had a deep knowledge of astronomy—manages to interweave many astronomical considerations in his *Divine Comedy*. He presents them, however, almost as a secret code in a work that is based on a variant of the above scenario.

The Church of Rome was more familiar with astrology than with scientific investigation. In this area, it followed the indications of Saint Isidore of Seville, who distinguished medical, meteorological, and political astrology from astrology that was prophetic and involved with black magic. If pure research touched on ecclesiastic elements, it was immediately punished, as in the case of Pietro of Abano, who dared to state that miracles could be explained naturally. For this, some time later, he was condemned to die at the stake. Since he had unfortunately already died of natural causes by then, his remains were exhumed and burned. It was worse still for one Cecco of Ascoli, a professor of astrology at the University of Bologna, who was burned at the stake for having tried to study the evil eye and necromancy beyond specific limits set by the Inquisition.

In most cases, however, astrologers enjoyed a relatively secure position in the eyes of the Church; popes and cardinals regularly asked their advice. Such innovative scientists as Bruno and Galileo would be the ones to pay for having strayed from the cosmological model imposed by the Church.

With the passing of the years, libraries expanded and more and more Greek literature, translated into Latin, was read. This wave of philosophy and mythology succeeded in lightening the heavy atmosphere of scholasticism and contributed enormously to the revolution of the Renaissance, which accepted the world as a place given to men and women to enjoy and make use of in the best way possible.

In Italy the mythological-pagan reaction was so strong that, for a time, it seemed that paganism would replace Christianity.

Aristotle

God as the architect of the universe. From Introduction au monde des symboles

Lucifer imprisoned in the frozen lake. Illustration by Gustave Doré

Celestial influences on the human body. From Sibyl, Key to Physick *(1790)*

Opposite: Virgil and Dante returning from Hell *under a starry sky. Illustration by Gustave Doré*

We mounted up, he first and I the second,
Till I beheld through a round aperture
Some of those beauteous things which Heaven doth bear;
Thence we came forth to rebehold the stars.

Dante, Inferno, 34.136–9

The rediscovery of heliocentrism

X
The Revolution of the Renaissance

The victorious entrance of Ottoman Sultan Muhammad II into Constantinople in 1453 marked the end of the last bulwark of the Roman Empire of the East. As a result of this collapse, many scholars and scientists who had maintained Constantinople as a center of knowledge emigrated to Italy. They found asylum in many of the city-states of the peninsula, above all, in Florence, which was the capital of the arts.

The Aristotelian-scholastic atmosphere that permeated the Middle Ages was too heavy a burden for the requirements of a society in need of new cultural stimuli. This explains the enormous impact of the philosophy of Plato—who brought liberalism and independence from dogma—on artists, scientists, and princes. This philosophy was based on the concept of the supreme harmony of the cosmos, a harmony that could be studied and explained rationally. The importance of Plato to the Italian Renaissance was not due so much to his scientific discoveries: it was that he demonstrated the method by which freedom of investigation and thought had to proceed. It was through his teachings that the attempt by the Church of Rome to enslave philosophy to theology was undermined at its very foundations. Although the Inquisition strenuously defended its positions, the most enlightened spirits could continue to conduct independent research.

Plato

Actually, the story of this new course had started before the fall of Constantinople, when the Byzantine emperor had participated in the Council of Ferrara in 1438, and had ordered Bessarion, the bishop of Nicaea, to bring as a gift about eight hundred manuscripts of Greek philosophy that were safeguarded in Constantinople. Bessarion, a man of great culture, decided to remain in Italy in order to make public this small library of knowledge that would become such an important factor in the establishment of the Renaissance. In Vienna a few years later, he met the astronomers Peuerbach and Regiomontanus; the latter followed him to Italy where he studied Greek to be able to read the ancient texts in the original. Peuerbach published the famous *Ephemerides*—the star tables for the years 1475–1506, which were used by such seafarers as Amerigo Vespucci and Christopher Columbus for their voyages.

The cultural situation in Italy was one of badly concealed revolt against the tyranny of dogmatic scholasticism. Petrarch, Boccaccio, and Dante had prepared minds and hearts for the transformations of the Renaissance in all the capitals, from Genoa to Venice, Florence, Naples, Bologna, and, with the papacy of Leo X, Rome. In this heated atmosphere, Plato had the effect of a welcome thunderstorm that drives the clouds away. Marsilio Ficino and Pico della Mirandola in Florence and, later, Annibale Caro in Rome were some of the intellectuals who indicated the road the artist of the Renaissance would take to look at nature with new and inquiring eyes, come to know new laws of perception, and rediscover classicism.

The discovery of perspective, the artifice that produces a three-dimensional effect on a flat surface, was made at this time. Paolo Uccello, Leon Battista Alberti, Sandro Botticelli, Domenico Ghirlandaio, and Michelangelo were all

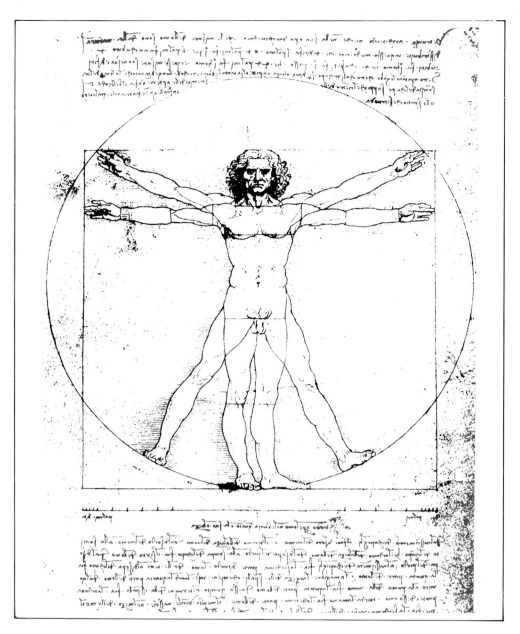

Leonardo da Vinci, proportions of the human body, Venice, Accademia (1492)

Agrippa, man and the macrocosm

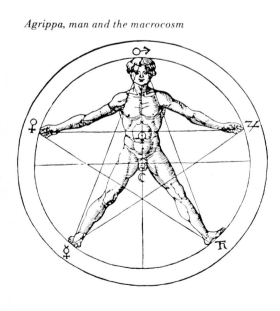

creators of the new science of harmonious vision, but Leonardo da Vinci stood out above all. The central figure of the Renaissance, he was able, with the same self-assurance, to paint the *Last Supper*, study the anatomy of humans and animals, and design war machinery or flying machines. In astronomy he was the first to explain why one can indistinctly see the rest of the moon's face when one observes the sickle of the new moon—because of the reflected light of the sun. In thinking about the problem of motion, he wrote, ''The sun does not move''; and with regard to the earth, ''It is not in the middle of the circle of the sun, nor is it in the middle of the world.'' To his creative mind we owe the drawing of the proportions of the human body where a man in the nude is drawn within a circle and a square. This drawing would become the symbol of modern science, replacing Aristotle's primum mobile.

Meanwhile, seafarers ventured out onto the vast and unknown oceans determined to demonstrate in practice that the earth was a sphere. Columbus discovered the Americas, Ferdinand Magellan circumnavigated the globe, and Amerigo Vespucci quietly navigated the southern hemisphere while drawing the first constellations of a new and mysterious sky.

Gradually the representations of the ancient constellations began to assume new personalities as they grew away from the model of the Arab records that had come to Europe with the *Alfonsine Tables*; they began to refer more closely to scenes of daily life or Greco-Roman mythology and art.

In the fourteenth century the walls of the Palazzo della Ragione in Padua were covered with frescoes of astrological allegories inspired by the *Astrolabium planum* of Pietro of Abano. These frescoes consisted of about three hundred figures shown in attitudes of daily life, distributed over twelve zodiacal cycles. In another work of this type, we can admire the frescoes that Francesco del Cossa painted in the Salone dei Mesi in the Palazzo Schifanoia in Ferrara; the style of these paintings, done in 1470, is freer than the more rigid medieval example of the Ragione building. We must place the marvelous ceiling that Baldassare Peruzzi painted in the Sala di Galatea in Rome's Villa Farnesina (1511) in the tradition of the classical-astronomical allegory. It is a symbolic interpretation of the horoscope of Agostino Chigi, prince and protector of the arts. (It is beautifully described in the thirteenth chapter of *Le Fede negli Astri* by Fritz Saxl.) What is remarkable about this cycle, apart from the artistic quality of the execution, is the use of the fixed stars in the compilation of the horoscope with Ursa Major and Pegasus in the center and surrounded by Crater, Corona Borealis, Lyra, Ara, Sagitta, Hydra, Corvus, etc.

Then, in 1573–75 the masterpiece of Renaissance astronomy, perhaps the most beautiful representation of the sky and its stars ever, was created. Unfortunately, we do not know the name of the artist who painted the ceiling of the Sala del Mappamondo in the Villa Farnese of Caprarola, near Viterbo. Whoever he was, he succeeded in giving life to the ultimate merging of science and art with a true sense for beauty and with geometric precision. This great celestial map, erroneously called zodiacal, represents all the constellations that are visible from the latitude of Alexandria in Egypt (which reveals the Ptolemaic origin of the design). This design is immersed in an atmosphere that is vibrantly alive, in which the figures, strewn with gilded stars, are harmoniously suspended in the cobalt blue of the sky. The elegance of the bodies and the execution of the faces and the animals in the drawings complement to perfection the general equilibrium of the entire fresco. For some reason this admirable work is not as well known as it should be. We are remedying this at once by presenting it in the color plates of this book.

Representations of the sky and its stars multiplied as they became more and more distant from the Arab tradition and ever closer to the Greco-Latin one. The most beautiful images are those engraved by Dürer, the German artist who came to Italy toward the end of the fifteenth century, who immersed himself in

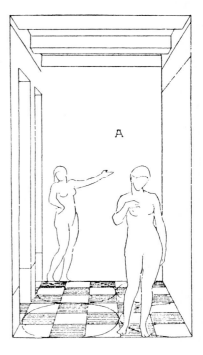

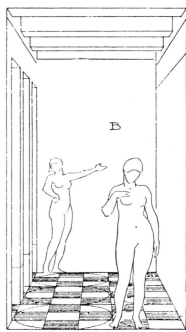

The effects of perspective: (A) short range, and (B) long range. From Hatton, Figure Composition

Marsilio Ficino

the Renaissance vision and became a versatile creator of the mode of Leonardo. In Nuremberg in 1515, Dürer published two splendid circular planispheres, one for the northern hemisphere and one for the southern. These celestial maps were of such high quality that Johannes Bayer copied the figures from Dürer with very few exceptions when he published his famous *Uranometria* in 1603.

The celestial vault was revisited with new zeal. The Latin translation of Aratus' *Phaenomena* by Germanicus and Cicero was republished under the name of *Aratea*. *Poetica astronomica*, an anthology of the myths connected with the constellations, written by Hyginus in the first century B.C., was also republished.

Translations of Aristarchus' works started several researchers thinking about possible theories about the earth's motion and the centrality of the sun. Celius Calcagnini (1479–1541) declared that it was the earth that turned, not the sun and the stars. In 1496 the young Nicolaus Copernicus (1473–1543) arrived in Italy from Poland. He spent ten years studying in Bologna and Padua, visiting Rome, and getting a degree in Ferrara. During this period the young man had the opportunity to soak up the cultural upheavals of the Renaissance. He studied Greek, read Plato and Aristarchus, and struck up a friendship with the astronomer Domenicus Maria from Novara with whom he conducted regular observations of the sky and stars. When Copernicus returned to his own country, he was convinced that the heliocentric theories of Aristarchus were correct and was determined to discover the evidence that would prove them to be true, and in 1543 he published *De revolutionibus orbium coelestium* (*On the Revolutions of the Celestial Spheres*). In addition to physically demonstrating

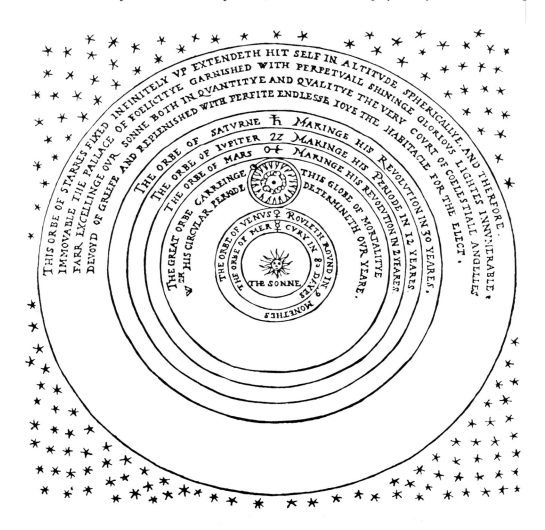

Copernicus' heliocentric system

heliocentric theory, he succeeded, with this book, in refuting all opposing arguments based on philosophical, religious, naturalistic, and scientific preconceptions. In so doing, he managed to transform Aristarchus' geometric model into a real and concrete theory that took into consideration important physical facts such as relative motion.

His announcement of heliocentric theory came at a particularly turbulent time in the history of the Church: the breaking away of the Protestants. This crisis forced the Vatican to take an especially strong stand against any theory contrary to official Aristotelian dogma. Copernicus' work was declared heretical and banned. Anyone who studied or practiced it would have to contend with the Inquisition. The Protestants, who were very preoccupied with the literal reading of the Holy Scriptures, condemned Copernicus' work, and Martin Luther called Copernicus "another mad astrologer who wants to overthrow the entire science of astronomy; but, as the Holy Scripture shows, it was the sun and not the earth that was ordered by Joshua to halt."

Partly due to fear and partly to the technical complexity of *De revolutionibus*, heliocentric theory was known to only a few scholars in Europe at first. It seemed almost destined for oblivion until a new philosophic course that took its inspiration from the thinkers of the school of Miletus and from Democritus came along. Known as Philosophic Naturalism, it had as its followers such southern philosophers as Bernardino Telesio of Cosenza, a student of optics, medicine, and mathematics; Tommaso Campanella of Stilo, an admirer and correspondent of Galileo; and Giordano Bruno of Nola. Their thinking was significant in the struggle to keep theology separate from science.

Copernicus

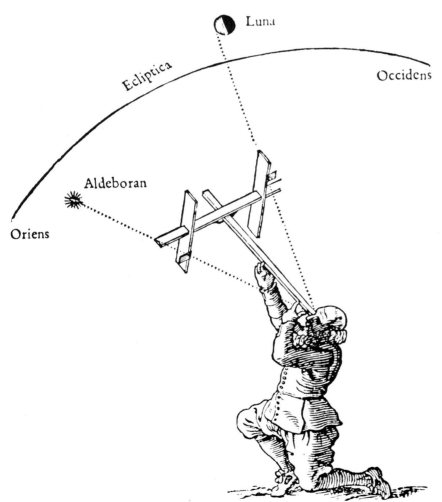

Calculating the angle between Aldebaran and the moon with respect to the ecliptic

Tycho Brahe

Galileo

Uraniborg, Tycho Brahe's observatory

The true public launching of Copernicus' theories in Europe and the beginning of their popularization came with the great charismatic figure of Giordano Bruno (1548–1600). Not only did he understand the implications of the heliocentric planetary system but, in applying them, he took the vision of the universe to its logical extreme. A man of great poetic and scientific imagination, unfettered by preconceptions, Bruno was very much like Anaximander; both rationally contemplated the Great Infinite—the beginning and end of all things in which the cosmological event occurs. Bruno applied the laws of relative motion to the solar system and noted that the laws were valid for all the stars, which had an imperceptible movement of their own. Bruno saw the entire universe as a physical entity based on valid principles, both in microcosm and in macrocosm. The result of this vision was that the earth not only lost its immobility but also ceased to be the center of creation: it became a small, negligible fragment mounted in a grandiose, infinite setting.

Confirmed by new data uncovered by the discoveries of Copernicus, this news had the effect of an earthquake in Europe, at that time dominated by the Catholic-Protestant duel. Bruno had the courage—and the impudence—to announce his theories in Naples, Geneva, Toulouse, Paris, London, Germany, and finally, in Venice. Everywhere he had to flee as he was violently accused of heresy. Finally the Venetian nobleman Mocenigo turned him in to the Inquisition. After years of prison and torture, refusing to retract his theories, Bruno was sentenced to be burned alive. The execution took place on February 17, 1600, at the beginning of a new century, in the Campo dei Fiori in Rome.

How far away was the freedom the Greek philosophers had enjoyed two thousand years earlier, and how petty was the exploitation of the infamous stake by the Protestants who accused the Inquisition of barbaric acts—despite the fact that they would have been glad to light the fire themselves. The widespread shame over the death of Giordano Bruno, in fact, saved Galileo's life, but he too experienced the heavy hand of religious censure: he was sentenced to the humiliation of silence and exile.

Thanks to *De revolutionibus* of Copernicus, the marvelously accurate observations done by Tycho Brahe in his observatory of Uraniborg ("City of the Sky"), Johannes Kepler's laws of motion, the ground-breaking discoveries of Galileo, and, later on, the new laws of Newton, astronomical research experi-

URANOMETRIA

Figurální atlas význačných souhvězdí
severní a jižní oblohy podle díla
Jana Bayera: URANOMETRIA z roku 1603.

Upravil a doplnil
JOSEF KLEPEŠTA

enced a prodigious change in quality, broadened by the new horizons that the invention of the telescope opened up. It became necessary to have better-organized representations of the constellations so as to undertake a more-detailed study of the stars. Voyages in the southern hemisphere had presented the problem of vast celestial zones with unnamed star groups, so astronomers began to invent new constellations.

In 1603 the German Johannes Bayer published a star atlas entitled *Uranometria*, in which twelve new southern hemisphere constellations appeared for the first time. There were a total of 709 stars labeled with—and this was new— Greek letters. This system, still in use today, marks the brightest star of the constellation with the letter alpha (α), the second brightest with beta (β), the third with gamma (γ), and so on. After the Greek letter follows the genitive of the Latin name of the constellation. Thus, Aldebaran in Taurus becomes Alpha Tauri, Merak in Ursa Major becomes Beta Ursae Majoris, and so on. Following Bayer's catalogue, new constellations were published in *Planishoerium stellatum* of 1624 by Jakob Bartsch (Bartschius), Kepler's *Rudolphine Tables* of 1627, the tables of Augustin Royer of 1679, and, in the same year, *Catalogue of Southern Stars*, published by Edmund Halley with observations compiled from St. Helena island.

In 1660 Andrew Cellarius published star maps that represented the constellations as seen from above, with a transparent, internal sphere that represented the earth. Prints of the celestial vault and celestial globes began to appear in the royal and noble houses all over Europe, their quality continually being perfected. Among the more interesting were certainly those published in 1690 by Johannes Hevelius with the title *Uranographia totum coelum stellatum*. It contained a catalogue of 1,564 stars compiled on the basis of visual observation; this is the most accurate catalogue in the history of stellar observation before the advent of the telescope. As his inspiration for this compilation, Hevelius used the *Zig Tables* that Ulugh-Beg had composed in Samarkand. Nine new constellations appear in Hevelius' atlas.

Johannes Hevelius and his wife observing the stars with Hevelius' machina coelestis *(celestial machine)*

Having founded the Royal Observatory at Greenwich, the English astronomer John Flamsteed produced an extremely beautiful *Historia coelestis* that was widely distributed in the Anglo-Saxon world and contributed to him being named the first Astronomer Royal.

The fashion of inventing constellations, unfortunately, showed no signs of abating. This practice reached truly absurd limits at times, as in the case of the French abbot Nicolas Louis de Lacaille (1713–1762). On a trip to southern Africa, he succeeded in determining the position of ten thousand stars of the southern sky; he decided to introduce in his *Coelum australe stelliferum* fourteen new constellations inspired by artists' instruments or scientific instruments: Telescopium, Microscopium, Horologium, and so on. These new constellations, unfortunately, were not relegated only to the virgin southern sky but were scattered just about everywhere, even among the ancient constellations, without logical continuity. So it happened that the area of the sky called the Sea in antiquity, where the rivers Eridanus and Aquarius flowed, was filled with constellations like Fornax Chemica, Machina Electrica, and Machina Pneumatica.

Bizarre, interesting, and certainly worthy of separate study was the attempt by certain Christian astronomers to eliminate completely the ancient pagan constellations and replace them with biblical figures. The first exponent of this school can be said to have been Bede the Venerable, but he and many others were dominated by the figures of the Germans Johannes Bayer and Julius Schiller. They were the creators of the beautiful maps drawn in the *Coelum stellatum christianum* (1627), in which the twelve signs of the zodiac became the twelve apostles, Ophiuchus became St. Benedict, Ursa Major became the Ship of St. Peter, Pegasus became St. Gabriel, and so on. Fortunately, the thousand-year-old charisma of the pagan constellations succeeded in suppressing this iconoclastic attempt. The Christian sky appeared for a time next to the classical representations and was then gradually abandoned.

In eighteenth-century France the astronomers Pierre Charles Lemonnier and Joseph Jérôme de Lalande published beautiful star maps. In *Astronomie* by the latter, there were eighty-eight constellations for the two hemispheres. In Germany, in 1800, Johann Elert Bode published a *Uranographia* with nine new constellations that were never adopted. In 1840 the astronomer Friedrich Wilhelm Argelander published the most complete catalogue of the sky of his time. It contained 210,000 stars—so many that he had to outline the constellations in order to separate them. This method was immediately accepted by all astronomers and remained in use until 1928 when the International Astronomical Union accepted Belgian astronomer E. Delporte's suggestion to define the borders of the constellations by the lines of right ascension and declination. This system is still in use today in modern star catalogues, which provide eighty-eight constellations accumulated by physicist-astronomers alone, without the advice of mythologists, who could organize the constellations in a way that would be consistent and harmonious with the ancient world of the stars.

Urania, the Muse of astronomy. From Flammarion, Astronomie populaire

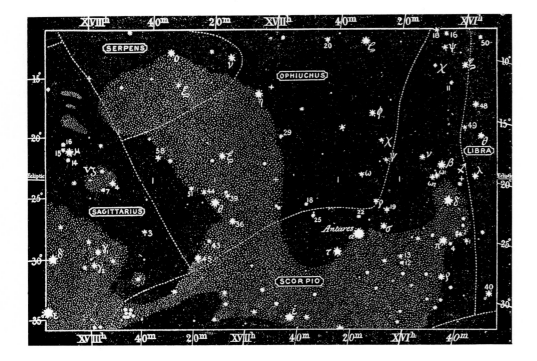

The borders between the constellations, according to Argelander

ALBRECHT DÜRER, CONSTELLATIONS OF THE NORTHERN HEMISPHERE (1515)

ALBRECHT DÜRER, CONSTELLATIONS OF THE SOUTHERN HEMISPHERE (1515)

NORTHERN HEMISPHERE

From W. Peck, The Constellations *(1884)*

SOUTHERN HEMISPHERE

From W. Peck, The Constellations *(1884)*

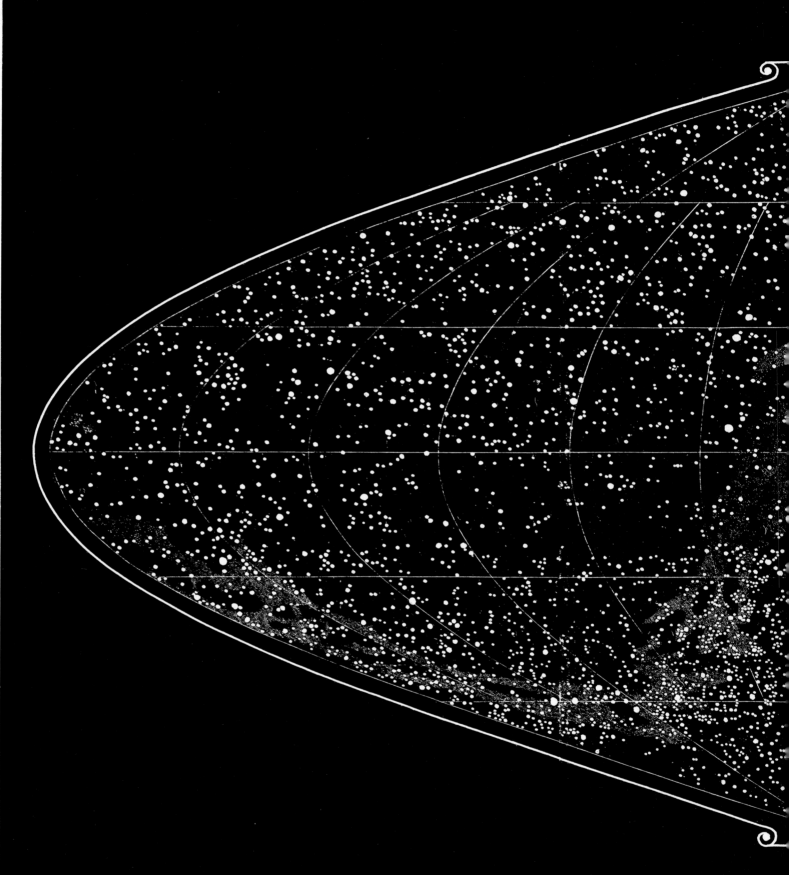

THE STAR – SPHERE ON FLAMSTEED S PROJECTION (

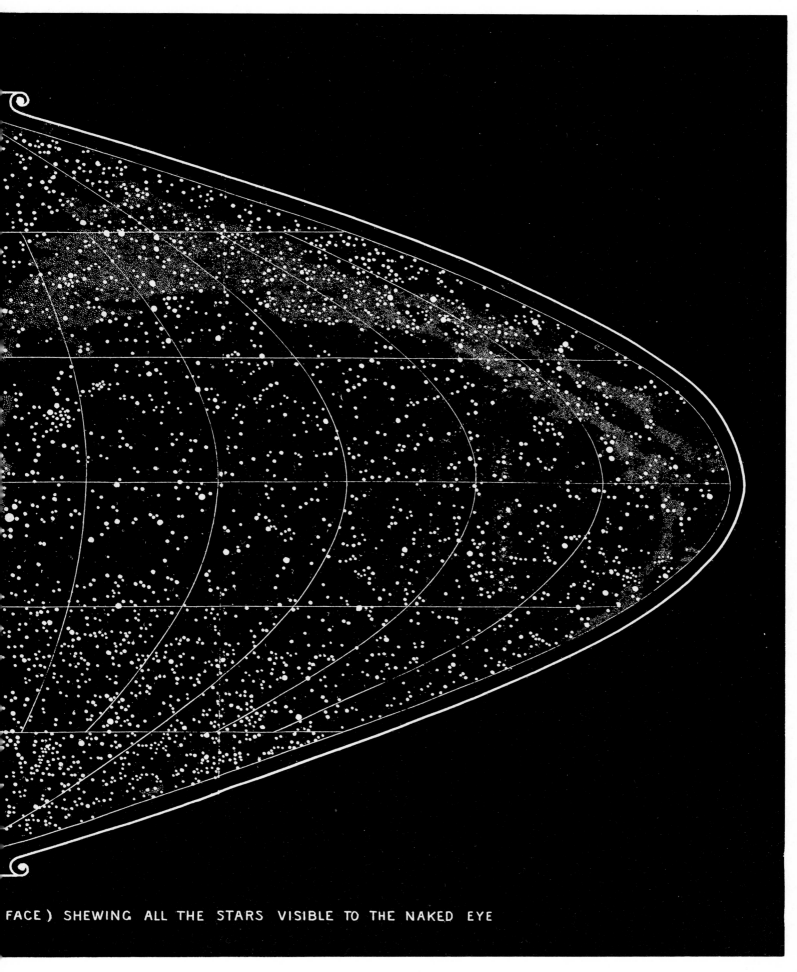

FACE) SHEWING ALL THE STARS VISIBLE TO THE NAKED EYE

FLAMSTEED'S PLANISPHERE, SHOWING THE STARS VISIBLE TO THE NAKED EYE

NORTHERN HEMISPHERE

The principal stars visible to the naked eye.
Stereographic projection by Proctor

SOUTHERN HEMISPHERE

The principal stars visible to the naked eye.
Stereographic projection by Proctor

NORTHERN HEMISPHERE

From Houzeau, Atlas de tous les étoiles
visibles, *Paris (1878)*

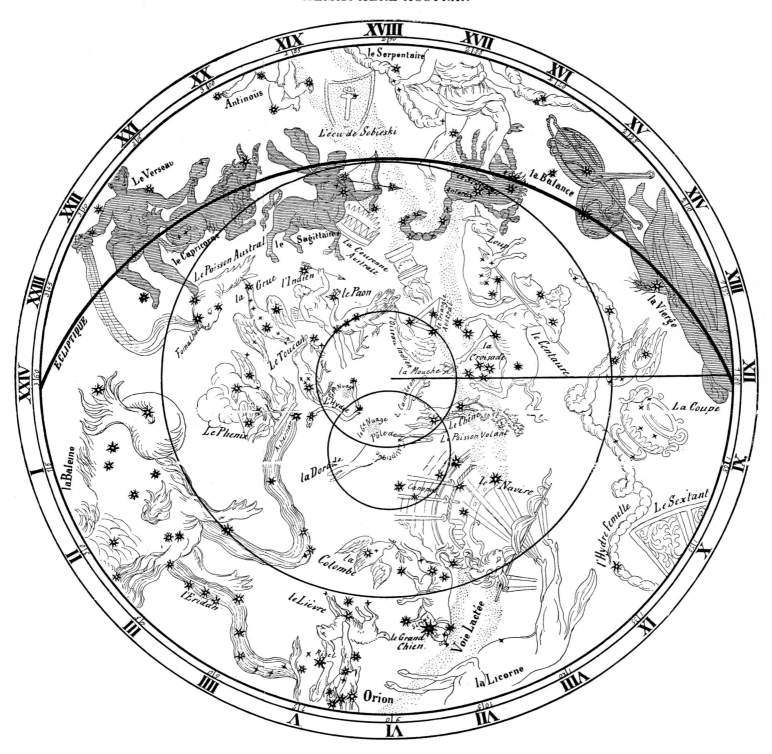

SOUTHERN HEMISPHERE

From Houzeau, Atlas de tous les étoiles
visibles, *Paris (1878)*

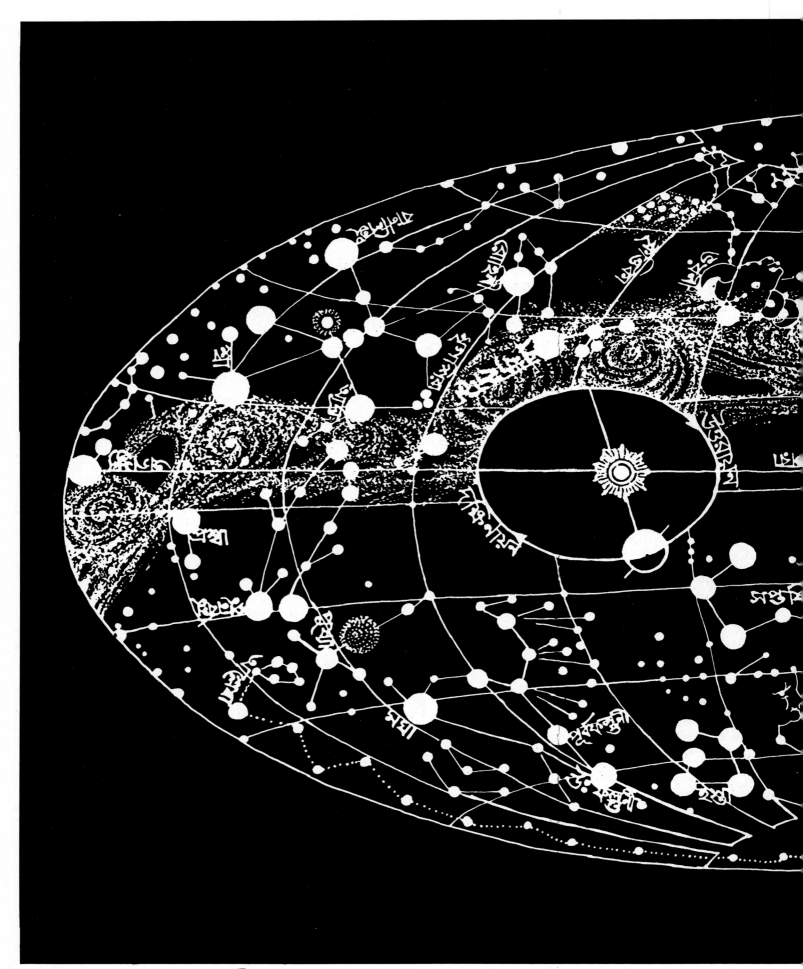

ব্রহ্মাণ্ডের নাক্ষত্রিক মানচিত্র

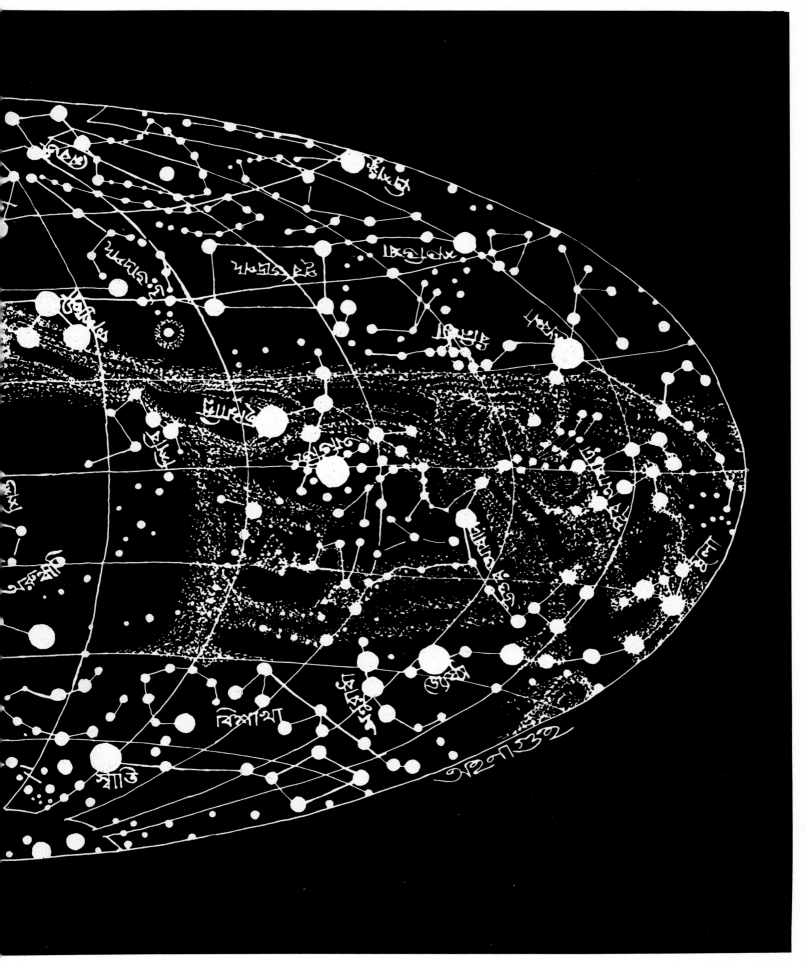

INDIAN PLANISPHERE

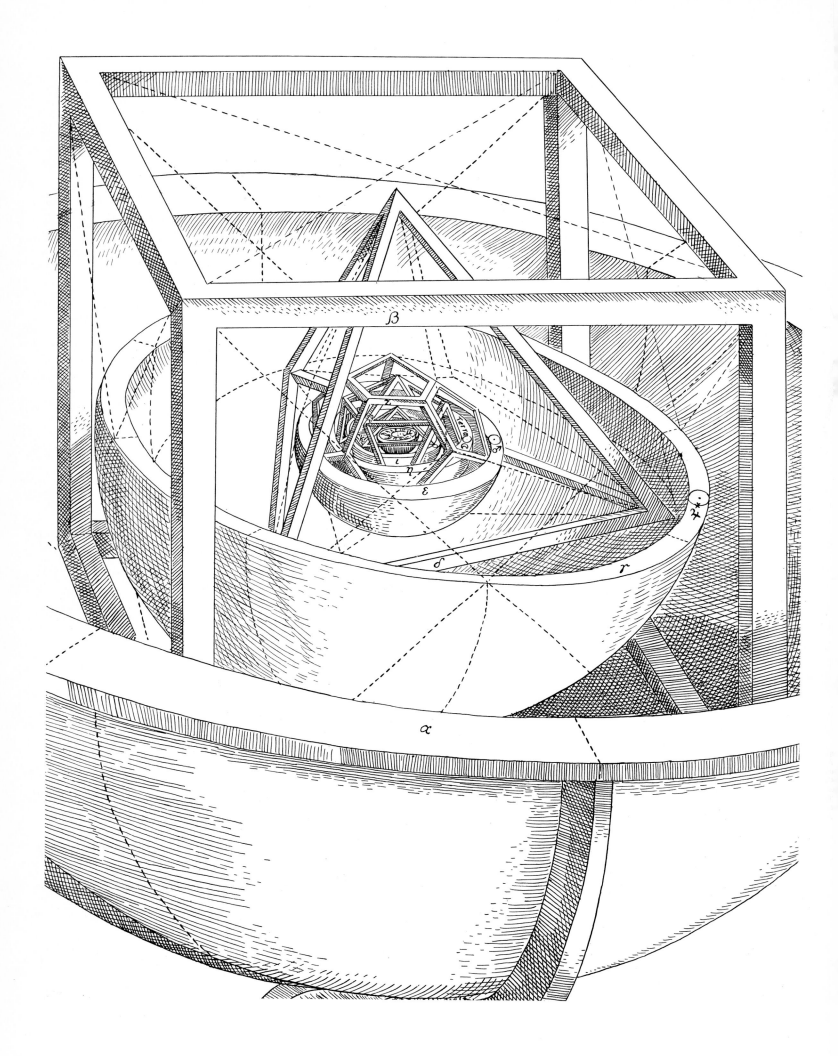

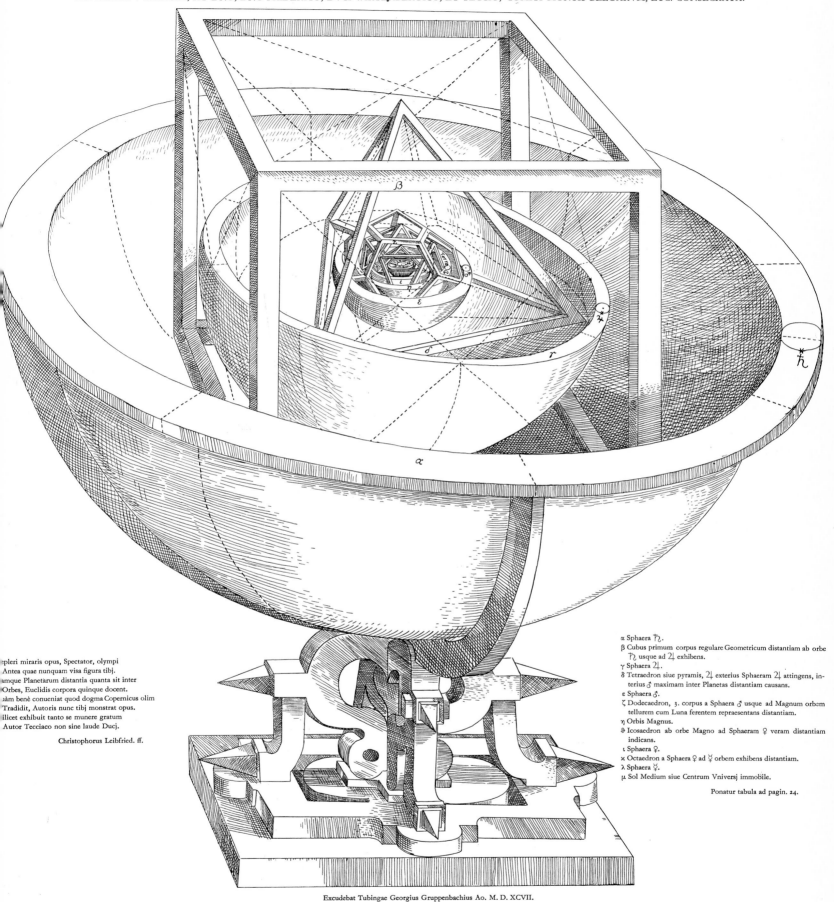

TABELLA III.

ORBIVM PLANETARVM DIMENSIONES, ET DISTANTIAS PER QVINQVE REGVLARIA CORPORA GEOMETRICA EXHIBENS.
ILLVSTRISSº. PRINCIPI, AC DŇO, DŇO FRIDERICO, DVCI WIRTENBERGICO, ET TECCIO, COMITI MONTIS BELGARVM, ETC. CONSECRATA.

epleri miraris opus, Spectator, olympi
Antea quae nunquam visa figura tibj.
amque Planetarum distantia quanta sit inter
Orbes, Euclidis corpora quinque docent.
uàm benè conueniat quod dogma Copernicus olim
Tradidit, Autoris nunc tibj monstrat opus.
ilicet exhibuit tanto se munere gratum
Autor Tecciaco non sine laude Ducj.

Christophorus Leibfried. ff.

α Sphaera ♄.
β Cubus primum corpus regulare Geometricum distantiam ab orbe
  ♄ usque ad ♃ exhibens.
γ Sphaera ♃.
δ Tetraedron siue pyramis, ♃ exterius Sphaeram ♃ attingens, in-
  terius ♂ maximam inter Planetas distantiam causans.
ε Sphaera ♂.
ζ Dodecaedron, 3. corpus a Sphaera ♂ usque ad Magnum orbem
  tellurem cum Luna ferentem repraesentans distantiam.
η Orbis Magnus.
ϑ Icosaedron ab orbe Magno ad Sphaeram ♀ veram distantiam
  indicans.
ι Sphaera ♀.
ϰ Octaedron a Sphaera ♀ ad ☿ orbem exhibens distantiam.
λ Sphaera ☿.
μ Sol Medium siue Centrum Vniversj immobile.

Ponatur tabula ad pagin. 24.

Excudebat Tubingae Georgius Gruppenbachius Ao. M. D. XCVII.

Kepler's application of the geometric models of
Pythagoras to the planet's orbits, according to the
heliocentric concept of the solar system

NORTHERN HEMISPHERE

From Andrew Cellarius, Harmonica
macrocosmica *(1660)*

SOUTHERN HEMISPHERE

From Andrew Cellarius, Harmonica
macrocosmica *(1660)*

NORTHERN HEMISPHERE

Coelum stellatum christianum *(1627)*

SOUTHERN HEMISPHERE

Coelum stellatum christianum *(1627)*

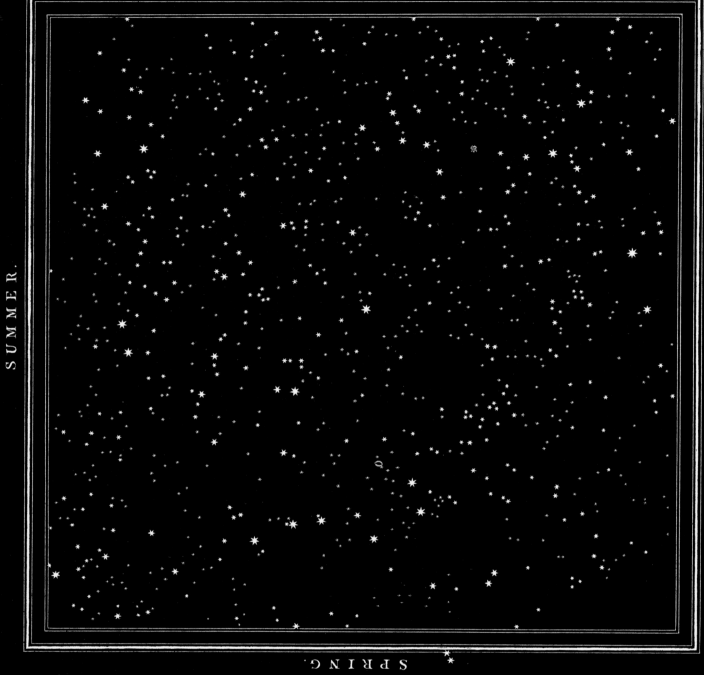

MIDDLETON CELESTIAL ATLAS (1843)

*Circumpolar constellations at nine o'clock
at night during each of the four seasons*
Opposite: *The constellations exactly as they
are seen in the sky—not inverted, as they are
on celestial globes*

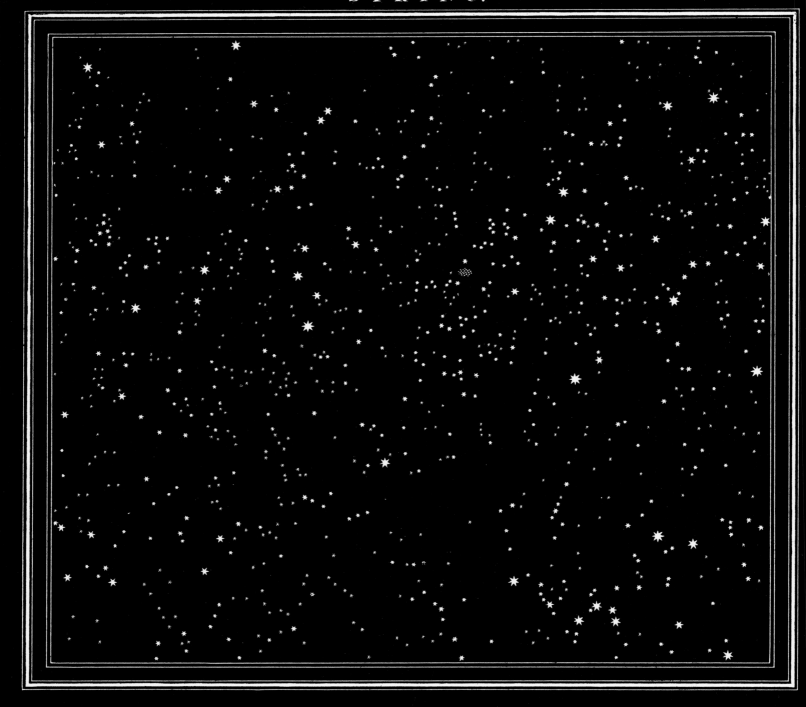

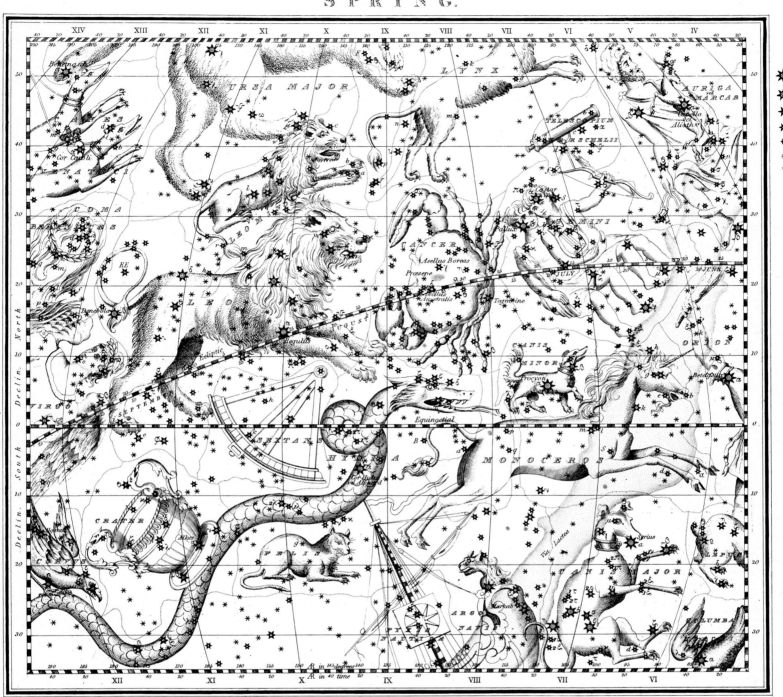

MIDDLETON CELESTIAL ATLAS (1843)   SPRING

*Constellations visible in the evening during
the spring*
Opposite: *The constellations exactly as they
are seen in the sky—not inverted, as they are
on celestial globes*

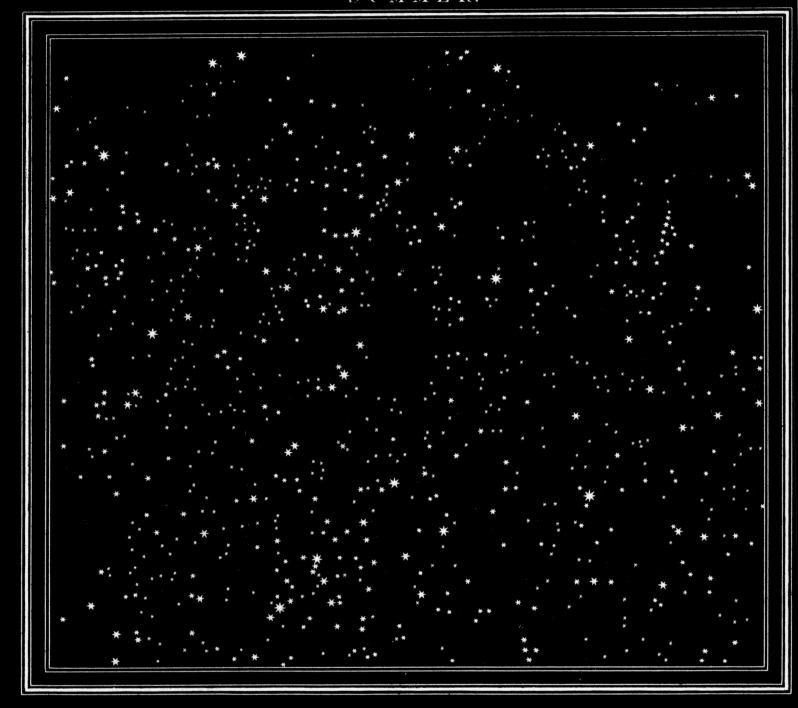

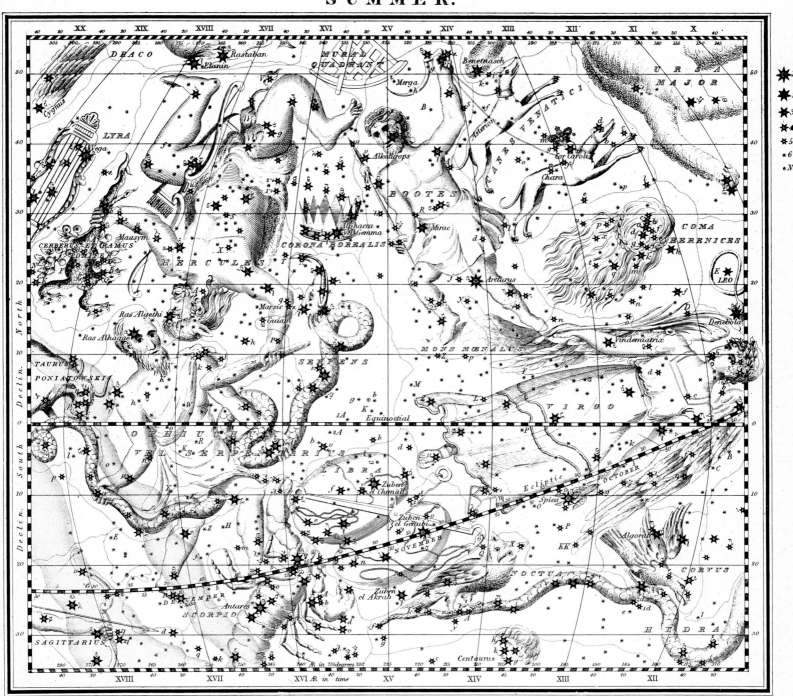

MIDDLETON CELESTIAL ATLAS (1843)   SUMMER

*Constellations visible in the evening during
the summer*
Opposite: *The constellations exactly as they
are seen in the sky—not inverted, as they are
on celestial globes*

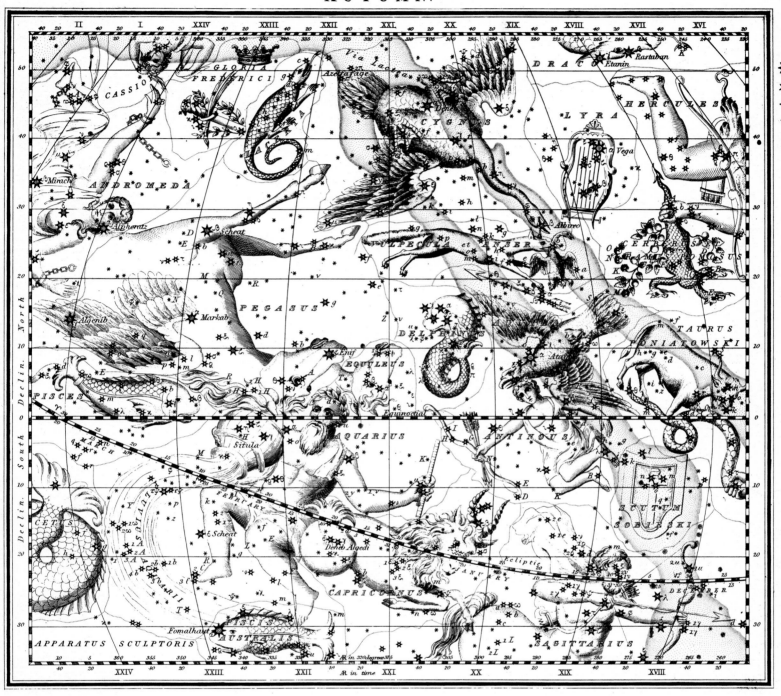

MIDDLETON CELESTIAL ATLAS (1843)   AUTUMN

*Constellations visible in the evening during
the autumn*
Opposite: *The constellations exactly as they
are seen in the sky—not inverted, as they are
on celestial globes*

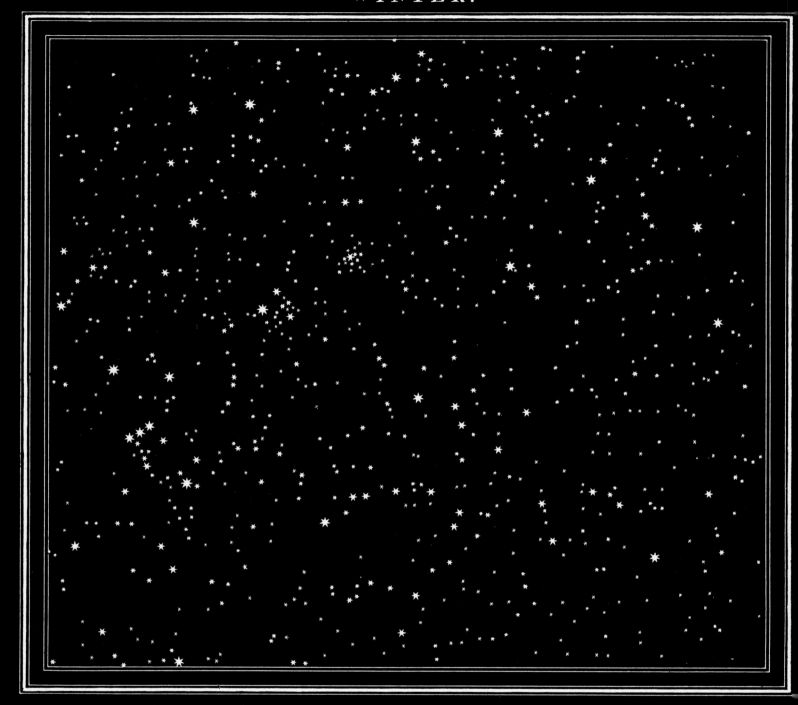

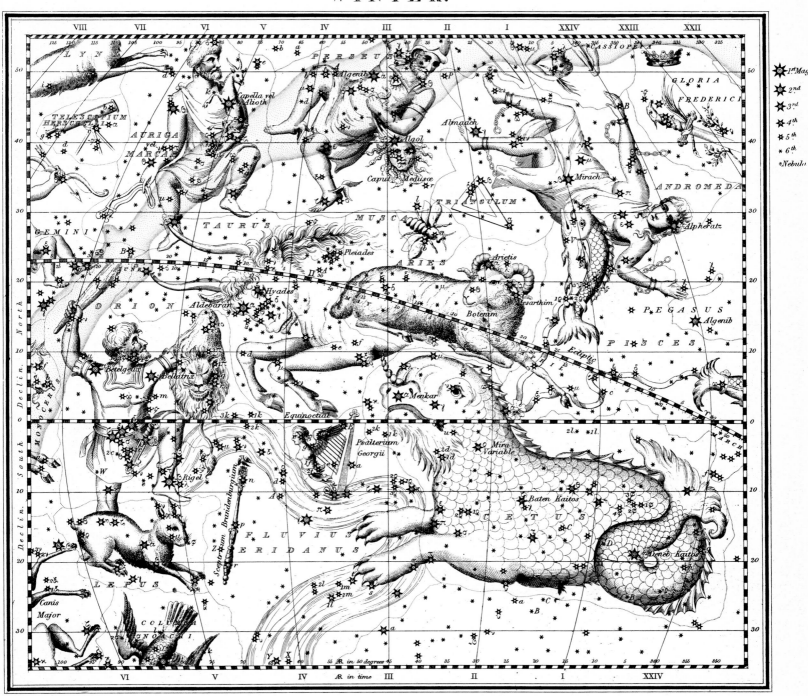

MIDDLETON CELESTIAL ATLAS (1843)   WINTER

*Constellations visible in the evening during
the winter*
Opposite: *The constellations exactly as they
are seen in the sky—not inverted, as they are
on celestial globes*

All color photographs of the fresco on the following pages were taken by Isidoro Genovese.

The Cosmography of the Sala del Mappamondo, Villa Farnese, Caprarola, Italy

The heavens are the imagination's ideal domain. There we can see depicted, with invisible threads tying one star to another, marvelous figures projected from our imagination. Indeed, cosmography resembles nothing so much as a great zoo in which animals and deities, people and ships are captured.

It took a painter to give shape to our projections, the slides our eyes superimpose on the sky's plane. It happened, and with precision, at the Villa Farnese in Caprarola, Italy, where the celestial sphere is represented, not symbolically, but graphically and anthropomorphically. If we think of its illustrious predecessors, such as the Salone dei Mesi in the Palazzo Schifanoia in Ferrara, where a nominal symbolism with no direct relationship to the sky dominates, we can appreciate the singular spirit that moved the animator and painter of the Caprarola project. Here, the heavens are peopled with human and animal figures that correspond exactly to the positions of the stars.

The bodies emanate from the stars. The intent to instruct is evident: certainly the vault, begun around 1573 for the Sala del Mappamondo in the Villa Farnese, provides the astrological key for the iconographical program of the room's decoration, which was completed in 1575, as we can read between the grotesques in the alcove of a window beside the map of Europe.

The program was dictated by Orazio Trigini De Marij, whom Ignatio Danti, in his *Commentari a le due Regole della Prospettiva Pratica* of Vignola, mentions as a designer of instruments used for drawing in perspective. In a letter of March 4, 1573, from Fulvio Orsini to Cardinal Alessandro Farnese, we read:

"I am sending your most illustrious excellcy my friend's lecture on the subject of the cosmography of the Caprarola room, so that, seeing it, you may determine what is to be done . . . . My friend's doctrine and practice is [*sic*] good and founded on good authors, besides the spice he brings by virtue of his being well-versed in Roman antiquities, whence he will derive many things for the celestial dreams, for which he also has an extremely old, handwritten Hyginus, with colored drawings as they are to be placed."

In another letter, of September 6, Orsini adds: "As regards the painter that yr excellcy wrote me to find, I have been most diligent, and there seem to be few who would come to Caprarola and that would satisfy yr excellcy." However, while the name of the painter of the maps is known—Giovanni Antonio da Varese, who about ten years earlier painted the cosmography in the third loggia of the Vatican Palace— and the authorship of the other wall decorations is divided between Raffaellino da Reggio and Giovanni De Vecchi, the painter of the ceiling remains unknown.

Roli suggests it might have been either Lelio Orsi or Bertoja. Certainly the question admits of no easy solution, even though the elegant learning of the Master of the Cosmography "appears, indeed, peculiarly Emilian, and more specifically, Parmesan." Photographs of the present work reveal it to have the same transparency, or thinness of material, as the Bertoja fragments in the Palazzo del Giardino in Parma, although the formal dynamic of the latter, even against the ethereal background of the sky, appears heavier and displays less evocative power. Our unknown painter cuts out his figures, isolating them like nomads, giving them no space to inhabit. They float, suspended by invisible threads, above us. What this candid artist so urgently desires to tell is that the world of the stars is not so distant, but rather directly related to us, familiar through the patient course of our anthropomorphizing.

Vittorio Sgarbi

The charming ceiling of the Sala del Mappamondo in the Villa Farnese in Caprarola, Italy. We know from documents of the period that it was painted in 1575; unfortunately, we do not know the name of the artist who painted it.

The figures of the constellations are here shown upside-down, as they appear on celestial globes.

The work's grandeur and the exquisite quality and astronomical logic of its execution make this fresco the finest representation of Western astronomy.

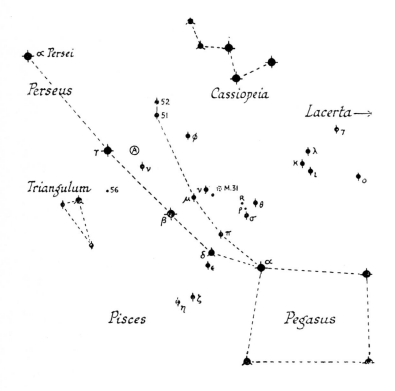

ANDROMEDA

Chain'd to a rock she stood; young Perseus stay'd
His rapid flight, to view the beauteous maid.
So sweet her frame, so exquisitely fine,
She seem'd a statue by a hand divine,
Had not the wind her waving tresses show'd,
And down her cheeks the melting sorrows flow'd.
Her faultless form the hero's bosom fires;
The more he looks, the more he still admires.
The admirer almost had forgot to fly,
And swift descended, fluttering from on high:
"O virgin! worthy no such chains to prove,
But pleasing chains in the soft folds of love;
Thy country, and thy name," he said, "disclose,
And give a true rehearsal of thy woes."

Ovid, *Metamorphoses*, 4.671–81

Plate 1
ANDROMEDA

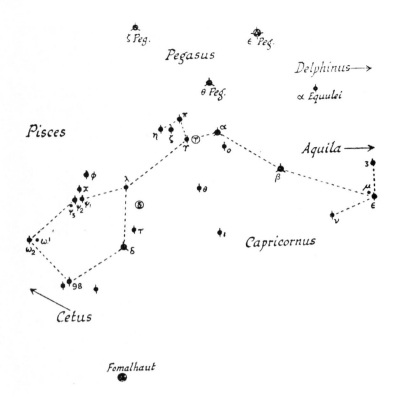

Pegasus
ζ Peg.
ε Peg.
θ Peg.
Delphinus→
α Equulei

Pisces

Aquila →

AQUARIUS

Cetus

Capricornus

Fomalhaut

Ganymede was the son of Tros, the king of Asia Minor from whom the city of Troy took its name. So beautiful was he that Zeus, enamored, transformed himself into an eagle and carried him off from Mount Ida to Olympus, where Ganymede became Zeus' companion and cupbearer to the gods. Zeus endowed the youth with immortality and placed his image among the stars as the constellation of Aquarius.

Plate 2
AQUARIUS

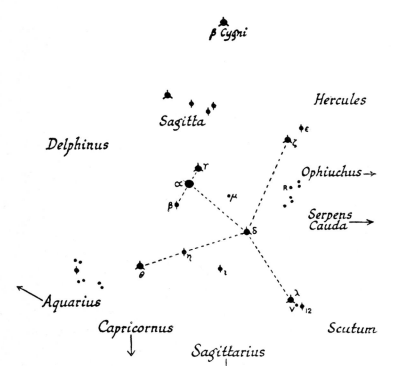

β Cygni

Hercules

Sagitta

Delphinus

Ophiuchus →

Serpens
Cauda →

Aquarius

Capricornus

Scutum

Sagittarius

AQUILA

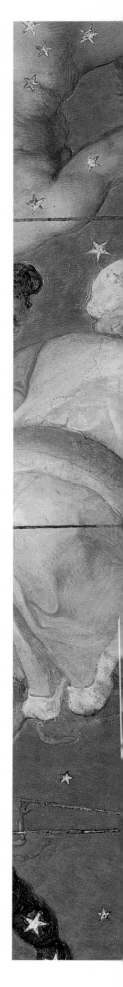

The king of gods once felt the burning joy,
And sigh'd for lovely Ganymede of Troy:
Long was he puzzled to assume a shape
Most fit, and expeditious for the rape;
A bird's was proper, yet he scorns to wear
Any but that which might his thunder bear.
Down with his masquerading wings he flies,
And bears the little Trojan to the skies;
Where now, in robes of heav'nly purple drest,
He serves the nectar at th'Almighty's feast,
To slighted Juno an unwelcome guest.

Ovid, *Metamorphoses*, 10.155–61

Plate 3
AQUILA
AND ANTINOUS

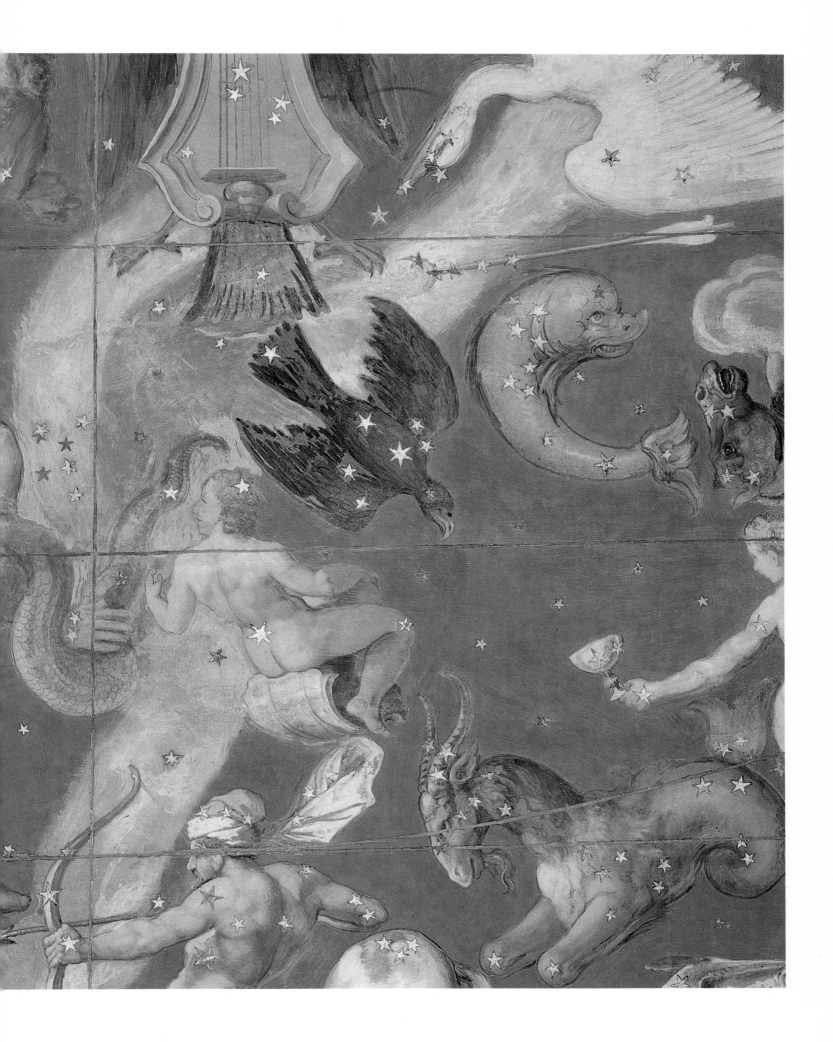

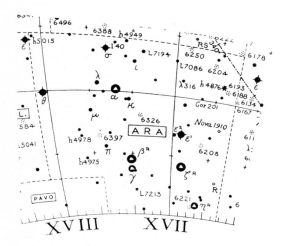

ARA

Then I threw everything open to the four winds, I made a
sacrifice and poured out a libation on the mountaintop.
Seven and again seven cauldrons I set up on their stands, I
heaped up wood and cane and cedar and myrtle. When the
gods smelled the sweet savour, they gathered like flies over
the sacrifice.

The Epic of Gilgamesh, The Story of the Flood

Plate 4
ARA

130   *The Glorious Constellations*

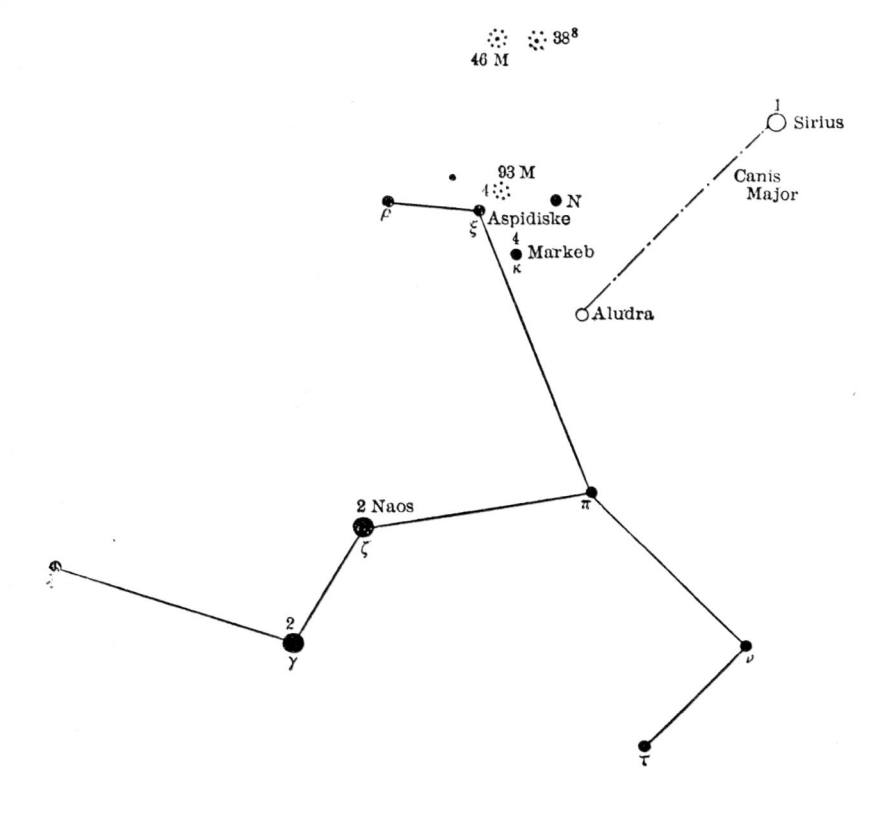

ARGO NAVIS

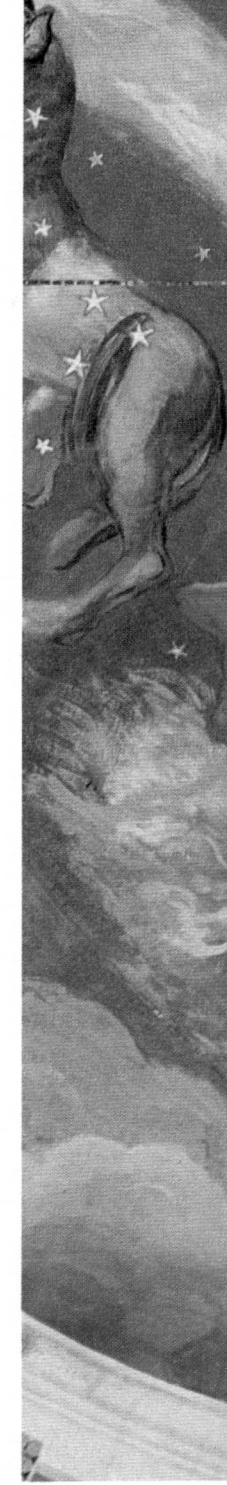

And their arms shone in the sun like flame as the ship sped on; and ever their wake gleamed white far behind, like a path seen over a green plain. On that day all the gods looked down from heaven upon the ship and the might of the heroes, half-divine, the bravest of men then sailing the sea; and on the topmost heights the nymphs of Pelion wondered as they beheld the work of Itonian Athena, and the heroes themselves wielding the oars. And there came down from the mountain-top to the sea Chiron, son of Philyra, and where the white surf broke he dipped his feet, and, often waving with his broad hand, cried out to them at their departure, "Good speed and a sorrowless home-return!"

Apollonius of Rhodes, *The Argonautica*, 1.544–556

Plate 5
ARGO NAVIS

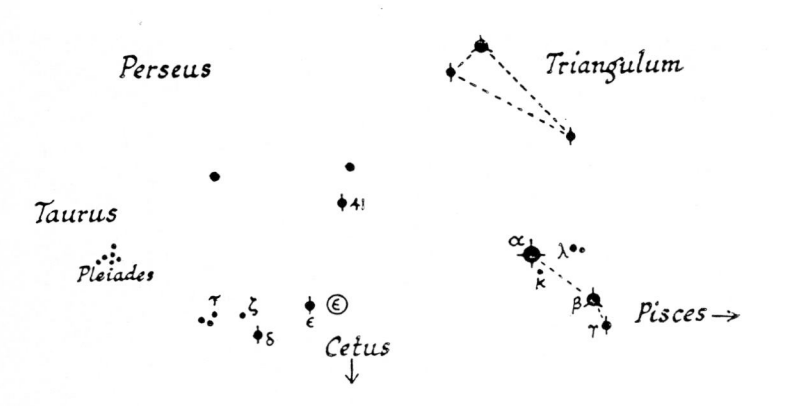

ARIES

While Phrixus and Helle under madness sent by Liber were
wandering in a forest, Nebula, their mother, is said to have
come there bringing a gilded ram, offspring of Neptune and
Theophane. She bade her children mount it, and journey to
Colchis to King Aeëtes, son of Sol, and there sacrifice the ram
to Mars. This they were said to have done, but when they had
mounted, and the ram had carried them over the sea, Helle
fell from the ram; from this the sea was called Hellespont.
Phrixus, however, was carried to Colchis, where, as his
mother had bidden, he sacrificed the ram, and placed its
gilded fleece in the temple of Mars—the very fleece which,
guarded by a dragon, it is said Jason, son of Aeson and
Alcimede, came to secure.

Hyginus, *Fabulae*, III

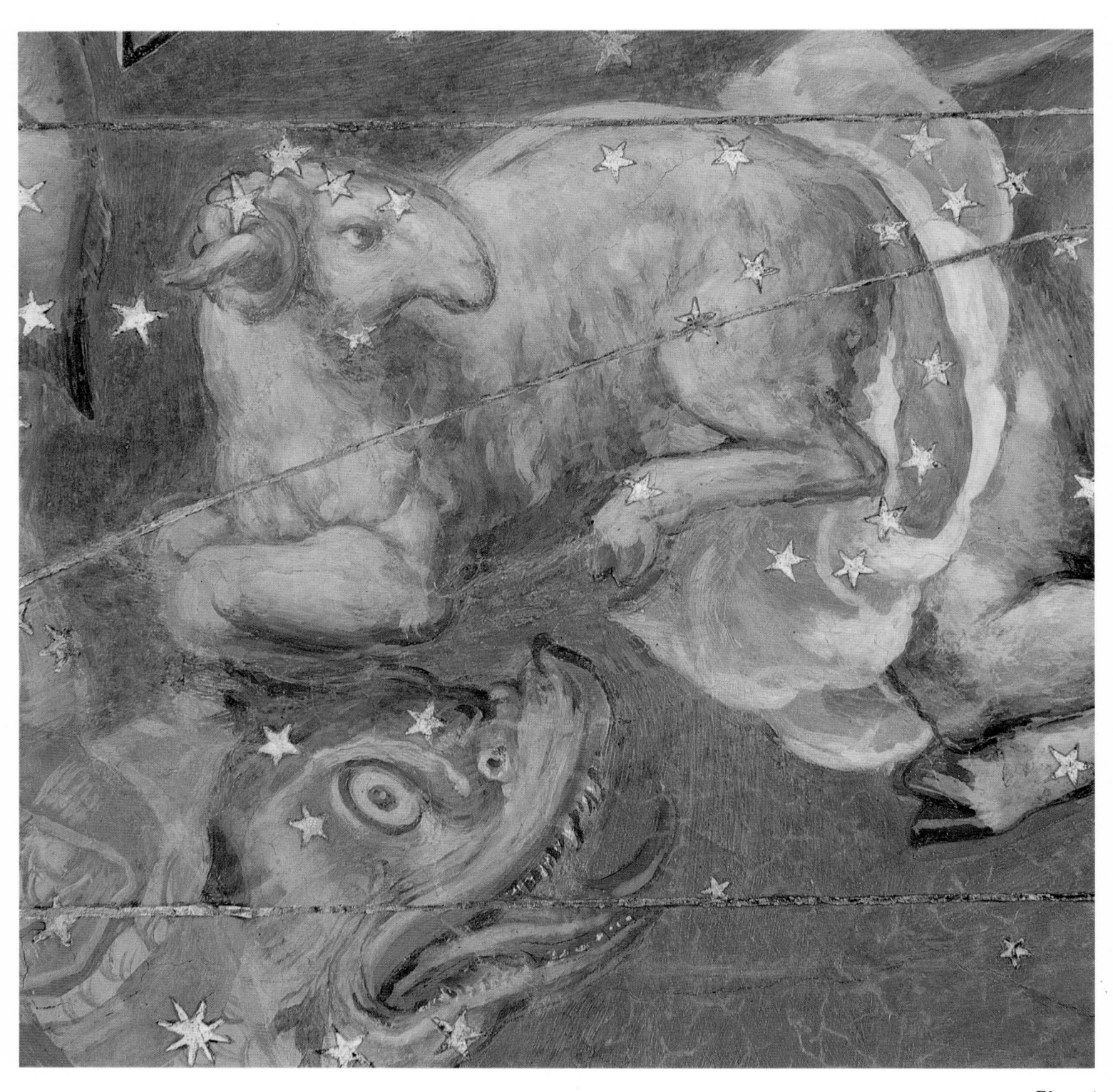

Plate 6
ARIES

AURIGA

On his left shoulder (the goat) Capra stands, and in his left hand the Kids seem to be placed. They tell this story about him. . . . A certain Melisseus was king in Crete, and to his daughters Jove was brought to nurse. Since they did not have milk, they furnished him a she-goat, Amalthea by name, who is said to have reared him. She often bore twin kids, and at the very time that Jove was brought to her to nurse, had borne a pair. And so because of the kindness of the mother, the kids, too, were placed among the constellations.

Hyginus, *Poetica astronomica*, II.13

Plate 7
AURIGA

136 *The Glorious Constellations*

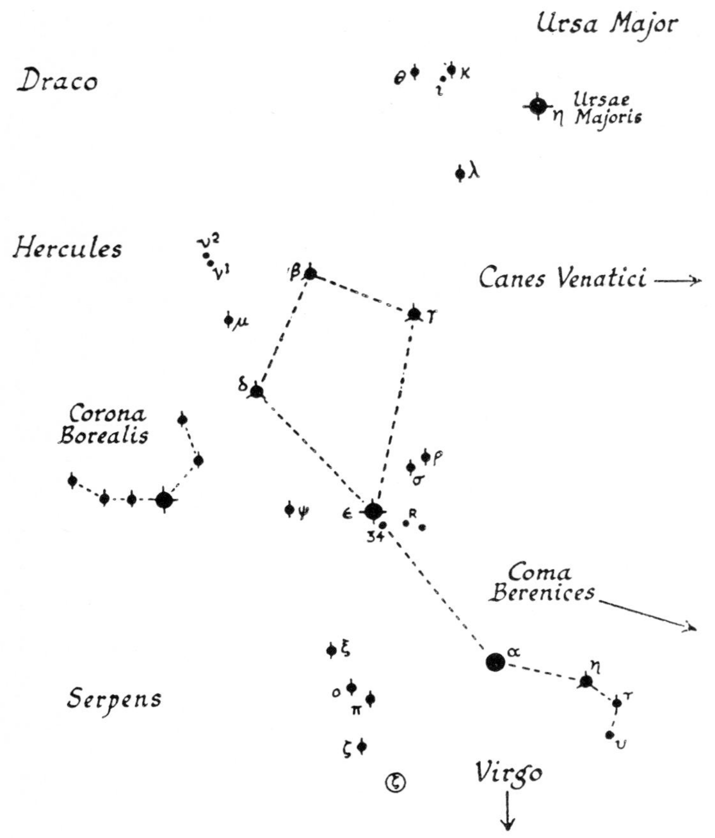

Ursa Major

Draco

η Ursae
Majoris

λ

Hercules

ν²
ν¹
β

Canes Venatici →

μ

τ

δ

Corona
Borealis

ρ
σ

ψ
ε
34
R

Coma
Berenices →

Serpens

ξ

o
π

α

η
τ
υ

ζ

ϑ

Virgo

↓

BOÖTES

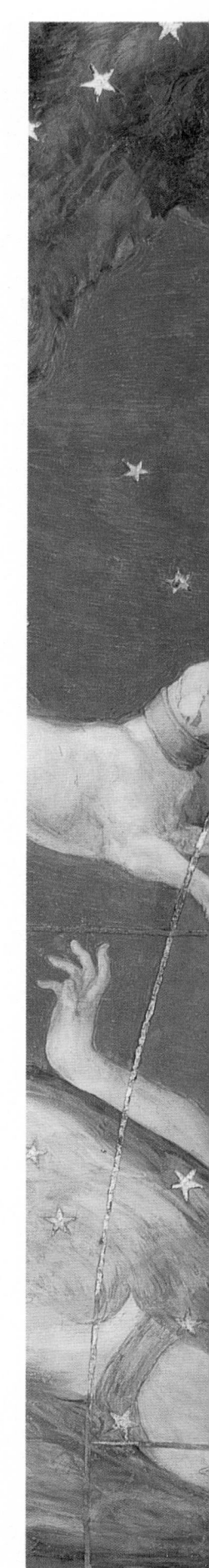

Some have said that he is Icarius, father of Erigone, to
whom, on account of his justice and piety, Father Liber gave
wine, the vine, and the grape, so that he could show men how
to plant the vine, what would grow from it, and how to use
what was produced. When he had planted the vine, and by
careful tending with a pruning-knife had made it flourish, a
goat is said to have broken into the vineyard, and nibbled the
tenderest leaves he saw there. Icarius, angered by this, took
him and killed him and from his skin made a sack, and
blowing it up, bound it tight, and cast it among his friends,
directing them to dance around it. And, so, Eratosthenes
says: "Around the goat of Icarius they first danced."

Hyginus, *Poetica astronomica*, II.4

Plate 8
BOÖTES

139

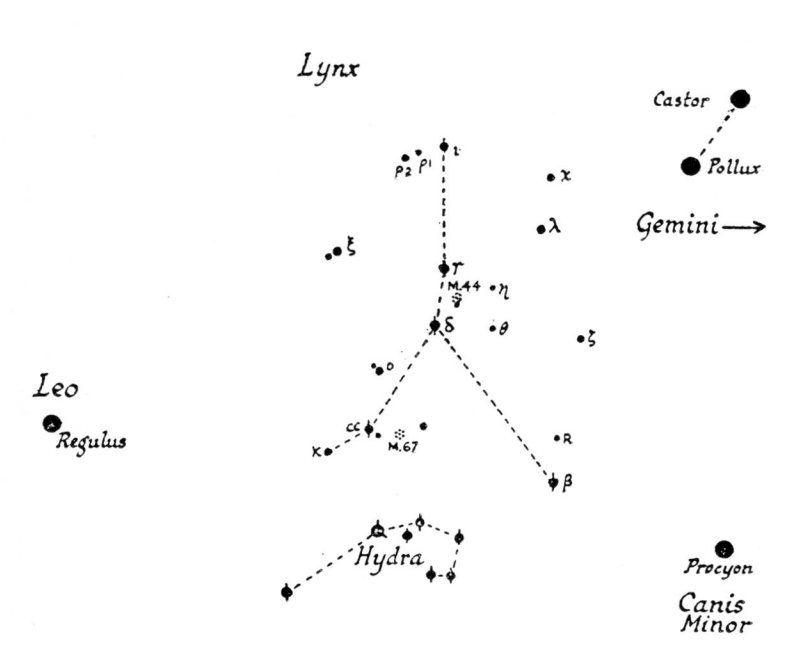

CANCER

This constellation represents the crab that bit the heel of
Hercules during his fight with the Lernean Hydra, and was
placed amongst the stars in gratitude by Juno, the enemy of
Hercules.

V. E. Robson, *The Fixed Stars & Constellations in Astrology*

Plate 9
CANCER

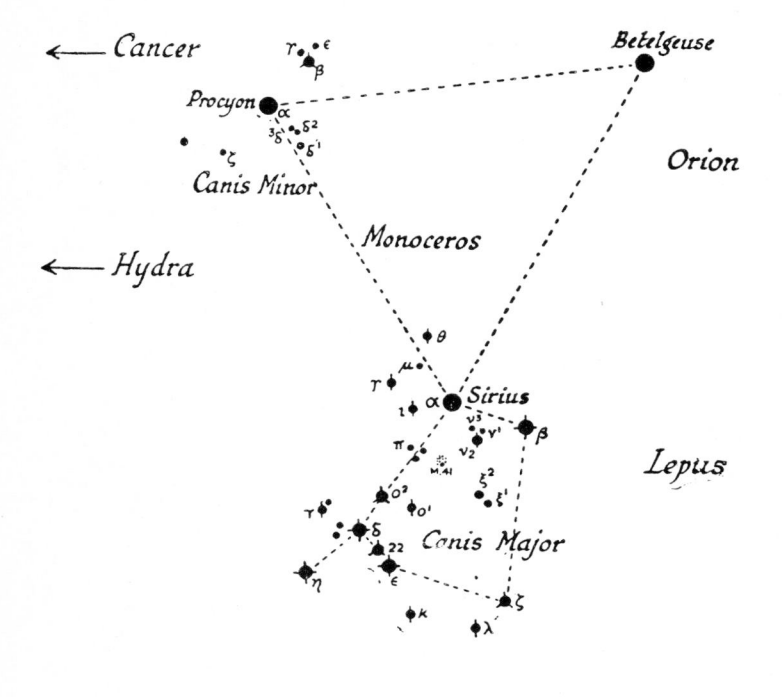

CANIS MAJOR

When the artichoke flowers, and the tuneful cicada, perched
on a tree, pours forth a shrill song oft-times from under his
wings, in the season of toilsome summer, then goats are
fattest, wine is best, women most wanton, and men weakest,
since Sirius parches head and knees, and body also is dried-
up by reason of heat. But then at last be thine the rocky
shade, and Biblian wine, a light-well-baked cake, the milk of
goats which-are-now-off-their milk, and the flesh of a heifer
browsing-the-forest, which has not yet calved, and of first-
born kids—then sit in the shade, and drink moreover dark-
hued wine (having your soul satisfied with viands, and
turning your face to catch the brisk-blowing Zephyr) and the
ever-running and forth-gushing spring, which is untroubled-
by-mud. Pour in three cups of water first, and add the fourth
of wine.

Hesiod, *Works and Days*, 582–596

Plate 10
CANIS MAJOR

142 *The Glorious Constellations*

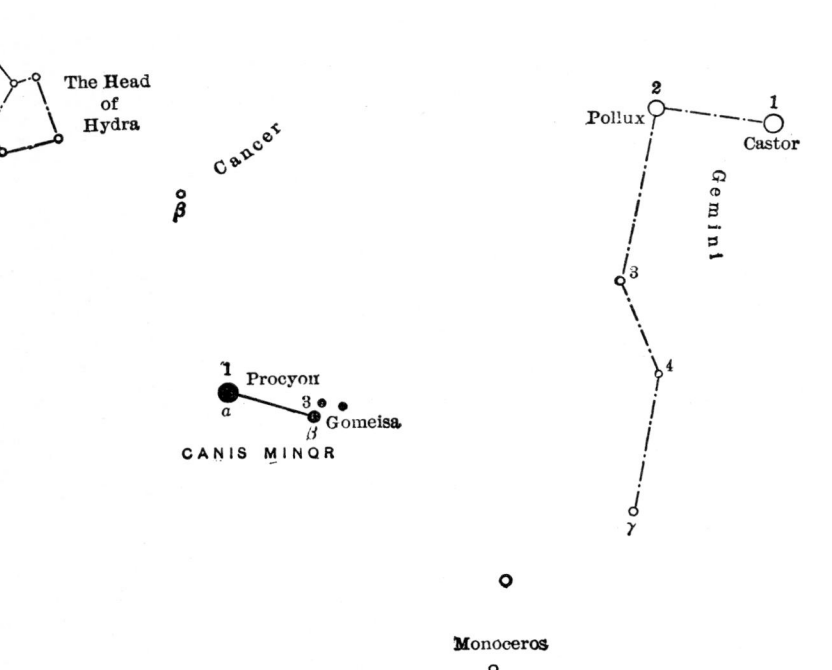

The Head
of
Hydra

Cancer

β

Pollux 2   1 Castor

Gemini

3

4

1 Procyon
α   3
β Gomeisa
CANIS MINQR

γ

Monoceros

Betelgeuze 1
in
Orion

CANIS MINOR

*[It] seems to rise before the greater Dog; for this reason it is
called the Fore-dog. By some it is thought to be Orion's dog,
and it is put in all the same tales in which the greater Dog is
numbered.*

Hyginus, *Poetica astronomica*, II.36

Plate 11
CANIS MINOR

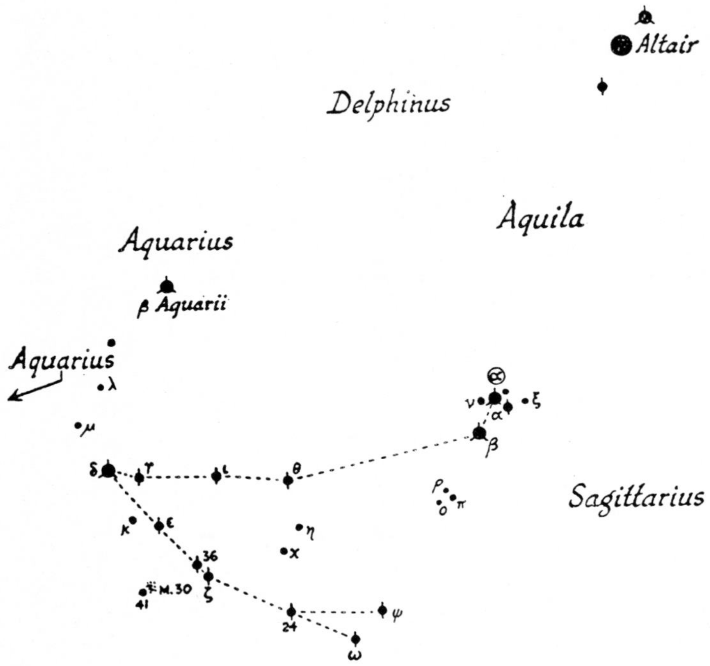

Altair

Delphinus

Aquila

Aquarius

β Aquarii

Aquarius
λ

μ

ν α ξ

β

Sagittarius

ρ
π
ο

δ τ ι θ

κ ε

η

χ

36

M.30
41 ζ

24 ψ

ω

CAPRICORNUS

Behind [Pegasus, the horse] is the Goat, standing farther
off where runs the Sun's path.
    In that month sail not upon the vast tempestuous ocean,
certainly not for any distance, since the days are very
short. . . .

Aratus, *Phaenomena*, 25–26

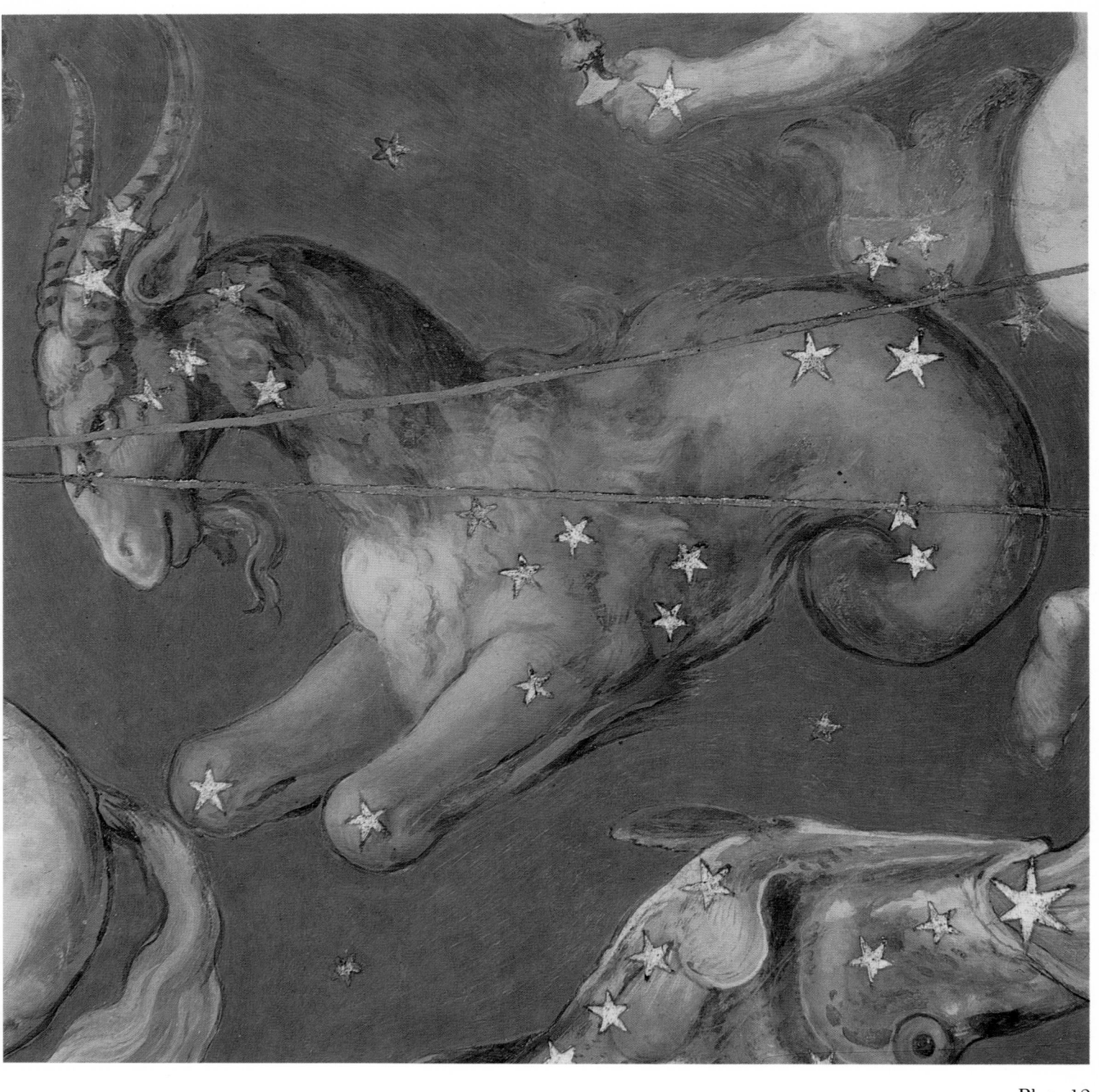

Plate 12
CAPRICORNUS

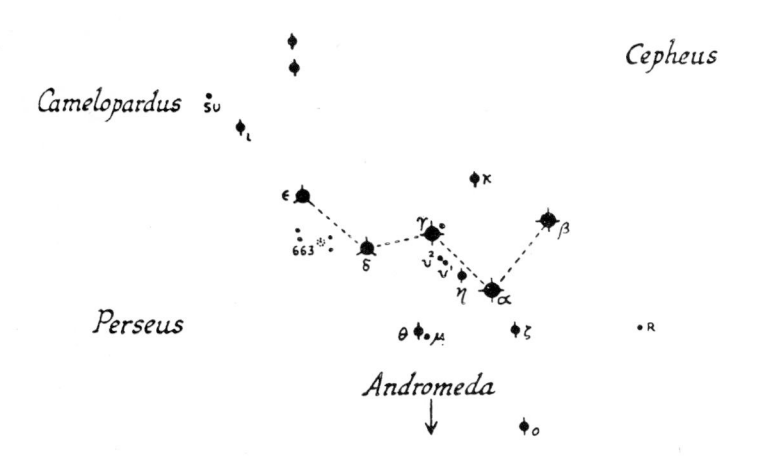

CASSIOPEIA

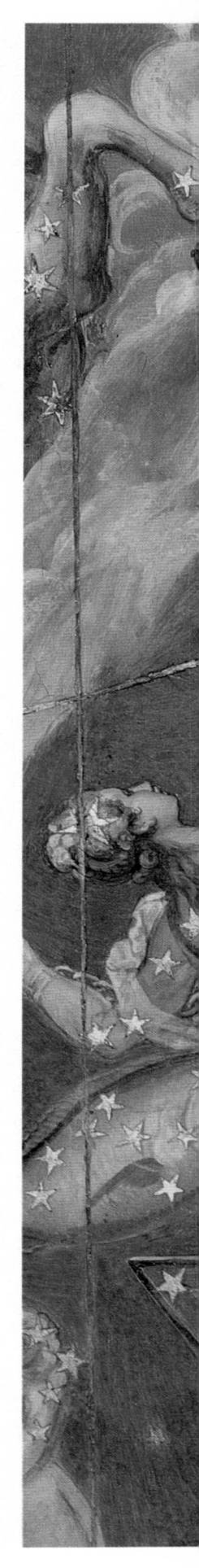

Seated on a beautiful throne of stars placed amid the Milky Way, there appears in the northern hemisphere of the sky a mysterious queen, engaged each night in a slow, untiring revolution around the North Pole.

Plate 13
CASSIOPEIA

CENTAURUS

Plate 14
CENTAURUS

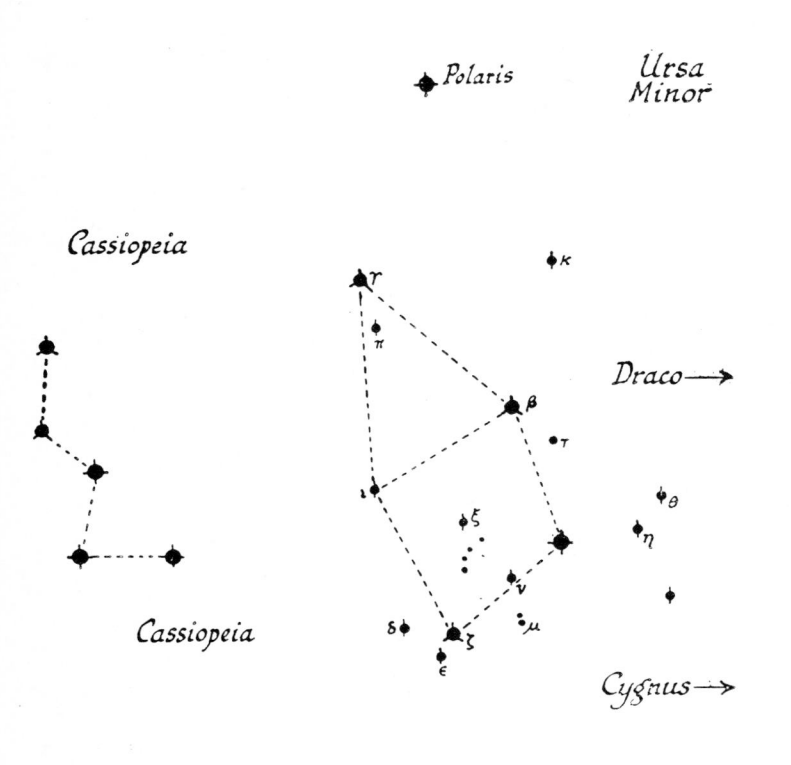

Polaris

Ursa
Minor

Cassiopeia

κ

γ

π

Draco →

β

τ

ι

θ

ξ

η

Cassiopeia

ν

δ

μ

ζ

ε

Cygnus →

CEPHEUS

"Hold! brother, hold! what brutal rage has made
Your frantic mind so black a crime conceive?
Are these the thanks that you to Perseus give?
This the reward that to his worth you pay,
Whose timely valour saved Andromeda?
Nor was it he, if you would reason right,
That forc'd her from you, but the jealous right
Of envious Nereids and Jove's high decree,
And that devouring monster of the sea,
That ready, with his jaws wide gaping, stood
To eat my child, the fairest of my blood."

Ovid, *Metamorphoses*, 5.12–19

Plate 15
CEPHEUS

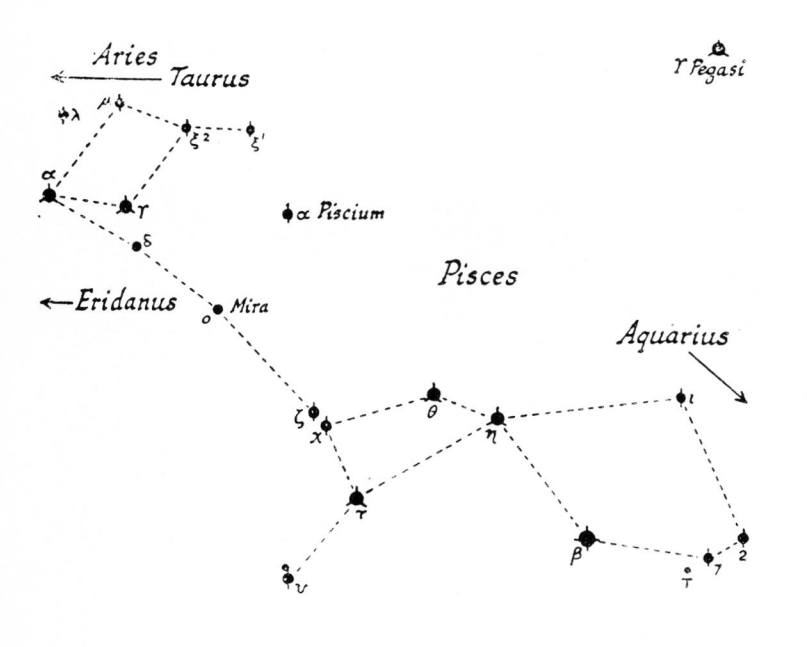

CETUS

As well-rigg'd galleys, which slaves, seating, row,
With their sharp beaks the whiten'd ocean plough;
So, when the monster moved, still at his back
The furrow'd waters left a foamy track.
Now to the rock he was advanced so nigh,
Whirl'd from a sling, a stone the space would fly.

Ovid, *Metamorphoses,* 4.706–10

Plate 16
CETUS

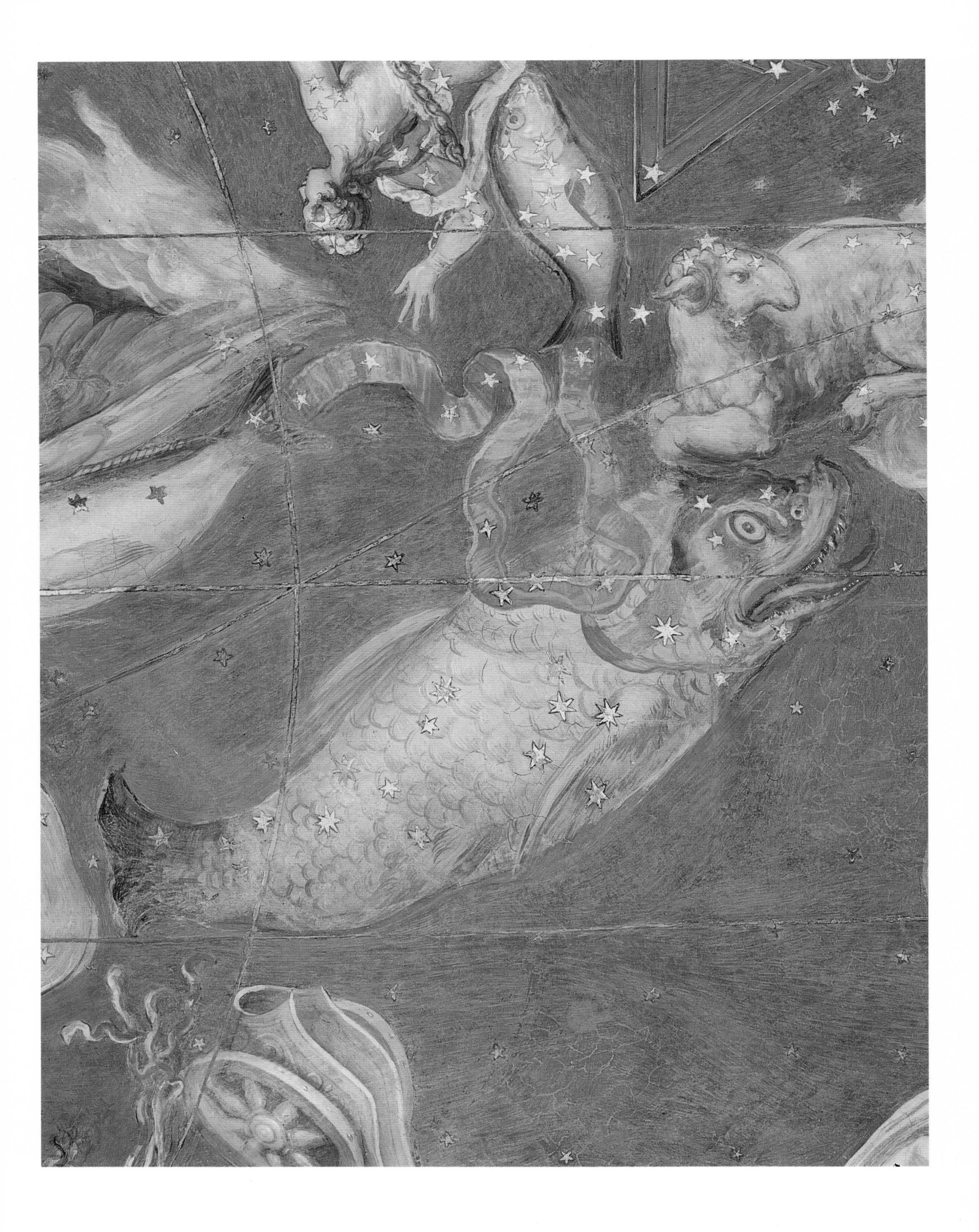

CORONA AUSTRALIS

Ixion's cosmic wheel
Turning in the heavens,
Eternally

Plate 17
CORONA AUSTRALIS

157

Hercules   Bootes

Serpens
Caput

CORONA BOREALIS

When Theseus, aided by the virgin's art,
Had traced the guiding thread through every part,
He took the gentle maid that set him free,
And, bound for Dias, cut the briny sea;
There, quickly cloy'd, ungrateful, and unkind,
Left his fair consort in the idle behind,
Whom Bacchus sees and loves; decrees the dame
Shall shine for ever in the rolls of fame;
And bids her crown among the stars be placed,
With an eternal constellation graced.
The golden circle mounts, and, as it flies,
Its diamonds twinkle in the distant skies;
There, in their pristine form, the gemmy rays
Between Alcides and the dragon blaze.

Ovid, *Metamorphoses*, 8.176–82

Plate 18
CORONA BOREALIS

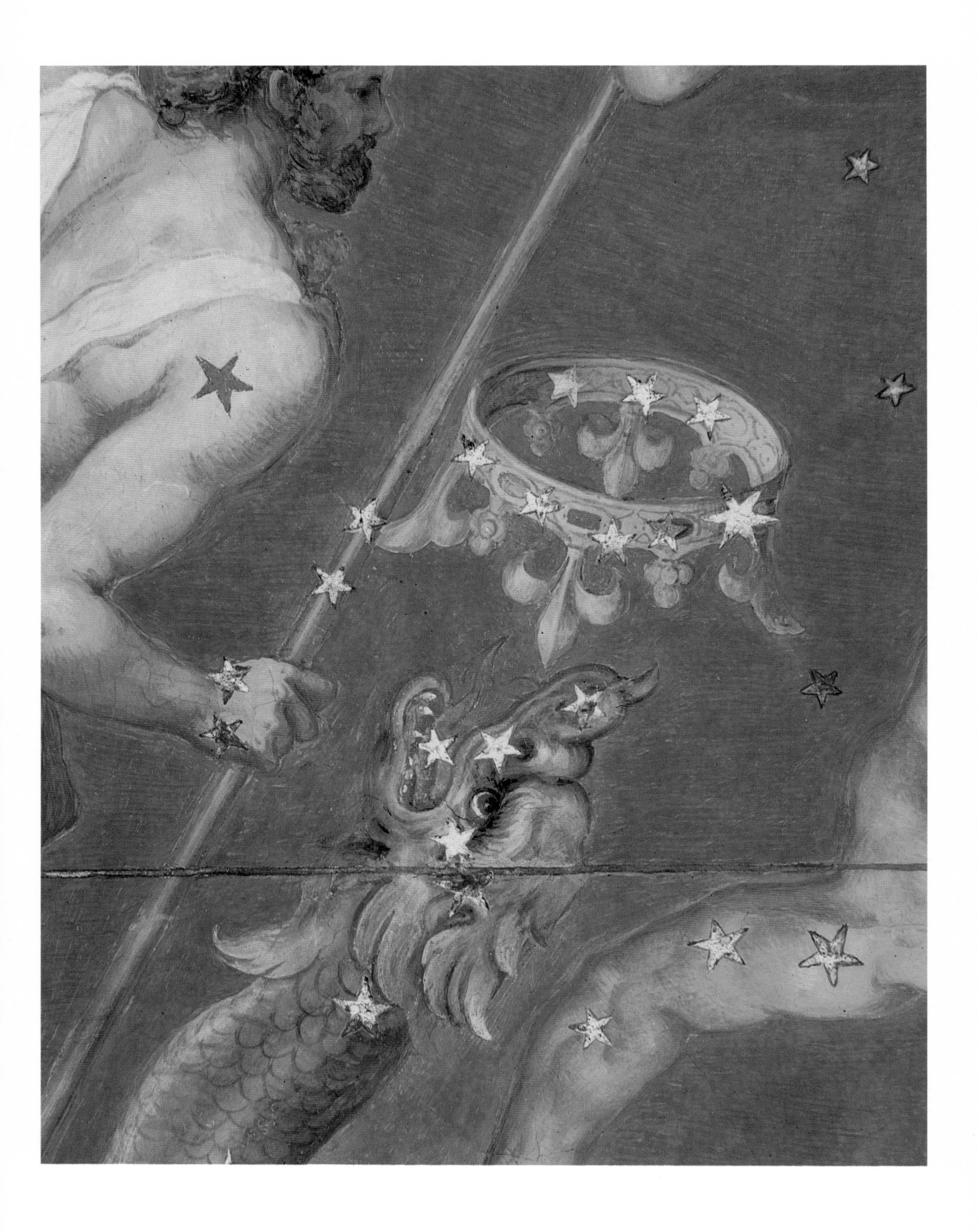

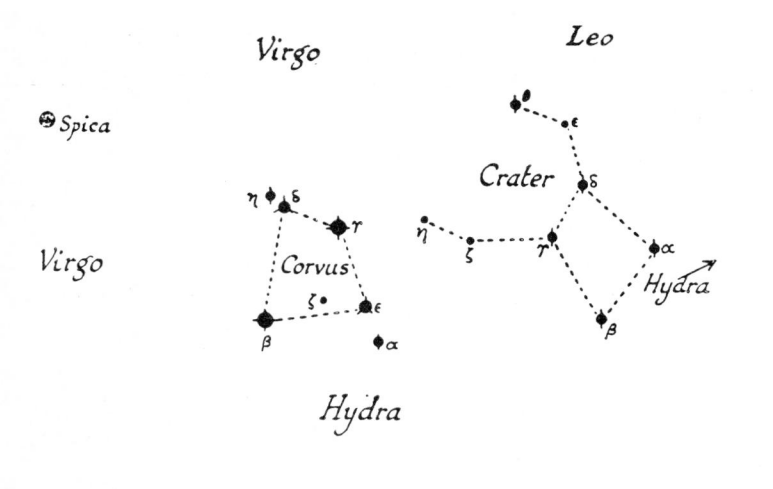

CORVUS

The raven once in snowy plumes was dress'd,
White as the whitest dove's unsullied breast,
Fair as the guardian of the capitol,
Soft as the swan, a large and lovely fowl;
His tongue, his prating tongue, had changed him quite
To sooty blackness from the purest white.

Ovid, *Metamorphoses*, II.534–41

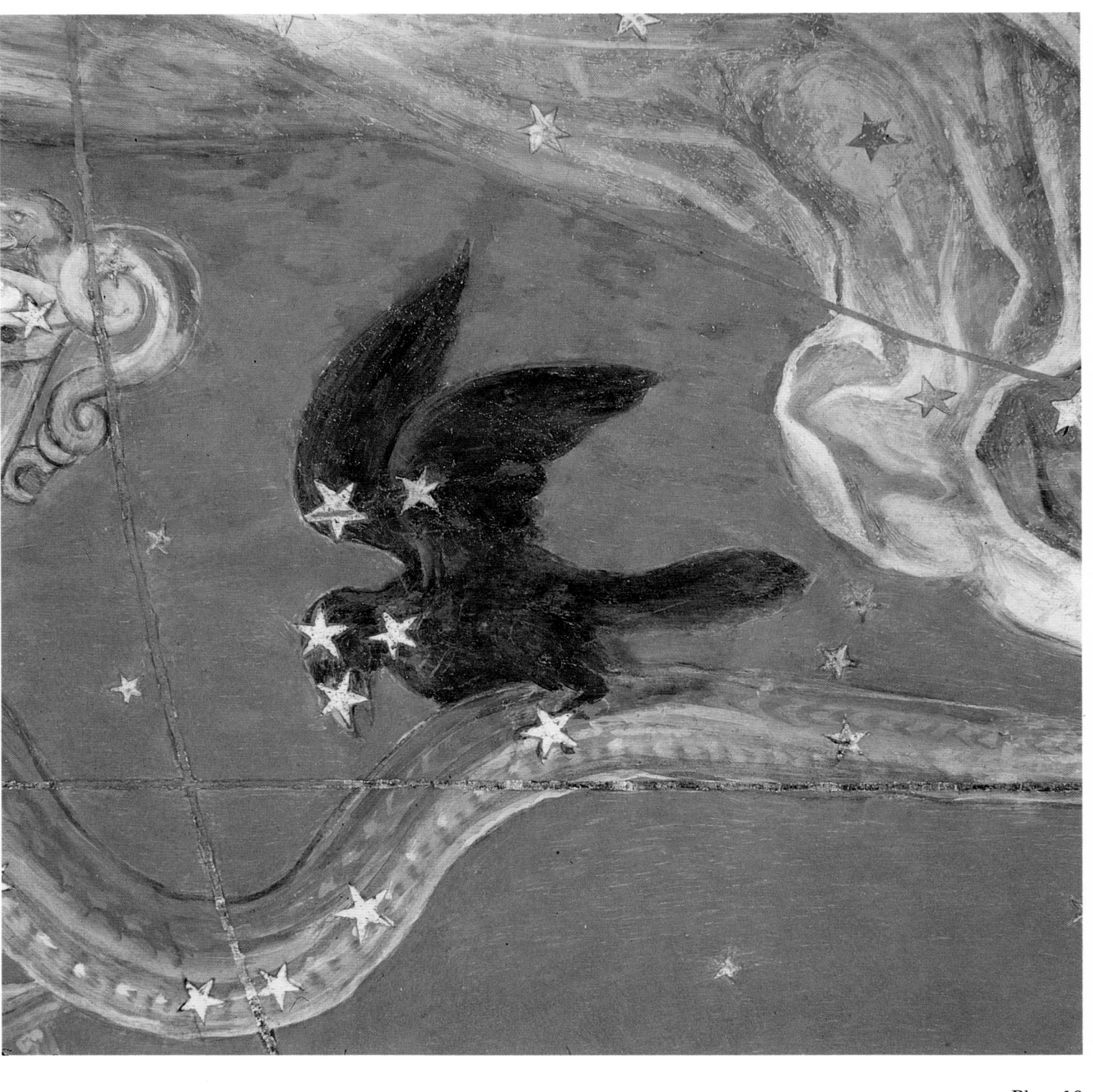

Plate 19
CORVUS

161

Corvus

η

CRATER

γ δ

Alkes

Hydra β

CRATER

We have drunk the Soma; we have become immortal; we have
gone to the light; we have found the gods. What can hatred
and the malice of a mortal do to us now, O immortal one?

Rig-Veda, VIII.48

Plate 20
CRATER

163

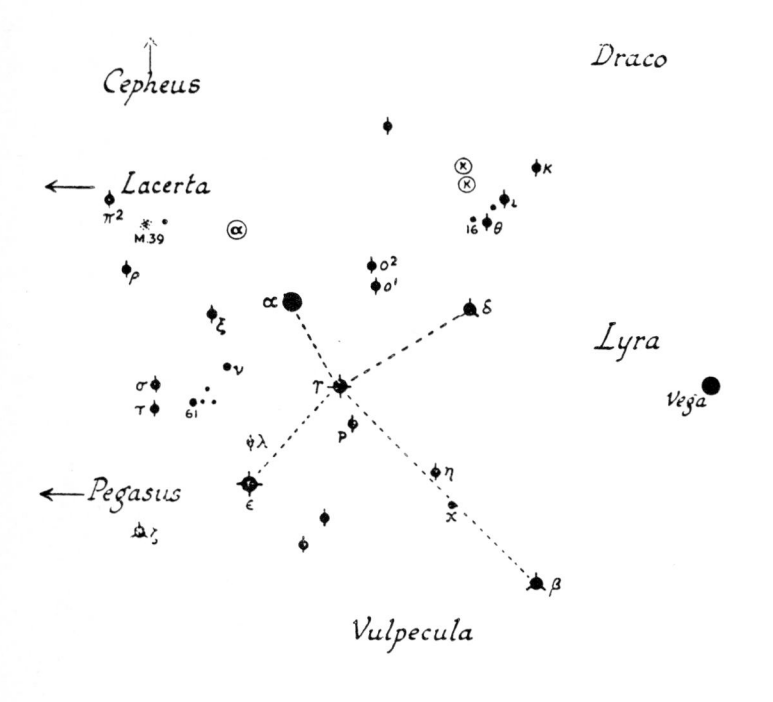

CYGNUS

*[Jove] bade Venus, in the form of an eagle, pursue him; he,
changed to a swan, as if in flight from the eagle, took refuge
with Nemesis and lighted in her lap. Nemesis did not thrust
him away, but holding him in her arms, fell into a deep sleep.
While she slept, Jupiter embraced her, and then flew away.
Because he was seen by men flying high in the sky, they said
he was put in the stars. To make this really true, Jupiter put
the swan flying and the eagle pursuing in the sky.*

Hyginus, *Poetica astronomica*, II.8

Plate 21
CYGNUS

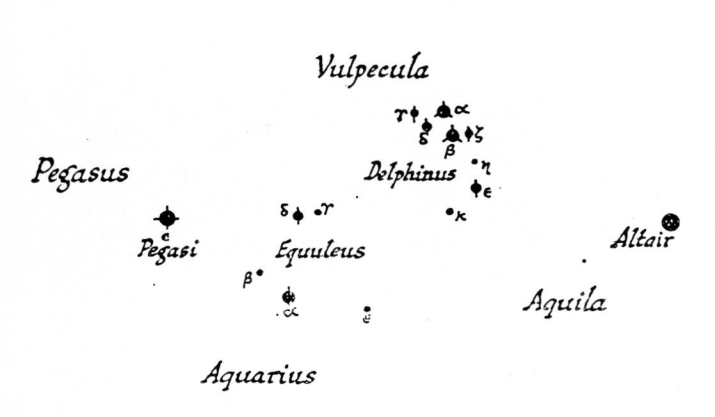

DELPHINUS

Amphitrite, when Neptune desired to wed her and she
preferred to keep her virginity, fled to Atlas. Neptune sent
many to seek her out, among them a certain Delphinus, who,
in his wanderings among the islands, came at last to the
maiden, persuaded her to marry Neptune, and himself took
charge of the wedding. In return for this service, Neptune put
the form of a dolphin among the constellations.

Hyginus, *Poetica astronomica*, II.17

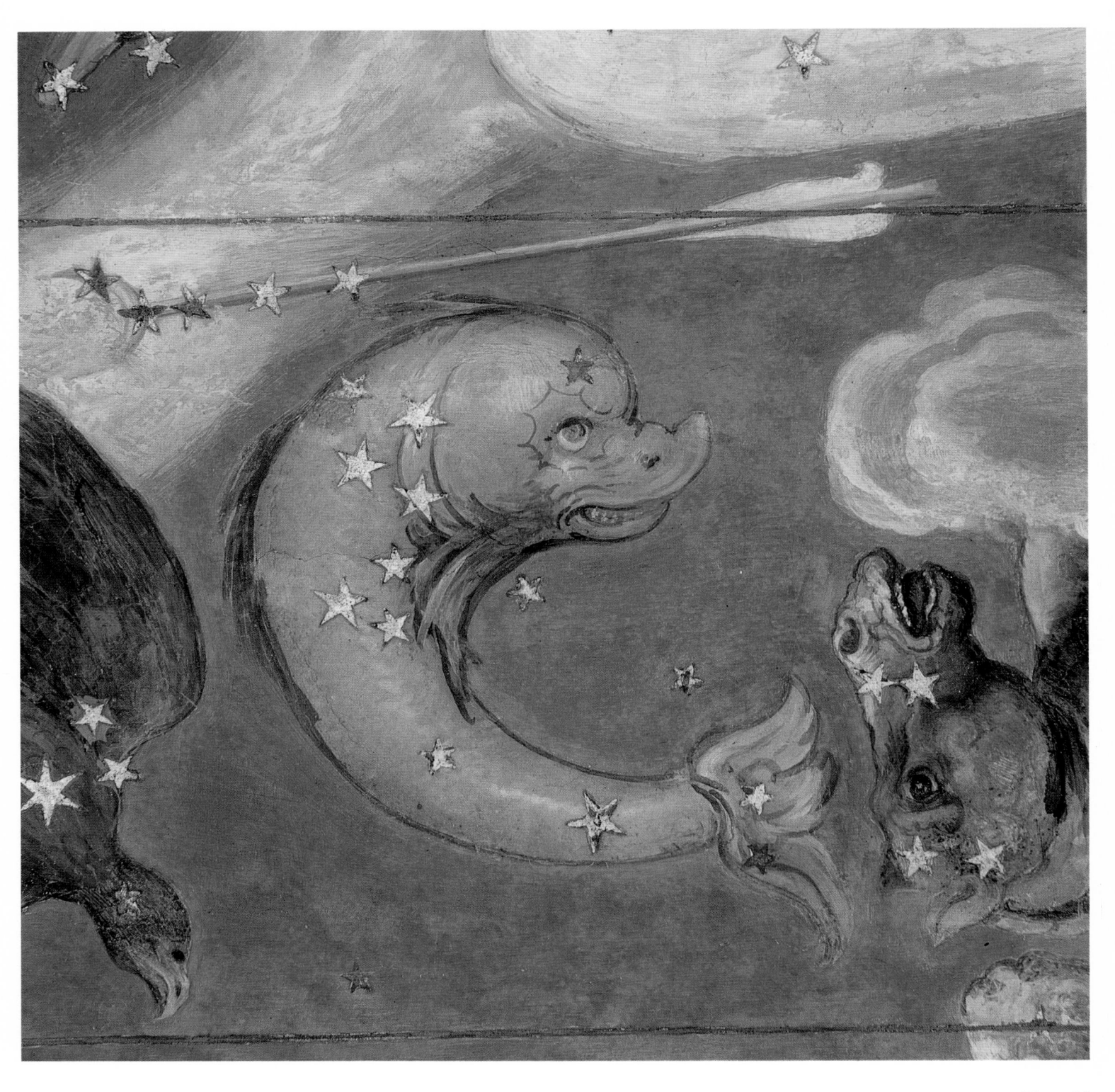

Plate 22
DELPHINUS AND SAGITTA

This huge serpent is pointed out as lying between the two Bears. He is said to have guarded the golden apples of the Hesperides, and after Hercules killed him, to have been put by Juno among the stars, because at her instigation Hercules set out for him.

Hyginus, *Poetica astronomica*, II.3

Plate 23
DRACO

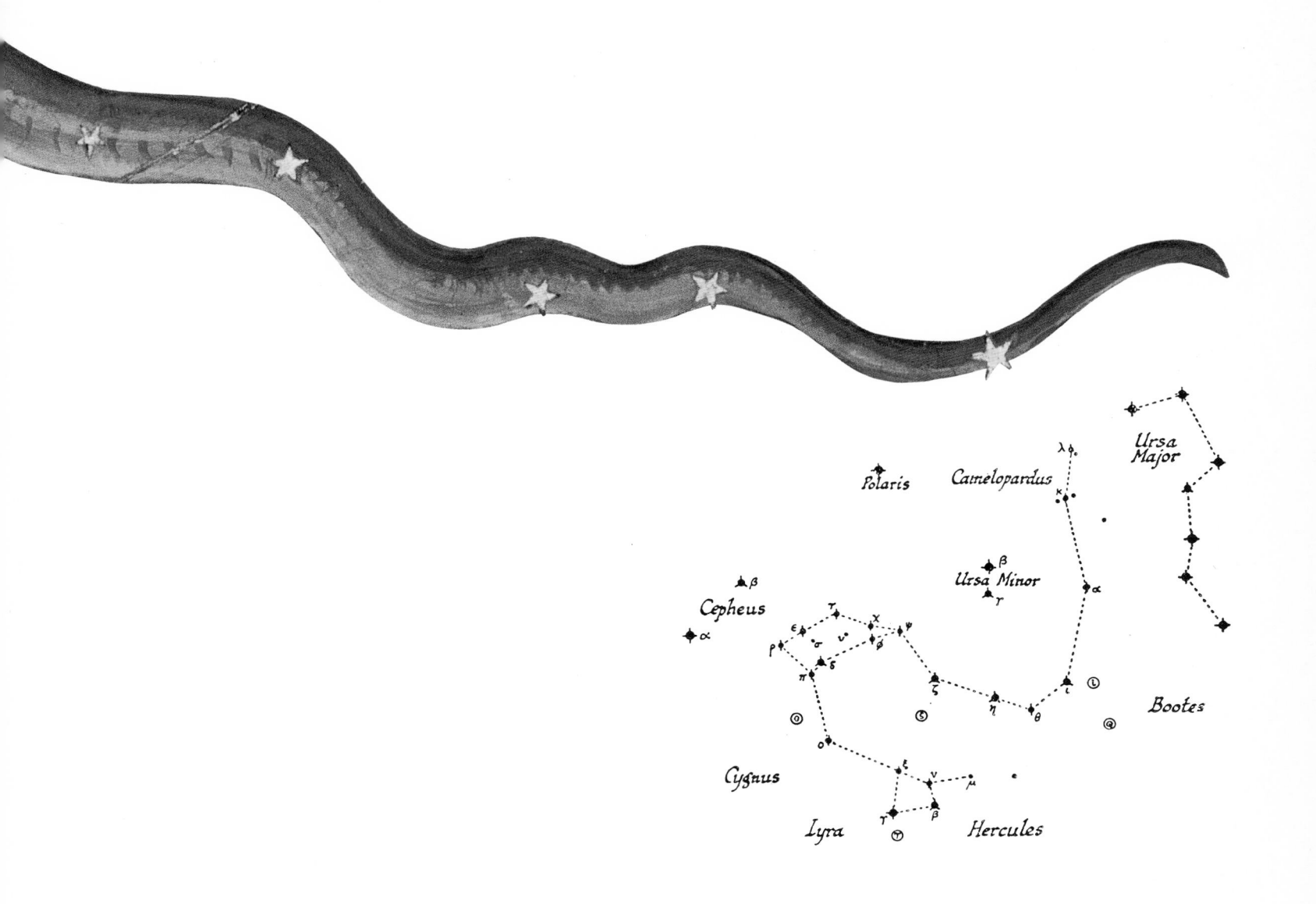

Ursa Major

Polaris   Camelopardus

Ursa Minor   β

Cepheus   β

Bootes

Cygnus

Lyra   Hercules

DRACO

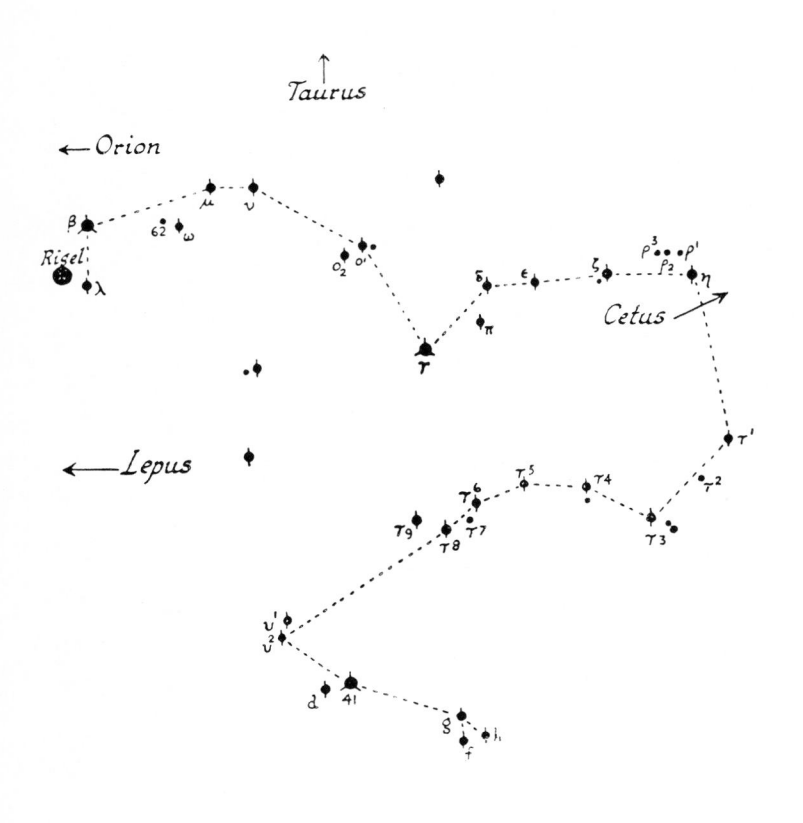

ERIDANUS

. . . Thus the almighty sire
Suppress'd the raging of the fires with fire.
 At once from life and from the chariot driven,
The ambitious boy fell thunder-struck from heaven;
The horses started with a sudden bound,
And flung the reins and chariot to the ground:
The studded harness from their necks they broke,
Here fell a wheel, and here a silver spoke,
Here were the beam and axle torn away,
And scatter'd o'er the earth the shining fragments lay.
 The breathless Phaeton, with flaming hair,
Shot from the chariot like a falling star,
That in a summer's evening from the top
of heaven drops down, or seems, at least, to drop,
Till on the Po his blasted corpse was hurl'd,
Far from his country, in the western world,
 The Latian nymphs came round him, and amazed,
On the dead youth, transfix'd with thunder, gazed,
And, while yet smoking from the bolt he lay,
His shatter'd body to a tomb convey. . . .

Ovid, *Metamorphoses*, 2.313–26

Plate 24
ERIDANUS

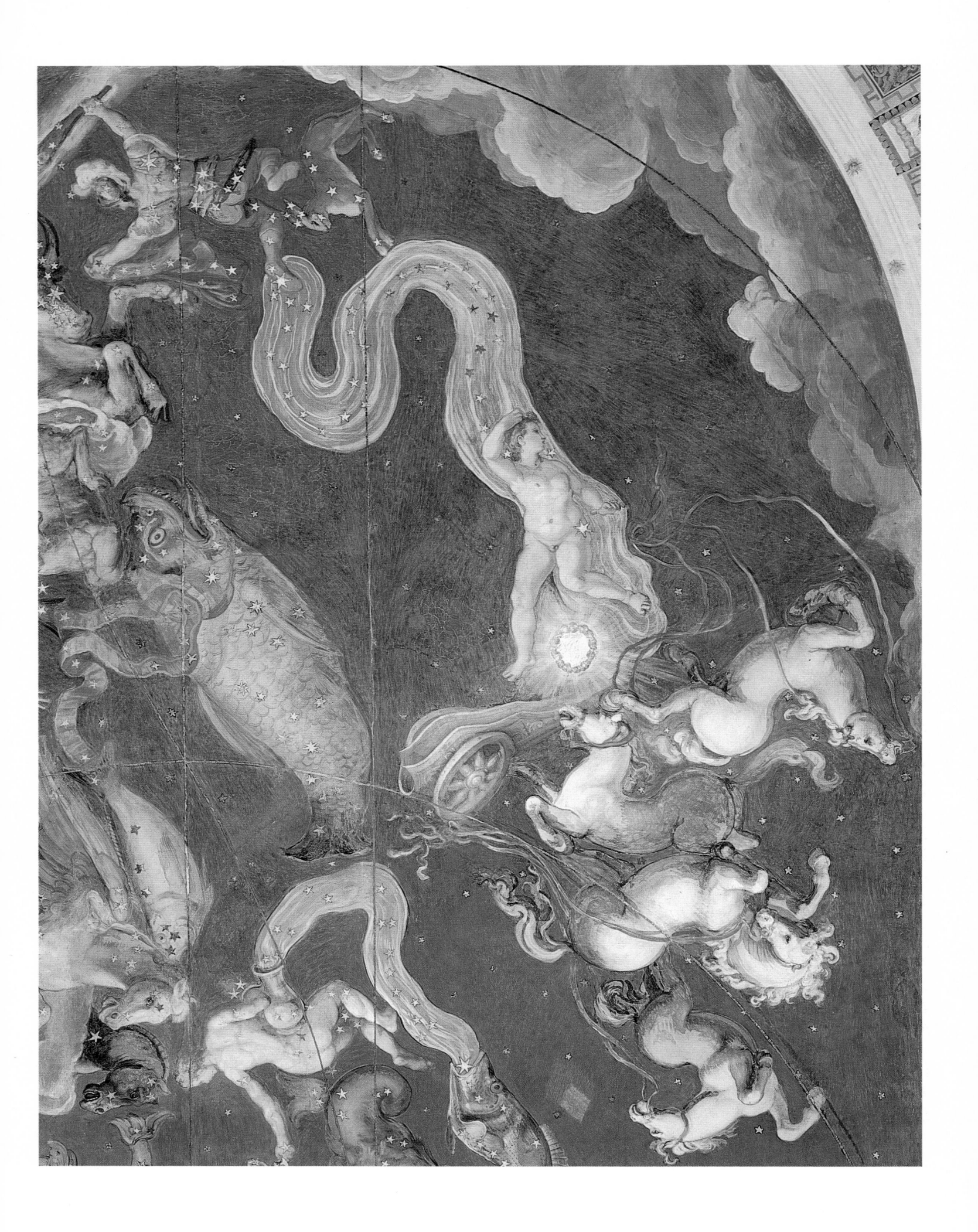

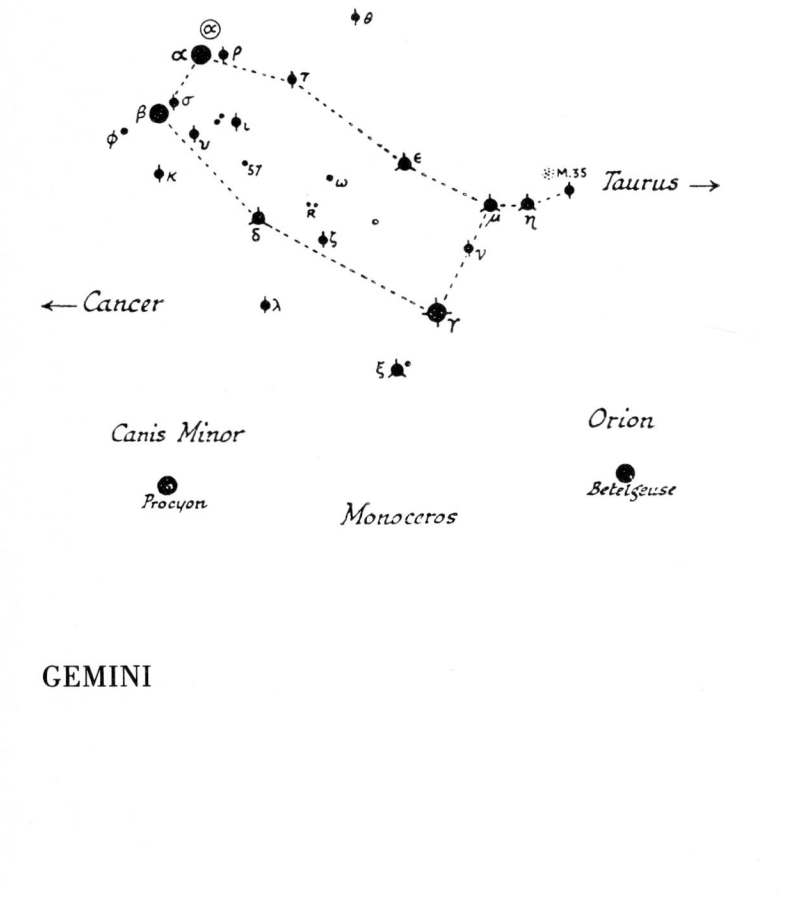

Lynx   *Auriga*

Taurus →

← Cancer

Canis Minor   *Orion*

Procyon   Betelgeuse

Monoceros

GEMINI

*They grew up together and their brotherly attachment
became legendary. They became famous for their skills in
competitions—there was no better horse-breaker than Castor,
and no one surpassed Pollux in the art of boxing—so much
so that the Olympic games were celebrated under their aegis.
They participated in the hunt for the Calydonian boar and in
the famous expedition of the Argonauts, who sailed in search
of the Golden Fleece.*

Plate 25
GEMINI

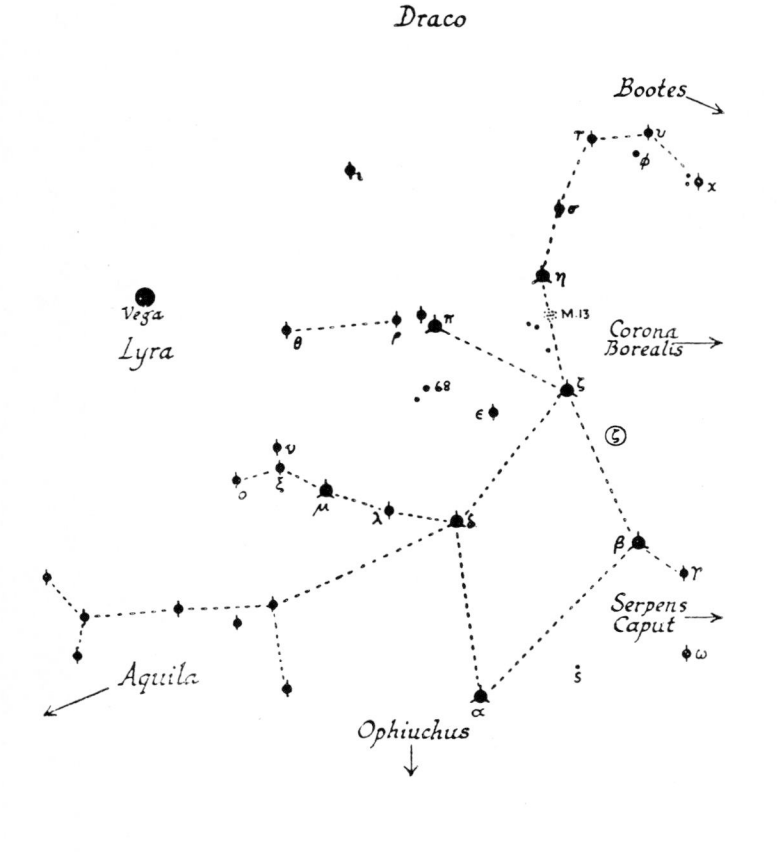

Draco

Bootes

Vega

Lyra

M.13

Corona Borealis

68

Aquila

Serpens Caput

Ophiuchus

HERCULES

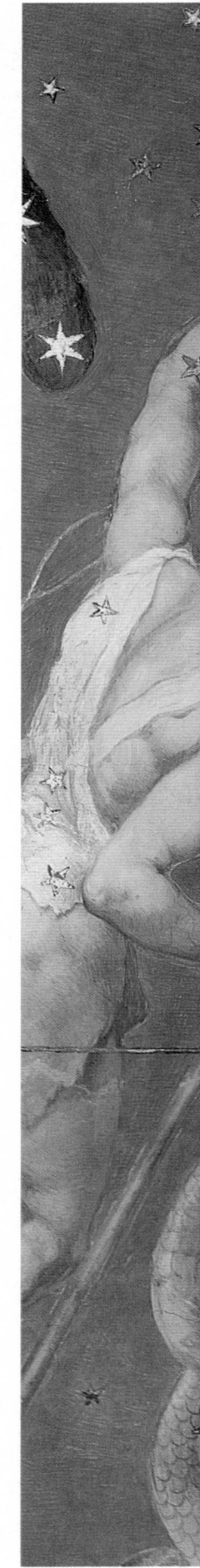

*"Look, my dear! What a wonderfully robust child!" said
Athena, pretending surprise as she stopped to pick him up.
"His mother must have been out of her mind to abandon him
in a stony field! Come, you have milk. Give the poor little
creature suck!" Thoughtlessly Hera took him and bared her
breast, at which Hercules drew with such force that she flung
him down in pain, and a spurt of milk flew across the sky and
became the Milky Way. "The young monster!" Hera cried.
But Hercules was now immortal. . . .*

Robert Graves, *The Greek Myths*, II, 90

Plate 26
HERCULES

[*Echidna*] *gave birth to the Lernean Hydra, subtle in*
destruction, whom Juno, white-armed goddess, reared,
implacably hating the mighty Hercules. And it Jove's son,
Hercules, named of Amphitryon, along with warlike Iolaus,
and by the counsels of Pallas the despoiler, slaughtered with
ruthless sword.

Hesiod, *Theogony*, 312–320

Plate 27
HYDRA

Cancer
Regulus
Leo
Canis
Minor
Monoceros
Libra
Virgo
Spica
Virgo
Crater
Corvus

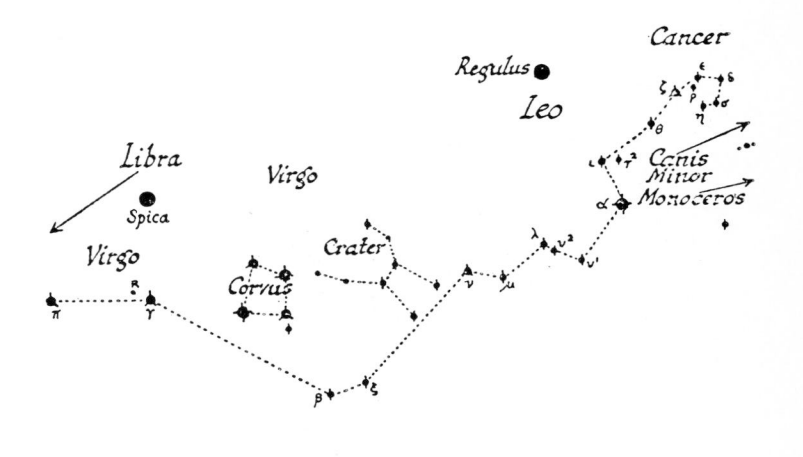

HYDRA

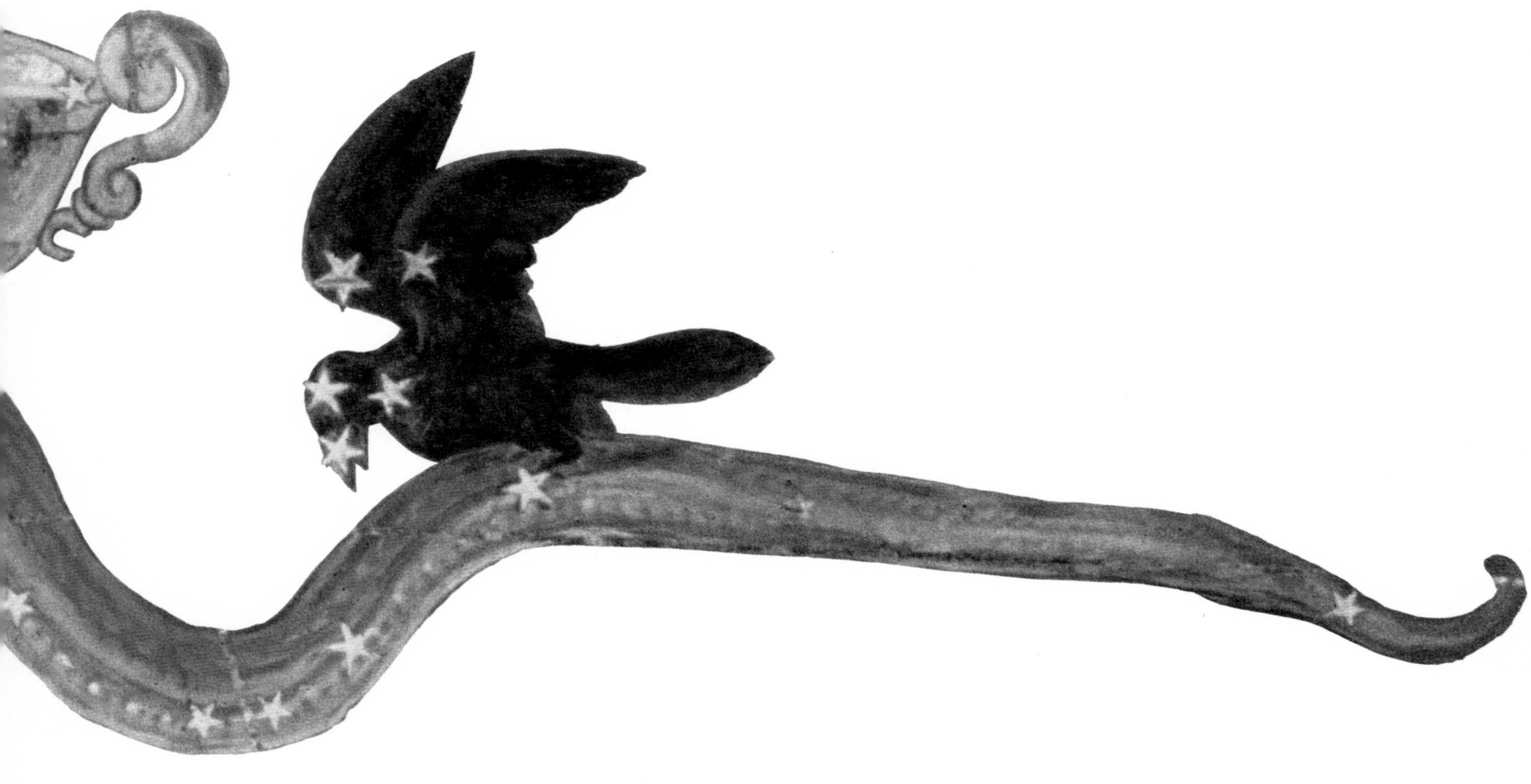

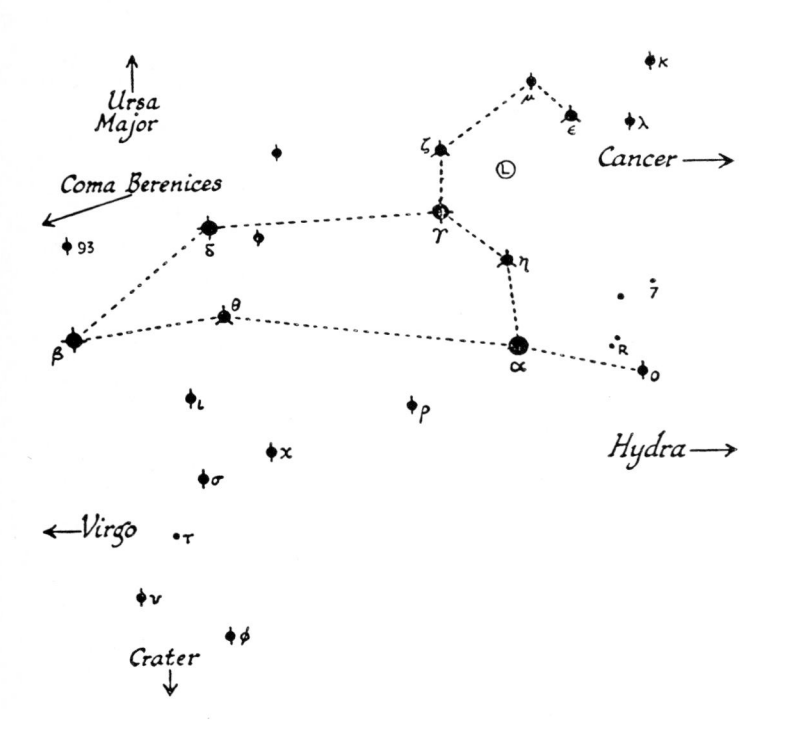

LEO

He is said to have been put among the stars because he is
considered the king of beasts. Some writers add that
Hercules' first Labor was with him and that he killed him,
unarmed.

Hyginus, *Poetica astronomica*, II.24

Plate 28
LEO

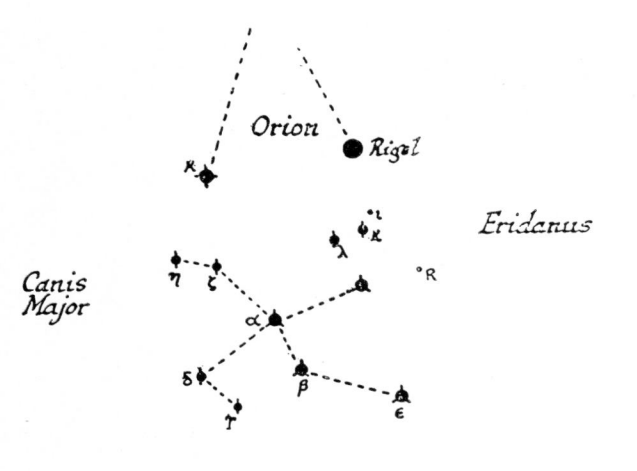

LEPUS

This hare is said to be fleeing the dog of the hunter Orion, for when, as was proper, they represented Orion as a hunter, they wanted to indicate what he was hunting, and so they put the fleeing hare at his feet. Some say that it was put there by Mercury, and that it had been given the faculty, beyond other kinds of quadrupeds, of being pregnant with new offspring when giving birth to others.

Hyginus, *Poetica astronomica*, II.33

Plate 29
LEPUS

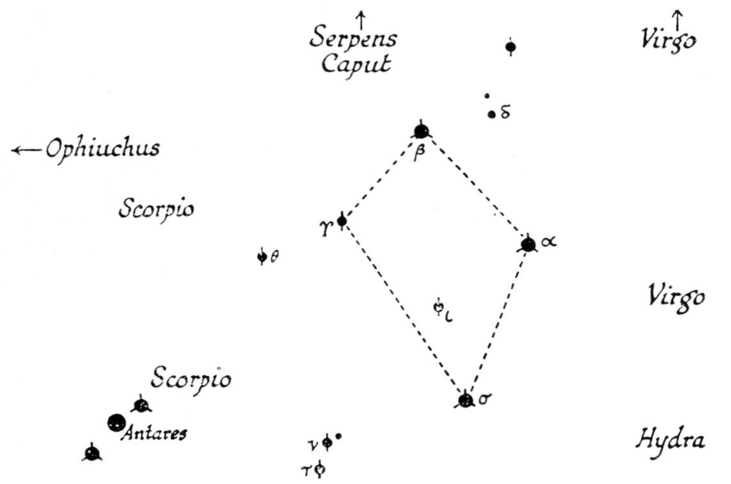

Serpens
Caput

Virgo

Ophiuchus

β

δ

Scorpio

γ

θ

α

ι

Virgo

Scorpio

Antares

σ

ν
τ

Hydra

LIBRA

*At the Virgin's feet, beside the menacing Scorpion, we find
the seventh sign of the zodiac, Libra, the Scales, marked by
two stars of similar magnitude. The first, slightly brighter, is
Alpha Librae, called Zubenelgenubi, from the Arabic* al-
Zuban al-Janubiyyah, *the Southern Claw. The second star,
Beta Librae, is correspondingly called Zubenschamali, from*
al-Zuban al-Shamaliyyah, *the Northern Claw.*

Plate 30
LIBRA

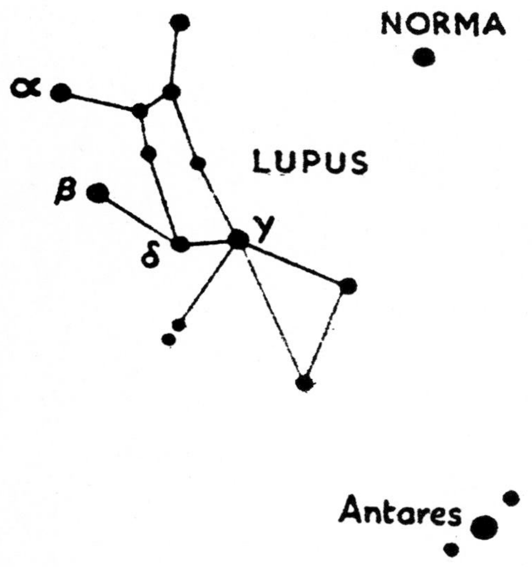

NORMA

α

LUPUS

β

δ γ

Antares

LUPUS

His mantle, now his hide, with rugged hairs
Cleaves to his back, a famish'd face he bears,
His arms descend, his shoulders sink away
To multiply his legs for chase of prey;
He grows a wolf, his hoariness remains,
And the same rage in other members reigns.
His eyes still sparkle in a narrower space,
His jaws retain the grin and violence of his face.

Ovid, *Metamorphoses*, 1.232–35

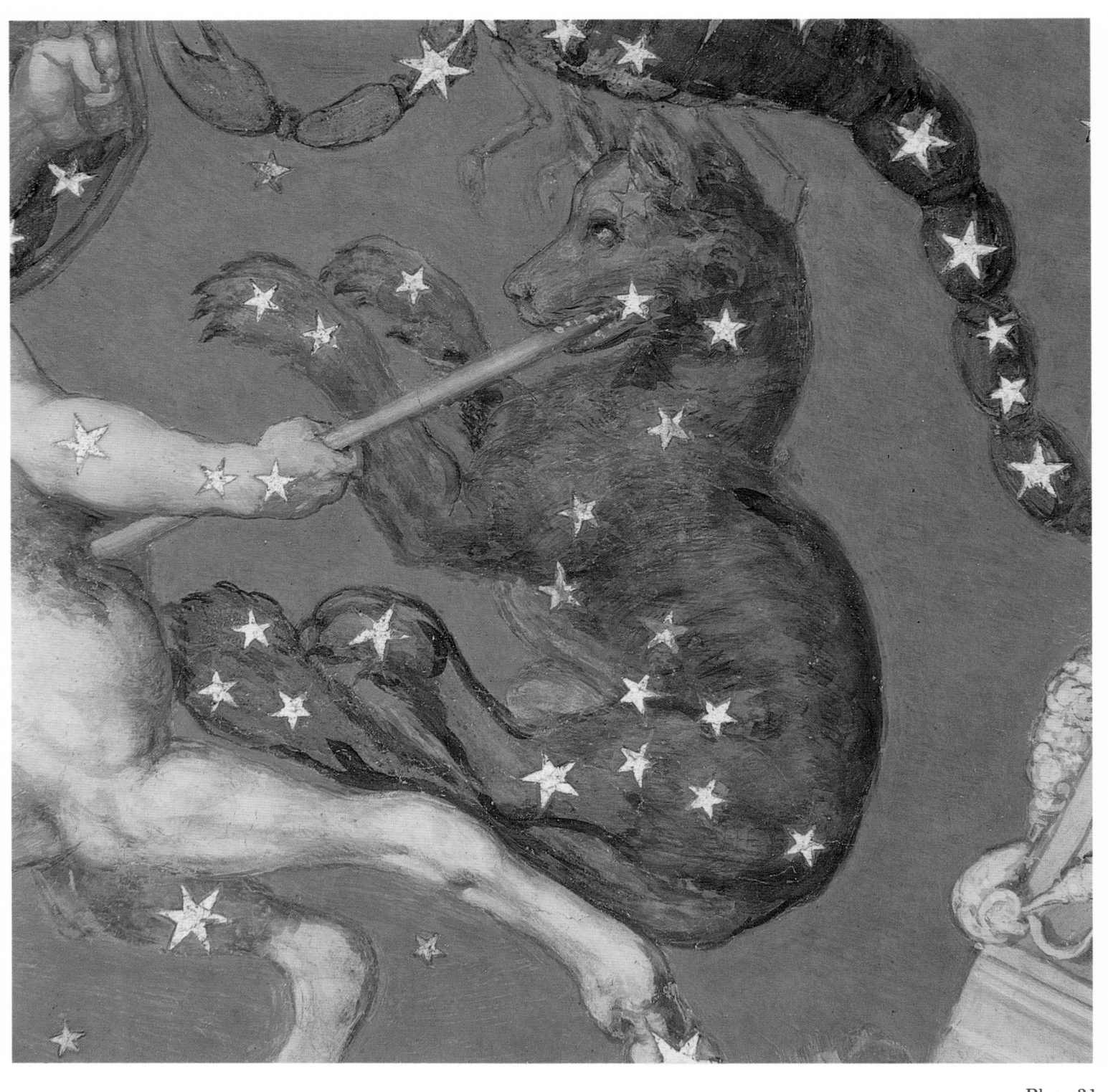

Plate 31
LUPUS

185

Draco

Cygnus

ε φ
φ η   ζ φ ●α
φ θ   (L)
δ φ
φ κ

Hercules

β
γ

β Cygni

Hercules

Aquila

Altair

LYRA

Thus, while the bard melodiously complains,
And to his lyre accords his vocal strains,
The very bloodless shades attention keep,
And silent seem compassionate to weep;
Ev'n Tantalus his flood unthirsty views,
Nor flies the stream, nor he the stream pursues;
Ixion's wondering wheel its whirl suspends,
And the voracious vulture, charm'd, attends;
No more the Belides their toil bemoan,
And Sisyphus, reclined, sits listening on his stone.

Then first ('tis said) by sacred verse subdued,
The furies felt their cheeks with tears bedew'd.
Nor could the rigid king or queen of hell
The impulse of pity in their hearts repel.

Now, from a troop of shades that last arrive,
Eurydice was call'd, and stood revived. . . .

Ovid, *Metamorphoses*, 10.40–47

Plate 32
LYRA

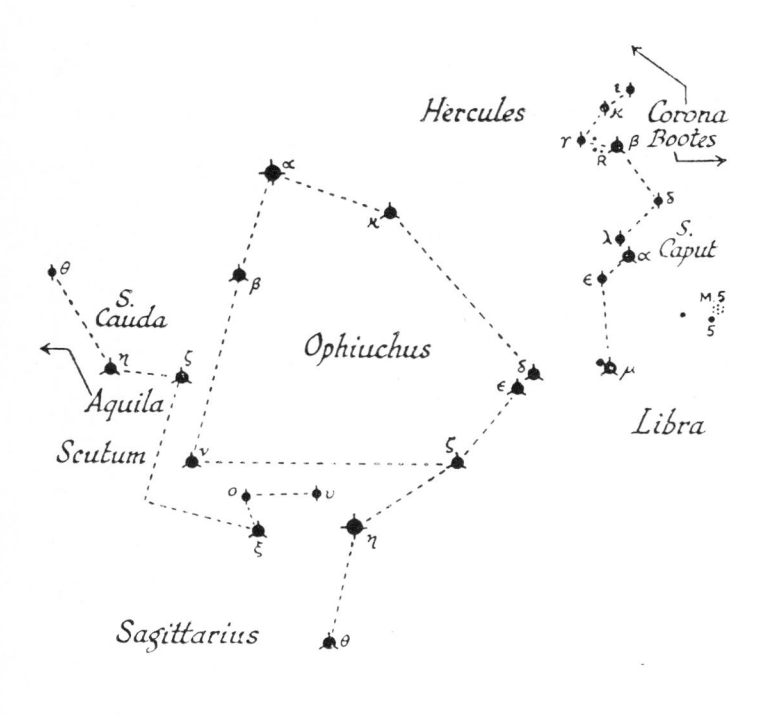

OPHIUCHUS AND THE SERPENT

*I begin to sing of Asclepius, son of Apollo and healer of
sicknesses. In the Dotian plain fair Coronis, daughter of King
Phlegyas, bare him, a great joy to men, a soother of cruel
pangs.*

Hesiod, *The Homeric Hymns*, XVI

Plate 33
OPHIUCHUS AND THE SERPENT

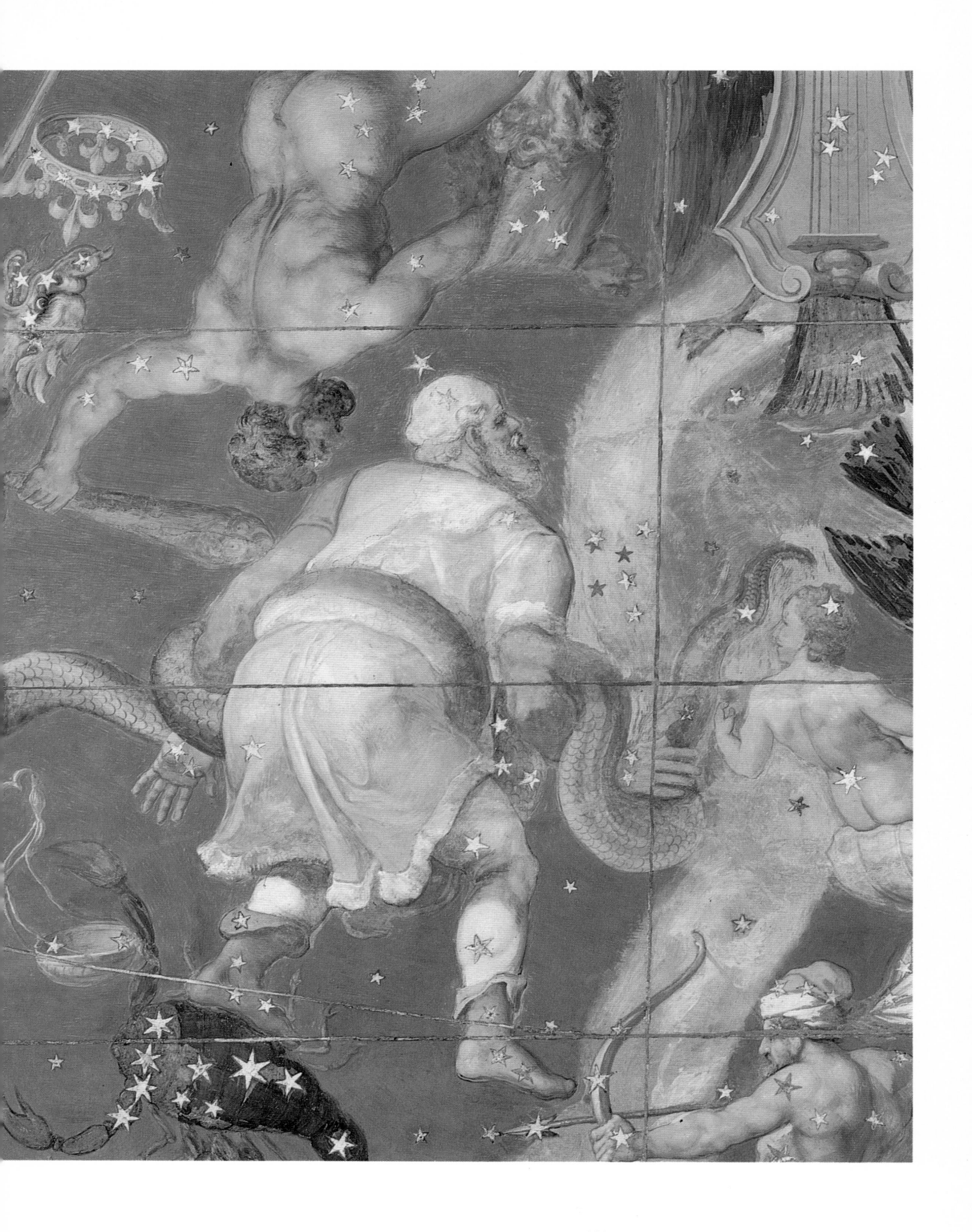

Gemini

x^2 x^1

Taurus $\longrightarrow$

ν
ξ

λ
μ
φ^2 φ^1
α
o^1
o^2
π^1
ϕ γ
π^2
π^3
ω
π^4
π^5
π^6

Monoceros

ϵ σ
ζ
η

θ M.42

Eridanus $\longrightarrow$

τ
β

κ

Lepus
μ Leporis

α Leporis

ORION

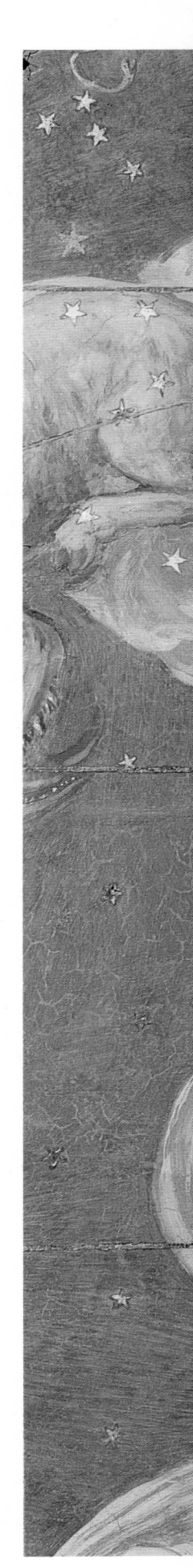

Istrus . . . says that Diana loved Orion and came near
marrying him. Apollo took this hard, and when scolding her
brought no results, on seeing the head of Orion who was
swimming a long way off, he wagered her that she couldn't
hit with her arrows the black object in the sea. Since she
wished to be called an expert in that skill, she shot an arrow
and pierced the head of Orion. The waves brought his slain
body to the shore, and Diana, grieving greatly that she had
struck him, and mourning his death with many tears, put him
among the constellations.

Hyginus, *Poetica astronomica*, II.34

Plate 34
ORION

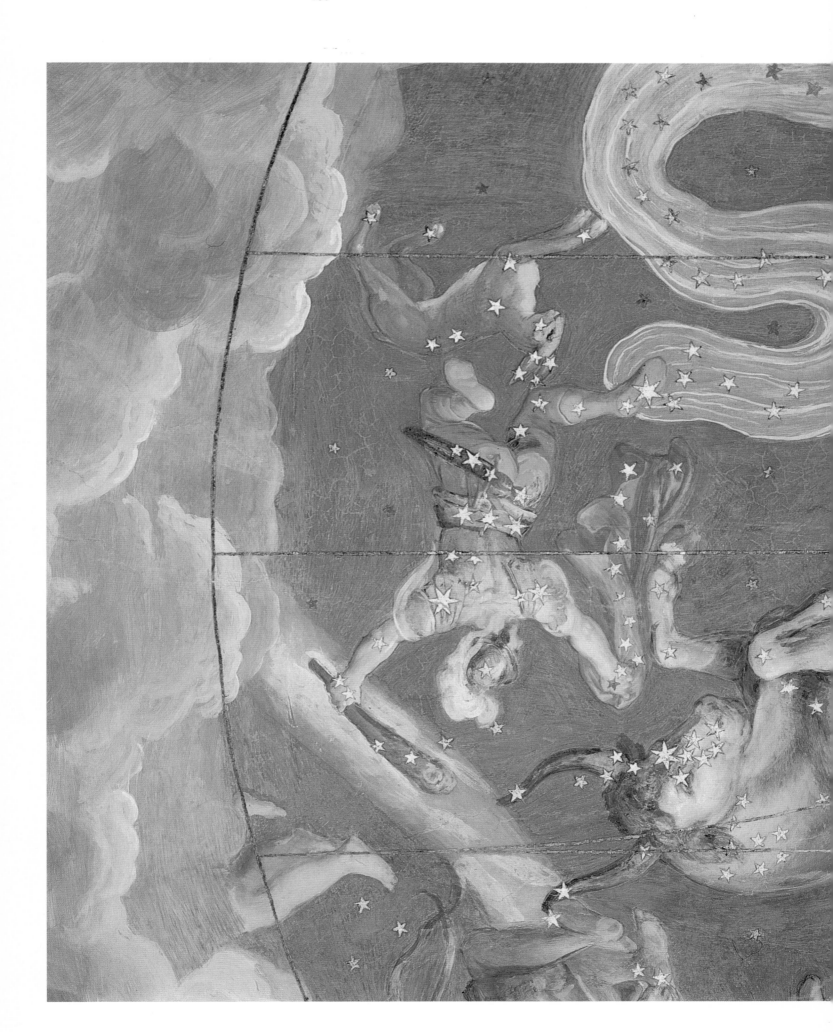

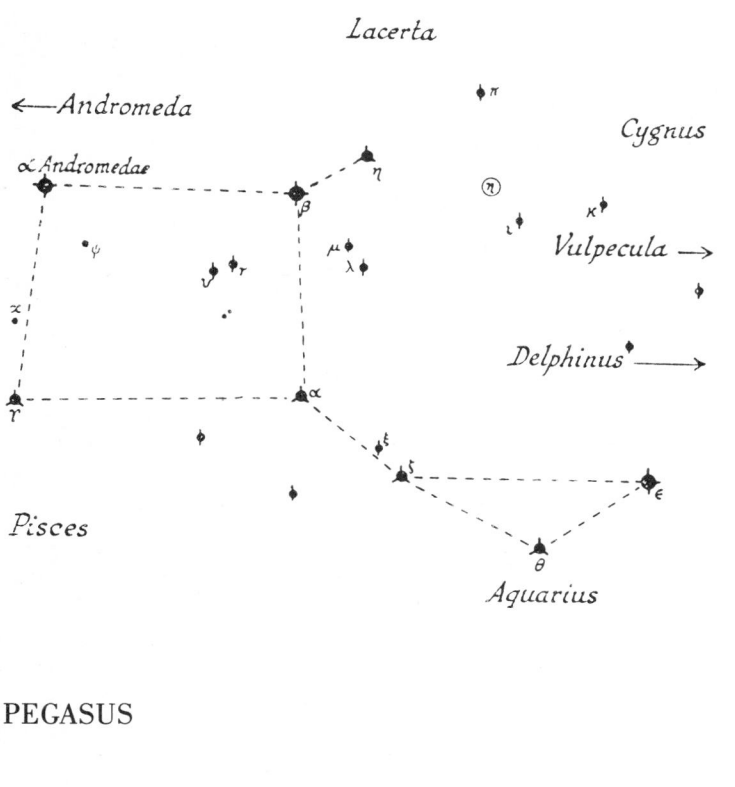

PEGASUS

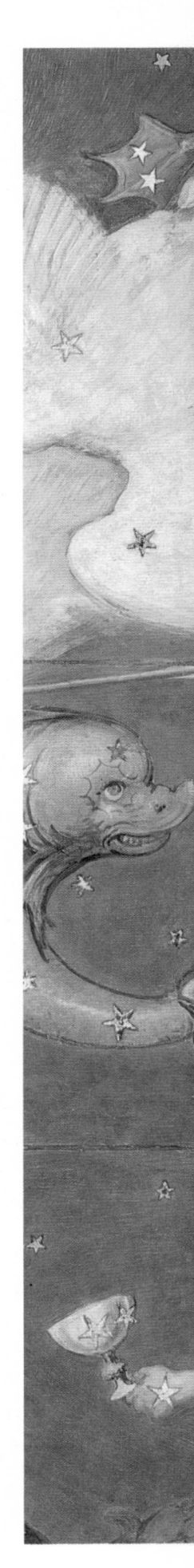

"We the strange tidings of a new-found spring,
Ye learned sisters, to this mountain bring.
If all be true that Fame's wide rumours tell,
'Twas Pegasus discover'd first your well;
Whose piercing hoof gave the soft earth a blow.
Which broke the surface where these waters flow.
I saw that horse by miracle obtain
Life, from the blood of dire Medusa slain;
And now this equal prodigy to view,
From distant isles to famed Boeotia flew."

The muse Urania said: "Whatever cause
So great a goddess to this mansion draws,
Our shades are happy with so bright a guest;
You, queen, are welcome, and we muses bless'd.
What Fame has publish'd of our spring is true;
Thanks for our spring to Pegasus are due."
Then with becoming courtesy, she led
The curious stranger to their fountain's head,
Who long survey'd, with wonder and delight,
Their sacred water, charming to the sight;
Their ancient groves, dark grottoes, shady bowers,
And smiling plains, adorn'd with various flowers.

Ovid, *Metamorphoses*, 5.256–66

Plate 35
PEGASUS

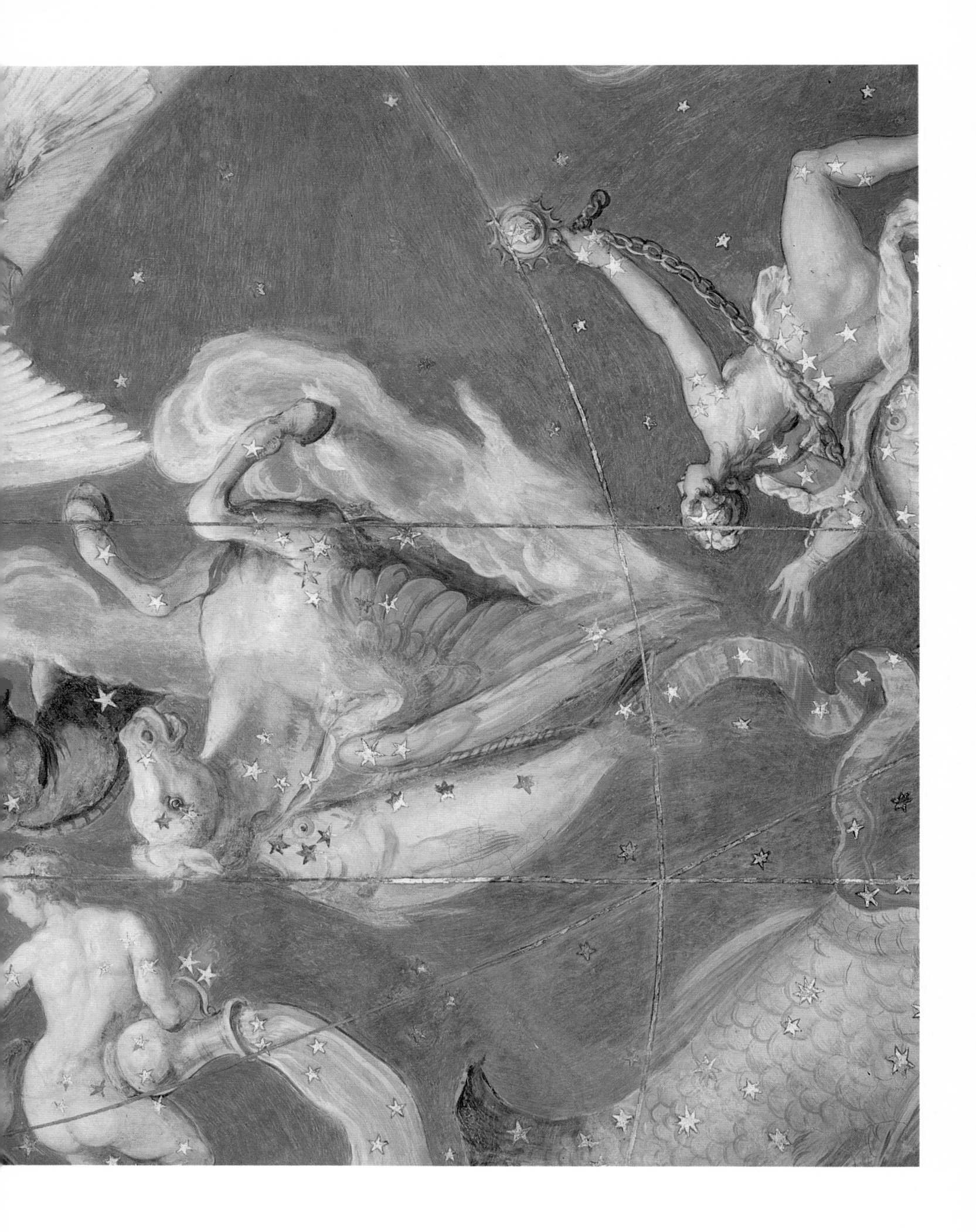

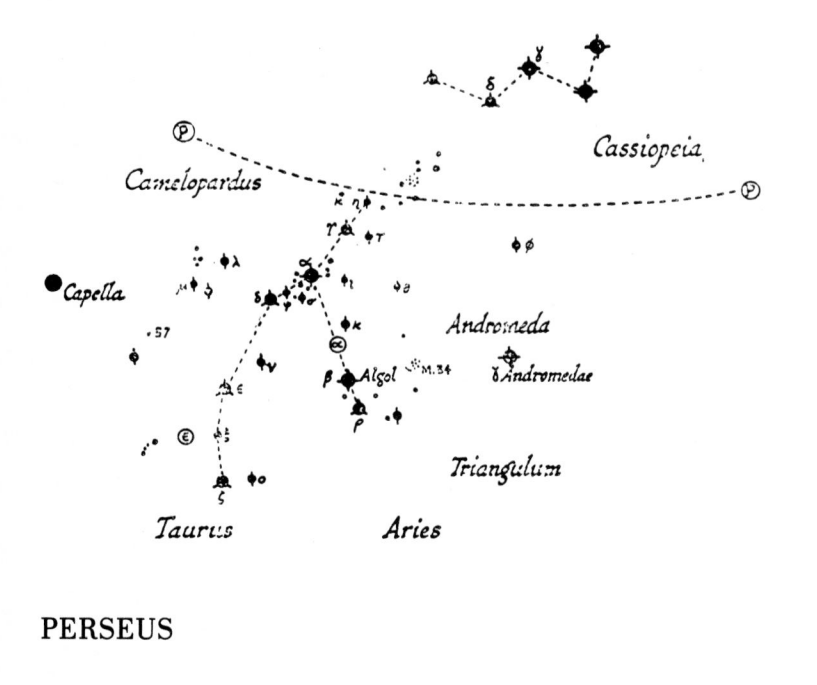

PERSEUS

"In me the son of thundering Jove behold,
Got in a kindly shower of fruitful gold:
Medusa's snaky head is now my prey,
And through the clouds I boldly wing my way:
If such desert be worthy of esteem,
And if your daughter from death redeem,
Shall she be mine? Shall it not then be thought
A bride so lovely was too cheaply bought?
For her my arms I willingly employ,
If I may beauties, which I save, enjoy."

Ovid, *Metamorphoses*, 4.697–703

Plate 36
PERSEUS

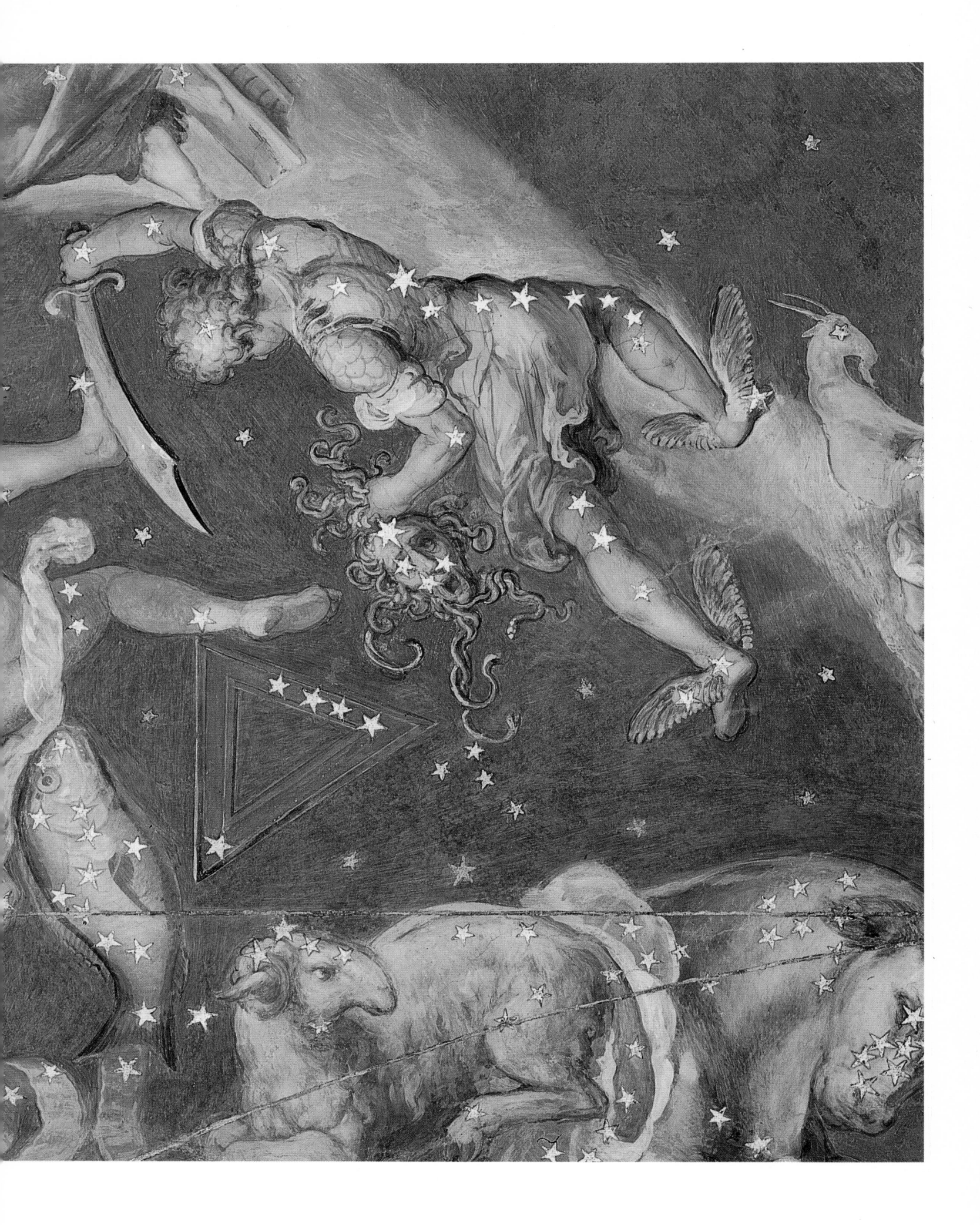

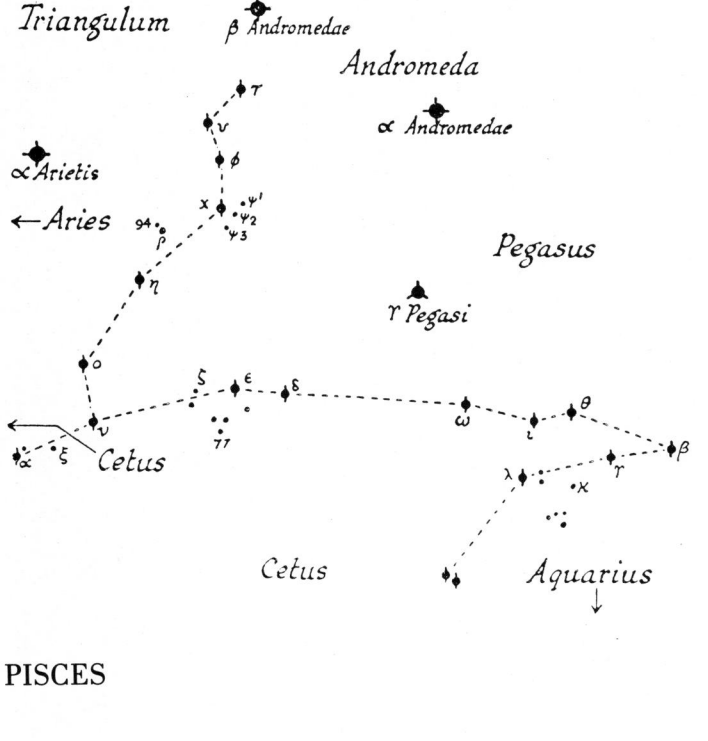

PISCES

Once Venus and her son Cupid, in Syria, came to the river
Euphrates. There Tryphon suddenly appeared. Venus and
Cupid threw themselves into the river and changed into
fishes, and by doing so, escaped danger.

Hyginus, *Poetica astronomica*, II.30

Plate 37
PISCES

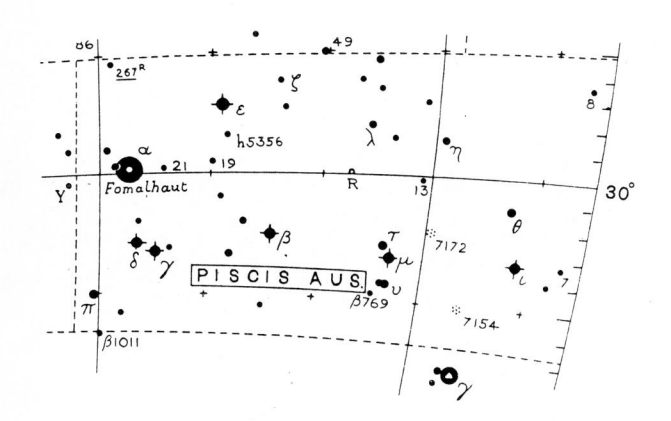

PISCIS AUSTRINUS

This is the Fish that is called Southern. He seems to take water in his mouth from the sign of Aquarius. Once, when Isis was in labor, he is thought to have saved her, and as a reward for this kindness she placed the fish . . . among the stars.

Hyginus, *Poetica astronomica*, II.41

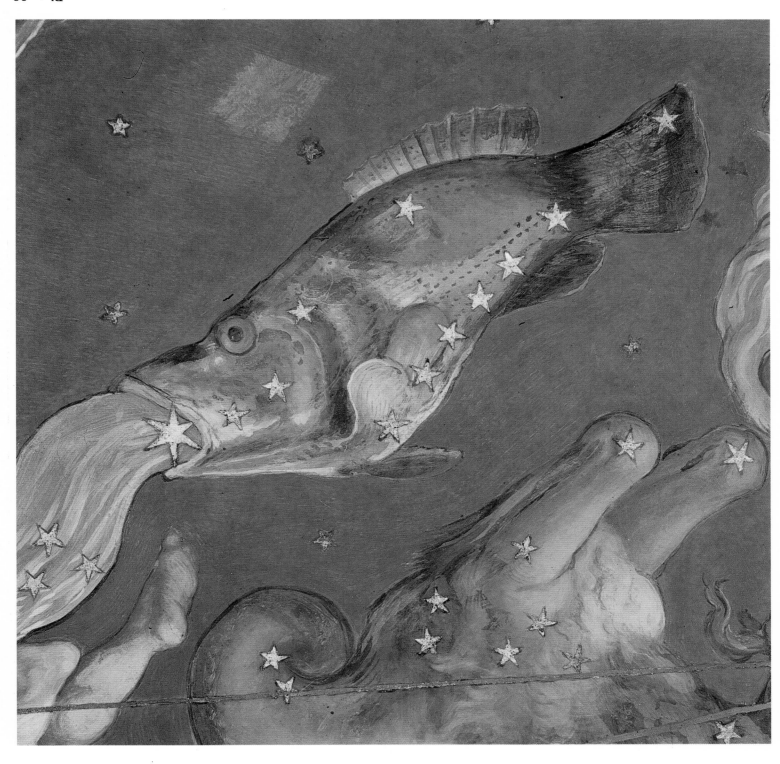

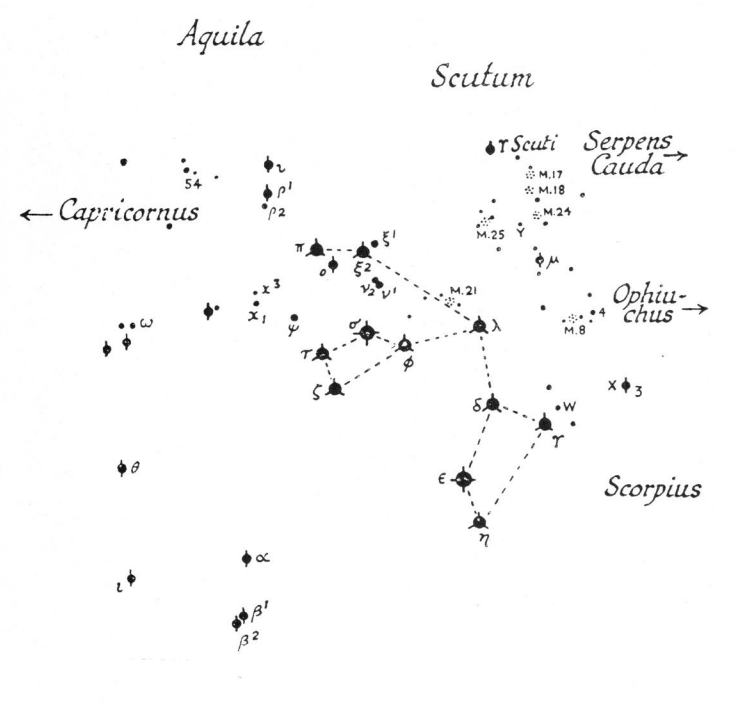

Aquila

Scutum

Serpens
Cauda →

← Capricornus

Ophiu-
chus →

Scorpius

SAGITTARIUS

Crotus, son of Eupheme, nurse of the Muses . . . had his home on Mt. Helicon and took pleasure in the company of the Muses, sometimes even following the pursuit of hunting. He attained great fame for his diligence, for he was very swift in the woods, and clever in the arts. As a reward for his zeal the Muses asked Jove to represent him in some star group, and Jove did so. Since he wished to display all his skills in one body, he gave him horse flanks, because he rode a great deal. He added arrows, since these would show both his keenness and his swiftness, and he gave him a Satyr's tail because the Muses took no less pleasure in Crotus than Liber did in the Satyrs.

Hyginus, *Poetica astronomica*, II.27

Plate 39
SAGITTARIUS

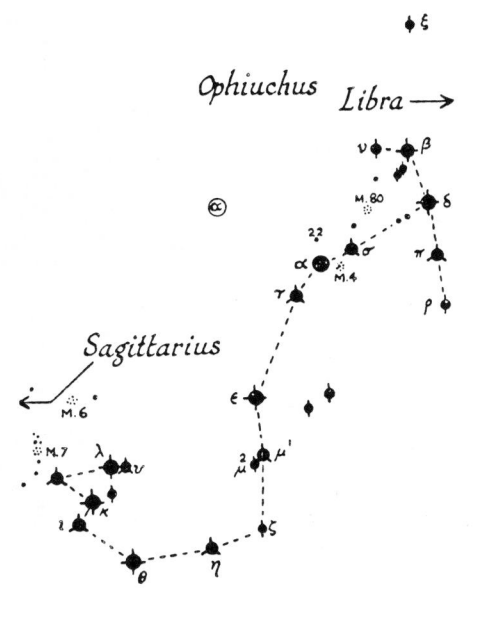

Ophiuchus Libra →

Sagittarius

SCORPIUS

Now all the horrors of the heavens he spies,
And monstrous shadows of prodigious size,
That, deck'd with stars, lie scatter'd o'er the skies.
There is a place above, where Scorpio bent
In tail and arms surrounds a vast extent;
In a wide circuit of the heavens he shines,
And fills the space of two celestial signs.

Ovid, *Metamorphoses*, 2.193–97

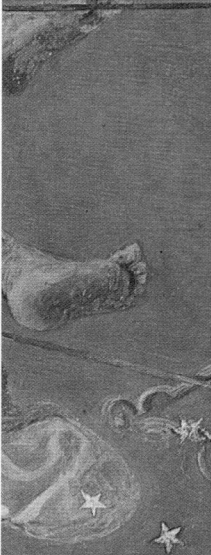

Plate 40
SCORPIUS

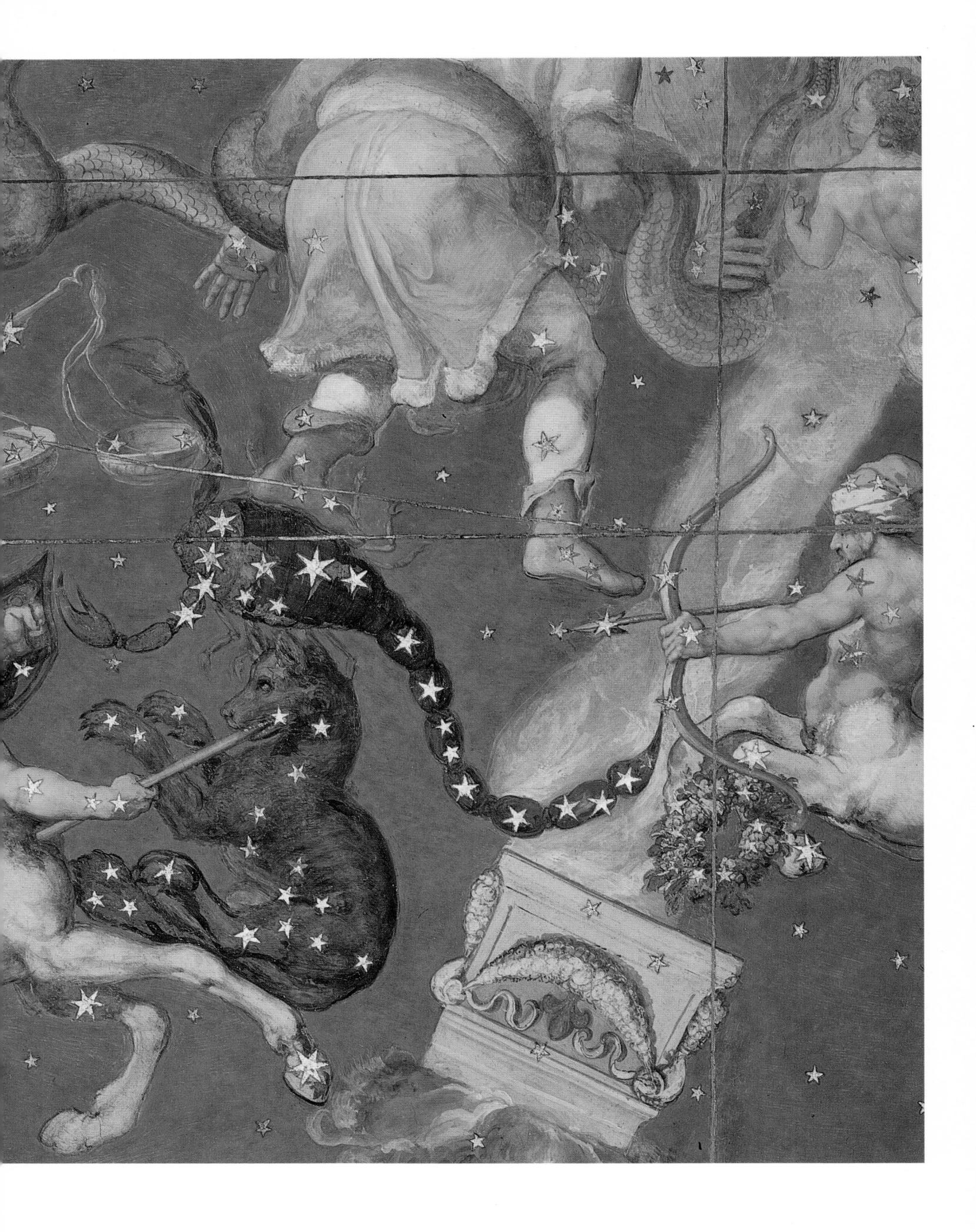

Auriga

Perseus

β

Aries →

ψ

φ

M.1

ζ

τ

ν
χ
ε

Pleiades

ω

ε φ

Gemini

α

δ

←

ρ

θ¹
θ₂

γ

λ

ξ
ο

Orion

μ

Cetus

ν

Eridanus

TAURUS

Large rolls of fat about his shoulders clung,
And from his neck the double dewlap hung;
His skin was whiter than the snow that lies
Unsullied by the breath of southern skies;
Small shining horns on his curl'd forehead stand,
As turn'd and polish'd by the workman's hand;
His eyeballs roll'd, not formidably bright,
But gazed and languish'd with a gentle light;
His every look was peaceful, and express'd
The softness of the lover in the beast.
    Agenor's royal daughter, as she play'd
Among the fields, the milk-white bull survey'd,
And view'd his spotless body with delight,
And at a distance kept him in her sight.
At length she pluck'd the rising flowers, and fed
The gentle beast, and fondly stroked his head.
He stood, well pleased to touch the charming fair,
But hardly could confine his pleasures there.

Ovid, *Metamorphoses*, 2.854–63

Plate 41
TAURUS

204   *The Glorious Constellations*

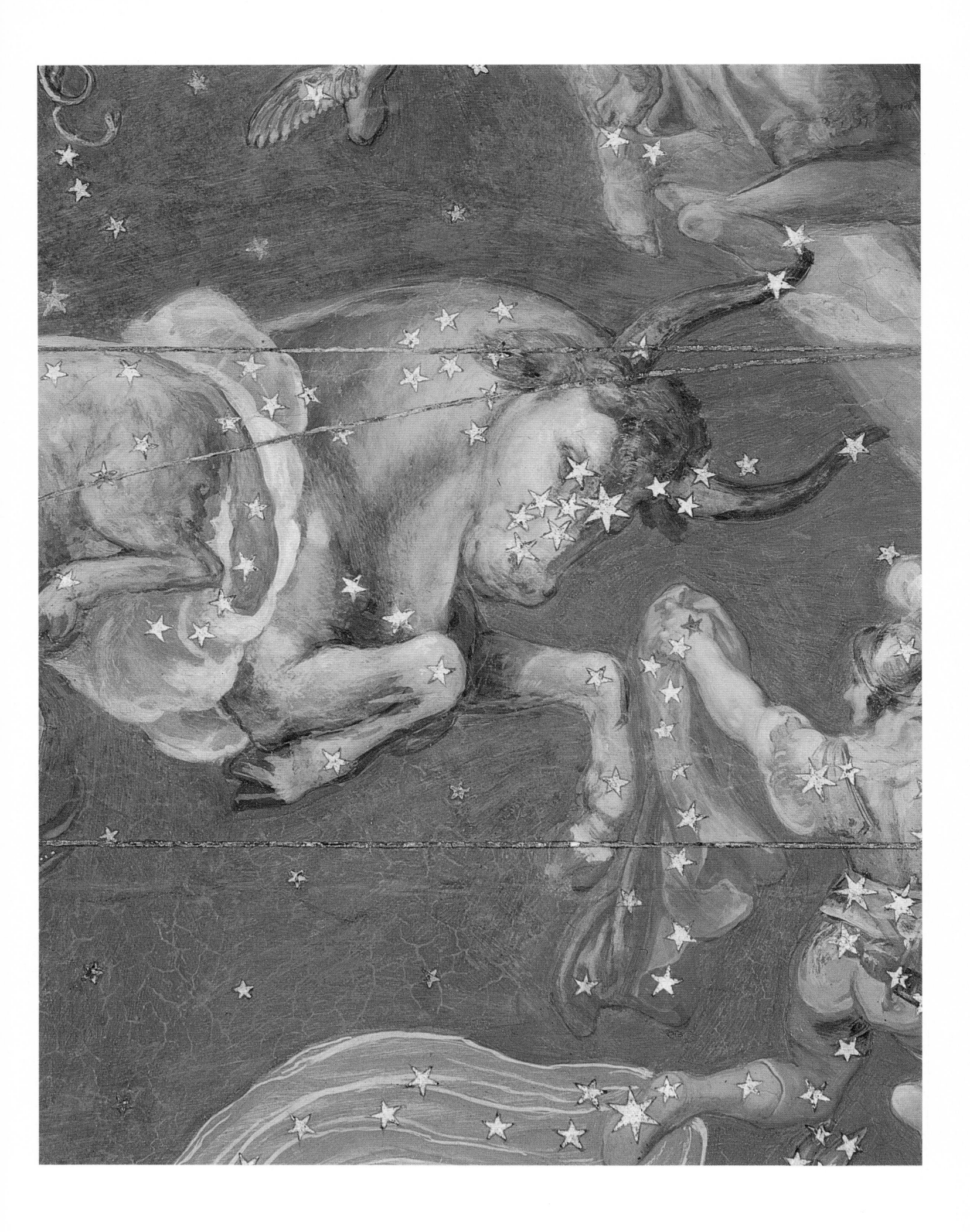

TRIANGULUM

*Some have said that it pictures the position of Egypt; others,
that of Aethiopia and Egypt where the Nile marks their
boundaries. Still others think that Sicily is pictured there;
others, that three angles were put there because the gods
divided the universe into three parts.*

Hyginus, *Poetica astronomica*, II.19

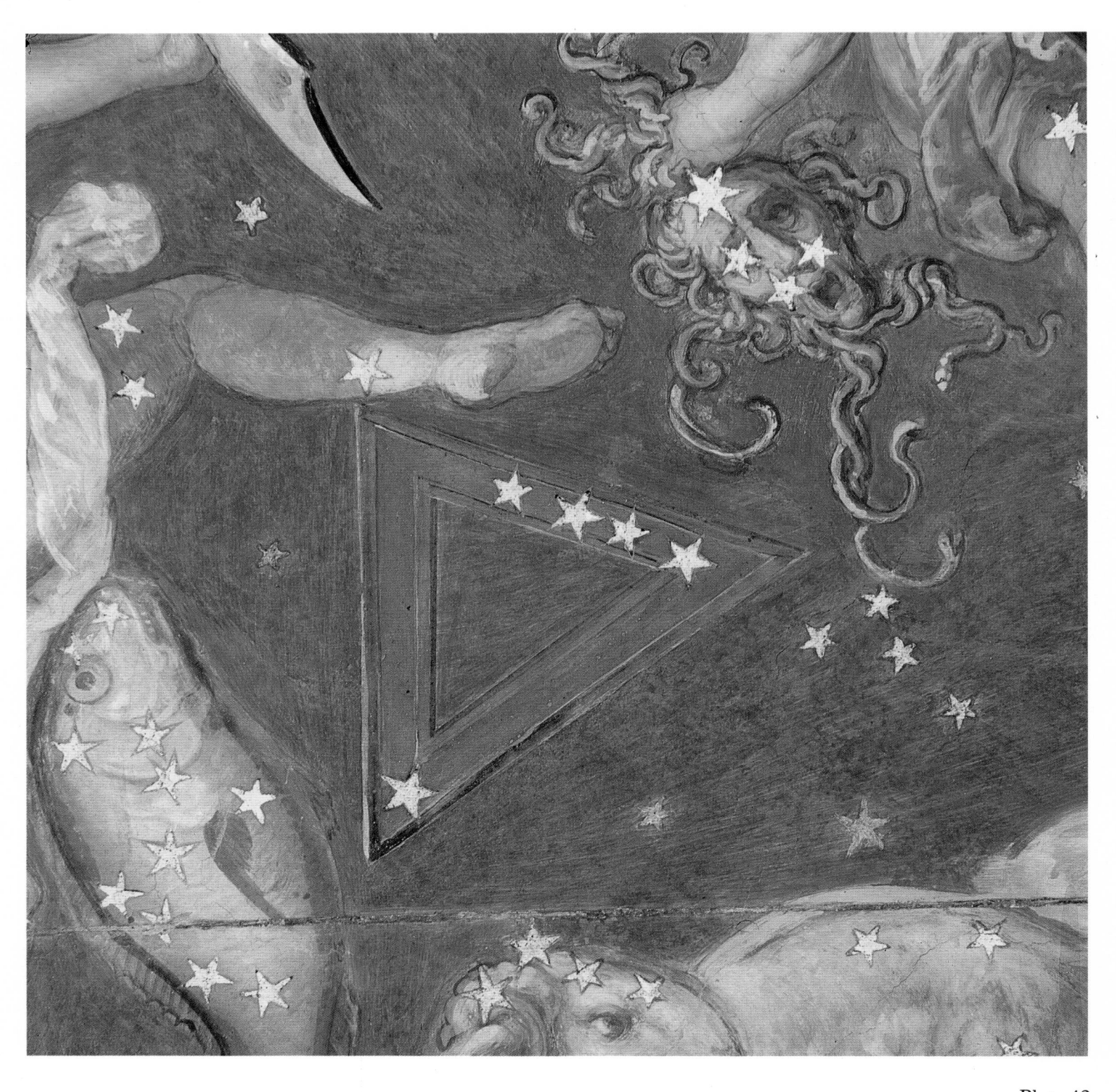

Plate 42
TRIANGULUM

Polaris

Camelopardus

Lynx →

Draco

α

Bootes

ξ
ε
δ
γ
η

β

θ
κ

Canes
Venatici

χ

Lynx →

ψ
λ
μ

Leo

ν
ξ

URSA MAJOR

The axis [of the earth] is always firm, and although it may
appear to shift a little, yet it is never much disarranged, while
the earth maintains its equilibrium in the centre; and around
it the sky turns itself. Also the two Poles terminate at either
extremity; one indeed is not visible, but the other to the
Northward rises high above the ocean surrounding it, two
Bears lie circularly, which are usually called the Wains. Each
has its head inverted upon the loins of the other, but always
borne along back to back while the shoulders are alternately
reversed.

[The ancients] would have us believe that they ascended to
heaven, from the island of Crete, by the powerful assistance
of Zeus himself, because these Bears, when they deceived
Saturn, placed him, while still an infant, in a place, odorous
with flowers, near Mount Ida, and nourished him for a whole
year. They called one of these Bears Cynosura [Ursa Minor]
and the other Helice [Ursa Major].

Aratus, *Phaenomena*, 18

Plate 43
URSA MAJOR

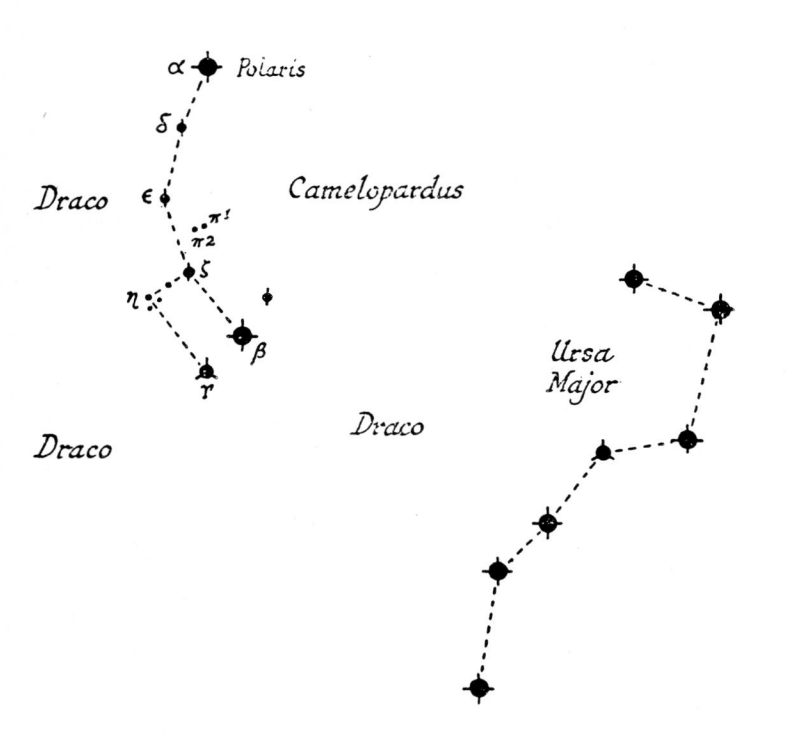

URSA MINOR

The Greeks place faith in Helice [Ursa Major] in respect of
their naval affairs and the direction of their shipping. The
Phoenicians have confidence in Cynosura [Ursa Minor]
during their voyages.

Helice is clear and readily observed shining brightly at the
commencement of the night. The other, Cynosura, is
comparatively obscure, but, nevertheless, more useful to the
sailor because it revolves in a lesser circle.

Aratus, *Phaenomena*, 18

Plate 44
URSA MINOR

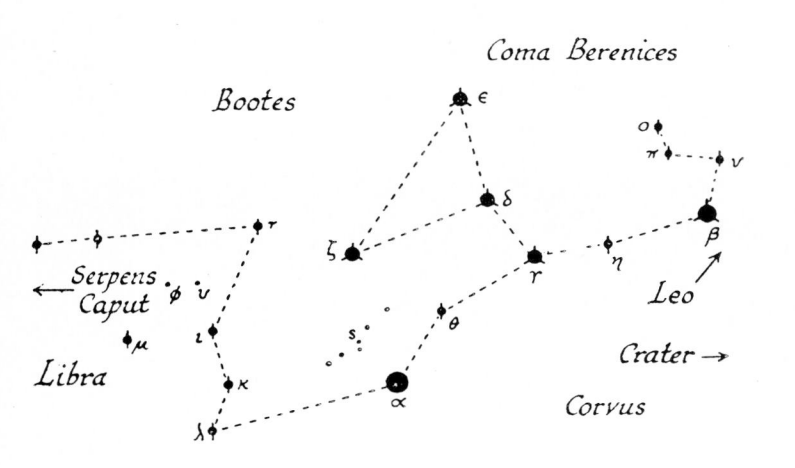

VIRGO

But when Erigone [Virgo, the Virgin], the daughter of Icarius, moved by longing for her father, saw he did not return and was on the point of going out to hunt for him, the dog of Icarius, Maera by name, returned to her, howling as if lamenting the death of its master. It gave her no slight suspicion of murder, for the timid girl would naturally suspect her father had been killed since he had been gone so many months and days. But the dog, taking hold of her dress with his teeth, led her to the body.

Hyginus, *Poetica astronomica*, II.4

Plate 45
VIRGO

213

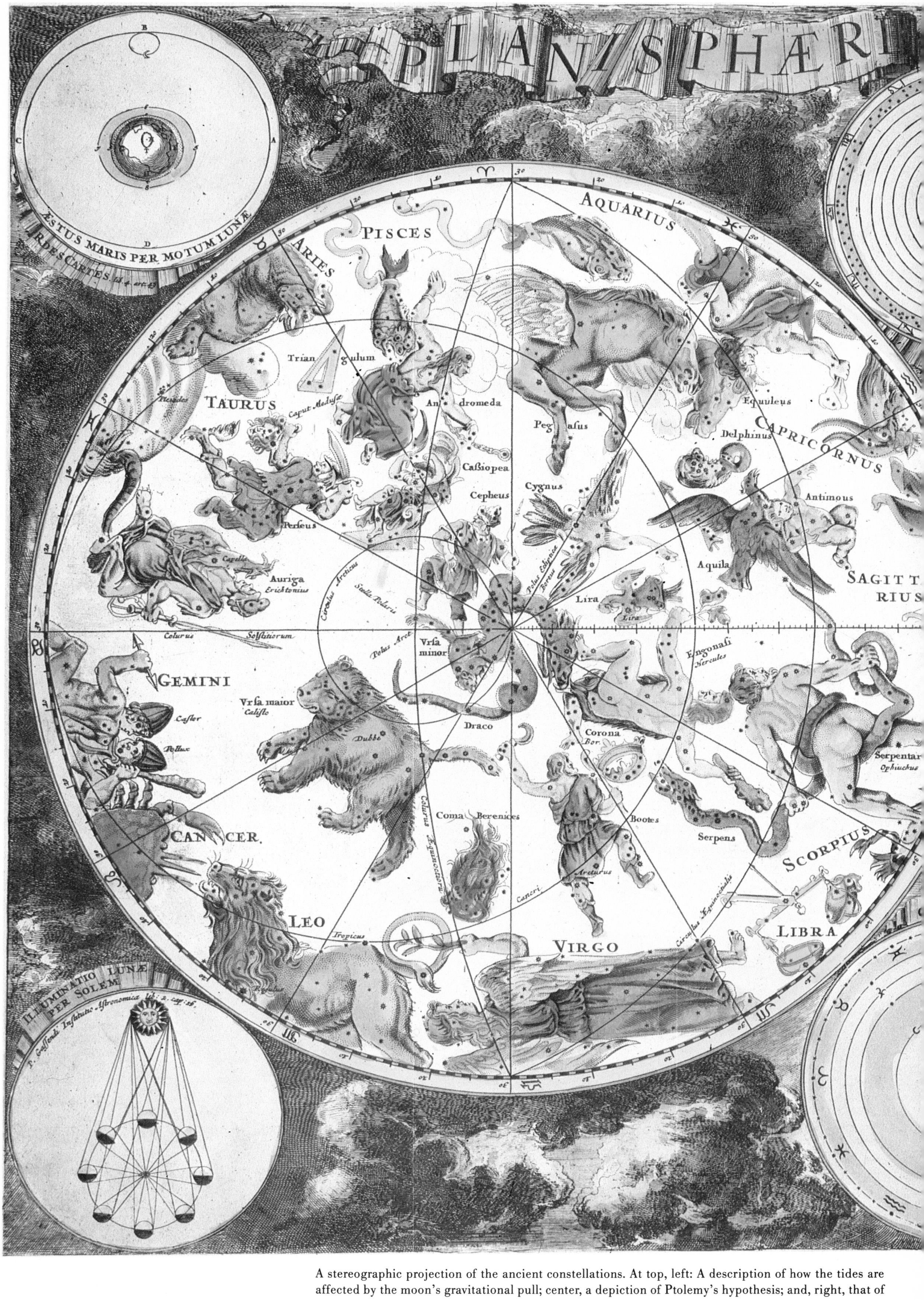
PLANISPHÆRI
ÆSTUS MARIS PER MOTUM LUNÆ
R. DESCARTES
ILLUMINATIO LUNÆ PER SOLEM
PISCES
ARIES
AQUARIUS
TAURUS
Triangulum
Andromeda
Pegasus
Equuleus
Delphinus
CAPRICORNUS
Caput Medusæ
Caßiopea
Cepheus
Cygnus
Antinous
Perseus
Aquila
Auriga
Erichtonius
Capella
SAGITTARIUS
Lira
Circulus Arcticus
Stella Polaris
Polus Eclipticæ Boreus
Colurus Solstitiorum
Polus Arct.
Vrsa minor
Engonasi
Hercules
GEMINI
Vrsa maior
Calisto
Castor
Pollux
Draco
Dubbe
Corona Bor.
Serpentarius
Ophiuchus
Coma Berenices
Bootes
Serpens
CANCER
Arcturus
SCORPIUS
Colurus Æquinoctiorum
Cancri
Circulus Æquinoctialis
LEO
Tropicus
VIRGO
LIBRA

A stereographic projection of the ancient constellations. At top, left: A description of how the tides are affected by the moon's gravitational pull; center, a depiction of Ptolemy's hypothesis; and, right, that of

COELESTE

Labels on the celestial map:

AQUARIUS

PISCES

ARIES

Cetus, Balena

TAURUS

Fomahant

Piscis notius

Phœnix

Orion

Fluvius Eridanus

Rigel

Grus

Indus

Pica Indica

Turnar

Colomba Noe

Lepus

Alldbaran

Hydra

Polus Ecliptica Australis

Canis maior Sirius

GEMINI

Corona australis

Pauo

Antar cticus

Circul'

Apous Indica

Cameleon

Congrus

Sirius

GEMINI

TTARIUS

Musca

Canicula Procyon

Argo Navis

Ara Thuribulum

ORPIUS

Fera Lupus

Centaurus

Hydra

CANCER

Antares Cor Scorp

El Crisio

Tropicus Capricorni

Cobra

LIBRA

Spica Virginis

Corvus

Crater Vas

LEO

Circulus Equinoctialis

VIR GO

HYPOTHESIS TYCHONICA
Sphæra Stellarum Fixarum

Cælum Saturni

P. LANSBERGII SCHEM

MOTUS TERRÆ ANNUI CIRCA SOLEM
Controversia Secunda

Magnitudines Stellarum
Prime   Quarta
Secunde Quinta
Tertie   Sexta

Amstelodami apud Fredericum de Wit

Tycho Brahe. Below, at left: the moon's reflection of the sun's light; center, the Copernican system; and, right, the earth's annual revolution around the sun.

The Constellations

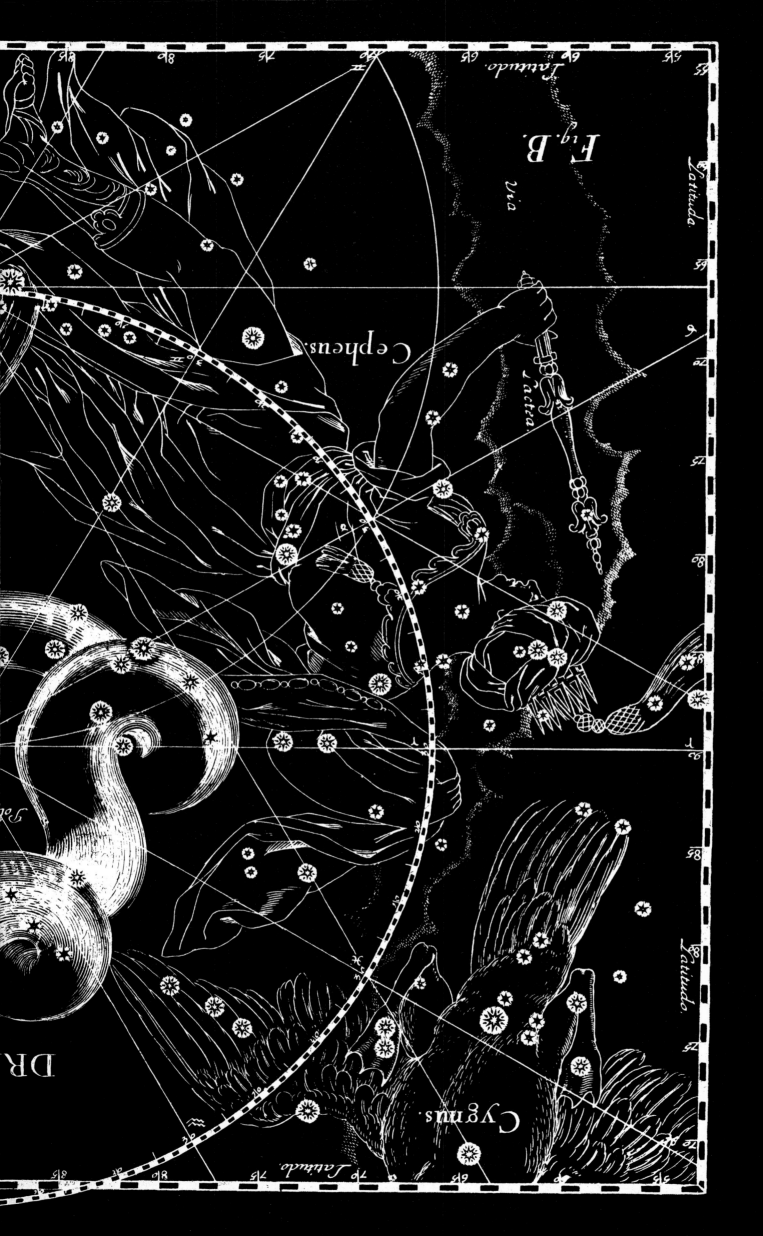

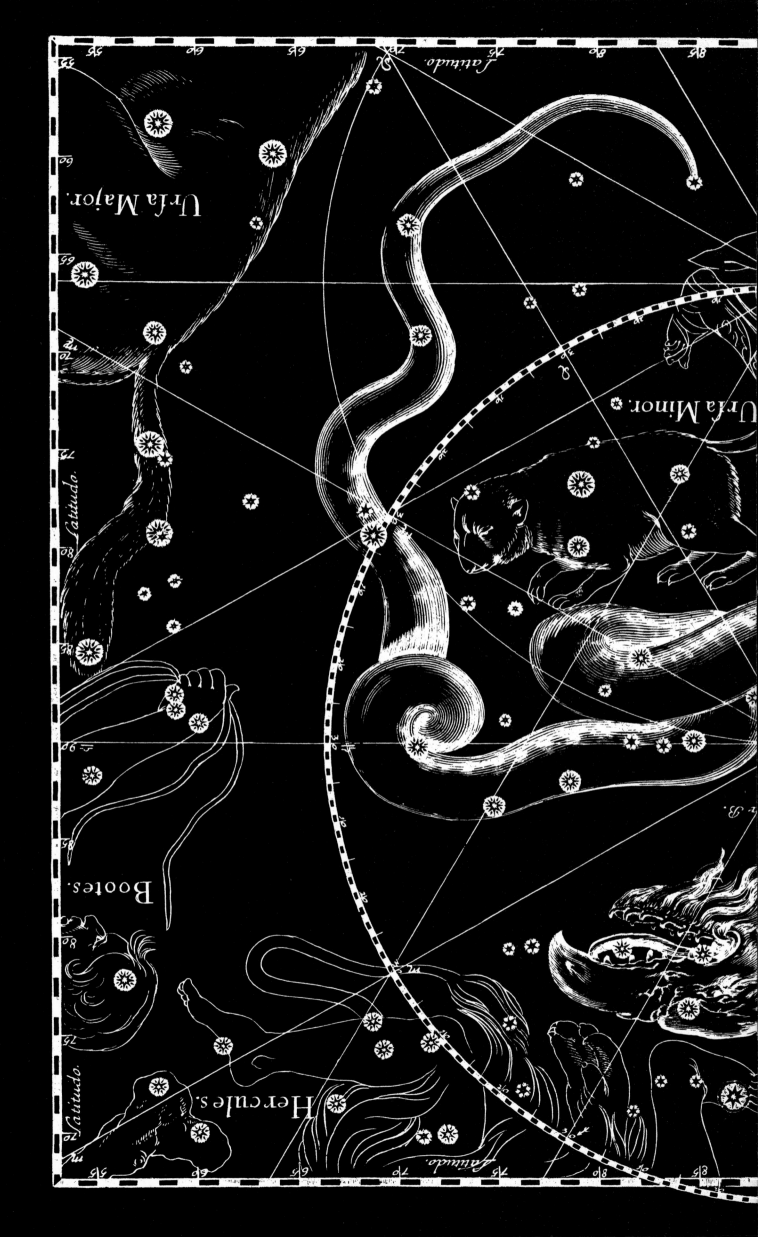

1
Andromeda

If we were to draw an imaginary line from Ursa Major through the Polar Star and Cassiopeia while observing the stars on a beautiful fall evening, we would arrive at Andromeda, next to Pegasus. The first star of the Square of Pegasus is, in fact, Alpha Andromedae, or Sirrah, and belongs to both constellations. Similarly, Beta Andromedae, or Mirach, was shared by Andromeda and the northern fish of the constellation Pisces in the ancient catalogues. Andromeda belongs to that large region of the sky that is dedicated to the epic of Perseus. This region is a vast mythological plot that all together involves as many as seven constellations. It is described in the chapter on Perseus.

The representation of this constellation in star atlases has undergone the most curious of transformations. Originally it was a young girl in the nude wearing jewelry. With the passing of the centuries, however, and with the arrival of less-permissive fashions, the girl was covered, more or less, with veils. Together with Cassiopeia, Cepheus, Pegasus, and Cetus, Andromeda is located on the opposite side of the ecliptic with respect to the sign of Virgo, where the solar expression of the Great Mother as queen of the summer solstice reigns. The Great Mother had, however, three manifestations (as is explained in the chapter on Virgo). As nymph she was Persephone (the seed, the young grain), as woman she was Demeter (the mature grain), as old woman she was Hecate (the harvested grain). The sky maps transmitted to us by the ancient inventors of constellations do not leave much choice for the identification of the three manifestations of the Great Mother. Indeed, the only female figures depicted on the stellar vault are Andromeda, Virgo, and Cassiopeia, the alter egos of Persephone, Demeter, and Hecate.

Andromeda was Ishtar-Kore-Persephone, the goddess of vegetation, who represented the period of the winter repose of the seed underneath the earth. It would return and sprout in the spring, warmed by the rays of the new sun, Tammuz-Perseus-Adonis. Over the stars of Virgo shone the summer sun of the harvest of the grain during solstice. This was the constellation of the triumph of matriarchy's science, agriculture. The ancient Hecate, on the other hand, goddess of many meanings, had her throne among the stars of Cassiopeia, the queen represented sitting with a stalk of grain in her hand.

The young Andromeda represents the danger that the Great Mother runs every year when the powers of the dark slowly reduce the sun to its seasonal minimum, the winter solstice. It is the time when vegetation halts, the time of trees devoid of leaves, the time of lethargy in nature caused by the abduction of Persephone to the realm of the dead by Hades—the black knight who is the possessor of the helmet that makes its wearer invisible, the same helmet that Perseus used to save Andromeda's life.

In his *The History of the Heavens* (1741) Noël Antoine Pluché maintained that the root of Cepheus and Cassiopeia in the ancient Phoenician language was *cepha*, which means stone, and that the coast of Palestine could be called *andromeda*, meaning bare and stony coast. The historian Strabo added to this

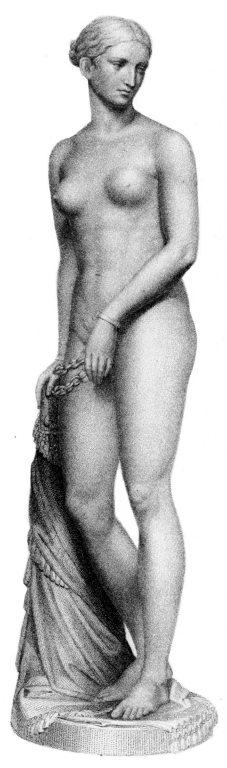

Andromeda
Opposite: *Andromeda. From Hevelius,*
Uranographia totum coelum stellatum *(1690)*

221

Andromeda. From the Alfonsine Tables *(thirteenth century)*

Al-Sufi's Andromeda

Andromeda. From Hyginus, Poetica astronomica *(1485 edition)*

the idea that, in jargon, every Phoenician ship was called *Perseu,* or *Racer,* and that they all had the figurehead of a winged horse, the symbol of navigation, on the prow. On the horse, there often was a knight holding in his hand the symbol of the city of Seis, which was the head of the Medusa.

In the third book of his *Asian Researches,* Wilford notes that, during his stay in India, he had a conversation with an astronomer pundit about the names of the Indian constellations. When requested to indicate Antarmada, the pundit immediately pointed to Andromeda. Later he showed Wilford a rare and curious manuscript in Sanskrit on the extrazodiacal constellations. It contained drawings of Capuja (Cepheus), of Casyapi (Cassiopeia) sitting with a lotus flower in hand, of Antarmada with the fish close to her, and, finally, of Parasica (Perseus) with the head of a serpent-haired monster in his hand.

Despite the Koran's prohibition against representing the human form, even the Arab astronomers called these stars *al-Mar'ah al-Musalsalah,* the Woman in Chains, a title that became Almara Almasulsala in the Chilmead catalogue. Later, however, when religious pressure became more intense, the maiden of stars became a marine seal.

In the *Alfonsine Tables* Andromeda was shown with a chain around her waist and with two fish, one on her breast and the other between her feet, which might point to an ancient tie to the sign Pisces. In the 1488 Venetian edition of Hyginus' fables she was shown chained between two trees. Julius Schiller, an astronomer and iconoclast, published a map of the sky in 1627 on which the young virgin, improbably enough, was transformed into the tomb of the Redeemer with the title of Sepulchrum Christi.

Ptolemy attributed to Andromeda the qualities of Venus, whose gifts were purity of thought, honor, dignity, and virtue, but who could also cause battles with chimeras and bestow the tendency to become easily discouraged. If, however, Mars influenced the stars of Andromeda, she caused death by hanging, decapitation, crucifixion, or impalement.

The cabalists assigned her the seventeenth trump card—the Stars.

The Stars of Andromeda

The brightest star of the constellation is Sirrah, also called Alpheratz. Both names derive from the Arabic name *al-Surrat al-Faras,* the Navel of the Horse, because, as previously seen, this star is shared by Pegasus and Andromeda. In the Arabic sphere inspired by Ptolemy, it was, in fact, described as *al-Ras al-Mar'ah al-Musalsalah,* the Head of the Woman in Chains. In the third century B.C. Aratus called it Common Star to specify that it belonged to two constellations, while in some modern catalogues it is called Caput Andromedae (Head of Andromeda). According to Ptolemy Sirrah was similar in nature to Jupiter and Venus, to whom Alvidas also added Mars. It bestowed independence, freedom, love, riches, honor, and intelligence.

Beta Andromedae, or Mirach, is also a star that belonged both to Andromeda and to the northern fish of the sign of Pisces, as can be seen in the twenty-sixth of the Arab lunar stations, or *manzil, al-Batn al-Hut* (the Belly of the Fish) or *al-Kalb al-Hut* (the Heart of the Fish). Late Arab astronomy assigned it the name *al-Janb al-Musalsalah,* the Side of the Woman in Chains. Confusion about its name is great because Mirach comes from the Arabic *Maragg ad-Dubb al-Akbar,* Back of the Great Bear, a title also assigned to Zeta Ursae Majoris. It was the sixteenth-century French astronomer Scaliger who made this mistake.

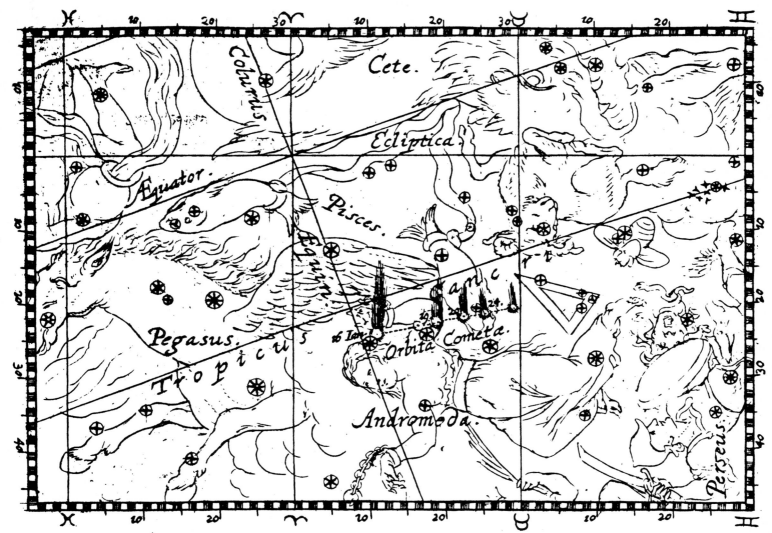

While compiling his map of the stars he erroneously assigned to the Ursa star the original name of Beta Andromedae, Mizar (from *Mi'zar*, Belt or Side), and vice versa. Since then all modern catalogues have scrupulously reproduced the error. All this could mean that the young Andromeda was once a less conspicuous stellar figure or that the division of her two main stars indicates an ancient relationship with the sign of Pisces and the Square of Pegasus.

Ptolemy assigned to Mirach the qualities of Venus, while Alvidas classified it as a dependent of Mars and the moon. This star bestowed great beauty, a brilliant mind, love of home, devotion, beneficence, forgiveness, love, gentleness, fame, and fortune in marriage.

The history of the name Gamma Andromedae, Alamac, which appeared in the *Alfonsine Tables* and in the *Almagest* of 1515, is also eventful. Elsewhere it was transcribed as Alamak, Alamech, Almak, or Almaack, all derived from *al-Anak al-Ard*, a small Arabian predator similar to a badger. It appears this way in the catalogues of Ulugh-Beg, in those of al-Tizini, and in all the preceding Arab catalogues. This calls for the hypothesis that the ancient astronomy of the nomads had another constellation in this place, different from Andromeda. To be noted also are the versions of Muhammad al-Achsasi al-Muwakkit, who called the star *al-Hamis al-Naamat*, the Fifth of the Ostriches, and the one recorded by Hyde, *al-Rijl al-Musalsalah*, the Foot of the Woman. In Chinese astronomy this star appears with the name of *Tien Ta Tseang*, the Great General of the Sky. Reputed to be of the same nature as Venus, Alamac brought honors, eminence, and artistic qualities.

Path of a comet through the constellation of Andromeda, as observed by J. C. Stumm in January, 1681

X. *Andromeda.*

ANDROMEDA proxime Caſſiepeiam, ſupra caput
Perſei, brevi intervallo diſſidente collocata perſpicitur, ma-

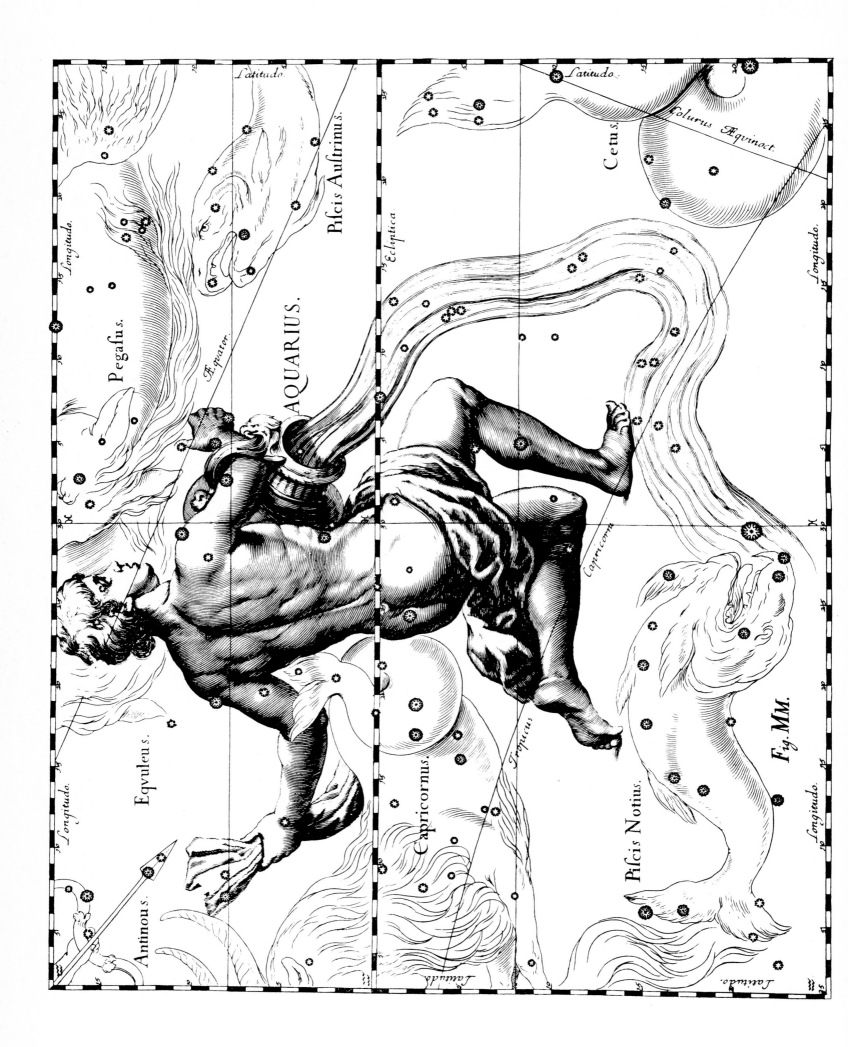

Latitudo.

Latitudo.

Piscis Austrinus.

Cetus.

Colurus Æquinoct.

AQUARIUS.

Pegasus.

Ecliptica.

Longitudo.

Æquator.

Longitudo.

Longitudo.

Capricornu.

Pisces Notius.

Fig. MM.

Equuleus.

Capricornus.

Tropicus.

Longitudo.

Longitudo.

Antinous.

Latitudo.

Latitudo.

2
Aquarius

Low on the southern horizon of the starry sky shine the stars of an ancient and complex constellation, Aquarius, the Water Carrier. On the star maps it can be found in the large region the ancient astronomers called the Sea. This region is filled mainly with marine or amphibious figures, and it is located on the ecliptic between the signs of Pisces and Capricornus.

Aquarius is composed of the figure of a man with one arm outstretched toward Capricornus with a cloak or small staff in his hand. He holds the pail or amphora from which the River Aquarius flows in his other arm. This small river, composed of a quantity of little stars, descends toward the south until it encounters a brilliant first-magnitude star, Fomalhaut—from the Arabic *fom al-hut* (the mouth of the fish); a fish, Piscis Austrinus, marks the river's end and seems to drink all its water.

The ancient astronomical literature gives us very few—almost no—explanations for the placement of the elements that make up the figure of Aquarius and the true identity of the person who holds the pail. What we do know is that the rising of the sun into this sign coincided with a time of abundant rainfall and that late Greek mythology saw Ganymede, the cupbearer of the gods, as the hero who held the receptacle. Between 4000 and 2000 B.C. the winter solstice occurred in Aquarius. This means that for thirty days Aquarius was made invisible at noon by the light of the sun shining in conjunction with its stars. At that period in history the spring equinox occurred in Taurus, the autumnal one in Scorpius, and the summer solstice in Leo.

Immediately above Aquarius is the constellation of Pegasus, the winged horse famous for having made the mythical spring of Hippocrene on Mount Helicon well up by kicking the spot with his hoof. As explained in the chapter on Pegasus, this figure is represented in a strange upside-down manner. If we should attribute this to a transcription error that probably occurred a couple of centuries B.C., and if we should then reestablish the horse in the erect position, we would find ourselves faced with an image of Pegasus touching the urn of Aquarius with his hoof, making the water overflow abundantly.

The original matrix of the myth of the winged horse and Aquarius comes from India in the time of the Vedas. Around 3000 B.C. it was possible to observe the full moon in the constellation of Aquarius every year around the summer solstice. This event was celebrated during a ceremony that took place during the full moon of the summer solstice, considered the most sublime mystical moment of the year. It was at this moment that Chandra—the god of the moon who was identified with soma, the magical drink of the gods—reached his maximum splendor and was triumphantly drunk by Indra, the Sun. The Sun had thus reconquered the throne of the solstice by winning the yearly battle against the demon of darkness and drought, Vritra (see the chapter on Hydra). In India the summer solstice corresponds exactly with the arrival of the monsoons. The association between Aquarius and the element water during the summer solstice can thus be easily understood.

Aquarius. From Hyginus, Poetica astronomica *(1485 edition)*

Opposite: *Aquarius. From Hevelius,* Uranographia totum coelum stellatum *(1690)*

225

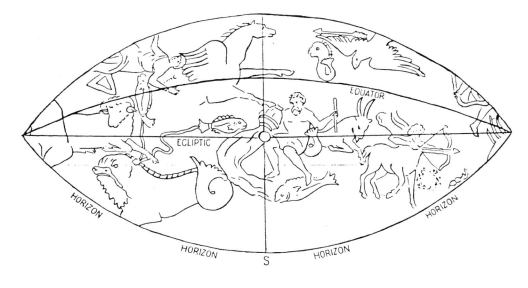

Position of the full moon during the night of the summer solstice in 3000 B.C. Pegasus is shown upright, not upside-down, as in the official maps

Triton and the conch shell

In the *Rig-Veda* there appears a figure who is associated with Indra to such a great extent that attributes of Indra in one hymn are repeated for him in the next. He is Trita Aptypa, or Trita of the Waters, who was considered the preparer of the soma that Indra had to drink. It may be, in fact, that he is the mysterious officiant who holds the vessel in Aquarius.

As is demonstrated by a reading of the *Zend-Avesta*, Trita was a pre-Vedic divinity. He subsequently emigrated to the pre-Greek Mediterranean with the

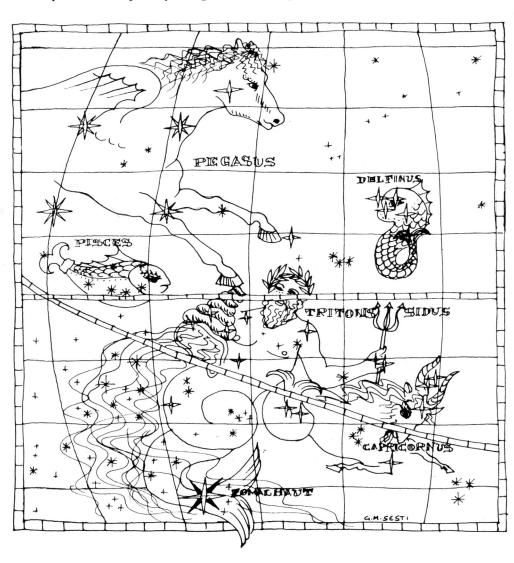

Reconstruction of the ancient figure of Aquarius as he might have been. Pegasus' hoof touches the pail out of which flows the soma of the full moon, the water of the monsoons, and the second heavenly river—Fluvius Aquarii—in which the tail fins of Trita (Triton) are immersed

title of Triton—a vigorous, bearded god who holds in his hand the spiral seashell whose sound calmed the sea or unchained the storms. His lower limbs consisted of a double fishtail of extraordinary length. Triton was the ancient god of the sea who was later dethroned by the Hellenes, who replaced him with Poseidon.

If at this point we replace Aquarius' legs hanging in the water with Triton's flippers and make them extend down to the bright star Fomalhaut, Triton appears to us in all his majesty—the master of the ocean, triumphant on the marine throne of the zodiac and surrounded, in the celestial Sea, by Pisces, Delphinus, the marine monster Cetus, Capricornus, and Pegasus, the horse sacred to Poseidon.

For two thousand years, the sun entered into this starry throne during the winter solstice, and the moon shone here during the summer solstice.

Ganymede and the Eagle

Ganymede

In antiquity, before the arrival of the patriarchal solar gods, the task of preparing and serving the nectar of the gods belonged to the beautiful Hebe, goddess of eternal youth and daughter of Hera, the Great Mother. When Zeus conquered the throne of the gods, he forced Hera to marry him and then constantly humiliated her with his infidelity. As a sign of his supremacy, he took the young Hebe's task away from her, using the fact that she had fallen as his excuse.

In her place he put the handsome Ganymede, with whom he had fallen in love. The love of Zeus for Ganymede and that of Apollo for Hyacinthus were the first examples of male homosexuality in the Greek religion. In the case of Ganymede, this form of amorous passion accentuated the victory of patriarchy over matriarchy because of the independence that the man acquired in obtaining pleasure without the help of a woman. Having been the guardian of the intellectual and the priestly life, women were now relegated to the condition of unpaid domestic worker and procreator of children. The young Ganymede was the son of Tros, the king of Asia Minor from whom the name of Troy is derived. Ganymede's beauty was such that when Zeus became enamored of him he transformed himself into an eagle and abducted the boy on Mount Ida. Zeus then took him to his home on Olympus to become his companion and cupbearer to the gods. Zeus gave the young man immortality and placed his image among the stars as the constellation of Aquarius. To console Tros for the loss of his son, Zeus had Hermes bring him as a gift a golden vine shoot sculpted by Hephaestus, along with two marvelous horses.

The Aquarius at Dendera

The association of Aquarius with rains, floods, rivers, and fountains occurs just about all over the world. In ancient Peru the entrance of the sun into this same group of stars was celebrated with the constellation of the Mother of the Waters. The Sumerians associated it with the eleventh month, *Shabatu*, which means Malediction of the Rain. In their creation epic the description of the universal deluge is written in the eleventh book, corresponding to the eleventh sign, just as each of the other books corresponded to a different zodiacal sign. In a more recent Babylonian calendar, Aquarius was called Gu or Amphora, and was sacred to the goddess Gula-Bau, the personification of the primordial black waters. In the Hebrew zodiac Aquarius corresponded to the tribe of Reuben, meaning unstable as water.

It was said that the ancient Egyptians imagined that the setting of Aquarius in the Nile caused its flooding at the moment he immersed himself into its waters. The Arabs called him *al-Dalw* (the Pail of the Well), but in one of their catalogues he appears as *Sakib al-Ma*, the One Who Pours the Water.

The Christians of the seventeenth century transformed him into the figure of Saint John the Baptist, but he also had the title of the apostle Judas Thaddeus, as well as that of Moses saved from the waters.

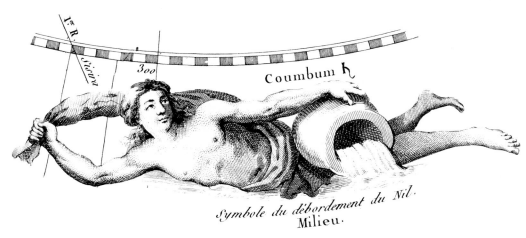

Symbole du débordement du Nil.
Milieu.

Astrology of Aquarius

With the beginning of the new millennium, we will officially enter what many have called the Age of Aquarius, characterized by the apparent entrance of the sun into the constellation Aquarius on March 22, the spring equinox. This means that the extremely slow shifting of the earth's axis that we call the precession of the equinoxes has completed another advance of two thousand years. These shifts were very important in antiquity and they were accurately recorded and interpreted. The myths and the archetypes had to take a subordinate position to the cosmic changes. The reigning sign of the preceding two thousand years would lose its strength of springtime energy and another would take its place on the throne.

So we have passed from the sign of Gemini, 6000–4000 B.C., to that of Taurus, 4000–2000 B.C., and, subsequently, Aries, 2000 B.C. to the birth of Christ. Upon arrival at Aries, something happened that caused a halt in the astronomical and astrological calculations. The creators of myths disappeared, the ancient religions and gods disappeared, Christianity became established and no one was able to manipulate the celestial vision. So it happened that instead of going from the era of Aries to that of Pisces at the beginning of the first millennium of our history, everything remained exactly as it had been before—everything except the apparent motion of the sun that shone, and still shines, in Pisces at the spring equinox.

When the Arabs rediscovered astronomy at the end of the first millennium and translated the Greek texts, they reproduced the error and accepted it calmly. Notwithstanding the fact that they were excellent astronomers and mathematicians, they lacked a class of philosophers and mythographers capable of installing the new values. So, having nonchalantly skipped two thousand years, we are now about to enter the Age of Aquarius even if there does not seem to be anyone interested in the changing of the signs. The reason for this is that Renaissance astronomers discovered that the sun actually had never been in Gemini, or in Taurus, and so on, due to the fact that the earth revolves around the sun; consequently, the sun seems to move, but in reality it does not.

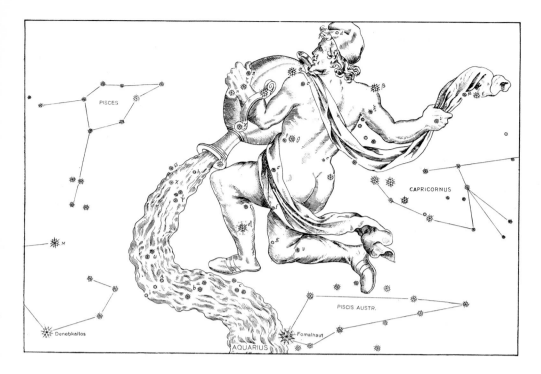

Bayer's Aquarius (1603)

A more in-depth analysis of this dilemma appears in the chapter on Aries and in the introduction to this book. For the moment we will proceed with the program assigned to this sign by the astrologers.

Aquarius is a fixed sign of air; the residence of Uranus and Saturn, it is marked by the color violet. In the human body, it influences the ankles, calves, circulation, breathing, vision, Achilles tendon, and fibula.

Ptolemy made the following observations: "The stars in the shoulders operate as Saturn and Mercury; those in the left hand and the face as well; those of the thighs execute an influence that is more consonant with Mercury and, to a lesser extent, with Saturn; those of the brook have a power similar to Saturn and, to some extent, similar to Jupiter."

The cabalists assigned to Aquarius the fourteenth trump card of the tarots, Temperance, but in recent times he has been associated with the seventeenth, the Stars.

Aquarians are humanitarians, humanists, and dreamers; they are altruistic, friendly, progressive, detached and abstract, romantic, utopian. Aquarians are often innovators, inventors, scientists, pilots, organizers, or public relations people.

Aquarius was the residence of two of the Arabic lunar stations, or *manzil.* The twenty-first, or *al-Sad al-Bula,* the Good Fortune of the Swallower, presided over the liberation of prisoners, divorce, and the healing of the sick. When the moon entered into this sign it was time to get married, to sow, to take medicine, or to command an army. The twenty-second *manzil, al-Sad al-Suud,* the Most Fortunate of the Fortunates, favored the happiness of marriages and military victories but impeded the formation of a government. With the moon here, one should build, get married, start a friendship, or travel.

In India the twenty-third lunar station was celebrated in Aquarius, *Catabhishaj,* or the Hundredth Medical Doctor, who was governed by Varuna, supreme god of the celestial and terrestrial waters, also called the Hindu Uranus. This lunar house was presided over by the Head of the Dragon, which was a mobile constellation relevant to the caste of the butchers, favorable to the beginning of work for fishermen, wine merchants, and bird sellers.

AQUARIUS

Latitudo.   Latitudo.

Delphinus.

Equuleus.

Vulpecula

ANTINOUS

Capricornus.

Sagitta

Cancri.

AQVILA

Scutum.

Sagittarius.

Anser.

Tropicus

Lacerta

Serpens

Cerberus.

Serpentarius.

Sobiesc.

Fig. R.

Æquator

Æquator

INRI

Longitudo.

Longitudo.

Longitudo.

Longitudo.

Latitudo.

Latitudo.

230   *The Glorious Constellations*

3
Aquila

Next to that vast portion of the starry sky that the ancient Sumerians called the Sea, there is another one we could call the Sky because it is inhabited exclusively by creatures of the air. It is dominated by the beautiful geometry of the quadrangle of Pegasus, the cross of Cygnus, Lyra (which has always been represented as being held by a raptor), and, finally, the queen of winged animals, Aquila, the Eagle. The only bird among the stars not in this location is the crow, perching on the long back of Hydra.

In 4000 B.C., when Taurus entered into the spring equinox, it so happened that both the equinoxes and the solstices were extremely well marked by the four famous stars known as the Royal Stars. They were: Aldebaran in Taurus for the spring equinox, Regulus in Leo for the summer solstice, Antares in Scorpius for the fall equinox, and Altair, which roughly indicated the winter solstice. This last marking was approximate because the solstice actually occurred in Aquarius but, since that constellation lacked conspicuous stars, the bright, nearby Altair was chosen to represent its position. It would have been astronomically more precise to use Fomalhaut, in Piscis Austrinus, but this star was not easily visible in 4000 B.C. on the latitude of 40° N.

In the ruins of Persepolis very ancient representations in bas-relief have been found in which a king slays a griffin. Observing this griffin closely, one sees that it has the hind legs and the wings of an eagle, the body and horns of a bull, the head and front legs of a lion, and the tail of a scorpion.

These astronomical symbols foreshadow the ritual depicted in the bas-reliefs of the Roman era—Mithras in the act of slaying the celestial bull surrounded by the zodiacal signs and various constellations.

In the Vedic version of the battle between Indra (the sun) and the serpent Vritra (the constellation of Hydra)—in other words, between the powers of light and darkness—Indra approaches the summer solstice, which occurred precisely above the stars of the serpent Vritra, thereby making it invisible with his light. Vritra, on the other hand, was the dominant constellation in the night of the winter solstice. During this summer solstice, the full moon always occurred in Aquarius and this moon, that is, soma—the mythical drink of the gods—was brought by the celestial Aquila. It was, in fact, by drinking this soma that Indra succeeded in finding all the energy lost in the winter and in taking possession of the solstice. At the time the *Rig-Veda* was written, the moon was, in fact, on the meridian of the Aquila during the night before the full moon of midsummer in Aquarius.

Meteorologically, this coincided with the arrival of the monsoons and the end of the dry season. This is why Aquila was known by the Greeks as the bird that brought rain, as well as the symbol of Zeus, god of lightning and clouds.

Aquila. From Proctor, Easy Star Lesson *(1883)*

Aquila. From Hevelius, Uranographia totum coelum stellatum *(1690)*

Etana's flight

The Legend of Etana

Etana, one of the Babylonian national heroes, was a friend of the god Shamash' eagle and had done some favors for him. In return, one day he asked the bird to bring him the plant that makes childbirth easier and relieves its pains. He needed this for his wife, Kisha, who could not deliver her child.

The plant was only to be found in the sky of Anu and was sacred to Ishtar, the goddess of the moon. It was necessary to go all the way up there in order to acquire it. The eagle proposed to Etana that he would take him up to that lofty height by hiding him among his feathers, thus avoiding the wrath of the gods who did not care for the idea of men entering their supreme kingdom.

The flight was very long and every once in a while the eagle pointed out to Etana how the earth was shrinking. Etana, dizzy and exhausted from the effort of clinging to the eagle, eventually let go and fell crashing to the ground.

This myth is the foundation upon which the Greeks later built the Zeus-Ganymede myth explained in the chapter on Aquarius.

The story of a king who climbs into the sky on the back of an eagle was used extensively in later religious literature. In the case of Etana, his punishment for attempting to gather the forbidden plant was death. In fact, Kisha was the mother earth and the magical herb that he had to find could have been the plant called mountain arnica, a poisonous plant that grows at high altitudes and is a great panacea for women in childbirth when taken in homeopathic doses.

The Shepherd and the Weaver

In China, Japan, and Korea, the star Altair is the principal character in a delightful story that also involves the star Vega, which is located on the other side of the Milky Way.

It involves the beautiful and modest She-niu and the young shepherd, who had a love that was the model for, and envy of, all lovers. She-niu was known to be the best weaver in the country; her name, which meant "the maiden who weaves," had actually been given to her because of the outstanding skill with which she wove the many-colored threads into cloth that was worthy of the emperor's court. Her lover, just as graceful and charming, did not neglect anything to make himself liked by the beautiful and virtuous girl. Only a river divided their two lands, so it was easy for the young man to cross it every night on his way to the place where the two lovers would meet.

But intrigues and jealousies took the young man far away from the weaver, who waited for him faithfully, renouncing all offers that came to her, until she finally died of sorrow, a fate she unknowingly shared with her lover. But the sublime Sovereign did not want such love and faithfulness to end up in nothingness, so he transported the two young people into the sky, where the Weaver, the star Vega, weaves threads to make marvelous cloth. Not far from her, the Shepherd, the star Altair, dedicates himself to his ancient work. Between the two of them flows, like a boundary, the river of the Milky Way.

Once a year, on the seventh day of the seventh moon, their work ceases, the constellations join, and the Shepherd makes his way to a lovers' tryst with the Weaver. To help him cross the river, magpies gather from all around the earth and fly over the Milky Way, forming with their feathers a bridge on which he can walk.

Aquila. From Hyginus, Poetica astronomica *(1485 edition)*

Aquila

As the poet says, "The scattered air comes together again, the shattered dew drops merge together; all things are decided by Fate and fixed by celestial laws" (Bussaghi, *I Miti dell'Oriente*).

The Star of the Shepherd was also mentioned in the fifth century B.C. by Confucius, in the ode She-King. While every year during the millennia the promise of eternal fidelity was renewed, Chinese girls can on that night receive the image of their future fiancé in a dream.

After the lovers' encounter, the magpies return to their woods with no feathers on their heads because the Shepherd's steps have worn them out. (This of course actually occurs when the birds molt.) If there should be an evening shower during the lovers' meeting the raindrops represent their tears of joy shed in happiness over their being together again. If it rains at dawn, the tears are shed for the sad separation.

In Japan it is believed that during the union (*tanabata*) the two star-lovers shine with five different colors.

The Eagle and the Serpent

The great collection of Indian fables, *Jatakas*, contains the story of Rukh, the giant bird, which can be dated to about the fourth century B.C. The enormous bird Roc of the *Thousand and One Nights* derives from this creature. Sindbad's

She-niu and the shepherd at the bridge made of magpies crossing the Milky Way

bird was like a cloud that obscured the Valley of Diamonds, frightening the serpents into scurrying for cover, which indicates the power of the day in the eagle and that of the night in the serpent.

The association of eagle and serpent can be found all over the world, even in those countries such as New Zealand and Bali where snakes do not exist. In Babylonian astronomy the constellation of Aquila represented the year that is born while that of Serpens is the symbol of the year that dies, "at the end of his life at the time of the winter solstice, Aquila magically recaptures life and strength."

In Psalm 103 it is written, "So that thy youth is renewed like the Eagle's." There is also a Persian story in which the symbol of resurrection is represented by the metamorphosis of wine:

Sultan Schemiram was sitting with his son Behiram and other dignitaries of

Aquila and Antinous

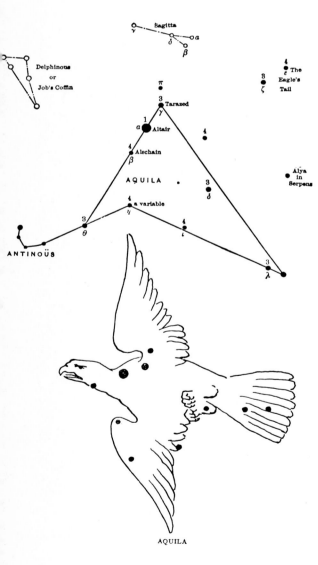

his realm on a tower of the castle when a large royal eagle appeared to him and began to fly in circles around his head to attract his attention. Looking at the bird carefully, the sultan noticed that a serpent was wrapped around the eagle's neck and was about to strangle him. Immediately the sultan ordered that his most skillful and courageous archer kill the serpent without wounding the eagle. It was his son Behiram who, with the speed of lightning, shot off an arrow that pierced the serpent's head, leaving the eagle unharmed. Having recovered, the eagle circled once more around Schemiram's head.

The following year during the same season, the sultan was again on the tower of his castle, and the eagle reappeared and let some seeds fall from his beak at Schemiram's feet.

The sultan gathered up this gift and, having examined them, ordered that the unknown seeds be sown in the sunniest spot in his gardens, that their growth be watched over, and that they be protected from bad weather, insects, and birds.

It was during the spring festivals that were the custom in Persia that the seeds sprouted, while being watched over by the sultan and his sages. The shoots grew rapidly and took on the aspect of an unknown plant on which first green, then red and brown, clusters appeared. After a while, they matured. But what to do with these clusters from which issued a strange liquid?

The sultan and his sages made their decision when they noticed that the juice fermented and, after bubbling and emitting vapors, became clear again. They thought at once of a drink, but they wanted to try it out and thus offered it to a prisoner who had been condemned to death. He drank a substantial amount of it, showed signs of joyfulness, began to sing and dance and asked for more until he fell asleep.

Was he dead? the sultan and the sages asked themselves.

When the condemned man finally woke up the following day and told them about all the sensations he had felt, the sultan decided to cultivate in his gardens a great number of the seeds that the eagle had given him.

Prometheus and the Eagle

Prometheus, the Provident One, was a Titan who was an expert in architecture, astronomy, mathematics, medicine, and navigation. His name is perhaps the Greek variant of the Indian Pramantha, which means swastika or torch. His legend belongs to that group of pre-Greek myths of which Iapetus, Chiron, Ixion, Perseus, and many others are a part. In Greece he became the god Hephaestus.

Like Chiron, he was a beneficent spirit to mankind. His most famous exploit was that of giving fire to men against the wishes of the gods. For this he was punished by Zeus who had him chained to the top of a mountain where, every day, an eagle pecked at his liver, which then grew back again.

The origins of the myth seem to date back to the time when the Hellenes migrated to Greece from the Caspian Sea. There was a legend of a frost-giant, recumbent on the snow of the peaks and attended by a flock of vultures. The allegory of the eagle who feeds himself with Prometheus' liver—the Greek word for liver is *hepatos*, from which the word epact may be derived—conceals a specific astronomical reference: the eagle-sun devours the *hepatos*-epact—the time added every year to the calendar to harmonize the lunar and the solar cycles—which then magically grows back the following year.

The Arabic name of the constellation is *al-Nasr al-Tair*, the Flying Vulture, from which Altair is derived.

According to Ptolemy the astrological influence of Aquila was similar to that of Mars and Jupiter. It bestowed a predisposition toward imagination, strong passions, indomitable willpower, domineering character, clairvoyance, and an aptitude for chemical research. The cabalists represent Aquila with the sixth trump card of the tarots—the Lovers.

The star Altair, on the other hand, is very controversial. Ptolemy thought it to share the qualities of Aquila while others assigned it to the spheres of Saturn and Mercury, to that of Uranus, and to that of Mercury.

Antinous

It would not be possible to finish with this discussion without talking about the star group created before the Christian era among the stars of Aquila—Antinous, a constellation included in all the atlases of the last two thousand years but deleted from the official star maps due to the sense of propriety of the astronomers of this century.

A young man of incomparable beauty, born at Claudiopolis in Bithynia (Turkey), Antinous became the lover of the Roman emperor Hadrian. During a voyage to Upper Egypt, Hadrian consulted the famous oracle of Besa, which predicted that either he himself or the person he loved the most would soon die. Antinous' love for Hadrian was so great that, without hesitation, the young man threw himself into the Nile and thus, by drowning, saved the emperor's life.

The news of his untimely death spread throughout Egypt. Hadrian had the city of Antinopolis built on the riverbank near where his lover had died. The city was inaugurated in A.D. 130 and here Antinous was worshiped as Osiris himself. With the help of the Alexandrian astronomers Hadrian immortalized Antinous by placing him as a constellation next to the Milky Way among the stars of Aquila.

Aquila was the symbolic representation of the coming of the new year and was also the symbol of resurrection. These stars, in fact, disappeared under the horizon as the winter solstice approached and then reappeared in the spring, climbing ever higher in the sky. They represented immortality through the eternal rebirth of youth and beauty in the spring.

Antinous was identified with the mysteries that were celebrated in regard to the death of the young Dionysus. A kind of religious drama, *The Passion of Antinous*, was presented annually at the start of the astronomical flight of Aquila. In this, the pathos of his premature death and the glory of his resurrection were re-created in ceremonial dances.

The cult of Antinous survived in the Greek world for two hundred years. Sculptors created a new, beautiful image for him, sculpting him with voluptuous lines, a low forehead crowned with little curls, fleshy lips, and dreamy eyes. It is with this as a model that later masterpieces such as Donatello's *David* were created.

Antinous represented the eternal sorrow for the transience of youth, for the beauty that disappears and the perfection that dies, but it also represents their continuing rebirth. His image was reproduced on amulets, medallions, and on coins minted by the governors of Egypt and the Asiatic cities.

A flower was dedicated to Antinous, the Lotus of Antinous, a rare pink lotus that was said to have been born from the blood of a lion killed by Hadrian.

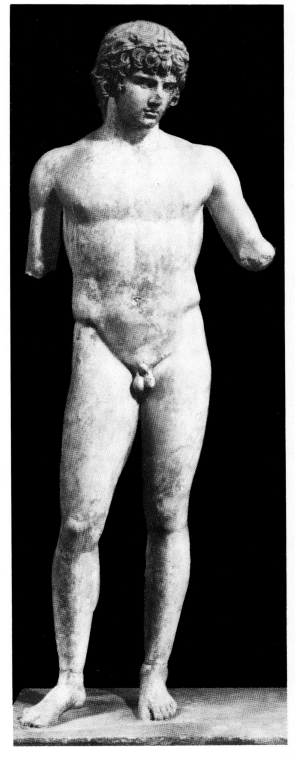

Antinous

4
Ara

Ara, the Altar, is a very ancient constellation. It was described in Aratus' *Phaenomena* as signaling danger for sailors when it appeared in the southern sky; it predicted heavy storms. The Latin name Ara was given to this group of stars by Cicero.

In the stellar mythology of Sumer, its position was slightly different and it was probably the twelfth zodiacal sign. Subsequently it was represented by Scorpius' claws, which the Greeks later transformed into the constellation Libra. Ara was identified with the seventh Sumerian month, *Tashritu*, and with the sign *Tul-Ku*, Sacred Altar or Famous Grave, perhaps in reference to the round altar-grave of the Tower of Babel. In fact, in the ancient catalogues, the stars of this constellation—Alpha, Mu, Xi, Delta, Beta, Chi, Zeta, and Nu Arae—looked very much like a circle or circular altar. The Sumerians also called this sign by two other names, the Censer—the officiating priest at the sacrifice—and, frequently, the Lamp or Beacon. This last name was related to the custom of always keeping a fire lit on temple altars close to the sea to show the way to sailors at night. This lamp is often represented between the claws of Scorpius on Babylonian border stones. The eighteenth-century French astronomer Lalande stated that in the Egyptian star map of Petosiris the stars that make up Ara were represented as a human figure with a dog's head. Ara is no longer completely visible at the horizon above 23° N., and where it is visible, then only for a brief period of four hours. In modern maps it is positioned upside-down, since it is visible in the southern hemisphere almost the entire year.

Near the shiny sting of the dreadful sign, Scorpius, there in the South, Ara is suspended. . . .

One myth of Ara involves a prediction that the end of the reign of Cronus, son of Gaea (Earth) and Uranus (Heaven), would be caused by one of his own sons. Terrified, Cronus devised a solution worthy of his cunning: every time Rhea, his wife and sister, gave birth, he swallowed the child. Rhea suffered unspeakably; she had already lost five children when she realized that she was pregnant again. With the help of her mother, Gaea, she gave birth in secret during a dark night on Mount Lycaeum in Arcadia. Having washed the baby in the river Neda, she then consigned him to Gaea who hid him in the forests of Crete. There the youngster was suckled by the divine goat Amalthaea and grew up under the protection of Adrasteia, nymph of the ash trees. To deceive Cronus Rhea pretended to give birth, wrapped a stone in the linen of a newborn, and let him swallow it.

Ara. *Engraving from Hyginus,* Poetica astronomica *(1485 edition)*

Opposite: *Ara. From Hevelius,* Uranographia totum coelum stellatum *(1690)*

237

Zeus and the giants

The years went by and the young Zeus, now strong and resplendent, disguised himself as a cupbearer one day with the help of Rhea, and mixed poison into his father's wine. Cronus vomited up first the stone and then, one after the other, all his children, Zeus' siblings. Cronus gathered his brothers, the Titans, to his aid and prepared to attack Zeus. Not all the Titans, however, would come since they remembered Cronus' earlier treachery: he had imprisoned them in Tartarus.

For ten years a dreadful battle raged between Zeus and Cronus. The son took up position on Mount Olympus with his siblings (Hestia, Demeter, Hera, Hades, and Poseidon), as well as some Titans who had become his allies (Hyperion, Oceanus, Tethys, Themis, and Mnemosyne). The father was positioned on Mount Orthrys with the Titans who had remained with him; they were led by the very ferocious Atlas, son of Iapetus.

The opposing forces were of equal strength until Gaea prophesied the triumph of Zeus who, in order to obtain victory, had to ally himself with the other sons of Uranus, namely, the Cyclopes and the Giants with the Hundred Hands, who were also locked up in Tartarus. Zeus succeeded in liberating them by killing the prison guard, Campe. The prisoners, however, were lethargic, exhausted from their extremely long imprisonment. Zeus restored their strength by giving them ambrosia and nectar, and they agreed to help him.

The Cyclopes, the great weaponsmiths, held the secret of fire and lightning. They made Zeus the scepter that gave him control over arrows and destruction by fire. For Poseidon they forged the trident, a magical weapon and symbol of victory and power. And for Hades they made the famous helmet that rendered the bearer invisible. Finally, they built a great altar, the first one that was ever seen, on which the first sacrifice was offered. The smoke that rose into the sky served to hide the power and direction of the shafts of lightning that Zeus hurled from Olympus.

The Giants with the Hundred Hands were able to take many Titans prisoner by hurling hundreds of rocks simultaneously. To overcome the others who were still fighting, the god Pan intervened: he frightened them so much with a blood-curdling scream that they fled in that state of mind that from then on was called panic.

The defeated Titans were again condemned to Tartarus, a dark abyss as deep underground as the earth is distant from the sky. If a bronze anvil were thrown into this chasm, it would fall for nine days before hitting bottom. The leader of the Titans, Atlas, was exiled to a mountain range at the edge of the world, where he was condemned to hold up on his shoulders the entire vault of the sky for all eternity. These mountains in Morocco are still called Atlas to this day.

The Altar built by the Cyclopes was eternalized by Zeus, who placed it as a constellation in the southern reaches of the sky, under the stars of Scorpius and at the beginning of the Milky Way, so that the Milky Way itself became the smoke of divine sacrifices.

The Deluge

The other myth of the constellation Ara is that of the universal deluge, whose first telling belongs to the Sumerian civilization. It tells the heroic tale of Utnapishtim (later transformed into the biblical Noah) and his wife, who having

Micyllus' Ara

The altar of thanksgiving after the universal deluge

been warned by the god Ea of the upcoming deluge that the god Bel was about to unleash to destroy mankind, built an ark and filled it with the "seeds of every kind of life."

The dreadful deluge came and the ark, lost in the leaden sky, wandered far and wide over an endless sea, until one day the rains ended and there was nothing but water as far as the eye could see. After twelve days a strip of land emerged from the water, a mountain of the country of Nisir, which restrained the ship and kept it from floating any further. When, after seven days, Utnapishtim let a crow out and set it free, he knew the waters had lowered because the bird did not return. He then let all the animals of the ark go and offered a sacrifice to the gods, with many vessels with fragrant reeds, cedar, and scented bark. The gods inhaled the smell and crowded "like flies" around the offering.

In the Sumerian cosmology the stars were considered gods and perhaps the beautiful description "the gods crowded around like flies" can be explained by observing the constellation Ara in the night sky and seeing the Milky Way— smoke and scent of the offering—wind through the center of the sky surrounded by thousands of stars.

Entering Noah's ark

The universal deluge

Ara 239

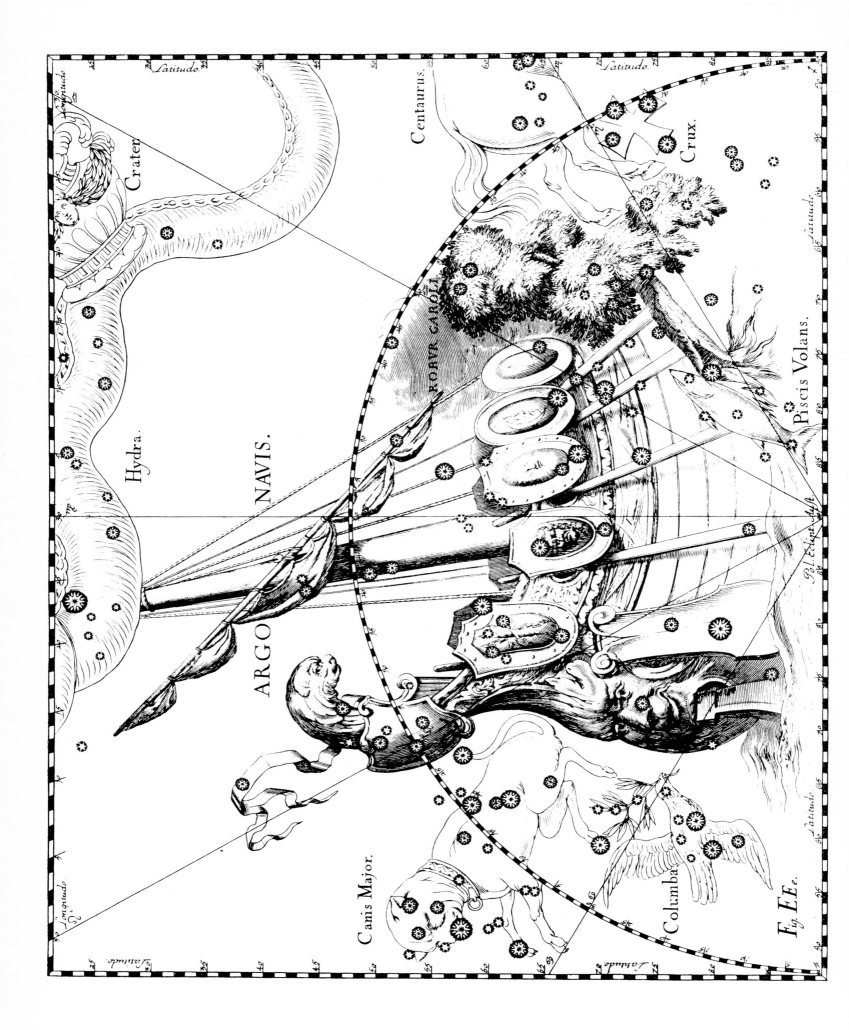

5
Argo Navis

In the region of the sky that in antiquity was called the Sea, there sails an enormous starry ship extending over as much as seventy-five degrees of arc. This is Argo Navis, the Ship Argo. Unfortunately, few of its stars are visible to the North American or European observer, due to its location in the extreme south, where the slow precessional shifting seems to have moved it further and further over the centuries.

Argo Navis, almost completely immersed in the Milky Way, is composed of stars of very modest magnitude, except for the legendary Canopus, a brilliant star and the subject of many ancient legends.

The great size of the heavenly ship caused the eighteenth-century French astronomer Lacaille to divide the original constellation into three distinct constellations, Carina (Keel), Puppis (Stern), and Vela (Sails), to make it easier to study. This division is still used in modern star catalogues. In almost all ancient maps Argo Navis was depicted as cut in half. It is not well known what the reason was for the disappearance of the bow with its figurehead, which was said to have been carved from the trunk of the talking oak of Dodona. This trunk had been a gift of Pallas Athene, and it endowed the ship with the gift of speech. It could, therefore, warn its crew of dangers, just as sonar and radar do today.

The constellation of the ship is definitely very ancient. Traces of it are found from the time of the first Sumerian civilization where it was called by the name of its lucida, Canopus. This star group was associated with the cult of Ea, king of the primordial waters and protector-god of fishermen and sailors, who directed, through his pilot, the ark of Utnapishtim (the Sumerian Noah) while the elements raged. Similarly, he guided the ship of Gilgamesh during his pilgrimage to the island of the blessed. It was believed that Ea swam in front of the ships in the form of a human bust ending in a fishtail, which was perhaps an ancient representation of the classical Triton. In an ancient hymn the ship is described on which Ea, with his wife Davkina, his son Marduk, other divinities, and a pilot, navigated the ocean. In the chapter on Capricornus we see that Ea had his Way in the sky and a star of his own; the former being the Tropic of Capricorn and the latter the sacred star of the city of Eridu, which was dedicated to him.

According to Eratosthenes Argo Navis represents the first ship that sailed the oceans and that, long before the expedition of the Argonauts, transported Danaus and his fifty daughters from Egypt to Rhodes and later to Argus.

In Egyptian mythology this constellation of a ship was presented as the ark that had carried Isis and Osiris during the deluge. In Hindu mythology, in an exceptional parallelism of names, this same ship was the ark of safety for Isi and Iswara; in a protohistoric Hindu tale, it was indicated by the name of the Ship Argha or the nomad sun, and it was piloted by Agastya or the star Canopus.

Isaac Newton dedicated many pages of his *Chronologia* to Argo Navis. He

Argo Navis. From Hyginus, Poetica astronomica *(1485 edition)*

Opposite: *Argo Navis. From Hevelius,* Uranographia totum coelum stellatum *(1690)*

241

based his observations on the tradition of the author of the *Gigantomachia*, who was cited by Clemens of Alexandria. According to this author, the constellations would have been designed by the centaur Chiron during the same period in which the expedition of the Argonauts took place. Under his guidance the Argonaut Musaeus, Orpheus' teacher, would have designed a globe on which the forty-eight constellations later described by Eudoxus would already have been represented.

Newton even goes so far as to add that Chiron and Musaeus had designed this globe for the use of the Argonauts and that the circles of the solstices and the equinoxes passed through the constellations of Aries, Cancer, Libra, and Capricornus. According to the English scientist, the construction of the ship would have taken place at approximately 936 B.C., forty years after King Solomon.

As can easily be imagined, in the Christian tradition, Argo Navis became *Arca Noachi* or *Archa Noae*, the Ark of Noah, or simply the Ark.

Canopus

During the return voyage from the Trojan War, while Menelaus was heading toward the island of Pharos with his fleet, he stopped in an inlet located twelve miles from the future city of Alexandria. There he lost his beloved helmsman Kanobus to a snakebite. Menelaus had a monument built in his honor and to him he also consecrated the star, subsequently called Canopus, that rose seven and one-half degrees above the horizon at that time. Around the monument arose the city of Canopus which reached its maximum splendor during the dynasty of the Ptolemaic pharaohs.

Today Canopus is a heap of ruins, but in its place arose the city of Abukir, which became famous for the defeat of Napoleon's fleet by Nelson in the famous Battle of the Nile in August, 1798, as well as for the French victory, the following year, over the Turkish fleet of Pasha Mustafa. In ancient Canopus stood the Temple of Serapis, the Serapeum, which was the seat of the famous observatory from which Ptolemy made his astronomical observations. Serapis was identified with the god Osiris, who was represented in the sky by the star Canopus.

The nomads who lived in the desert especially venerated Canopus, who represented to them the camel *al-Fahl*, which was the subject of superstitions, stories, and proverbs. It was also believed that the blue reflections of the star endowed precious stones with their brilliance and imparted an immunity against illnesses.

The heliacal rising of *al-Fahl* is still used today for the computation of the year, the ripening of dates, the end of the summer heat, and the weaning of young camels. In addition, the rising of this star has the same significance as that of the Polar Star in the north.

Canopus shining-down over the desert, with its blue diamond brightness (that wild blue spirit-like brightness, far brighter than we ever witness here), would pierce into the heart of the wild Ishmaelitish man, whom it was guiding through the solitary waste there.

Carlyle, *On Heroes and Hero Worship*, 247

The great devotion of the Arabs for Canopus is reflected in the title by which the star was known from Morocco to Persia, *al-Suhail*, a name derived, according to Buttman, from *al-Sahl*, meaning the Clear One or the Evident One. Al-Suhail indicated everything that was brilliant, glorious, and beautiful. The word is still used today in some regions as a synonym for beauty. In Persia it

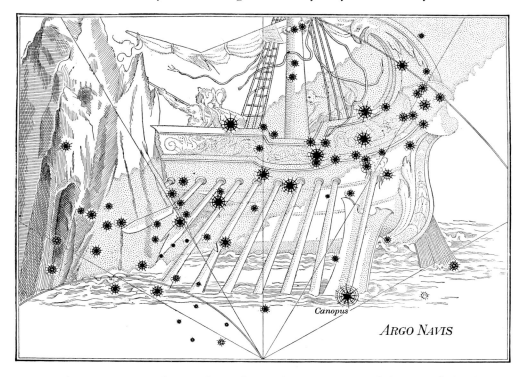

was used as a synonym for wisdom; there, the expression *al-Anwar i Suhaili*, the Lights of Canopus, indicated the lights of spiritual thought.

In the European star maps the name Suhail has been corrupted to Suhel, Sohil, Suhil, Sohayl, and Sohel, and many other variations. In the *Alfonsine Tables* it was Ponderous Suhel, a translation of the Arabic *al-Suhail al-Wazn*. In some sources it was called *al-Suhail al-Yamaniyya*, or Suhail of the South, to distinguish it from the one in the north that was represented by Capella.

From the sixth century on the faithful who were adherents of the Christian Orthodox religion would set out on pilgrimages from Russia and Greece to Palestine in order to visit the sanctuary of the convent of Saint Catherine of Alexandria at Sinai. On these voyages to the south, they were guided by Canopus, and they therefore called it the Star of Saint Catherine.

The Argonauts and Their Ship

The construction of *Argo*, meaning Fast, had been the wish of Jason, son of Aeson. In order to reconquer his father's realm, which had been usurped by Pelias, Jason had to retrieve the Golden Fleece of the Heavenly Ram, which was being guarded in the wood of Hades, in the realm of Aeëtes, in Colchis at the foot of the Caucasus.

To accomplish this task Jason assembled a total of some fifty Greek heroes and gods who went down in history as the Argonauts. The shipyard was set up on the beach of Pagasae in Magnesia. The wood used to build the ship was from pine trees felled on Mount Pelion and rolled down to the Bay of Pagasae. The figurehead, however, was made from the trunk of one of the sacred oaks of Dodona.

Opposite: *Argo Navis. From Cicero's* Aratea

The helmsman of the *Argo* was the Boeotian Tiphys, who would lose his life during the voyage even though it was Athene herself who had induced him to participate in the undertaking. Tiphys is another addition to the long line of mythical helmsmen such as Ursanabi, who guided the ship of Gilgamesh, Palinurus of Aeneas' ship, and Canobus of Menelaus'. According to Apollonius, this is how the launching of the Argo, from the beach of Pagasae, was accomplished:

First of all, by the command of Argus, they strongly girded the ship with a rope well twisted within, stretching it tight on each side, in order that the planks might be well compacted by the bolts and might withstand the opposing force of the surge. And they quickly dug a trench as wide as the space the ship covered, and at the prow as far into the sea as it would run when drawn down by their hands. And they ever dug deeper in front of the stem, and in the furrow laid polished rollers; and inclined the ship down upon the first rollers, that so she might glide and be borne on by them. And above, on both sides, reversing the oars, they fastened them round the thole-pins, so as to project a cubit's space. And the heroes themselves stood on both sides at the oars in a row, and pushed forward with chest and hand at once. And then Tiphys leapt on board to urge the youths to push at the right moment; and calling on them he shouted loudly; and they at once, leaning with all their strength, with one push started the ship from her place, and strained with their feet, forcing her onward; and Pelian Argo followed swiftly; and they on each side shouted as they rushed on. And then the rollers groaned under the sturdy keel as they were chafed, and round them rose up a dark smoke owing to the weight, and she glided into the sea; but the heroes stood there and kept dragging her back as she sped onward. And round the thole-pins they fitted the oars, and in the ship they placed the mast and the well-made sails and the stores.

Now when they had carefully paid heed to everything, first they distributed the benches by lot, two men occupying one seat; but the middle bench they chose for Hercules and Ancaeus apart from the other heroes, Ancaeus who dwelt in Tegea. For them alone they left the middle bench just as it was and not by lot; and with one consent they entrusted Tiphys with guarding the helm of the well-stemmed ship.

Next, piling up shingle near the sea, they raised there an altar on the shore to Apollo, under the name of Actius and Embasius. . . .

Apollonius of Rhodes, *Argonautica*, I. 367–403

And now the hawsers were being slipped and they poured wine on the sea. But Jason with tears held his eyes away from his fatherland. And just as youths set up a dance in honour of Phoebus either in Pytho or haply in Ortygia, or by the waters of Ismenus, and to the sound of the lyre round his altar all together in time beat the earth with swiftly-moving feet; so they to the sound of Orpheus' lyre smote with their oars the rushing sea-water, and the surge broke over the blades; and on this side and on that the dark brine seethed with foam, boiling terribly through the might of the study heroes. And their arms shone in the sun like flame as the ship sped on; and ever their wake gleamed white far behind, like a path seen over a green plain. On that day all the gods looked down from heaven upon the ship and the might of the heroes, half-divine, the bravest of men then sailing the sea; and on the topmost heights the nymphs of Pelion

wondered as they beheld the work of Itonian Athena, and the heroes themselves wielding the oars. And there came down from the mountain-top to the sea Chiron, son of Philyra, and where the white surf broke he dipped his feet, and, often waving with his broad hand, cried out to them at their departure, "Good speed and a sorrowless home-return!"

Hylas, the young Argonaut and favorite of Hercules, is carried off by the nymphs of the spring

(ibid., 533–555)

The story of the conquest of the Golden Fleece is told in the chapter on Aries.

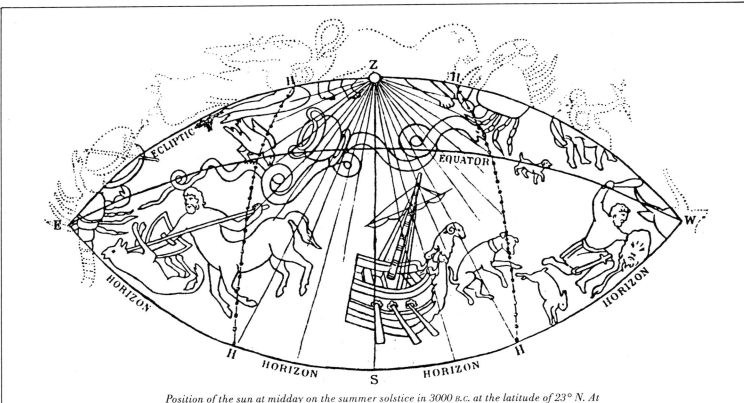

Position of the sun at midday on the summer solstice in 3000 B.C. at the latitude of 23° N. At this time Argo Navis was on the meridian of the solstice. The same constellations were visible in the same positions at midnight on the winter solstice during this period

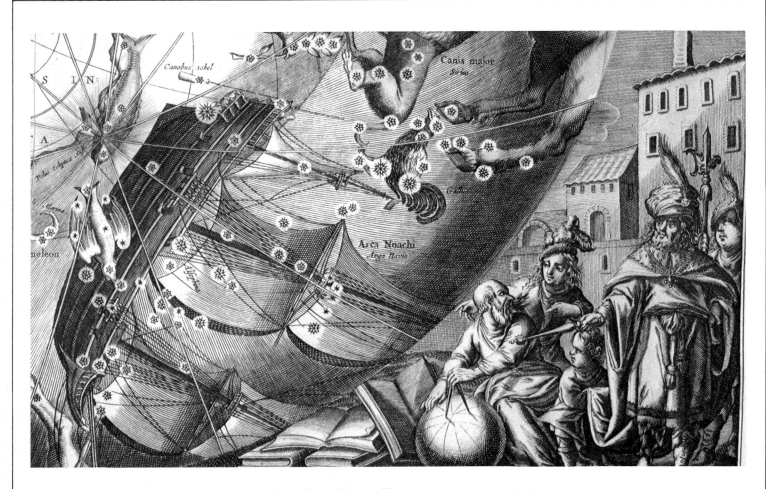

Argo Navis. From Cellarius, Harmonica macrocosmica *(1660)*

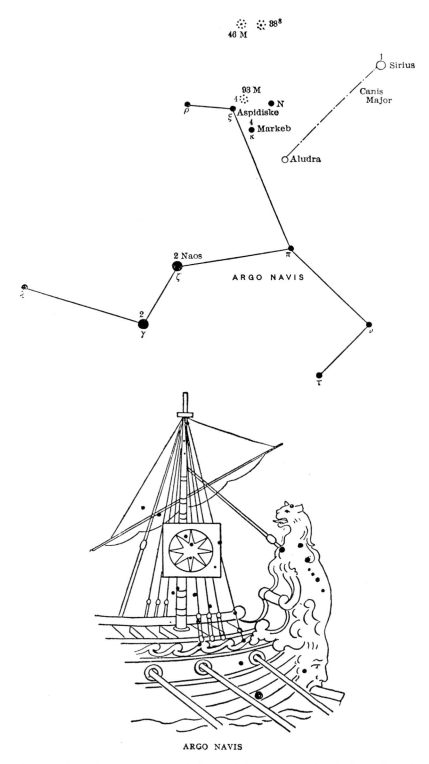

ARGO NAVIS

The tales in the *Argonautica* originated in ancient ballad cycles that, as Homer states in the *Odyssey*, were on everyone's tongue in his time. They were later transcribed, but almost all the texts were lost until the time that the poet Apollonius of Rhodes rewrote them in the third century B.C. This is the only complete version of the voyage of the *Argo* that remains.

Apollonius had been a pupil of Callimachus, the tutor of Ptolemy III as well as the director of the famous library of Alexandria before Eratosthenes. His second name, Rhodius—of Rhodes—seems derived from the fact that the first version of the *Argonautica* was not appreciated in Alexandria; he therefore moved to Rhodes where he rewrote the story and, at last, received general acclaim.

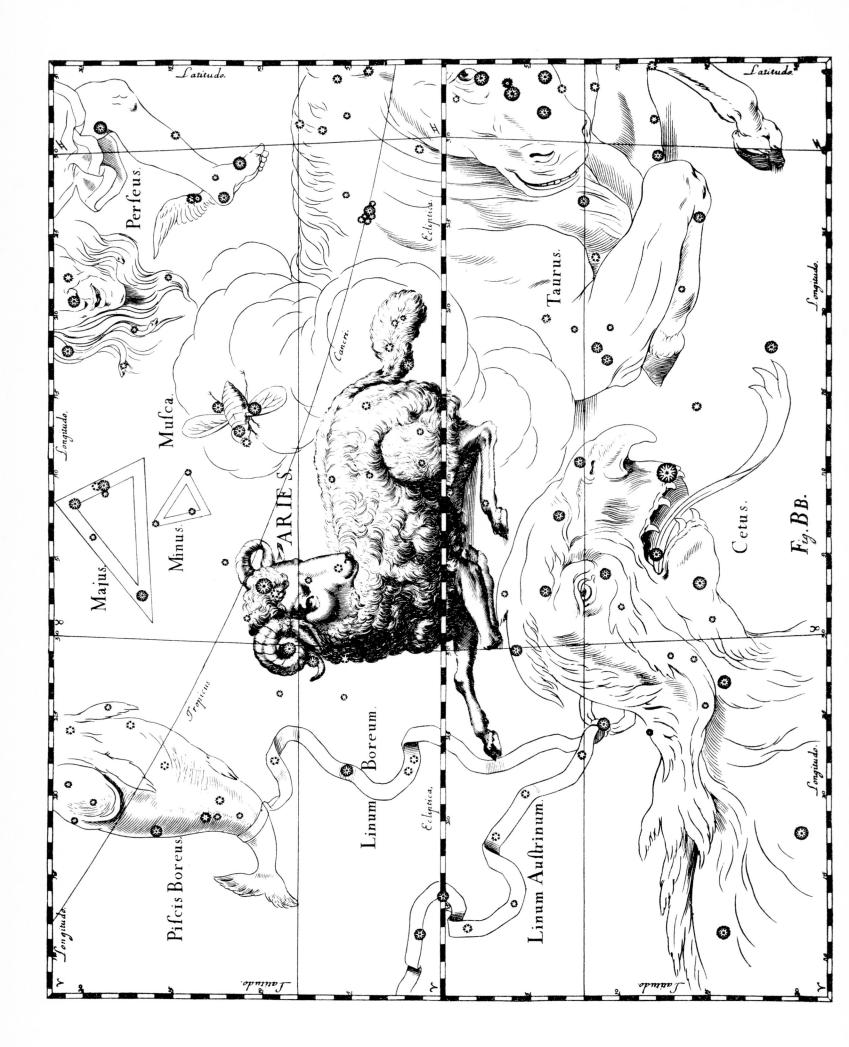

Latitudo.

Latitudo.

Perfeus.

Taurus.

Ecliptica.

Cancri.

Mufca.

Majus.

Minus.

A R I E S.

Cetus.

Fig. BB.

Tropicus

Pifcis Boreus.

Linum Boreum.

Ecliptica.

Linum Auftrinum.

Longitudo.

Longitudo.

Longitudo.

Longitudo.

Latitudo.

Latitudo.

6
Aries

During the months from October to February, it is possible to observe along the southern edge of the ecliptic a faint constellation composed of three main stars. This is Aries, the Ram. In order to find it, all one has to do is draw an imaginary line from the star Scheat of the Great Square of Pegasus and pass through Alpheratz—the star of the head of Andromeda—to arrive at the stars of Aries' head, Alpha, Beta, and Gamma Arietis.

Even though this constellation is not very spectacular, Aries is perhaps the most famous zodiacal sign because, during the two thousand years preceding the birth of Christ, the sun entered among these particular stars at the spring equinox. Previously, from 4000 to 2000 B.C., Taurus had been the sign of the equinox, but the slow shifting due to the precession of the equinoxes caused the meridian to move toward the sign of Aries—which became, together with Capricornus, Libra, and Cancer, one of the four cardinal signs.

Subsequently no one was able to manipulate the combination of the cardinal points, which should have been the following from the Roman era on: spring equinox, Pisces; summer solstice, Gemini; autumnal equinox, Virgo; and winter solstice, Sagittarius. This means that modern astrologers use a zodiacal model that has been outdated for almost two thousand years.

The succession of the sign of Aries to that of Taurus has entered into the legends and myths of every culture. This symbolism is evident in the biblical allegory of Moses who goes up onto Mount Sinai (mountain of the moon) to receive the new laws for the future country of Israel and comes down with the commandments in his hands and two budding ram's horns on his forehead. He then catches the Israelites in the act of worshiping the golden bull—symbol of the old zodiac—and, enraged, he orders the idol to be destroyed.

Despite the Sumerian origin of the Old Testament and the creation myths, such as the story of the deluge, the Hebrews were fierce iconoclasts when it came to Mesopotamian symbols and traditions.

The Sumerians called the sun *Subat*, the Ancient Sheep (or Ram), while the collective name given to the planets was either Stars of the Ancient Sheep or Celestial Herd. In the *Table of the Thirty Stars*, Aries appears under the name of Gam, the Scimitar, which stretched from Okda in Pisces to Hamal in Aries, where the three brightest stars formed its blade. This was the weapon that protected the realm against the Seven Diabolic Spirits or Spirits of the Storm. Other Mesopotamian names for Aries were Rubu or I-ku-u or, more simply, Ku. These names all mean Prince or Military Leader, perhaps in the sense of Leader of the Heavenly Host—a title that was also assigned to the star Capella, located in the constellation of Auriga.

The Egyptians were the supporters and creators of the cult of Aries, a very important sign for them because its zenith coincided with the rising of the star Sirius, which determined the time of the flooding of the Nile. A significant indication of the importance of Aries to the Egyptians is the triumphal road at

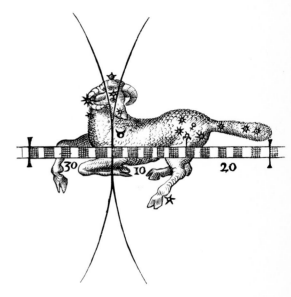

Aries. From Robert Flud, Cosmi historia *(1612)*

Opposite: *Aries. From Hevelius,* Uranographia totum coelum stellatum *(1690)*

249

Karnak, which is formed of two wings of granite sphinxes bearing the heads of Aries. The road led to the Temple of Amon, or Amen-Ra, the supreme sun-god of the Egyptian pantheon, which was shown with ram's horns and sitting on a processional boat.

Having grown up in the house of the Pharaoh and having been educated by the Egyptian high priests, Moses had absorbed the symbolism of that religion, the notorious enemy of the Mesopotamian civilization. This provides an insight into the Jews' moralistic legends such as the one about the Tower of Babel, which was none other than the city of Babylon's ziggurat Esagila, astronomical observatory and religious temple.

The cult of Aries spread from Egypt to the entire Mediterranean sphere, where the earlier cult of Taurus was gradually abandoned in favor of the new course.

The Golden Fleece

The Greeks, the great alchemists of the Mediterranean myths, succeeded in implanting Aries into their culture in this way.

Taking advantage of Zeus' hospitality, Ixion had fallen in love with his wife, Hera. Having noticed this, the king of the gods created a cloud in the image and likeness of Hera, which Ixion impregnated and so generated the first Centaurs. This cloud was given the name Nephele, or Nubes in Latin.

Ixion was condemned by Zeus to roll forever tied to a fiery wheel, which has often been compared to the circle of the ecliptic, the path of the sun in the sky. Poor Nephele remained alone and sad, roaming around Olympus until Hera, moved by compassion, had her marry Athamas, brother of the famous Sisyphus and king of Boeotia. From this union Phrixus and Helle were born.

Athamas was not faithful to Nephele, and after some time he became the lover of Ino, who gave him other children and forced him to hate Phrixus and Helle to the degree that Athamas condemned them to die in a sacrifice.

However, Hera watched over her protégés and ordered Hermes to send a ram to their aid. So it happened that, before the sacrifice could be performed, a ram in a golden fleece descended from the sky and the youngsters climbed on its back. It flew away in the direction of Colchis where Helios, the sun, kept his chariots locked in a stable during the night.

Dazed by the height and seized by dizziness, the young Helle lost her grip and fell in that arm of sea that separates Europe from Asia and which, from then on, has been called Hellespont in her honor.

Only Phrixus reached Colchis, located in the eastern area of the Black Sea, the realm of Helios' son, Aeëtes. The moment he arrived, the young man sacrificed the ram to Zeus the Liberator and placed its fleece in a sacred wood.

In the myth of Athamas, Nephele, and Phrixus, there appears the ancient motif of the annual sacrifice of the king and his companion, a boy who went to the sacrificial altar wearing a ram's fleece and who was later replaced by the ram itself. This rite was celebrated by the shepherds on the mountains, at the beginning of spring, during the festivities for the new year. Nephele was the cloud that brought rain. Helle was the ancient goddess of the moon. Her death by drowning represents the decline of the lunar cult in favor of the solar cult of Zeus, who was often identified with Aries under the name of Zeus-Amon.

The Golden Fleece, therefore, was to be found in the sacred wood of Ares, guarded day and night by a dragon who never slept. It became so famous a myth in all of Greece that it can be compared with the legend of the Holy Grail or Holy Sepulcher. In fact, as we will see, the moment a pretext arrives to conquer it, the best of all the youth in Greece will set out on one of the most famous transcendental voyages of antiquity.

Jason

Pelias, son of Poseidon, seized Aeson's throne and had him locked up in the palace with his wife, Polymele. Pelias ordered that, if Polymele should become pregnant, the child to be born should be killed immediately because an oracle had predicted that he would be killed by a descendant of Aeson.

After a time Polymele gave birth to a child by the name of Diomedes. In order to save his life, she made him fall asleep by giving him a sleep-inducing herb and had her maidservants weep over his apparently lifeless body. The child was taken to Mount Pelion where he was taken care of and raised by the centaur Chiron, and he grew up under the name of Jason.

The course of destiny could not be stopped, and so it was that one day Pelias and Jason met. The young man claimed the throne that was rightfully his and Pelias accepted on the condition that the remains of Phrixus, who had died but was never buried, be returned to his homeland together with the Golden Fleece so the hero could be given the proper burial.

Jason accepted. The voyage of the ship *Argo* was long and marked by storms, battles, duels, and monsters. In the end, however, heroism, magic, and the help of the gods enabled the Argonauts to land in Colchis.

The genealogy of the house of Aeëtes is particularly interesting due to the multitude of astronomical figures it contains. Nephele was the meteorological manifestation of Hera, the ancient Great Mother of the universe. Her son Phrixus had ridden celestial Aries toward the land where the ancient mythical roots of so many Greek legends were to be found, that of Prometheus, for example. Aeëtes was a son of the sun who had first been married to Asterodeia, the One of the Starry Way, which is the name of the lunar goddess who gave birth to Calciope and Medea. Calciope had married Phrixus who, at this point in the story, however, is already dead. In a second marriage, Aeëtes had married Eidyia, the Wise, who bore him a son, Apsyrtus.

According to Diodorus Siculus, Aeëtes had instead married Hecate, the moon, and with her he had fathered Medea and Kirke, the great lunar sibyls. These figures, ancient and distant even at the time of the Greeks, represented genealogies of extinct gods reborn with other names in other regions. In Greece, Medea and Kirke most probably became Demeter and Persephone.

While Jason and the Argonauts were deciding on the best way to ask Aeëtes for the Golden Fleece, Hera was preoccupied with the safety of her protégé, now exposed to the great magic force of the royal house of Colchis. She therefore decided to ask for the help of Aphrodite, with whom she agreed that the young man's efforts would be to no avail without an ally in that family.

They chose Medea, an extraordinary lunar magician who knew the wood of the Golden Fleece thoroughly. Aphrodite went to Eros and asked him to pierce Medea with one of his arrows to make her fall in love with Jason. To persuade him, Aphrodite gave him the golden ball encircled by azure circles that had been given by Amalthaea (Capricornus) to the infant Zeus when he was in her custody. Much has been said about this golden ball; some claim it was a celestial globe with the motions of the planets and the stars drawn on it.

Jason went to see Aeëtes accompanied by the Greek sons of Phrixus and asked the king diplomatically to give the Golden Fleece back. Aeëtes agreed, with only one condition: that the Greek pass two very dangerous tests.

First, Jason would have to yoke the wild bulls of Hephaestus who had bronze hoofs and whose nostrils breathed fire. With them he would have to cut four furrows in the field of Mars and then sow some serpent's teeth there; these were the few that were left of those that Cadmus had sown in Thebes. Jason had to accept, but he was terrified by the difficulty of the test.

The princess Medea, who had observed the hero during his meeting with Aeëtes and had immediately fallen in love with him, introduced herself that same night to Jason, who was anxiously pondering what to do. She proposed to help him with the bulls of Hephaestus and the Golden Fleece on condition that he would take her with him to Greece and marry her.

Jason agreed and Medea at once handed him a salve that would keep him from being burned by the bulls' flames. This medicine, called Unguent of Prometheus, was obtained from the sap of the flower that had sprouted in the Caucasus valleys from the blood of Prometheus' liver. This flower, the crocus of Corico, has roots that are the color of blood.

With Medea's salve and advice, Jason yoked the bulls, cut the furrows, and sowed the serpent's teeth, from which armed warriors were immediately born who hurled themselves against the Greek. He threw a rock among them, and they proceeded to kill each other.

Enraged by this success, Aeëtes refused to keep his word and secretly prepared to assault the Argonauts and destroy the ship *Argo*. However, the all-knowing Medea quickly conducted Jason to the wood of Ares, cut some juniper branches, immersed them in a magical liquid, and then approached the Dragon with the Hundred Eyes while chanting magical mysteries. Circling around him, she sprinkled the sleep-inducing drops over him.

Once the monster was asleep, Jason took the Fleece from the oak, quickly returned together with Medea to the *Argo* before Aeëtes' guards could reach them, and escaped during the night. The golden coat of celestial Aries, sent by the Great Mother and guarded by the son of the sun, was from that moment on in Greek hands.

The conquest of the Golden Fleece by Jason ties into the tradition of new solar heroes who with the help—through love or force—of the ancient goddess succeeded in achieving victory over fantastic animals or monsters with profound astronomical meaning. So Perseus overcame Medusa and Cetus to save Andromeda; Bellerophon conquered the Chimera; Theseus slew the Minotaur; Hercules took possession of the golden apples of the Hesperides (see chapters on Perseus, Pegasus, Corona Borealis, and Hercules).

Celestial Aries replaced celestial Taurus (the one that was allegorically slain by Gilgamesh and Mithras) as symbol of the resurrection at the spring equinox. In so doing, it brought a new element to the ancient cult, the end of human sacrifice, which had until then been practiced throughout the Mediterranean.

If the hypothesis that Aries was added to the zodiac by the Egyptians is accepted as true, a discussion on how the insertion of this sign may have occurred would be timely here. What is most remarkable when one looks at the layout of the constellations in this area of the sky is that in one relatively restricted area there are two constellations that are only half-figures. Only the head, forelegs, neck, and horns of Taurus can be seen, and Pegasus is also represented by only the anterior part of its body. It gives the impression that Taurus has been halved to make way for the new figure. In fact, Aries occupies exactly the space that would have been the posterior part of the body of Taurus.

What we have here is a case that is analogous to that of Scorpius, a zodiacal constellation that is widely spread out and to which two interpretations were given in antiquity. The part that contained the poisonous stinger had very different meanings from those of the pincers, almost as if it were a different sign. It is also a fact that, in order to obtain the optimum number of signs—twelve—Caesar cut off Scorpius' pincers and invented the sign Lyra. Similarly, Taurus has traces of being divided into three parts in antiquity. Taurus, the Pleiades (in the area of Taurus' neck), and Hyades (the stars of its forehead) were discussed as if they were separate signs.

The case of Pegasus is more difficult. As explained in that chapter, the horse was probably turned over, and the second horse, Equuleus, was definitely added.

However, in the ancient astronomy of India in particular, there seems to be a very strong connection between Pegasus and Aries. In the *Rig-Veda* the divine twins Aswin, in many aspects similar to our Dioscuri, had the horse of the Aswameda called Pagas in their possession. They were also the ones who ruled the first *nakshatra* of the Indian lunar zodiac, that is, the one that opened the year. Furthermore, they were identified with the two stars in Aries' head, Beta and Gamma Arietis.

Zeus Amon

In his *Poetica astronomica* Hyginus records the stories of Hermippus and Leon about the origin of the sign Aries. In both, the principal figure was Dionysus.

The first one tells how, at the time of Dionysus' African campaign, he came with his troops to a sandy desert called Ammodes. The army was in great danger because it was sinking further and further into the sand, and it had completely exhausted its drinking water.

Completely worn out, the soldiers had halted when a ram approached and flew up into the air. Encouraged by this sight, all followed the animal until it landed behind a dune. When they arrived at the spot, they found, instead of the ram, a freshwater spring. Dionysus then ordered them to build in that spot a temple which was dedicated to Zeus Amon. A statue of the god was sculpted that represented him with ram's horns.

Subsequently, he placed the ram among the constellations, in a place where the sun would return each year and nature would be renewed by the young, springtime sun.

Leon's version tells how, at the time of Dionysus' reign over Egypt and while he taught the arts to men, someone by the name of Amon came from Africa bringing a flock of sheep with him. Dionysus rewarded him by giving him the land located opposite Thebes and decreed that all statues of Amon should have ram's horns in remembrance of the fact that he had been the first to teach men the use of flocks. Furthermore, to commemorate the event, a ram was placed among the constellations in the sky.

The temple of Amon at Karnak, built in conjunction with the sun, Amen-Ra, was reached by means of a triumphal road along the sides of which there were dozens of giant sphinxes sculpted with ram's heads standing guard. When, in the spring, the sun entered into the sign, the statue of the god Amon was carried in procession over the triumphal road to the necropolis, from where the stars of Aries could be observed. Preparations for this great celebration began before the full moon following the spring equinox. Thus, on the fourteenth day of that moon, all of Egypt rejoiced in the dominance of the sun in the sign of Aries.

Amon, from a funerary papyrus of the twenty-first dynasty, Museum of Cairo

Astrology of Aries

Along with Leo and Sagittarius, Aries formed the famous Trigon (Triangle) of Fire, which was the residence of Mars. In the human body it influenced the head, cerebral hemisphere, blood vessels of the brain, cranium, bones of the face, teeth, pineal gland, and optic nerve.

Aries produced the primary force of new initiatives and it was, therefore, the sign of combatants, pioneers, voyagers, artists, and bandits.

Mars was the god most worshiped among the ancient Romans. He presided over the art of war, but he also represented the power of the resurrection of vegetation that was reborn with the young, springtime sun. So despite the classical association of the color red with Mars, he was often represented in sculptures with his face painted green, just as the Egyptians did with Osiris.

The cabalists assigned to Aries the fifth trump card of the tarots—the Pope—while today others associate him with the fourth—the Emperor.

The Stars

The name that has come down to us for Alpha Arietis is Hamal, a contraction of the Arabic name *al-Ras al-Hamal*—the Sheep's Head. In the catalogues of al-Kazwini, al-Tizini, and Ulugh-Beg, it was also called *al-Natih*, the Butting Horn. In Mesopotamia it had various names, including *Arku-sha-rishu-ku*, literally, the Backside of the Leader's Head, *Dil-Kar*, She Who Announces the Dawn, and *Dilgan*, She Who Is the Messenger of the Dawn.

The astronomer Brown has associated Hamal with Aloros, the first of the ten mythical kings of Mesopotamia of the period preceding the deluge. The time span of their reigns coincided proportionally with the distances of the ten major stars of the ecliptic, which actually began with Hamal. Brown assumes a derivation of Aloros from the Assyrian name *Ailuv*, which in Hebrew became *Ayil*. The other stars corresponding to the other mythical kings were Alcyone, Aldebaran, Pollux, Regulus, Spica, Antares, Algedi, Deneb Algedi, and Sheat.

Beta Arietis has come to us with the name of Scheratan, from *al-Sharat*, meaning the Sign, since it marked the spring equinox in Hipparchus' time. Gamma Arietis was called Mesarthim from the Hebrew *Mshartim*, or Ministers. Delta Arietis was Botein, from *al-Butain*, the Belly. The lunar stations of India began their course with the *nakshatra* Aswin, ruled by the twin knights and marked by the stars Sheratan and Mesarthim. In the Arab lunar stations the same stars marked the twenty-seventh *manzil*, *al-Sheratain* (the Two Signs), while the twenty-eighth, *al-Butain* (the Belly), was marked by the stars Delta and Epsilon. The Chinese stations, too, marked the twenty-seventh and twenty-eighth *sieu*. The first was called *Leu*, the Trail of the Dress; the second was called *Oei*, the Belly.

XIX. *Aries.*

Nᴜɴᴄ protinus XII. fignorum figurationem dicemus, quorum eft princeps Aries.

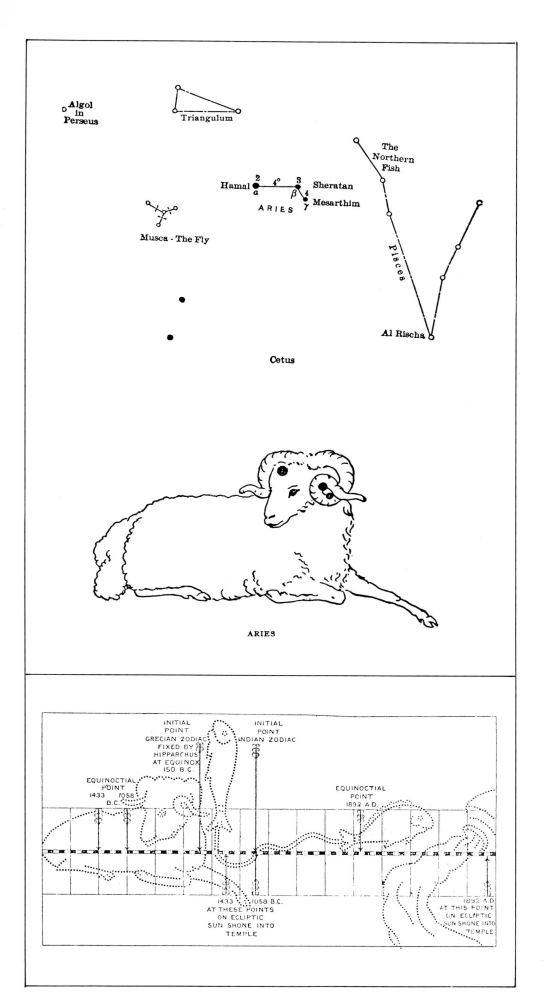

Algol
in
Perseus

Triangulum

The
Northern
Fish

Hamal **2** 4° **3** Sheratan
a *β* 4
ARIES *γ* Mesarthim

Musca - The Fly

Pisces

Al Rischa

Cetus

ARIES

INITIAL
POINT
GRECIAN ZODIAC
FIXED BY
HIPPARCHUS
AT EQUINOX
150 B.C.

INITIAL
POINT
INDIAN ZODIAC

EQUINOCTIAL
POINT
1433 1058
B.C.

EQUINOCTIAL
POINT
1892 A.D.

1433 1058 B.C.
AT THESE POINTS
ON ECLIPTIC
SUN SHONE INTO
TEMPLE

1892 A.D
AT THIS POINT
ON ECLIPTIC
SUN SHONE INTO
TEMPLE

Shifting of the spring equinox relative to its
orientation with the Temple of Amon-Ra.
From E. Plunket, Ancient Calendars and
Constellations *(1903)*

7
Auriga

A very ancient star figure, Auriga, the Charioteer, is remembered in Greek mythology as the coachman Erichthonius. He was represented as half-man and half-serpent, probably in memory of the invasion of Attica by a race of healer-priests—perhaps the Celts—who used snake venoms for their therapies. He is remembered as the inventor of the carriage and the chariot. The ancient royal family of Athens prided themselves on having descended from Erichthonius, and its members called themselves Erechtheides. They customarily carried golden serpents as amulets and worshiped a sacred serpent on Mount Erechtheion.

Micyllus' Auriga

At one time during the Trojan War, Athene asked Hephaestus to make her a set of arms. Hephaestus said coyly that he would undertake the work for love. Missing his point, she entered the smithy to watch him beat out the red-hot metal, and he suddenly turned around and tried to caress her. Hephaestus was the victim of a malicious joke: Poseidon had told him that Athene was hoping to have violent love made to her. As she tore herself away, Hephaestus ejaculated on her thigh. Disgusted, she wiped off the seed with a handful of wool and threw it away. It fell to the ground near Athens, and accidentally fertilized Mother Earth. Revolted at the prospect of bearing this child, Mother Earth declared that she would accept no responsibility for its upbringing, so Athene said she would. She took charge of the infant, named him Erichthonius, and hid him in a sacred basket which she gave to Aglauros, eldest daughter of the Athenian King Cecrops, to guard carefully.

Cecrops, a son of Mother Earth and, like Erichthonius, part-man, part-serpent, had married Agraulos and they had three daughters, Aglauros, Herse, and Pandrosos. One evening the women looked under the lid of the sacred basket, and seeing a child with a serpent's tail, they screamed in fear and leaped from the Acropolis. On learning of this tragedy, Athene was so grieved that she dropped the enormous rock she had been carrying to the Acropolis; it became Mount Lycabettus.

Erichthonius then took refuge with Athene, and she treated him so tenderly that some mistook her for his mother. Later, he became king of Athens, where he instituted the worship of Athene. His image was set among the stars as the constellation Auriga, since he had also introduced the four-horse chariot (Robert Graves, *The Greek Myths*).

For the Athenians, Athene's virginity was the symbol of the impregnability of Athens, and they often manipulated various myths so as to keep her a virgin.

Opposite: *Auriga. From Hevelius,*
Uranographia totum coelum stellatum *(1690)*

257

This is the case with the legend of Boreas (northern wind with its body ending in a serpent's tail). Having transformed himself into a black stallion, he impregnated the three thousand mares of Erichthonius, generating the twelve fillies who, yoked to three chariots, represented spring, summer, and fall. One of Athene's attributes was *Polias*, meaning filly.

The other coachman figure connected with this constellation is that of the legendary Myrtilus, son of the Amazon Mirto and Hermes (the god whom Pausanias saw represented in a sculpture in the temple of Athene-Polias in which he was completely entangled in myrtle branches). In preagricultural civilizations, the myrtle cult was extremely important because a heady and aphrodisiac wine was obtained from the myrtle. It was drunk until cultivation of the grapevine began in the Mediterranean. Myrtle wine was an important ingredient in rituals of a combined erotic and funerary nature.

In Greek legend Myrtilus is the charioteer of Oenomaus during the marriage contest to which those who vied for the hand of the beautiful Hippodameia had to submit. Oenomaus, son of Ares and Asterope, had married Euarete and fathered Hippodameia, a girl of extraordinary beauty; Oenomaus did not want to give her in marriage because an oracle had predicted that he would perish by the hand of his son-in-law. In order to keep the suitors away, Oenomaus had established that whoever could beat him in a chariot race would obtain the hand of his daughter while those who failed would die by decapitation.

Many attempted the undertaking without success since Oenomaus had the fastest horses in the world. One day Pelops—son of Tantalus and Dione—came to try his hand at it. However, when he saw the heads of the suitors hanging over the entrance, he became afraid. With subterfuge, he succeeded in convincing Myrtilus (secretly in love with Hippodameia) to sabotage the course. In exchange he would allow Myrtilus to lie with Hippodameia one night and also give him half of Pelops' realm, the Peloponnesus.

Before the race Myrtilus took out the bolts holding the wheels of Oenomaus' chariot so that it came apart in the middle of the race. Having received his reward, Myrtilus—inflamed with love—tried to flee with Hippodameia while traveling with her and Pelops toward Peloponnesus. Pelops slew him and threw him in the sea that from then on was called Myrtoan Sea. His body, buried in Arcadia, was honored with an annual nocturnal sacrifice that, according to the custom of the heroic cult, was placed on his tomb.

Capella

The constellation Auriga is represented by the figure of a man leaning one foot on one of the horns of the constellation Taurus. In his right hand, he has the reins, symbol of his mastery of horsemanship. On his left arm, he has a female goat, and in his left hand, two kids. The principal star of the goat, the brightest of the constellation, is the famous Capella. This is one of the most important stars of the sky because of its brilliance, its position, and the arcane complexity of its myths.

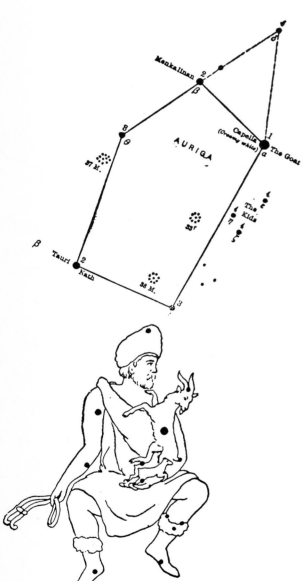

AURIGA

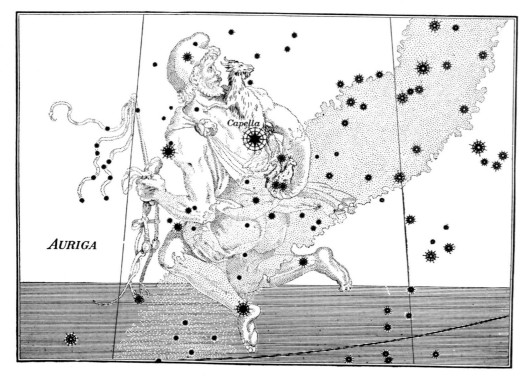

Bayer's Auriga (1603)

The presence of the female goat with its kids in this figure does not correspond to anything in the stories of either Erichthonius or Myrtilus. It is therefore very likely that this myth was superimposed on another more ancient one. Most probably it is the representation of a shepherd god of the nomadic tribes during the time of the preagricultural civilizations.

In Sumerian mythology Capella was called Dilgan, from *Dil-gan-I-ku*, the Messenger of the Light, and also *Dil-gan-babili*, the Protector Star of Babylonia, or *I-ku*, the Military Leader. Its most ancient written record is Sumerian and is to be found on a clay tablet in cuneiform: "When, on the first day of the month of Nisan the star of stars [Dilgan] and the moon are parallel, it is a normal year. When, on the third day of the month of Nisan, the star of stars and the moon are parallel, the year will be abundant."

This made Capella the star that determined the beginning of the year. This could only happen in 1730 B.C. and in the two thousand preceding years, that is, when this star—along with Taurus—indicated the spring equinox.

In the Egyptian zodiac at Dendera, Capella is represented by a mummy of a cat carried in the hands of a man adorned with a crown of feathers. The star had a special place in the cult of Ptah, the One Who Opens (the year), who is the Egyptian representation of the Greek god Hephaestus. The temples dedicated to Ptah were oriented toward Capella, like the temple of Karnak at Thebes.

In India Capella was worshiped as Brahma Ridaya, the Heart of Brahma, the Aryan god of the four heads who holds in one of his hands the rosary of pearls symbolizing the phases and stations of the moon in the lunar calendar.

Fifteenth-century engraving

8
Boötes

From April to September, the stars of the constellation Boötes, the Herdsman, follow those of Ursa Major in the eternal circle that these stars trace around the Polar Star. The brightest of the group is the beautiful Arcturus, that is, Guardian of Ursa. This is from the Greek *artos* (bear), from which the word arctic also derives.

A springtime constellation, Boötes is the protagonist of various legends, either because of its proximity to the Pole or to the importance of the star Arcturus. The name Boötes derives from the Sumerian *Riv-but-sane*, the Man Who Drove the Great Cart. It was also identified with a farmer who plows the land in the spring. The Romans called it the Herdsman of the Septemtriones, that is, of the seven oxen represented by the seven stars of the Great Cart. Septemtriones became, in fact, the root of the now-obsolete word septentrion, meaning north.

In order to truly understand this personality, it is necessary to look at him as he appeared in the sky during specific moments in the development of pre-Greek astronomy. In the third millennium B.C., Boötes was a circumpolar constellation that was visible every night very close to Thuban, the Polar Star at the time. Boötes gave the impression of following the seven stars of Ursa which, in those days, were actually called the cart or the plow.

It is thus an agricultural civilization that conceived this image representative of the farmer's most complex operation, plowing. There remains, however, a certain lack of symmetry, which makes this figure not completely credible. This is especially evident at the culmination points of the map of the stars, the equinoxes and the solstices, so the impression lingers that the label of Plowman or Wagoneer was superimposed on a previous figure. To discover who this was, it is necessary to first discover when these stars fell naturally on the equinoxes and solstices. To obtain that information, we must take the constellation back another three thousand years, to the year 5744 B.C., when the North Pole was extremely close to the head of Boötes and his figure seemed to be perfectly aligned with the meridian of the summer solstice at midnight. In addition, Boötes was also aligned with the meridian during the winter solstice and at the spring and fall equinoxes.

Gradually, from that date on, the slow shifting of the precession of the equinoxes has deprived Boötes of this position of ruler of the Pole and indicator of the seasons.

Finally, it is very important to consider the motion of Arcturus, an authentic pearl for naked-eye observation of the sky and its stars, and the first star to appear in the sky right after sunset. Arcturus' own motion was discovered by the English astronomer Edmund Halley, who calculated it to have one of the fastest movements to be found among the fixed stars. Arcturus moves 2.28″ per year toward the south, which is the equivalent of almost one lunar diameter every eight hundred years. This fact is extremely important because, if we backdate this star's position by a few thousand years, we can see it gloriously situated near the head of the constellation.

Boötes *. From Hyginus,* Poetica astronomica *(1485 edition)*

Opposite: *Boötes. From Hevelius,* Uranographia totum coelum stellatum *(1690)*

Constellations that were visible at 45° N. at midnight on the summer solstice in 5744 B.C.

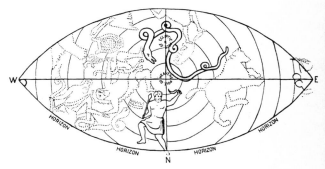

Atlas, the celestial Titan, was a protohistoric
constellation at the pivot of the ancient North
Pole. During the classical period, his right arm
was amputated to create the new constellation
of Corona Borealis

Atlas

The Celestial Titan

What remains to be discovered is the identity of this prehistoric person
described as being at the most important point in the sky.

The only mythological figure worthy of occupying this position is the Titan
Atlas, who holds on his shoulders the vault of the sky at its most meaningful
point—the fixed pivot of the North Pole, around which all the known stars
gravitate. The position of the figure is just right, that is, almost kneeling from
the effort of supporting the weight of astronomical knowledge. However, what is
missing is the right arm lifted in the classical pose of the Titan. This is because
this arm was originally represented by the arc of stars the Greek astronomers
amputated in order to create the constellation known as Corona Borealis, the
crown given to Ariadne by Dionysus (see the chapter on Corona Borealis).

All the writers of myths agree that the Titans were foreign to Greek civilization. Iapetus and Atlas came from far away, but it is difficult to establish exactly
from where.

New archaeological discoveries made in the Sahara Desert, as well as the excavations done along the fossil river at Uadi Berging, have clearly shown that around 10,000 B.C. the desert there was covered by luxuriant tropical forests. Great streams coursed through this region, providing a comfortable habitat for animals like the giraffe, the elephant, the hippopotamus, and the zebra.

The northwestern boundary of the Sahara is ringed by the chain of the Atlas Mountains and it is here that, in the Greek myths, the Garden of the Hesperides was located. Here the mythical daughters of Atlas guarded in their garden the golden apples, that is, the stars Atlas supported. According to legend, the Greek hero Hercules came here to capture them, an allegory of the fact that Hercules went to Atlas in order to learn astronomy. Atlas himself symbolized a people that were very advanced in their knowledge of the sky.

Having said this, the following question naturally presents itself: couldn't it be that the lost continent of Atlantis was the land of the Sahara, which after the last ice age was transformed into a desert due to the sudden change in climate? To justify this hypothesis, there is the firmly rooted presence of Atlantis in ancient European culture, the geographical proximity of this area, and the reality, by now demonstrated, of an enormous cataclysm. We are talking about a vast expanse of land, larger than all of Europe with Russia included, that, within a couple of millennia, was transformed from tropical forests into a desert in which official maps presently list only about ninety oases large enough to support a small population.

Bayer's Boötes (1603)

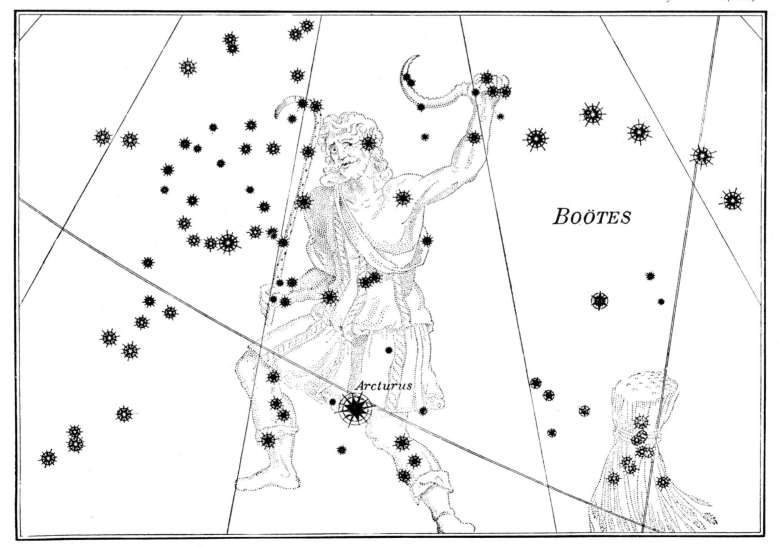

BOÖTES

Arcturus

Boetes

In later times the most commonly recorded myth relating to Boötes was linked to the arrival of the cult of the grapevine in the Mediterranean and the erotic-funereal and resurrection rituals that characterize the cult of Dionysus. According to many, these may be connected with the birth of tragedy and in this regard the constellation offers the figure of Icarius, father of Erigone. Dionysus made Icarius the first among men to plant the grapevine and make wine. Icarius learned the art of pruning, and he also invented the wineskin, made of goatskin, meant to carry wine. It is around this mythical wineskin that "for the first time men danced," as Eratosthenes tells us.

But let's get to the tragedy: Icarius had loaded a cart with wineskins filled with wine and was passing through the woods of Marathon near Mount Pentelicus when he encountered some shepherds and gave them a wineskin of his wine. They drank it without diluting it, as Oenopion later advised doing, and began to show signs of drunkenness, speaking nonsense and walking around foolishly. Other shepherds, thinking that Icarius had poisoned their companions, killed him and buried his body under a pine tree. Later, when the shepherds who had been drinking awoke from the torpor caused by the wine, they asked for Icarius so they could reward him for the divine state in which he had immersed them. Overcome by remorse, the assassins then escaped to a faraway island. Icarius' dog, Maera, returned mournfully home to Icarius' daughter Erigone and, pulling her by her dress, she led her to the pine where Icarius was buried and began to dig the earth with her paws. In despair at the sight of her dead father, Erigone committed suicide by hanging herself from the same tree. Before dying, she intoned a prayer to the sky asking that the

Erigone and Maera find Icarius' body

maidens of Athens should follow her example until her father's death had been avenged. It was thus that many mysterious hangings among Athenian girls began to occur. The oracle of Delphi was consulted, the cause was revealed, and a group of armed men set off in search of the killer shepherds, who were found and slain.

From these events, the ceremonial grape harvest was born during which Icarius, Erigone, and Maera were worshiped with libations. In remembrance of the hangings, the girls of Athens invented the swing, on which they swung back and forth during the harvest. In so doing, they would draw a sickle in the air, symbol of both the moon and the cutting of the clusters of grapes. From the branches of pines, trees that were always present in the ancient vineyards of Attica, masks were hung to twist in the breeze; they were meant to guarantee the fertility of the vineyard. The resin of the pine was often added to the fermentation to give the wine a specific taste.

The bitch Maera, who had alerted Erigone to the fate of her father, was immortalized among the stars in the constellation of the dog Procyon, which rises before the Dog Star, Sirius. Some even say that Maera became Ursa Minor.

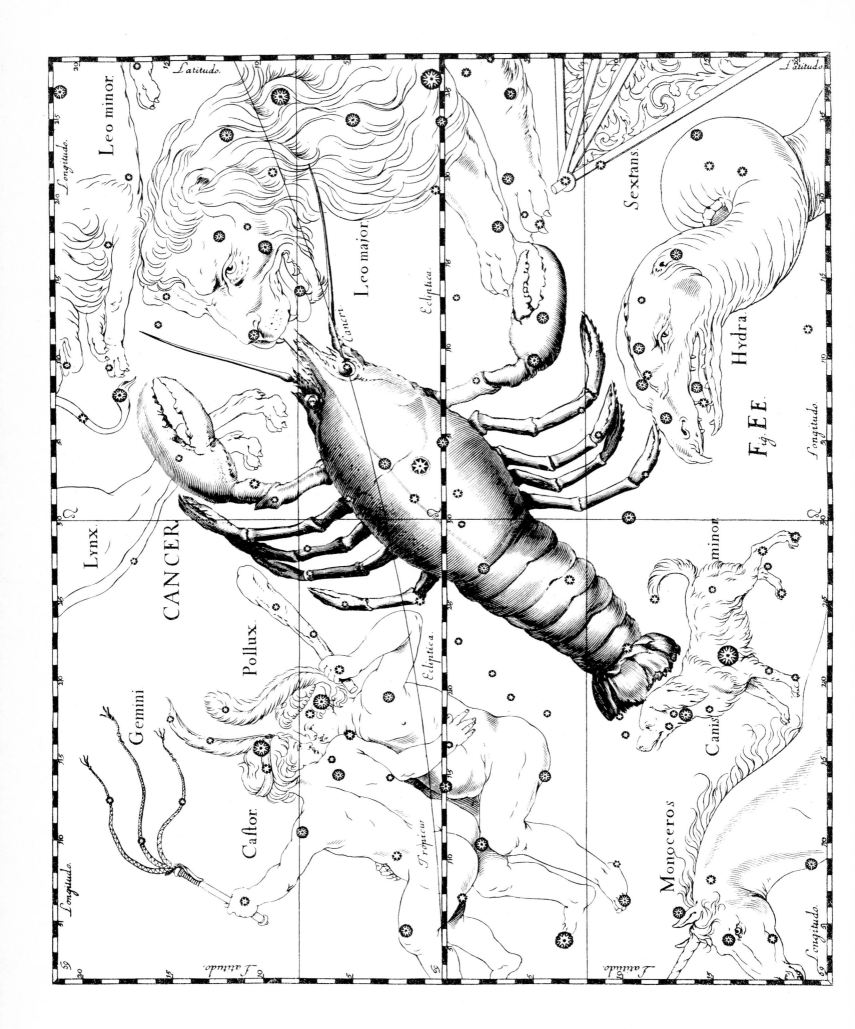

Leo minor.

Latitudo.

Leo major.

Cancri

Ecliptica.

Sextans.

Hydra.

Fig. EE.

Longitudo.

Lynx.

CANCER.

Gemini

Pollux.

Castor.

Ecliptica.

Tropicus.

minor.

Canis

Monoceros

Latitudo.

Latitudo.

266   *The Glorious Constellations*

9
Cancer

Located between Leo, where Regulus is enthroned, and Gemini, with Castor and Pollux, there is a region of the sky that is dark and devoid of stars brighter than the fourth magnitude. In this void there is one of the most important constellations of the zodiac—Cancer, the Crab (or Lobster). In order to find it we can draw an imaginary line starting at Castor and passing through Pollux. If we then extend this line slightly more than twice that distance, we will find the star Zeta Tegmen, the Shell. With the help of the map reproduced here, we can then reconstruct the entire figure.

Cancer can be observed during the period between December and June, but it is best to choose very dark moonless nights with good visibility and to stay far from light-producing centers.

The choice of the crab or lobster to represent the apparent entry of the sun into this part of the zodiac could not have been more appropriate given the very peculiar motion of these animals. They walk backward or sideways, exactly as the sun does when it enters Cancer and reaches its maximum northern declination. It then seems to remain stationary for some days before descending obliquely toward the south. It is the "sun standing still" of the summer solstice.

In Greece it was said that Hera had placed this crab among the stars because it had pinched Hercules on the foot while he was fighting the Hydra in the Lernean marshes. Even more ancient than this legend is the one regarding the central stars of the constellation, Gamma and Delta, among whom the star group of the Manger glimmers with such a faint light that it is just barely visible with the naked eye. The name manger makes us think immediately of a Christian origin: its Latin root, *praesepe*, indicates the crib in which Jesus was born. From this word the scenic representation of that event, introduced by Saint Francis of Assisi at Greccio (near Rieti) in 1223, takes its name.

We find the Manger in the writings of Pliny the Elder: "In the sign of Cancer, there are two small stars, called the donkeys, that are separated by a small space in which a nebula called Praesepia can be seen."

According to this ancient tradition, the two donkeys are the stars Delta and Gamma, still to this day called Asellus Australis and Asellus Borealis, respectively, while Praesepe is the star cluster called M44 in modern catalogues. The story of the two donkeys occurs in an episode of the life of Dionysus when he was crazed by desire for Hera, the jealous wife of Zeus, who was hostile to Dionysus because while Zeus was his father, Semele, the moon, was his mother.

Accompanied by Silenus, the ancient divinity of wine in the Mediterranean, and followed by satyrs and maenads, he wandered around in search of the oracle of Zeus of Dodona—the only one that would be able to help him regain his senses. The story goes that, when he arrived at a large marsh, two donkeys offered to let them cross on their backs and carried the god (and his alter ego Silenus) to the other side without allowing him to touch the water. Having reached the temple of Zeus Dodona and, freed from his madness, Dionysus rewarded the two donkeys by placing them among the constellations.

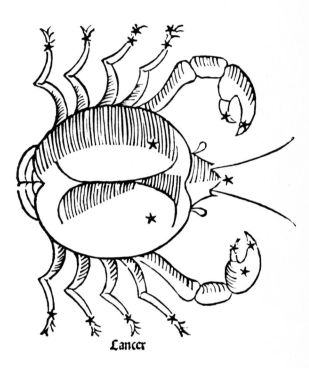

Cancer. From Hyginus, Poetica astronomica *(1485 edition)*

Opposite: *Cancer. From Hevelius,* Uranographia totum coelum stellatum *(1690)*

267

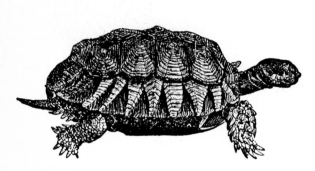

The association between Silenus and donkey, the animal on which he was represented in a perennial state of drunkenness, is a classic of the artistic iconography of Greece, Rome, and the Renaissance. Silenus sometimes appears in hybrid form, a man with the ears and legs of a donkey, much like his friends the fauns and satyrs, who are men with horns and the legs of goats.

The antiquity of Silenus is considerable, dating back to the preagricultural period of the Mediterranean—before the introduction of the grapevine—when wine was made with myrtle berries boiled in a three-legged kettle (see the chapter on Boötes). His cult was integrated into the cult of Dionysus with its three manifestations relating to three age periods: Dionysus first as child, then mature, and finally as an old man. In the first period, he was torn to pieces by the Titans, which symbolized the pruning of the vines. In his mature period, Dionysus was represented as the ripe grapes at the time of harvesting. In his last manifestation, he was Silenus, the wine, the state of drunkenness.

According to a story transmitted to us by Eratosthenes (*Catasterismi* II) and Panyassis (*Heracleias*), Zeus declared war on the Titans and called all the gods to his aid so as to be able to do battle with them. Dionysus, Hephaestus, the satyrs, and Silenus came riding on asses who, frightened at the sight of the Titans, began to bray so loudly in their fear that the Titans, in turn terrorized by a sound they had never heard before, pulled back, allowing Zeus to defeat them. In recognition of their contribution to his victory, the donkeys were placed among the stars.

Still other metamorphoses have occurred to the stars of this constellation. In Mesopotamia a turtle often appeared in place of the crab (see the border stones

Above and below: *Khepri, the sacred scarab, was the Egyptians' symbol for Cancer. The Assyro-Babylonians used a turtle*

Khepri rises from the primordial tumulus (left), pushes the sun out from the world of the dead (center), and (right) sails on the monster of the water

in the British Museum). In Crete these stars were represented by the *Octopous*, or Octopus. In Egypt the constellation appeared in the zodiacs of Dendera and Esna as the god Khepri, the sacred scarab whom the priests of Heliopolis had transformed into a solar divinity or, more precisely, the early morning aspect of the sun. "I am Khepri in the morning, Ra at noon, and Atum in the evening." This trinity suggests that of Dionysus.

Khepri was called "scarab of the heart" because its image, carved in stone, was placed on the mummy in a spot corresponding to the heart. On it were incised the thirtieth and seventy-fifth formulas of the *Book of the Dead* (Boris de Rachewiltz, *I Miti Egizi*).

This connection with the hereafter introduces another very popular metamorphosis of this "black sign" of the zodiac. The adherents of the Orphic and

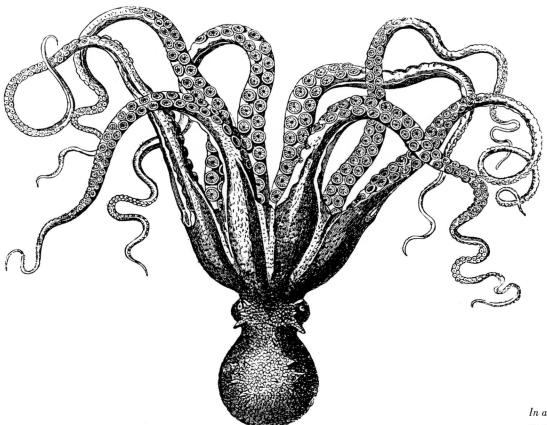

In ancient Crete Cancer was portrayed as an octopus

Platonic doctrines have called it the Gate of Men, meaning the gate through which it was believed that souls descend from the sky to become incarnate in the bodies of human beings.

Notwithstanding their variety, it must be noted that all the creatures chosen to represent this sign are very slow moving—the crab, the donkey, the turtle, the scarab, the octopus—which seems to symbolize the apparent slowing down of the sun when it reaches Cancer.

In the meteorology of Homer, Aratus, and Pliny, the Manger was of great importance because its appearance meant the arrival of good weather. Pliny said, "If Praesepe is not visible in a clear sky, it can be considered a warning of a violent storm."

Chinese astronomy had placed the lunar station *Kwei* or the Specter, and earlier *Kut*, the Cloud, among the stars of Cancer. Both referred to the Manger.

In India it indicated the sixth lunar station, *Pushya*, the Flower, represented by a crescent moon on the point of an arrow, which was the residence of Brihaspati, the teacher of the gods. This flower has a strange parallel in the

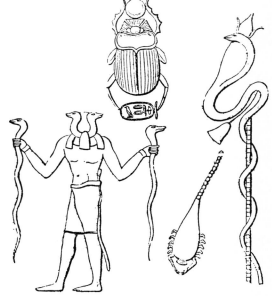

Egyptian constellations

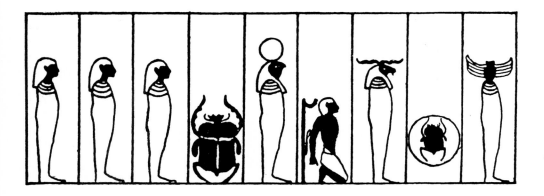

Khepri, along with other gods, in the second corridor of the tomb of Seti I

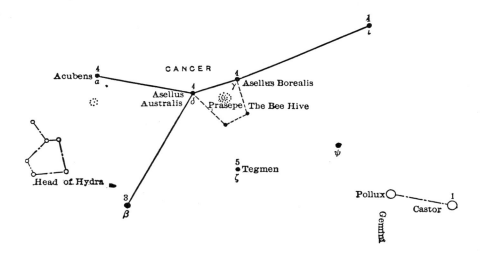

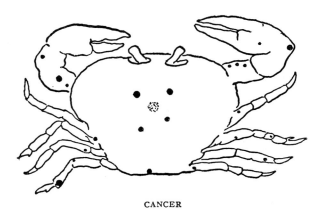

CANCER

astronomy of Peru where Cancer was known as *Cantut Pata*—the Terrace of the *Cantut*, the sacred flower of the Incas, which had an intense red color. During July and August the fields around Cuzco become red with this flower.

Astronomer Julius Schiller's attempt to Christianize the constellations in the seventeenth century transformed the twelve zodiacal signs into the corresponding twelve apostles of Christ and, in so doing, Cancer became Saint John the Evangelist.

In 1531 the comet that is presently called Halley's appeared in the constellation of Cancer.

The Astrology of Cancer

Cancer is traditionally the domain of the moon. This derives from the ancient belief that our satellite was situated in Cancer at the moment of creation. This probably means that, in ancient oral tradition, astrology began during the time when the sun entered into Cancer at the spring equinox, which happened during the two millennia between 8000 and 6000 B.C.

The moon—in its Greek manifestation of Artemis, goddess of the hunt and the woods—is the absolute mistress of the sign. She has as symbols the stone amber, the metal silver, the Orphic egg (an egg with a serpent wrapped around it), the color reddish yellow, and the eighteenth trump card of the tarots—the Moon (although today some consider it to be the Chariot).

The influence of this sign on the human body manifests itself on the esophagus, stomach, diaphragm, pancreas, nipples, chylous vessels, upper lobes of the liver, thoracic duct, uterus, ribs, sternum, and armpits.

Cancer is the sign of the unconscious, fertility, the mother, home, family life, dreams, the need for protection, and life's end. Ptolemy observed that "the two stars of the eyes of Cancer have the same influence as Mercury and, to some extent, Mars. Those of the claws are like Saturn and Mercury."

Berossus, the Chaldean priest of the fourth century B.C. who was a naturalized Greek, asserted that the earth would be submerged by a deluge when all the planets joined each other in Cancer, and would be destroyed by fire when they met in Capricornus. The opportunity presented itself in June, 1895, when they joined in Cancer, which gives us hope for the upcoming encounter in Capricornus.

If the empirical nature of astrology is to be preserved, all those born under Cancer today would belong to the sign of Taurus, due to the precession of the equinoxes. For almost two thousand years the apparent entry of the sun on the first day of spring has occurred in the sign of Pisces, which moves each of the signs back to the preceding one.

The Orphic egg

Bayer's Cancer (1603)

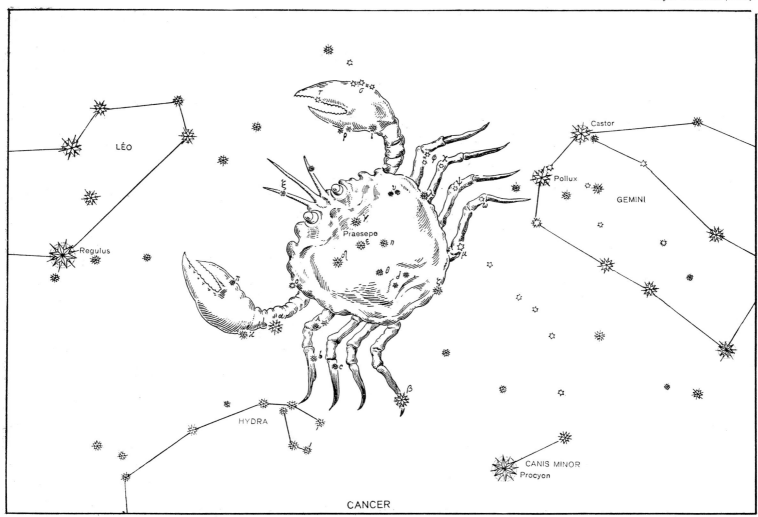

CANCER

Argo Navis.

Monoceros.

CANIS MAJOR.

Orion.

Lepus.

Columba.

Eridanus.

Fig. DDd.

10
Canis Major

If we draw a line connecting the three stars of Orion's belt and continue south, we encounter the most brilliant star in the entire firmament, Sirius. This star begins to appear in October, toward the southeast, after midnight. From then on it rises ever earlier until, in December, it rises at ten P.M., in January at eight P.M., etc. We see it first shine at the feet of the giant Orion and then disappear among the western fogs, toward the southwest, during the last evenings of April. The name Sirius derives from *seir*, to shine; in Aratus' astronomical poem Seirios defined a brilliant, fiery star. However, the Greek word *seir* comes from the Sanskrit *swar*, which has the same meaning but was also used by the ancient Indians to indicate the sky itself.

In the Egyptian calendar the new year began with the solar rising of Sirius, when the star rose at dawn with the sun during the summer solstice. The flooding of the Nile began with the first day of the month of Pachon and, due to its apparent function as the source of information on the level of the river, this star was compared to a watchdog or Anubis, the dog-god (Flammarion). From this custom originated the name for the entire constellation—Canis Major, the Greater Dog. The flooding of the Nile was always preceded by the Etesian winds (periodic winds that occur annually and blow in opposition to the monsoons) that would blow from north to south during the passing of the sun through Cancer. They would drive the clouds toward the south and then, by accumulating them over the marshes where the river's sources were, would cause abundant rains and, consequently, flooding. Prediction of this event was of the utmost importance to the population so that they could prepare themselves by storing supplies of food, protecting their tools, and so on.

The Egyptian calendar did not use the concept of the leap year. Therefore, the extra fragment of time that was left at the beginning of the new year—each year was always 365 days—was added up until, after 121 years, it became a month. After 1,460 years, it became a year and this year was called the Sothic year, from Sothis (another name for Sirius); this is the period of time needed by Sirius to return again to the same date in the Egyptian civil calendar. When this happened, the greatest festivities were celebrated throughout the country. At Heliopolis—the biblical On—in the biggest temple of the sun in Egypt, an

273

The Egyptian god Thoth

Opposite: *Sirius is low on the horizon, to the right of the Milky Way*

Canis Major. From Cicero's Aratea
(British Library)

eagle in a nest of palm fronds was sacrificed alive in a fire. The eagle represented the sun-god and was the symbol of the resurrection; the palm was sacred to the Great Goddess, his mother. In some texts the Sothic year was called the Period of the Phoenix. In 238 B.C., under the reign of the pharaoh Ptolemy Euergetes, a group of priests met at Canopus, in the Nile Delta, to modernize the calendar by adding one day to it every four years. However, the attempt was in vain; the thousand-year-old tradition, and a symbol of stability of the Egyptian world, did not permit it. In the year 26 B.C. Julius Caesar introduced the Julian calendar in Alexandria, Egypt, which was by now a Roman province, but the country continued to use the old 365-day year of the civil calendar. The star map carved in the red sandstone of the Temple of Esna ceiling at Dendera in 36 B.C. shows the star Sirius between the horns of the celestial cow Hathor, whom Ra—the sun—had forbidden to mate with her brother during all of the 365 days of the year. However, having won several games of cards while playing with the moon, Thoth added up various fractions of time and created the five intercalated days during which Hathor was able to conceive Osiris, Isis, Nephtis, and Set, who hold up the four cardinal points (see the chapter on Gemini).

The soul of Isis finally found peace in this star and the temples dedicated to her were oriented toward Sirius. Osiris, on the other hand, rested in Orion.

Sirius

In the star maps of the Greeks, Canis Major was one of the two dogs of the hunter Orion. It was shown standing on its two hind legs ready to jump onto the constellation of Lepus, which was located at the feet of its master. The second dog was made up of the stars of Canis Minor, with the beautiful lucida Procyon. Hyginus associates this constellation with Icarius' dog, Maera. Its fame is tied to the torrid weather that it brings for a period of about forty days. Various remedies for the dog days were listed by the official medicine-prescribing books of the time, but the best was perhaps the one prescribed by Hesiod, who, in *Works and Days*, counsels:

Anubis

When the green artichoke ascending flowers,
When, in the sultry season's toilsome hours,
Perch'd on a branch, beneath his veiling wings
The loud cicada shrill and frequent sings. . . .
Sit in shade of rocks; with Byblian wine,
And goat's milk, stinted from the kid, to slake
Thy thirst, and eat the shepherd's creamy cake;
The flesh of new-dropt kids and youngling cows,
That, never teeming, cropp'd the forest browse.

274   *The Glorious Constellations*

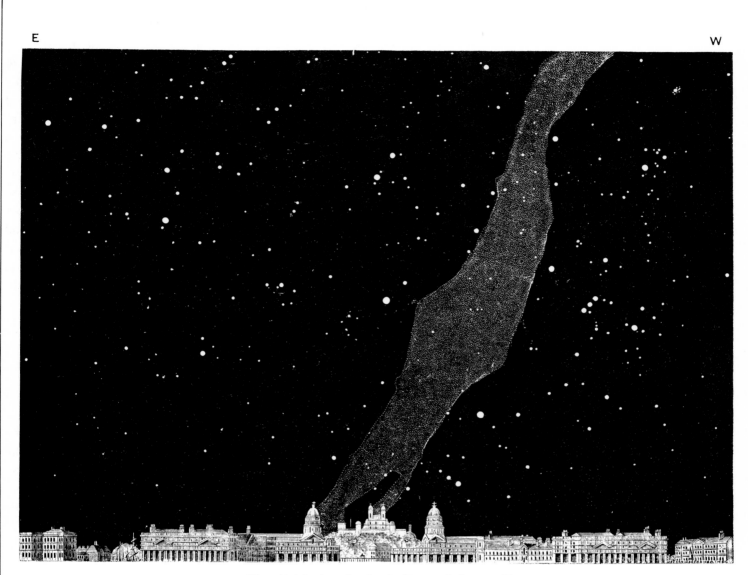

The midnight sky at London, looking south, January 15

With dainty food so saturate thy soul,
And drink the wine dark-mantling in the bowl:
While in the cool and breezy gloom reclined
Thy face is turn'd to catch the breathing wind;
And feel the freshening brook, whose living stream
Glides at thy foot with clear and sparkling gleam:
Three parts its waters in thy cup should flow,
The fourth with brimming wine may mingled glow. . . .
When Sirius and Orion the mid-sky
Ascend, and on Arcturus looks from high
The rosy-finger'd morn, the vintage calls:
Then bear the gather'd grapes within thy walls.
Ten days and nights exposed the clusters lay
Bask'd in the lustre of each mellowing day:
Let five their circling round successive run,
Whilst lie thy frails o'ershaded from the sun:
The sixth in vats the first of Bacchus press;
Of Bacchus gladdening earth with store of pleasantness.
But when beneath the skies on morning's brink
The Pleiads, Hyads, and Orion sink;
Know then the ploughing and the seed-time near:
Thus well-disposed shall glide the rustic year.

In the very ancient carvings of the atlas on the celestial globe held up by the Titan, the star Sirius stands out among the various constellations represented. It is surrounded by rays that indicate its particular brilliance.

Some astrologers treated those who were born under the influence of this star rather harshly. But Ptolemy assigned to the entirety of the constellation, excluding Sirius, the gentle qualities of Venus, who predisposed men to kindness, charity, and fidelity. These qualities, however, are often marred by violent passions and an atavistic fear of the dark. To the temperament of Sirius, Ptolemy assigned Jupiter and Mars, who generate devotion in their subjects, which meant that they would become perfect guardians, tutors, and guards.

The Star Named Arrow

In Sumer the ancient astronomers created a constellation that brought some of the stars of Argo Navis together with those of Canis Major. They called it *Ban Kak Si Di*—Bow and Arrow—and it represented, in fact, a bow and an arrow pointed toward Orion (see the chapter on Orion). The Babylonian name is also similar, *Kakkab-Kasti*, the Star named Bow. Bow and Arrow are found also in ancient Iran with the name of *Tistrja* and in various star maps of China. Even in the starry ceiling of Dendera in Egypt, the divine archer Sothis is shown pointing her bow at the star between the horns of the cow, Sirius.

The famous Arab astronomer al-Sufi described Sirius with the name *al-Schira al-Abuz*, Sirius Who Has Passed Through. Al-Sufi spoke of a very ancient myth of the nomads of the desert in which Sirius had traveled south across the Milky Way, in the direction of the star Suhail (Canopus). This myth has caused some astonishment among modern astronomers—having studied the slow motion peculiar to Sirius, which can now be calculated with our very accurate modern instruments, they have demonstrated that, in effect, during the last sixty thousand (!) years, this star has indeed passed from one side of the Milky Way to the other.

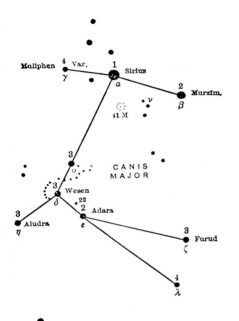

CANIS MAJOR

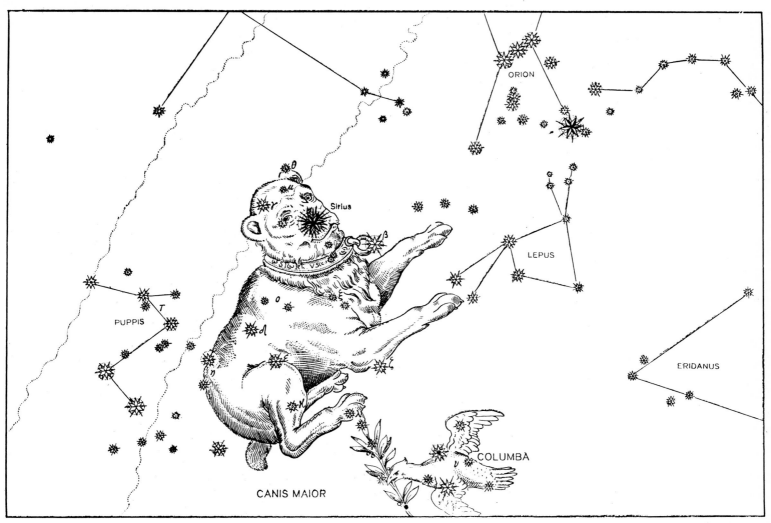

Bayer's Canis Major (1603)

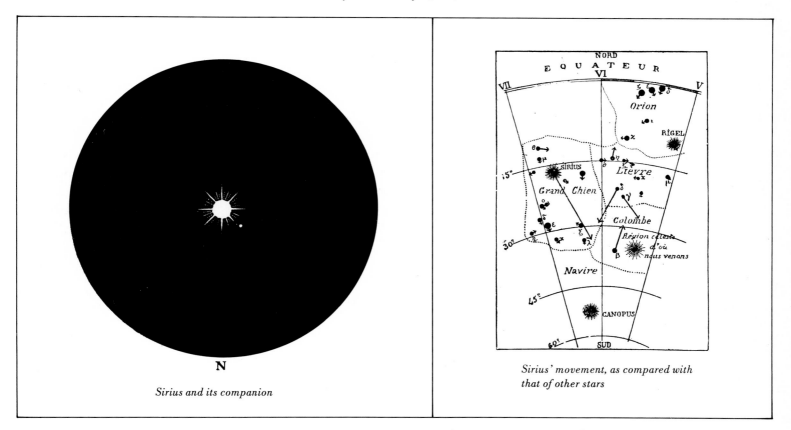

N

Sirius and its companion

Sirius' movement, as compared with that of other stars

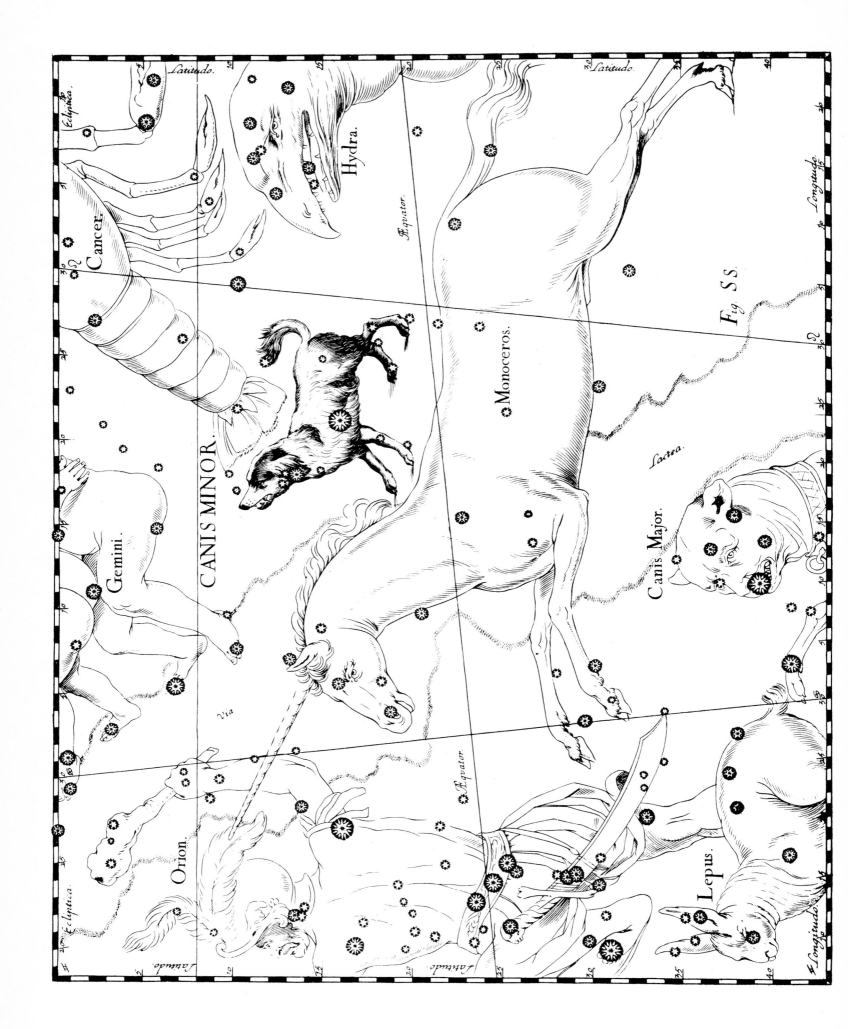

Latitudo.

Ecliptica.

Hydra.

Cancer.

Aequator.

Longitudo.

Fig. SS.

CANIS MINOR.

Monoceros.

Gemini.

Lactea.

Canis Major.

Via.

Orion.

Aequator.

Canis Major.

Lepus.

Ecliptica.

Latitudo.

Longitudo.

11
Canis Minor

Under the stars of Gemini a little dog trots along toward the west. He can be recognized from his lucida, the star Procyon. A little farther toward the south sparkles his better-known companion, Canis Major, where the beautiful Sirius glitters.

Due to the fact that it rises before Canis Major, Canis Minor, the Lesser Dog, had earned itself such Latin names as Antecanis, Antecedens Canis, Antecursor, Praecanis, and Procanis. Vitruvius called it Canis Septentrionalis; as well as (for the first time) Canis Minor, in comparison to the magnitude of Sirius; Canis Parvus (Small), in comparison to Sirius' brilliance; and Canis Primus because it rose first.

Its heliacal rising forewarned the Egyptians of the rising of Sirius, which in its turn marked the beginning of the flooding, the end of the dry period, and the arrival of the new year. It is exactly because of this quality of forewarning, much like guard dogs, that Procyon and Sirius have been associated with this animal.

Greek tradition considered this constellation to be one of the dogs of the hunter Actaeon, son of Aristaeus, who was leaning against a rock near Orchomenus when he happened to see Artemis in the nude while she was bathing in a stream. Offended at having been seen by a mortal man, Artemis transformed Actaeon into a deer, and he was at once torn to pieces by his own dogs.

Much older than this myth is that of Icarius, his daughter Erigone, and their dog, Maera, personalities adopted from the primitive cults of the Greek peninsula. They are remembered in three different constellations. In their stories mythographers see the first representation of the classic tragedy of Icarius, the first man to plant a grapevine and to produce wine (see chapter on Boötes).

In the chapter on Leo we discuss that incredible constellation, created by the imagination of the desert nomads, which consisted of the figure of a giant lion stretching from Gemini to Scorpius. It was called Asad and it had one front leg extended over the stars of Gemini. The other, bent back, ended above Canis Minor and was called *al-Dhira al-Asad Makbudah*, Asad's Bent Leg. The post-Ptolemaic Arabic texts called it *al-Kalb al-Asghar*, the Smaller Dog, or *al-Kalb al-Mutakaddin*, the Dog Who Precedes.

Even greater than the lion Asad itself is the mystery presented by a very ancient legend that might date back to the original inhabitants of the Sahara at the time when this region of Africa was covered by luxuriant forests. This fable tells of the sisters al-Ghumaisa (Procyon) and al-Shira (Sirius) who both fell desperately in love with the handsome al-Jauzah (Orion). Unfortunately, he resided on the other side of a river, which was represented by the Milky Way. So the sisters set out on a quest to reach their beloved. However, only al-Shira succeeded in crossing the great river and was therefore called *al-Shira al-Abur*, Sirius Who Has Passed Through, while the other sister was *al-Ghumaisa* or She Who Weeps (Houseau, *Bibliographie Générale de l'Astronomie*). In another

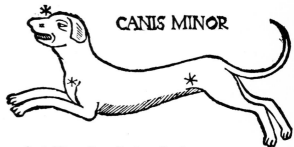

Canis Minor. From Hyginus, Poetica astronomica *(1485 edition)*

Opposite: *Canis Minor. From Hevelius,* Uranographia totum coelum stellatum *(1690)*

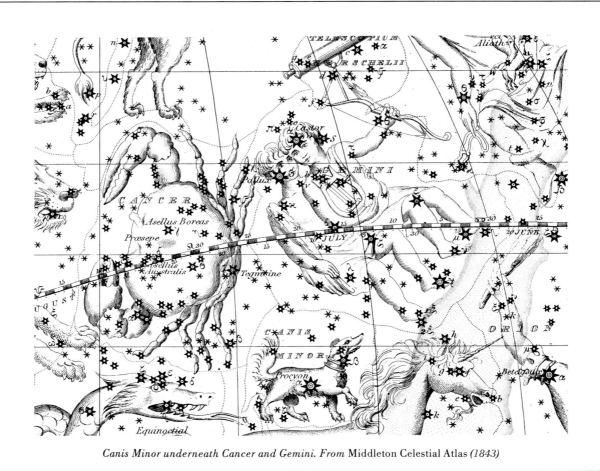

Canis Minor underneath Cancer and Gemini. From Middleton Celestial Atlas *(1843)*

हनुमान्

The warrior Hanuman carries the trisula of Shiva, the sword of Kali, the club of Vishnu, the cord of Varuna, the Parijata tree of Indra's paradise, the sacrificial vessel of Brahma, the Mahendra Mountain, etc. Hanuman represents the defender of Hindu tradition. From Morretta, Miti Indiani (1982)

version, by al-Sufi, the beloved was not Orion but the star Canopus in the constellation Argo Navis.

So far this is an apparently normal story. The incredible part arises when we take into consideration the movements of Procyon and Sirius. These two stars move through the sky at a speed that is greater than that of many other fixed stars. From an analysis of these movements, it has been calculated that over the past sixty thousand years Sirius has actually passed through the Milky Way and that Procyon will do so over the next sixty thousand years. This evidence has us assume that someone at the time of the Stone Age knew the movement of these two stars and so the knowledge of their positions was conveyed orally down through the ages.

The French astronomer Dupuis discovered that Procyon had been worshiped by the Hindus under the name of Hanuman, the extremely popular monkey-god of India, who had the god of the wind as his father and the monkey Anjana as his mother. Hanuman was the nephew of the Vedic Maruts, the terrible spirit manifestations of the monsoons of India. This relationship placed him in the context of the most ancient of traditions. He moved like the wind, he uprooted and swept the mountains along, he had the magical power to grow immeasurably big or become extremely small. Above all he was a formidable warrior, having been of great help to Rama in defeating Ravana and occupying Lanka.

He was the symbol of the union between the Aryans and the Dravidians during the time of the great mergers between the north and the south. The Aryans of Rama called those peoples monkeys but later popular imagination dissipated the negative connotation of the word and raised Hanuman to a divine rank. From then on the actual monkeys became almost as sacred as the cows (Morretta, *Miti Indiani*).

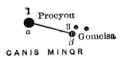

CANIS MINOR

CANIS MINOR

Pegaſus.

Latitudo.

Latitudo.

Longitudo.

Equuleus.

Aquarius.

Pifcis Notius.

Æquator.

Aquarius.

Eclyptica.

Capricorni.

Longitudo.

CAPRICORNUS.

Antinous.

Ecliptica.

Tropicus.

Sagittarius.

Fig. LI.

Longitudo.

Longitudo.

Latitudo.

Latitudo.

12
Capricornus

During the period from August to October, we can see Capricornus, the Goat, in the southern hemisphere of the sky. It is the tenth constellation of the zodiac, and it is composed of rather dim stars. In fact, Cancer is the only zodiacal constellation that is less brilliant.

The absence of first-magnitude stars in Cancer and Capricornus, together with the fact that during the two thousand years before the birth of Christ the sun reached its highest declination in Cancer and its lowest in Capricornus, had resulted in Cancer being considered the northern gate of the sun and Capricornus, the southern.

In Porphyry's essay "In the Cave of the Nymphs" (300 B.C.) he states that the souls that descend from the heavens to become incarnate on earth pass through the celestial gate of Cancer and that upon completion of their life cycle they return to the heavens through the gate of Capricornus.

Also, the two circles that run parallel to the celestial equator, located at 23° S. and 23° N., got their names from the two signs that marked the declination of the solar solstices—the Tropic of Cancer and the Tropic of Capricorn. By now the centuries-old movement of the precession of the equinoxes has shifted that part of the sky where Capricornus is located toward the north and, in so doing, has made visible to us stars our ancestors were not able to observe. Today it is Sagittarius who receives the sun in the winter solstice and therefore occupies the southernmost position in the zodiac.

For a number of reasons scientists have never wanted to change the names of these lines to the actual ones, that is, the Tropic of Gemini and the Tropic of Sagittarius. In the same way astrologers have not wanted or known how to change the equinoxes and the solstices that were correct during the two thousand years before Christ (Aries, Libra, Capricornus, and Cancer) to those that are correct today (Pisces, Virgo, Sagittarius, and Gemini).

Capricornus is a hybrid with the form of a goat for the upper part of its body and the shape of a fish from the shoulders down. Its amphibious nature is understandable if its position in the sky is taken into consideration. Capricornus is located in the celestial zone the ancient astronomers called the Sea. For the part of its body that is a goat, we may suppose that the goat—an animal used to climbing rocky mountains to feed—may have seemed the right symbol for the sun which, having reached its lowest declination at the solstice, resumed its climb along the ecliptic in Capricornus. This interpretation was, of course, only valid for the period when these stars marked the winter solstice. However, our Capricornus is much more ancient and the explanation of this figure is perhaps lost in the mists of time.

While translating some Sumerian inscriptions in cuneiform, the nineteenth-century English historian A. H. Sayce found a reference to Capricornus as the Father of the Light—a title that priests usually gave to the sign of the summer solstice. This could have happened only around the year 13,000 B.C. Incidentally, the goatskin was the magic garment of the Sumerian astronomer-priests.

Capricornus. From Hyginus, Poetica astronomica *(1485 edition)*

Opposite: *Capricornus. From Hevelius,* Uranographia totum coelum stellatum *(1690)*

Alignment for finding Capricornus

283

Ea

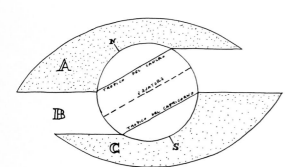

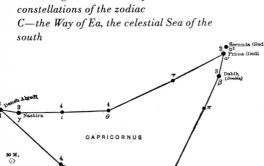

A—the Way of Enlil, the northern sky
B—the Way of Anu, the heavenly band
containing the sun, moon, planets, and
constellations of the zodiac
C—the Way of Ea, the celestial Sea of the
south

CAPRICORNUS

If, in conclusion, we shift this sign backward in time in order to determine when it had an important position in relation to the solstices and the equinoxes, we obtain the following dates: from 14,000 to 12,000 B.C., the summer solstice occurred in Capricornus; from 8000 to 6000 B.C., the autumnal equinox; and from 2000 B.C. until the beginning of our era, the winter solstice.

Among the archaeological finds of Mesopotamia we often find the symbol of Capricornus with a ram's head above it. This animal has nothing to do with the sign of Aries, but belongs to Ea—the principal god of the most ancient phase of the Sumerian religion (Gleadow, *The Origin of the Zodiac*). This makes it possible to state that Ea was the lord of the sign of Capricornus when the Sumerian astronomers drew the map of the sky as we know it today.

Ea was the only god of the Mesopotamian pantheon who was considered utterly good. One of his ancient names was Dugga, Good or Beneficent. He was invoked as Spirit of the Land and Water Surface, but he was also the sovereign of that region of the atmosphere in which life took place in all its various and manifold forms.

The ideogram of the name Ea means abode of the waters. In actuality, the god had as his abode the abyss. This explains his condition of god-fish, which is often represented as fish-man or fish-goat. It was said that he had emerged four times at long intervals from the ocean in order to teach men, each time withdrawing into the waters of the night.

Capricornus, his symbol, represented his land-water ambivalence. In those days his association with Saturn was entirely unknown. This god was instead depicted with a dragon with a lion's head and by the god Nergal, the scorching sun of summer.

Ea was also often invoked with the name of *Kusarikku*, Fish-Ram. This explains why a ram was often represented on the back of Capricornus. He was the supreme protector of men and of all of nature; even the gods called for his help when they were threatened by some danger. He has often been called Oannes but it seems that this name is a Greek adaptation of the name *Eaganna*, Ea, the Fish.

Since he was god of the waters of the seas and the oceans, the southern region of the earth and the southern zone of the sky were sacred to him. We must point out that for people living in Mesopotamia the south corresponded to the sea (Persian Gulf) and that the celestial region the astronomers called the Sea was also located in the south.

It would seem natural for Ea to have been assigned to the sign of Aquarius at the time when the sun entered into this sign during the winter solstice (4000–2000 B.C.). With the solstice subsequently passing on to Capricornus, we can suppose that the astronomers would have created the link between Ea and Capricornus for convenience' sake. However, the judgment of the best experts as well as the ancient cuneiform texts confirm that, from time immemorial, not

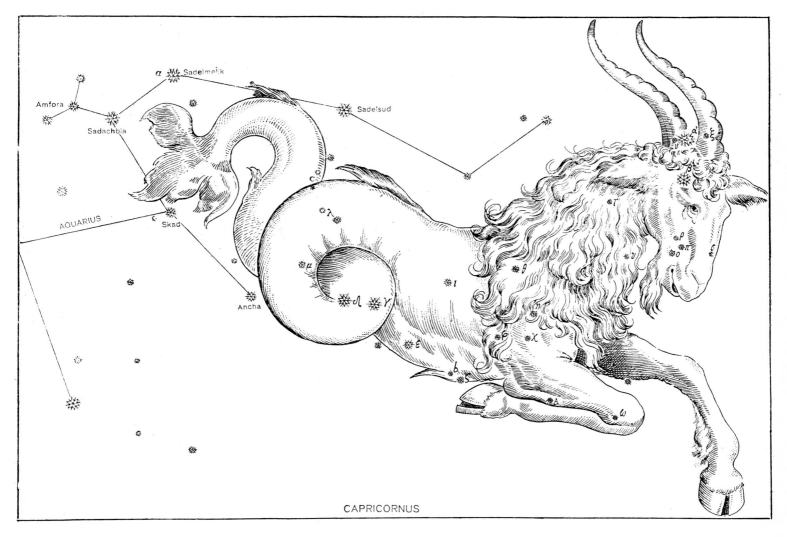

CAPRICORNUS

Bayer's Capricornus (1603)

only were the figure and the sign of Capricornus dedicated to Ea but so was that area in the sky that corresponds to the southern celestial region defined by the Tropic of Capricorn and is called Way of Ea.

Pan

In antiquity the Greeks worshiped the great phallic god with horns and goat's legs who was named Pan and who originated in Arcadia and Peloponnesus.

It was said of him that he was a son of the goat Amalthaea. At the time she was nursing him Rhea entrusted her with her own infant—Zeus—to save him from his father, Cronus, who was looking for him in the sky, the sea, and on the land in order to kill him.

Amalthaea had hung the crib from the branch of a tree so that the baby was neither in the sky nor on land nor in the sea. In addition, to keep Cronus from hearing his son's wails she called young boys to come and play with bronze shields and lances, and she had them dance noisily around the tree. These boys were called curetes or corybantes.

Amalthaea fed the baby from her celestial horn—the cornucopia—from which flowed inexhaustible nourishment. Later on the legend developed that Zeus, in gratitude to Amalthaea, placed her among the stars as the constellation of Capricornus.

There are several versions of the myth that identifies Pan's parents. It was said, for example, that Hermes lay with the nymph Dryope (nymph of the oak)

The Curetes

Capricornus 285

Pan

Cybele, the Curetes, the goat Almathaea, and the infant Zeus

and that from this union a marvelous baby boy was born who had horns and goat's legs and was very outgoing and cheerful. Hermes took him at once to be introduced to the gods of Olympus. They enjoyed him so much that they called him Pan, which means All in Greek. For this reason he was subsequently identified with the universe. In another version of the myth, it was said that Callisto—the nymph seduced by Jupiter and transformed into the constellation of Ursa Major—was the mother not only of Pan but also of his twin, Arcas.

The figure of Pan is tied to the famous myth of the battle between Typhon and Zeus. This myth tells the story of how that monstrous dragon had succeeded in defeating the king of the gods and had cut off the sinews of his legs and arms. He then hid him in a cave in Cilicia and gave the sinews to Pythia, the high priestess of Apollo at Delphi, for safekeeping. With the help of Hermes, and using subterfuge, Pan succeeded in returning the sinews to Zeus. Healed, Zeus ascended to the sky again on a chariot drawn by winged horses in order to continue the battle with Typhon. He succeeded in defeating him and buried him under Mount Etna, which was from then on a volcano.

It is easy to determine the astronomical meaning of these myths. Zeus was the sun who, during his yearly voyage, reached the winter solstice (minimum declination of the year) in Capricornus. At that point the forces of darkness and chaos were about to defeat him, but then he was aided first by the she-goat Amalthaea and then by Pan—allegories of this zodiacal sign—who enabled him to be reborn by nourishing him and freeing him from the dark cave. This could, of course, only happen when the winter solstice fell in Capricornus, that is, during the two thousand years preceding the birth of Christ. Even the image of Zeus, who rises up from the dark cave on a celestial chariot drawn by winged horses, is symbolic of the chariot of the sun which resumes its seasonal ascent.

The astronomer-mythologer Burritt proposed another interpretation of the myth of Amalthaea which says that on the island of Crete there existed a small territory in the shape of a horn that was exceptionally fertile. Amalthaea was not a she-goat but the daughter of the king of Crete, and the infant Zeus was given to her for safekeeping. She did this by hiding him in this particular fertile terrain from which the image of the cornucopia derives.

The symbolism of the nourishment that the young sun took from the figure of the goat derives also from the association with the ancient southern and Mediterranean custom of feeding newborn children goat's milk, which was considered the most complete and easily digestible food.

Pan was famous for his amorous exploits both with nymphs and with young boys. On three occasions, however, the same thing happened to him that happened to Apollo with Daphne. While he was pursing the nymph Pitys, she transformed herself into a pine tree in order to escape from him. From then on one of the symbols of Pan was the thyrsus of the pinecone—a ritual staff surmounted by a pinecone (see the chapter on Centaurus). The nymph Syrinx similarly escaped from him by transforming herself into a reed from which Pan made the first syrinx, or panpipe, which was composed of reed segments held together by pieces of string. The nymph Echo also managed to escape and was transformed into a voice—only the echo, that is. Pan's great love, however, was Selene, the moon. In order to seduce her the goat-god hid himself under the white fleece of a sheep.

When the cult of Dionysus became dominant throughout Greek civilization, Pan's attributes were acquired by this god of drunkenness. From then on he became associated with the constellation of Capricornus and the winter solstice, during which great quantities of wine were imbibed as celebration of the rebirth of the sun in the ecliptic.

Dionysus and a maenad

The Astrology of Capricornus

It was the Greeks who assigned to Saturn the house of Capricornus, generally called "abode of the gods." When Greek civilization moved to Alexandria in Egypt and grafted itself onto the Egyptian civilization, Saturn was identified with the god Set, who represented the aridity of the desert and the destructive force of the sandstorms.

In Roman times Capricornus became the favorite of the astrologers because it was the auspicious sign under which Caesar and Vespasian were born. Saturn was considered by the Romans to be the god of agriculture and his allegory was, in fact, the cornucopia. The Saturnalia were the great festivities for the winter solstice that later became our Christmas. They were surpassed in ostentation and merriment only by the Bacchanalia, or festivities of Bacchus (who, like Dionysus, was also associated with Capricornus), and these later became our Carnival.

For the Romans, Saturn was not the only one who reigned over the house of Capricornus. There was also a beneficent goddess by the name of Fortuna—a word that derives from the Latin *Vortumnia*, She Who Turns—called this because the new year began at this time. This dating system had been established by Numa Pompilius (715–673 B.C.), second king of Rome, whose

Fortuna

Capricornus. From the planisphere at Dendera

calendar was adopted and used until the revisions made by Julius Caesar. Fortuna is the Roman transposition of Tyche, the Greek goddess who was worshiped in the constellation of Virgo.

In Roman culture there was a great conflict between the masculine puritanism and the joyful matriarchy of Etruscan origin. From the time of Rome's foundation, the puritan wing celebrated the greatest goddess of the Latin pantheon—Vesta—in whose temple burned the sacred fire that was always kept alive by the vestal virgins. Vesta was the symbol of the faithful, pure, sacrificing, and submissive woman who renounces the pleasures of life. It is to her the sign of Capricornus was dedicated and was therefore also called Vestae Sidus, the Seat of Vesta, a name therefore that conveyed the exact opposite character of the sign's Dionysiac nature.

A significant number of gods have been associated with this constellation. We can also add to these the Christian revision of the sky and its stars that had transformed the twelve zodiac signs into the twelve apostles. With this revision our fish-goat became for a short while Saint Simon.

Along with Taurus and Virgo, Capricornus formed the Terrestrial Trine, or threesome. Its astral influences made themselves felt on the skin, the knees, the bones, the joints, and the kneecaps. The lands of Greece, India, Macedonia, Thrace, Spain, France, and Germany were dedicated to this constellation.

The cabalists assigned it the tenth trump card of the tarots, the Wheel of Fortune, but today some have instead adopted the fifteenth—the Devil.

Ptolemy observed that the stars of the horns of Capricornus have a similar effect to that of Venus and, partially, to that of Mars; those of its mouth are like Saturn and, in part, Venus; those of the feet and the belly act like Mars and Mercury; those of the tail like Saturn and Jupiter.

The Arabs celebrated in this sign their twentieth *manzil*, or lunar station—
al-Sad al-Dhabih, the Fortune of Those Who Sacrifice (Alpha and Beta
Capricorni)—which referred to the sacrifice of the she-goats that is still celebrated today by all Moslem families during the feast of *Id-al-Adha*, which falls
around the time of our Christmas. This *manzil* provided aid to slaves and
prisoners in their struggle for freedom as well as to people seeking to rid
themselves of bodily illnesses. With the moon in this constellation, it was the
right time to take medicine and to travel, although it was not a good time to
make loans or get married.

In the list of the Hindu stations this is the place for the twentieth
nakshatra—Abhijt, the Victorious—whose symbol was a triangle. Under its
influence, the gods had defeated the Asuras, the Indian titans.

In China this was the abode of the twentieth *sieu—Nieu*, the Ox—which was
governed by the planet Venus. This constellation was dedicated to the cultivation of silk berries.

Among the stars of Capricornus the composition of the two main stars is
unusual: they are so close to each other that they were often considered to be
one. At the time of Ptolemy the distance between them was calculated to be
four minutes; at the beginning of this century, it was six and one-quarter
minutes. Therefore, their distance grows by about seven seconds every hundred
years. In the catalogues these two stars are called Alpha One and Alpha Two
Capricorni. However, their common name is Gedi or Algedi, which derives from
the Arabic *al-Jadi*, the Goat, which was also the name for the entire constellation. Another one of its names was Dabih, a contraction of the lunar *manzil*
discussed earlier—*al-Sad al-Dhabih*, the Fortune of Those Who Sacrifice.
Consequently, the name for Beta Capricorni is Dhabih for the same reason.
Gamma Capricorni gets its name of Nashira from *al-Sad al-Nashirah*, She Who
Brings Glad Tidings. Deneb Algedi was instead the name of Delta Capricorni
and is derived from *Dhanab al-Jady*, the Tail of the Goat.

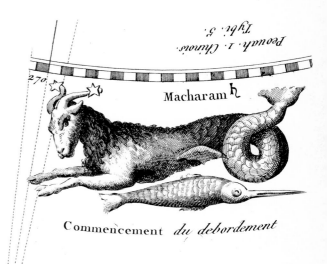

13
Cassiopeia

In the Milky Way a mysterious queen sits on a beautiful throne of stars. Every night, slowly and tirelessly, she revolves around the North Pole.

It is easy to find her because she is as far from the Polar Star to one side as the Big Dipper is to the other, and also because her five main stars, second and third magnitude, look like a W when they are above the Pole and like a slightly distorted M when they are below it. The movement that this constellation makes in its rotation allows this queen to remain seated when the stars are in the position of a W, but turns her upside-down every day when the stars assume the shape of an M. Perhaps this is the reason why she was associated with Cassiopeia, the powerful protohistoric queen-goddess who was punished by Poseidon and turned to marble by Perseus. In his *Poetica astronomica* Hyginus even described her as being tied to her throne with ribbons to keep her from falling off every time she turns upside-down.

Her story and that of her family are told in the chapter on Perseus. It would be helpful to read them before continuing with this constellation.

The ancient constellation-makers drew only three female figures among the stars; Cassiopeia is one of them. From the discussions of Perseus and Andromeda, it is evident that these three figures were the transpositions of the Great Mother—the universal symbol for woman and creator, which dates back to prehistory—to the world of the stars. This principle is represented by the actual triad of Persephone-Demeter-Hecate that, in antiquity, appears in innumerable other combinations of goddesses but always in a threesome. According to this interpretation Cassiopeia is the celestial transposition of Hecate—the oldest of the three—while Demeter is to be found in the constellation of Virgo, and Persephone in that of Andromeda.

Being of extremely ancient origin, Hecate must have had the highest position in the protohistoric pantheon. She was sovereign of the sky, the earth, and Tartarus, as well as the supreme representative of the creativity of that matriarchal priesthood that gave life to botany, medicine, and agriculture.

With the arrival of the Hellenes the image of Hecate underwent a remarkable transformation. All her attributes of creativity and justice were abolished and the emphasis was put on her destructive capacities; it eventually came to the point where she was invoked only during the clandestine rites of black magic. Despite this fact, her power was so great that Zeus himself honored her to the extent that he did not take away from her the ancient prerogative of bestowing on or removing from mortals any gift whatsoever. The story of Cassiopeia meets with the same fate. She is powerful and so beautiful and irresistible that the vengeance of the Hellene Poseidon is unleashed against her. Not only does he let loose the marine monster upon the land where she is worshiped, but he actually demands her daughter Andromeda as a sacrifice.

Cassiopeia. From Hyginus, Poetica astronomica *(1485 edition)*

Opposite: *Cassiopeia. From Hevelius,* Uranographia totum coelum stellatum *(1690)*

291

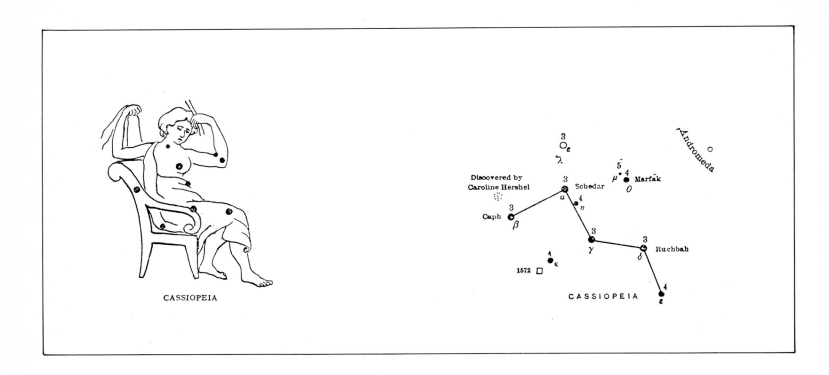

CASSIOPEIA

CASSIOPEIA

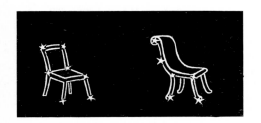

Variations in the design of Cassiopeia's chair

Hecate

Quassio-peaer, meaning Rose-Colored Face in Phoenician, is the name of a queen who reigned over a world far from Greece, where they still called her Ethiopian Queen. She was therefore often imagined to be a black woman, as were Cepheus and Andromeda. Recently it has, however, been ascertained that during the classical period the word Ethiopia was used to designate all the faraway lands to the south, including India and Arabia.

In Assyrian clay tablets she is referred to as the Mistress of Grain (W. T. Olcott, *Star Lore*). This confirms the ancient link with the Virgin. Cassiopeia was often depicted with a palm frond in her left hand. Before it came to be considered a symbol of martyrdom by the Christians, the palm frond had been a powerful symbol of fertility and victory. Carl Jung considered it also a symbol of the soul.

In this part of the sky the ancient Arabs saw a large hand, which they called *Kaff al-Habib,* Broad Hand Dyed with Henna, or simply the Dyed Hand. It must have been a conspicuous constellation because the five most brilliant stars marked the tips of the fingers. After Muhammad, the Dyed Hand became the Hand of Fatima, who was the prophet's daughter, and spouse of her cousin Ali. The Fatimids attributed a divine origin to this couple. The imagination of the inhabitants of the desert had not stopped at just the hand of stars. In al-Tizini's star catalogue there appears the nomadic figure of a Crouching Camel and two more, Two Dogs, one assigned to Cepheus and one to Cassiopeia. It is a more widely accepted fact, however, that the majority of Arab astronomers referred to Cassiopeia as *al-Dat al-Kursivy,* the Lady on the Throne, a title that, upon reaching Europe, became Dhath Alcursi or Dath Elkarti.

The Christian reconstruction of the sky and its stars by Julius Schiller in 1627 proposed the personality of Mary Magdalene as the candidate to replace Cassiopeia. However, others were worried about the stormy past of Jesus' friend and replaced her with Deborah sitting under a palm tree on the mountain of Ephraim, or with Bathsheba, the mother of Solomon, seated on the royal throne.

To Cassiopeia was assigned the second trump card of the tarots, the Great

Priestess, while Ptolemy attributed to her the qualities of Saturn and Venus—meaning power, respect, and command. When the combination was negative, however, it generated exaggerated pride and great presumption.

The Main Stars

In the last century young astronomers were made to memorize "bagdei" to help them remember the order in which the stars of Cassiopeia are arranged: Beta, Alpha, Gamma, Delta, Epsilon, and Iota. The lucida is called Schedar (this name appears for the first time in the *Alfonsine Tables*) and Shadar, Schidar, and Shedis, all derived from *al-Sadr*, the Breast—which the star's position marks in the figure. Burritt, differs on this point, citing Ulugh-Beg's star catalogue, in which the entire constellation was indicated by the name *El Seder*, the Seder Tree. The next star is Beta Cassiopeiae or *Caph*, the Hand. A different form is found in al-Tizini's catalogue: *al-Sanani al-Nakar*, the Hump of the Camel. No Middle Eastern name for the star Gamma has reached us. For Delta we find Rucbar, from the Arabic *al-Ruk Bah*, the Knee.

Theta and Mu Cassiopeiae were known as *al-Marfik*, the Elbow. The star Mu is interesting because it is one of the fastest-moving stars known; it will make a complete turn around the sky in three million years.

Cassiopeia, tenth-century Arab drawing

Bayer's Cassiopeia (1603)

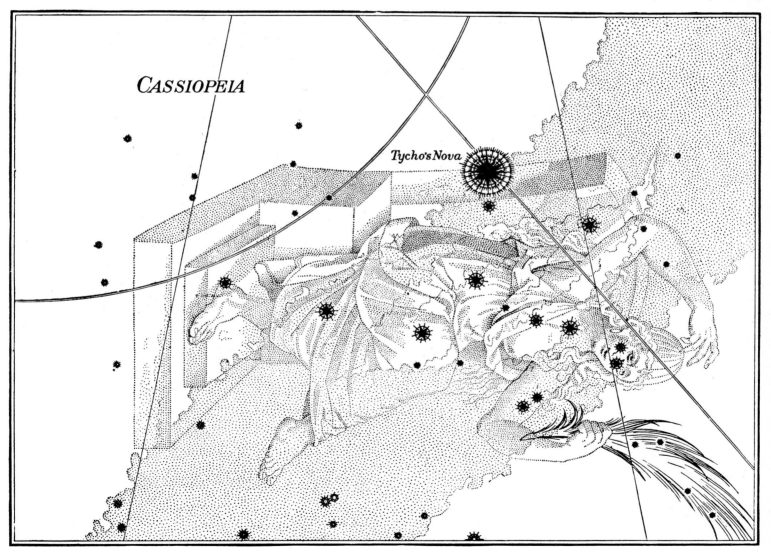

CASSIOPEIA

Tycho's Nova

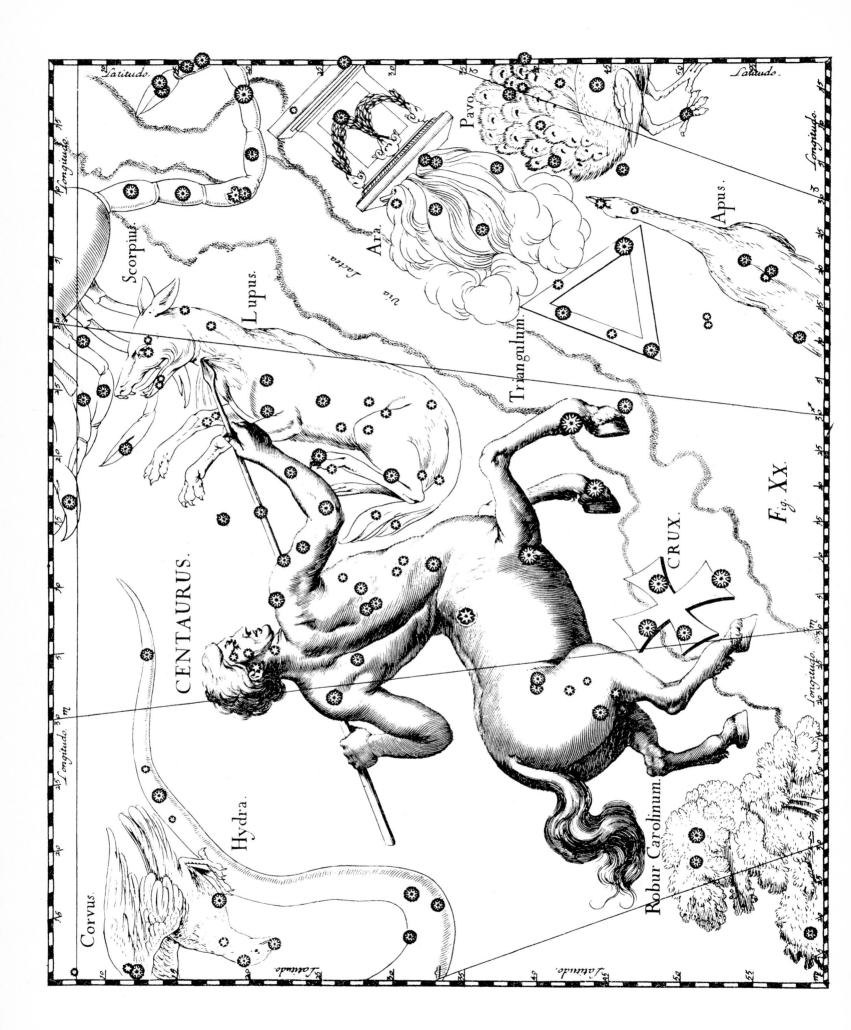

14
Centaurus

Below the stars of Hydra and Scorpius there is the erect figure of a fantastic animal with the body of a horse and the torso, arms, and head of a man. His name is Centaurus and at the time of his creation he stood on the southern horizon of the sky. He was the last visible constellation of the Mediterranean, on the edge of the great mystery only a few adventurous sailors had witnessed—the southern hemisphere.

Centaurus is turned toward the east and gives the impression that he will soon encounter the other centaur of stars—Sagittarius—who is galloping westward, toward him. In his hands he holds a strange pole that looks like a lance which he is using to kill the she-wolf of the stars, Lupus, in front of him.

Centaurus is a legendary creation brimming with myth and poetry. In earlier times his progenitor was represented by the hybrid figure of the goat, donkey, and bull as manifested in Pan, Dionysus, Silenus, the fauns, the Minotaur, and Priapus himself. All these were the ancestors of this figure that appeared in Hellas after the introduction of the horse from the Asian continent. It is easy to reconstruct the imaginative process of the Mediterranean people when, from the Orient, there arrived the first warriors mounted on horseback who looked like creatures that were half-horse and half-men.

The Babylonian priest Belriusciu (known to us by the Greek variant Berossus) wrote for the Greeks a history of Babylonia from its origins until the time of Alexander the Great. In this work he says, as he describes the primordial chaos of the period of Scorpius and the Dragon:

One saw other human figures with the legs and horns of goats; some had horses' hooves, and others joined the hindquarters of a horse with the body of a man, so resembling hippocentaurs. Similarly, bulls were portrayed with a man's head or a dog's, with the body of a four-footed animal ending with the tail of a fish.

Brown, *Law of Cosmic Order*

The first satyr of whom we have a description is probably the unforgettable Enkidu, the friend of Gilgamesh described in the chapter on Orion, who is shown in the bas-reliefs with goat's horns and often with the legs and tail of a bull. In Greece the satyrs were considered sylvan spirits, as were the nymphs. They were descended from Phoroneus of Argos—the first man who used fire—represented by the alder tree, who was a son of Melia, nymph of the ash tree, and the river-god Inachus (Graves, *The White Goddess*).

Next to the satyrs, there were representations of sileni—spirits friendly to men—with the ears, tail, and sometimes the hooves of a horse or a donkey. Great lovers of wine, they were always pictured as drunk. In his work *Cyclops*, Euripides made a distinction between the satyr, who was younger and sensual, and the silenus, who was older and more like a donkey.

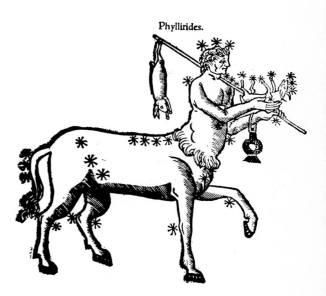

Phyllirides.

Centaurus. From Hyginus, Poetica astronomica *(1485 edition)*

Opposite: *Centaurus. From Hevelius,* Uranographia totum coelum stellatum *(1690)*

295

Battles between centaurs and Iapyths

The Centaurs

Centaurus and Lupus (seventeenth century)

Ixion, king of the Lapiths, had committed the crime of killing a relative. The gods requested that Zeus punish him for this; however, Zeus not only forgave him but invited him to his table after he had him purified. During the meal Ixion fell in love with Hera—the wife of Zeus—and, intoxicated by the wine, thought of seducing her. When Zeus understood his intentions, he bestowed upon a cloud the likeness of Hera; Ixion lay with it. To punish him Zeus had him tied to a burning wheel, condemned to roll forever in the sky.

The symbolism of this legend is clearly astronomical. Ixion was a local god of the sun whose cult was integrated into that of Zeus. He was identified with the burning wheels that were rolled down from the hills during the festivities of midsummer as a token that the sun had reached its zenith and was beginning its decline toward the winter solstice (Graves, *The Greek Myths*).

The cloud of the feigned Hera was named Nephele. Impregnated by Ixion, she gave birth to the first centaur, who subsequently coupled with the mares of Magnesia, thus generating the other centaurs. These beings were frequently associated with wedding rites, where they often had the orgiastic and anarchic characteristics of the satyrs. At the wedding of Pirithous and Hippodameia, they drank so much wine that they proceeded to capture the bride when she appeared and, in so doing, forced the Lapiths and Theseus to do battle with them. This was the beginning of the hatred between the Lapiths and centaurs which inspired many illustrations called "centauromachies." The pediment of the Parthenon shows such an illustration.

Chiron

Chiron, son of Saturn and Philyra, was the most famous and wisest of the centaurs. In his youth he had often participated in the hunts of Artemis and it seems that he acquired from her his knowledge of the art of medicine and medicinal herbs, which he taught to Asclepius. In contrast to the other centaurs, Chiron was peace-loving. He had set his dwelling at the foot of Mount

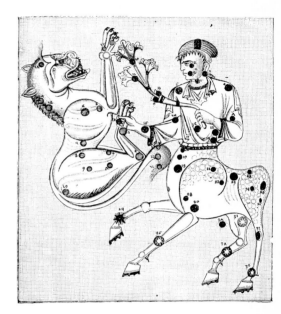

Centaurus and Lupus, Farnese globe

Centaurus and Lupus, Arab (fourteenth century)

Pelion and it was esteemed as the best school in all of Greece. The list of his most famous pupils includes, in addition to Dionysus, whom he raised from childhood, Hercules, Jason, Theseus, Castor and Pollux, Nestor, Aeneas, Hippolytus, Odysseus, Diomedes, Cephalus, and Achilles. He taught them all astronomy, surgery, and medicine. Eratosthenes associated him with the stars of Centaurus, and Aeschylus praised him as the inventor of the sky's constellations of stars. The fables spoke of him being the first to teach men the practice of laws, the inviolability of an oath, and the worship of the gods. To him were attributed the knowledge of the various properties of the celestial bodies as well as the practices that might avert their maleficent influences on human beings.

Despite being immortal, this sage unfortunately died by the unwitting hand of his disciple Hercules, who accidentally struck Chiron in the knee while he was trying to hit Elatus with one of his poisoned arrows. In despair Hercules tried to heal the wound with the powerful medicines of his teacher, but his efforts were in vain. The terrible poison advanced inexorably until it caused the poor immortal centaur such excruciating pain that Hercules himself beseeched Zeus to let him die; subsequently, Zeus placed Chiron's image among the stars to keep his memory alive forever.

It was Hercules who suggested that the immortality of Chiron be transferred to Prometheus who then could be freed; he thereby inherited the astronomical knowledge of Chiron. Ovid narrates the wise man's end, with Achilles at his pillow, as follows:

. . . but the gnawing poison defied all remedies, and the bane soaked into the bones and the whole body. The blood of the Lernean Hydra, mingled with the centaur's blood, left no time for rescue. Achilles, bathed in tears, stood before him as before a father; so would he have wept for Peleus at the point of death. Often he fondled the feeble hands with his own loving hands; the teacher reaped the reward of the character he had moulded. Often Achilles kissed him, and often said to him as he lay there, "Live, I pray thee, and do not forsake me, dear father." The ninth day was come when thou, most righteous Chiron, didst gird thy body with twice seven stars.

Ovid, *Fasti*, V. 403–414

The Thyrsus and the She-Wolf

In recent star maps Centaurus is depicted in the act of killing the wolf of the constellation of the same name with a lance. However, if we carefully observe more ancient maps, we notice that the weapon that Centaurus holds in his hand is not a lance, but a staff from which ivy or vine leaves grow. We have here an authentic case of image reversal: the lance is not a weapon; it is instead the legendary thyrsus, a magic rod of very ancient origin on which grew grape or ivy branches or that had a pinecone on its tip. The ivy that often encircles the thyrsus was the magic plant whose sap was an essential component of nectar, the beverage of the gods that was drunk in rituals throughout the Mediterranean in the preagricultural period (see the chapter on Crater). Another ingredient of nectar was the resin of the pine tree that was added to wine, a process still in use in Greece today. This joining of the two elements is revealed in the thyrsus with the pinecone, a symbol of fertility and cosmology about which Philostratus speaks in the third century B.C. Dionysus most probably inherited the thyrsus with the pinecone from the god Pan, who had attempted to violate the nymph Pitys. Pitys, in order to escape from him, transformed herself into a pine tree which then became sacred to Pan and his followers. The thyrsus, the pine tree, the ivy, and the vine were an integral part of the nuptial, rebirth, and orgiastic rites of antiquity. Centaurus, therefore, is not engaged in the act of killing the wolf, but, along with the wolf, is executing a mysterious act with the thyrsus.

In the *Alfonsine Tables*, for example, the centaur holds in his hands a flowering branch that looks completely innocuous. Earlier, Ptolemy had described Centaurus holding the wolf up with one hand and grasping the thyrsus with the other. In the ancient sculpture of the celestial globe shouldered by Atlas, Centaurus is simply pointing toward the wolf. According to the testimony of Geminus, the great astronomer Hipparchus, father of the Greek conception of the sky and its stars, had considered the thyrsus of Centaurus as a separate constellation. In Greek the word wolf was *lycos* and Lycaon was the name of the legendary king who had brought civilization to Arcadia and had been the first to introduce the cult of Zeus at Lycaeus (Zeus of the She-Wolf). Lycaon and his fifty sons (the Olympic year consisted of fifty lunar months) had maintained the tradition of cannibalism, which provoked the vengeance of Zeus when they sacrificed a newborn child to him. Disgusted, Zeus transformed them all into wolves and condemned mankind to death by sending the deluge.

The true meaning of the myth of Zeus of the She-Wolf is to be found in his identification with the ancient god Chiron, propitiator of rain and servant of the Divine She-Wolf who makes wolves howl during nights of full moon. Apollo had to transform himself into a wolf so as to be able to couple with the moon-nymph Cyrene. From this union was born the famous Aristaeus, who was educated in the cave of the centaur Chiron. Due to his intercession, the Etesian winds, which blow during the forty dog days when the Dog Star Sirius reigns at night, were generated. It was Aristaeus who also invented apiculture, the production of cheese, and the oil press.

These considerations remove us far from the representation of Centaurus killing a wolf. Instead there appears a ritual scene, framed among the stars of the southern hemisphere, in which the hybrid Dionysiac-satyric-orgiastic figure is represented with his lover, the moon–she-wolf–Selene, performing an erotic ritual symbolized by the nuptial thyrsus.

Alpha and Beta Centauri

Bundula, Alpha Centauri, is the most famous star to today's astronomy aficionados because it is the closest to our sun. But in the last century astronomer Sir John Herschel tried to describe the distance to the star by saying that if a traveler dropped a pea every mile of the journey there, he would need a fleet of ten thousand galleons' worth of peas. The catalogue of Ulugh-Beg called this star Rigil Kentauros, the Foot of Centaurus. The Chinese assigned it the important role of *Nan Mun*, the Southern Gate.

Together, Bundula and Agena—Beta Centauri—take the name of Indicators because they point to the nearby Southern Cross. The nomads of the desert called them *Hdar* and *Wazn*—the Terrain and the Weight. The hunters in South Africa saw them as Two Men Who Were Once Lions. The Australian aborigines called them the Two Brothers, who had killed Tchingal with a lance represented by the stars of the Southern Cross.

Ptolemy divided the astrological influence of this constellation by giving to the stars of the human part the qualities of Venus and Mercury. To those of the part represented by the horse he gave the qualities of Mars and Jupiter, which induce in their subjects' hearts a passion for arms and revenge. Bundula (in antiquity also called *Toliman*, the Hereafter) and Agena were assigned to Venus and Jupiter. However, Alvidas assigned the former to Mars, with the Moon and Uranus in Scorpius and the latter to Mars in conjunction with Mercury.

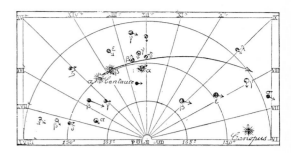

Alpha Centauri's rapid movement

Bayer's Centaurus (1603)

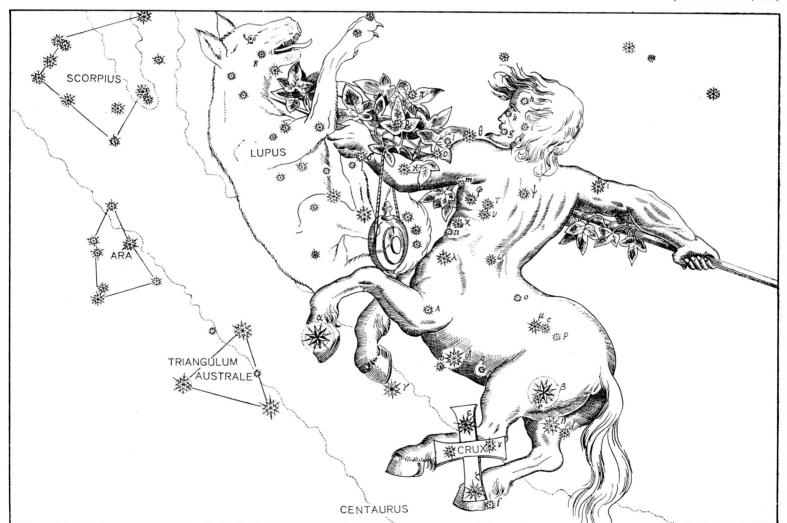

15
Cepheus

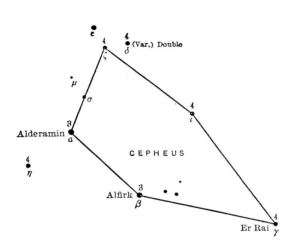

CEPHEUS

Cepheus. From Hyginus, Poetica astronomica
(1485 edition)

About twenty-two thousand years ago, the North Pole was in the stars of Cepheus, King of Ethiopia, and it remained there for approximately two thousand years. Today the Pole is once again slowly approaching Cepheus, whose foot almost touches the Polar Star.

Perhaps it is for this reason that the figure of a king was set in this extremely dark part of the northern hemisphere. Its stars are not very bright, and reconstructing its figure remains something of a problem. From the time the constellations were invented, however, there has always been a king in this region.

In China this constellation was called the Secret Throne of the Five Emperors, while the Arab astronomers called him *al-Multafab*, the Blazing One.

According to the Greek myth-writers Cepheus was an Argonaut and appeared in the saga of Perseus as Cassiopeia's husband and the father of Andromeda (see the chapter on Perseus). The information about him is as vague as his stars. He was called king of Ethiopia, but in classical times all the lands to the extreme south were referred to as Ethiopia.

King Cepheus is depicted with one foot on the Polar Star and the other on the Lesser Bear. He wears a turban as well as a crown on his head; in one hand he has his cloak, in the other, his royal scepter.

The nomadic shepherds of the Middle East saw in this region of the stars a shepherd who guarded his grazing sheep with his dog. In the adaptation of the sky and its stars to the Christian tenets, which was proposed by Julius Schiller in 1627, Cepheus became Saint Stephen.

According to Ptolemy Cepheus had the qualities of Saturn and Jupiter. He conveyed authority and a balanced mind, but he exposed those under his influence to the risks of severe and cruel processes. If Mars intervened, he could cause death by hanging, decapitation, or crucifixion. The cabalists associate this constellation with the twenty-second trump card of the tarots—the Fool.

Opposite: *Cepheus. From Hevelius,*
Uranographia totum coelum stellatum *(1690)*

301

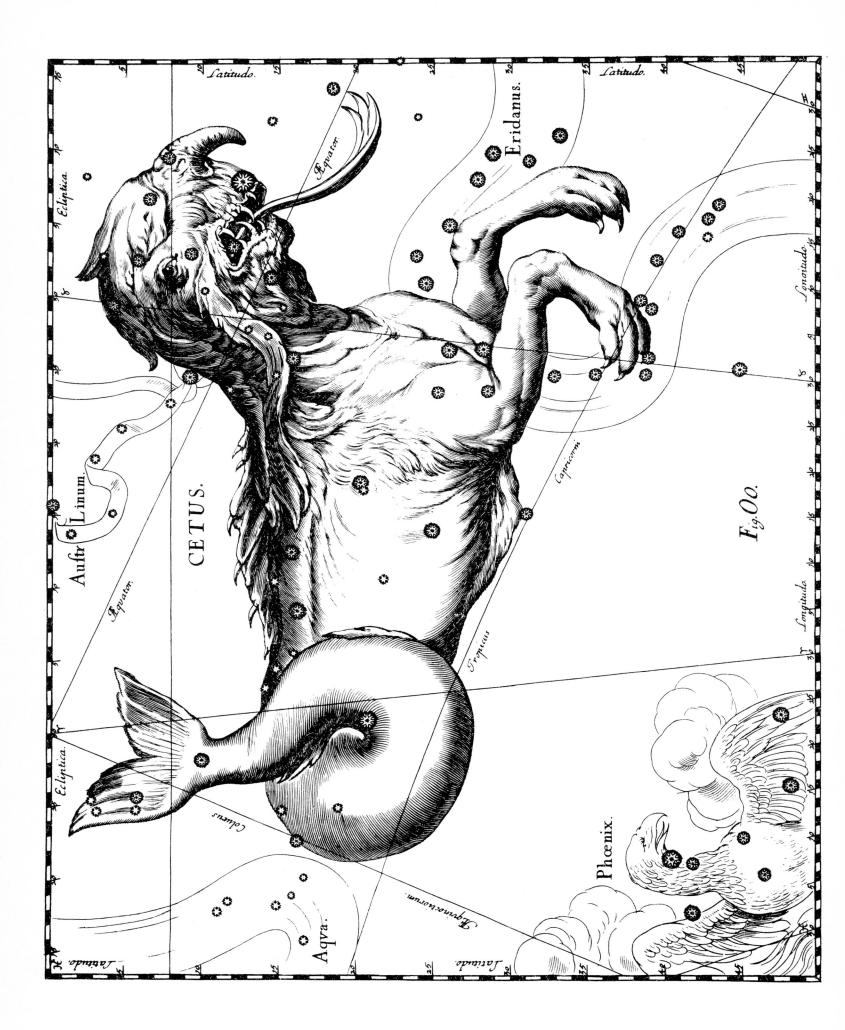

CETUS.

Eridanus.

Phœnix.

Aqva.

Fig. Oo.

16
Cetus

In the region of the sky that is called the Sea there floats a huge whale composed of stars of which none are brighter than the second magnitude. Its body extends for about fifty degrees and is located underneath the zodiacal signs of Aquarius, Pisces, Aries, and Taurus. Its forelegs are immersed in the river Eridanus while the fin of its tail touches the river that streams out of the pail of Aquarius. Its name is Cetus, and it is linked to the legend of Perseus and Andromeda, even though its origin is known to be much more ancient.

Cetus was the spouse of the ancient sage of the sea, Phorcys, brother of Nereus. From their union the Phorcids, who had such an important role in the composition of the myths of the stars, were born. Ladon was the serpent-guard of the Garden of the Hesperides after whom the biblical serpent was modeled. Echidne, half-woman and half-serpent, was spouse to the terrible Typhon and mother of Cerberus, the dog of the underworld, as well as the Marine Hydra, the Chimera, and Orthrus, the two-headed dog of Geryon. The other daughters of Cetus were the three Gorgons, whom we discuss in the chapter on Perseus, and the three Graeae, the gray-haired, swanlike sisters who had a soothsaying tooth and an eye that saw everything.

The layout of the stars of Cetus allows for the formation of many figures, but the most classical one takes the shape of a kite and, somehow, the entire constellation resembles a prehistoric ichthyosaur.

Cetus was known by the ancient Sumerians as a constellation and they probably identified it as Tiamat, the monster depicted also as the Dragon, the Hydra, and the Serpent of Ophiuchus. In the Hebrew myth it became the legendary Leviathan, the sea monster God destroyed in some versions.

Other legends narrate that God spared the Leviathan since he considered him one of his creatures and that, after completely domesticating him (or having ordered the archangel Jahoel to do so), he deigned to play with him on the sea for as much as three hours a day.

The monster drank from a tributary of the Jordan, at the point where it flows into the ocean through a secret canal. When it was hungry it let off a thick smoke that darkened a large expanse of water. When it was thirsty it caused such an increase in the waters that they disturbed the calm of the abyss for seventy years and even Behemoth, on the thousand mountains, showed signs of terror.

In the seventeenth century Cetus was identified with Jonas' whale, and Julius Schiller placed Saint Joachim and Saint Anne among these stars.

Ptolemy assigned to Cetus saturnine qualities that encouraged idleness and laziness, but also an emotional and charitable nature with a strong inclination to command.

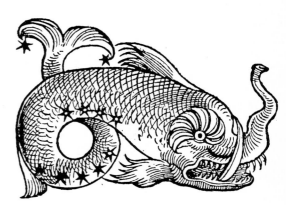

Cetus. From Hyginus, Poetica astronomica *(1485 edition)*

Opposite: *Cetus. From Hevelius,* Uranographia totum coelum stellatum *(1690)*

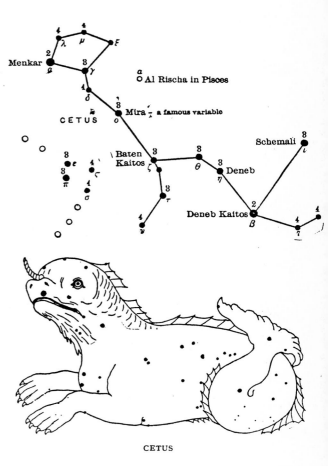

CETUS

17
Coma Berenices

Discreetly located above Virgo between Leo and Boötes, these small stars called Berenice's Hair require concentrated attention to identify.

The early identity of the group is unknown. Many think that it first was the bushy tip of the tail of Leo, and others propose that it was part of the sheaf of grain that Virgo carried on her arm. When the sun passes through these constellations it is certainly at its hottest, and Leo's tail as well as the sheaf of grain are part of the theme of the summer heat. In his 1603 star catalogue Bayer has an olive branch in this location. However, Ptolemy called these stars Hair and, in the tenth century, al-Sufi called them *al-Dhafira*, the Braid of Hair.

For many centuries its names were Hair, Mane, or Tresses. It is in the 1590 star catalogue by Tycho Brahe that the complete title of Coma Berenices appears for the first time in a map.

In 247 B.C. Berenice—daughter of Maga, the king of Cyrene—married the pharaoh of Egypt, Ptolemy III, with whom she was very much in love. Berenice was famous for her beauty and especially famous for her amber-blond hair, so rare in North Africa.

In 245 B.C. Ptolemy had to set out on a long war campaign against Seleucus II, king of Syria. Afraid that something might happen to her spouse, Berenice went to the temple of Venus-Arsinoe at Zephyrium and there she made a solemn vow to give up her hair if Ptolemy would return victorious and unharmed. This came to pass, and Berenice's hair was cut off and placed on the altar of the goddess.

Inauspiciously, some days later, the amber braids disappeared from the altar to the consternation of the priests and the rage of Ptolemy and Berenice. The astronomer Conon of Samos intervened, explaining that Venus herself had performed a metamorphosis that had transformed the queen's hair into stars. Conon then drew a mane of hair on the celestial globe of Alexandria and from then on it remained a constellation.

In other, less-documented versions the stars of the hair belonged to the distaff, or spinning staff, that was said to be in Virgo's hand. Others saw them as belonging to the caduceus of Mercury because he, in fact, had his astrological house in Virgo.

In the Dresden globe a garland of ivy appears in this position and, in explanation, the astronomer Hyde cited ancient codices in which those stars were called *Kissin*, which is a type of vine—*Convolvulus* (Allen, *Star Names*). Some consider this to be the constellation of the Shroud of Veronica, which has the image of Christ on it. This is perhaps due to the fact that this constellation was identified with Herod's Berenice (Beronica in Latin, and therefore Veronica), who was converted to Christianity by the suffering of Christ (Eastlake-Jameson, *History of Our Lord*). In the *Coelum stellatum christianum*, these stars are designated as the constellation Flagellum.

Astrologically Coma Berenices bestows gentle, aristocratic manners and great charm, which, however, can degenerate into laziness and dissipation.

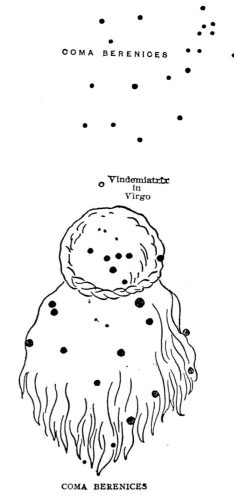

COMA BERENICES

Opposite: *Coma Berenices. From Hevelius,* Uranographia totum coelum stellatum *(1690)*

St. Veronica's Veil, a seventeenth-century constellation

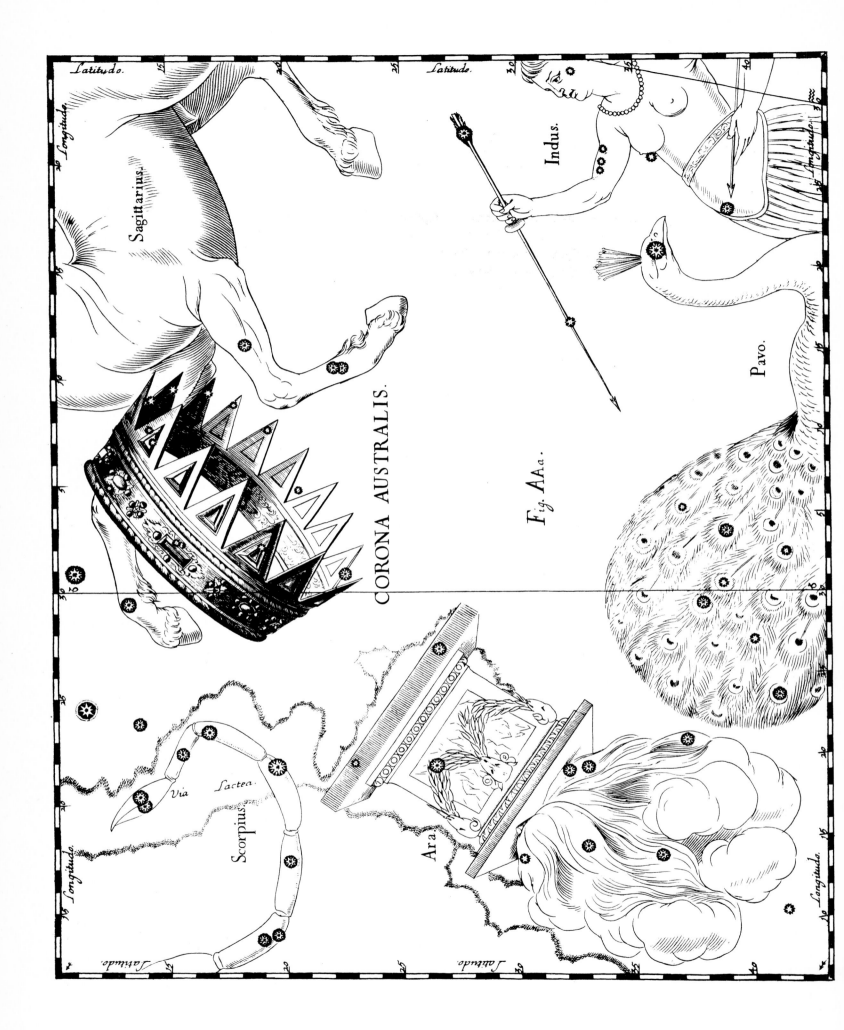

Latitudo. 15 20 25 *Latitudo.* 30 35 40

Sagittarius.

Indus.

Pavo.

CORONA AUSTRALIS.

Fig. AAa.

Via Lactea.

Scorpius.

Ara.

Latitudo. 15 20 *Latitudo.* 25 30 35 40

18
Corona Australis

Underneath the bow and arrow of Sagittarius and along the edge of the Milky Way, there is a circle of stars that has been known ever since Hipparchus' time by the name of Corona Australis, the Southern Crown. The Arab astronomer al-Kazwini, who has recorded for us the legends of the ancient stellar landscape of the desert nomads, states that they called this circle *al-Udha al-Naam*, or the Ostrich Nest. The ostriches would gather in order to drink from the waters of the Milky Way and so they were represented by the stars of Sagittarius and Aquila.

In al-Sufi's catalogue Corona became *al-Kubbah*, the Turtle, while others called it *al-Hiba*. The Chinese saw a Turtle (*Pee*) here as well.

The proximity of Corona to Sagittarius is not accidental because, in many ancient texts, we find this constellation under the name of Corona Centauri or Corona Sagittari. These names are most probably reminders of the crowns consisting of rays of sunlight that adorned the *gandharvas*, or celestial horses of Aryan myths, who were probably the forerunners of the centaurs.

For a confirmation of the interdependence of these two figures compare the symbol of the Assyrian gold Assur, who was represented in a circle with wings in the act of shooting an arrow, with that of the god of the Medes Ahura-Mazda (see the illustrations in the chapter on Sagittarius).

Astronomically speaking, the origin of this symbol could date back to the two millennia during which the stars of Corona and those of Sagittarius indicated the meridian of the autumnal equinox, 6000–4000 B.C.

However, it is even more significant that at about 4000 B.C. there occurred a series of coincidences relating to the position of the moon during the equinoxes and solstices:

1. at the beginning of spring the full moon always occurred between the stars of Corona and Sagittarius' bow;

2. on the other hand, at the autumnal equinox it was the new moon that occurred in Corona-Sagittarius;

3. at the winter solstice it was the waning half-moon that coincided with these same signs;

4. finally, still in Corona-Sagittarius, the waxing half-moon indicated the summer solstice.

Another confirmation of the link between Corona and the centaurs is the other name of this constellation, *Rota Ixionis*, Ixion's Wheel, which is a reminder of what happened to Ixion, the king of the Lapiths (see the chapter on Centaurus).

Subsequently, Ixion's wheel, symbol of the apparent course of the sun around the zodiac, is supposed to have been placed among the stars in the location of Corona Australis next to the zodiacal centaur Sagittarius.

Ptolemy attributed to this group the qualities of Saturn and Jupiter which bestowed a predisposition for hidden problems but also a propensity for positions of authority.

Bayer's Corona Australis (1603)

Opposite: *Corona Australis. From Hevelius,* Uranographia totum coelum stellatum *(1690)*

Ixion tied to the solar wheel, depicted between Sisyphus and Tantalus

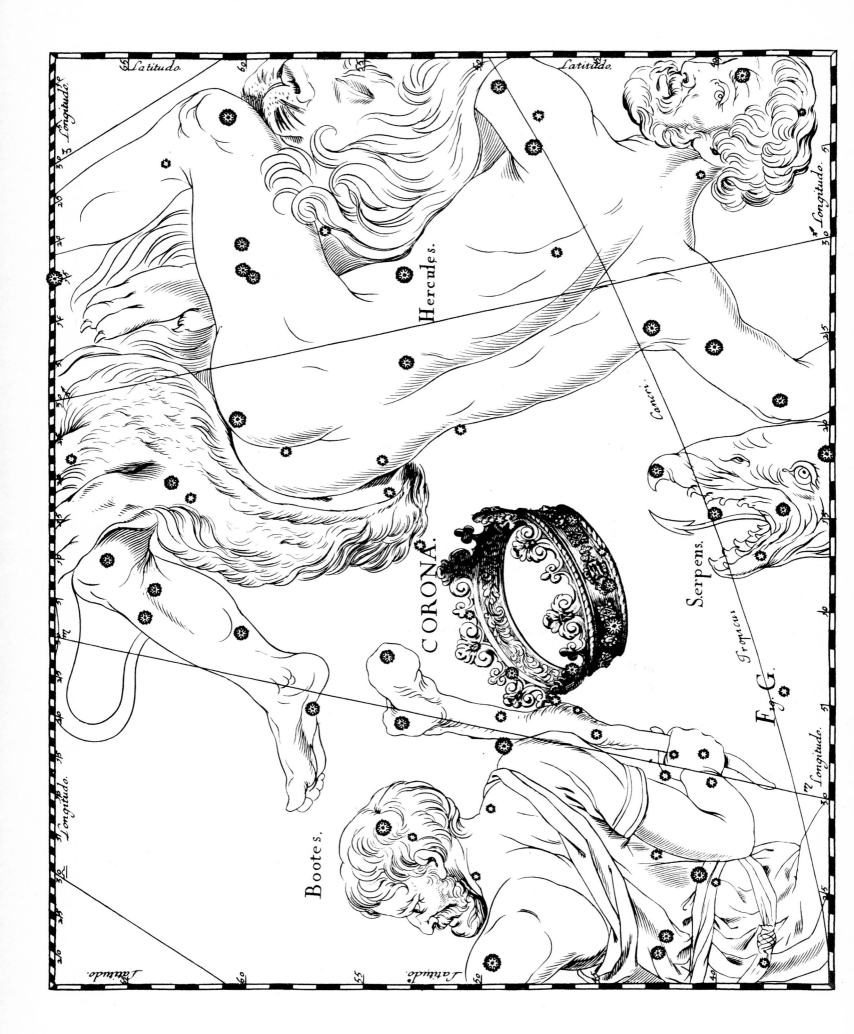

19
Corona Borealis

Corona Borealis is a small but important constellation of the northern hemisphere situated between Boötes and Hercules. It is composed of a group of stars that is famous for having the shape of a crescent moon. The lucida of the group is Alphecca, or Jewel, and is located in the center of the anterior part of the crown, just like the most precious stone in a crown.

Greek mythology attributes this crown to Ariadne, the Cretan princess who was the beloved of Theseus and Dionysus. When Minos, son of Zeus and Europa, was fighting a battle against the Athenians, his son, Androgeus, was killed on the battlefield. The Cretans won, and Minos, in revenge for the death of his son, imposed on the Athenians the sentence of having to send seven boys and seven girls to Crete every nine years. The children would be given in sacrifice to the terrible Minotaur. This monster was the son of Pasiphae, wife of Minos, who had fallen desperately in love with the white bull that Poseidon had sent to her husband.

In despair over the practical impossibility of a union, Pasiphae had asked for help from Daedalus, the famous architect who delighted Minos and his family during the time of his Cretan exile with animated dolls that he cut out of wood. Daedalus made a wooden sculpture of a young cow and placed it in a meadow where the bull was grazing. He then showed Pasiphae how to get into the artificial cow through a sliding panel and left discreetly.

It wasn't long before the white bull approached the feigned cow and mounted her. Pasiphae was thus able to satisy her desire and she subsequently gave birth to the Minotaur, a monster with the head of a bull and the body of a man. In order to imprison this force of nature, Daedalus was required to construct the extremely intricate labyrinth of Cnossus; Minos took charge of feeding to the Minotaur slaves and prisoners who had received the death sentence.

It was the third time that the Athenian hostages were about to leave for Crete among the lamentations of the entire population when Theseus—who was half-son to both Aegeus and Poseidon—offered himself as the one who would protect the youngsters and put an end to Athens' humiliating predicament.

When Theseus arrived in Crete, Ariadne, daughter of Minos and Pasiphae, fell in love with him to the point that she betrayed her stepbrother by giving the Greek hero a magic ball of string, made by Hephaestus, with which Theseus could not only reach the Minotaur but also find his way back out of the insidious labyrinth. In exchange for this favor Ariadne asked the hero to take her away with him once he had accomplished the feat. So it was that Theseus, having slain the Minotaur, escaped from Crete with the Athenian hostages and headed toward the island of Naxos. There, however, he abandoned Ariadne, who had fallen asleep on the beach.

When she awoke the princess found herself desperately alone and began to wander the island. At some point she heard the sound of singing and, as it came

Corona Borealis. From Hyginus, Poetica astronomica *(1485 edition)*

Opposite: *Corona Borealis. From Hevelius,* Uranographia totum coelum stellatum *(1690)*

309

Cup of Epictetus: Theseus and the Minotaur

closer, it wasn't long before Dionysus appeared with his band of maenads. The god saw her and was suddenly overcome by love. Soon the wedding was celebrated and Dionysus gave Ariadne as a wedding present a splendid crown which Hephaestus had made with gold and rubies from India, arranged in the shape of roses.

Unfortunately, as in all relationships between mortals and immortals, Ariadne became old and eventually died. To eternalize their love story, Dionysus placed the crown among the stars (Eratosthenes, *Catasterismi*).

Ariadne gave Dionysus six children, Oenopion, Thoas, Staphulus, Latromis, Euanthes, and Tauropolus, who were the eponymous ancestors of the tribes of Hellenic culture living in Chios, Lemnos, and the Thracian Chersonese.

In another version of this myth it is said that the crown was found during a confrontation between Theseus and Minos. When the Greek hero arrived in Crete with the hostages, Minos became infatuated with one of the newly arrived girls, and he was about to take possession of her when Theseus confronted him, introducing himself as the son of Poseidon. Minos challenged the hero to demonstrate his divinity by a sign from his father and, throwing his ring into the sea, he bade Theseus return it to him.

Theseus threw himself into the water without hesitation and at once a large school of dolphins appeared and conducted him to the underwater palace of the Nereids—the fifty daughters of Poseidon—who gave Theseus not only Minos' ring but also the crown which Venus and the Hours had given to Tethys on her wedding day (Hyginus, *Astronomical Fables*). In this version Theseus married Ariadne and gave her the crown as a pledge of his love.

At this point it would be appropriate to note a chronological clarification about the Cretan and Greek civilizations. Before the Hellenic civilization, Crete had already been for many hundreds of years an economic and cultural power right in the middle of the Mediterranean world and it was through Crete that the Mesopotamian, Syrian, and Egyptian mythologies arrived in Greece.

The Cretan civilization had its beginnings at about 3000 B.C., and it reached such heights that its reputation as the pearl of the Mediterranean was thoroughly justified. Subsequently, for reasons that today are attributed to a catastrophic earthquake, its dominance suddenly ended around 1400 B.C.

Many of the myths that have reached us were originally Cretan and were later elaborated upon by the Greeks for their use. Ariadne was the ancient Cretan goddess of the moon and the harvests, as indicated by her name, *Ar-ri-ad-ne*, meaning the Very Fruitful Mother of Barley. She was also the Lady of the Labyrinth, the goddess who reigned over the world represented by the labyrinth, namely, Hades. Before Homer, the netherworld was imagined to be a labyrinth in the form of a spiral, and it was possible to ask its queen for mercy and be granted a return from that world. In this netherworld the Lady of the Labyrinth reigned under the guise of Ariadne, who was also called by her pre-Greek name of Persephone (Kerenyi, *Nel Labirinto*). The origin of the name of Persephone comes from much farther away, all the way from Mesopotamia: *Phe'er* meaning Crown, and *Serphon* meaning of the North (Dupuis, in Lalande, *Astronomie*).

In the most ancient Cretan mythology, Ariadne's brother was Deucalion who, together with his wife, Pyrrha, survived the deluge and gave life to a new mankind. Deucalion was the father of Orestheus and it was during his reign that a white dog gave birth to a shoot that was planted by Orestheus and grew into the first grapevine.

Both the biblical Noah and his Sumerian ancestor, Utnapishtim (see the chapter on Orion), were said to be the first men who planted the vine and made wine. The roots of the names Deucalion and Pyrrha are interesting: *Deuco-shalieus* means Sailor of the New Wine, while *Pyrrha* means Flaming Red, an adjective used to designate the vine (Graves, *The Greek Myths*).

It is obvious that there existed a pre-Greek link, beyond the classical myth as we know it, between the moon goddess Ariadne-Persephone and the god of the wine Dionysus-Deucalion-Zagreus. We must keep in mind that viticulture reached Greece and the Aegean through Crete. *Oinos*, the Greek word for wine, was originally a Cretan word.

Dionysus himself took the place of Zagreus, the ancient Cretan wine god who, like him, was at once torn to pieces upon birth and whose mother, to complete the circle, was Persephone.

The Lady of the Labyrinth

The throne room in the Palace of Knossus, Crete

It is quite clear that after the decline of the Cretan civilization, the Greeks not only absorbed the extensive mythology inherited from Crete but also imposed their own heroes as conquerors. In so doing they created in the case of Theseus and Ariadne a parallel with Perseus and Andromeda.

The Mythical Wreath

Corona Borealis is one of the few constellations whose stars actually represent the object they are meant to depict.

The first classical author who mentions it is Pherecydes, in the fifth century B.C. (Allen, *Star Names*). Two centuries later, the constellation is referred to by Apollonius of Rhodes in his *Argonautica*. It is also mentioned in *Phaenomena*, the astronomical poem by Aratus of Soli of the third century B.C.

When one observes the position of Corona Borealis between the constellations of Hercules and Boötes, it naturally comes to mind that Hercules could be Theseus. In actuality, as reported by Aratus in the *Phaenomena*, the Greeks did not know who this figure represented before they assigned these stars to Hercules. At that time they had named it Engonasi (see the chapter on Hercules). Identifying Boötes with Dionysus is easier, as we have seen in our discussion of Boötes, where the other great pairing—that of Corona and Boötes—is also presented. This consisted of the identification of Boötes with a very ancient constellation, dating back to 6000 B.C., in which the giant Atlas was represented with his head close to what at that time was the North Pole. In order to make this figure, all we have to do is add the right arm, formed by the semicircle of Corona Borealis, to the body of Boötes, who already has one arm raised in the typical position of the Titan (see the chapter on Boötes).

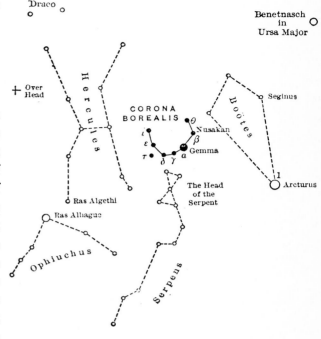

The Circular Path of the Prairie

Corona was called by various names, including Crown of Vulcan, Corona Cretica, Minoia Virgo, and Wreath of Flowers. The ancient Arabs called this constellation *al-Fakkan*, or Bowl; as a consequence, the name of its most brilliant star, Alphecca, is a contraction of *al-Munir al-Fakkah*, Brilliant One of the Bowl. The Australian aborigines had imagined in the semicircular shape of these stars a *woomera*, a name that was subsequently anglicized into boomerang. The Shawnee called this group the celestial sisters. These ancient North Americans tell a story about White Falcon, a mythical hunter who, while pursuing his prey, came upon a large prairie where he noticed a perfect circle traced in the grass. What puzzled him was that there was no path leading to the circle. While pondering this mystery he saw a silver basket descending from the sky in which twelve beautiful maidens were standing. As soon as the basket touched ground, the maidens began to glow with an internal light and dance around the circular path while beating out the rhythm of the dance on a ball made of silver.

Enchanted by so much beauty, White Falcon decided to capture the most beautiful of the maidens in order to marry her. However, as soon as he approached the path, the young women suddenly leaped back into the basket, which quickly climbed back into the sky. Being a good hunter, White Falcon decided to wait and camouflage himself. So he returned to the vicinity of the path the following night disguised as a rabbit. However, this scheme proved unsuccessful because the young women were faster than he. Undaunted, he disguised himself the next night as a mouse and thus finally captured the most beautiful of the maidens and took her to his tent as his bride.

Time went by, but life on earth did not suit the young woman, who looked at the night sky where her sisters shone in the stars of Corona with such melancholy. Her longing was so great that one night, while White Falcon was out hunting, she made herself a silver basket and intoned a magical song that had the power to lift her into the sky. However, since she was far from the circular path, she did not end up among the stars of Corona; she became the star Arcturus, in the constellation Boötes.

Some other North American peoples see in the arrangement of these stars a council meeting of great chieftains sitting in a semicircle, while the small star in the center of the circle represents the servant busily preparing the food.

In the tradition of the Algonquins and the Iroquois, Corona Borealis is the den out of which, every spring, the Bear (who is represented by the four stars of the square of the Big Dipper) appears. She is pursued by various celestial hunting birds, depicted by the stars of the Dipper's handle and the stars of Boötes. In this case Arcturus is the Owl (see the chapter on Ursa Major).

In the Christian reinterpretation of the ancient stars, Ariadne's crown is transformed into Christ's crown of thorns.

For the preparation of horoscopes, Ptolemy attributed to Corona Borealis the qualities of Venus and Mercury. This constellation bestowed artistic ability, a love of flowers, apathy, and disillusionment, and it also gave to those born under its influence positions of command. The cabalists associated the constellation with the fourth trump card of the tarots, the Empress.

CORONA BOREALIS

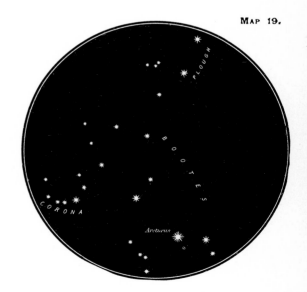

MAP 19.

Corona Borealis and Boötes

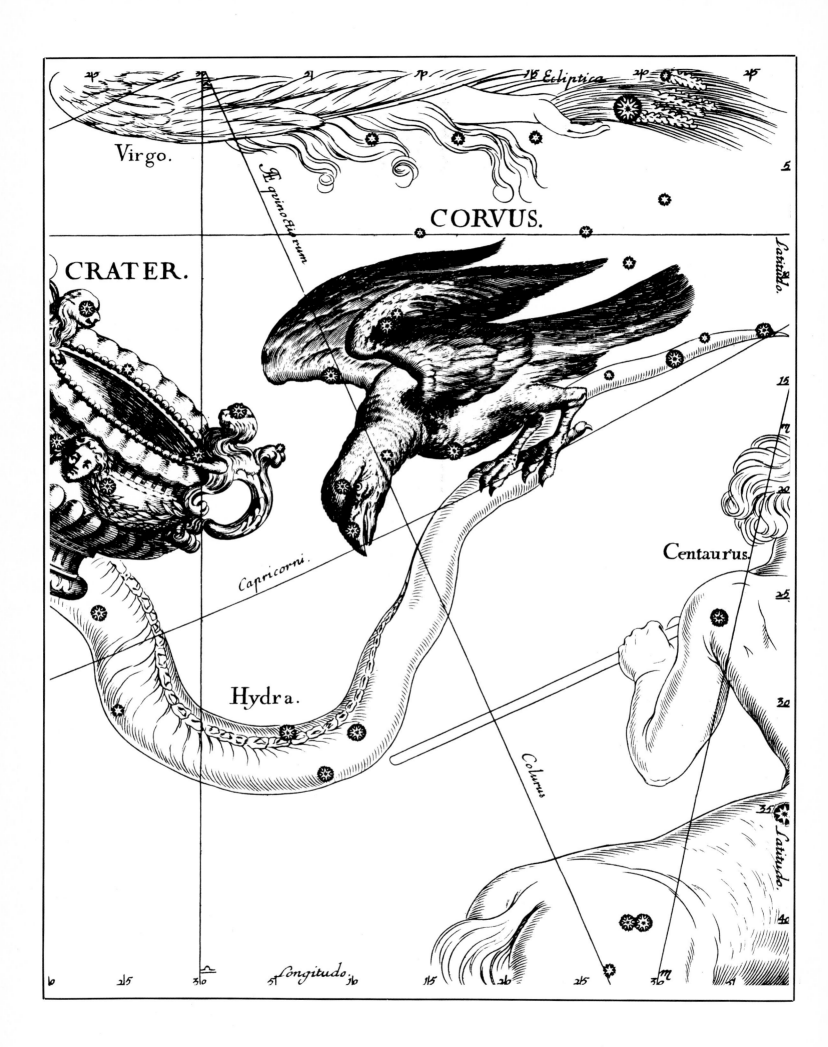

Virgo.

Ecliptica

CORVUS.

CRATER.

Latitudo.

Æquinoctiorum

Capricorni.

Centaurus

Hydra.

Colurus

Longitudo.

Latitudo.

20
Corvus

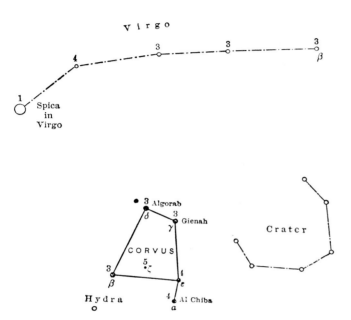

CORVUS

Perched on the stars of the aquatic Hydra sits Corvus, the Raven sacred to all the sibyls. These prophetesses were able to predict the future by interpreting the birds' song. Their goddess was Coronis, who was worshiped in pre-Olympic Greece and whose name was later usurped by the Hellenic Athene. It was Coronis-Athene whom Apollo married in order to impose himself as oracular god and inherit the raven as his symbol. In paragraph forty of the *Poetica astronomica*, Hyginus tells this anecdote about the Raven's—or Crow's—appearance among the stars:

When Apollo was sacrificing, the crow, who was under his guardianship, was sent to a spring to get some pure water. Seeing several trees with their figs not yet ripe, he perched on one of them waiting for them to ripen. After some days when the figs had ripened and the crow had eaten some, Apollo, who was waiting, saw him come flying in haste with the bowl full of water. For this fault of tardiness Apollo, who had had to use other water because of the crow's delay, punished him in this way. As long as the figs are ripening, the crow cannot drink, because on those days he has a sore [?] throat. So when the god wished to illustrate the thirst of the crow, he put the bowl among the constellations, and placed the water-snake underneath to delay the thirsty crow.

It was said that at one time the Raven had been as white as a dove, but that he was changed into a blackbird by Apollo because he had brought the sad news that Coronis had been unfaithful to him with the young Ischys.

Opposite: *Corvus. From Hevelius,*
Uranographia totum coelum stellatum *(1690)*

315

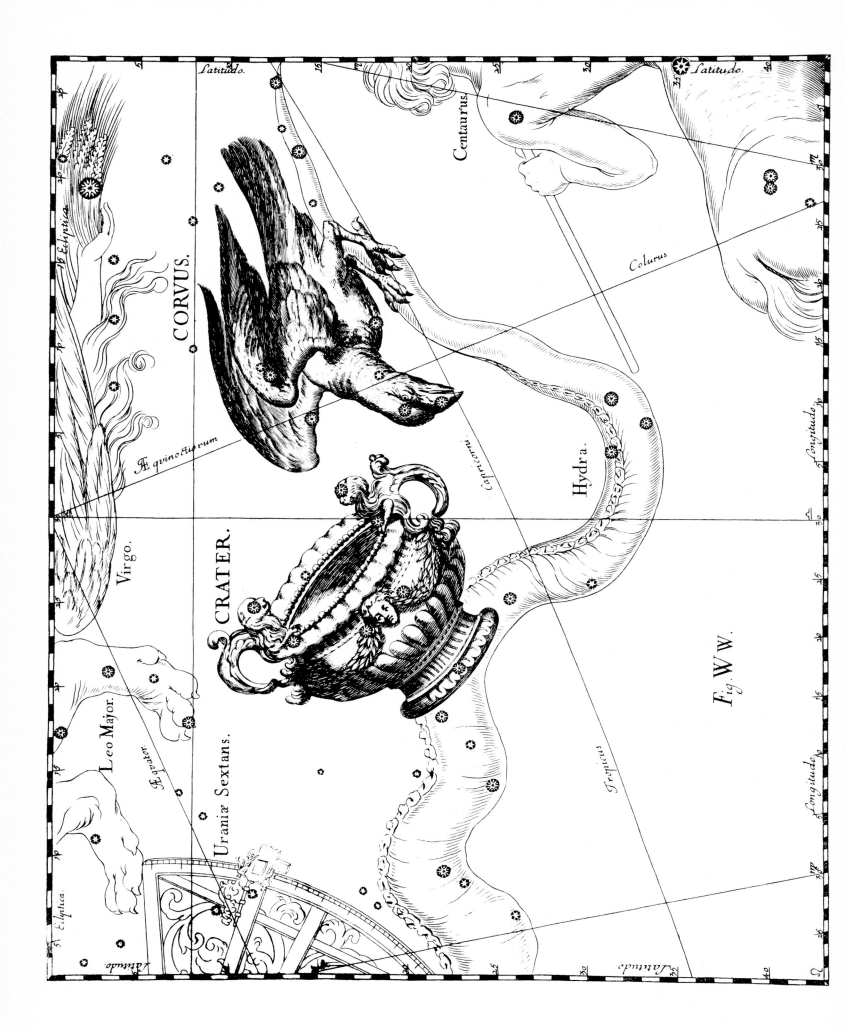

CORVUS.

Latitudo.

Centaurus.

Colurus.

Virgo.

Æquinoctiorum.

Hydra.

Capricorni.

CRATER.

Leo Major.

Æquator.

Uraniæ Sextans.

Tropicus.

Fig. WW.

Latitudo.

Latitudo.

21
Crater

When we look toward the south in the starry springtime sky, we see Crater, the Cup, underneath the constellation Virgo. Sitting on the tail of Hydra, it consists of six very bright stars that seem to describe the outline of a goblet. In Greece a crater was the terra-cotta receptacle in which wine and water were mixed in equal parts. This was done because Greek wine was too strong to be drunk pure. Eratosthenes mentions Oenopion, son of Dionysus and Ariadne, as the inventor of the crater, which prevented the excessive use of pure wine (see the chapter on Boötes).

In Hyginus' *Poetica astronomica*, there is a moralistic story the author attributes to the historian Phylarchus (272–220 B.C.). Near Troy, where Protesilaus' tomb is said to be located, there was a city called Eleusis. During the time of Demophon's reign there, the land was hit by a plague that caused the death of many citizens. Concerned about this, Demophon turned to Apollo's oracle to find a remedy. The answer was that a maiden of noble blood must be sacrificed to the gods of the city every year. Excluding his own daughters, Demophon drew lots among the daughters of his nobles and this continued to be done year after year until the noble Mastusius objected to this situation. He refused to submit his daughters to the drawing of lots if the king did not include his own. In anger, Demophon had one of the daughters of the nobleman sacrificed without even having the drawing. Sadly, Mastusius pretended not to take offense and accepted the punishment.

Time went by and the episode seemed to be forgotten; the king and the nobleman became friends again. One day, however, Mastusius invited the king and his daughters to a solemn sacrifice. Not suspecting anything and busy with the affairs of state, the king sent his daughters ahead saying that he would join them later. This was exactly what Mastusius had suspected would happen and, as soon as the young women arrived, he killed them. He then mixed their blood with wine in a crater and gave it to the king to drink when he finally arrived. Demophon inquired where his daughters were and, when he found out about the tragedy, he ordered Mastusius and the crater to be thrown into the sea. The sea became known as Mastusius and the harbor was called Crater. The ancient astronomers placed him among the stars to remind men that no one can commit diabolic acts without being punished, and also that offenses are not often forgotten.

The Myrtle and the Lebes

Crater was a constellation even before the time of the Greeks. The Sumerians called it the Cup of the Serpent and all the legends associate it with wine and with orgiastic and funerary rituals. This takes us back to the time of the pre-agricultural cultures of the Mediterranean, a time that preceded the introduction of the grapevine. At that time, wine was made by boiling myrtle berries in

CRATER

Opposite: *Crater. From Hevelius,* Uranographia totum coelum stellatum *(1690)*

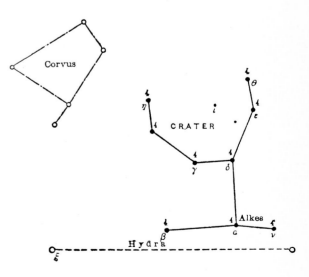

Myrtle (Myrtus communis)

the *lebes*, a cauldron made of bronze or terra-cotta often mounted on a tripod.

Myrtle is an original Mediterranean plant and has existed in this area for over one million years, having survived the ice age. It was of considerable economic importance to those primitive cultures just reaching the end of the hunting and gathering stage that Jensen defines as belonging to the so-called *Knollenkultur*, the cultivation of tuberous plants, which can historically be placed in the recent Paleolithic. All the plants that humans found a use for during this period were thought to take their origin from a demon, a primary divinity that dies in order to undergo a transformation so that the plants could sprout from its body. This was the case with the fig, the pomegranate, the daffodil, the hyacinth, and many other plants. This relationship with death—in which the divine and the human, the natural and the supernatural touch, eliminating the differences among humans, animals, and plants—entirely removed from death the absoluteness of nonexistence and returned to it the aspect of an accident or an event. In his *Politeia* Plato refers to the simple ancient Mediterranean meal whose delights were myrtle berries, bulbs, various types of greens, figs, chick-peas, broad beans, and acorns. In his comedies Aristophanes often talks about myrtle berries as choice food and Athenaeus tells of the Theban Matris who ate them all his life. Pliny records that these berries were used to season game, especially boar.

Diodorus Siculus describes the myrtle-Amazon Myrina in the act of honoring the funeral pyres of her three companions who died in battle. The Amazons, warrior women of the myrtle, were heroines foreign to the Greek/Indo-European tradition. Linked to a myth of death and rebirth of the myrtle, they are the ancient demons of the Mediterranean. They originally came from Lybia, a country that was recognized by ancient tradition as the birthplace of the cultivation of the myrtle. Boiling the berries in the *lebes*-crater produced a highly aphrodisiac wine that was much used in the orgiastic and matrimonial rituals (Ileana Chirassi, *Elementi di Culture Precereali*). The *lebes* also was used in the preparation of another very famous drink, nectar.

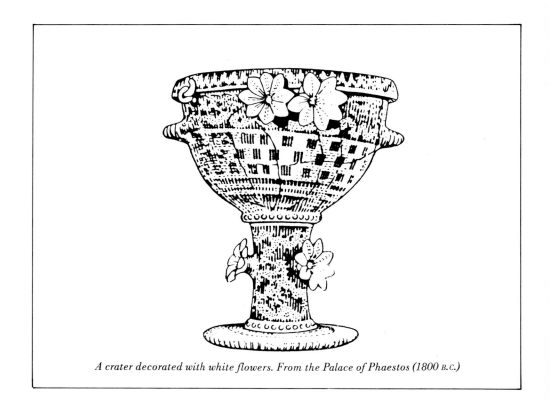

A crater decorated with white flowers. From the Palace of Phaestos (1800 B.C.)

Grape (Vitis vinifera)

Nectar of the Moon

Crater is also linked to the goblet of soma, the mythical drink of ancient India that was associated with the moon. It was represented by a male god, Chandra, who was shown as a young man on a chariot drawn by an antelope. In one hand he carried a conch shell, which had multiple meanings: prosperity, marine tides, female cycles, and death. In the other hand he held the pearly wheel of the lunar rotations. In astronomical symbolism soma was identified with the waning moon whose gradual diminishing and eventual disappearance was explained by the fact that the gods "drank" it. Soma was therefore a drink that was strictly reserved for immortals, while men drank goblets of sura. Sura, the wife of Varuna, later became the goddess of wine.

In the *Rig-Veda*, the god of the summer solstice, Indra-sun, is reinvigorated with several goblets of soma and in so doing finds the energy to battle and defeat the serpent demon Vritra, who is the Indian version of the constellation Hydra (see the chapters on Hydra and Aquarius).

In 4000 B.C. the sun shone exactly over Crater at noon on the summer solstice while this constellation's stars shone over the meridian of the winter solstice at midnight on the same date.

Chandra

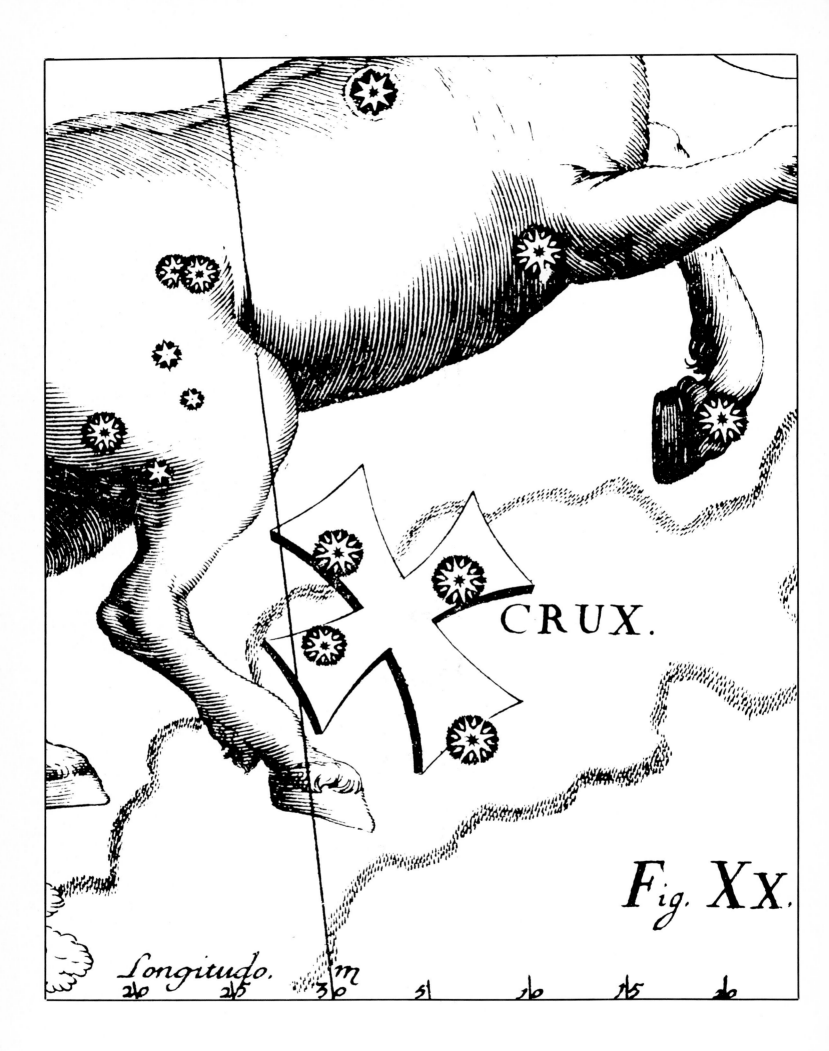

CRUX.

*F*_{ig.} *XX.*

Longitudo.

22
Crux

Although it does not belong to the forty-eight constellations that have come down to us from antiquity, Crux, the Southern Cross, has been a part of our constellation myths since Dante, who, never having seen it with his own eyes, described it as being located in the vicinity of the mountain of Purgatory:

> To the right hand I turned, and fixed my mind
> Upon the other Pole, and saw four stars
> Ne'er seen before save by the primal people.

Divine Comedy, I.21–24

Perhaps the poet was able to observe some celestial globe of the Arabs, with whom the people of Pisa and Florence had continuing relationships, or perhaps he had heard about this constellation upon the return (in 1295) of Marco Polo, who had gone as far south as Java and Madagascar. Among other things, Dante had attributed to these four stars the emblematic values of the four virtues, Justice, Temperance, Strength, and Prudence. There are frequent allusions to stars and constellations in the *Divine Comedy*, and it is not surprising that the last word of "Hell," as well as of "Purgatory" and "Paradise," is actually "stars." One must go as far south as 30° N., down to Cairo, to begin seeing the Cross. Today, Hipparchus and Ptolemy would no longer see its stars from their observatories (Alexandria is at 31°12′) as they did twenty centuries ago, because the age-old shifting caused by the precession of the equinoxes has moved them farther south. The earliest reference to its present name was made in 1515 by the Florentine Andrea Corsali. He called it Marvelous Cross and described it as "the most beautiful among all the southern constellations." In 1520 it was referred to by Antonio Pigafetta of Vicenza, who accompanied Magellan's crew on their circumnavigation of the globe (1519–22).

In 1501 Amerigo Vespucci created a constellation of his own, which he called the Almond. This name was used in artistic jargon to describe the halo that was drawn around portraits of saints. Vespucci was a capable astronomer who contributed to the systematizing of the sky. He became a living legend and his contemporaries exaggerated his exploits. Gerolamo Cardano even asserted that he had catalogued ten thousand southern stars, something that was clearly impossible.

The Southern Cross made its entrance into the official astronomical maps with Bayer's star atlas of 1603. Bayer himself stated that he had added twelve new constellations based on what had been observed and recorded by Amerigo Vespucci, Andrea Corsali, Pietro di Medina, and Pietro Theodori.

Pliny tells us that when Caesar conquered Egypt the stars of the cross were dedicated to him under the name of *Thronos Caesaris*, the Throne of Caesar, but in all ancient traditions the cross had always been an integral part of the constellation Centaurus.

According to the astrologers, these stars confer perseverance in the face of difficult tests, as well as responsibility and suffering.

The Southern Cross. From E. Dunkin, Midnight Sky *(1869)*

Opposite: *Crux. From Hevelius,* Uranographia totum coelum stellatum *(1690)*

321

23
Cygnus

In that part of the sky and its stars that is inhabited by such winged creatures as Pegasus and Aquila, a cross of very bright stars can be seen immersed in the creamy splendor of the Milky Way. These stars represent the mythical white swan, the bird sacred to Venus. The origin of this constellation is very ancient. In Mesopotamia it was called Bird of the Forest and the Greeks called it *Ornithos*, meaning Bird, until Eratosthenes named it Cygnus.

It has been proposed that this was the constellation dedicated to Orpheus, the divine musician immortalized here next to his beloved Lyra, the star group next to Cygnus. Although there is not enough evidence to validate this idea, it is a fascinating hypothesis because, in the world of symbols, the swan, the harp, and the sacrificial serpent are always associated with the mystical voyage to the hereafter that Orpheus undertook in search of Eurydice, who had died from the bite of a serpent (Cirlot, *Diccionario de simbolos tradicionales*). To this we must add that the other constellation next to Cygnus is, in fact, Draco, the great northern serpent who counted the North Pole and the center of the ecliptic among his stars.

Cygnus. From Hyginus, Poetica astronomica *(1485 edition)*

Leda and the Swan

Zeus had fallen in love with Leda, wife of Tyndareus, and had transformed himself into a swan in order to lie with her. His deception was successful, and Leda laid an egg from which Helen, Castor, and Pollux were born. Leda was subsequently deified under the name of Nemesis (Hyginus, *Fabulae*).

In another version of the same myth, Zeus attempted to copulate with Nemesis, but she transformed herself into a fish. He then promptly became a beaver, and Nemesis transformed herself into various other animals. Finally, she transformed herself into a wild goose and Zeus, having turned himself into a swan, seduced her at Rhamnus in Attica. Nemesis then proceeded to Sparta where she gave the egg that she had produced to Leda for safekeeping. From that egg Helen was born. Helen, Helle, and Selene are local variants of the Middle Eastern moon goddess. This was an orgiastic divinity to whom the Helenephoria festivities were dedicated, a time during which women carried baskets filled with phallic objects (Graves, *The Greek Myths*). The original myth of the love goddess who is born from an egg is, however, a Mesopotamian myth. In this legend the egg fell directly from the moon into the Euphrates River, where two fish pushed it onto the riverbank, after which it was hatched by doves. From it Ishtar was born who, in gratitude to the fish, transformed them into the constellation Pisces while the doves were transformed into the Pleiades (Hyginus, *Fabulae*).

There existed in Greece another legend concerning the origin of the mythical bird, that of Cycnus, son of Apollo and Hyria. Cycnus had imposed on the hero Phylius the task of strangling a lion, slaying a wild bull, and capturing alive some monstrous man-eating birds. When Phylius succeeded in passing

Opposite: *Cygnus. From Hevelius,*
Uranographia totum coelum stellatum *(1690)*

Providence, a Mesopotamian symbol of the moon

these tests, Cycnus took his own life by throwing himself into a lake, which was later called the Cycnean Lake. His mother, Hyria, followed him to his death and both were transformed into swans (Graves, *The Greek Myths*).

Ovid and Virgil attributed the origin of this myth to Cygnus, brother of Phaethon, who roamed in search of his brother's body after Phaethon died, having precipitated from the sky into the river Eridanus. After Cygnus threw himself repeatedly into the waters of the river, the gods took pity on him in his sorrow and transformed him into a swan. This is thought to explain why ever

Saint Helena's Cross, a seventeenth-century constellation

since then swans wander over the water as if deep in thought and every so often immerse their long necks (Ovid, *Metamorphoses*).

The Northern Cross

The stars of Cygnus form a large cross that is clearly identifiable even in the brightness of the surrounding Milky Way. Its beauty is such that it is small wonder that in his 1627 Christianized system, Schiller replaced this ancient pagan constellation with a cross carried by Saint Helena, the mother of Constantine. According to tradition, she found the true cross on which Jesus had drawn his last breath, which had been lost for three centuries.

This cross is formed by the stars Alpha, Gamma, Eta, and Beta Cygni for the long arm, located along the Milky Way for approximately twenty degrees, while the crosswise arm is formed by Zeta, Epsilon, Gamma, and Delta Cygni.

The Northern Cross is certainly more beautiful and perfect than the Southern Cross. Many Christians believe that this constellation can be seen as a divine sign because on the night before Christmas at nine o'clock, it stands erect and shines brightly over the western hills.

In the world of astrology Cygnus is the patron of an adaptable, intellectual, contemplative, and dreamy nature. It generates disorderly and unstable relationships, it causes talents to mature late, and it creates an attraction for both the element water and for the arts.

The trump card number twenty, Judgment, represents it in the tarots.

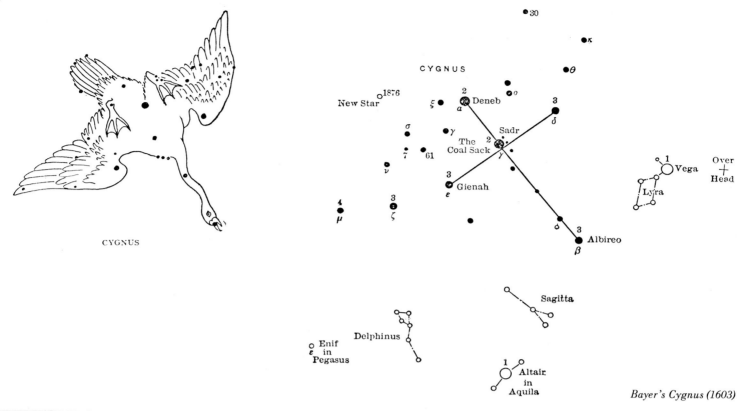

CYGNUS

New Star 1876 °
ξ ●
σ
γ
The
Coal Sack
7 ● 61
ν
Deneb
2
a
Sadr
2
γ
3
ε Gienah
μ
3
z ζ
Vega
1
Lyra
Over
+
Head
3
δ
3
ο
Albireo
β

Sagitta

Delphinus

Enif
e in
Pegasus

Altair
1
in
Aquila

Bayer's Cygnus (1603)

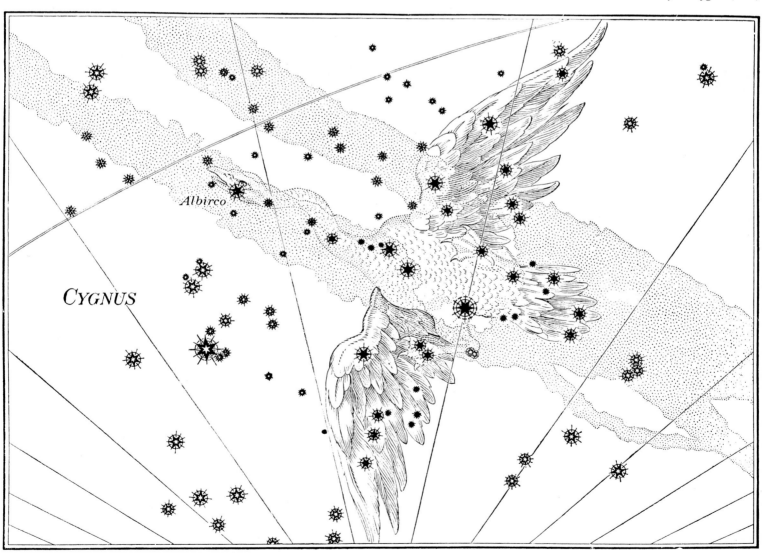

Albirco

CYGNUS

Cygnus   325

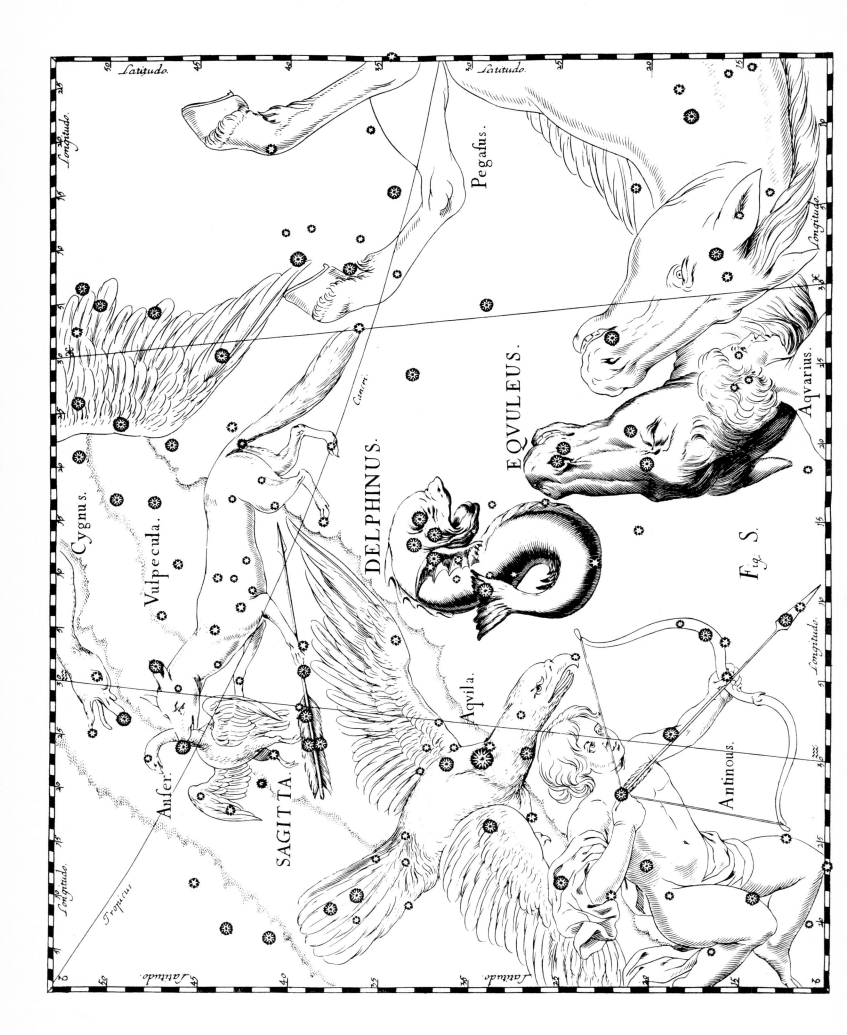

24
Delphinus

Delphinus. From Hyginus, Poetica
astronomica (1485 edition)

Between Aquila and Pegasus at the beginning of the vast stellar region called the Sea in antiquity, there is an extremely small constellation, Delphinus, the Dolphin. This animal is referred to very often in the ancient myths because it formed attachments to man and because it would gather in schools when music would be played on the beach.

The quintessential marine symbol, the dolphin appears in very ancient myths as mediator and peacemaker among both gods and men. These qualities were attributed to the dolphin because it almost always appeared after the passage of storms.

At the time when Poseidon, god of the sea, was looking for a wife, his first choice was Thetis, the Nereid over whom hovered the prophecy that she would bring forth a son who would become more famous than his father. The god's favors therefore turned to Amphitrite, another Nereid. However, she disdained his advances and took refuge on the Atlas Mountains in present-day Morocco. Poseidon then sent a dolphin to her to try and dissuade her from her obstinacy. This animal was so clever that it succeeded in convincing Amphitrite to marry Poseidon.

Having become pregnant, the goddess gave birth to three daughters: Triton, Rhode, and Benthesicyme. Poseidon was so grateful to the dolphin that he placed its image among the stars. In his comments about this myth, Robert Graves explains that Thetis, Amphitrite, and Nereis were different names of the same triple moon-goddess in her aspect of ruler of the sea.

Amphitrite, whose name means sea, was the ancient matriarchal goddess of the sea. Her priestesses controlled the fishing industry but, with the arrival of the patriarchal system, this control passed to male priests. This explains why Amphitrite was reluctant to marry.

Her daughters, who symbolized the goddess herself, were another indication of her lunar character: the triple aspect of Triton, the lucky new moon; Rhode, the full harvest moon; and Benthesicyme, the dangerous waning moon. At a later date Triton was masculinized (Graves, *The Greek Myths*).

Arion and the Dolphin

Like Zeus, Poseidon had many extramarital love affairs. One of these united him with the nymph Oneaea who bore him Arion, the bard, a beautiful young man, famous musician, and poet. He was, among other things, the inventor of the dithyramb, the emotional and orgiastic choral hymn that was used in the Dionysian rites.

Arion, who was protected by Periander, the tyrant of Corinth, succeeded in convincing his king to give him a ship with which to travel to Taenarus in Sicily, where he had been invited to participate in a music competition.

He not only won first prize, but his new admirers heaped gifts upon him rich

Opposite: *Delphinus. From Hevelius,*
Uranographia totum coelum stellatum *(1690)*

327

enough to provoke the greed of the sailors who were taking him back to Corinth. The sailors decided to kill him during the return voyage. Arion tried in vain to dissuade them by offering them all his riches. When he realized the inevitability of his death, he asked to die as a bard, and his request was granted.

He dressed in a tunic of gold and purple cloth, with jewelry around his arms; he perfumed his long hair and set a gilt diadem on his head. With his lyre in the left hand and the ivory plectrum in the right, he then went to the prow of the ship where he sang his last, sweet, passionate song to the sea.

When he finished his song, he threw himself into the waves and the ship

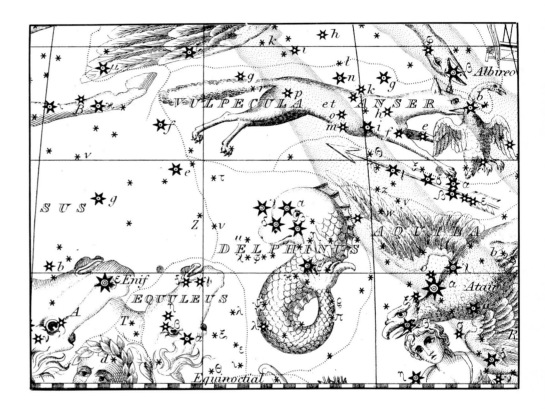

The constellation and the stars of Delphinus.
From Middleton Celestial Atlas *(1843)*

rapidly sailed away. However, his music had been heard in the depths of the sea. A school of dolphins came and gathered him up and, riding on the back of one, he reached Corinth even before the ship sailed into its harbor. The dolphin ran aground on the beach and died, despite Arion's attempts to push it out into the open sea. Delighted with the return of his protégé, Periander had a monument erected in honor of the savior dolphin, and when the ship arrived in Corinth he had the sailors crucified in front of the monument.

Arion was not the first man saved by a dolphin. In fact, a dolphin saved Enalus when he leaped overboard in order to reach his beloved Phineis who, as ordered by an oracle, had been thrown into the sea to placate Amphitrite. Phineis too was saved by a dolphin, and a fourth dolphin saved Phalanthus from drowning in the Crisaean Sea while on his way to Italy.

One final Greek story about the birth of Delphinus is an episode in the life of Dionysus at the time when he was still a child and traveling on a ship directed toward Naxos. Not knowing the identity of the god and struck by his beauty, the sailors decided to sell him as a slave and shifted their course toward Asia. Dionysus then caused a grapevine to grow around the main mast. While the plant encircled the rigging, he transformed the oars into serpents and himself into a lion. The ship became populated with wild animals who moved to the sound of flutes until the pirates flung themselves in terror into the sea and became dolphins (Graves, *The Greek Myths*).

The original constellation of Delphinus probably also included the stars that today belong to Equuleus, a constellation created by Hipparchus (Allen, *Star Lore*) in the form of a horse's head, perhaps in memory of the widespread ancient sacrifices of horses.

In China this constellation was called *Tien-Kion*, Celestial Stable. Every spring this stable was cleaned and then smeared with the blood of a horse that had been sacrificed (Flammarion, *Le Stelle*). Horse sacrifices were also used by the Indo-Parsees under the name of *aswamedha*, derived from *aswa*, or horse, and *medha*, or sacrifice (see the chapter on Pegasus).

In India these stars were called *Shi-shu-mara*, which was later changed to *Zizumara*, the Porpoise or Marine Serpent. The twenty-second *nakshatra*, or lunar node, *Cravishtha*, meaning the Favorable, was assigned to these stars.

Al-Biruni records the name given by the desert nomads to this sign, *al-Kaud*, the Camel. However, al-Kazwini stated that the scholars of his time called the rhombus of Delphinus' stars *al-Ukud*, meaning the Pearls, and the stars of the fish's tail *al-Salib*, meaning the Cross. The constellation's star Epsilon was called *al-Amud al-Salib*, or the Pole of the Cross. Later on these names were abandoned by the Arab astronomers in order to take on the Greek name of *al-Dulfin*, or the Dolphin.

Ptolemy assigned Delphinus to the guardianship of Saturn and Mars. It conveyed simplicity of appearance, a jovial nature, love of the hunt and sports, an attraction to pleasures, ecclesiastic affairs, and traveling; however, it also exposed its subjects to the dangers of suffering as a result of ingratitude.

Sualocin and Rotanev, the names assigned to Alpha and Beta Delphini, appear for the first time in the 1814 catalogue of Palermo. The search for the source of these names kept the keen mind of Admiral Smyth engaged for a long time; in vain he conducted research at the observatory of Palermo. But it was Webb who, at a later date, unveiled the mystery by reading the letters of the names backward, producing Nicolaus Venator, the Latinized name of Nicolo Cacciatore, who was the assistant to and successor of the astronomer Piazzi, director of the observatory at Palermo.

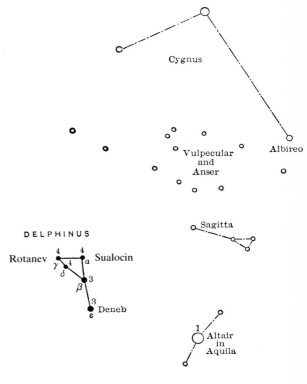

DELPHINUS

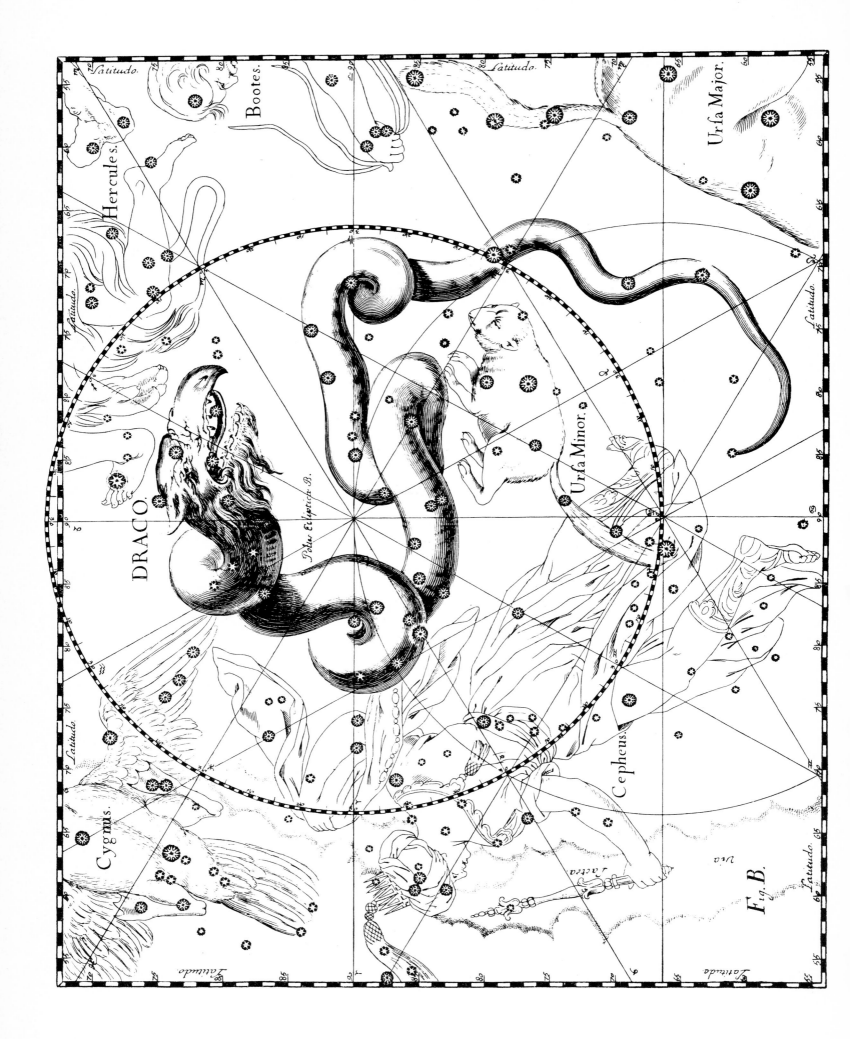

25
Draco

In the remote time when the constellations were created by unknown astronomers who populated the nighttime sky with winged horses, dolphins, centaurs, scorpions, and goats, the Polar Star was not our Polaris, located in the tail of Ursa Minor. Instead it was the legendary Thuban, in the body of that immense dragon of stars that is Draco. This sinuous monster of the sky was located exactly as if it were the pivot for the revolutions of the entire heavenly vault. Due to the precession of the equinoxes, the Pole has slowly moved until it has reached today's Polar Star.

Why was the figure of a dragon chosen to represent such an important point in the sky? Draco contained not only the North Pole, but also the pole of the equator and that of the ecliptic, on which the twelve signs of the zodiac are located.

Draco often occurs among the many stellar symbols on Mesopotamian boundary stones that carry bas-reliefs of historical and astronomical subjects. On the top part of the stone Draco uncoils; on the lower part there is always the long aquatic serpent, Hydra; in the center there is the serpent who is bent at a right angle and held in Ophiuchus' hands.

Hydra delineated the equator, and Ophiuchus' serpent followed the celestial equator until it intersected the meridian of the fall equinox. It then bent in a right angle and followed the meridian until it marked the zenith with the star placed on its head.

The names Dragon's Head and Dragon's Tail stand for the lunar nodes—the points at which the moon crosses the ecliptic. The interval necessary for the moon to pass through one of these nodes and return is called the Month of the Dragon or Draconic Month. In astronomy Dragon's Head generally means the ascending node of any orbit, whether it is the orbit of the moon, a planet, or a comet; Dragon's Tail refers to the descending node. These symbols appear in contemporary astronomy as well as, identically, in four-thousand-year-old Mesopotamian boundary stones.

An eclipse of the sun or the moon can occur only when these two bodies are close to one of the nodes, either the Dragon's Head or Tail. This relationship was expressed by the saying "the dragon causes the eclipses." In fact, in many myths throughout the world, eclipses are represented by a dragon who devours the sun or the moon.

In ancient times the prediction of eclipses was considered the most sophisticated ability an astronomer could have. Whoever designed the constellations left us clues that allow us to establish that the knowledge of the time was such that it did allow prediction of eclipses. After a long voyage in Mesopotamia Thales of Miletus (c. 624–546 B.C.) had learned so much about celestial matters from his studies with Chaldean mathematicians that he did not hesitate to predict a total eclipse of the sun. This eclipse occurred punctually in May, 585 B.C., and interrupted, as Herodotus narrates, the war that was going on between the Lydians and the Medes.

The dragon Kala Rahu causes an eclipse by swallowing the moon. From M. Covarrubias, Island of Bali *(1942)*

Opposite: *Draco. From Hevelius,* Uranographia totum coelum stellatum *(1690)*

Dragon's Head, or ascending node

Dragon's Tail, or descending node

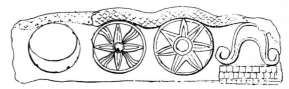

The most frequently occurring astronomical symbols in Sumerian art: the moon, Ishtar (Venus), the sun, the dragon (Draco), and the scissors used to cut the umbilical cord. The scissors represented the intersection point (node) of the orbits of two celestial bodies

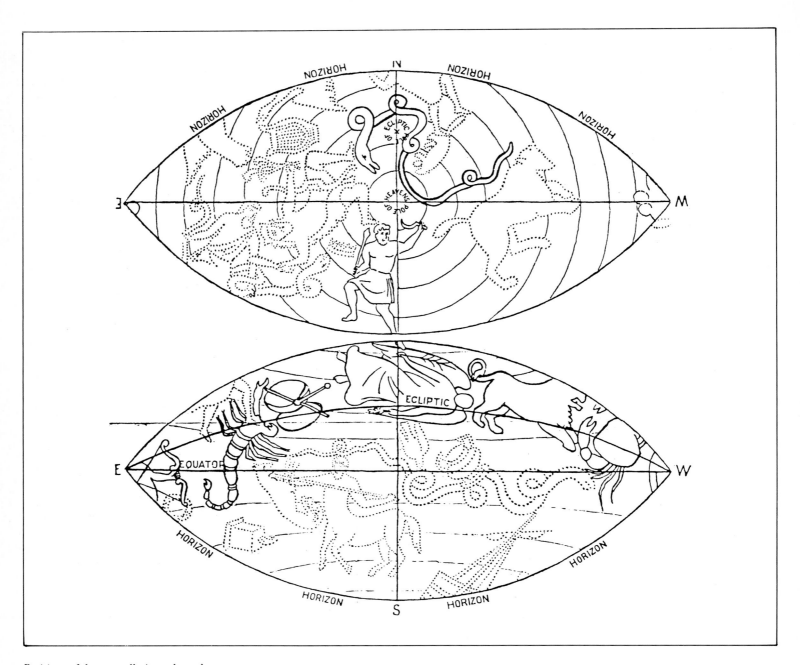

Positions of the constellations along the
meridian of the summer solstice in 5700 B.C.

Knowledge of the draconic or serpentine figures provided the key to the laws of the star-filled sky, which was represented by a tree whose fruits were the stars and whose trunk was their axis of rotation. The supreme guardian of this Tree of Knowledge was, of course, none other than he himself—Draco, Cronos, the Ourobouros—symbol of all cyclical processes. One of his qualities was untiring vigilance; his sight was exceptional and he never slept. These same characteristics were attributed to astronomers. It seems that the root of Draco comes from the Greek *derkein*, to see.

Of all creatures, the serpent is historically the most interesting since it appears in myths and legends more often than any other creature and, being connected with the biblical Eden, it is linked with man's ancient history.

The Sumerians considered Draco the female monster Tiamat, symbol of the primordial chaos, who was defeated by Marduk in an epic duel at the end of which she was cut into two pieces. One half became the constellation of Draco, and the other became the constellation of Hydra. (For more details on the

Tiamat-Marduk duel, please turn to the chapters on Hercules and Hydra.)

The fact that Draco's stars not only never set, but also occupied the central throne among the constellations, made this creature the true symbol of eternity, consciousness, and vigilance.

As keeper of the tree of the golden apples—the stars—we find him in the Garden of the Hesperides under the name of Ladon. Again it is a dragon who tirelessly guarded the Golden Fleece in the Garden of Ares, the much longed-for destination of the Argonauts, who set out from Greece to accomplish an exploit that had a profoundly astronomical character. The Golden Fleece represented, in fact, the sign of Aries and at that moment the Greeks were performing the great astronomical feat of the arrival of Aries—and the removal of Taurus—as the springtime sign (see the chapters on Aries and Argo Navis).

A total of fifty gods, half-gods, and heroes set out on this allegorical voyage toward Colchis, close to the Caucasus Mountains where Prometheus had been chained and from where so many myths and so much knowledge had come to Greece. Jason, the solar commander of the expedition, succeeded in the task of defeating the dragon only with the help of the magician Medea. By using the ancient herbs of the priestesses—one of which was the crocus that sprang from the blood of Prometheus—she put the dragon to sleep, thus making it possible for the Greek hero to capture the Golden Fleece. With this exploit the Greek Aries officially replaced the Middle Eastern Taurus as the sign indicating the spring equinox.

Various interpretations of the figure of Draco. In the drawing above the wings were obtained by adding the stars of Ursa Minor.

The Hesperides

Hespere, Aegle, and Erytheis, daughters of the Night, and Atlas, guarded the tree of the golden apples in a garden that belonged to Mother Earth located on the slopes of the Atlas Mountains. Atlas represented the astronomical knowledge of peoples who preceded the Greek culture. He is always depicted as a Titan who holds up the entire vault of the heavens and its stars, and he is represented among the stars by the constellation Boötes. The Hesperides were identified with the sunset, which painted the sky with the marvelous colors of the golden apples (Graves, *The Greek Myths*).

As the solar disk was disappearing behind the horizon, Hesperus, who was the evening star sacred to Aphrodite, appeared. The golden apples, which are often thought to be simply apples, were actually an allegory for the stars. In Greek the word *melon* indicated any round fruit; the fruits of the land that the legends referred to were probably the mythical pomegranates that are always present in the rituals of the early Mediterranean cultures (Ileana Chirassi, *Elementi di Culture Precereali*).

The task of fetching the golden apples was the eleventh labor of Hercules. Following Nereus' advice, he killed the dragon Ladon with an arrow and then persuaded Atlas to gather the apples while, in exchange, he held up the vault of the sky. As a token of his gratitude, Atlas not only gave him the apples but taught him astronomy. (Atlas, in fact the first astronomer, knew so much about this science that he carried the globe of the sky on his shoulders.) This is why it was said that Hercules relieved him temporarily of that weight. Ladon was later placed among the stars by his mother, while Hercules, upon accomplishment of the twelve labors, and with the newly acquired knowledge, became the ruler of the zodiac.

The serpent, guardian of the tree of knowledge in the biblical paradise

The Fall of Man

The biblical serpent of the Old Testament who lives in the tree of knowledge and life is very close to the religious spirit of the West. However, this serpent is a very ancient being that existed before man. Eve is his confidant and an initiate into his mysteries; she eats the apple of knowledge and, in so doing, she incarnates the lunar prophetess, symbol of the religious matriarchy. In contrast, Adam does everything that she advises him to do. He is also frightened by his God who personifies the new solar being, Zeus or Shamash, and brings an end to both the priestly hierarchy of women and the matriarchy.

When God questions Adam he does not share the sin with Eve, but accuses her and the serpent who, as a result of the subsequent punishment, becomes the tempting devil. Having driven all of them out, God remains as lord and master of the flowering garden.

All the Gardens of Earthly Delights of antiquity were originally governed by female deities; these gardens were usurped by male solar gods in order to do away with this matriarchy that prevailed over the patriarchal system. Hera was the goddess of the flowering garden and the Lady of the Pomegranate before the arrival of Zeus, whose resigned wife she became.

The bejeweled Sumerian paradise where Gilgamesh went was the dominion of Siduri, goddess of knowledge. Shamash, the sun-god, dethroned Siduri and reduced her to a slave who served in a tavern.

In the wood of Ares, where the Golden Fleece was guarded, it was once again a woman—the disconcerting lunar magician Medea—who ensured the successful conquest of astronomical knowledge with her incantations. This was also done by Ariadne, who offered Theseus the solution to the labyrinth (see the chapter on Corona Borealis).

When Apollo, the quintessential solar god, was still a child, he set out with his bow and arrows for Mount Parnassus, where the serpent Python, who was the most important oracle of Greece, lived. The young god slew him and went at once to the oracular companion of Python in Delphi, the serpent-woman Delphyne, also called Pythoness, and forced her to serve him. To purify himself he then started the funeral games in honor of Python, the Pythian Games.

The biblical myth of the fall compels man to despise woman for all the evils that come from her, to demand that she work upon his order, to exclude her from religious functions, and to forbid her to occupy herself with moral problems. Adam is always awkward in his role of God's favorite, even after the fall. Having become a patriarch, he does not know how to make decisions on his own while Eve seems to be much more at her ease in the mystery of the new reality. Loyal to her matriarchal nature, she is unfaithful to Adam and couples with Samael, the serpent; then she travels alone to the ocean, where she builds herself a hut. Only when the labor pains begin does she ask the sun and the moon to call Adam to come and help her with the birth.

What follows contains an element of the fantastic for those who know only the biblical version. Adam comes to her aid and invokes God; he sends the archangel Michael with two virtues and twelve angels and they all surround her and help her. Michael even sits next to her and assists her lovingly by caressing her forehead and her breasts until a baby boy, shining like an angel, is born. Eve at once recognizes his divine origin: he is the son of the dragon. She calls him Cain, which means stalk, because the baby had gotten up onto his feet to go and gather a stalk of grain as soon as he was born; this he then gave to Eve (Graves-Patai, *Hebrew Myths*).

These elements make it possible for us to read this famous myth for its astronomical message. Cain, who is the first farmer and who represents the new science of cultivation, in contrast to the nomadic pastoral peoples represented by Abel, offers the stalk of grain to the great goddess who is the mother of the farmers, Demeter. In the sky Demeter was represented by Virgo who, at the time, was the most important constellation of the zodiac. It showed a winged woman with a stalk of grain in one hand and a sickle in the other.

The apotheosis of the constellation of Virgo occurred when the sun entered into this sign and marked the beginning of the barley and wheat harvests. The summer solstice fell in Virgo as early as the year 5744 B.C. and remained there for two thousand years. This gives us an indication of the antiquity of both this myth and the constellation.

Draco, Ursa Major, and Ursa Minor. From Hyginus, Poetica astronomica *(1485 edition)*

Cain's birth assisted by twelve angels, symbolizing the entire zodiac, has a purely astronomical reference. It symbolizes the fact that agriculture brought the need for a more sophisticated calendar, and this resulted in a refinement of the science of the sky.

In Alexandrian astrology Ptolemy assigned to Draco the qualities of Saturn and Mars that produce an artistic and emotional nature, a penetrating and analytical mind, and a desire to travel and to have many friends. However, they also expose their subjects to the risks of being robbed or accidentally poisoned. It was commonly thought among astronomers that the world would be permeated with poison if a comet should travel through Draco.

The cabalists have assigned Draco the thirteenth trump card of the tarots, namely Death.

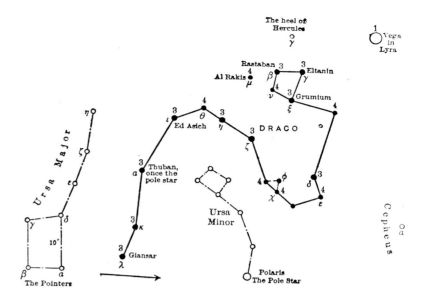

DRACO

Thuban

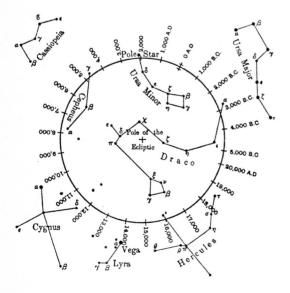

The pole of the ecliptic among the stars of Draco. The circle represents the anomalous rotation of the terrestrial axis over a period of 25,765 years, the Platonic Year. From J. Jeans, The Stars in Their Courses

Thuban was the first Polar Star of the historical period and, as the pivot and heart of the northern hemisphere, it has attracted particularly flamboyant names. In the cuneiform texts dealing with astronomical subjects that were compiled by Sargon, the first Sumerian king, this star was called *Tir-an-na*, meaning Light of Paradise, or *Dayan-Same*, meaning Judge of Paradise, or *Dayan-Sidi*, meaning Favorable Judge or Crown of Paradise. These titles confirm that Draco belonged to a paradise that preceded the Christian one.

The cult of Enlil, the god of storms and winds, was also linked to this star. He was the god to whom the Way of the Sky, which stretched over the Tropic of Cancer, was dedicated.

According to Berossus, Enlil had formed the sky and the earth and created humans and the luminous celestial bodies. He was called God of Light, and the biblical god of the ancient testament was modeled after him.

The star of the city of Nippur was dedicated to Enlil as well. It appears in several texts under the name of Margida; it was probably the star Thuban.

Several Egyptian pyramids at Abousseir and Giza were oriented toward Thuban. The most famous is the pyramid of Cheops, in which a narrow passage was built that had a length of one hundred and twenty-six meters and an inclination of 26° 17′ over the horizon. Every night Thuban shone directly through this passage into the chamber of the sarcophagus.

The Five Camels

The nomads of the desert called the group of stars that form the head of Draco the Five Camels Trotting Along in the Desert. In Ulugh-Beg's star catalogue we find, instead, that they were called *al-Awwad* (Lute Player) and *al-Rakis*, modernized into Arrakis (Principal Dancer). Since various names have been assigned to some of the stars of Draco it seems appropriate to analyze them separately.

Beta Draconis is listed in today's star atlases under the name of Alwaid, derived from *al-Awaid*, or the Mother Camel. It was also called Rastaban, which was derived from *al-Ras al-Thuban*, or the Head of the Dragon.

Gamma Draconis is now called Etamin, from *al-Ras al-Tinnin*, also meaning the Head of the Dragon. This star was worshiped in particular by the Egyptians, who knew it by the name of Iris. It marked the head of the hippopotamus, an Egyptian substitute for Draco. Since Etamin is located almost exactly on the zenith at Greenwich it has also been called Zenith Star.

Nodus Secundus marks the second node of the figure of Draco. Al-Tizini called it *al-Tais*, or the Goat. Zeta and Eta together were *al-Dhibain*, the Two Hyenas, who were lying in wait for the passage of the camels and were ready to attack the small camel marked by the star *al-Ruba*.

Bayer's Draco (1603)

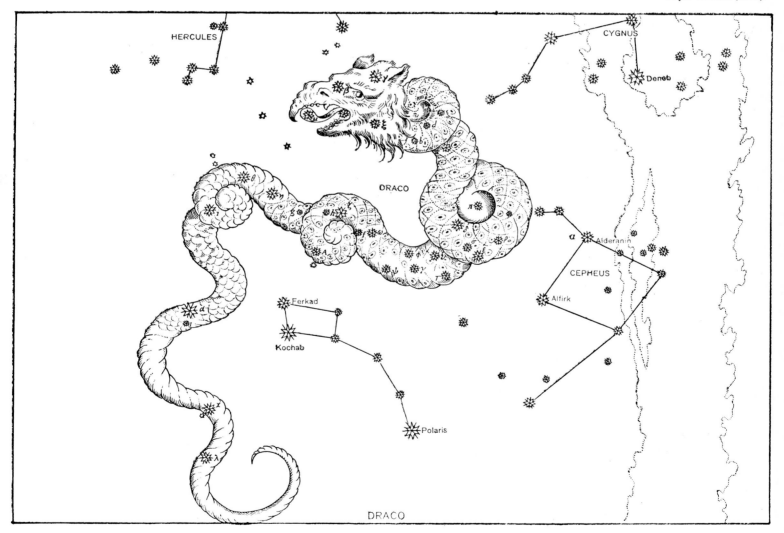

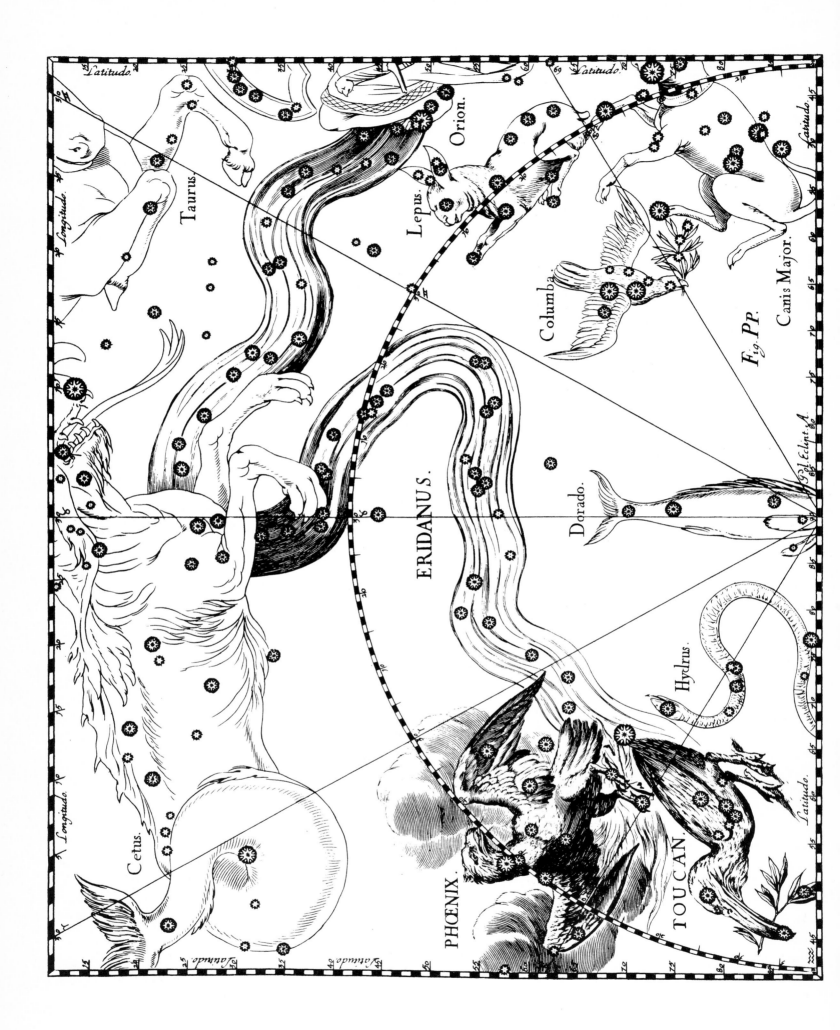

26
Eridanus

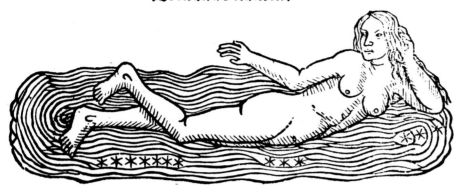

Eridanus flumen.

The river Eridanus. From Hyginus, Poetica astronomica *(1485 edition)*

A very large part of the southern hemisphere's starry sky was called the Sea by the ancient Sumerian astronomers. The waves of this sea seem to lap on a hypothetical celestial beach over which Sirius, the Dog Star, announced the upcoming flood of the Nile. Farther up we see the constellation of Gemini, protector of sailors, next to Cancer, the amphibious crab.

In this southern ocean there flows a great river of stars that starts at the star Rigel, located on Orion's foot. This river is called Eridanus, and it is the longest of all the constellations. Composed of rather dim stars, it can best be observed on a clear winter night with no moon; the feeling of a river can easily be perceived as a great horseshoe southwest of Orion.

Many hypotheses have been advanced for the corresponding terrestrial identity of this river. Most agree that it is the celestial representation of the Nile; some identify it as the Po, and still others look at it and think they see the Euphrates.

The Po must be excluded because it is located too far north from the latitude in which the constellations were originally designed and, as we will see later, this is definitely a Greek interpretation. As far as the theory of the Nile is concerned, it is very probable that Eridanus was called Nile by the Egyptians. The fact that Sirius is nearby would demonstrate this to be true. However, we must keep in mind that, in antiquity, the Milky Way was also considered a heavenly river and is also close to Sirius (see the chapter on the Milky Way).

In order to find out which river is represented by Eridanus we must find out which river on earth has the same characteristics of this river in the sky. First of all the river flows south into a great sea. The sea follows the southern horizon of the sky. This excludes the Nile, because it flows from south to north.

The only territory with the appropriate latitude and a south-flowing river is Mesopotamia, with the Tigris and Euphrates, which empty into the Persian Gulf. (There is, in fact, among the stars another river—the one that flows out of the vase of Aquarius and in which Piscis Austrinus, indicated by the beautiful star Fomalhaut, swims.) The name Eridanus comes from the Sumerian *Ariadan,* which means Strong River.

Opposite: *Eridanus. From Hevelius,* Uranographia totum coelum stellatum *(1690)*

Geruvigus' Eridanus

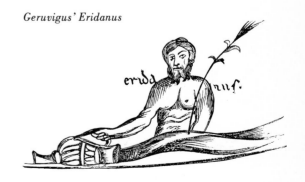

339

Al-Ahir al-Nahr

In today's star maps Eridanus starts at the star Rigel and ends at Achernar, whose name derives from *al-Ahir al-Nahr*, the End of the River. It is well documented that it was the eighteenth-century astronomers who moved this star in order to stretch the river Eridanus all the way to the Clouds of Magellan in the vicinity of the South Pole. In ancient maps Eridanus ended much earlier, at the star Theta Eridani, today called Acamar. The English astronomer Edmund Halley speaks of it as "the last one of the rivers in the old catalogue." Today's Acamar was called Achernar in antiquity.

The ancient Achernar was located exactly on the horizon in 1500 B.C., if observed from a point of view of at least 35° N., which corresponds approximately to the latitude of Mesopotamia. In Manilius' *Astronomica*, an epic poem in Latin, after reaching the ancient Achernar the river Eridanus continues along the celestial horizon until it meets, in Piscis Austrinus, the river that flows out of the pail of Aquarius.

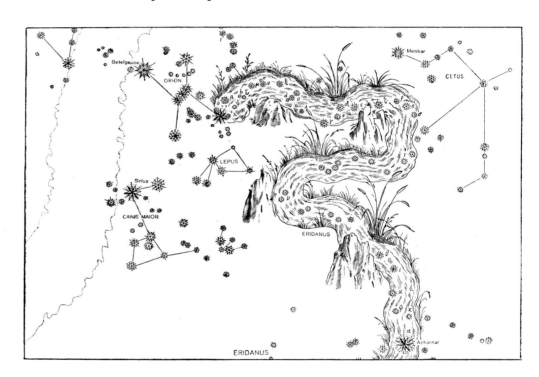

Bayer's Eridanus (1603)

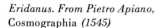

Eridanus. From Pietro Apiano,
Cosmographia *(1545)*

The Legend of Phaëthon

Phaëthon, a young man of rare beauty, son of Clymene and Helius, had been challenged by his sisters to show proof of his divine origin. In order to do so he went up into the sky to meet with his father who, about to set out in his chariot, was with Hours, Days, Months, and Seasons. Helius recognized his son and magnanimously offered to grant any request of his. Without hesitating Phaëthon asked to be allowed to drive the chariot of the sun for a day. The god reacted bitterly because, on the one hand, he could not retract his offer and, on the other, he understood that this would mean certain death for the young man.

In vain he tried to dissuade Phaëthon, but the young man was determined and, trembling, he approached the divine chariot, decorated with jewels and drawn by four magnificent white stallions. He took the reins in his hands, climbed on board, and flew off into the sky. The horses at once felt the inexperienced hand that guided them and took fright. Phaëthon lost the reins, and the chariot of the sun shot through the sky like a comet.

It distanced itself so far from the earth that cold and frost descended upon the world. Then it reappeared and descended so low that the snow melted and the woods went up in flames. In Africa and India people were so burned by its rays that they have had dark skin ever since. All men sent long prayers up to Zeus asking him to bring an end to the terrors. Compelled to contain the cataclysm, he hit Phaëthon with lightning and put the sorrowing Helius back into his chariot, who at once restrained the stallions and brought the sun back to its natural path. After a long fall, similar to that of a falling star, Phaëthon's tormented body fell into the river Eridanus. The gods placed the river among the stars to commemorate this event.

The astronomical origin of this young solar god who appears in the morning sky only to disappear immediately helps us to recognize him in the planet Venus in her guise as the Morning Star or Phosphorus, who rises at dawn but disappears with the arrival of the sun. From this astronomical allegory derives the myth of the fall of Lucifer; in fact, the Latin translation of Phosphorus is Lucifer, the Brilliant One.

Poplars were trees sacred to the moon and the symbols of resurrection as well. The metamorphosis of the nymphs is the indication of a funeral island that was inhabited by a group of priestesses who were worshipers of Persephone (Graves, *The Greek Myths*). The identification of Eridanus with the Po derives from the fact that, in the time of classical Greece, the Amber Way, the absolute realm of the poplars (the nymphs), passed over this river.

The fable containing the moral demonstrating that fathers should never give in to the will of their sons probably refers to the annual sacrifice of the royal prince, held on the only day that was calculated as belonging to the terrestrial year but not to the star year. The king feigned death at sunset; the interim boy-king at once took over his function and titles and married the queen, only to be killed twenty-four hours later. The old man then emerged from the tomb where he had hidden and ascended to the throne (Graves, *The Greek Myths*).

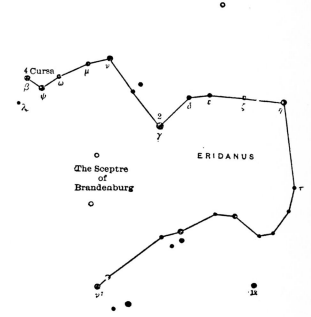

Rex Fluviorum

As explained earlier, the Sumerian name *Aria-dan*, or Strong River, is the most ancient root of Eridanus which, in its turn, has given names to other rivers such as the Rhine and the Rhone.

In his *Theogony* Hesiod called this river Phasis and had it flow into the sea of Euxinus near the place where the Argonauts took possession of the Golden Fleece of Aries. Phasis is the *Fosch* of the Turks, which derives from the Sanskrit *Phas*, or water.

Bayer's *Uranometria* (1603) calls this river Guagi, which is a contraction of the Moorish *Xadi al-Kabir*, the Great River, which later became the name of a real river, the great Spanish Guadalquivir.

Ptolemy assigned to the river of stars the qualities of Saturn, who imbued a passion for knowledge and science, travels, changes, and authority. But it also meant the risk of incidents relating to water, among those drowning. In the Christian revision of the constellations, Eridanus was changed from river to sea and became the Red Sea.

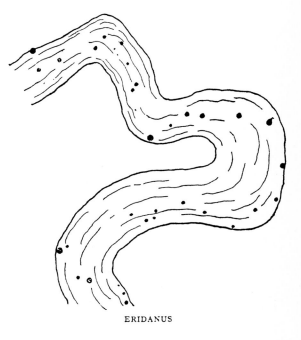

ERIDANUS

27
Gemini

An imaginary line drawn from the star Aldebaran and passing between the horns of Taurus brings us to the two stars that belong to the constellation of Gemini. The higher one is Castor and the lower one, which is brighter, is Pollux.

Gemini is the third sign of the zodiac, and it is clearly visible from December to May. Navigators attached great importance to it because the sun's entrance into Gemini marked the end of the winter storms, when ships could take to sea again. Altars and statues were raised to Castor and Pollux on ships to ensure a tranquil voyage. The bronze statues of Riace that were found on the bottom of the sea near the coast of Calabria were most probably statues of the twins. Many harbors of the classical period, such as Ostia and Alexandria, had statues of Castor and Pollux on either side of the entrance to the sea.

Between 6000 and 4000 B.C. the sun entered into Gemini at the spring equinox (March 21); this gave great importance to the sign, both for its cult and for the calendar. In fact, it was at about that time that the new science of agriculture was being refined, so there was an ever-greater need for an accurate calendar that would precisely establish the succession of the various agricultural operations with respect to the seasons. In the most ancient texts, the sign was symbolized by two newborn kids; this was in accordance with the natural sequence of the order in which domesticated animals were born: first the lambs, then the calves, then the kids. And so there was Aries, then Taurus, then Gemini.

In Sumerian iconography a series of three stellar symbols regularly appears. These have been called Triad of Stars by Assyrologists; they depict a crescent moon with two stars next to it. For the longest time this symbol remained a mystery. Then studies were done on the formation of primitive lunar calendars, and calculations were performed that showed that for hundreds of years—around 4000 B.C.—the very first visible crescent of the new moon appeared next to the stars Castor and Pollux. In those days the first crescent moon was the official beginning of the month. The same thing would have occurred next to the star Capella during the following two thousand years (Maunder, *The Astronomy of the Bible*).

The Triad of Stars is the representation of what people saw, year after year, in the sunset sky, at the beginning of every month, six thousand years ago. It is the most ancient description of an astronomical observation that has reached us. Furthermore, the ancient astronomers who calculated the zodiac, in noting that the spring equinox passed two stars that were almost identical, adopted twin creatures to symbolize the division of the day and the night into an equal number of hours.

Castor and Pollux. From Smith, Classical Mythology

Opposite: *Gemini. From Hevelius,* Uranographia totum coelum stellatum *(1690)*

343

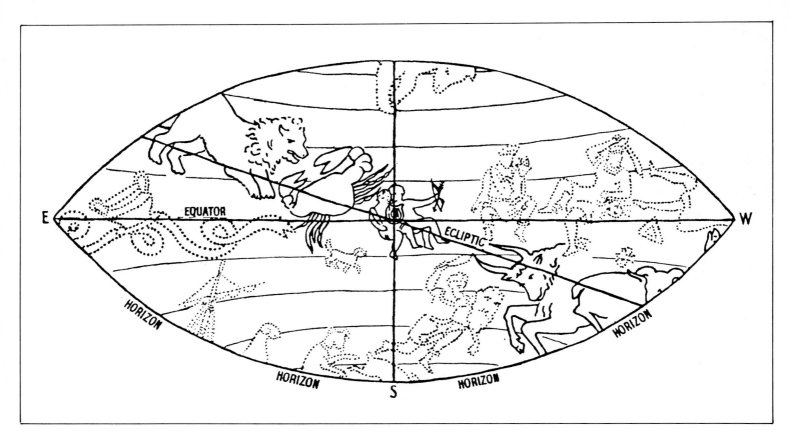

*Position of Gemini on the meridian of the
spring equinox in 5744 B.C.*

Castor and Pollux

Greco-Roman mythology identified the two main stars of this constellation with
Castor and Pollux, also called the Dioscuri, or sons of Zeus. Having fallen in
love with Tyndareus' wife, the beautiful Leda, Zeus transformed himself into a
swan in order to seduce her. Leda became pregnant and laid an egg from which
Helen and Pollux were born. At the same time she gave birth to Castor and
Clytaemnestra, who had been, however, conceived from the seed of Tyndareus.
Pollux, as son of the god, was therefore immortal, but Castor was mortal.
Originating in Sparta, their cult spread throughout Greece and Italy, where the
Romans worshiped them as principal gods of their Olympus.

They grew up together, and their brotherly love became legendary. They
became famous for their abilities in sport competitions: no one was a better
horse tamer than Castor and no one could defeat Pollux in the art of boxing.
Their sportsmanship resulted in the Olympic games being celebrated under
their aegis. They participated in the hunt for the Caledonian boar and in the
famous expedition of the Argonauts, who set out on the conquest of the Golden
Fleece (see the chapter on Argo Navis).

Linked with their destiny was another set of twins, their cousins Idas and
Lynceus. Tyndareus, the mortal father of Castor, had a stepbrother by the name
of Aphareus, whose wife had given birth to the twins Idas and Lynceus.
However, only Lynceus was the son of Aphareus because Idas was born from the
seed of the god Neptune. Like the Dioscuri, they excelled in the martial arts
and in athletics. Lynceus was even endowed with such good sight that he could
see in the dark, while Idas succeeded in taking the beautiful Marpessa away
from Apollo in a horse race; he subsequently married her. The twins were also
involved in the hunt for the Caledonian boar and the expedition of the

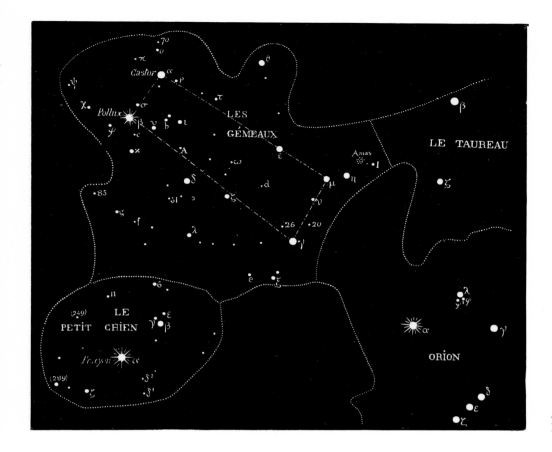

Region of Gemini. From Flammarion,
Les Etoiles

Argonauts. The relationship between the two sets of twins was friendly until the priestesses Phoebe and Hilaeira were betrothed to Idas and Lynceus. Castor and Pollux, who were also in love with the two women, captured and married them. This gave rise to an intense rivalry between the twins, which seemed to end with Aphareus' death.

To seal their newly regained friendship they decided to go on a cattle raid together. The undertaking was a success, and when they had to divide the booty they agreed that each of the four would receive an equal portion of the meat to eat. They then determined that the right to choose the most valuable animals would go to the one who finished eating his portion first. The others would then take their turn in choosing according to the order in which they finished eating their parts.

Idas finished first and helped Lynceus to finish his part. Without waiting for the others, they then took the entire herd and left. Castor and Pollux, feeling cheated, decided to go and take the animals back. They found them grazing in a clearing. While Idas and Lynceus were making a sacrifice to Neptune on a hill, Castor and Pollux captured the animals and then hid inside a hollow oak to wait for their rivals. With his extremely sharp eyesight, however, Lynceus had seen everything and Idas came running down and hurled his javelin against the tree. It penetrated the wood and Castor was killed instantly. Pollux' revenge came at once: beside himself with rage, he hurled himself against the two brothers and succeeded in killing Lynceus, while Zeus, who came to his aid with an arrow, struck Idas. Prostrate with grief, Pollux begged his father to let him die since his brother could not share his immortality. Touched by this attachment, Zeus offered to have his brother leave the realm of the dead and take his place on alternate days. Pollux accepted and, to reward their brotherly love, Zeus placed their image among the stars as the constellation of Gemini.

Symbole des productions naissantes.

The Astrology of Gemini

Astrologers believe this sign to preside over the arms, hands, fingers, shoulders, lungs, thymus, upper ribs, collarbone, humerus, bronchial tubes, nervous system, speech organs, windpipe, spine, and ulna. The sign is ruled by Mercury; its color is orange, its animal the magpie.

Those born under Gemini have as character traits intense devotion, genius, open-mindedness, kindness, and generosity. If the normal advancing of the stars due to the precession of the equinoxes had been respected, those who were born between May 21 and June 21 would actually have been born under the stars of Taurus. However, no modern astrological school seems able to accomplish the change with all the implications it would require.

According to Ptolemy the star Castor, which is Alpha Geminorum in today's catalogues, was of the nature of Mercury. Under his influence, it favored intelligence, success in legal and editorial matters, many voyages, love of horses, and sudden success, often followed, however, by misfortune, disgrace, and illness. If present at the time of birth, it bestowed a spiteful character with a tendency toward violence.

Pollux, which is Beta Geminorum, is one of the lunar stars used in navigation. Ptolemy assigned it to Mars who imparted an elusive, able, audacious, cruel character with a fondness for fighting and a tendency to gossip.

The Egyptians identified in these two stars the very ancient solar god Horus, whose eyes were considered the sun and the moon. In the texts of the pyramids there are narrations of the cosmic battle between Horus and Set during which Set succeeded in ripping out one of his opponent's eyes. Horus succeeded in finding it again and, having purified it, he called it *Udiat*, or He Who Is in Good Health. This symbol, often used in various cults, has been translated into that of the eye of God enclosed in a triangle. The Eskimos believed that these stars were the upright posts of an igloo. The Arabs called them, in addition to the Twins, the Two Peacocks.

In India they marked the fifth *nakshatra* of the lunar calendar, *Punarvarsu*, or the Two Good Ones, which was under the aegis of the goddess of the sky Aditi, or Infinity. She was the Great Mother, who had given birth to the twelve sun-gods, the Aditya, each of whom represented one month of the year. This myth probably originated in the fourth millennium B.C., when Gemini marked the spring equinox.

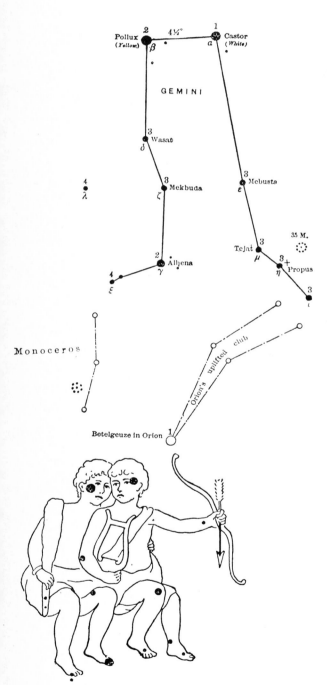

GEMINI

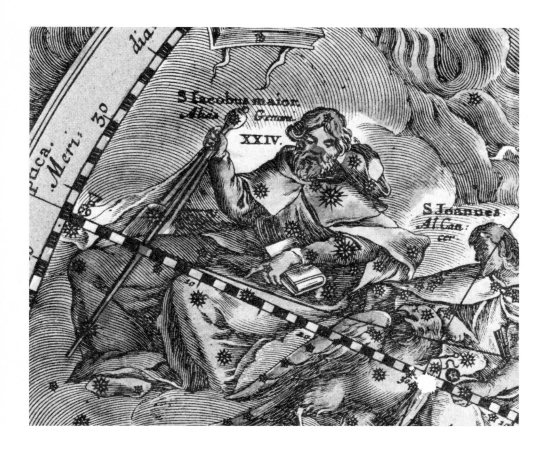

In the Christian version of the constellations,
Gemini was replaced by Saint James

Bayer's Gemini (1603)

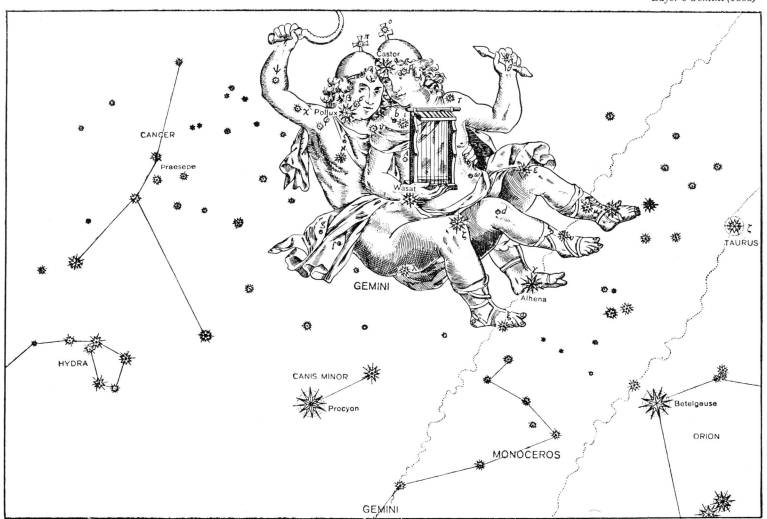

Cygnus

Vulpecula

Sagitt

Anser

Aquila

Lyra

Cerberus

Serpentarius

HERCVLES

Corona Borealis.

Serpens.

Fig. H.

28
Hercules

Hercules. From Hyginus, Poetica astronomica
(1485 edition)

Between Vega and Corona Borealis stretches the constellation of Hercules, whose kneeling figure seems to be upside-down when observed in the northern hemisphere. The lowest star marks the figure's head, which is near the head of Boötes; the horizontal line of stars somewhat higher up is the arm; the three stars near Vega form the bent leg; and the long curved line to the left is the outline of the other leg and the back. The constellation is clearly visible from May to October, when the sun seems to travel toward Hercules.

Despite the fact that these stars are called by the name of the most famous hero in Greek mythology, the constellation's past is wrapped in the darkest of mysteries. The first Greek astronomers named it Engonasi, or the One Who Kneels. As such it was recorded by Eudoxus, Aratus, Eratosthenes, Hipparchus, Ptolemy, and then by Manilius, al-Sufi, and Ulugh-Beg. It is certainly disconcerting to have so little information about a constellation that in 2700 B.C. was close to the Polar Star of the time, Thuban.

Manilius describes it with the following disparaging remark: "Close to the polar bear and the icy north there is a figure that leans on one knee and he himself is the only one who knows the reason for this position."

In the *Phaenomena* of 300 B.C. Aratus, who says this figure is a mystery, describes it as "a phantom turning round and round" with both arms raised and his right foot leaning on the head of the Dragon.

This acceptance without understanding or knowledge is another demonstration that the science of astronomy was created elsewhere and only imported by the Greeks. Over the centuries they succeeded in restructuring it with their mathematical and geometric contributions as well as enriching it with their great mythological fantasy. The stars of Hercules actually have an extremely ancient history which is not always well documented. The constellation's figure, which today appears to be completely upside-down to us, was in the correct position in the fourth millennium B.C., when it culminated on the northern meridian at midnight during the spring equinox. At that time the North Pole was close to Thuban, as we have seen.

Opposite: *Hercules. From Hevelius,*
Uranographia totum coelum stellatum *(1690)*

Marduk

In Mesopotamia the stars of Hercules were identified with Marduk, the powerful Assyrian god who had supplanted the ancient cult of Bel, the god of the sky to whom the North Pole was dedicated. After the Assyrian conquest, Marduk became the most celebrated god of Babylonia and we find him depicted on numerous clay tablets and bas-reliefs, always performing his great cosmological feat: the duel with the celestial Dragon, the goddess Tiamat.

Tiamat, She Who Created Everything, the Chaos of the Sea, had mated with Apsu, the Cosmic Ocean, and from this union the sun, moon, gods, and all the creatures that populated the sky were born. This entire creation was, however, chaotic and senseless. Apsu was enraged with his son Anu because he was producing too many gods and he succeeded in persuading Tiamat to kill them. Frightened and unable to oppose the goddess, they asked Marduk for help. He offered to save them in exchange for their divine birthrights. Aided by the winds, smeared with red ocher as a defense against magic spells, and encircled by lightning, he then set off for the huge battle. While the winds blew in all directions so as to stop the allies of the goddess, Marduk hurled the wind Uraganus into Tiamat's mouth. It entered her stomach with such violence that it took her strength away. He then let fly an arrow which, speeded by the force of the wind, entered the goddess' throat and, penetrating her heart, killed her (Domenico Bassi, *Mitologia Babilonese-Assira*).

Marduk then began to arrange and order the primordial chaos. First he took the allies of Tiamat, the eleven star creatures, and set them out in the sky. In so doing he formed the first zodiac.

Next Marduk set out to remove the enormous mass of the body of Tiamat. He drew out the blood and "had the north wind carry it to hidden places." Perhaps the goddess' blood was the substance that the Sumerians called bitumen. It occurred naturally in their country, flowing out of the ground in certain places; it was nothing more than oil. The hero-god cut the great body into two parts; one part he suspended in the air—this became the sky—the other he put down under his feet to make the land. Thus the world was formed. Marduk built a wall around the land and made the heavenly vault out of a hard and shiny metal. He opened the two doors of the sky (east and west), and he regulated the entrance and exit of the sun, the moon, the planets, and the stars. He set up the year and divided it into twelve months by assigning to each three decades of days. At this point Marduk created man by pasting together, with clay, the blood and bones of the giant Qingu, ally of Tiamat, and to this new creature was given the task of serving the gods.

All ziggurats, the towers that functioned as temples and astronomical observatories, were dedicated to Bel-Marduk. The best-known ziggurat, Esagila, located in the city of Babylon, became famous as the Tower of Babel.

The Labors of Hercules

Avenio says that the first to assign Hercules to these stars was Panyassis (fifth century B.C.), uncle of the great historian Herodotus. He wrote fourteen books about the hero and had wanted to insert another Argonaut into the sky. Even if this were true, it certainly was not taken up by anyone else—as we have seen, all the Greek astronomers from Eudoxus to Ptolemy, as well as the Arab ones from al-Sufi to Ulugh-Beg, called this man of the stars Engonasi.

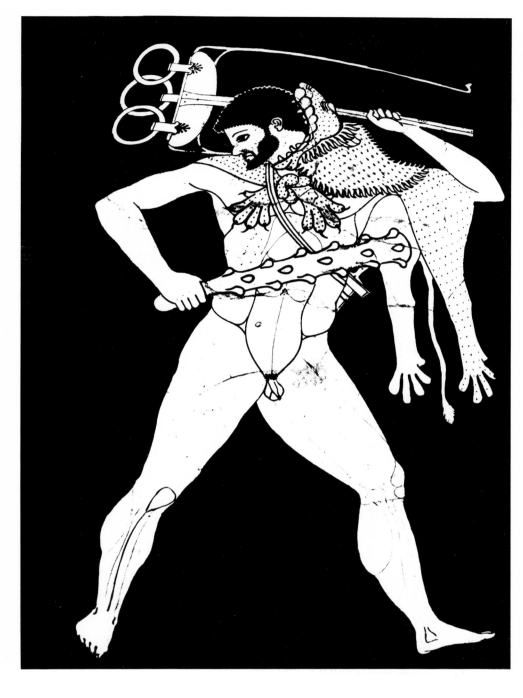

Hercules captures Apollo's tripod

The Farnese Atlas, the famous sculpture of the Titan who holds up the globe of the constellations that, without a doubt, is more than two thousand years old, represents these stars with the figure of a nude man in a kneeling position. It is not until 1485, when the Venetian edition of the astronomical fables of Hyginus was published, that we find the first depiction of Hercules with a club and a lion's skin, trying to slay a serpent that is wound in the biblical way around a tree. And this notwithstanding, the text still calls him Engonasi.

In 1603 the astronomer Johannes Bayer compiled a star atlas in which Hercules appears with club, lion's skin, and a branch full of apples in his hand. Finally, in 1690, Hevelius replaced the branch with the three heads of the dog Cerberus, who was the last victim in the labors of Hercules.

It would seem appropriate to consider how the astronomical character of the Greek hero might allow us to attribute to his twelve labors the task of representing the course of the sun through the signs of the zodiac. The concept is that Hercules, the Ruler of the Zodiac, slays the Nemean lion at the time of the

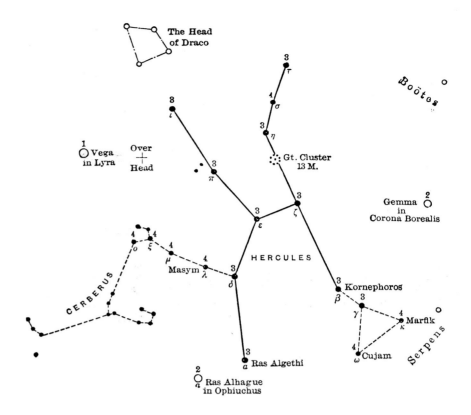

summer solstice in the sign of Leo. He then goes on to Virgo when the constellation of Hydra sets, and there kills the Lernean Hydra. In the third labor the sun enters into Libra (the ancient claws of Scorpius) and he captures the Ceryneian deer (?). In Scorpius he confronts the Erymanthian boar, but he has to battle the centaurs before he can reach it (the constellation of Centaurus is relatively close to Scorpius); however, there is no trace of a celestial boar. In the fifth labor, in Sagittarius, he cleans the stables of Augeias and, with a little imagination, we can connect the stables with the hybrid horse-man.

In Capricornus he does battle with the Stymphalian birds (?). In Aquarius he confronts the Cretan bull (?). In Pisces he captures the mares of Diomedes, perhaps because Pegasus is nearby. In Aries he wins Hippolyte's girdle (?). In Taurus he takes the cattle of Geryon, which does make sense. In Gemini he takes the golden apples from Atlas; this is more obscure. Finally, in the sign of Cancer, Hercules defeats Cerberus, the guardian of the world beyond the grave, perhaps because the constellation of Cancer was considered the gate of the souls that returned from the beyond to be reincarnated and, upon death, returned through the exit gate—Capricornus.

The placement of the northern constellations with respect to the legends of Hercules, Atlas, and the Garden of the Hesperides is interesting. As explained in that chapter, Boötes is a very strong candidate for the position of representative of Atlas. All we have to do is add the half-circle of Corona Borealis as the right arm and we obtain the classical image of the Titan holding up the celestial pole. A little higher up there is the constellation of Draco, or the dragon Ladon, who stands guard over the gardens where the tree of the golden apples grew. Apart from the incidental similarity to the biblical Eden and the tree of the forbidden fruit, the earthly reflection of this situation would be as follows: In western Africa where the sun sets, there lived the wise Atlas who knew the stars so well that he supported them all, allegorically, on his back. Having slain the dragon who guarded the tree, Hercules asked Atlas to do him

HERCULES

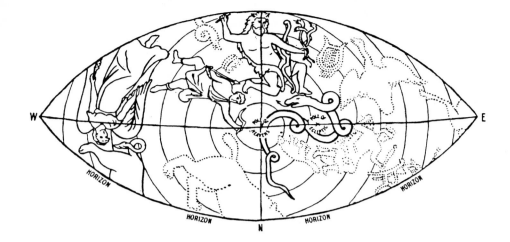

Position of the constellations with respect to the meridian of the autumn equinox in 4667 B.C.

the favor of picking the apples for him while he himself held up the sky. In this way Atlas' astronomical knowledge was transmitted to him.

The Shepherds of the Sky

Robert Graves theorizes that there may be a rational explanation for the myth of the golden apples. He states that the apples may have been beautiful sheep (*melon* means both sheep and apple) with such tawny fleece that they seemed to be made of gold. They were guarded by a shepherd, called Dragon, whose food was brought by the daughters of Hesperus, the Hesperides. Hercules carried off the sheep and killed the shepherd.

We must acknowledge that this could be the correct interpretation of the myth, if we compare it with the constellations created in antiquity by the nomadic shepherds of north Africa. They called this region of the sky that was so devoid of bright stars *Raudah*, the Pastures, complete with fences, sheep, and dogs.

Bayer's Hercules (1603)

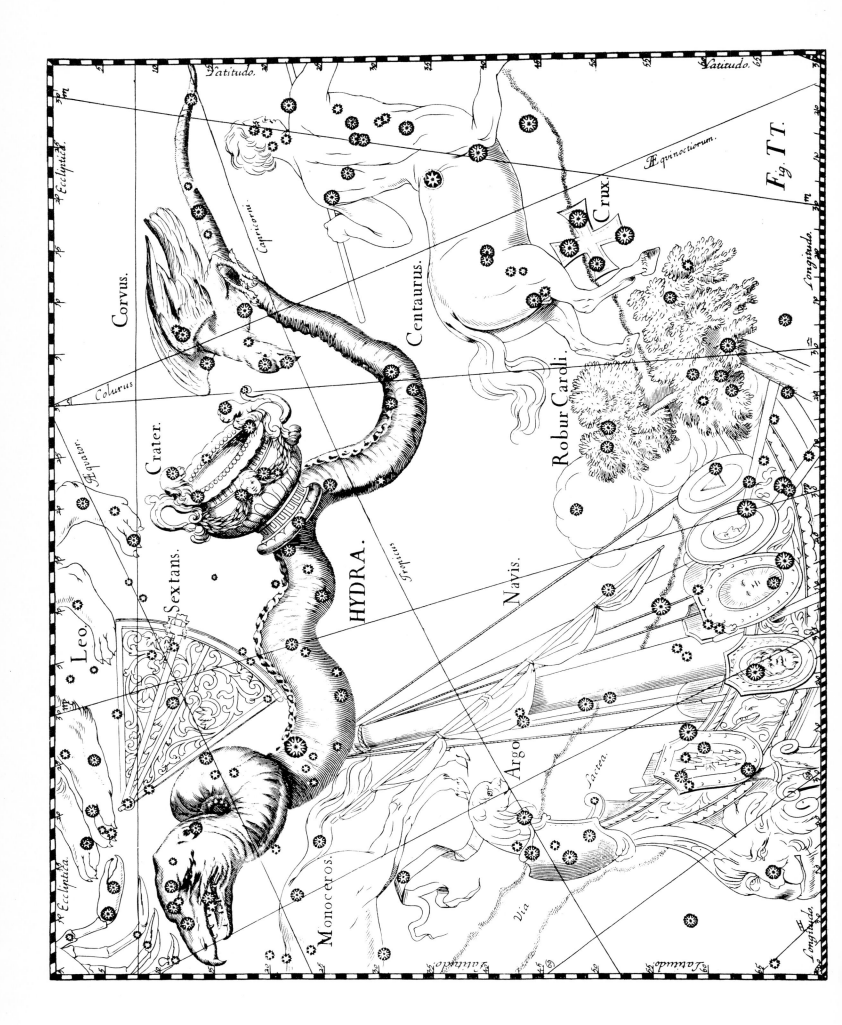

29
Hydra

This famous water snake is one of the most ancient constellations in the heavenly sphere. With respect to its length it can be compared to the river Eridanus and even to Draco. The constellation is characterized by a very long series of stars that stretches over as much as ninety-five degrees of arc and gives the impression of an enormous serpent upon which the constellations Corvus and Crater lean. Hydra is so long that to its north we can observe the zodiacal signs of Cancer, Leo, Virgo, and Libra.

There is a large region of the sky the ancient astronomers called the Sea, which contained many aquatic constellations. One of the boundaries of this region actually consists of the stars of Hydra.

Unfortunately, modern astronomers have done little to respect this beautiful heavenly sea. When they wanted to add new constellations to this area, instead of adding tritons, fish, submarines, or forms of that nature, they ruined everything by adding constellations such as the Furnace, the Sculptor, the Compressed Air Pump, and Horologium, the Clock. It is a pity.

As stated in the introductory chapter, we want to use a kind of golden rule in order to better understand the reasons for the arrangement of the constellations. This rule consists of backtracking to see how the stars appeared in the sky during time periods prior to our own from the regions around 40° N. It enables us to note how certain constellations that today appear to be designed haphazardly, obliquely, or even upside-down actually turn upright or follow the horizon faithfully as soon as they intersect with an equinox or a solstice. The serpentine figures in particular contain very important astronomical patterns. Draco, for example, contains in the center of the sky, in its spiral, the Polar Star and the center of the ecliptic. Another example is that of the Serpent in Ophiuchus' hands who diligently follows the celestial equator with its body, but raises itself the moment it touches the meridian of the autumnal equinox to follow it, until it finishes with its head actually on the star marking the zenith.

Similarly, in 4000 B.C., Hydra appeared to be centered in the sky at midnight on the winter solstice. Its entire length rested on the celestial equator, and it took seven out of twenty-four hours to pass the meridian.

Hydra. From Hyginus, Poetica astronomica *(1485 edition)*

Opposite: *Hydra. From Hevelius,* Uranographia totum coelum stellatum *(1690)*

The four cardinal points of the Egyptian Hydra

Position of Hydra in relation to the celestial
equator and the meridian of the summer
solstice in 2700 B.C. From Maunder, Astronomy
of the Bible
Below: Position of the solar disk at midday on
the meridian of the summer solstice in
4000 B.C. The body of Hydra precisely follows
the celestial equator

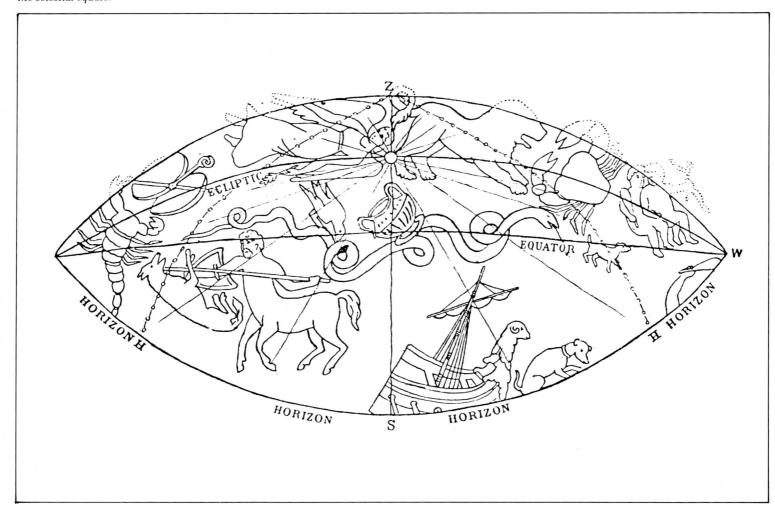

Indra and Vritra

This astronomical fact can be traced in the Sanskrit poems of the *Rig-Veda*. Herein the Indian bards tell the allegorical epic of the sun god Indra, who is overcome by the heavenly monster Vritra (the constellation of Hydra) at the winter solstice when, in fact, the sun is at its annual minimum and the stars of Hydra rule during the night. Slowly, however, as he approaches the summer solstice, Indra is aided by Aquila, who brings him several goblets of soma (that is, the moon; see the chapter on Crater) to drink. Thus, the sun-Indra succeeds in conquering the monster Vritra, thereby making him completely invisible at the moment of his own maximum splendor—the summer solstice, which, in India, corresponds to the arrival of the monsoons. For this reason Indra was considered master of rains and lightning, just as Zeus was. It must be added that when this myth was conceived the full moon of the summer solstice fell in the constellation of Aquarius, another indication of the beginning of the rainy season.

Also in Sumerian astronomical mythology, the sun-god Marduk defeated the dragon-goddess Tiamat, who was mistress of the dark primordial chaos, and created the sky with half of her body; he then reorganized the sky by placing Hydra on the celestial horizon with her center in the summer solstice so that the sun could reconquer her every year, thus perpetuating the eternal battle between the forces of light and darkness (see the chapter on Hercules).

Ancient Sumerian star map, clearly showing the equatorial function of Hydra

Indra on the white elephant Airvata, with his attendants, the Maruts. From Morretta, Miti Indiani *(1982)*

In a Babylonian inscription of 1200 B.C. Hydra was also identified with all the springs that originated in the depths of the earth.

In antiquity the constellation of Draco represented the oblique course of the stars while Hydra symbolized the path of the moon (Allen, *Star Names*).

Along the body of Hydra, the Chinese represented as many as three *sieu*, or lunar nodes: the seventh, the eighth, and the ninth. The seventh, called *Lieu*, or Willow Wreath, was located on the head of Hydra and ruled the planets. It was worshiped at the summer solstice as the emblem of immortality and was also considered the dwelling of Saturn. The eighth was *Sing*, or Star, namely the star Alphard, which is the lucida of the constellation and the house of the sun. The ninth was *Chang*, or the Bow, house of the moon.

Alphard is the contraction of *al-Fard al-Shuja*, or the Solitary One of the Serpent. This star is also known as *Cor Hydrae*, or the Heart of the Hydra, a title created by the astronomer Tycho Brahe.

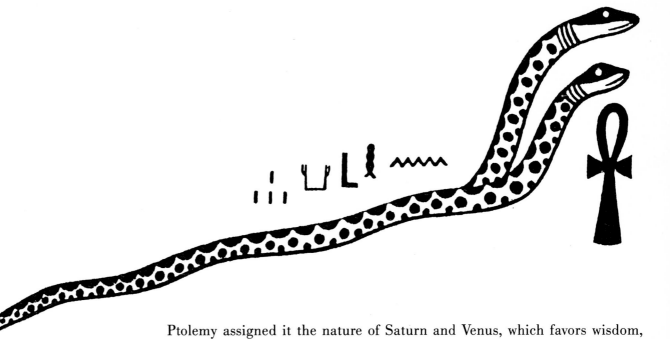

The Egyptian cosmic serpent

Ptolemy assigned it the nature of Saturn and Venus, which favors wisdom, artistic and musical expression, knowledge of human nature, and the capacity for strong passions. On the other hand, when negative, it favors dissoluteness, immorality, and the possibility of dying by asphyxiation, poisoning, or drowning. The astrology of this star is the same as that of the rest of the constellation.

Bayer's Hydra (1603)

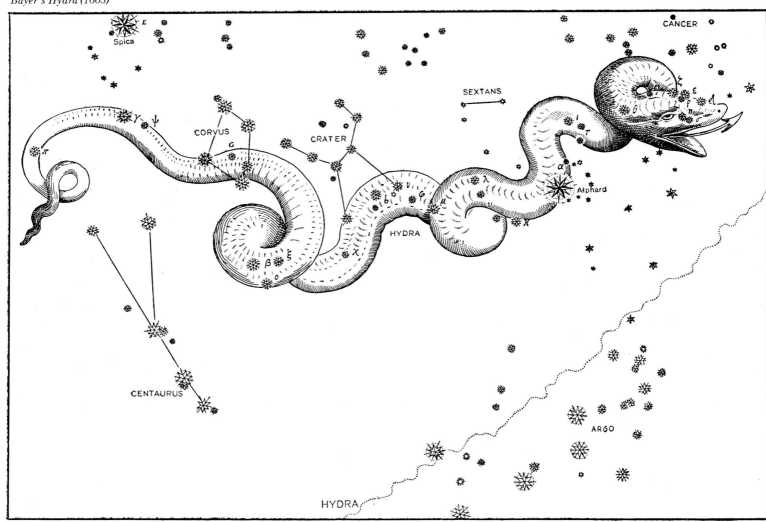

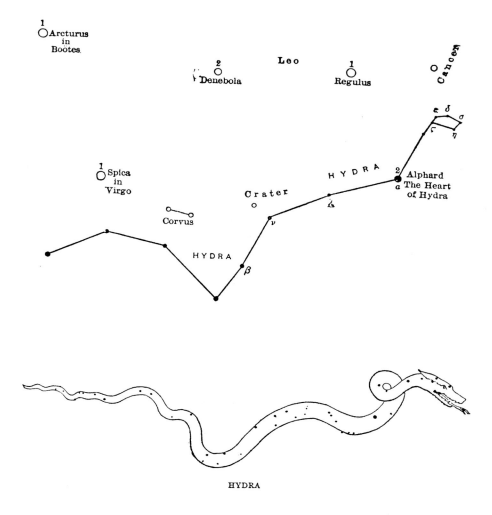

HYDRA

Springs and Marshes

The Greeks associated Hydra with the Lernean Hydra. On his search for his dead mother, Semele, Dionysus found her "in the region of the deep spring of Lerna where the mysteries of Demeter were also celebrated" (Kerenyi, *Die Mythologie der Griechen*).

It was Hercules who slew the Hydra with the many heads that grew back as soon as they were cut off. Many have seen in this labor of the hero an initiation symbol. Others have explained the exploit by affirming that the marshes of Lerna were infested by a great multitude of serpents who seemed to multiply with the same speed with which they were killed. This brings another labor of the hero to mind—the cleaning of the enormous stables of Augeias: he removed their accumulation of years' worth of manure by deviating a river through the stables. This could have cleared that region of snakes as well.

Yet another myth was told that involved Hydra, along with Corvus and Crater. Preparing to make a sacrifice to Zeus, Apollo gave a cup (Crater) to the Raven, who in those days was as white as a dove, and asked him to go get some pure water from a spring. Flying to a spring, the raven saw a fig tree whose fruit was almost ripe. He decided to perch on it and wait for the fruits to ripen so he could eat them. Afterward, fearing the wrath of the god, he caught an aquatic serpent (Hydra) to create an alibi for himself and, returning with it in his beak, he accused the snake of having been the cause of the delay. Guessing that it was a trick, Apollo changed the color of the Raven's feathers to black and then placed Hydra, Corvus, and Crater among the stars as a reminder and warning.

Summer solstice, 2700 B.C.

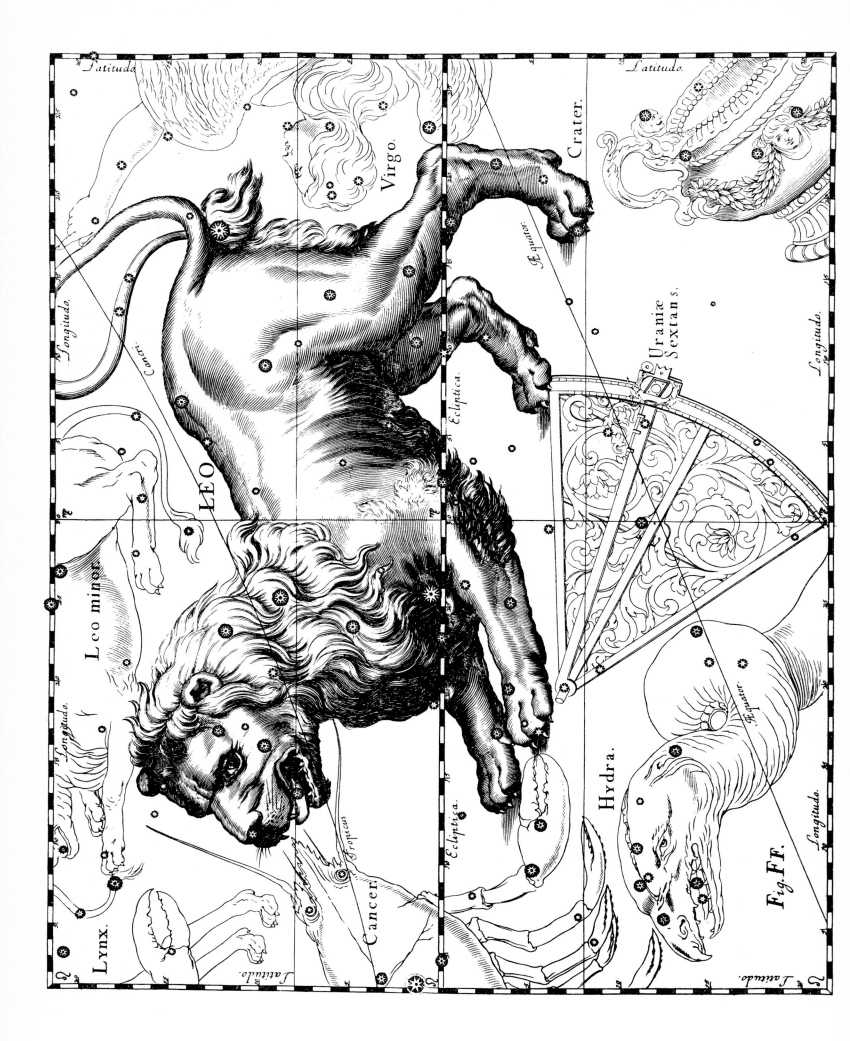

30
Leo

A straight line from the Polar Star through the pointers of Ursa Major, the stars Dubhe and Merak, brings us to the fifth constellation of the zodiac, Leo, the Lion. It can be identified by the famous sickle, formed by the stars of his mane, and by Regulus, his lucida.

Visible from December to June, Leo is one of the largest figures in the sky. In fact, it covers sixty degrees of longitude and thirty of latitude. Its main stars are of approximately second and third magnitude, and Regulus is a first-magnitude star. The polygonal figure traced by their position truly gives the impression of an animal of great strength who looks toward the west. Leo occupied a position of primary importance when the constellations were created in about 3000 B.C. because it marked the summer solstice, which symbolized the supreme victory of the light over the forces of darkness. Leo later lost this position to Cancer, but it was his from 4000 to 2000 B.C.

To escape the dry season, the lions of the desert came close to the valley of the Nile when the river flooded, which happened when the sun was in Leo; some have seen in this the origin of the name of the constellation. The head of a lion was always carved on the gates that opened the irrigation canals of the Nile Valley. This symbol was later perpetuated on fountains which carried representations of lions from whose mouths gushed jets of water, such as the ones that can still be seen today in Athens, Ephesus, Olympia, Agrigento, and many other Mediterranean cities. Also, the water clock, which was used in antiquity during public trials, had the shape of a lion and was called the Guard of the River. In ancient Egypt the solstice, the heliacal rising of Sirius, and the arrival of the lions from the desert coincided with the flooding of the river and marked the beginning of the new year. In the planisphere at Dendera, the constellation is represented by a lion standing on a serpent, which was intended as a symbol of the victory of light over the serpent of darkness. The situation in the sky and its stars is similar to the extent that the stars of Leo are actually above the constellation of the celestial serpent Hydra.

There are those who have seen in the Egyptian Sphinx the symbol of the zodiacal Leo and, certainly, this figure is quite ancient. The Sphinx of Giza dates back to the fourth dynasty, that is, to the period between 2600 and 2500 B.C. The Sphinx and its variant, which the Egyptians called Sirian (a lion with wings and the face of a woman), undoubtedly has a relationship with the sign of Leo. However, as we will see, the origin of the hybrid is more ancient.

At the beginning of the fourth millennium B.C. a special astronomical situation occurred: the solstices and the equinoxes were marked by four stars of the first magnitude. This remained so during the next two thousand years. To the eyes of the astronomers of the time this could only appear to be a divine plan. The spring equinox in Taurus was marked by the star Aldebaran, the summer solstice in Leo by Regulus, the fall equinox in Scorpius by Antares, and the winter solstice in Aquarius by Fomalhaut. These stars have passed into history under the name of the Royal Stars. It so happened, however, that for the

Leo. From Hyginus, Poetica astronomica *(1485 edition)*

Opposite: *Leo. From Hevelius,* Uranographia totum coelum stellatum *(1690)*

361

The Egyptian guardian lions of the solar disk.
From Myth and Symbol in Ancient Egypt

people who lived above a certain latitude, Fomalhaut was hard to see because it was too low on the horizon, and therefore preference was given to the nearby Altair in Aquila. Thus it was that in Mesopotamia the griffin was formed, the astronomical hybrid with the hind legs and wings of an eagle, the body and horns of a bull, the head and forelegs of a lion, and the tail of a scorpion with a poisonous stinger at the tip. This figure was the prototype of the sphinxes and the chimeras, composite figures whose meaning was both astronomical and calendrical and which were used throughout most of the Middle East and the Mediterranean.

Leo appears in all of the cultures and calendars while the other figures occur irregularly. In the three-season year the trio of animals later united in the Chimera were either the Lion, Goat, and Serpent or the Bull, Lion, and Serpent, who corresponded to the seasonal metamorphoses of Dionysus. In some cases they were Lion, Horse, and Dog, like the three heads of Hecate. At Thebes the goddess Sphinx ruled over a year of two seasons, while in the Greek year of four seasons we have Bull, Lion, Scorpion, and Marine Serpent (Graves, *The Greek Myths*).

*The lion of Echternach (*A.D. *690)*

A variant of the Royal Stars appeared in the vision that Ezekiel had "in the land of the Chaldeans." The image that appeared to him had four faces: those of a Man, a Lion, an Eagle, and a Bull. They appeared on a "wheel with four faces" and "above the heads of the animals there was the figure of the Firmament" (Ezekiel 1:1–28). John had a similar vision in the Apocalypse: to him appeared "four beasts full of eyes before and behind. And the first beast was like a lion, and the second beast like a calf, and the third beast had a face as man, and the fourth beast was like a flying eagle" (Revelation 4:6–7). These four figures later became the four evangelists: Matthew, the Man; Mark, the Lion; Luke, the Bull; and John, the Eagle.

The lion became the symbol of absolute sovereignty as well as the male solar hero, like Gilgamesh (see the chapter on Orion), who was represented with a club in one hand and a young lion in the other, just like his Greek equivalent, Hercules, a native of Thebes, where the Sphinx was worshiped. It was, in fact, in conquering the Nemean lion that the hero completed the first of his twelve labors. This lion was the son of the two-headed dog Orthrus and Echidne. Its sisters were the Chimera, the Sphinx, and the Hydra. Orthrus was actually the constellation of the Dog. He had two heads because the revised year of Athens had two seasons (Graves, *The Greek Myths*).

Others say that at Hera's request Selene (the moon) created the lion from sea foam and that Iris used her belt as a leash to guide him to her cave on the Nemean Mountains, from which he took his name. It was in this cave that the terrible duel between Hercules and the beast took place. It ended with a victory for the hero under circumstances that were similar to Theseus' victory over the Minotaur. From then on Hercules wore the lion's skin, which became his symbol.

Asad

Even before the introduction of Greek astronomy, the ancient Arabs had created a mythical constellation of which we have some knowledge. It was an enormous lion that began on one side with the stars of Gemini; it stretched over Cancer, today's Leo, and Virgo up to Libra; it reached the stars of Ursa Major to the north and those of Hydra to the south. It is without a doubt the largest star figure ever created. This hyperbolical constellation was given the name Asad, or the Lion, which later Arab astronomers changed to Leo, thus keeping the same name.

The sickle of stars with Regulus as the handle and the stars of the mane as the curved blade is quite well known. Doubtless it was a popular symbol for the farmers of the time when the solstice occurred in Leo and the time to cut the grain had arrived. In Mesopotamia it was called *Gis-mes*, or the Curved Weapon. The people of Sogdania and Chorasmia called it *Khamshish*, or the Scimitar. Little known and irreparably lost, however, is a constellation that was located between Leo and Virgo. Calling it *Fahne*, or Flag, Ideler mentions it in the forty-seventh volume of his *Archaeologia*. It probably was the tail of Leo (now seen as curled over onto itself) standing straight up and ending in a cluster of stars. In the time of Ptolemy it was amputated in order to form the new constellation of Coma Berenices, as discussed in that chapter.

In the seventeenth-century book *Coelum stellatum christianum*, Julius Schiller replaced the zodiacal signs with the twelve apostles and, for a short time, Leo became Saint Thomas.

The king's battle with the heavenly griffin, a hybrid composed of a bull, lion, scorpion, and eagle. Persepolis. From Histoire de l'art dans l'antiquité

Leo. From Proctor, Easy Star Lesson (1883)

Indra

There are 250 hymns in the *Rig-Veda* that are dedicated to the solar god Indra—more than to any other deity in the Indian pantheon. Indra was the king of rains, lightning, and the solstice. As happened in Egypt with the solstitial flooding of the Nile, so too in India, the dry period ended with the entrance of the sun in Leo when the monsoons arrived that brought rain and the rebirth of plant life. As the personification of the summer solstice, Indra was described as "he who placed the sun so high in the sky." "Indra stopped the course of the sun" is a reference to the apparent slowing of the sun at the time of the solstice. In the chapter on Hydra there is an explanation of the conflict between Indra (the sun) and the serpent Vritra (Hydra). This duel was the astronomical representation of the eternal conflict between light and darkness, with the final victory of Indra occurring at the summer solstice.

Leo with the moon and stars, Mercury, Mars, and Jupiter

The Lunar Zodiac

Three *nakshatras*, Indian lunar stations, were located in Leo. The first is *Magha*, the Great, which is a star cluster of the Shudra caste that contains the star Regulus and has a house as its symbol. The second is *Purva Phalguni*, the First Evil One, which was represented by a Bed or Stretcher; it belonged to the Brahmin caste and had as its rulers the Aditias, namely Ariman and Baga. The third is *Uttara Phalguni*, the Other Evil One, which had the same symbol and the same rulers as the previous one but belonged to the caste of the Kshattrija.

The Arabs also had three stations, *manzils*, among these stars: *al-Jabhah*, or the Front (of the Lion); *al-Zubrah*, or the Mane; and *al-Sarfah*, or He Who Varies (the Weather).

The Chinese did not have any lunar station, or *sieu*, in Leo. They preferred to place the houses of the moon in the constellation of Hydra. In the place of Leo they had the constellation of the Horse, previously the Red Bird. In the sixteenth century they officially introduced Leo under the name of *Sze-Tsze*.

Opposite: *Leo. From Cellarius,* Harmonica macrocosmica *(1660)*

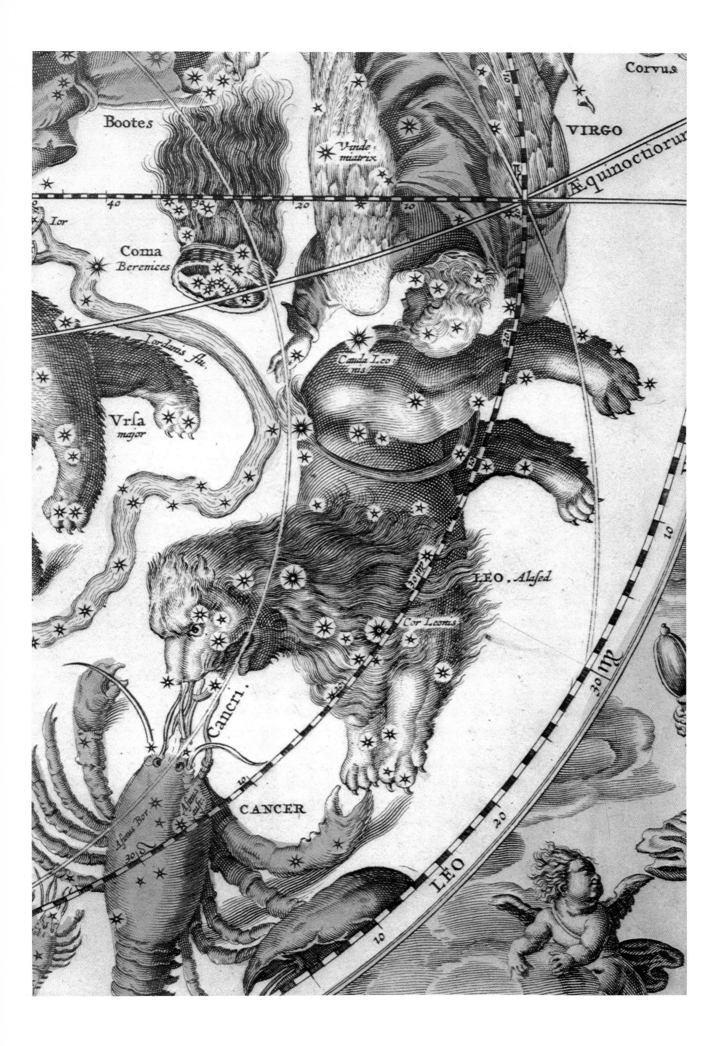

Bootes

Corvus

VIRGO

Æquinoctiorur

Vinde matrix

Coma Beremices

Ior

Iordanis flu.

Vrſa major

Cauda Leonis

LEO. Alaſed

Cor Leonis

Cancri.

CANCER

LEO

Leo 365

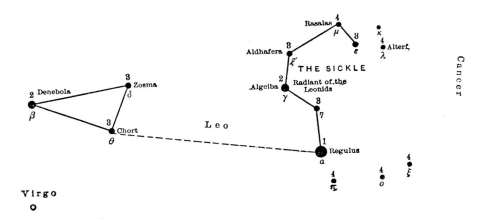

The Astrology of Leo

LEO

At one time it was believed that the sun was in Leo and the moon in Cancer at the moment of creation. The House of the Sun, also known as the House of the Lions, was the undisputed seat of the king and the nation in general.

Before astrology was popularized and applied to private individuals, it was conceived of as a science for the state. It involved the study of the behavior of the gods as represented by the planets that moved in the twelve houses of the zodiac. Furthermore, unlike today, the fixed stars were seen in terms of their relationship to the ecliptic. These stars were deemed very important for the calculation of the horoscopes that were originally done for the nation and the individual who represented the nation, the king. The Chaldeans introduced astrology into the Mediterranean—until then the dominion of the sibyls—during the second half of the first millennium B.C. A sign of fire, fixed and masculine, Leo presides over psychic strength, love, sexuality, magnetism, creativity, command, gambling, pleasure, and athleticism. It governs the heart, spinal column, nerves, bone marrow, circulation, spleen, and vital forces.

The sun-Leo was often depicted in its destructive sense—which is reflected in the vulnerability of some solar heroes: Gilgamesh is overwhelmed by leprosy, Hercules performs the twelve labors in order to cure himself from madness and subsequently dies from poison, and Orion becomes blind.

In antiquity doctors believed that medicines became poisonous when the sun was in Leo and also that taking a bath could be dangerous. The electrical storms of August would spoil milk and disturb the blood, and wine could not be poured from one receptacle into another during this entire period.

Ptolemy assigned different qualities to the stars of this constellation: "The two stars of the head are like Saturn and, partly, Mars. The three in the neck are like Saturn and, partly, Mercury. The ones on its flanks are like Saturn and Venus, and the ones in its thighs like Venus and, partly, Mercury."

It was said that the stars of the neck, back, and flanks would bring misfortune, problems, and illness relating to the parts of the body influenced by the sign, especially if the moon had been in conjunction with the sign. The beautiful lucida of the constellation, Regulus—from the Latin *regulus*, little king—which was called *Basiliscos* in Greece and *Cor Leonis* in the Middle Ages, belonged to Mars and Jupiter, according to Ptolemy.

Whoever was born under the influence of this star was magnanimous, liberal, ambitious, and independent. However, the star could also bring violence, short-lived success, failure, imprisonment, and violent death. The cabalists recognized in Leo the eleventh trump card of the tarots, Fortitude.

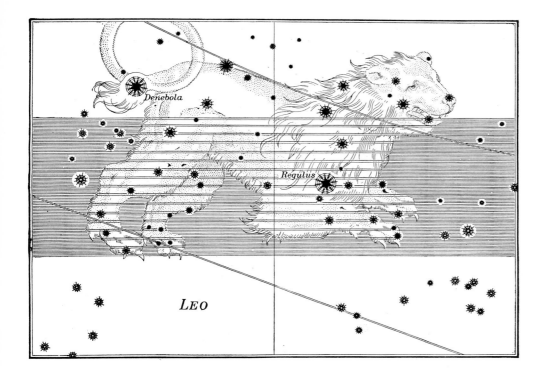

Bayer's Leo (1603)

Leo. From Petrus Apianus, Cosmographia *(1545)*

Leo 367

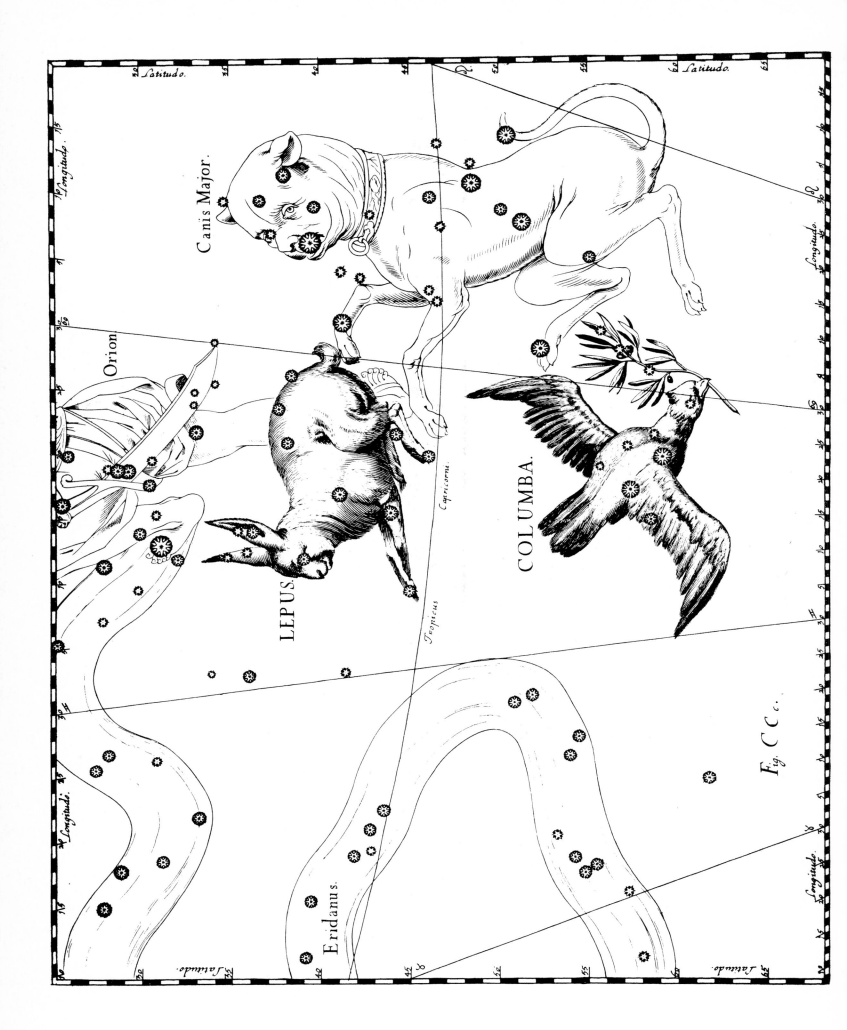

31
Lepus

Immediately underneath Orion there appears the modest constellation of Lepus, the Hare, with its head under the star Rigel and its back pressed under the right foot of the giant. Its four main stars, Alpha (Arneb), Beta (Nihal), Gamma, and Delta form a quadrilateral. They rise at almost the same time as Canis Minor and slightly earlier than Canis Major. The two Dogs, marked by the stars Procyon and Sirius, seem to pursue the Hare during the slow heliacal ascent of their stars. The chase lasts for the entire arch of the night until the Hare sets in the western horizon, the two dogs still in hot pursuit.

It is not unusual to find behavior marked by conflict among the figures depicted in the stars: Hercules is about to slay the Dragon with his club while he restrains its head with his foot, Orion is about to attack the celestial Bull, Ophiuchus attempts to subdue the contortions of the Serpent with his hands while one of his feet squashes the Scorpion, who in turn threatens him with his poisonous stinger, and so on.

The Greeks called this star figure *Lagos* and the Arabs called it *al-Arnab*, both of which mean Hare. However, al-Sufi, the astronomer of the ninth century, describes the four stars of the square as *al-Nihal*, or the Four Camels, who, parched with thirst, are about to drink from the river that flows out of the star Rigel—Eridanus. In the more ancient Egyptian tradition they represented a boat on which Osiris (Orion) made his star voyage. On more recent star maps, however, there is the figure of a serpent, also to be found on some Persian maps. In this case there would be four giants in the sky engaged in subduing serpents or dragons: Hercules, Perseus, Ophiuchus, and Orion.

The hare is a symbol that is widely used throughout the world for its association with the moon, and the moon is always associated with a female divinity, for example, Diana. The reason would be that the docility and shyness of this animal correspond to an aspect of traditional femininity that is similar to the light of the moon: in contrast to that of the sun, it is gentle, fresh, and beneficial to the sprouting of seeds (Herodotus stated that the hare is able to conceive while still pregnant).

The constellation of the Hare, therefore, symbolized the moon, and the sun was represented by the Eagle. These analogies are astronomically reflected in the fact that the stars of Lepus rise when those of Aquila set, just as in the case of the sun and the moon.

Lepus. From Hyginus, Poetica astronomica *(1485 edition)*

Opposite: *Lepus. From Hevelius,* Uranographia totum coelum stellatum *(1690)*

369

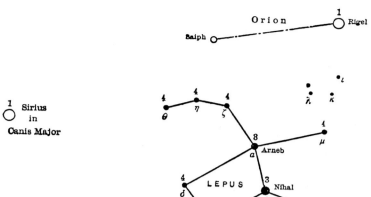

Orion

Saiph   Rigel
1

Sirius
in
Canis Major
1

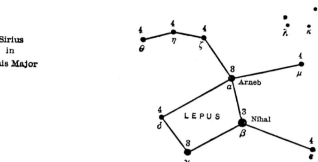

θ   η   ζ

Arneb
α   μ

λ   κ   ι

LEPUS

δ   3 Nihal
β

γ   ε

Eridanus

Columba
Phaet
β   α   ε

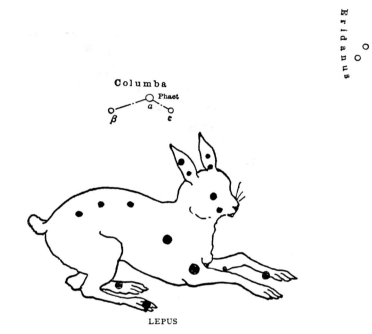

LEPUS

*In Egypt the stars of Lepus were identified
with the boat in which Osiris (Orion) traveled
across the sky. Here, the sacred boat is
supported by the four gods of the equinoxes
and the solstices*

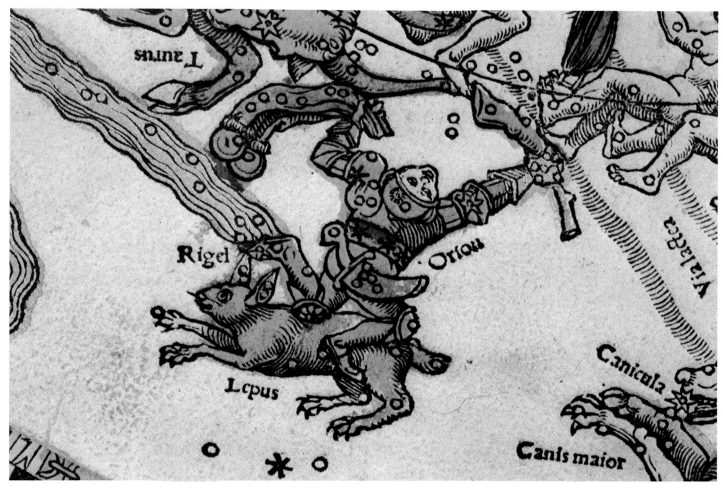

In his second astronomical fable Hyginus attributes the birth of this constellation to the inhabitants of the island Leros. They had imported a pregnant hare and started breeding these animals. Before long their land was totally infested by the pests who completely ruined the grain harvest. Faced with this disaster, the island dwellers organized a long and difficult hunt that ultimately did succeed in exterminating the animals. In memory of this event they placed the hare among the stars.

An interesting chronicle is the Indian legend about one of the first manifestations of Buddha. Before he became Gautama, meaning Illuminated, he incarnated himself as various beings and succeeded in accomplishing a holy act in each one of these forms. Under the name of Sakyamuni, he became incarnated as a hare. One day, while in the company of a monkey and a fox, he met the ruler of the firmament, the god Indra. Disguised as a beggar so as to put their hospitality to the test, the god asked for some food. The three at once set out in different directions in search of something to eat. The hare was the only one who returned with empty hands. Without hesitating he had a fire lit and then leapt into it, offering himself as a meal to the poor beggar. To reward him, Indra placed his image on the moon. This figure, visible when the moon is full, is recognized as a hare by almost all mythologies on earth.

The astronomer Ptolemy attributed to Lepus the astrological value of Saturn and Mercury. Similarly, Manilius identifies those born under this influence with the metal mercury.

The sun-god with the Morning Star and the moon with the Hare

Lepus 371

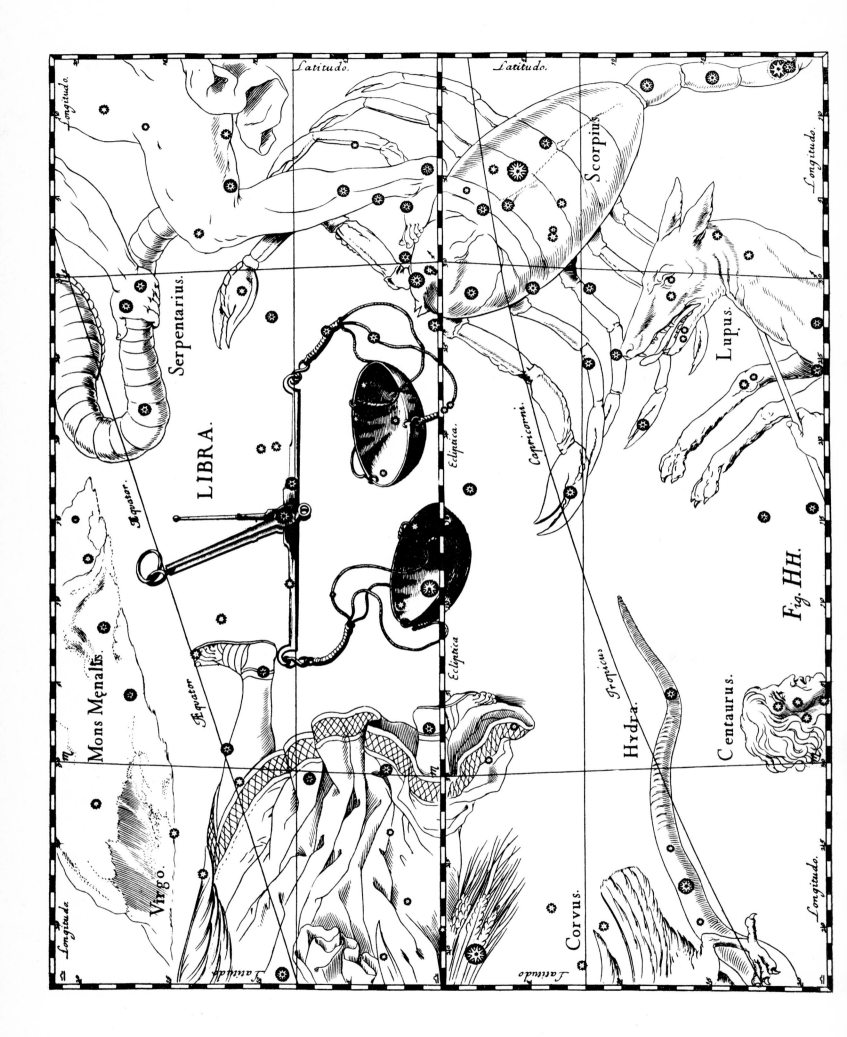

32
Libra

At Virgo's feet, next to threatening Scorpius, we find the seventh sign of the zodiac, Libra, the Scales, marked by two stars of similar magnitude. The first, slightly brighter one is Alpha Librae and carries the name Zubenelgenubi, from the Arabic *al-Zuban al-Janubiyyah,* meaning the Southern Claw. The second, Beta Librae, is instead called Zubenschamali, from *al-Zuban al-Shamaliyyah,* the Northern Claw.

The Arabic names of these two main stars are the literal translation of the Ptolemaic Greek names. This derivation means that, until the time of Ptolemy, this sign was not represented by the two plates of a scale, but by the claws of the adjacent Scorpius. In fact, Scorpius was originally a much larger stellar figure and it contained two zodiacal signs: the Body, with the poisonous stinger, and the Claws.

The first appearance of Libra in the classical era is in the Julian calendar, which was devised in 46 B.C. by Julius Caesar as Pontifex Maximus with the help of Flavius, the Roman scribe, and Sosigenes, the Alexandrian astronomer.

Actually, the symbol ♎ and the model for Caesar's calendar had already been created in Alexandria by Greek astronomers and only later on were popularized by Caesar Augustus.

Our knowledge of this is based on the studies of Lepsius, who, in 1866, discovered, in Sanor Tanis, the "Decree of Canopus," written in 238 B.C. under Ptolemy Euergetes, where the same intercalation methods were used as in the Julian calendar.

Notwithstanding the widespread opinion that the twin stars of the sign were the symbol of the equinox—the moment of the year in which there are the same number of hours in the day as in the night—Alpha and Beta Librae have not always been identical.

We know from the *Catasterismi* of Eratosthenes that, at that time, Zubenschamali was the brightest star of the great Scorpius, "the most brilliant of all [the stars]," superior even to Antares. Three hundred and fifty years after this observation Ptolemy assigned the same magnitude to Zubenschamali and Antares. What happened in subsequent centuries has been easily analyzed on the basis of Arab and Renaissance observation. From these records it becomes obvious that the luminosity of Beta Librae has lessened to its present state, while that of Antares has grown substantially (see the table on the changes in magnitude of Antares included in the chapter on Scorpius).

Between the Claws shone the brightest star of the sign, then called Lamp, Light, Censer, or Solar Lamp. In Mesopotamia it was associated with the seventh month, *Tashritu,* and with the seventh sign, *Tul Ku,* which marked the biblical tower of Babel, where the sacrificial fire burned.

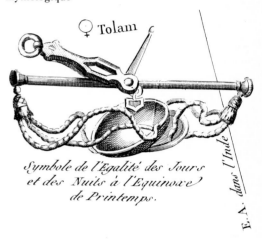

Libra. From Zodiaque chronologique et mythologique

Opposite: *Libra. From Hevelius,* Uranographia totum coelum stellatum *(1690)*

373

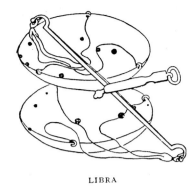

LIBRA

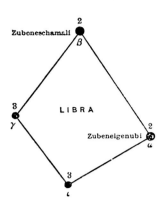

The Astrology of Libra

"Those stars on the tips of the claws of Scorpius operate like Jupiter and Mercury; those in between the Claws, like Saturn and a little like Mars." Thus Ptolemy analyzed these stars when they still belonged to the claws of Scorpius. Later they were amputated and the Scales appeared in the Mediterranean, with the name Libra, as the seventh sign of the zodiac, the "circle of animals." Libra is the only inanimate sign. Its promoter, Julius Caesar, even had himself represented on some coins with a scale in his hand as dispenser of justice.

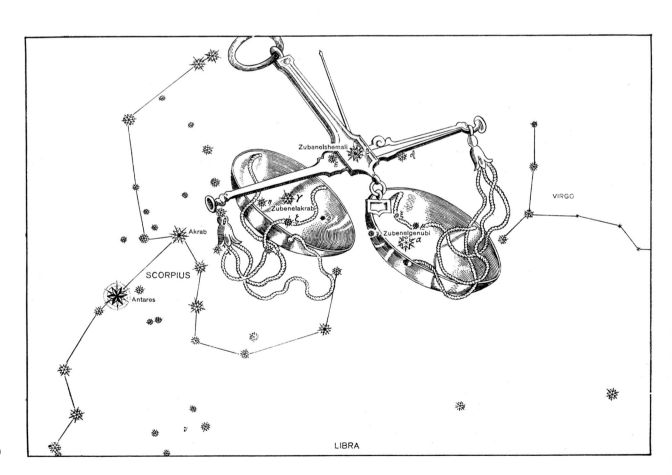

Bayer's Libra (1603)

A sign of air, a cardinal point, and masculine, Libra was governed by Venus, the goddess of love, who originally shared it with Vulcan, her spouse. Its influence on the human body was directed toward the kidneys, the suprarenal and lumbar glands, the vasomotor system, the adrenaline, the skin, the distillation of urine, the external genital organs, the lumbar nerves, and the buttocks.

The cabalists assigned to it the eighth trump card of the tarots, Justice. In the Christian zodiac it was for a short period replaced by the apostle Philip.

In Libra, only one lunar station was celebrated, called *al-Jubana* by the Arabs, *Visakha* by the Indians (both words refer to the Claws), and *Ti*, the Bottom, by the Chinese.

Painting on the inside of an Egyptian sarcophagus cover. Nut, goddess of the sky and the stars, is in the center, and the sign of Libra, at left, is portrayed on a column with the solar disk Aton

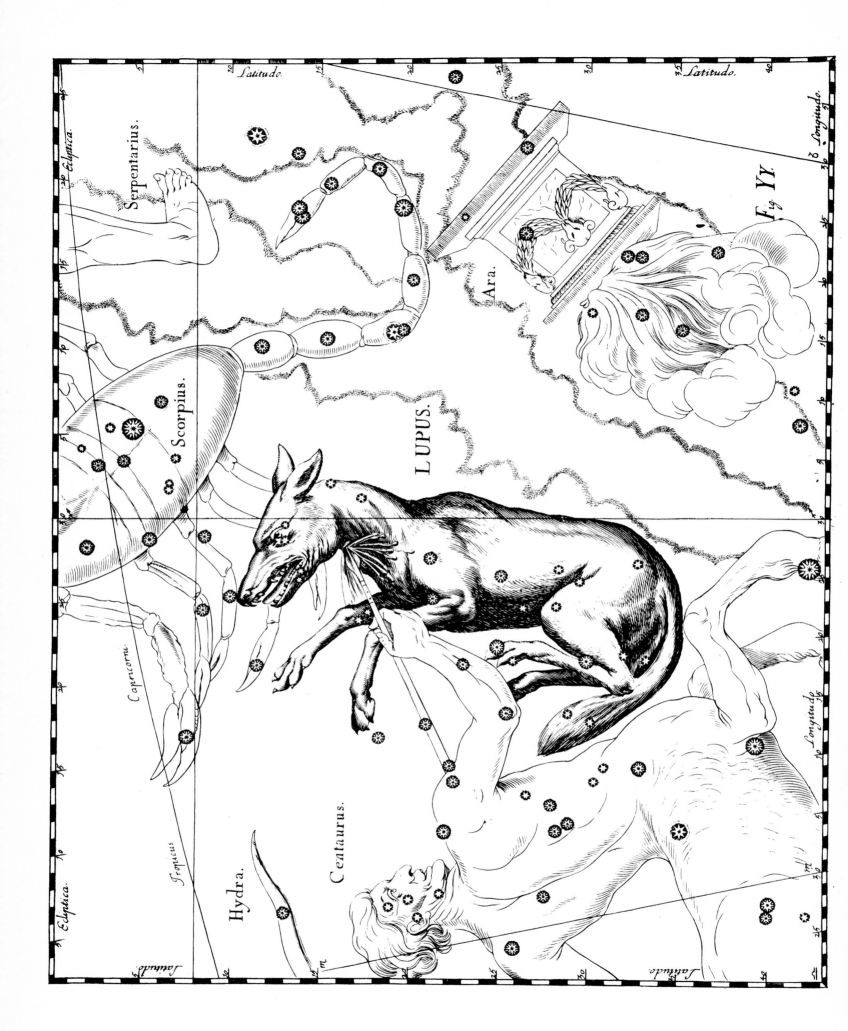

33
Lupus

Despite its antiquity Lupus, the Wolf, is not a conspicuous constellation. It is partly immersed in the Milky Way, below Libra and Scorpius, and to the east of Centaurus, whose disposition toward Lupus is apparently hostile. As we discuss in that chapter, however, Centaurus does not kill Lupus with a lance (as is shown on maps starting at the time of the Renaissance). Instead, he is holding the magical thyrsus in his hands, and he and Lupus (goddess of the moon, represented by a she-wolf) perform an erotic rite together.

In pre-Olympic Arcadia, the mythical wolf-king Lycaon (*lycos* meaning wolf) was worshiped; he was the allegorical father of fifty wolf sons (fifty lunations composed the year, subsequently called the Olympic year).

Their cult required human sacrifices, cannibalism, and the trancelike symbiosis of the wolf-priests with the Divine She-Wolf, or lunar goddess, through the practice of the werewolf cult on nights with a full moon (Graves, *White Goddess*). In order to be worshiped in Arcadia, Zeus had to submit to the ancient cult using the name of Zeus Lynceus (Zeus of the She-Wolf). Also, Apollo transformed himself into a wolf so that he could become united with the lunar goddess Cyrene. The cult of the she-wolf was very important to the Romans, who were descendants of Romulus and Remus—sons of the she-wolf. This was the subject of the important annual celebrations called the Lupercalia.

Comparing these stars with the Serpent of Ophiuchus, Aratus describes them in the *Phaenomena* as follows: "Another creature that is kept well-restrained . . . the animal that Centaurus holds back with his right hand."

Above and left: *Greek wolf-men. Illustrations by Holmes Grimes in* Gods of the Cataclysm

Opposite: *Lupus. From Hevelius,* Uranographia totum coelum stellatum *(1690)*

34
Lyra

In the spring, during the beautiful, mild evenings that make us want to go out at night to observe the stars, a splendid blue star shines brightly to the east (May–June). It rises and stays enthroned on the zenith (July–August) and then, descending toward the west (September–October), it shines near the western horizon (November–December). At last it lightly touches the northern region from January to April only then to rise back again toward the east and retrace the same route.

This star, one of the brightest in our sky (along with Arcturus and Sirius), is Vega—the lucida of the constellation Lyra, the Lyre. Situated among the constellations of Hercules, Cygnus, Aquila, and Draco, Vega is located along the imaginary circle that the terrestrial axis describes in the sky during the course of 25,000 years, in accordance with the law of the precession of the equinoxes. On this circle the various Polar Stars succeed each other. While today we have Polaris in Ursa Minor, three thousand years ago it was Thuban in Draco, and twelve thousand years ago the fixed center of the sky and its stars was actually Vega. The spectacle of such a bright Polar Star, surrounded by Aquila with its star Altair and Cygnus with its star Deneb, must have been quite a sight to behold at the time when the sun entered the spring equinox in the sign of Virgo.

The lyre was the mythical instrument that was invented by the infant Mercury. He used the shell of a turtle over which he stretched strings made from the intestines of a cow. This lyre as well as a pipe were later given to Apollo in exchange for the golden thyrsus, a thin staff with which Mercury separated two serpents engaged in a mortal duel. From that moment on they became a part of the staff as the symbol of peace; this is how the caduceus was created (Hyginus, *Poetica astronomica*).

The musical origin of the constellation is very ancient. Originally it was known as *Chitara* or *Kitara*, meaning Turtle, from the sound box of the instrument, which is the root from which both the words guitar and zither are derived. It is also called Little Turtle in Aratus' astronomical poem, and this name is also the source of various later versions such as Testudo, Galapagus, Belua Aquatica, and Testa.

In Persia the poet Sciams Ud-Din Muhammad praised in these stars the lyre of Zurah, while other Persian writers called the instrument *Sanj Rumi*. This name was transformed by the Arabs into *al-Sanj,* from which various names of the European Middle Ages, such as Asange, Asanges, Asangue, and Sangue, are derived. According to Assemani, on the other hand, it was derived from *Azzango,* or the Cymbal (Allen, *Star Names*). In Bohemia Lyra was *Hanslicky na Nebi,* or the Violin of the Sky. The Teutonic and Anglo-Saxon peoples called it, respectively, Harapha and Hearpe. The sixth-century bishop-poet Fortunatus of Poitiers used this title to coin the name *Arpa Barbara.*

The exchange of gifts between Apollo and Mercury is evidence of a historic event that Robert Graves has appropriately interpreted as the arrival of the

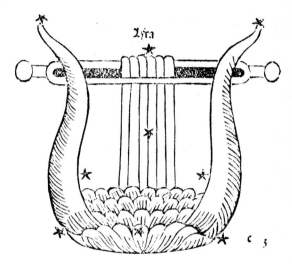

Lyra. From Hyginus, Poetica astronomica *(1485 edition)*

Opposite: *Lyra. From Hevelius,* Uranographia totum coelum stellatum *(1690)*

379

From the title page of Johannes Bayer's Uranometria *(1603)*

Hellenes and their god Apollo in a Greece where civilization was flowering and the people were already familiar with weights, measures, music, the cultivation of olives, and astronomy; in addition, the amazing Hermes-Mercury had succeeded in both deceiving the new conqueror-god with his tricks and surprising him with his clever inventions (Graves, *The Greek Myths*). Having obtained the lyre, Apollo gave it to Orpheus, son of the Thracian king Oeagrus and the Muse of poetry, Calliope.

Orpheus was taught music by the Muses themselves and he became such an expert at playing the instrument and so persuasive with his song that wild animals became tame and even trees and rocks moved in order to be able to listen in enchantment to his music. In short he seems to have been a kind of preliterate Saint Francis, an inspiring force for the movement of Orphism. Orphism was a philosophy inclined toward rejecting the city and repositioning man at the center of creation, which was seen as mysterious and wild, the natural dwelling of gods and men. In this respect Orphism comes very close to the Dionysian cult. In fact, some see the same principle as the inspiration for both movements and assume Orpheus to be the alter ego of Dionysus. One exponent of this view was Apollodorus, who even designated Orpheus as the one who instituted the Dionysian rites.

According to Diodorus Sĭculus, Orpheus used the ancient alphabet of thirteen consonants, and the legend of both the taming of wild animals and the trees that moved was actually a reference to the seasonal changes affecting the trees and animals. As we will see further on, the entire legend of Orpheus is full of astronomical symbolism.

The first Greek alphabet was a secret that was jealously guarded by the priestesses of the moon. Its letters were not written signs, but twigs of different trees that symbolized the different months of the year. In *The Greek Myths* Robert Graves has reconstructed its sequence and compared it to the ancient Irish alphabet of Phrysian origin.

The Sun and the Nightingale

According to legend Orpheus traveled to Egypt, where he was initiated into the monotheistic cult of Akhenaton, which held the sun as father of all things. This is why all the Orphic priests in the Greek world wore Egyptian costume.

We also find Orpheus among the Argonauts, who set out to conquer the Golden Fleece, which, as explained in the chapters on Aries and Argo Navis, was the allegory of the sun shifting the spring equinox from the constellation of Taurus to that of Aries.

The most famous of Orpheus' undertakings was that of descending into the world of the dead in order to convince Persephone to return Eurydice to him. Eurydice was Orpheus' young wife, always pictured in a springtime meadow in the act of gathering flowers, like Eve in Eden or Europa before her abduction. In this flowering meadow appears Aristaeus, the divine beekeeper, who tries to rape her. As Eurydice tries to flee, a serpent bites her on the ankle and the young woman dies. Her companions, the dryads, priestess-nymphs of Thrace, come running in consternation and weep at her death. When Orpheus arrives, Eurydice's soul has already entered Persephone's realm. In desperation he begins his disconsolate song and, with his lyre in hand, he starts out on the dark path that leads to the realm of the dead. Here Cerberus is hypnotized by his song, Charon abandons his boat so he can listen to him, Ixion's wheel stops, Tityus' liver is no longer lacerated, Danaus' daughters do not carry water anymore, Sisyphus sits down on his stone, Tantalus forgets his thirst, and the judges of the dead weep. Persephone herself is moved and breaks the barrier between life and death, thus permitting Eurydice to ascend back into the world of the living—on the condition that Orpheus walk ahead of her without turning around. However, when the two young people reemerge into the light of day, Orpheus fails to control his curiosity and turns around. He is just in time to see Eurydice become as smoke in the air while the voice of fate thunders three times.

The myth of the goddess of the underworld who allows the souls of the dead to reappear every year during the flowering of the springtime meadow originates in the ancient myths of the Mediterranean. It was still celebrated in the classical calendars of the Greeks and the Romans, whose funeral rites, grouped around the *dies violae,* were the matrix onto which the Christian Easter celebrations were grafted (Ileana Chirassi, *Elementi di Culture Precereali*).

It is here that there is a natural analogy for the astronomical meaning of the eternal battle between the forces of light and darkness, represented by the sun-god Orpheus, and the goddess of dusk and dawn—impersonated by Eurydice and the serpent of the night.

It starts with the serpent who, with his bite, kills the light that disappears in the darkness of the night. Here in the depth of the woods, however, begins the song of the nightingale, the little bird that the Greek bestiary identifies with Orpheus. He intones an uninterrupted and sweet love song, always the inspirer and hypnotizer of the souls of poets and lovers. This song is so persuasive that the serpent and his priestess, the lunar goddess of Hades, give the light back (Eurydice-dawn, who is born again with the sun in the new day). However, as soon as the sun gathers strength, its shining rays make the light of dawn disappear. Eurydice will return at the end of the day in her manifestation of Hesperus, the Dusk, and this cycle repeats itself day after day.

The specific detail of the promise demanded of Orpheus—not to turn around—was an integral part of the cult of the souls of the dead. To them, and only to them, sacrifices were made with the face averted, since no glimpse was

Orpheus and Charon

Orpheus

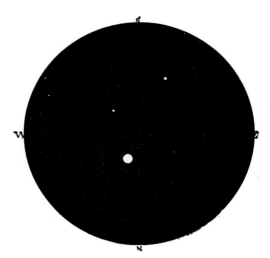

Vega and its companion

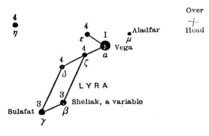

LYRA

permitted into the realm of the beyond (Kerenyi, *Eroi della Grecia*).

That a marriage between Orpheus and a woman had only allegorical value can be confirmed in Orpheus' reputation as a homosexual. He had intimate relationships only with young boys, and it was said that it was he who introduced love between men in Thrace.

It is, in fact, this love that would cause the end of the divine musician. He had attracted so many young men to his rites that the Thracian women, the maenads, became jealous to the point that they set a trap for him and killed him savagely and scattered his limbs in all directions. The only parts that were salvaged were the poet's head and his lyre. The head rolled into the river Ebrus and, never ceasing to sing, was carried by the current to the sea. Floating there, it arrived at the island of Lesbos where it was picked up and deposited in the sanctuary of Dionysus, thus becoming a famous oracle. The lyre, on the other hand, was placed in the sky as a constellation.

It is significant that Orpheus' head ended up in the Temple of Dionysus, evidence of a pairing of the two that is rich with other revealing examples, such as the dismembering of Dionysus when, as a child, he was captured by the Titans, savagely torn into pieces and subsequently roasted at the spit and boiled in a pot. In his case as well, a part of his body is salvaged: the heart, with which the gods were able to execute the magic of his resurrection.

The dismemberment of the young Dionysus is an allegory of the mutilation undergone by the grapevine (the plant that is sacred to him) during pruning. More complex, instead, is the ritual of roasting and then boiling, two sacrificial customs that are symbols of two time periods. The ancient period, that of hunting and gathering, is represented by the spit, and the new one by the technique of boiling (Detienne, *Dionisio e la pantera profumata*). In the case of Orpheus, his sacrifice could be explained with the ritual of the grape harvest since he died as a fully grown man.

Finally, Dionysus also descended into the world of the dead in search of his mother, the lunar goddess, Semele; he succeeded in convincing Persephone to set her free and brought her back with him to Olympus.

In Alexandrian astrology Ptolemy assigned to the stars of the Lyre the characteristics of Venus and Mercury, causing those who are born under this constellation to be by nature harmonious and poetic, lovers of music, the sciences, and the arts, but exhibiting a tendency toward kleptomania. The cabalists assigned to the Lyre the fourth trump card of the tarots, the Emperor.

Vega

The lucida of the constellation is the beautiful Vega, a very bright blue star that is inferior only to Sirius and Arcturus. Its name derives from the Arabic name of the constellation, *al-Nasr al-Waki,* or Flying Vulture, which was contracted to Waghi, Wega, and, finally, Vega.

In China, Korea, and Japan this star is associated with the legend of the divine weaver She-niu, represented by Vega, and her shepherd lover, the star Altair, who are divided by the heavenly river, the Milky Way. The complete story of the two lovers is to be found in the chapter on Aquila.

Along with Epsilon and Zeta Lyrae, Vega marked the twentieth Indian lunar station, called *Abhijit,* the Victorious One. This *nakshatra* is the northernmost of all; it is, in fact, located far outside the course of the moon (which in this node is in the sign of Capricornus). An exception was clearly made specifically to include this benevolent star.

Alvidas assigned to Vega the nature of Saturn as a triad with Jupiter and the sign of Capricornus, favoring idealism, hope, positiveness, elegance, change, sobriety, and seriousness, but lasciviousness as well. Ptolemy saw it in a different light and gave Vega the same nature as Lyra, namely that of Venus and Mercury.

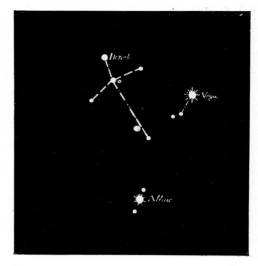

The relative positions of Vega, Altair, and Deneb

Bayer's Lyra (1603)

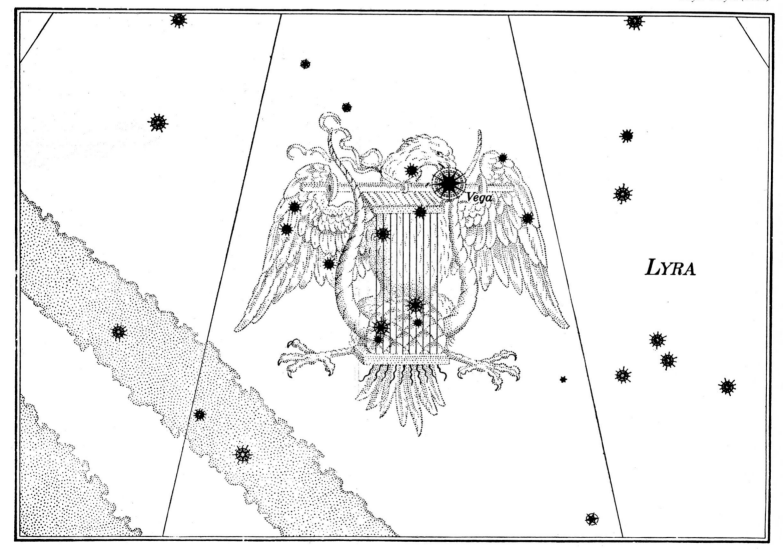

LYRA

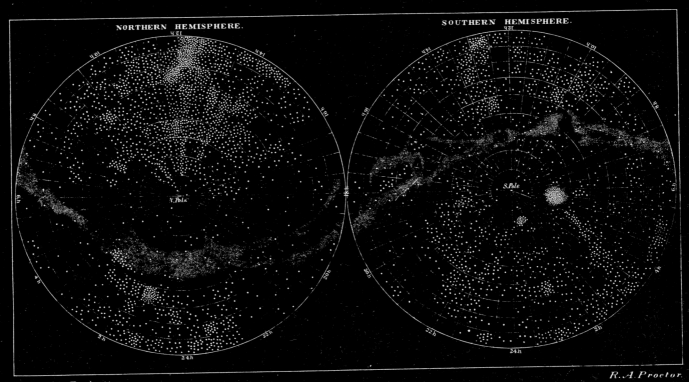

NORTHERN HEMISPHERE.   SOUTHERN HEMISPHERE.

Isographic Projection.   R.A.Proctor.

I. DISTRIBUTION of the NEBULÆ.
The Northern & Southern Nebulæ.

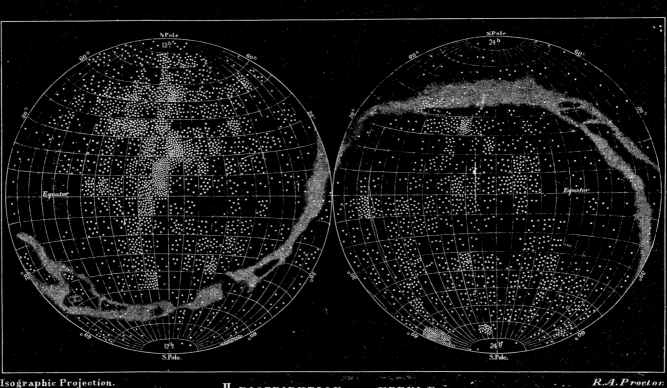

Isographic Projection.   R.A.Proctor.

II. DISTRIBUTION of the NEBULÆ.
The Great Nebular Groups.

35
Milky Way

In order to observe this faint and ever so precious brilliance in the sky, we must choose a moonless and particularly clear night. Even the far-off glow of the lights of a small city can obliterate the Milky Way, or Galaxios, as Eratosthenes and Plutarch called it. Its surface covers more than one-tenth of the visible sky and contains more than nine-tenths of the visible stars. It looks like a great circle of light that has its poles in Coma Berenices and Cetus.

This whitish stripe, unwinding like an arch in the sky, has some visible irregularities. At some points a river runs through it; in other places it divides into two branches that gradually separate, seeming to come apart like a skein of wool. It is like a large scar left by the fire started by Phaëthon when the chariot of the sun broke away under his inexperienced hands.

What kind of substance could make up such an impalpable cloud? And above all, what is the meaning of such a regular circle which is so out of place with respect to the circles of the equinoxes and solstices? These questions constituted an inexhaustible subject for the Greek philosophers to debate. Anaxagoras thought that it was a large collection of stars whose light was partially obscured by the shadow of the earth. In a similar argument Pythagoras said that it consisted of thousands of suns that were extremely far away and therefore not very luminescent. In 460 B.C. Democritus said that the cloudy appearance of the Milky Way was due to the presence in that part of the sky of numerous small stars that were so small that they illuminated each other. Aristotle thought that Galaxios was a great mass of luminous vapor higher than the region of the ether but lower than that of the planets. Parmenides believed that it was made up of a mixture of rarefied and dense air. Metrodorus and Oenopides conceived of the science fiction–like idea that the Milky Way marked a former path of the sun—its original course at the beginning of the world. Tying in to the myth of Phaëthon, this theory was also espoused by some of the Pythagoreans. (We must keep in mind that the shifting of the sun from its orbit, which occurred at a time beyond memory, is as common a myth in many parts of the world as that of the universal deluge.) Another theory was the one proposed by Theophrastus, who imagined the Milky Way to be the line that connects the two hemispheres that form the heavenly vault. He assumed this suture to be imperfect enough to allow us to see some of the light that, according to his hypothesis, existed in the infinite space beyond.

From the above, it is clear that in addition to very practical intuitions, some errors were made, but they were made in good faith and so should not detract from the efforts that produced them. As we all know, Greek philosophical speculations are the basis of modern scientific thinking, which, during the last four centuries, has made use of powerful instruments that have widened our range of perception of the universe. Even with these, there still remain limits to a complete knowledge of cosmic phenomena. Modern scientists' theories on the universe are constantly either being disproved or being put aside due to lack of evidence, in anticipation of the day when further updates will prove them.

The Milky Way. From Hyginus, Poetica astronomica *(1485 edition)*

Opposite: *Distribution of the Milky Way and the main nebulas, as seen from the North and South Poles (above) and from the equatorial band (below). Charts by the nineteenth-century English astronomer R. A. Proctor*

All this is said not to criticize the indisputable and welcome human zeal for research. Instead it is to dismantle the assumptions held by a substantial number of modern scholars who see themselves as the bearers of absolute truth and consequently look down on the authentic and extraordinary accomplishments achieved by so-called primitives. Their only limit was that they did not possess the technology of modern-day scientists who, in their turn, have this same limit with respect to tomorrow's scientists.

The Sacrificial Smoke

In contrast to the way it looks today, a few millennia ago the constellation Ara could be seen on the southern celestial horizon, perfectly upright, and totally immersed in the Milky Way.

For those populations who devotedly offered sacrifices to their gods, the altar and the offerings that were burned on it as well as the smoke that rose all the way to the heavenly abode of the gods represented the supreme means of communication between god and human.

The image of the Milky Way as the heavenly smoke of offerings curling up into the sky is certainly very beautiful, and, from the records known to us, it is one of the most ancient interpretations. Originally it probably was the altar built by Utnapishtim (the Sumerian Noah) when, immediately after the deluge, the ark was stranded on Mount Ararat. This altar was erected to thank the gods for having saved a small group of animals and people from total extinction.

In the Punjab the Milky Way was actually associated with the name of *Bera da Ghas,* meaning Path of the Ark. In a strange coincidence Australian aborigines believed it to be the smoke of the fire of an ancient race.

Lowering Ara to its position underneath the southern horizon due to the precession has caused it to be redesigned. From the time of Bayer's work (1603) on, it is shown upside-down, so that it could be seen in an upright position by the populations of the southern hemisphere.

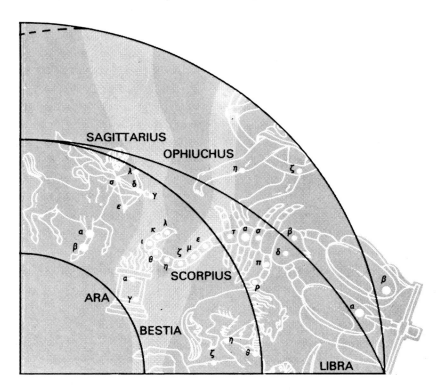

A powerful means of communication existed between men and gods—the sacrificial altar—whose smoke, some said, rose into the sky and became the Milky Way

The Milky Way as seen in the southern hemisphere, with the main stars visible to the naked eye

The River

In mythologies throughout the world, it often happened that the Milky Way was imagined as a great heavenly river. In Mesopotamia it was called the Serpent River, or *Nahru Tsiri*; in two other versions it was known as *Hid-in-ni-na*, meaning River of the Divine Lady or River of Nana—the goddess who was the spouse of the sky just as Hera was in the Greek myth.

At some point it was even called by the name of river Eridanus in a blurring of distinctions between it and the constellation of the same name. The Arabs called it *al-Nahr*, the River. The Semites and Hebrews gave it the name *Nhar di Nur*, meaning the River of Light, despite the fact that Rabbi Levi had reestablished the link with Sumerian tradition by calling it the Winding Serpent. In China it was *Tien Ho*, or the Heavenly River. In Japan it was the Silver River whose fish were frightened by the crescent moon, which they thought to be a fishhook. Al-Biruni cited a Sanskrit tradition that called it *Akash Ganga*, or the Bed of the Ganges. On the other hand in northern India it was *Nagavithi*, meaning the Path of the Serpent. The Hindus considered it to be the Path of Ariman that led to his throne at Elysium.

In the ancient world of the shepherds the Milky Way was the Great River, while the stars that surrounded it were the flocks of sheep that populated the sky. The shepherd was indicated by the star Capella, which portrayed him sitting on the bank of the river watching his sheep as they drank. In Egypt it was associated with the Nile and with Isis who, in fleeing the monster Typhon, sprinkled thousands of stalks of grain among the stars. These became the Milky Way.

The Beyond

The two points at which the circle of the Milky Way intersects the ecliptic are, to use an expression of Santillana's, "crisis proof" because they are not subject to any shifting due to precession; one coincides with Sagittarius and the other with Gemini. In the analysis of these two signs and the stars of Pegasus, we explain that, if we look back approximately seven thousand years to the time in which Gemini marked the spring equinox and Sagittarius the fall equinox, we are faced with a rare situation of great harmony in the combined placement of the stars. The axis of the solstice starts out at Virgo, passes through Draco (which at the time was the North Pole), and meets the Milky Way exactly in the center. This makes it appear to be a bow whose tips are Sagittarius and Gemini while the tightly strung cord between the tips of the bow is the meridian of the equinoxes. Continuing along the solstitial meridian, we find the Square of Pegasus enthroned above the center of the Milky Way. Continuing even further along this line, we finally arrive at Pisces on the winter solstice (see the illustration on page 408).

All this occurred between 6000 and 4000 B.C. and it had an enormous influence on the compilation of the cosmology of the beyond. The Milky Way was believed to be the river into which the souls of the dead entered at the end of their lives through the door guarded by Sagittarius. Here they waited until the time came for a new reincarnation on which they would embark by leaving through the other door—the door of Gemini.

In the ancient Mediterranean this reincarnation was symbolically celebrated every year with the ritual of the Spring Meadow whose flowers represented the souls of the dead who returned, after their winter absence, to salute the living. This springtime meadow, much beloved by the classical painters and poets, had direct links to the beyond. The unsuspecting maiden who gathers flowers and weaves garlands does not know what ambush resides within the seductive hypnosis of the flowering meadow (I. Chirassi, *Elementi di Culture Precereali*).

"We played and gathered perfumed flowers with our hands, the soft crocus, the flowers of the iris, the hyacinth, roses with large buds, lilies wonderful to behold, and the daffodil which the wide earth caused to rise like the crocus."

It was a serpent that inflicted the mortal bite upon Eurydice while she was gathering violets and, again in a field adorned with flowers, Persephone was abducted by Hades while she gathered daffodils.

"I picked it joyfully, but the earth opened up from below. Out came the powerful lord, ruler of many people, and carried me to the underground world in his golden chariot" (Anonymous, *Hymn to Demeter*).

Similarly, Europa was carried off by the white, perfumed bull as she was weaving garlands with her maidenly companions.

In this great cosmological framework, the Square of Pegasus was the island of the blessed, the Sumerian paradise where the gods and the souls of immortal men resided. Here Siduri reigned among flowers and trees made of gems; here also reigned many other manifestations of the Great Mother.

Giorgio De Santillana asserts that the interpretation of the Milky Way as a River of Souls is common to many cultures where the soul of the deceased had to await the occurrence of the divine coincidence in order to be able to enter the river of the beyond. Subsequently, once the meridian moved away as a result of the precessional shifting, this perfect arrangement disappeared, together with what had been called the Golden Age and, in so doing, produced the confused state of the later cosmologies (Santillana, *Il Molino d'Amleto*).

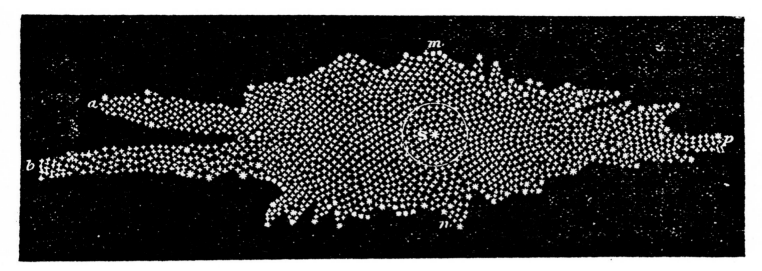

The Way of Hera

The name of the Milky Way originated in ancient Greek and Mediterranean mythology and was linked to the Great Mother, who at that time had the same divine stature that was later accorded to the Judeo-Christian god and Allah. Everything connected with her was replete with symbolism, allegories, and elements on which the creation myths were based. In his discussions of the Milky Way Eratosthenes remarked that even the sons of the gods would not have had any honor in their lives if they had not drunk milk from the breasts of Hera and that a mortal being would become immortal if allowed to drink just one sip of it.

This brings us to the early childhood days of Hercules, who was begotten by Zeus on a mortal—Alcmena—who, fearing Hera's possible revenge, had abandoned the little boy in the fields. At Zeus' suggestion Athene pretended to stumble upon the baby and said to the goddess, "His mother must have lost her mind to have abandoned him like this in such a stony field! You have milk, give some to this poor creature!" Hera took the baby boy and bared her breast, but Hercules grasped it with such force that the goddess pushed him away from her. A stream of milk flew up into the sky and became the Milky Way.

In another version it was the newborn Hermes (another name with the same root) who was given to Hera to be nursed. However, as she nursed him, she realized that the youngster was the son of Maia, Zeus' mistress, whereupon she violently pulled him away from her breast. So much milk was spilled that it formed the Milky Way.

Establishing which of the two versions is the original is complicated. There may have been a transfer of this myth. It was necessary for Hermes, a very ancient god of the world beyond the tomb, to learn Hera's knowledge, and so the latter myth was generated first. Subsequently, after the arrival of the Hellenic solar gods, Hercules in turn needed the ancient knowledge and therefore took over the events of the myth.

In his *Poetica astronomica* Hyginus also narrated the legend of the birth of Zeus. Cronus, the sky, regularly swallowed all the children Rhea, the earth, bore, until one day she decided that one—Zeus—would survive. She therefore decided not to give Cronus the child, but a rock wrapped in its swaddling clothes, as a meal. Before he swallowed it he asked Rhea to nurse it one more time and, when she pressed her nipple onto the hard rock, the milk that spurted out became the Milky Way.

The astronomer Herschel's theory on the form of the Milky Way in 1784 (below) and in 1785 (above). The sun is marked in the center with the letter S. From Knowledge *(January, 1884)*

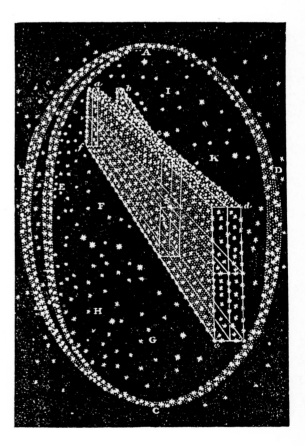

Latitudo.   Latitudo.

Anser.

Aquila.

Antinous.

Scutum.

Cerberus.

SERPENTARIUS.

Sobiescianum.

Sagittarius.

Æquator.

Ecliptica.

Hercules.

Scorpius.

SERPENS

Mons Mænalis.

Libra

Bootes.

Fig. P.

390   *The Glorious Constellations*

36
Ophiuchus and the Serpent

From May to September a giant holding a poisonous Serpent in his hands stands precariously in the southern hemisphere with his feet on the Scorpion, also poisonous. He is Ophiuchus, and his name derives from the Greek *Ofi-Okos*, which means the Man Who Holds the Serpent.

This is a very attenuated constellation, and we will divide it into three parts to make it easier to study: the head of the serpent to the west, Ophiuchus in the center, and the tail of the serpent to the east. To find it, draw an imaginary line from the star Antares in Scorpius to Vega in Lyra and another one from Altair in Aquila to Arcturus in Boötes. There are two stars where these lines cross; the brighter is Rasalhague, or the Head of the Snake-Charmer, the lucida of the constellation. The other star is Rasalgethi, or the Head of the Kneeling One, who is Hercules. Knowing these stars, one can reconstruct the entire figure.

The conception of these two giants in the sky is among the most complex in the design of the ancient constellations. The two heads are almost united but Hercules, who stands completely upside-down, has his feet planted on the great serpent Draco, just as Krishna is often represented after his victory over the serpent Kaliya. They are both heroes whose pre-Greek origin has been amply demonstrated, but whose stories are difficult to decipher and very complex (incidentally, Ophiuchus and Serpens are the only example of two constellations that intersect each other).

Once again we have to resort to analyzing the movement of the constellation's stars in order to verify over time if and when Ophiuchus had a position as well as a function that were interesting enough to justify his creation. Doing this, we obtain two dates that are important in the life of this constellation. The first is that of 3500 B.C. at the latitude of 35° N. (It might be helpful to know that this corresponds to the Upper Euphrates' location.) At this time Ophiuchus was in opposition to the sun during the night of the spring equinox. Thus he symbolically triumphed at midnight over the lords of darkness, who were represented by Scorpius, whom he squashes with his foot, and Serpens, whom he holds firmly in his hands.

Even if at this particular date the position of Hercules in the northern hemisphere was not well balanced or symmetrical—as it was a thousand years earlier (see the chapter on Hercules)—still, observed from the thirty-fifth parallel, the heads of Hercules and Ophiuchus were exactly on the zenith. Thus these heavenly brothers presented themselves—one in the northern region of the sky and the other in the south—in positions of command and conquest over the forces of winter and darkness at the time of the spring equinox.

The other important date is 2700 B.C. At this time the body of the Serpent in Ophiuchus' hands followed the celestial equator, but changed direction as soon as it intersected the meridian of the equinox; it then followed this meridian and ended with its head exactly on the zenith.

This suggests the bold hypothesis that perhaps Ophiuchus was originally a giant with a weapon in his hand, represented by the stars of the Serpent's head (much like Hercules with his club and Orion), with which he dominated the

Serpentarius

Ophiuchus and the Serpent. From Hyginus, Poetica astronomica *(1485 edition)*

Opposite: *Ophiuchus and the Serpent. From* Hevelius, Uranographia totum coelum stellatum *(1690)*

391

Bayer's Ophiuchus (1603)

dark scorpion. This probably occurred at about 3500 B.C. while seven hundred years later, when his position with respect to the equinox had changed, the astronomers (Sumerian, probably) invented the Serpent, who was able to provide the coordinates of the equinoctial meridian and the zenith so perfectly.

For the ancient astronomers who planned the constellations, serpentine figures have always had an important position rich in astronomical meanings. Thus it was for Draco and Hydra (respectively, the celestial North Pole and the southern horizon)—particularly for Draco, who became the absolute center of all the creation myths.

In ancient mythology the relationship between human beings and serpents was an extremely popular subject, and this sentiment has been handed down over the generations since time immemorial. It was possible to obtain power and the control of cults through knowledge of the mystery of the snake, its astronomical implications (see the chapter on Draco), and its pharmaceutical lore (consisting of the various poisons used to cure mortal illnesses with the doctrine of "like cures like," from which modern homeopathy derived).

In the pre-Hellenic Greek world this ritual was presided over by the priest-esses of the moon in sanctuaries with oracles where heroes were reincarnated into serpents or ravens. Famous examples of this practice are Erichthonius and Phoroneus. However, the one whose fame exceeded all others was the first doctor—the divine Asclepius or Esculapius, son of Coronis, a niece of Ixion.

While she was pregnant, Apollo had to go to Delphi and, during his absence, Coronis was unfaithful to him with the young Ischys. When Apollo discovered the liaison, he punished the raven whom he had left to guard Coronis (see the chapter on Corvus) and, with the help of the moon, his sister, he killed Coronis.

After the young woman had been put on the funeral pyre and the fire had been lit, Apollo was seized by remorse and, before the flames consumed his lover, he extracted a baby boy from Coronis' body. Apollo named him Asclepius and entrusted him to the centaur Chiron for his education.

Chiron was a divinity who was greatly worshiped in ancient Thessaly. He was so powerful, especially in the region of Pelion, that his sanctuaries occupied the most important centers of magic. As a result, Zeus, upon his arrival from Crete,

In 2700 B.C. the Serpent followed the celestial equator, curving up at a 90° angle on meeting the meridian of the autumn equinox, and then ending with its head on the zenith

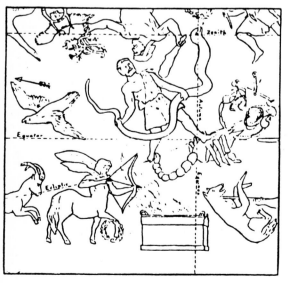

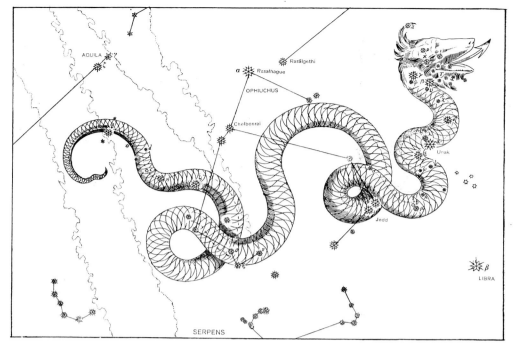

Bayer's Serpent (1603)

and Apollo Karneios had to regulate their places of worship in accordance with his sanctuary (Philipson, *Thessalische Mytologie*).

Asclepius learned the centaur Chiron's skills so well that he became the greatest surgeon and expert on poisons and pharmaceuticals of his time, so much so that he is still considered the father of medicine. He took part in the expedition of the Argonauts in conquest of the Golden Fleece, and he was the father of Podaleirius and Machaon, the doctors who cared for the Greeks during the siege of Troy.

With a few drops of blood from the Gorgon Medusa (probably a mixture of snake poisons), he concocted a remedy that enabled the dead to come back to life. This unleashed the wrath of Hades, king of the underworld, who compelled Zeus to call a halt to Asclepius' activities, which were contrary to the established order of things. Zeus struck the unfortunate Asclepius with lightning just as he was about to cure a new patient. In remorse, however, Zeus subsequently restored him to life, thus fulfilling a prophecy made by Euippe, daughter of Chiron, that Asclepius would become a god by first dying and then assuming his divinity. In fact, Zeus placed his image among the stars with a healing serpent in his hand.

According to Robert Graves, Asclepius is a composite name meaning He Who Hangs from the Esculent Oak, that is, mistletoe. The mistletoe was identified with the genitals of the oak, which the Druids ritually cut off with their golden sickle in performing a symbolic emasculation. It was believed that the sticky liquid of the mistletoe's berries was the sperm of the oak and that it was endowed with great curative powers. Ischys, Coronis' lover, has the same root in his name, indicating that, by suppressing the cult of the priestesses of the raven (coronids) and lovers of mistletoe, Apollo mastered the medicinal techniques of the mistletoe and the soothsaying qualities of the raven, who remained sacred to Apollo as symbol of the oracular art. Ischys, Asclepius, and Ixion are, in reality, the same mythical personality, the personification of the curative power hidden in the genitals of the sacrificed hero (Graves, *The Greek Myths*).

In ancient Arab astronomy of the time before the Greek influence had its

Asclepius, or Esculapius

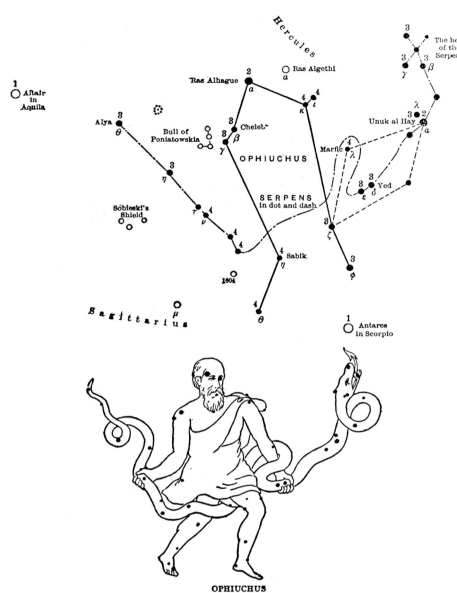

OPHIUCHUS

Anguis autem habet in summo capite duas, sub capite

effect, there was a completely different constellation in Ophiuchus' place, namely *al-Raudah*, the Pasture. In this pasture the stars Beta and Gamma, together with Gamma and Beta of Hercules, formed the *Nasak Shamiyy*, the Northern Boundary. On the other hand Delta, Alpha, and Epsilon of the Serpent with Delta, Epsilon, Beta, and Eta of Ophiuchus were *Nasak Yamaniyy*, or the Southern Boundary.

The sheep confined here were the stars that now compose Hercules' club. They were guarded by *al-Rai*, or the Shepherd, along with *Kalb al-Rai*, his Dog, represented by the stars Rasalhague in Ophiuchus and Rasalgethi in Hercules.

Zodiacal Ophiuchus

As we saw earlier the constellation of Ophiuchus is very close to the zodiacal belt and it is possible that at one time it was considered part of the zodiac. Actually, of the twenty-five days—November 21–December 16—that it takes the sun to pass from Libra to Sagittarius, only nine are spent in Scorpius. The other sixteen are all spent in Ophiuchus—more precisely, in the Serpent.

In connection with the hypothesis advanced earlier that Ophiuchus held a weapon, not the Serpent, in his hand, it is possible to develop a theory about this fascinating constellation. In the creation myths of the ancient Sumerians, there appeared a mythical race of scorpion-men. These are the hybrids that Gilgamesh meets in his desolate pilgrimage in search of Utnapishtim (see the chapter on Orion). They were probably an ancient people who used the scorpion's poison as medicine. In this interpretation Ophiuchus would not be holding a serpent but would be the transposition into the sky of a representative of this mythical race, that is, a giant composite man whose body was represented by the stars of Scorpius (who included, at that time, today's Libra). This would be one of the largest constellations ever created.

We cannot close the discussion of this constellation without noting a myste-

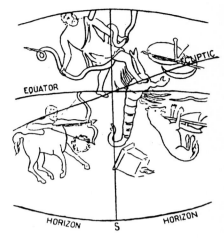

Constellations above the southern horizon during the fall equinox in 3589 B.C. at the latitude of 35° N.

The stars of Ophiuchus, the Serpent Bearer. From Easy Guide to the Constellations (1916)

rious sequence of constellations that are strangely connected with each other but lack a true legend to unite them. It is like hearing the music of an opera of which the libretto is lost. Such a libretto exists for the great cycle of Perseus, which includes the Gorgon, Andromeda, Cassiopeia, Cepheus, the Marine Monster, and Pegasus.

We can start from the center of the sky, the North Pole, where we find the winged serpent, Draco, upon whom Hercules-Marduk has placed his feet as the victor over the serpent Tiamat. In front of him stands Ophiuchus with his Serpent, his feet on the poisonous Scorpius. Underneath the Scorpion there is the centaur Chiron, who is the great healer-god and spiritual father of Ophiuchus. Centaurus has his left arm stretched out touching the stars of Corvus, the oracular bird who, in his turn, leans on the immense serpent of stars that is Hydra. For some reason, ravens, snakes, scorpions, doctors, and one hero —Hercules—seem to be united by one destiny.

As far as the astrological influence of the fixed stars is concerned, Ophiuchus was judged separately from the Serpent. Ptolemy considered Ophiuchus to have the nature of Saturn and to benefit moderately from the presence of Venus, who favors passion, blind generosity, a nature that is susceptible to seduction and wastefulness, scant happiness, hidden dangers, enemies, conflicts, and slander. Pliny asserted that the influence of this constellation caused many deaths by poisoning. The cabalists associated Ophiuchus with the sixteenth trump card of the tarots, the Tower Split by Lightning. Ptolemy assigned to Serpens the nature of Saturn and Mars, which conveyed wisdom, ability, shrewdness, and malice, but also little willpower and danger of poisoning.

Below: *Ophiuchus. From Geruvigus' planisphere*

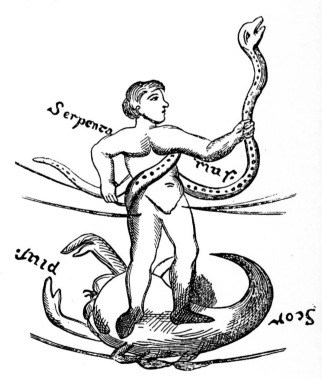

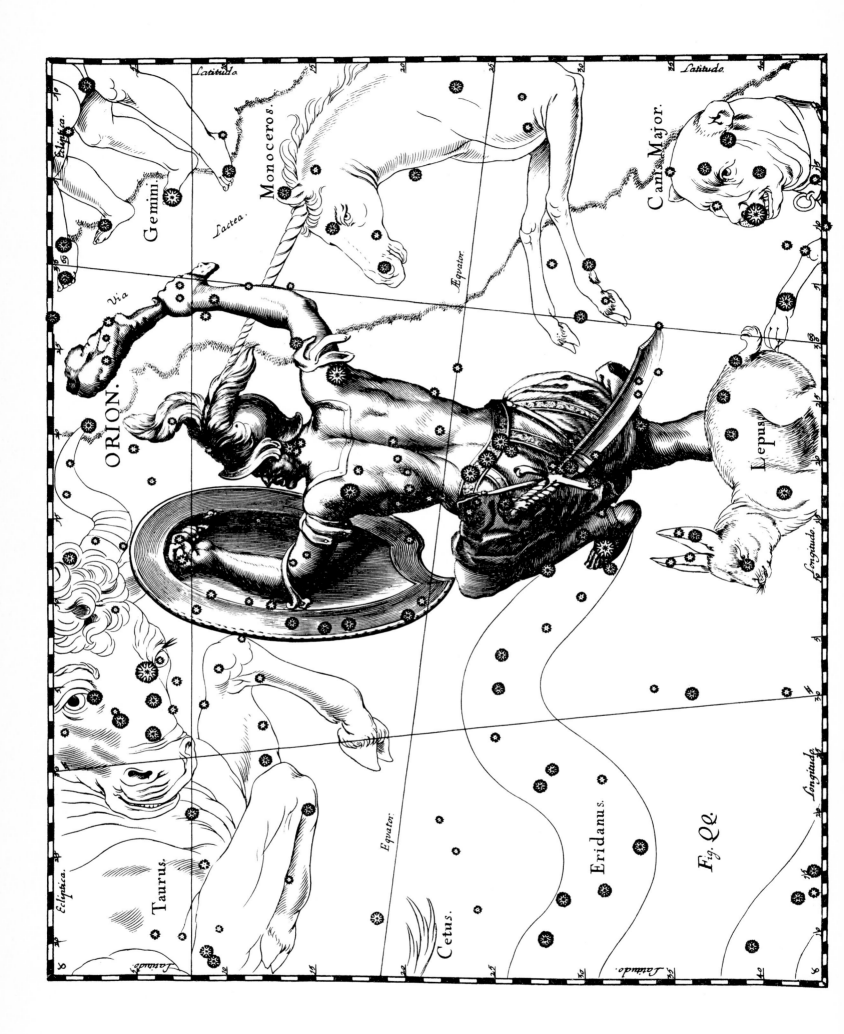

Via

Lactea

ORION.

Gemini.

Monoceros.

Canis Major.

Lepus

Taurus.

Eridanus.

Cetus.

Fig. QQ.

Æquator.

Equator.

37
Orion

The entry of the stars of Orion into the autumnal sky, joining Sirius and the stars of Taurus and Gemini, is without a doubt the most spectacular of all the stellar events that we can observe. Queens of the night, Orion's stars shine like diamonds that are mounted on the black velvet of a sky wiped clean by the north wind and the frost. At the time of the origin of the constellations, 4000–2000 B.C., this group coincided exactly with the spring equinox (March 21), which at that time also marked the first day of the year.

Adjacent to the Milky Way, Orion stretches over both sides of the celestial equator and is therefore visible in every part of the globe. Its stars represent a kneeling warrior who, with his raised right arm, brandishes a club or a sword seemingly about to strike the celestial bull in front of him. His left arm holds a lion's skin; the row of three stars is the belt around his waist; his right foot rests on the constellation of Lepus, the Hare, symbol of the moon; and his left foot is indicated by the splendid star Rigel, the source of the grand heavenly river, the constellation of Eridanus.

The origin of the name Orion may be found in the Sumerian *Uru-anna*, Light of the Sky, also known as Tammuz, which became Adonis in classical times. In Egypt Orion is represented by the solar god Horus, who is shown on a boat surrounded by stars, as Sirius, in the form of a cow, follows him on another boat. The souls of Osiris and Isis were immortalized in Orion and Sirius, respectively. Indian mythology shows here the figure of the lord of all creatures, the god Praiapati, in his metamorphosis as the deer Mriga. Insanely in love, he pursues his daughter, the beautiful Roe Rohini (the star Aldebaran), and is stopped by the heavenly hunter Lubdhka (the star Sirius); Lubdhka's arrow stuck in the deer's body is represented by the three stars of his belt.

In ancient astrology Orion's stars, with the exception of Betelgeuse and Bellatrix, were considered to have the same astrological qualities as Jupiter and Saturn. They bestowed a strong and proud nature, self-confidence, arrogance, violence, ruthlessness, success in travel and business, but also betrayal and poisoning.

In the *Metamorphoses* Ovid recounts how Orion was born to Jupiter, Neptune, and Mercury who, during a voyage, had been invited in by Irieus, a poor shepherd who was a childless widower. Without knowing the divine identity of his guests, he offered them hospitality and sacrificed the only animal he had, an ox. Before leaving the house, the gods asked Irieus what he wanted most in the world and the poor shepherd revealed that, above all else, he wanted a son. The three gods urinated in unison into the skin of the ox that had been offered to them and told Irieus to bury it. A few months later, Urion—which, in fact, means urine but which later became Orion—was born. As a young man he came to Chios, to the court of Oenopion, who took him on as hunter. There he fell in love with the daughter of the king, the beautiful Merope. During some festivities he became excessively drunk and raped the young princess. To punish this outrage to the laws of hospitality, Oenopion had him blinded. In

Orion. From Hyginus, Poetica astronomica *(1485 edition)*

Opposite: *Orion. From Hevelius,* Uranographia totum coelum stellatum *(1690)*

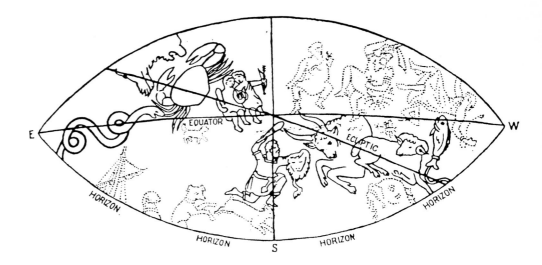

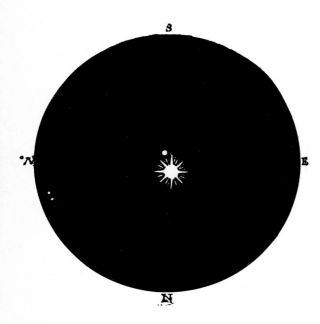

Orion on the meridian of the spring equinox in 4667 B.C. at the latitude of 40° N. Below: Rigel and its satellite. From Flammarion, Les Etoiles

despair Orion set out on a pilgrimage to Lemnos. The god Vulcan, pitying his helpless state, gave Orion a guide by the name of Cedalion to accompany him to the end of the world—the island of Delos—which was the nightly dwelling of Helius, the sun, the only one who could restore his sight. When Helius saw Orion, he fell in love with the handsome young man and was pleased to restore the light to his eyes. He then lay with him for the rest of the night. While the lovers were still embracing, Dawn came upon them and blushed so deeply at this sight that she has become red every morning since then.

Diana, the hunter-goddess, also fell in love with Orion. She loved to go on long deer hunts with him, but her brother, Apollo, plotted revenge because Orion had made love with Helius on the island sacred to him. So he set the celestial Scorpion against him and Orion, taken by fright, was unable to stand up against him and leapt into the sea. Apollo quickly went to visit Diana and, while they were sitting on the shore, he teased her about her skill with the bow and arrow. Spotting Orion swimming back, he then challenged the goddess to hit that faraway black dot among the waves. Furious about her brother's sarcasm, Diana picked an arrow from her quiver, took careful aim, and hit the target. How great was her sorrow when the waves brought to shore the lifeless body of Orion! After long laments, the goddess placed her lover among the most brilliant stars of the sky.

The astronomical basis of this myth is the fact that, in Greece, the constellation of Orion sets into the sea in the west exactly when the constellation Scorpius rises in the east, just as if it were pursuing the hero.

The Stars of Orion

Orion's belt is easily recognizable, composed of the stars Alnitak, Anilam, and Mintaka. Collectively they were called by various names, such as the Arabic *al-Nijad,* meaning belt, *al-Alkat,* meaning the Nuggets of Gold, or the Indian *Isus Trikanda,* meaning the Three Arrows Tied Together. In Greenland they were called *Siktut,* or the Seal Hunters, who, according to legend, were scattered during a hunt and then transferred as a trio to the sky. In Australia the aborigines called them the Dancing Young Men busily dancing the dance called *corroboree* in order to attract the attention of the girls, represented by the stars of the Pleiades in the neck of Taurus. The right shoulder of the giant is marked by the star Betelgeuse, the lucida of the constellation, whose name is a contraction of *Ibt al-Jauzah,* or the Armpit of He Who Is in the Center. In astrology this star was the bearer of civil and military honors. In India it marked the sixth lunar station, *Andra,* or Humid One, which related to the fact that the rising of this star coincided with the beginning of the rainy season. The left shoulder is the star Bellatrix, or the Amazon, but Ulugh-Beg and al-Sufi called it, respectively, *al-Murzim* and *al-Razam.* These two names mean the One Who Roars, referring to the fact that the left arm holds the lion skin.

In astrology Bellatrix was of the nature of Mars and Mercury and bestowed great military honors, famous friends, or, according to its position in the horoscope, blindness and dishonor. Women with this star in their sign were chatterboxes and had high-pitched, shrill voices. The brightest star of Orion is Rigel, a name derived from *Rijl,* or Foot. In the poetic literature of Norway, this star represents the thumb of the giant Orwandil; his other thumb, which had frozen, was cut off by the god Thor and thrown among the stars of the north where it became the little star Alcor, the companion of Mizar in the tail of Ursa Major. In astrology it indicated glory, honors, riches, and happiness. The cabalists associated it with the first trump card of the tarots, the Magician.

Orion. From a fifteenth-century engraving

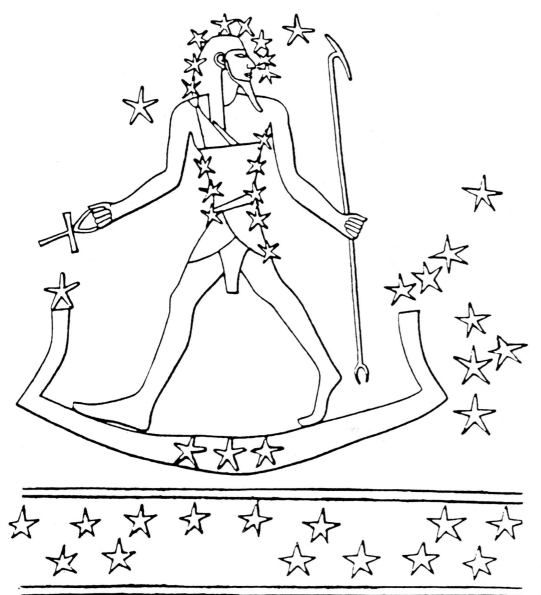

Osiris-Orion travels across the sky on the sacred boat (the stars of Lepus). From a star map in the tomb of Montemhet at Luxor (c. 650 B.C.)

Gilgamesh subdues two bulls in this decoration on a Sumerian harp from the first half of the third millennium B.C. University Museum, Philadelphia. Drawing from The Ancient Near East, Bellerophon Books

The Epic of Gilgamesh

The stars of Orion have always inspired myths and legends, and it is difficult to choose the most meaningful. The most ancient and certainly the most captivating, based on its content, its sense of drama, and the novelty of its mythological elements, is the Sumerian Epic of Gilgamesh and his companion, Enkidu. This myth is narrated in twelve chapters, written in cuneiform script on clay tables that were found among the ruins of the library of Assurbanipal in Nineveh. The most ancient part of the text dates back more than four thousand years.

Gilgamesh was an actual historical person, king of the Sumerian Uruk in the first half of the third millennium B.C. According to legend his mother was the goddess Aruru, niece of Utnapishtim, who survived the deluge and later became the biblical Noah (see the chapter on Ara). Although he was mortal, he was so strong that he could subdue a lion without any weapons. It is, in fact, with a lion in his arm that he is portrayed in bas-reliefs. He was the idol of the young men of Uruk who admired his strength, his dissoluteness, and his irresistible beauty. It was said that "he does not leave a single virgin for her mother, not a single daughter for the warrior, not a single bride to her groom." He was untamed—wild and despotic. The elders of Uruk complained about him to the gods, who ordered his mother to create a double of her son and set him against Gilgamesh, as a rival. Aruru obeyed: she took some clay, threw it on the ground, kneaded it, and so gave life to Enkidu. Enkidu was similar to the satyrs, the fauns, and Priapus (see the chapter on Centaurus). "His whole body is shaggy with hair, and his head-hair is like a woman's. . . ." (Kirk, *Myth*).

Orion. From the Alfonsine Tables *(thirteenth century)*

Enkidu was immensely strong; he certainly would have been a worthy opponent for Gilgamesh had not the sun-god Shamash intervened by concocting a plan to make the two become friends. Shamash ordered his messenger, Sadu, to conduct Enkidu to Uruk. However, when Sadu saw him he was so terrified that he returned to Shamash in a panic.

The god of the sun then thought of another strategy for drawing him out peacefully. He sent the same Sadu to Uruk to choose the most beautiful of the priestesses of Ishtar. Using the art of feminine seduction, she was to bring Enkidu under her spell (the priestesses of Ishtar practiced ritual prostitution and were, therefore, great experts in the art of lovemaking). Sadu and the priestess waited three days for Enkidu at a spring before he finally arrived. As soon as she saw him, she too was panic-stricken but Sadu commanded her to do her duty, whereupon she managed to be so seductive that Enkidu, completely bewitched, made love to her for six days and six nights. Satiated, he then went in search of his flock, but the animals escaped; he was too weak to keep up with them. He was so weak, in fact, that he fainted, but he regained his senses at the sweet words of the prostitute: "Why, Enkidu, do you, who are superb like a god, live among the wild beasts? Come, I will take you to Uruk—to the radiant house, the dwelling of Anu and Ishtar—the place where Gilgamesh lives who is supremely strong and who has the temperament of a wild bull."

Now the harlot continues Enkidu's acculturation; she clothes him, leads him to the house of the shepherds, teaches him to take solid food instead of the milk of wild creatures. He drinks strong drink, becomes cheerful, rubs the hair from his body and anoints his skin, and as a final service to his new friends he chases off, or captures, some of his old ones, the lions and wolves. When he hears from a passerby about Gilgamesh' riotous and immoral behavior in town he is deeply shocked. Finally he goes to Uruk; the people, recognizing him as Gilgamesh's natural counterpart, feel relieved. That night he intercepts the king on his way to an amorous assignment, and they wrestle. (ibid.)

Gilgamesh managed to win this fight, and the two young men came to understand the mystery of their being like twins and became intimate friends. The loss of his wild nature had made Enkidu melancholy and lonely, and he found in the irresponsible Gilgamesh a friend with the same nature as his. The reversal of their roles underlines the twin aspects of the two opposites: Enkidu rejected the animals and became wise as a god; but Gilgamesh, a king who should be wise, behaved like a wild animal.

Happy to have found a companion as strong as himself, Gilgamesh decided to undertake an extremely difficult exploit: to slay the giant of the cedar wood, the undefeatable Humbaba. Enkidu explained to Gilgamesh that he had known the giant when he was still living in the wild and knowing the giant's strength he tried to dissuade Gilgamesh. But Gilgamesh answered that since it isn't possible for him to obtain immortality the only thing he can do is to perform a deed for which he will be remembered forever.

After his initial euphoria Gilgamesh had moments of disheartenment and weeping, and the elders advised him to follow Enkidu, who had more experience with the forest. If he defeats the giant he was instructed to take off his battle clothing and put on new garments to purify himself.

Orion. From Hyginus, Poetica astronomica *(Venetian edition)*

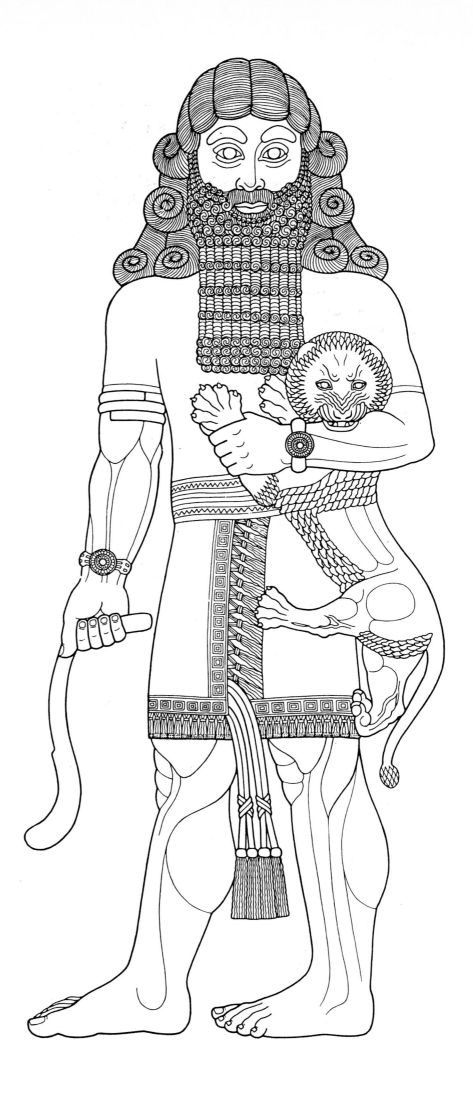

Gilgamesh, from a relief in the throne room of the Palace of Sargon II (721–705 B.C.). Drawing from The Ancient Near East, *Bellerophon Books*

The two friends left for the cedar forest, which seems to have been be-witched; they were assailed by unknown fears and incomprehensible dreams. However, Shamash came to their aid, spurring them on, urging them not to give up. At last they succeeded in rousting Humbaba and after a long battle the monster was killed. Mindful of the advice to purify himself, Gilgamesh removed his weapons, donned white garments with the royal insignia, and covered his head with a crown. He was so magnificent that Ishtar, the goddess of love, became consumed by desire for him and offered herself as his bride:

"Come to me Gilgamesh, and be my bridegroom; grant me seed of your body, let me be your bride and you shall be my husband. I will harness for you a chariot of lapis lazuli and of gold, with wheels of gold and horns of copper; and you shall have mighty demons of the storm for draft-mules. When you enter our house in the fragrance of cedar-wood, threshold and throne will kiss your feet. Kings, rulers, and princes will bow down before you; they shall bring you tribute from the mountains and the plain. . . . Your oxen shall have no rivals, and your chariot horses shall be famous far-off for their swiftness."

(Sandars, *The Epic of Gilgamesh*)

However, Gilgamesh rudely refused, reminding Ishtar of the end to which all her lovers had come:

"There was Tammuz, the lover of your youth, for him you decreed wailing, year after year. You loved the many-coloured roller, but still you struck and broke his wing; now in the grove he sits and cries, "kappi, kappi, my wing, my wing." You have loved the lion tremendous in strength: seven pits you dug for him, and seven. You have loved the stallion magnificent in battle, and for him you decreed [death]; and for his mother Silili lamentations. You have loved the shepherd of the flock. . . . Now his own herd-boys chase him away, his own hounds worry his flanks. And did you not love Ishullanu, the gardener of your father's palm-grove? . . . You struck him. He was changed to a blind mole deep in the earth, one whose desire is always beyond his reach. And if you and I should be lovers, should not I be served in the same fashion as all these others?"

(ibid.)

Furious about these insults Ishtar ran to her father, Anu, asking for ven-geance, and she compelled him to send the celestial Bull (the constellation of Taurus, adjacent to the stars of Orion) against Uruk. Gilgamesh and Enkidu armed themselves and set out to hunt him down. They succeeded in rousting him near the marshes of the Euphrates. Enkidu managed to force him to the ground while Gilgamesh planted a dagger in the animal's heart. Enkidu then quartered the Bull and threw the pieces into the sky at Ishtar, who, with her priestesses, wept over the limbs of the celestial Bull. Gilgamesh took the horns to Uruk to consecrate them to the god Shamash.

The dismemberment of the Bull explains perhaps why all star maps, includ-ing the most ancient ones, depict the constellation of Taurus with only the front part of the animal.

Here we have an allegory of the Sumerians' astronomical conquest of the calculation of the spring equinox, which occurred in Taurus for two millennia. Gilgamesh's conquest of the heavenly horns and his consecrating them to the sun-god can be compared to the conquest of the Golden Fleece by the Argonauts when, during the following two thousand years, the spring equinox shifted from Taurus to Aries.

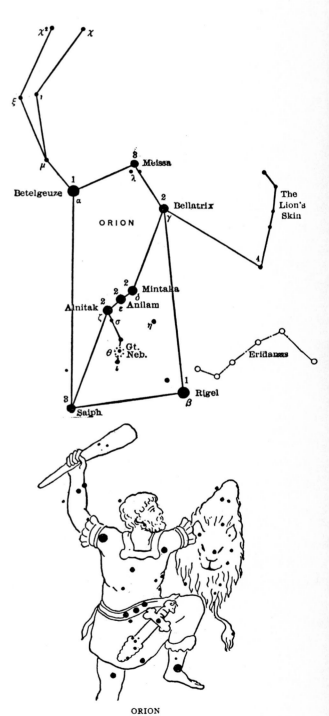

ORION

Gilgamesh battles a lion, on a cylindrical seal from the second half of the third millennium B.C. British Museum. Drawing from The Ancient Near East, *Bellerophon Books*

The stars of Orion. From Easy Guide to the Constellations *(1916)*

Ishtar's revenge was terrible. After boasting about his beauty in the exultation of his victory, Gilgamesh was struck with leprosy while Enkidu first had a premonition in a dream, then became ill, and finally died. Having nursed him day and night, Gilgamesh first thought that his friend had dozed off, but then he noticed that Enkidu's heart was no longer beating. He covered his friend's face and gradually began to become crazed with sorrow. He did not leave Enkidu for several days, until a worm fell from the corpse's nose. Gilgamesh then fled into the desert where he roamed in despair. His hair grew long, and he dressed in a lion skin: the thought of death terrified him.

Instead of accepting fate, Gilgamesh became determined to attempt something—anything—to become immortal. He undertook a voyage to the ends of the world in search of his great-uncle Utnapishtim, the hero of the universal deluge (see the chapter on Ara), to whom the gods had given immortality.

The voyage brought many dangers. Gilgamesh had to cross the Masu Mountains and the desert west of the Euphrates that ends in the Persian Gulf. To do this, he had to ingratiate himself with the terrifying scorpion-men, confront the blackest darkness, and arrive, somehow, at the shore of the sea that surrounds the world. There he found a marvelous wood where the trees produce gems and precious stones instead of fruit—Eden.

Here Gilgamesh encountered Siduri, "the divine maiden who sits on the throne of the sea," who explained to him that, in order to cross the Sea of Death and reach the Island of the Blessed where Utnapishtim resided, he would need the help of Ursanabi, helmsman and snake charmer. Siduri tried in vain to dissuade Gilgamesh from his dream of immortality—she told him that the only happiness for man is to be found in music, dance, festivities, and a loving wife and children. But the hero was determined; he went in search of Ursanabi and persuaded him to make the frightful voyage over the Sea of Death; after a very

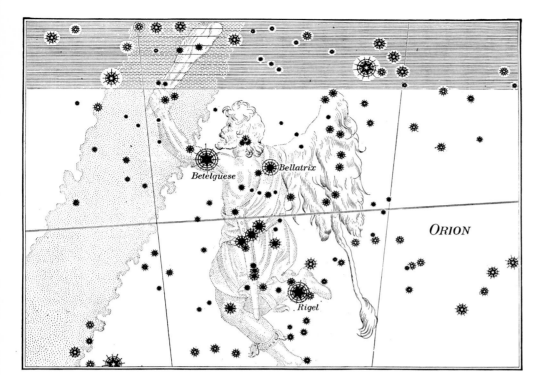

long and desperate crossing, they reached the Island of the Blessed. There Gilgamesh encountered Utnapishtim, who was willing to discuss how he succeeded in obtaining immortality from the gods. Utnapishtim told Gilgamesh the story of the deluge and the Ark (see the chapter on Ara), but confirmed that, unfortunately, only such exceptional events as the deluge could make the gods agree to raise a man to the condition of immortality. All men must die.

However, Utnapishtim's powers were great, and he decided to cure his great-nephew's leprosy in a complicated ceremony lasting seven days. He then told him about a certain tree. If Gilgamesh kept a branch of this tree with him, he would enjoy everlasting youth until his death.

So Gilgamesh took to sea again and reached the island where the tree grew. He succeeded in removing a branch, but when he was returning with his trophy he stopped to wash himself in a spring. While he was in the water, a serpent flung itself onto the branch and swallowed it.

Gilgamesh' sadness was profound, but in the end he learned that youth and eternity were not for him, and he decided to return to Uruk. There he prepared a great funeral ceremony for his beloved friend during which he invoked the god of the dead, Nergal, to allow him to speak once more with Enkidu. The extraordinary request was granted and Enkidu's spirit appeared. To Gilgamesh' questions about the world of the dead, he responded, "The soul of he who dies in battle, with his weapons in his hand, and whose body was buried, has some comfort in the world of the beyond; but the soul of he whose body was abandoned in the fields after death does not find rest; its only nourishment is the refuse thrown in the dirt from the tables of men."

The Epic of Gilgamesh goes through the various attitudes one can take when confronted by death. The infinite melancholy of Gilgamesh is skillfully contrasted with his image at the beginning of this legend, when he is the symbol of anarchical youth—beautiful as a god, irrational as a wild beast, and an insatiable lover. Heroism, love, and death distance him from the state of grace; he is conscious, suffering, trying to fight the inevitability of destiny by becoming savage again; his hair grows long, he roams the plains, he wears animal skins just as Enkidu did before his arrival in Uruk.

Orion. From the planisphere
at Dendera, Egypt

38
Pegasus

Pegasus. From Hyginus, Poetica astronomica *(1485 edition)*

Pegasus, a large constellation located just above the signs of Pisces and Aquarius, is visible every night from July through January. It is formed mainly by the four stars delineating the square that astronomers have always called the Square of Pegasus, located on the other side of the Polar Star from the Great Bear. A curved line of three brilliant stars is grafted onto this square in such a way that this figure approximately reproduces the general look of Ursa Major and Ursa Minor, but on a larger scale.

Despite the great size of the constellation, it depicts only half of a horse—the front half. A pair of great wings sprouts from its shoulders. The peculiar characteristic of Pegasus is that it was designed completely upside-down, with its feet up in the air and its head below.

The origin of this figure is uncertain and very ancient. Therefore, it is essential to study what celestial positions it has had in the past; we must follow the shifts in the precession of the equinoxes. As we slowly shift the sky and its stars backward in time, we reach at a latitude of 40° N. an extremely interesting situation in the faraway fifth millennium B.C. At that time the spring equinox occurred in Gemini and the autumnal one in Sagittarius. Both signs are situated on the Milky Way, which seemed like a drawn bow above the Polar Star, at that time located on the tail of Draco. The summer solstice occurred in Virgo, and the winter solstice in Pisces—amid which our Square was enthroned, exactly on the meridian of the solstice.

The perfect geometric placement of the Square on the axis of the solstices, together with the other coincidence between equinoxes and Milky Way, resulted in its being identified as the charismatic center of the sky—the merging point of the harmony of the universe. For this reason it was called Paradise, the mythical primordial garden in which creation occurred. This Paradise, placed in the center of the arch of the Milky Way (the evanescent abode of the souls), offered the eschatological model from which the magical unit of measure used in Sumer, the *iku*, derived. With this, Utnapishtim (the Sumerian Noah) built his Ark in a cubic shape; it is also the measure of the plan of the temple of the god Marduk in Babylon.

When Gilgamesh wanted to reach the Paradise of Siduri during his voyage in search of eternal youth, he had to cross the great sea on Ursanabi's boat. This region at the ends of the earth is surely that portion of the sky the Sumerian astronomers knew by the name of the Sea. Although the presence of a horse in the Sea may seem strange, we must remember that it was the creature of Poseidon par excellence and that Phoenician sailors had figureheads that repre-

407

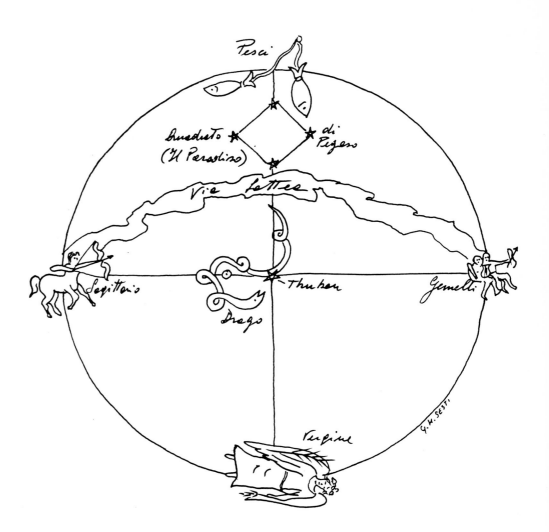

The position of the constellations in 5000 B.C. with respect to the solstices and equinoxes was considered the expression of the harmony of the great divine plan for the heavenly bodies. Paradise, represented by the Square of Pegasus, was located above the Way of the Souls—the Milky Way—exactly on the meridian of the solstice

sented the winged horse as the symbol of navigation on the prows of their ships.

In the chapter on Virgo it becomes clear that Paradise was the dominant element of the matriarchal priesthood of protohistory. The fact that it is located on the meridian of the solstice of Virgo confirms and qualifies this concept. The only thing left to discover, as a curiosity, is the true identity of the female figure, Andromeda, who is depicted between Pegasus and Pisces, with whom she shares two important stars. Perhaps originally she was Medea, Circe, Hesperide, or Eva, the goddess and female guard of that *Paradaisos* from which she was brutally deprived by the new male solar gods (see the chapter on Virgo).

Little is known about the metamorphosis of the Paradise into a winged horse, but it surely happened in very ancient times. Aratus called him the Divine Horse in the third century B.C.; Eratosthenes described him without wings; Nonnos called him the Lybian Horse That Is Half Visible; he appeared on stones, jewels, and coins in Mesopotamia, at Corinth, at Carthage, and in Sicily; the Hebrews considered him the great Horse of Nimrod; but, above all, in the mythology of the Mediterranean, he was the horse of Poseidon, the god of the sea.

The great mystery of Pegasus' position remains. He is completely upside-down; no explanation for this strange position exists. The only vague reason could possibly be found in the attempt of Bellerophon who, riding Pegasus, tried to reach Olympus. In order to stop him, Zeus sent a horsefly to bite the animal. Startled, the horse jumped and threw Bellerophon out of the saddle.

Is it possible that Zeus, in placing Pegasus among the stars, depicted him in

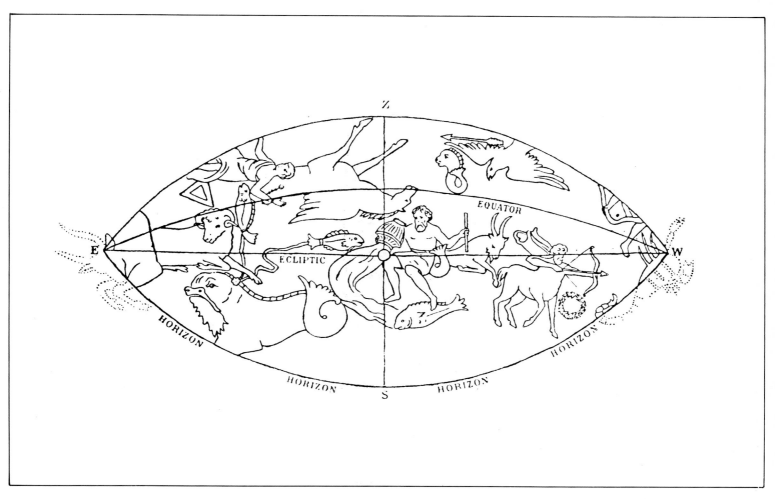

Position of the sun with respect to the constellations at midday during the winter solstice in 3000 B.C.

the act of kicking, upside-down? It's difficult to say. The fact remains that Pegasus was shown upright until the time of late Greek astronomy. It seems therefore legitimate to ask if perhaps it was an erroneous transcription by some astronomer or the whim of a local legend that, at some point, turned Pegasus over.

So many coincidences support this hypothesis that an in-depth analysis seems justified. In classical Greece Pegasus was the favorite horse of the Muses. With his hoof, he struck the earth on Mount Helicon and thereby caused the fountain of Hippocrene, sacred to poets, to gush forth.

The present position of Pegasus' hooves in the sky does not suggest anything that could be connected with this myth. In fact, the region where the legs of the horse are to be found is almost totally devoid of bright stars. However, if we turn Pegasus over so that he stands upright, his hoof magically rests on the pail of Aquarius from which streams the Fluvius Aquarii in which Piscis Austrinus is swimming.

This hypothesis is decidely enticing, due to both the logical conclusiveness of this scheme's agreement with the myth and the evidence provided by an analysis of the stars' earlier position. This takes us far back into time and onto another continent: the protohistoric India of 3000 B.C., which has left traces in the *Rig-Veda*. There, the glories of many Vedic gods are recounted, among them the twin divinities—the Aswin, or Indian dioscuri—who are gods with horse's heads. They are sons of Dyaus, the Sky, and brothers of Usha, the Dawn. The frequency with which they were praised attests to the importance of their cult. They are extolled in more than fifty complete hymns and in parts of

many others; their names are written in the sacred book more than four hundred times. Ancient Indian astronomy recognized the Aswin in the stars Alpha and Beta Arietis, and a story was told in which they owned a horse called Pagas who "had filled a hundred vessels with a sweet liquid" with his hoof—an explicit reference to the magical lunar drink of the gods called soma.

The meaning of their prodigious nature may be determined from the magical and universal virtues that the horse possessed in the ancient Indian culture. It was not by chance that the most important rite of Vedic civilization was the *Aswameda*, or Sacrifice of the Horse (*aswa* meaning horse, *meda* meaning sacrifice), officiated over by the Great Lord of the Supreme Cult, Brihaspati, symbol of the planet Jupiter and always depicted on horseback. It should be noted that the word *meda* is a part of the name of the nearby constellation Andromeda, the young woman offered in sacrifice to the marine monster. This could indicate an ancient link between the two constellations.

Having said this, it is possible to reconstruct the sky and its stars as it appeared in the year 3000 B.C. and, more precisely, during the night of the summer solstice. At this time the full moon was celebrated, year after year, in perfect conjunction with the sign of Aquarius. The horse (overturned) kicked the moon with his hoof, thereby causing the soma to gush forth, which filled the vessel of Aquarius and then flowed out into the heavenly river.

This coincided exactly with the arrival of the monsoons. Thus an explanation is now also provided for the ancient legends of the horse as the son of Poseidon, creator of springs and central figure in the propitiatory rites of the rains (Plunket, *Ancient Calendars and Constellations*).

Constellations that were visible at midnight of the summer solstice in 3000 B.C. The full moon occurred at that time every year on the pail of Aquarius. In this drawing the horse has been turned over, in accordance with its mythological qualities

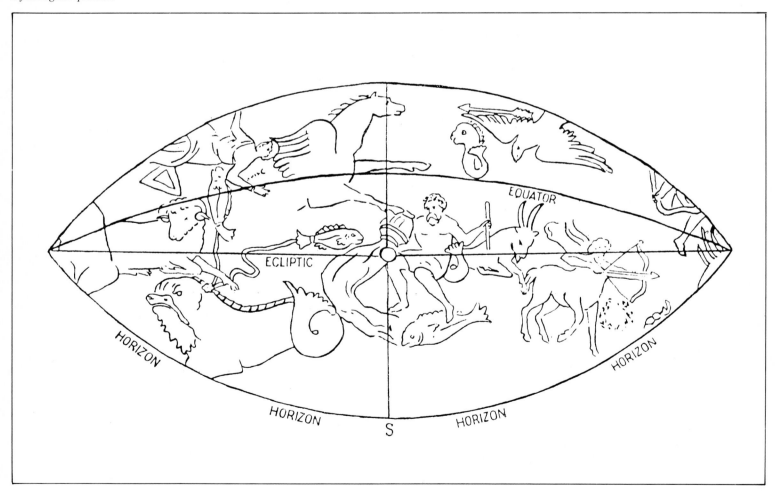

Bellerophon

Poseidon, king of the sea, had fallen in love with the beautiful Lybian princess Medusa, and he had copulated with her on the sacred soil of the Temple of Athene. Enraged by this profanity, the goddess transformed Medusa and her two sisters into horrible Gorgons with hair of serpents and bodies of birds.

Medusa was later killed by Perseus who, with the help of the magic of several gods, succeeded in decapitating her. Immediately, Pegasus and the warrior Chrysaor, who had been conceived inside Medusa from Poseidon's seed, jumped out of her open neck. Perseus did not ride Pegasus, as some believe (due to a confusion created by later pictorial representations). He was already endowed with the winged sandals that allowed him to fly.

The myth of Medusa refers to the religious practices of the Lybian priestesses, who wore masks that made them look horrible, with serpentlike hair and dangling tongues. The purpose of these masks was to keep curious onlookers away as they celebrated their secret rites.

After his birth Pegasus went to live on Mount Helicon, where he became the favorite of the Muses. It was there that he caused the spring of Hippocrene to well up. He remained there, untamed and wild, for many years, until he was tamed by a hero with an unusual story—Bellerophon, grandson of Sisyphus.

Bellerophon got his name from having killed the warrior Bellerus, but it seems that earlier his name was Chrysaor, or He Who Has the Golden Sword (Kerenyi, *Gli dei e gli eroi della Grecia*).

To purify himself after the death of Bellerus, the young man went as a suppliant to the court of Proetus, king of Tiryns, but fate would have it that Anteia, wife of Proetus, fell in love with him. He rejected her so as not to violate the duties of hospitality. Taking revenge, Anteia told her husband that Bellerophon had attempted to seduce her. In order not to soil himself with the killing of a suppliant, Proetus plotted another end for him. He sent him to his father-in-law, Iobates, king of Lycia, with a sealed message in which he asked him to kill the young man.

Pegasus. From a fifteenth-century engraving

Equus

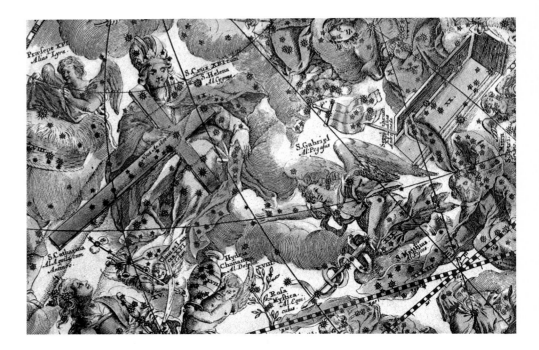

However, Iobates was also reluctant to kill a guest. He therefore asked him to do him the favor of fighting the mythical Chimera, the fire-breathing monster with the head of a lion and the body of a she-goat. The king knew that no man could survive such a duel. Bellerophon turned for advice to the seer Polyeidus, who told him to capture and tame Pegasus. Only in riding such a steed would he be able to get the better of the monster.

There are many versions of the capture of Pegasus by our hero. Some say that it was Minerva who inspired him to forge the first bit; others say that Poseidon consigned him the horse already tamed; others still that it was Bellerophon who tamed him with a golden bridle. However, riding Pegasus, Bellerophon rousted the Chimera, wounded it with his arrows, and succeeded in jamming a piece of lead between its jaws that, melted by its burning breath, flowed down into its stomach, and killed the monster.

The Chimera, sacred to the Great Mother, was the symbol of the tripartite year: the lion represented the spring, the she-goat the fall, and the serpent the winter. It was fire-breathing because it was identified with the Chimera Mountain, or Mountain of the She-Goat, an active volcano near Phaselis, Lycia (Pliny, *Natural History*). Its slaying is to be understood as the suppression of the ancient Carian calendar by the Hellenic invaders.

After the Chimera, Bellerophon was asked to do battle with the Solymians and their allies, the Amazons. His zeal was such that Iobates began to suspect that perhaps Proetus had been wrong in his estimation of the hero. He therefore decided to show him the letter. Having been told the truth, he then embraced Bellerophon as a son, gave him in marriage his daughter Philonoë, Anteia's sister, and appointed him heir to the throne of Lycia.

Unfortunately, Bellerophon became so elated with his resounding success and great renown that he conceived the idea of trying to reach Olympus on his winged horse. This ambitious enterprise was reminiscent of those of Icarus and Phaëthon. Hearing of it, Zeus sent a horsefly that bit Pegasus under this tail and startled him. Bellerophon was thrown into a bramble bush, which made him blind and lame, and he was condemned to live the rest of his life without seeing other men.

Pegasus' fate, however, was different. He continued his flight into the sky,

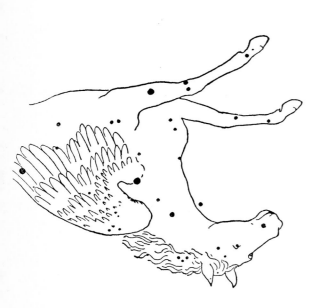

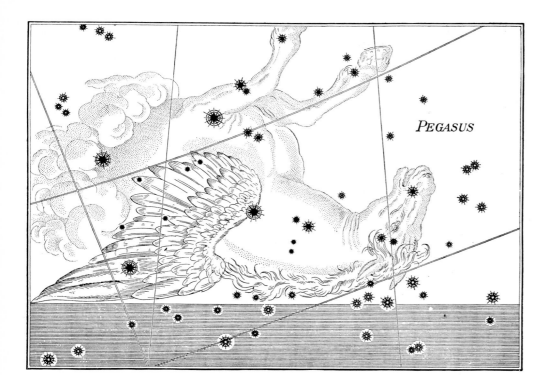

PEGASUS

Bayer's Pegasus (1603)

where he was received by Zeus, who quartered him in the ancient stables of Mount Olympus and gave him the duty of transporting for him the flashes of lightning forged by the Cyclopes. For this reason, his image was immortalized among the stars as the constellation of the winged horse.

The Stars

The name of Alpha Pegasi is *Markab*, which is an Arabic word meaning Saddle, Ship, or Vehicle. The astronomer al-Kazwini maintained that Alpha and Beta together formed *al-Arkuwah*, or the Well-Beam, the instrument that is used in hauling water from wells; it consists of a pole with a counterweight at whose end the rope is attached that holds *al-Dalw*, or the Pail, which may be depicted by the pail of Aquarius. Ptolemy assigned it the nature of Mars and Mercury, and Simmonite, that of Mars and Venus. It bestowed honors, riches, and fortune, but also the risk of fevers, cuts, beatings, fire, and violent death.

Beta Pegasi is called Scheat, which seems to be a contraction of *al-Said*, the Thigh. It was, however, more popular among the Arabs under the name of *Mankib al-Faras*, or the Shoulder of the Horse. It appears thus in Ulugh-Beg's catalogue. It is not a lucky star. Ptolemy considered it to have the worst nature of Mars and Mercury. To these, Simmonite added Saturn, with its predilection for misfortune, homicide, suicide, or drowning.

Gamma Pegasi is known to us by the name of Algenib, derived from either *al-Janah*, meaning the Wing, or, more probably, *al-Jamb*, the Side. Being of the nature of Mars and Mercury, Algenib conveyed notoriety, dishonor, or misfortune, and was considered to be the star of beggars. The fourth star of the Square of Pegasus is described in the chapter on Andromeda since it belongs to that constellation.

Ptolemy assigned to Pegasus in general the qualities of Mars and Mercury, ambition, intuition, and enthusiasm, but also eccentricity and irresponsibility. In the Christian sky Pegasus was replaced by Saint Gabriel, the archangel.

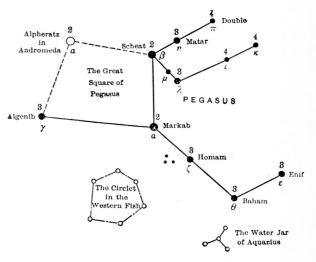

Camelopardalus.

Auriga.

Via.

Lactea.

Taurus.

PERSEUS.

Fig. W.

Casfiopeja.

Andromeda.

Triangulum Majus.

Musca.

Minus.

Aries.

39
Perseus

The myth of the son of Jupiter and Danaë gathered into one story the destinies and the stars of seven mythological figures and as many constellations. It is therefore the greatest epic ever written by the ancient inventors of constellations in the nighttime sky.

Starting at the center of the ecliptic, in the constellation of Draco, and going toward Aries and Pisces, we encounter the first figure of the Royal Family of the Stars: King Cepheus, standing upright, with a crown on his head and a scepter in his hand. The stars that give him shape are not very bright and it takes considerable imagination to reconstruct his figure. Leaving Cepheus behind, we come to Queen Cassiopeia. This constellation is considered to be one of the most famous in the sky due to the ease with which its stars, which are in the shape of a W, can be identified. Cassiopeia is seated on her throne and holds a stalk or palm frond in her hand. Next to her are the stars of the young Princess Andromeda, who is chained to rocks in front of what the ancient astronomers called the Sea, a vast region of the sky inhabited exclusively by marine constellations.

The star on Andromeda's head, Sirrah, is also one of the four stars that make up the great Square of Pegasus, the winged horse depicted upside-down, of whom only the front part is visible. Under Andromeda's feet are the stars of the magical hero Perseus, who is fitted out with all the trappings of his invincible strength: the helmet that makes him invisible, the winged sandals that allow him to fly, the mirror-shield, and the magic sickle. His bag (*kibisis*) is also a work of magic. With one hand he holds the head of the horrendous Medusa, which, at one time, was considered a separate constellation (Caput Medusae) and which is marked by the sinister star Algol, famous for its maleficent influence.

At this point we encounter the ecliptic with the sign of Pisces. The Fish are linked by a long cord that is tied near the large constellation of Cetus —the whale or marine monster—with which they swim in the heavenly Sea.

The legend known to us about these stars is the one we find in the writings of Apollodorus, Homer, Herodotus, Clemens Alexandrinus, and Ovid. It is basically about the creation of an Argive kingdom, onto which is grafted the fight against a Lybian queen—impersonated by Medusa. In this legend there are also elements of Phoenician legends, the birth of quarrelsome twins (common to so many mythologies), and links with the Assyrian-Babylonian myth of Marduk-Bel and Tiamat.

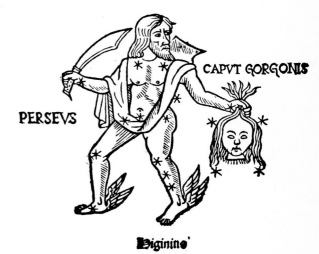

Perseus. From Hyginus, Poetica astronomica *(1485 edition)*

Opposite: *Perseus. From Hevelius,* Uranographia totum coelum stellatum *(1690)*

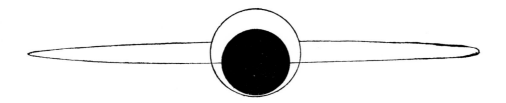

Algol and its motion. From Flammarion, Les Etoiles

415

The Wondrous Legend of Perseus

There once ruled over Argolis a king who was famous for his strength, Abas the Invincible. His fame was so great even after he died that a glimpse of his shield would provoke an enemy to flee in terror. By his wife, Aglaia, Abas had two sons—Acrisius and Proetus. They had such quarrelsome and violent natures that it was said they had quarreled even in their mother's womb. These disputes continued after their father's death since he had commanded them to rule the kingdom alternately, not to divide it in half. Of all the reasons for hatred between the two brothers, one created an irreversible crisis. Proetus had fallen in love with Acrisius' daughter, the beautiful Danaë, and he had secret meetings with her. It was not long, however, before the incest was discovered and a violent argument erupted, which degenerated into civil war. The armies of the two brothers confronted each other many times but no one succeeded in winning until the twins reluctantly decided to divide the kingdom: Acrisius took Argos, and Proetus, Tiryns and the coast of Argolis.

Seven gigantic Cyclopes, the Gasterocheires, were called by Proetus to fortify Tiryns with rocks so enormous that two mules were unable to move one. Acrisius also strengthened Argos, but he was tormented by the fact that he did not have any sons. To whom would he leave his kingdom? So he decided to consult an oracle to find out what fate had in store for him. The response was ever-so-inauspicious: not only would his wife not conceive again but a son would be born of Danaë who one day would be the cause of his death.

Frightened by such a prophecy, the king decided to fight his destiny and ordered that Danaë be locked up in the highest tower of the city. Everything was provided for: the wooden doors were exchanged for doors made of bronze, ferocious packs of dogs presided at every entrance, the windows were completely barred so as to prevent indiscreet glimpses of the unhappy girl who, assisted by a female slave, was condemned to oblivion.

However, the absolute isolation of Danaë's prison did not prevent the immortal gods from observing what went on in her cell. Zeus had set his eyes on the young princess and had fallen so much in love that he decided to make her his own. So he transformed himself into a fine golden rain that fell from the sky, penetrated the seals of the tower, settled on Danaë's lap, and took her.

From this divine love a son was born, Perseus, whose crying revealed his birth to Acrisius. Perhaps believing that this was the incestuous son of Proetus—and unable to commit a barbarous act against his own daughter—the king decided to entrust the god of the sea, Poseidon, with the fate of both mother and baby. Thus Danaë and Perseus were enclosed in a wooden ark and abandoned at sea.

After many days the capricious marine currents pushed the boat toward the island of Seriphos, over which Polydectes reigned. This king had a brother, Dictys, who noticed the boat drifting as he was fishing. He pushed it onto the beach and found the two bodies, unconscious but still alive. Having quenched their thirst and massaged them, he took them to the royal palace where Polydectes, struck by Danaë's beauty and the torment in her face, as well as by the presence of the baby, guessed at the mysterious sign of destiny and offered them hospitality in his palace.

Thus Perseus grew up in Seriphos. He played with boys of his own age and excelled in discus throwing and wrestling. Despite his young age, he often had to defend Danaë from the constant advances of Polydectes, who had fallen in love with her and wanted to marry her at all costs, despite her refusal. As the

Perseus. From the Alfonsine Tables *(thirteenth century)*

presence of Perseus prevented the king from using force, he conceived of a plan to free himself of the young man. Feigning love for Hippodameia, daughter of a king on the continent, he gathered his closest friends, among them Perseus, and explained to them that, although the island was poor, he did not want to cut a poor figure with the princess' parents. So he asked that each of them offer a beautiful horse to be donated to the family of Hippodameia. All consented except Perseus who, not having any possessions of his own, found himself in the embarrassing situation of not being able to honor the request of the person who had been his benefactor. He therefore told the king he would accomplish any exploit, even the most arduous, requested of him.

Polydectes, who had foreseen this, astutely asked Perseus to bring him the head of the Gorgon Medusa. This Medusa once was a beautiful Lybian princess who lived near Lake Tritonis. She had two sisters, also daughters of Phorcys and Cetus, who were also very beautiful.

Medusa, who had had very fine golden hair, aroused Poseidon's desire and, having transformed himself into a bird to trick her, surprised her while she was officiating in the temple consecrated to Athene; there, heedless of their profanity, he seduced her. The revenge of the goddess was not long in coming: she turned Medusa and her two sisters into monsters, a kind of hybrid of a bird—with wings and feet of a raptor and nails of bronze—and a woman—with breasts, a frightful face, big teeth, protruding tongue, and hair consisting of tangles of serpents. Their gaze was especially lethal—it transformed those who dared to intercept it into stone.

The task of defeating such a powerful monster presented itself to Perseus in all its enormity. No mortal could kill such a powerful creature. As he pondered his lot, Athene appeared to the young man, for she had decided to help him. She took him with her to the island of Samos and taught him the use of a magical mirror-shield in which he could look at the Gorgon's reflected image and avoid being turned into stone. Also, Hermes came to Perseus' aid by giving him a small, very sharp sickle endowed with special powers. He also told Perseus that he would need winged sandals that would enable him to fly, the helmet of Hades that would make him invisible, and the *kibisis*—the magical bag—to hold the head of the Medusa once it was cut from the body. He told him that this bag could only be obtained from the nymph Styx, but that no one knew where she lived except the three Graeae, nymphs with the bodies of swans who lived in a large royal palace on the mountain where Atlas reigned.

Sisters of the Gorgons, the three Graeae shared between them only one eye and one tooth which they continually passed back and forth. The eye bestowed the ability to perceive and the tooth had divinatory powers.

The voyage to the realm of the night was long and tiresome but Perseus at last came in sight of the three great thrones on which the swan-nymphs sat. Staying out of sight, he patiently waited for the moment when they would exchange the eye and the tooth and, when this happened, he quickly grabbed them. With the new qualities conferred upon him by these two organs he was able to find out where the nymph Styx lived. She was the sinister daughter of Oceanus and Thetis who acquired her name from her role as the guardian of the icy river Styx, where Mercury delivered the souls of the dead to Charon. She dwelt on the top of a high rock which was supported by columns of silver, and it was here that she consigned to Perseus the helmet of Hades, the winged sandals, and the magical bag.

Finally equipped, Perseus undertook the long voyage to the land of the Hyperboreans in search of the Gorgons. The closer he came to the fatal

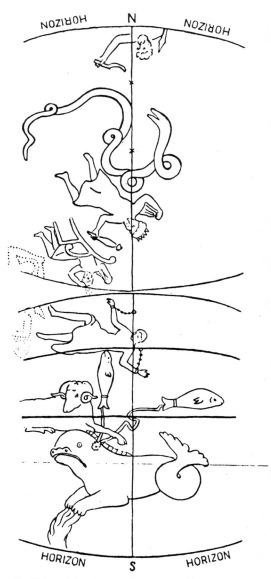

Meridian of the winter solstice at midday in 5744 B.C. In addition to Cetus, Andromeda, and Cassiopeia, Perseus can be seen in the dotted lines to the left of center. These constellations were visible at midnight of the summer solstice during the same period

dwelling place the more dramatically the landscape changed. The green of the plants increasingly changed into a marble gray, and the forest seemed petrified by a spell; the atmosphere was terrifying.

As he proceeded, the young man began to see some statues of human beings that looked perfectly real. They all depicted people with terrified expressions who had been caught in the act of covering their eyes with a raised arm or uttering a scream that would never be heard. They were the victims of the Gorgons, petrified by their lethal look.

Made invisible by the helmet, and walking backward so as to see only the image reflected in the mirror-shield, Perseus approached the frightening figure of Medusa with his heart in his throat. The variety and the colors of the serpents that sprouted from the monster's head formed a head of hair that was horrendously alive. The mouth was an obscene wound from which a swollen tongue hung, and pointed, yellow teeth like those of a wild beast could be seen.

Having approached this being so closely that he could hear both its ill-omened breathing and the hissing of the serpents, Perseus gathered his courage and, with one blow of the magical sickle, cut off Medusa's head. To his great amazement, there came jumping out of the wound the winged horse Pegasus and the warrior Chrysaor with a golden sickle in his hand. These two creatures had been generated in Medusa by Poseidon before her metamorphosis when he had seduced her in Athene's temple.

Not understanding this wonder before him, Perseus decided not to confront them; instead, taking advantage of his invisibility, he quickly picked up the head of the Gorgon, slipped it into the bag, and made off as fast as he could since he feared the revenge of the other sisters.

Tired but happy to have escaped the danger, he decided, while flying over northern Africa, to make a stop and rest at the Garden of the Hesperides, dwelling of Atlas. There he asked the Titan for asylum and hospitality, but Atlas was reminded of a prophecy by Themis who had predicted the arrival of a son of Jupiter who would rob him of his golden apples. Not knowing that the oracle referred to Hercules, he rudely refused to offer hospitality to Perseus. Offended, Perseus pulled the head of the Medusa out of the *kibisis* and showed it to the enormous Titan. The metamorphosis was instantaneous: the hair and beard of Atlas became forests, his body and head changed into a mountain chain and, above these, settled the sky with all its stars.

Continuing his voyage and flying over Lybia, Perseus dropped the eye and tooth he had taken away from the Graeae into Lake Tritonis. However, as he was closing the *kibisis* again, a few drops of Medusa's blood fell onto the desert and were instantaneously transformed into a population of reptiles, monsters, scorpions, and poisonous serpents. Later, one of these would kill the Argonaut Mopsus.

Now, the wheel of fortune had not stopped turning in favor of the young Perseus. While flying over the coast of Philistia, a strange sight unfolded before his eyes: on the seashore, chained to the rocks, stood a young woman, naked, of such beauty that Perseus had never seen before; her sinuous body was decorated with precious gems—necklaces of pearls and sapphires, bracelets mounted with rubies, and, in her black hair, diamonds that shone like stars in the night. She was Andromeda, daughter of King Cepheus and Queen Cassiopeia, and destined to an unusual fate because of her mother's vanity.

Cassiopeia, a woman of great beauty, had dared to declare that she was more beautiful than the Nereids, the fifty sirens who were daughters of Nereus and Doris, whose duty it was to assist the goddess of the sea, Thetis, in her mythical palace on the bottom of the sea.

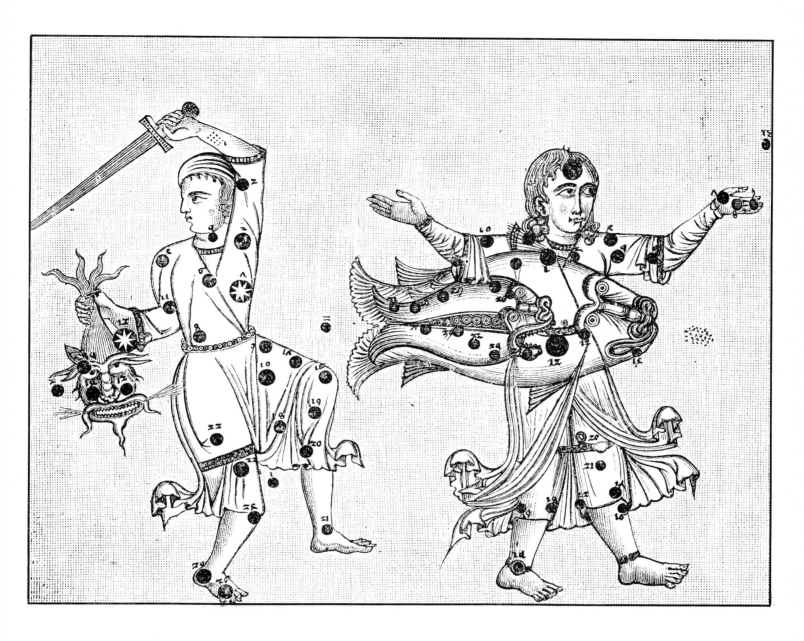

These Sirens had subsequently complained to Poseidon. To punish Cassiopeia for her vanity he sent the huge marine monster Cetus, against Philistia. This creature, a female, was the daughter of Pontus and Mother Earth; in turn, she was the mother of the serpent Ladon, Echidne, the three Gorgons, and the three Graeae.

In a short time Cetus had devastated the coast, the harbors, the ships, and the cities of the kingdom with such force that Cepheus and Cassiopeia went to the oracle in order to find out the reasons for this calamity. The reply of the wizard was cruel: the monster was Poseidon's revenge against the queen's vanity and, to free themselves of it, they had to sacrifice their daughter Andromeda—dressed only in her jewelry—to it, on the seashore. With death in their hearts, the parents had to have their daughter chained to a rock and, at a distance, they anxiously awaited the arrival of the terrible Cetus.

Moved by the tears of the young princess and taken by love for her, Perseus flew to Cepheus and Cassiopeia and proposed an exchange: he would slay the monster, thus saving them from the scourge, and they would give him Andromeda in marriage so he could take her with him to Greece. Having obtained their consent, he prepared himself for the duel. It was not long before Cetus appeared: the waters of the sea parted and the enormous mass of the monster showed itself in all its horror.

Having pulled out the head of Medusa, Perseus flew high in the sky, ready to transform Cetus into stone by showing her the head of the Gorgon. But this did not come to pass; seeing Perseus' shadow on the water, the monster attacked it, exposing its undefended neck. At once the hero swung his sickle in the air and the severed head of Cetus floated on the waves. To get a good look at the monster as it was slowly sinking, Perseus went to the shore and placed Medusa's head face down on a patch of seaweed. When he picked the head back up, the seaweed had changed into a strange plant that had never been seen before—red coral, which took its color from Cetus' blood.

Great was the relief of Andromeda's parents and the inhabitants of Philistia. In gratitude, festivities and sacrifices were celebrated and the wedding of the two young people was prepared in an atmosphere of joy. However, not everyone rejoiced. The warrior Agenor (or Phineus, in some versions), Andromeda's fiancé, had been forgotten as a result of the disastrous events and Perseus' incredible exploit. He was plotting to take revenge on the foreign hero and to regain his right to the woman. In these plans he was aided by Cassiopeia and together they prepared a stratagem.

While the wedding was being celebrated with balls and banquets, Agenor lowered himself, along with a group of men who had remained loyal to him, among the celebrators, and so Perseus was surrounded. Cepheus attempted in vain to persuade the warrior not to desecrate the nuptial rite, and so the battle began. Although he had already killed many of the enemy, Perseus realized that his forces could not hold out much longer. He asked the guests to turn their backs and, revealing the head of Medusa, he transformed Agenor, Cassiopeia, and their followers into statues. He then put on his winged sandals, took Andromeda in his arms, pulled her up with him into the sky, and headed back toward the island of Seriphos.

Danaë's situation on the island was precarious. Believing Perseus dead, Polydectes had thrown away his mask and now tried to marry her by force. She had taken refuge on the sacred soil of Athene's temple, where she could not be captured, and Polydectes had had the temple surrounded and gave orders not to let any food enter until the woman had come out of her own volition.

Having seen this, Perseus went to Polydectes' court, where he was entertaining his friends. Great was the general dismay when they saw him. In keeping the promise made before his departure Perseus pulled his trophy out of the bag and showed it to the king—who was instantly changed to stone, along with the others present. Perseus then returned to Argos with Danaë and Andromeda to reclaim that kingdom. Acrisius, mindful of the oracle, fled to Larissa. Once he had reorganized and consolidated Argos, Perseus went to live in Tiryns, where he succeeded in reuniting the two territories.

One day he was invited to Larissa for the funeral games in honor of the king of that city. He participated in several competitions and in one he threw the discus badly. It fell into the crowd and accidentally killed Acrisius who was there, unaware of his grandson's presence. The oracle's prophecy was fulfilled.

Subsequently Perseus fortified the walls of Midea and Mycenae. From then on, the Mycenaeans, forgetting that the true founder of their city had been the heroine Mycene, proclaimed him as its founder. Among other things, they narrated how he had succeeded in making a spring well up for the city by pulling up a mushroom (*mykes*), from which water gushed forth that nourished the fountain of Perseus.

It was said that Perses, son of Andromeda and Perseus, was the founder of the dynasty of the Persian kings. Later, when they claimed the country of the Hellenes, they referred to Perseus as one of their progenitors.

Al-Sufi's Perseus

Diodorus Siculus has recorded for us the legend of Dionysus and Ariadne's arrival in Argos and the conflict that Perseus had with the god of wine. He even narrates how Ariadne and her crown were transformed into stone by Perseus before the crown became a constellation.

It is said that it was Poseidon who transformed Cepheus and Cassiopeia into constellations, and Athene created Andromeda.

Marduk or Horus?

The mythological elements that compose the legend of Perseus are among the most beautiful in all of classical literature, but they derive from preexisting models. These were admirably woven together by bards of great genius whose work was, in turn, reinterpreted or assimilated by other religions.

Thus Perseus already existed in the Sumerian cuneiform writings about Marduk's battle against the monster of the chaos, the goddess Tiamat. In that legend Andromeda was Ishtar (traditionally depicted as naked and covered with jewels), whom Marduk had chained to the rocks so he would be able to confront her emanation—Tiamat (Graves, *The Greek Myths*).

In Christian iconography Perseus and Cetus became Saint George and the Dragon; Perseus and Medusa were changed into David and Goliath. Proetus and Acrisius are the typical set of twins like Jacob and Esau, Pharez and Zarah, or the Palestinian Mot and Aleyn. Proetus, as lover of Danaë, is evidence of the great popularity of love between blood relatives in antiquity.

Robert Graves narrates that, in a more ancient version of the myth, Proetus, Danaë, Perseus, Acrisius, and the floating ark appear to be linked with the tradition of Isis, Osiris, Set, and the infant Horus. According to this interpretation Proetus (the Argive Osiris) was united with Danaë (his sister-wife, Isis), who bore him Perseus (Horus). Acrisius was the jealous Set who killed his twin Osiris and was punished for this by the revenge of Horus. The ark was the boat, made of acacia wood, that was used by Isis and Horus to search for the body of Osiris in the delta (Graves, ibid.).

Also Semele and Dionysus were locked up in an ark by Cadmus and arrived at the island of Brasiae in it. Similarly, when Rhoeo (Pomegranate)—daughter of Staphylus (Grape Cluster) and Chrysothemis (Golden Order)—was pregnant with Anius, she reached the island of Delos on a craft shaped in the form of a sickle. (Rhoeo was the aunt of the three mythical winegrowers, Olive Oil, Grain, and Wine, an ancient triad of the Great Mother of Cretan origin. Their cult survives today in the orthodox element of the triple receptacle—the *kernos*—used for the offering of oil, grain, and wine.)

As emanation of the new solar god, Perseus represented the Argolid conquest of Lybia, a land where matriarchy was dominant. Here the goddess Neith—who had been identified as the ancestor of Athene by Plato in his *Timaeus*—was worshiped. The aegis of this goddess was a goatskin containing a snake and protected by the mask of the Gorgon. It had belonged to Neith long before Athene sprung from Zeus' brain. The original myths about Athene were all manipulated by the Athenians, who made sure to delete all previous loves or marriages of their first goddess, whom they wanted *Pallas*, a virgin.

The Gorgon's head with the serpents was in reality a mask that was used by the priestesses of the moon, the followers of Neith, during the mysteries; it served to scare away curious onlookers. According to more ancient narratives the Medusa had the body of a horse or a mare and, in this form, she had married Poseidon in one of the marriages he had contracted while in the form of a stallion. This would justify Polydectes' request that Perseus donate a horse

Perſeus.

as a gift for Hippodameia. Here appears a link with Lybia, where, before the arrival of the Argolids, the lunar goddess Neith was worshiped. Her marine emanation, Cetus, had mated with the god of the sea, Phorcys, and given birth to her priestess-daughters—the Phorcids, or Graeae, and the Gorgons—who were forced to marry the Argive followers of the stallion-god Poseidon. In so doing they took possession of the rites for rain and the cult of the sacred horse (Graves, ibid.).

Intriguing linguistic similarities often turn up, complicating the myth and its uncertain origins. Being so similar to Hermes in all his attributes, Perseus could have been confused with the god who, as the messenger of death, was called *Pterseus*, or the Destroyer. Cepheus (*cepha*) meant Stone and, in Phoenician, *Andromeda* indicated a rocky cliff. Strabo wrote that all Phoenician ships had a winged horse on the bow as a figurehead and a symbol of navigation. On the horse there was often a rider with, in his hand, the symbol of the city of Sais—the head of the Medusa. In addition the typical Phoenician ship was called *Perseu*, or Runner, by the sailors.

The origin of Cassiopeia from *Quassiu-Peaer*, or Pink Face, is also Phoenician (see Brown). In many versions Cassiopeia is an Ethiopian queen, but we must remember that in classical Greek texts all the lands far to the south—including India and Arabia—were called Ethiopia.

In the *Rig-Veda* there is mention of Pagas, the swift horse of the Aswin twins (represented by the stars Alpha and Beta Arietis).

Bayer's Perseus (1603)

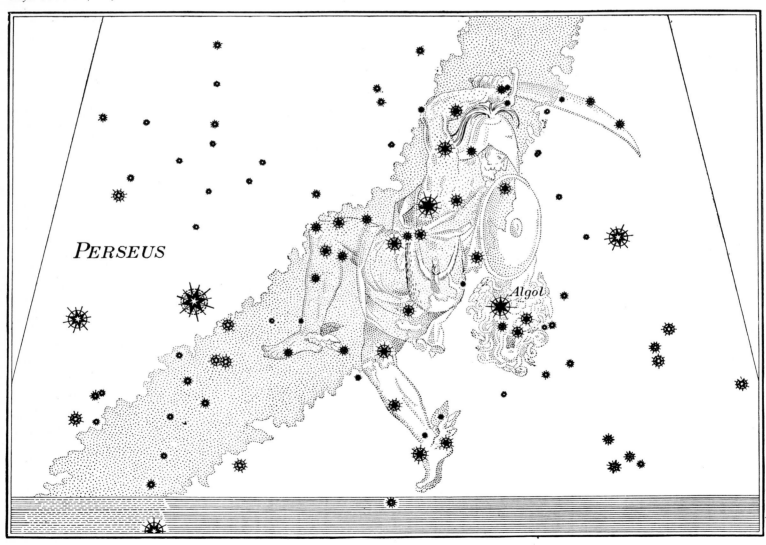

PERSEUS

Algol

The Constellation

The stars of Perseus occupy the region of the sky that is adjacent to Cassiopeia, Andromeda, Triangulum, Aries, Taurus, and Auriga. Perseus is partially immersed in the Milky Way and because of this he was called the Stirrer of Heavenly Dust by Aratus in the third century B.C. The force of his battling agitated the stardust in the sky, which formed the Milky Way.

Autumn is the best time of the year to observe this constellation. The heliacal rising of its stars precedes that of Andromeda, which has given some people the impression that Perseus saves Andromeda by taking her up into the sky far from the dark monster. The constellation is one of the widest, spanning twenty-eight degrees. Its main stars form a curve sometimes called Perseus' Segment.

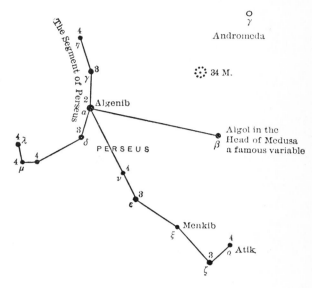

Ancient illustrations show the hero as young, wearing only his *talaria* (winged sandals) and a light cloth around his hips. With his left hand he holds the *gorgoneion*, head of Medusa, marked by the star Algol (a star that has been identified with the devil due to the extraordinary variations of its light), and in his right hand he holds the *falx*, which is the sickle he received from Mercury, a weapon of the Titans. His story must have been known in Greece before the fifth century B.C. because Euripides and Sophocles wrote about his exploits.

His name may have been derived from the epithet of Hermes, Pterseus, or from the Phoenician *Parash*, or Rider. In the fourth century B.C. Ctesius referred to a stellar figure, originating in Babylonia, by the name of Parsondas. The name *Parasica* found in Indian astronomical texts is a corruption of the Greek name.

The Arab astronomers called him *Hamil Ras al-Ghul*, or He Who Holds the Head of the Devil, a name that came to Europe by way of Moorish Spain. There it became Almirazgual, while Bershawish, Fersaus, and Siaush are Arabic spellings of the Greek name since their alphabet lacked the letter P.

According to the nineteenth-century scholar Kazimirski, Gul was a female demon or monster of the desert that assailed travelers and devoured them beginning at their feet. The Hebrews called her *Rosh ha Satan*, the Head of Satan, and also Lilith, who was the legendary first wife of Adam. She was a nocturnal vampire of the world of the abyss who reappeared in medieval demonology as the witch Lilith—one of the personalities of Goethe's *Walpurgisnacht* in *Faust*.

PERSEUS

Herodotus maintained that Perseus and Andromeda had a son by the name of Perses, from whom Persia got its name and from whom the Persian kings descended, calling themselves Cephenes, descendants of Cepheus—son of Belos—who some have identified with the Cepheus of the stars.

In the *Coelum stellatum christianum*, Perseus became the apostle Paul while, strangely, the Caput Medusae with its demoniacal star became the Holy Book. The lucida of the constellation is called Algenib, derived from *al-Janb*, the Side; in some catalogues it appears as Marfak, Mirfak, or Mirzak.

The classical astrologers assigned this constellation the qualities of Jupiter and Saturn, which bestowed a courageous nature, strength, and intelligence, but with a tendency toward lying. The cabalists assigned it the twelfth trump card of the tarots, the Hanged Man.

Although Algol also had the nature of Saturn and Jupiter, this star caused misfortune, violence, decapitation, hanging, and incitement to murder. It was the most diabolical and maleficent star of all the stars in the sky. Its name derives from *Ras al-Ghul*, the Head of the Devil.

40
Pisces

The Fish, Pisces, comprise the twelfth zodiacal constellation. Like Libra and Gemini they present a double figure, and their design is so extravagant that it makes them one of the most interesting constellations in the sky.

On the star maps we find ourselves in the celestial region called the Sea in antiquity. In this marine atmosphere the Fish swim in different directions, and they are at some distance from each other as well as from the ecliptic. In order to make them belong to it, their designers had to resort to the artifice of tying their tails with ribbons which are joined just below the ecliptic in the node marked by the star Alrisha.

The fish that looks toward the north is located to the left of the Square of Pegasus and grazes Andromeda's chest or, as on the Arab maps, actually ends right on the maiden's breast, marked by the star Mirach. The fish that looks toward the west in the direction of Aquarius is located under Pegasus' mane and is given its shape by a group of stars in the form of a trapezoid.

Two ribbons start out in one node and tie together two fish that are located at the two sides of a square. We almost seem to have here the work of a surrealist astronomer who is excited by the view of the stars on the black carpet of the night. The reality, however, could lead us to a no less fantastic, scientific incident that occurred long ago.

Between 6000 and 4000 B.C. the four cardinal constellations were Gemini, Virgo, Sagittarius, and Pisces. During this period the astronomers—who in their study of the stars had already discovered not only the movements of the sun along the ecliptic and its daily position with respect to the constellations but also the meridians, zeniths, and many heavenly laws—were confronted with a perfect pattern of forms due to a strange coincidence. This perfect design was formed by the four cardinal points along the zodiac and the Polar Star. The most surprising aspect was the fact that the ecliptic, the celestial horizon, the meridian, and the Milky Way all coincided in the equinoctial signs—Sagittarius and Gemini. The meridian of the solstices went from Virgo to the Polar Star, Thuban in Draco; continued through the center of the Milky Way with respect to the equinoxes; crossed the Square of Pegasus; and arrived at last in the constellation of Pisces, which marked the winter solstice.

The harmony of this arrangement was enhanced even further by Gemini (the guards at the entrance for the souls who were ready for reincarnation), the Virgin-Demeter (with the stalk of grain and the sickle that marked the summer solstice as well as the time of the grain harvest), Sagittarius (guard of the door through which passed the souls of the dead who were waiting in the Milky Way for the moment of their upcoming reincarnation), and the Square of Pegasus. This last constellation was identified with the jeweled paradise of the goddess Siduri and was the unit of measure with which Utnapishtim, the Sumerian Noah, constructed the rescuing ark (see the chapter on Pegasus).

During later times the slow progression of the precession of the equinoxes gradually moved the cardinal points away from this perfect picture. As this happened the Fish lost the charismatic force they once had until they even almost lost their name in the third century B.C., when they were simply called

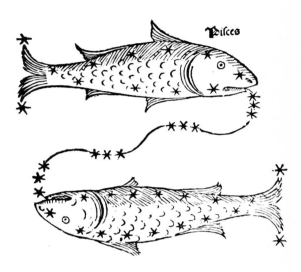

Pisces. From Hyginus, Poetica astronomica *(1485 edition)*

Opposite: *Pisces. From Hevelius,* Uranographia totum coelum stellatum *(1690)*

Position of Pisces along the meridian of the winter solstice c. 5000 B.C.

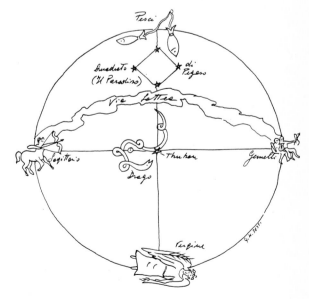

425

Water. However, as is known, astronomers and writers of myths are very conservative and the Fish thus succeeded in retaining their title even if the legends about their origin changed.

Al-Biruni maintained that, etymologically, the name of the sign was the Fish—singular, not plural—and for this reason he asserted that it was originally represented by a single creature. He had probably read Eratosthenes, who recounted that this sign was the stellar transposition of the Syrian goddess Derceto who was worshiped in particular at Ascolano. The legend says that Aphrodite, in revenge for Derceto's offending her, inspired in her a violent passion for the priest Siron or Sirio, who made her the mother of Semiramis.

Once the spell had worn off, Derceto castrated and murdered her lover, abandoned her daughter in the desert, and threw herself into a lake in Palestine. There the gods supposedly changed her into a fish who, in turn, was transformed into a constellation. In Syria she was worshiped as a goddess and depicted with the body of a fish and the head and arms of a woman.

The best-known Greek myth about the origin of this sign is the one about Typhon's pursuit of Aphrodite, goddess of love modeled on the Middle Eastern goddess Ishtar, who had unleashed the universal deluge. The monster Typhon was infatuated with Aphrodite and pursued her. However, the goddess and her young son, Eros, escaped, taking refuge along the banks of the Euphrates. To hide them from Typhon, the obliging river nymphs transformed the two gods into twin fish who became a zodiacal constellation to commemorate this miracle (Ovid, *Fasti*, II. 457–474).

The Abandoned Sign

After the glorious position Pisces had in the long-ago sixth and fifth millennia B.C., the slow precessional movement shifted the winter solstice into Aquarius (from 4000 to 2000 B.C.) and then into Capricornus (from 2000 to the birth of Christ). At that point the celestial clock ticked off the great moment of this sign: the Fish found themselves in the prestigious role of being in the house of the sun at the spring equinox. Succeeding Aries in this role, they were to keep it for the next two thousand years. However, due to a series of unfortunate circumstances this did not take place (see page 54). Why not? The climate for renewal of the skies existed already. Caesar was recompiling the calendar; the Alexandrian school was in full bloom; the secret symbol of the first Christians was a fish; knowledge of geometry and mathematics had never been so sophisticated; and the understanding of the precession of the equinoxes had passed from practical to mathematical knowledge. Still, no one was able to place the spring equinox in the sign where it belonged. This shows that a reactionary immobility existed in the culture of the time, comparable to the position of the Catholic Church with respect to the heliocentric theories of Bruno and Galileo.

The calculation of the apparent motion of the sun in the zodiac had been the great conquest of protohistoric astronomy around which civilizing sciences such as agriculture and navigation flourished. For millennia astronomers had known how to calculate with great precision the point on the zodiac at which the sun stood at noon. Great progress was made in geometry and mathematics by the Sumerians, the Egyptians, and individuals such as Thales, Hipparchus, Ptolemy, the Pythagoreans, and many others. Was it that the stability of a lasting government that could sponsor such a change was lacking? The Romans, practical and pragmatic, needed only a good calendar to decorate their year with the dozens of festivities that the empire had created, as is shown by

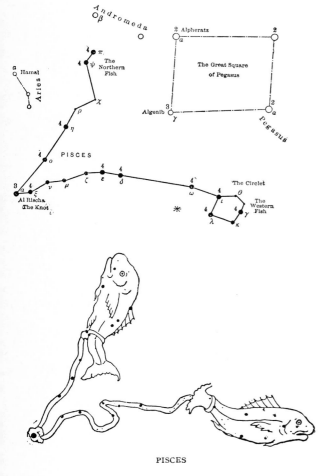

PISCES

Ovid's *Fasti*. They were never really interested in the change. The Greek philosophers had quarreled with each other in sterile personal battles. The only remaining cultural center was Alexandria, Egypt, where the Ptolemaic pharaohs had created three hundred years of continuity and stability, accumulating all the scientific, poetic, and religious written literature of the Middle East and Greece. It was here, however, that, with tragic destiny, fire destroyed the library where eight hundred thousand volumes had been collected. This accident can certainly be called the most serious cultural catastrophe of all time. There was a lack of myth-writers capable of readjusting the symbolism of the myths about seasons and characters. Astronomy entered into a kind of identity crisis that lasted until it was rediscovered by the Arab sultans after the eighth century.

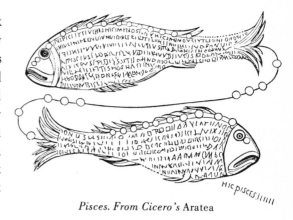

Pisces. From Cicero's Aratea

Thus it happened that after having marked the spring equinox for two thousand years, the sign of Aries erroneously maintained its position for the next two thousand years, thereby depriving Pisces of its rightful place. Yet the Age of Pisces had been announced as the blessed age when Virgo also would have returned to a cardinal position as the seat of the autumnal equinox, which made Virgil dream—in his fourth eclogue—of the return of the Golden Age: "Now the Virgin returns, the reign of Saturn returns; now a new generation descends from heaven on high. Only do thou, pure Lucina, smile on the birth of the child, under whom the iron brood shall first cease, and a golden race spring up throughout the world!"

The only thing that these verses accomplished was that Virgil was named honorary Christian by the followers of the new religion.

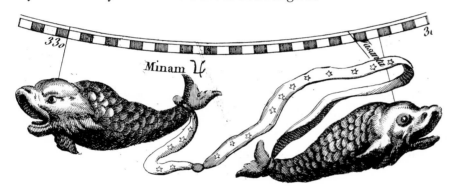

The Astrology of Pisces

A sign of water, changeable and feminine, the Fish are governed by the god of the sea, Neptune. Their influence on the human body was exercised on the feet, lymphatic system, synovial fluids, and gastro-abdominal system. A sign to dissolve material boundaries, Pisces influenced emotional receptivity, self-sacrifice, rhythm, impressionability, the isolated and the vague, the psychic and the sensitive, whatever relates to karma. As a result a large number of people born during this period have been mystics, poets, sufferers, drug addicts, and doctors.

The cabalists assigned Pisces the seventeenth trump card of the tarots, the Stars, but nowadays some seem to be more inclined to attribute to it the eighteenth, the Moon.

In the seventeenth century the apostle chosen for the formation of the Christian zodiac was Saint Matthew.

The ancient astrologers considered the joining of the slow planets, Jupiter and Saturn, in Pisces as a determinant of history. In the year 6 B.C. Jupiter and Saturn were also joined by Venus and this produced an exceptionally brilliant star, which tradition has recorded under the name of the Star of Bethlehem.

41
Piscis Austrinus

Piscis Solitarius, as the Southern Fish was sometimes called to distinguish it from Pisces, is a small constellation with one large star, the legendary Fomalhaut, which in Arabic means the Mouth of the Fish. Piscis Austrinus is located underneath Aquarius and Capricornus, rather isolated along the southern horizon of the sky. It can be observed around eleven at night in September, around nine in October, and seven in November. It is at its height on October 25.

This fish swims in the river of little stars that flows out of the urn of Aquarius. Ovid called it Piscis Aquosus, but it was also called Piscis Magnus and Piscis Capricorni due to its being near this sign.

Lalande and Dupuis associated the Southern Fish with the Syrian fish-shaped god Dagon, who is depicted on bas-reliefs as having the body of a fish with human shoulders and a head crowned with a tiara. He was also referred to by the name of Ea or Oannes and, according to legend, he had come from the sea at the time when men were uncivilized barbarians. It was he who had instructed them in reading, the sciences, and agriculture.

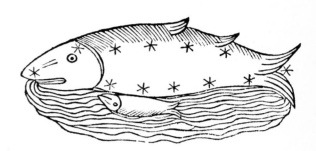

Piscis Austrinus. From Hyginus, Poetica astronomica *(1485 edition)*

Piscis Austrinus. From Cicero's Aratea

In the classical period the Greeks had two myths about the Southern Fish, both identical to those about the sign of Pisces. The first was about Aphrodite, who transformed herself into a fish in the river Euphrates in order to flee from Typhon. The second was that of the goddess Derceto, who was, against her will, driven by Aphrodite to love a mortal man. Once the effect of the spell was gone, Derceto killed her lover and, having abandoned her daughter Semiramis, whom she had conceived with him, she threw herself into a lake where she was transformed into a fish.

The lucida Fomalhaut, a star of first magnitude, is very famous in ancient astronomy since it was one of the Royal Stars that indicated the four cardinal points of the solstices and equinoxes between 4000 and 2000 B.C. (The other three stars were Aldebaran for the spring, Regulus for the summer, and Antares for autumn.)

The nineteenth-century French astronomer Camille Flammarion maintained that its ancient name was Hastorang. In the terminology of the desert nomads there are two names, *al-Difdi al-Awwal*, the First Frog, and *Thalim*, the Ostrich. For some reason, Cicero called Fomalhaut Stella Canopus, perhaps because he identified both stars by one name.

Ptolemy assigned it the influences of Venus and Mercury, whose powerful, positive, and fortunate charge it possessed.

Opposite: *Piscis Austrinus. From Hevelius,* Uranographia totum coelum stellatum *(1690)*

429

42
Sagitta

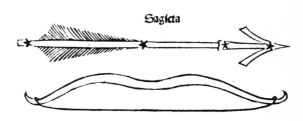

In the center of the Milky Way, above Aquila in the direction of Cygnus and Lyra, there is a small constellation, the smallest in the sky. It consists mainly of three stars in a straight line, followed by two other minor ones. This is Sagitta, the Arrow, which is visible every evening from July to October.

Although minuscule, this figure is very ancient. It is recorded by Aratus in the *Phaenomena* and Eratosthenes justifies its presence by identifying it with the arrow shot by Apollo against the Cyclopes, who forged the lightning with which Zeus had cut off the life of his son Asclepius, the divine doctor (see the chapter on Ophiuchus). Apollo had buried this arrow in the mountains of the Hyperboreans and, when Zeus finally forgave him, the wind brought the arrow back to Apollo with some stalks of wheat, a plant that was not yet known to the Hellenes. For this reason it was transformed into a constellation.

In Greek mythology there is another version—more famous and ancient—of this myth. It has to do with Prometheus, the Titan who was in chains where a vulture pecked at his liver every day. There existed a prophecy that said that Prometheus' suffering would last until one of the immortals agreed to descend voluntarily into Tartarus in his stead. The opportunity presented itself when the centaur Chiron was accidentally wounded with an arrow dipped into the poisonous blood of Hydra. The wound was incurable and since Chiron was immortal his agony was endless. Hercules himself asked Zeus to grant Chiron death, to release him in exchange for Prometheus' freedom. So it was that Hercules, invoking Apollo the Hunter, struck the vulture with an arrow and thereby put an end to the torture of the Titan (see the chapter on Centaurus). Thus it would be this arrow that was subsequently placed in the sky.

However, it is actually the association between Sagitta and Hercules that brings to mind the origin of the constellation of Hercules, which has had this name only in recent times. In antiquity it was still called Engonasi, or the One Who Kneels, and the Greeks did not know anything about him (see the chapter on Hercules). Earlier, in Sumerian astronomy, he was the god Marduk who, in a terrible battle, faced the monster of the primordial chaos, Tiamat. He shot an arrow into her heart and killed her.

In classical times Sagitta was also identified with the arrow of Cupid. Later it took the Greek name *Oistos*, Arrow, perhaps from the Turkish name of the constellation, *Otysys Kalem*, meaning the Straight or Smooth Arrow, and also the name *Toxon*, Bow. Later still the Arabs called it *al-Sahm*, or Arrow.

Many centuries later in 1627, when Julius Schiller reorganized stars into Christian constellations, this constellation became the Lance—the lance with which the Roman centurion Gaius Cassius penetrated Christ's ribs. In another version it became the nail of the crucifixion.

Ptolemy gave Sagitta the nature of Saturn tempered by some of Venus' influence. She supported abstract thought, teaching, and writing; but she also caused irritability, jealousy, and the risk of accidents.

Battle between Marduk and Tiamat

43
Sagittarius

Visible during summer nights and beautiful fall evenings, Sagittarius, the Archer, occupies the lowest region of the ecliptic, toward the south. Celestial maps depict him as having the body of a horse and trunk of a man in the act of shooting an arrow at the zodiacal Scorpius. Next to his forelegs there is the circle of the constellation of Corona Australis. The part of the constellation that represents a horse is completely immersed in the Milky Way, while the stars that form the bow touch only its border.

Except for the Indian descriptions of the sky, in which the constellation was represented with only a bow and an arrow, Sagittarius is present in all ancient sky maps as an archer who is half-man and half-animal. Originally the animal was mainly a goat, but it was subsequently changed into a horse.

The most ancient written description of Sagittarius appears in the *Catasterismi* of Eratosthenes, where the sign shows up not as a centaur but as a satyr, which was the ancient hybrid that preceded the arrival of the centaurs in the Mediterranean. Most probably the first satyr whose legend is known to us was the unforgettable Enkidu of the Epic of Gilgamesh, whom we discuss in the chapter on Orion. All the necessary mythical and uranographic background actually exists to enable us to hazard a guess that the first and original Sagittarius was Enkidu. He would have been transformed into a constellation along with Gilgamesh (Orion) due to the fame the two friends earned in their victory over the celestial Bull.

When we observe the location of the constellations of Taurus, Orion, and Sagittarius, we notice that Orion-Gilgamesh is depicted in the act of attacking the Bull with his club while, on the other side of the ecliptic, Enkidu-Sagittarius rises in the east just as the stars of Taurus set in the west. This gives the impression that the appearance of one constellation determines the disappearance of the other.

The proof of the existence of a faunlike creature used as the ancient figure of Sagittarius is carved on the marble celestial globe held by the Titan Atlas. On this sphere, which is more than two thousand years old, we can distinguish, as the ninth sign of the zodiac, a satyr who stands erect with a bow and arrow in his hands.

In the chapter on Centaurus we explain how the ancestor of the centaur in the Mediterranean was a hybrid of the goat, the donkey, and the bull. Pan, Dionysus, Minotaur, Silenus, the fauns, and Priapus himself anticipate the figure of the centaur, who appeared only after the introduction of the horse from Asia.

The presence of two centaurs in the stars of the sky has inevitably created some confusion about the identification of the character each represents. Certainly the centaur Chiron was originally attributed to the stars of Centaurus. However, even during Alexandrian and, later, Roman times, some authors confused Chiron with Sagittarius. In actuality, the character who originally represented Sagittarius in Greek mythology was the legendary Crotus, son of the goat-god Pan, and Eupheme, the famous nurse of the Muses.

Sagittarius. From Hyginus, Poetica astronomica *(1485 edition)*

Opposite: *Sagittarius. From Hevelius,* Uranographia totum coelum stellatum *(1690)*

433

Sagittarius. From the Durham manuscript

As the son of a goat-hybrid, he was probably a satyr and not a centaur, and therefore both Eratosthenes and the unknown sculptor of the Atlas were right. Crotus was reared on Mount Helicon with the Muses, and he became their companion and admirer. It was he who invented applause to express admiration for and joy in his foster sisters.

He was an infallible hunter, quick in the pursuit of his prey, and versatile in all the arts. To reward him for his skills and his friendship, the Muses entreated Zeus to transform him into a constellation suitable to his fame. So Zeus, in an effort to sum up all his qualities in one body, endowed him with the flanks of a horse because he was a great rider, a bow and arrow to celebrate his skill in the hunt, and the tail of a satyr because "the Muses experienced as much pleasure with Crotus as Dionysus did with the satyrs" (Hyginus, *Poetica astronomica*).

Bayer's Sagittarius

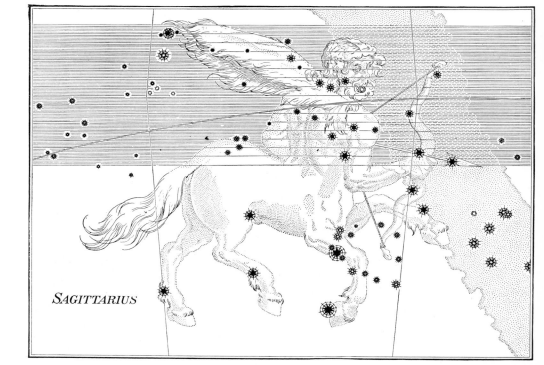

SAGITTARIUS

The stars of Sagittarius. From Easy Guide to the Constellations *(1916)*

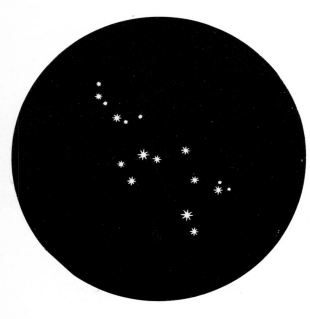

The Divine Door

In the fifth century B.C. a singular coincidence occurred in the pattern of the stars: the spring and fall equinoxes were exactly at the intersection of the Milky Way with the equinoctial meridian, the ecliptic, and the celestial equator. The two signs that occupied these positions at that time were Gemini for the spring equinox and Sagittarius for the fall equinox.

At that time the Milky Way was considered to be the abode of souls in between reincarnations. Upon death the soul of the departed had to wait for the autumnal equinox, when the heliacal rising of Sagittarius announced the Divine Junction, to be able to reenter the Milky Way. In order to be reincarnated, the same soul had to reenter the world through the "door" of Gemini. The only souls that were not subject to this law were those chosen for paradise, which was located between the four stars of the Square of Pegasus (see the chapter on Pegasus and the relevant illustration).

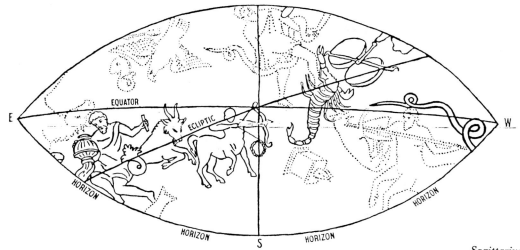

Sagittarius, on the meridian of the spring   equinox in 4667 B.C.

Sagittarius. From Cellarius, Harmonica macrocosmica *(1660)*

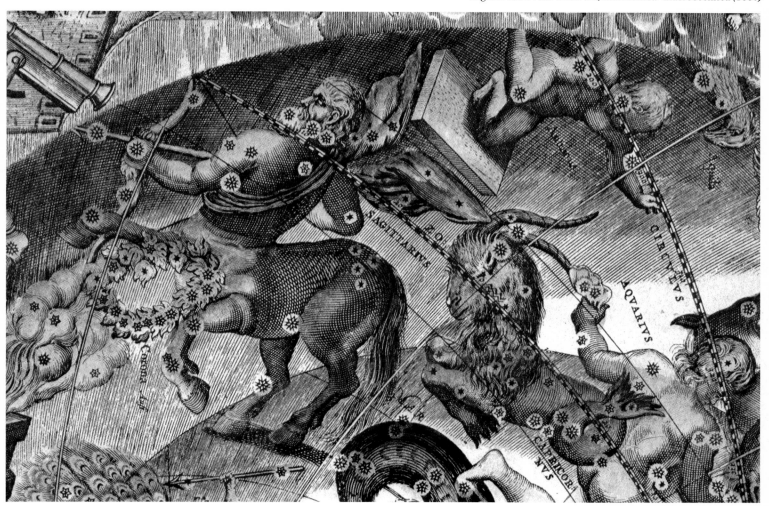

Sagittarius   435

SAGITTARIUS

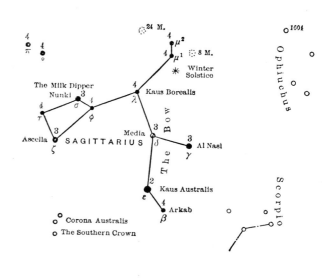

In the Coelum stellatum christianum (1627)
Sagittarius was replaced by the evangelist
Saint Matthew. Corona Australis, at his feet,
became the crown of King Solomon

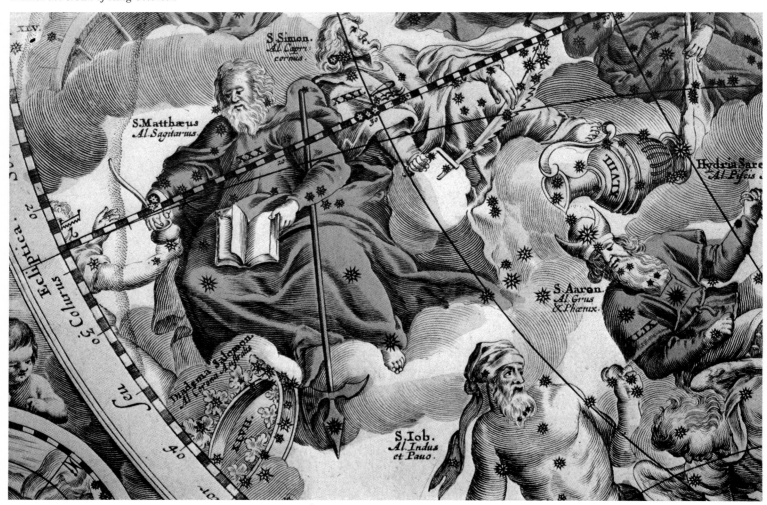

Sagittarius and Corona Australis

In observing the placement of the stars of Sagittarius, one is struck by the nearness of the circle of Corona Australis to the zodiacal sign. This stellar intimacy did not, of course, escape the notice of the ancient astronomers, who integrated it into representations of Sagittarius. The most obvious example is that of the major god of the Assyrian pantheon, the supreme father of the gods and the king of the sky and the earth, Assur, whose cult survived the destruction of Nineveh for at least eight centuries.

Generally depicted as a bearded figure in the center of a winged disk in the act of shooting an arrow from his bow, Assur is carved onto the majority of the Assyrian bas-reliefs. Sometimes he holds a circle in his hand in the place of a bow. The eagle's wings symbolize the royal characteristics of the god inside the flaming circle—which emphasizes his solar character. The bow is an expression of power and dominion (Cicero's Sagittipotens) while the circle in his hand represents the annual voyage of the sun through the zodiac, astronomically represented in Corona Australis.

Assur served as a model for the supreme god of the Medes, Ahura-Mazda, who was also depicted in a winged disk and with the circle of Corona Australis.

The Assyrian god Assur

Ahura-Mazda, god of the Medes

The Astrology of Sagittarius

A sign of fire, changeable and masculine, Sagittarius is governed by Jupiter. It influences the conscience, profundity of thought, achievement, expansion, meditation, literature, voyages, extravagance, and free-spiritedness. It is therefore not difficult to find among Sagittarians philosophers, psychologists, poets, musicians, priests, critics, travelers, and sports aficionados. In the human body its influence is manifested on the hips, thighs, sciatic nerve, arterial system, the sacrum, the gluteus, the pelvis, and the femur. The cabalists associated it with the sixth trump card of the tarots, the Lovers, although nowadays some believe it closer to the fourteenth, Temperance. Two lunar stations were located in Sagittarius, the eighteenth and the nineteenth, which the Arabs called *al-Na'am*, the Ostriches, and *al-Baldah*, the City. In India they were *Purva Ashadha*, the Ancient Inviolate One, and *Vitara Ashadha*, or the Present Inviolate One. In China they had the name of *Ki*, Sieve, and *Tow*, or Ladle.

If the placement of the zodiac signs were brought up to date with the precession of the equinoxes (an operation of the greatest importance for the ancient astrologers), Sagittarius would occupy the period from December 21 to January 21 in our calendar; it would contain the winter solstice and thus would become one of the four cardinal signs, along with Pisces, Gemini, and Virgo.

The Assyrian god Assur

44
Scorpius

Few constellations can boast an actual resemblance to the object they represent. The leading one among these is the star group of the Scorpion, which reminds even the layperson of the shape of the poisonous insect. Its stars are at their peak in June; they are located in the south, very low on the ecliptic. They are so low that it is no longer possible to see the curved line of its tail from most northern latitudes.

Although the Scorpion is nominally a part of the zodiac, the sun spends only nine days passing through its stars. The remaining two-thirds of the solar month are spent in the constellation of Ophiuchus—more precisely, in the Serpent that the giant holds in his hands.

The origin of this situation dates back to the time when the complete figure of the animal included the two stars that today mark the two plates of Libra. From the Sumerian time until Ptolemy two constellations belonged to Scorpius: the Body, with tail and stinger, and the Claws, which were cut off by Julius Caesar to create the sign of Libra.

The primitive Scorpion extended up to the feet of Virgo, with whom it shares not only the area of the sky, but, seemingly, a symbol as well: ♍ represents Virgo and ♏ stands for Scorpius. It was still this way at the time of Eratosthenes who, in *Catasterismi* (a work we know as his, but which seems to be an extract of a more important astronomical work), wrote: "Due to its great size the Scorpion was divided into two signs: in the one, the claws remained, in the other, the body and the stinger; each claw has two stars, one brilliant and the other dark; three more brilliant stars are located up front, two at its belly, five at the tail, four at the stinger. These stars are headed by the most beautiful of them all, the very brilliant one of the northern claw."

According to this description the star Beta Librae, marking the extremity of the northern claw, had to be more brilliant than Antares, which, today the lucida of the constellation, was once only of the second magnitude. This is the reason why it was seen as one of the two marking the belly, which undoubtedly are Alpha and Pi Scorpii.

The following is a table of observations made of the magnitude of Antares over the past two thousand years. It clearly shows how its low luminosity suddenly began to increase in the fifteenth century and then declined to 1.7:

127 B.C.	A.D. 960	1430	1590	1603	1667	1700	1750	1800	1840	1860	1880
2	2	2	1	1	1	1	1	1	1	1	1.7

Today its magnitude varies fairly regularly between 1.2 and 1.8 over a period of 1,733 days.

Perhaps it was this situation that inspired the Sumerian astronomers to imagine a light they called Lamp or Beacon between the claws of Scorpius.

When we look at the overall picture of the placement of the constellations above Scorpius, we notice that Ophiuchus, in addition to holding the Serpent in his hands, seems to be squashing the Scorpion with one foot. His companion, Hercules, squashes another reptilian figure—the Dragon.

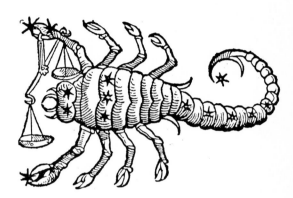

Scorpius. From Hyginus, Poetica astronomica *(1485 edition)*

Opposite: *Scorpius. From Hevelius,* Uranographia totum coelum stellatum (1690)

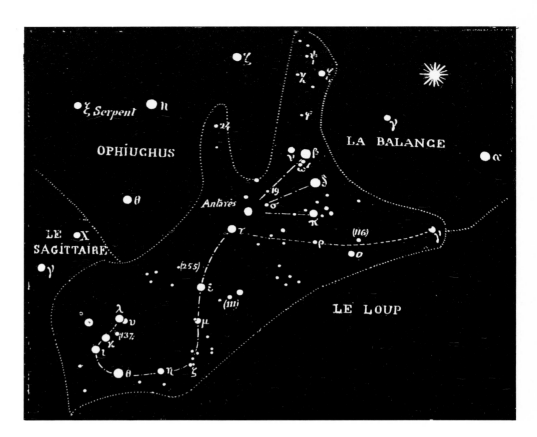

Reconstruction of the ancient constellation of Scorpius. At the center of the body is the first-magnitude star Antares. Antares was once much fainter, and Zubenschamali (Beta Librae), today in Libra, was the first-magnitude star that marked the northern claw of Scorpius. (Montage by the author from a map in Flammarion's Les Etoiles)

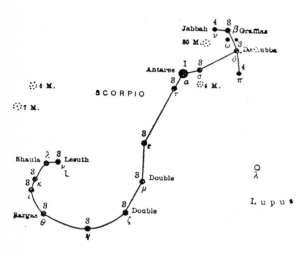

SCORPIO

These two heavenly brothers, typical solar heroes, are present on the part of the ecliptic that the sun traverses when its strength is waning in the fall. They symbolically reconfirm the future victory of the sun over the forces of the winter and dark, represented by the Dragon, the Serpent, and the Scorpion.

However, there is a more fascinating aspect of these figures revealed when we analyze their position 4,700 years ago. From this reconstruction it becomes clear that in 2700 B.C. the equinoctial meridian, the celestial equator, and the ecliptic joined at the point where Ophiuchus' foot pressed on the head of Scorpius during the autumnal equinox. Furthermore, the body of the serpent followed the equator but, when it reached the equinoctial meridian, it curved in order to follow it instead, until it reached the zenith with its head. This logical cycle is another demonstration of how the constellations are not a gratuitous fantasy but follow patterns prepared by competent astronomers.

Scorpius was considered to have played an instrumental part in the murder of several solar figures. It was in order to escape from him that the giant Orion dove into the sea and started swimming toward Delos. Before he could reach his destination, Apollo flew to the beach of the island, where Artemis—Orion's lover—was resting, and persuaded her to show her skill with the bow by hitting the small black dot that was approaching through the waves. Proudly the goddess shot an arrow, which hit its target, and the blood froze in her veins when she discovered that she had killed her lover (see the chapter on Orion).

In the astronomical allegories that are linked with the cult of Mithras, there is always a representation of the sacrifice of the celestial Bull surrounded by the symbols of the zodiacal and extrazodiacal constellations, the equinoxes, the sun, the moon, and a Scorpion who clasps the Bull's genitals with his claws (see the chapter on Taurus).

The famous tale of Phaëthon tells of the inexperienced son of Apollo, who rashly tried to drive the chariot of the sun along the zodiac. At the sight of the

Scorpion he was taken by such panic that he lost control of the horses and thereby caused the sun to swerve from its course. The incident cost the young man his life; he died as he plunged into the stars of the river Eridanus.

> Now all the horrors of the heav'ns he spies,
> And monstrous shadows of prodigious size,
> That, deck'd with stars, lie scatter'd o'er the skies.
> There is a place above, where Scorpio bent
> In tail and arms surrounds a vast extent;
> In a wide circuit of the heav'ns he shines,
> And fills the space of two celestial signs.

Ovid, *Metamorphoses*, II. 224–30

In these allegories there appears a simple astronomical symbolism that is based on the rising and setting of the stars. When Scorpius rises in the east, Orion, Taurus, and Eridanus set on the western horizon; this makes it seem as if Scorpius caused the disappearance of these stars.

Orion and Phaëthon are both synonymous with the sun as it enters the constellation of Scorpius, becomes weak, and starts its winter battle against the forces of darkness. This battle will not conclude until the sun's victorious climb back up onto the ecliptic starting in the sign of Taurus at the spring equinox.

Bayer's Scorpius (1603)

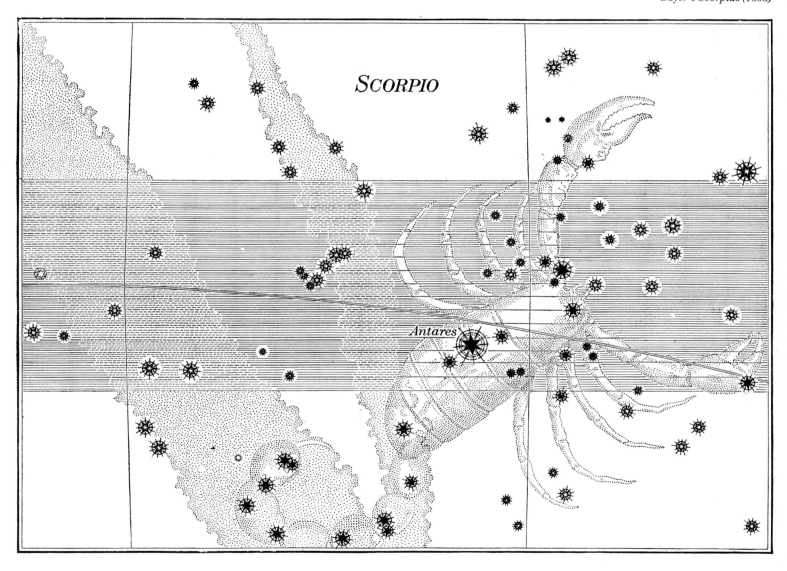

The midnight sky at London, looking south, May 15

In the history of the zodiac of the last six thousand years, Scorpius has a primary and influential position as the sovereign sign of the autumnal equinox. Between 4000 and 2000 B.C. the meridian moved slowly from the stinger to the body. During the next two thousand years it entered between the claws until these were changed into the sign of Libra.

Due to an anomalously static phase in the culture the cardinal signs did not pass on to the new combination of Pisces, Sagittarius, Virgo, and Gemini but remained frozen in the superseded order of Aries, Capricornus, Cancer, and, with the metamorphoses of Scorpius' claws, Libra.

Opposite: *The stars of Scorpius as seen on London's horizon. Because of the latitude it is not possible to see the stars of the tail and the stinger*

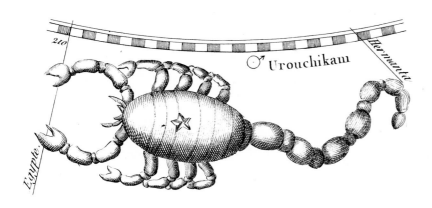

The Astrology of Scorpius

The eighth sign of the zodiac, Scorpius is a sign of water, fixed and feminine. Governed by Mars and Pluto, it presides over metaphysical thought and processes of putrefaction, fermentation, death, and resurrection. It produces passions, lust, violence, intuition, and profundity of thought. As for the human body, it exercises its influence on the sexual organs and urinary system.

Ptolemy assigned to Beta, Delta, and Pi the qualities of Mars and, to some extent, Saturn. Alpha, Tau, and Sigma were similar to Mars and also, to a lesser degree, to Jupiter. The stars of the junctures of the tail were similar to Saturn and also, somewhat, to Venus. Those in the stinger were like Mercury and Mars.

The Christian astronomers of the eighteenth century saw in Scorpius the apostle Saint Bartholomew. The cabalists associated it with the sixteenth trump card of the tarots, the Tower, but recently it has been assigned the thirteenth—Death—considered in its aspect of transformation and rebirth.

Scorpius was host to as many as three stations—the fifteenth, sixteenth, and seventeenth—in the ancient lunar zodiac. In the Arab *manzil* they were called *Iklil al-Jabhah*, or the Crown of the Forehead (Beta, Delta, and Pi Scorpii); *al-Kalb*, or the Heart (Antares); and *al-Shanlah*, or the Stinger (Iota and Epsilon Scorpii). In the Indian *nakshatra* we have Anaurada (Delta Scorpii), a positive and musical star that governed flowering meadows as well as the stomach. Then there is *Jyestha*, or the Most Ancient One (Antares), which is a sign of the deserts as well as of the right side of the body, and *Mula*, or the Root (Iota Scorpii), which is a sign of the stars and the left side of the body.

The three Chinese *sieu* were: *Fang*, or the Room (Pi, Beta, Delta Scorpii); *Sin*, or the Heart (Antares with Sigma and Tau Scorpii); and *Wei*, or the Tail (Mu, Eta, Epsilon, Nu, Theta, Iota, Kappa, Epsilon, and Lambda Scorpii).

The star Antares derives its beautiful name from *Anti Ares*, or Rival of Mars, for its reddish cast. Another name for this star was *Calbalacrab* from the Arabic *Kalb al-Akrab*, or the Heart of the Scorpion.

Scorpius. From a fifteenth-century engraving

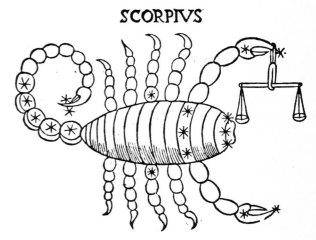

45
Taurus

Underneath the feet of Auriga stands Taurus,
robust, provided with menacing horns;
his head is surrounded by numerous stars.

Cicero, *De deorum natura*, II.XLIII

To Cicero's description we must add that the constellation of Taurus, the Bull, is enthroned in one of the richest regions of the firmament. Here shine the stars of the divine twins Castor and Pollux, Procyon with its golden reflections, the many-tinted Algol which indicates the head of the Medusa, and, above all, the greatest constellation of the sky—the giant Orion—at whose feet blazes the dazzling Sirius. Taurus rises in the east in October, immediately after sunset; it reaches his height in the south during December and January; it then descends toward the west and completely sets in April.

The figure of Taurus, as we know it, shows only the front part of the animal, which is turned toward the east and is composed of two distinct groups of stars. One, located on his forehead, is the V-shaped Hyades, including the star Aldebaran, and the other group is the Pleiades, located on his neck.

Originally the entire figure of a bull was included. From the time of Eratosthenes and Eudoxus on, however, only the front half was depicted. Most probably this was done to make room for the constellation of Aries, invented in Egypt to indicate the new course of the sun in the spring.

Taurus was the queen of the constellations for the Sumerians from the time of the fourth millennium B.C., when (4000–2000 B.C.) it marked the spring equinox. At that time the other three cardinal signs were Leo for the summer solstice, Sagittarius for the fall equinox, and Aquarius for the winter solstice.

When the astronomical knowledge of the Sumerians spread throughout the world, the Bull became the primary symbol of holiness everywhere, from the cow Vishavandevas in India to the ox Apis in Egypt, from the Cretan Minotaur to the tauromachy of Mithras. Even the Hebrews built themselves the Golden Calf as soon as they felt free of the power of Moses, who had climbed up Mount Sinai; this happened right at the moment when two goat's horns budded from Moses' forehead as the symbol of the new sign for spring—Aries.

It is difficult to establish exactly how and when this reformulation of the zodiac occurred. The fact remains that two zodiacal signs were cut in order to obtain four. Scorpius, who originally was considered double (that is, the body with the stinger and the two claws), was changed into two distinct constellations: the part with the body continued to be Scorpius, while the two stars that marked the claws became the two trays of the new sign of Libra.

Much more ancient is the halving of Taurus, whose hindquarters were transformed into the celestial Ram. This does not mean that previously there existed only ten zodiacal signs, because there were two signs that belonged to today's Scorpius and in the place of Taurus and Aries, there were the two distinct constellations—the Hyades and the Pleiades.

Taurus. From Hyginus, Poetica astronomica *(1485 edition)*

Opposite: *Taurus. From Hevelius,*
Uranographia totum coelum stellatum *(1690)*

The Hyades

The Hyades were daughters of Atlas and were therefore stepsisters of both the Pleiades and the Hesperides. With them they shared the name Atlantides, but they were also called Nysaean nymphs because they lived on Mount Nysa in Helicon. It was to them that Zeus entrusted the infant Dionysus, whom he had transformed into a kid so as to hide him from Hera. These sisters raised him, keeping him hidden in a cave. To reward them for their faithfulness, Zeus placed their images among the stars.

The Hyades form a V in the sky that is composed of six stars; the main one is Aldebaran. This name derives from the Arabic *al-Dabaran*, or the Next One, and is based on the fact that it rises after the Pleiades. The rising and setting of the stars was very important to the ancient cultures.

Some scholars maintain that the name Hyades derives from the Greek *uein*, meaning to rain, because their appearance coincided with the season of the autumn rains. It was also said that this was their name because they were the sisters of Hyas, the young hunter who was killed by a boar during a hunt. The sisters' sorrow for the loss of their brother was so great that they died of grief. In recognition of such great sisterly love they were transformed into the rainy constellation of the Hyades.

As in the case of Adonis, who was also killed by a boar, Hyas represents the young spring sun that caused the vegetation to be reborn, but was then killed by the sun of the summer solstice whose symbol was, in fact, the boar (see the chapter on Virgo).

Hyas and the boar

The Pleiades

No constellation has ever excited fantasy as universally as this small group of stars. Temples have been oriented to their direction the world over; great nations have worshiped them and people who live great distances apart have

Bayer's Taurus (1603)

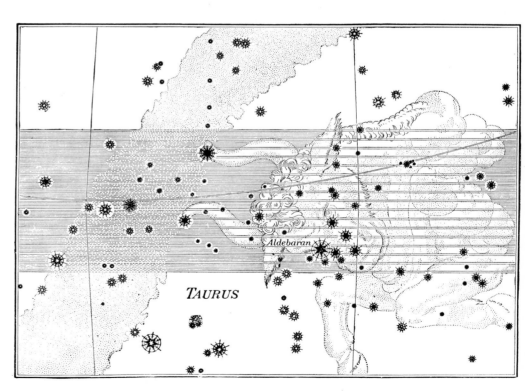

TAURUS

Aldebaran

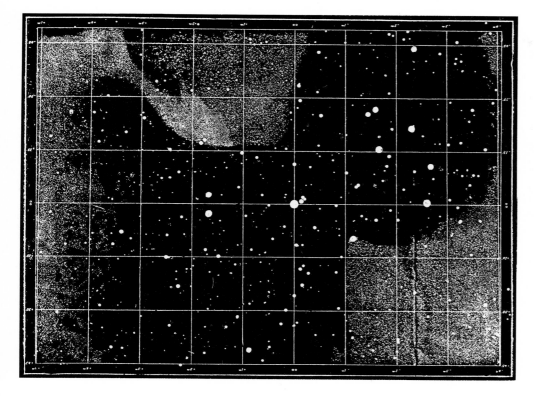

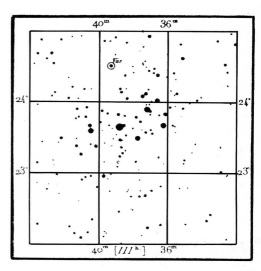

Maps of the Pleiades: Wolf (1874), at left, and Argelander (1885), above

considered the Pleiades the center of the universe—the place of the origin of souls.

In antiquity, before the solar year was determined and established, the year began with the early-morning appearance of the Pleiades, and the winter started with their evening rising. The year was divided into two parts and the reappearance of the Pleiades in November brought back the celebration of the dead—the moment of encounter with one's ancestors that is still celebrated as All Saints' Day, All Hallows' Day, and Souls' Day.

The ancient Egyptians gave to the month of November the name *Athar-aye*, which is equivalent to "Month of the Pleiades." We find the same custom among the Chaldeans and the Israelites.

The same division of the year is also found among the inhabitants of Polynesia, who give the name *Matarii i Nia*, meaning Pleiades Above, to one-half of the year and *Matarii i Raro*, the Pleiades Below, to the other. Similar customs were common the world over. Even the Mayas, the Aztecs, and various North American Indians used similar designations.

The precessional year, which was calculated by Hipparchus to consist of 25,765 years, was originally given the name of Great Year of the Pleiades. Later, when astronomy became fashionable again in Renaissance Europe, it became known as the Platonic Year.

The pyramid of Giza, which was oriented exactly to the four cardinal points and was used as observatory and tomb simultaneously, has two tunnels that were dug at an angle into its thickness. The one directed to the north is pointed toward the Polar Star of that time (Alpha Draconis). The one to the south has an inclination that corresponds precisely to the height of the meridian of the Pleiades whose passing through that opening, at midnight, marked the beginning of the year.

One of the Greek authors, Hesiod, linked the labors in the fields to the course of the Pleiades. The Latins called them *Vergiliae*, Stars of the Spring.

The spring equinox, which today occurs at Alpha Andromedae, passed through the Pleiades four thousand years ago. In the annals of Chinese

The Sumerian god El standing on his attribute, the bull

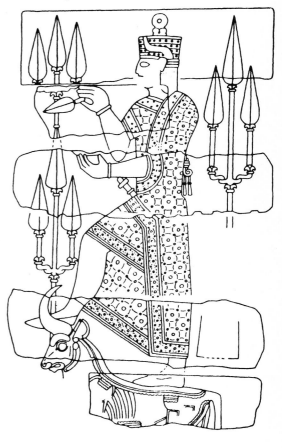

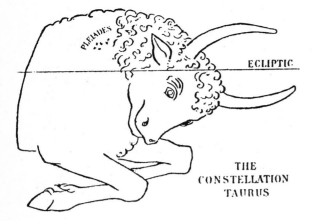

THE
CONSTELLATION
TAURUS

astronomy there exists the record of an observation of this group of stars that was made in the year 2357 B.C. Around 570 B.C. Anaximander calculated their early-morning setting to have taken place on the twenty-ninth day after the fall equinox.

Thirty centuries ago, sailors waited for the spring rising of the Pleiades before setting out onto the seas; this fact inspired etymologists to hypothesize that their name derives from *plein*, meaning to navigate. Likewise, the ships were taken out of the water for the winter at the Pleiades' setting in the fall.

However, the Pleiades are called thus because they were daughters of Pleione, the nymph—whose parents were Oceanus and Thetis—who became the lover of Atlas. There were names for seven, but only six could be seen as stars. In one version of the myth this was explained by the fact that six of them were spouses of immortal gods while Merope married Sisyphus—a mortal—and, out of shame, the light of her star is so weak that it cannot be seen.

In another interpretation the Lost Pleiad (the name with which this star has gone down in history) was not Merope, but Electra, the mythical mother of Dardanus, the founder of Troy. Unable to bear the sorrow of seeing her descendants massacred in the sack of Troy, Electra escaped to the Arctic Circle, totally disconsolate. From there she returns periodically with her long hair still hanging loose behind her as a sign of despair; this is how she became the Great Comet. The legend of the Lost Pleiad occurs in the myths and legends of so many different cultures on earth that there seem to be grounds for the hypothesis that a star just as brilliant as the other Pleiades suddenly disappeared at the time of the Trojan War.

The names of the seven Pleiades, which we know from mythology, are Taygete, Merope, Alcyone, Celaeno, Electra, Asterope, and Maia, the last of whom was the mother of the god Hermes. Aratus mentions them all in his *Phaenomena*, saying:

Seven in number are placed on record, but to our sight only six appear. It is not known for certain at what period the missing star disappeared and its pre-existence is considered fabulous. . . . Their light is by no means brilliant, but they are of fair renown, and rise and set at the will of their father Jupiter, who teaches them to observe the summer and winter seasons and the proper time for making preparations for the advent of the plough.

A similar version is presented by Ovid in the *Fasti*, (IV.165), while in the *Georgics* (IV.232) Virgil says the following about Taygete:

Twice they gather the teeming produce; two seasons are there for the harvest— first, so soon as Taygete the Pleiad has shown her comely face to the earth, and spurned with scornful foot the streams of Ocean, and when that same star, fleeing before the sign of the watery Fish, sinks sadly from heaven into the wintry waves.

Finally, in the *Metamorphoses* (III.594), Ovid says:

> Learn'd the fit havens, and began to note
> The stormy Hyades, the rainy goat,
> The bright Taygete, and the shining bears . . .

Modern astronomers have kept the names of the Pleiades, but they have also added the names of their parents, Atlas and Pleione. The most brilliant is called Alcyone.

CAPITAL
FROM SUSA

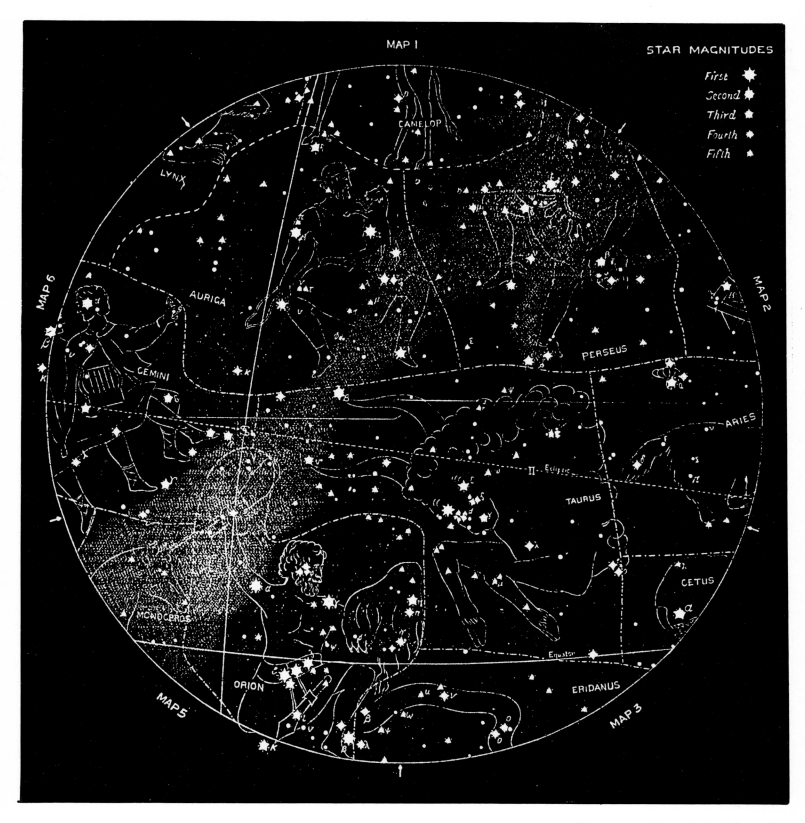

MAP I

STAR MAGNITUDES

First
Second
Third
Fourth
Fifth

MAP 6

MAP 2

LYNX

CAMELOP

AURIGA

PERSEUS

GEMINI

MAP 5

ARIES

TAURUS

Ecliptic

CETUS

ORION

MONOCEROS

Equator

ERIDANUS

MAP 3

The astronomer Proctor's celestial map of the southern hemisphere of the sky in the month of December

   In the pages of Athenaeus, Hesiod, Pindar, and Simonides, the Pleiades were identified with a flock of doves. In his *Poetica astronomica*, Hyginus narrates that Pleione, while traveling to Boeotia with her daughters, was attacked by the giant Orion. The young women succeeded in escaping because Zeus, moved by their prayers, transformed them into doves. Orion pursued them for seven years, until both birds and hunter were set among the stars. There the hunt continues during winter nights when the stars of the Pleiades perform their starry flight westward, followed at a slight distance by the constellation of Orion.

The tauromachy of Mithras

Tauromachy

Among the ruins of Persepolis, an enormous bas-relief has been found that depicts a man with a royal diadem in the act of thrusting his sword into the belly of an animal similar to the Chimera and the Sphinx. The creature is a combination of four animals: its hind legs and wings are those of an eagle, its tail ending in a stinger is that of a scorpion, its mane and forelegs are those of a lion, and the body and horns are those of a bull.

The composition of this griffin is basically astronomical and was meant to indicate the four cardinal signs, Taurus, Leo, Scorpius, and Aquila. There has been much discussion about the arbitrary assignment of the winter solstice to Aquila when it actually occurred in Aquarius—a sign without prominent stars, however. At that time the cardinal points were marked by the Royal Stars—Aldebaran, Regulus, Antares, and Altair. First of all, the star Fomalhaut, which should have marked the winter solstice, is not located in Aquarius but in Piscis Austrinus. Secondly, in those days and at that latitude, Fomalhaut was too low on the horizon to be easily observed, while the nearby Altair offered the perfect brightness to be the Royal Star (see the chapter on Leo).

The meaning of the tauromachy described above refers to the time during which the year began with the entrance of the sun into the constellation Taurus. On that occasion the king performed the most important rite of the calendar, the sacrifice of the bull, whose blood was collected and then sprinkled over the furrows to fertilize the fields. The ritual required that the king lie with the chief priestess of the temple on a recently plowed field. Even today plant cultivators in nurseries consider the blood of the ox an efficacious fertilizer.

The tauromachy is present everywhere in the Mediterranean. Its components change at times but essentially it remains the primitive allegory that can be found in the cults of Mithras, Gilgamesh, the slaying of the Minotaur in Crete, all the way to today's Iberian bullfight.

Theseus and the Minotaur

The Bull and the Moon

In Egypt the cult of the bull sacred to Apis existed from the time of the first dynasty. In Memphis a spotted ox was worshiped as the living symbol of Apis, and when he died the priests searched for a substitute who was chosen based on certain specific characteristics including a white triangle on its forehead, a white spot in the shape of a moon crescent on its flank, and another one similar to an eagle on its neck. The body would be embalmed and placed in a gigantic sarcophagus. The largest Apis tomb known is the mausoleum called Serapeum.

In Greek mythology the Bull was associated with Zeus in his metamorphosis as a bull when he fell in love with the young Europa (She Who Has Wide Eyes), the daughter of Telephassa (She Who Shines Far Away). Both these names mark mother and daughter as goddesses of the moon.

While Europa was gathering flowers near the seashore in Phoenicia, a herd of cows approached, among them Zeus in the form of a splendid bull who was white as the snow, whose breath was saffron-scented, and who had two small horns similar to gems. Struck by the beauty and the gentleness of the animal, Europa decorated him with flowers and sat on his back, holding onto one of his horns with one hand and carrying a basket full of flowers in the other. The white bull suddenly plunged into the waves of the sea and swam to the island of Crete, carrying Europa with him. There the young woman became his lover and produced three sons, Minos, Rhadamanthys, and Sarpedon.

Perhaps the origin of this myth is the pre-Hellenic Cretan portrayal of the priestess of the moon who appeared triumphantly seated on the solar bull, her victim, in the fertility rite during which Europa's springtime garland was carried in a procession (Graves, *The Greek Myths*).

Having become king of Crete, Minos married Pasiphaë (She Who Illuminates All) who gave birth to Ariadne (the Very Fertile Mother of Barley). Pasiphaë also had at one point coupled with a white bull with whom she had fallen in love, and from this union the Minotaur had been born.

Telephassa, Europa, Pasiphaë, and Ariadne are all manifestations of the lunar goddess who copulates ritually with the celestial Bull. We must keep in mind that, in the case of Ariadne, she did not consummate her marriage with Theseus but with the bull-god Dionysus. Europa's garland of flowers corresponds to the nuptial crown that was given by Dionysus to Ariadne and later transformed by the god into the constellation of Corona Borealis (see the chapter on this constellation).

The abduction of Europa

Taurus. From Star Stories

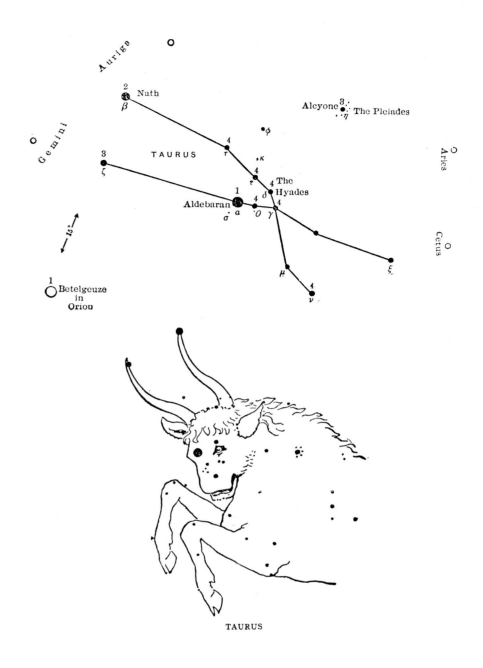

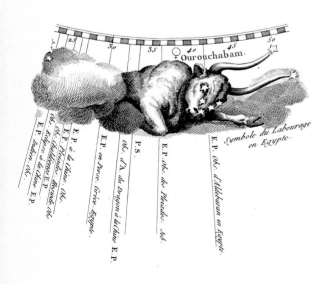

TAURUS

Continuing with the myth of the celestial Bull and the Lunar Cow, we will follow the tracks of Europa's brother, Cadmus, who set out in search of his kidnapped sister. The story goes that, on his arrival in Egypt, he founded the city of Thebes in the spot indicated to him by a cow whom he had set free; the cow had spots in the shape of a full moon on both flanks.

However, the most famous wandering Lunar Cow was Io, another mistress of Zeus, who had been changed into a cow by the jealous Hera and with whom Zeus had mated under the guise of a bull. Under the protection of Argus with the thousand eyes, Io had taken to traveling in order to escape from Hera's searches and so she arrived in Egypt where she gave birth to Epaphus—the future pharaoh, identified by many with the divine bull Apis. Some have thought to see Epaphus, son of the moon, as a synonym for epact—the period of eleven days astronomers added to equalize the lunar and the solar year. From the same root, perhaps, *epatos* (liver) refers to the meal the eagle of the stars consumed from the body of Prometheus. The eagle-sun allegorically devoured the *epatos*-epact and so generated the myth of Prometheus' liver, which regrew magically every time it was devoured.

The Astrology of the Bull

The house of the Bull is the domain of Venus (Veneris Sidus) who, in an ancient and complete sense, must be seen as the Great Mother, or Ephesian Artemis, or Ishtar, all of whom encompass the lunar and feminine universal principle.

A sign of earth, fixed and feminine, Taurus presides over the organs of the throat and the neck. It represents pure substance, hidden force, natural physical beauty, riches, lust, agriculture, pragmatism, and property. Typical of it are artists, people famous for their beauty, financiers, and jewelers.

The cabalists identified the sign with the first letter of the Hebrew alphabet, *aleph*, and the first trump card of the tarots, the Magician.

Ptolemy maintained that the Hyades were under the influence of Saturn and Mercury and that they were not at all favorable. To the Pleiades he assigned the influence of the moon and Mars, with the disastrous effects of blindness, disgrace, and violent death.

The ox Apis

The lunar stations were more favorable. The name of the first Indian *nakshatra*, which was centered on the star Alcyon, was *Krittika*, or General of the Heavenly Hosts, symbolized by a flame and governed by Agni, god of fire. Those born under this star group would love flowers, make sacrifices, and become musicians, metaphysicists, miners, potters, priests, or astronomers. However, if the moon were there at the moment of birth, it would stimulate gluttony and adultery and also make its subject beautiful and famous.

The second *nakshatra*, centered on the star Aldebaran, was *Rohini*, or the Red Deer, symbolized by a temple and governed by *Prajapati*, the Creator. This star cluster was favorable to coronations, expiatory ceremonies, the building of cities, planting of trees, and the sowing of seeds. The fortunate ones born under this influence would be devoted, rich, military leaders, merchants, and pilots.

The star Alcyon also marked the first Arab *manzil, al-Thurayya*, or the Small Numerous Ones (referring to the Pleiades), which was favorable to sailors, hunters, and alchemists. In addition it marked the first Chinese *sieu—Mao*, or the Constellation. Aldebaran marked the second *manzil, al-Dabaran*, or the Follower, and the second sieu, *Pi*, the Net.

To Aldebaran Ptolemy attributed the qualities of Mars, who favored intelligence, honors, eloquence, tenacity, integrity, popularity, ferocity, courage, positions of responsibility, public honors, and the conquest of power. He warned, however, that these benefits were rarely lasting.

In Julius Schiller's seventeenth-century Christian zodiac, which substituted the apostles for the pagan signs, the Bull was represented by Saint Andrew.

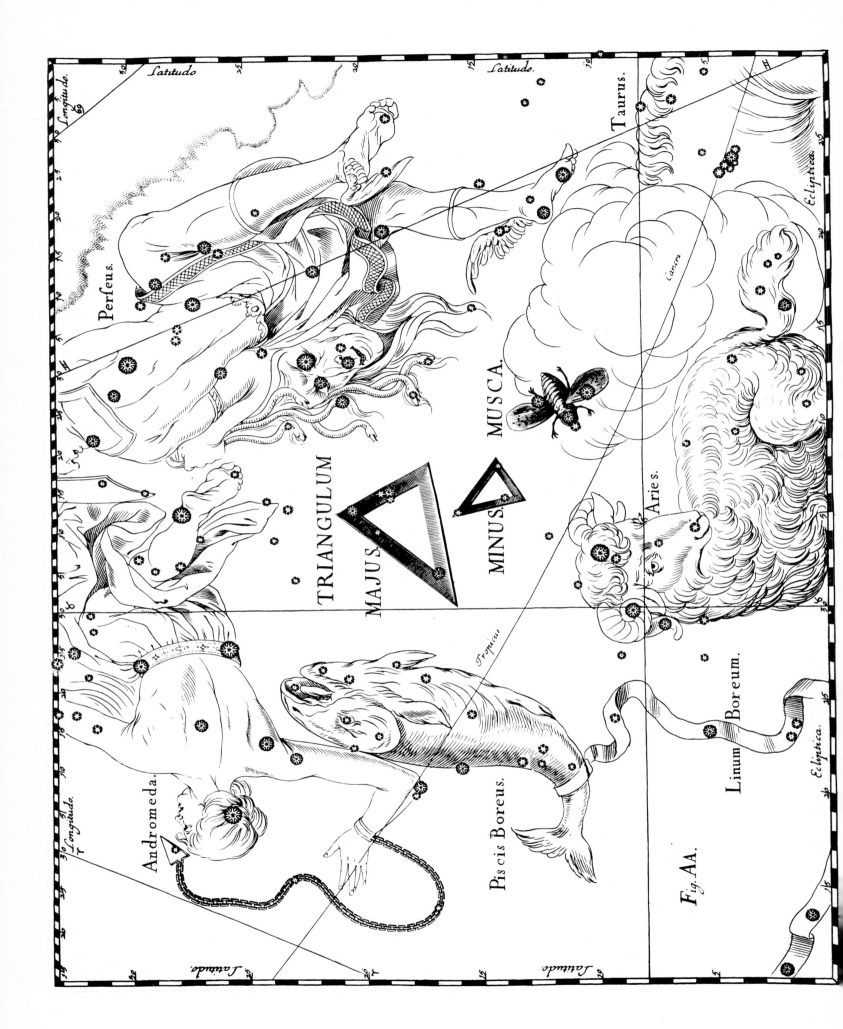

46
Triangulum

At the edge of the vast region of the starry sky that in antiquity was called the Sea, there is a rocky coast where the young Andromeda lies chained. She is the frightened virgin who waits to be devoured by the marine monster represented by the large constellation of Cetus. Directly underneath Andromeda and one of the fish of Pisces there are the stars of a small constellation that is easily identifiable because it has the shape of a right-angle triangle. It is especially visible during fall nights.

Despite the modesty of its dimensions, Triangulum, the Triangle, is a very ancient constellation that is present in all the star catalogues known to us. The legends that have been told about it are manifold. In the *Phaenomena*, which is the third century B.C. description of the stars by Aratus, it was called Deltoton in honor of the Greek letter delta.

It was said that Mercury had placed it among the stars so that it would indicate with its sharp angle the constellation of Aries, which was not very bright, and also because it would show the first letter of the name of Zeus, which in Greek was *Dis* (Hyginus, *Poetica astronomica*). During the Alexandrian era it was associated with the river Nile under such names as Nilus, Delta, and Nili Donum, which referred to the mouth of the river that terminated in the famous delta. Despite these attributions to the letter of the alphabet and the estuary of the river, Triangulum is not an equilateral triangle, as these figures are, but a right-angle triangle, as can be seen from the actual placement of its stars.

In the works of such authors as Homer, Eratosthenes, and Callimachus, we actually find it under a very different name—Thrinakie or Trinakria—a name used for Sicily in antiquity in reference to an important geographic characteristic of the island. It was, in fact, Phoenician and Greek sailors who called this island Land of the Three Capes for its three geographic points: Peloris to the northeast, Pachinos to the southeast, and Lilybaion to the west. Nowadays Peloris is called Cape of the Lighthouse, Pachinos has retained its name in the form of Pachino, and Lilybaion has become Cape Boeo or Lilibeo.

Trinacria was the island sacred to Ceres, the lady who ruled over grain and barley. Homer referred to the island as the land where the mythical oxen of the sun-god grazed; it was the "sacred land of the oxen" recorded by the Latin geographer Mela.

During the period preceding the Greek colonization, Sicily was inhabited by the Sicani and later by the Siculi, people who had conceived a mythology that revolved around the powers located underneath the soil. This was understandable on an island that—land of tremors, caverns, and deep holes from which springs of hot water gushed—was the seat of the largest volcano known at the time and featured such other volcanoes as Stromboli and Maccaluba. All signs clearly indicated that the forces of nature manifested themselves in the mysterious world of the underground from which everything seemed to generate. Fire, water, even plants and the beneficent barley had their roots in the dark cellar of the world.

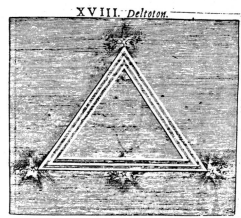

XVIII. Deltoton.

DELTOTON autem in triangulum deformatur, æquis lateribus duobus, uno breviore, sed prope æquali

Triangulum. From a fifteenth-century engraving

Opposite: *Triangulum. From Hevelius,* Uranographia totum coelum stellatum *(1690)*

The triscele, *Sicily's three-legged coat of arms*

The Sicani worshiped the giant shepherds of Mount Etna, the admirers of the god of fire Hadranus, who, in Greece, became the Cyclopes. Under the guidance of Vulcanus they forged the arrows with which Jupiter succeeded in defeating the Titans and the terrible Typhon. The body of this monster was buried in Sicily with its head directly under Mount Etna.

This primordial and animistic Olympus was dominated by a supreme divinity who was the mythical Hybla, the Great Mother, ruler of Avernus, the harvests, and the moon, whose priestesses read the future by interpreting dreams. The triple nature of Hybla was symbolized in what became the symbol of Sicily—the *triscele*. Pertinent to the Triangle under discussion in this chapter, it was a figure similar to the swastika in which three legs stretched outward from one central point. In another version it is portrayed by a head surrounded by three legs with stalks of grain between them. The *triscele* is a symbol of the moon, the sun, and motion in general. It appeared on many ancient Sicilian coins and it continued to be used as a representation of Sicily until the time of Emperor Hadrian.

The Iblei Mountains were dedicated to Hybla and so were various cities such as Ibla Erea near Ragusa, Ibla Magna to the north of Siracusa, and Ibla Galeotide near Catania (which later became today's Paterno). Here Hybla's temple was situated next to the volcano and several hot springs, which is an obvious demonstration of the relationship of the goddess to the underground. Her cult survived the Greek invasion of Sicily, which resulted in Hybla being worshiped as Ceres or Demeter. Like Hybla, Ceres was the Great Mother of the fertility of nature, with a particular focus on barley and wheat. She was identified with the summer solstice when the sun reaches its highest declination and the crops are golden in the fields, ready for harvesting. She was also worshiped as a phase of the seed (Proserpina) that was sown and, after a period of absence, returned to the world as the young plant ready to continue a new cycle of the calendar.

Proserpina was captured by the prince of darkness Pluto, the black rider

Proserpina, or Persephone

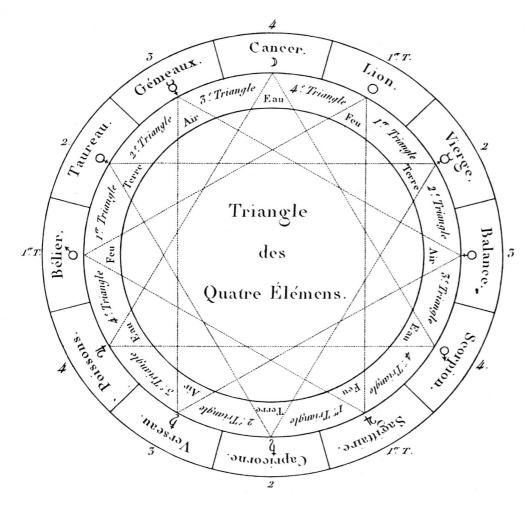

The four triangles that indicate the four elements of water, fire, earth, and air in the zodiacal circle

without a face who, on his chariot drawn by dark stallions, emerged from the underground world, took her by force upon his chariot, and disappeared with her into an underground chasm. The girl was abducted close to Lake Pergus, near Enna, while she was gathering daffodils with the nymphs. One of them attempted to struggle against the god and was, as a result, transformed into the spring that came to be known by the name of Kyana. Ceres' sorrow for the loss of her daughter was so great that the entire world of plants stopped producing flowers and seeds, which would have condemned the living to certain death if it had not been for the intervention of Jupiter. With the help of Hecate, he succeeded in convincing Pluto and Ceres to conclude a pact by which Proserpina would marry the king of the netherworld, thereby becoming the ruler of Avernus. However, this would only last for three months out of the year; she would spend the rest of the year in the company of her mother.

As a wedding present she was given the island of Sicily, which, in memory of this pact, was transferred to the sky as the constellation of Triangulum.

In actuality, Proserpina, Ceres, and Hecate were the Great Mother in her three aspects of nymph, woman, and venerable old woman. The first was the symbol of the seed and the young grain, the second was the mature grain, while Hecate represented the harvested grain. The allegory of the seed that was interred during winter, when plants do not sprout, and then reappeared transformed into a plant was expressed by the brief marriage between Proserpina and Pluto. In the countryside a custom was practiced in which a doll made of stalks was ritually buried in winter and then dug up in spring.

In the works of Homer, Diodorus Siculus, and Hesiod, there are references to a love affair between Ceres and a Titan named Iasion, who is not clearly

Ceres, or Demeter

Between the constellations of Pisces and Aries in the celestial planisphere at Dendera, we find the sacred eye of Horus in the place of the Triangle. Symbol of the full moon, this eye was ripped from Horus by Set but was later found again by Thoth; it became the subject of a cult and was worshiped under the name of Udjat (Uzat).
The illustration below represents the fourteen gods of each of the days of the waxing moon paying homage to Udjat. Horus' eye was later assimilated into Christianity, where it was inserted in the triangle as a symbol of the eternal vigilance of the trinity

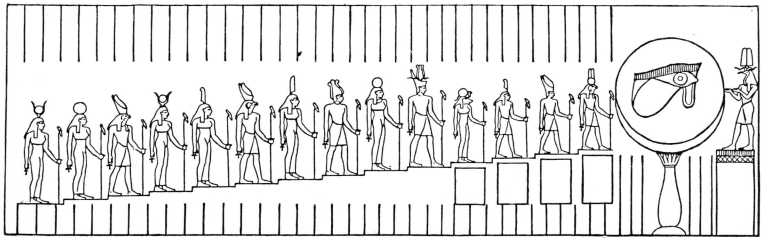

identified. The goddess lay with him on a field that had been plowed three times. As a result of this she bore two sons: Plutus, the rich, and Philomelus, the inventor of the cart and the plow, who is now represented by the constellation of Boötes (Hyginus, *Poetica astronomica*). Most likely Iasion is the Greek transposition of the Titan Hadranus, the Sicilian god of fire, with whom Hybla (Ceres) lay every year in a ritual copulation and so gave birth to Plutus, the allegory of abundance, and Philomelus, the allegory of agriculture.

Returning to the celestial Triangulum and its position in the sky, there immediately come to mind some considerations of a mythical-geographical character with regard to the placement of the constellation. The ancient astronomers who designed the map of the sky as we know it today portrayed Ceres in the constellation of Virgo in her glorified position as queen of the harvest at the time when the sun entered into this sign during the summer solstice (see the chapter on Virgo). But it is too far away; Triangulum is on the other side of the ecliptic from Virgo. This would seem to exclude all relationships with the patron of Sicily until we notice that Triangulum is located right next to the constellation of Andromeda, where Robert Graves sees the manifestation of Ishtar or Astarte. She is the Mesopotamian goddess who, in her lunar symbolism, is the ruler of both the world beyond the grave and that of the seeds. She is the black moon, the Core, Persephone, and Proserpina, who brings the sign of Triangulum close to the underground metamorphosis of its divine protector—Ceres (see the chapter on Virgo).

458   *The Glorious Constellations*

Interesting Information about Triangulum

On January 1, 1801, inaugurating the new century, the astronomer Giuseppe Piazzi, director of the observatory of Palermo, discovered the first minor planet in our solar system. A heavenly body with a diameter of about five hundred miles, it was just next to the constellation of Triangulum that night, due to a strange coincidence. This asteroid was rightfully named Ceres, in honor of the goddess who was the patron of the island.

Almost two centuries earlier, in his attempt to eliminate from the sky and its stars all traces of paganism, the Catholic astronomer Julius Schiller published a new star map in which Triangulum became the miter of Saint Peter, the official headdress of popes and bishops.

The Hebrews called Triangulum *Shalish*, from the name of a triangular musical instrument mentioned in the first book of Samuel. The Chinese saw in these stars *Tsien-Ta-Tseang*, or the Great Celestial General. The tenth-century Arabs called these stars *al-Muthallath*, or the Triangle, and even today the lucida of this constellation—Alpha Trianguli—has the name of Ras Muthallath, which in Latin is *Caput Trianguli*, or the Top of the Triangle. In pre-Greek Arab astronomy Alpha Trianguli and Beta Trianguli formed the constellation *al-Mizan*, meaning the Scales, or Beam of the Scales.

In his astrological catalogue on the fixed stars the astronomer Ptolemy assigned to Triangulum the same qualities as Mercury, a righteous, friendly, sincere, generous, and benevolent nature with a love of architecture.

Triangulum and Andromeda. From Cellarius, Harmonica macrocosmica (1660)

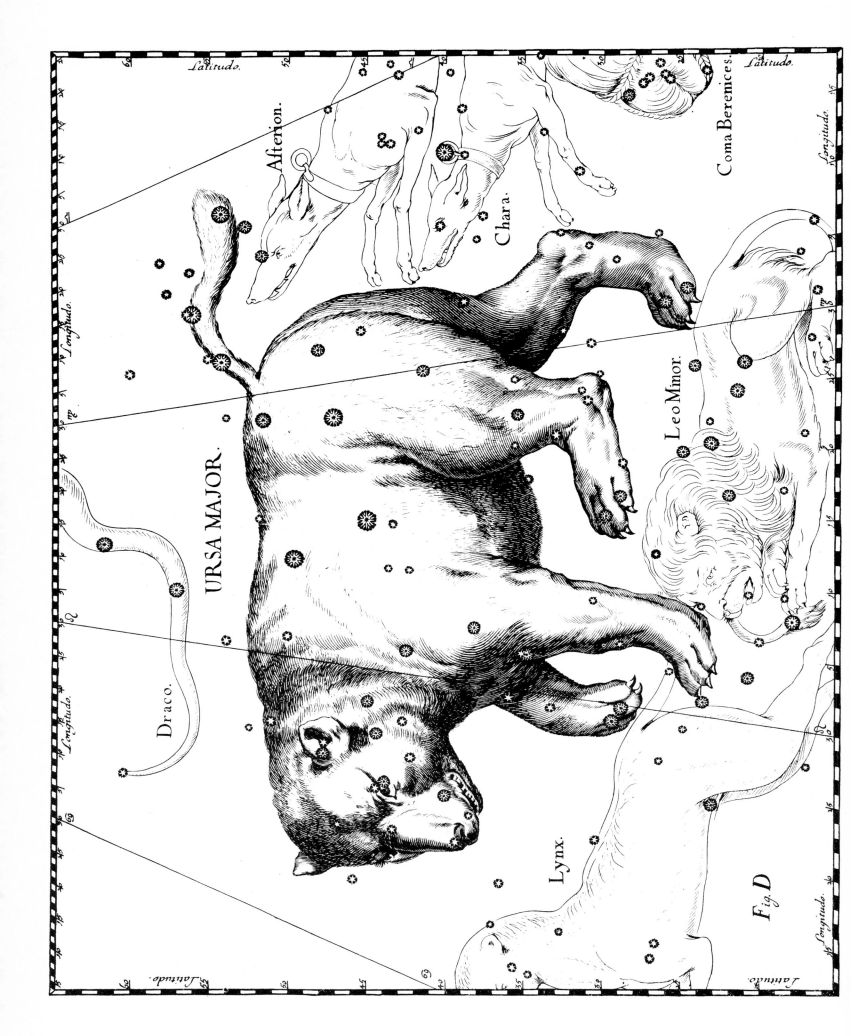

47
Ursa Major

No statistics exist about people's familiarity with the stars today, but we can estimate that eight out of ten individuals know only the three stars of Orion's belt, the stars of Taurus, and the seven stars that make up the back and tail of the Great Bear. These last are the most famous because they never set in their slow and tireless revolution around the North Pole.

Known as the Big Dipper, Bear, Great Wagon, and Plow, these seven stars offer one of the most beautiful spectacles in the starry sky. They are, at the same time, extremely useful because they have always shown which direction is north. In order to find the exact position of the Polar Star, a not-very-prominent star of third magnitude, all we have to do is draw an imaginary line through two stars at the end of the Big Dipper's cup, from Merak through Dubhe; extending this line will take us to Polaris in Ursa Minor. For this reason the two stars are also called the Pointers.

In the millennia preceding our time period, however, the arrangement of the stars in the sky was different. Due to the phenomenon of precession, the Pole slowly shifts its position so that, in 3000 B.C. for example, the Polar Star was Thuban, in Draco, and the Great Bear was much closer to the Pole than it is today.

The fact that it has been in a strategic position for such a long time has given rise to numerous legends, poems, and symbols about this figure. The best known of all these is of the Bear itself—almost always a female—the animal always associated in the popular imagination with the cold and the north. The Greek name for bear was *artos* and from this root comes the word arctic.

As we will see in the Greek myth the Great Bear was the stellar transposition of the nymph Callisto, who was transformed into a bear. However, it seems that the original and more ancient word comes from the Phoenician name for the constellation, *Kalitsah*, which means Security. Since the Phoenicians were a seafaring people, the observation of this stellar figure helped them to make their voyages with precision.

There are those, however, who give another version of the origin of the name Artos or Arktos, in which Callisto is described as heavenly mother of the Arcadians, the bear-people. Ovid describes them as having a primitive way of life, which justified their name: "They ran naked, proud of their skin. . . ."

In 300 B.C. the constellations of Ursa Major and Ursa Minor were described as follows in Aratus' *Phaenomena*:

The axis [of the earth] is always firm, and although it may appear to shift a little, yet it is never much disarranged, while the earth maintains its equilibrium in the centre; and around it the sky turns itself. Also the two Poles terminate at either extremity; one indeed is not visible, but the other to the Northward rises high above the ocean surrounding it, two Bears lie circularly, which are usually called the Wains. Each has its head inverted upon the loins of the other, but always borne along back to back while the shoulders are alternately reversed.

Opposite: *Ursa Major. From Hevelius,* Uranographia totum coelum stellatum *(1690)*

Ursa Major and Ursa Minor surrounded by Draco. From Hyginus, Poetica astronomica *(1485 edition)*

Dubhe and Merak, the Pointers, mark the position of the Pole Star

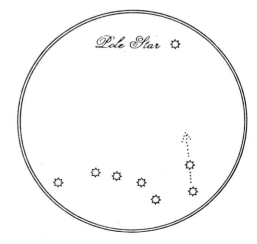

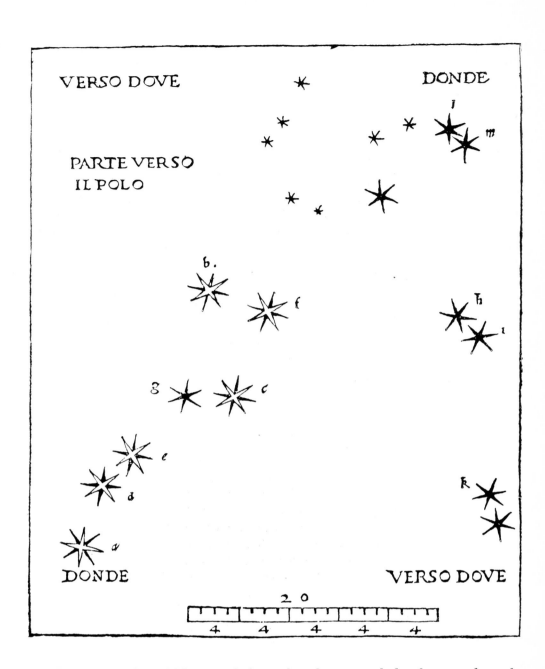

Ursa Major. From Piccolomini, De le Stelle
fisse *(1548)*

[The ancients] would have us believe that they ascended to heaven, from the island of Crete, by the powerful assistance of Zeus himself, because these Bears, when they deceived Saturn, placed him, while still an infant, in a place, odiferous with flowers, near Mount Ida, and nourished him for a whole year. They called one of these Bears Cynosura [Ursa Minor] and the other Helice [Ursa Major].

The Greeks place faith in Helice [Ursa Major] in respect of their naval affairs and the direction of their shipping. The Phoenicians have confidence in Cynosura [Ursa Minor] during their voyages.

Helice is clear and readily observed shining brightly at the commencement of the night. The other, Cynosura, is comparatively obscure, but, nevertheless, more useful to the sailor because it revolves in a lesser circle.

Aratus, *Phaenomena*, 23–43

The legend of the she-bears who nursed Zeus originated on the island of Naxos while, in the Greek myth, it was the she-goat Amalthaea who suckled the god and who was therefore transformed into Capricornus.

Aratus' position is interesting because he lived in the middle of two cultures:

the island where he lived, Soli, was very close to today's Turkey and therefore close to Phoenician culture; on the other hand, his education was Greek.

Callisto

It all started the day Helius allowed his son Phaëthon to drive the chariot of the sun. Not having had much experience in controlling the celestial stallions, the young man lost control over the reins when he was high in the sky. The result was that the sun swerved out of its path and came so dangerously close to the earth that it caused fires and devastation. At that point, in order to save the world, Zeus hurled a lightning bolt and Phaëthon plunged, dying, into the river Eridanus.

Zeus subsequently quickly checked the damage caused by the sun and he paid particular attention to his favorite land, Arcadia, where his eyes fell on Callisto—the beautiful nymph who was a hunter, friend, and follower of Diana.

This is how things proceeded, as described in Ovid's *Metamorphoses*:

> She flung herself on the cool grassy bed;
> And on the painted quiver rais'd her head.
> Jove saw the charming huntress unprepar'd,
> Stretch'd on the verdant turf, without a guard.
> "Here I am safe, he cries, from Juno's eye;
> "Or should my jealous queen the theft descry,
> "Yet would I venture on a theft like this,
> "And stand her rage for such, for such a bliss!"
> Diana's shape and habit straight he took,
> Soften'd his brows, and smooth'd his awful look,
> And mildly in a female accent spoke.
> "How fares my girl? how went the morning chase?"
> To whom the virgin, starting from the grass,
> "All hail, bright deity, whom I prefer
> "To Jove himself, tho' Jove himself were here."
> The god was nearer than she thought, and heard
> Well pleas'd himself before himself preferr'd.
> He then salutes her with a warm embrace;
> And, ere she half had told the morning chase,
> With love enflam'd and eager on his bliss,
> Smother'd her words, and stopp'd her with a kiss;
> His kisses with unwonted ardour glow'd,
> Nor could Diana's shape conceal the god.
> The virgin did whate'er a virgin could;
> (Sure Juno must have pardon'd, had she view'd)
> With all her might against his force she strove;
> But how can mortal maids contend with Jove?
> Possest at length of what his heart desir'd,
> Back to his heav'ns th' exulting god retir'd.
> The lovely huntress, rising from the grass,
> With down-cast eyes, and with a blushing face,
> By shame confounded, and by fear dismay'd,
> Flew from the covert of the guilty shade,
> And almost in the tumult of her mind,
> Left her forgotten bow and shafts behind.
> But now Diana, with a sprightly train
> Of quiver'd virgins, bounding o'er the plain,
> Call'd to the nymph; the nymph began to fear
> A second fraud, a Jove disguis'd in her.

But, when she saw the sister nymphs, suppress'd
Her rising fears, and mingled with the rest.
How in the look does conscious guilt appear!
Slowly she mov'd, and loiter'd in the rear;
Nor lightly tripp'd, nor by the goddess ran,
As once she us'd, the foremost of the train.
Her looks were flush'd, and sullen was her mien,
That sure the virgin goddess (had she been
Aught but a virgin) must the guilt have seen.
'Tis said the nymphs saw all, and guess'd aright:
And now the moon had nine times lost her light,
When Dian, fainting in the mid-day beams,
Found a cool covert, and refreshing streams
That in soft murmurs thro' the forest flow'd,
And a smooth bed of shining gravel show'd.
A covert so obscure, and streams so clear,
The goddess prais'd; "And now no spies are near
"Let's strip, my gentle maids, and wash," she cries.
Pleas'd with the motion, ev'ry maid complies;
Only the blushing huntress stood confus'd,
And form'd delays, and her delays excus'd;
In vain excus'd: her fellows round her press'd,
And the reluctant nymph by force undress'd.
The naked huntress all her shame reveal'd,
In vain her hands the pregnant womb conceal'd;
"Begone!" the goddess cries with stern disdain,
"Begone! nor dare the hallow'd stream to stain;"
She fled, for ever banish'd from the train.
This Juno heard, who long had watch'd her time
To punish the detested rival's crime;
The time was come: for, to enrage her more,
A lovely boy the teeming rival bore.
The goddess cast a furious look, and cry'd,
"It is enough! I'm fully satisfy'd!
"This boy shall stand a living mark, to prove
"My husband's baseness and the strumpet's love:
"But vengeance shall awake: those guilty charms
"That drew the thunderer from Juno's arms,
"No longer shall their wonted force retain,
"Nor please the god, nor make the mortal vain."
This said, her hand within her hair she wound,
Swung her to earth, and dragg'd her on the ground:
The prostrate wretch lifts up her arms in pray'r;
Her arms grow shaggy, and deform'd with hair,
Her nails are sharpen'd into pointed claws,
Her hands bear half her weight, and turn to paws;
Her lips, that once could tempt a god, begin
To grow distorted in an ugly grin.
And, lest the supplicating brute might reach
The ears of Jove, she was depriv'd of speech:
Her surly voice thro' a hoarse passage came
In savage sounds: her mind was still the same,
The furry monster fix'd her eyes above,
And heav'd her new unwieldy paws to Jove,
And begg'd his aid with inward groans; and tho'
She could not call him false, she thought him so,
How did she fear to lodge in woods alone,
And haunt the fields and meadows, once her own!
How often would the deep-mouth'd dogs pursue,

*Looking at Arcturus and the stars
of Ursa Major*

Whilst from her hounds the frighted huntress flew!
How did she fear her fellow-brutes, and shun
The shaggy bear, tho' now herself was one!
How from the sight of rugged wolves retire,
Altho' the grim Lycaon was her sire!
But now her son had fifteen summers told,
Fierce at the chase, and in the forest bold;
When, as he beat the woods in quest of prey,
He chanc'd to rouze his mother where she lay.
She knew her son, and kept him in her sight,
And fondly gaz'd: the boy was in a fright,
And aim'd a pointed arrow at her breast,
And would have slain his mother in the beast;
But Jove forbad, and snatch'd 'em thro' the air
In whirlwinds up to heav'n, and fix'd 'em there:
Where the new constellations nightly rise,
And add a lustre to the northern skies.

When Juno saw the rival in her height,
Spangled with stars, and circled round with light,
She sought old Ocean in his deep abodes,
And Tethys, both rever'd among the gods.
They ask what brings her there: "Ne'er ask," says she;
"What brings me here, heav'n is no place for me.
"You'll see, when night has cover'd all things o'er,
"Jove's starry bastard and triumphant whore,
"Usurp the heav'ns; you'll see 'em proudly roll
"In their new orbs, and brighten all the pole.
"And who shall now on Juno's altars wait,
"When those she hates grow greater by her hate?
"I on the nymph a brutal form impress'd,
"Jove to a goddess has transform'd the beast;
"This, this was all my weak revenge could do:
"But let the god his chaste amours pursue,
"And as he acted after Iö's rape,
"Restore th' adultress to her former shape;
"Then may be cast his Juno off, and lead
"The great Lycaon's offspring to his bed.
"But you ye venerable pow'rs, be kind,
"And, if my wrongs a due resentment find,
"Receive not in your waves their setting beams,
"Nor let the glaring strumpet taint your streams."

Ovid, *Metamorphoses*, II.518–657

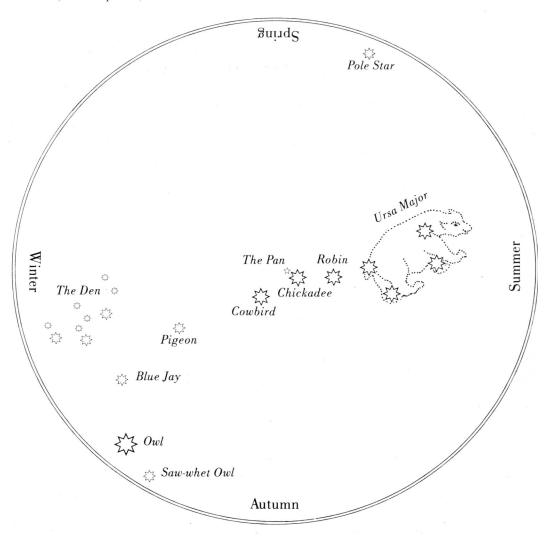

An American Indian Story about the Great Bear

North American Indians have a large repertory of legends about the stars. The importance of these legends derives from, among other things, their age.

What follows is a myth common to the Algonquins and Iroquois. In addition to the stars of Ursa Major, it also concerns the nearby stars of Boötes and Corona Borealis.

The story developed in the form of a play with the following players:

THE BEAR: Alpha, Beta, Gamma, Delta Ursae Majoris

THE HUNTERS: *Robin*, Epsilon Ursae Majoris; *Chickadee*, Zeta Ursae

Stylized bears in Native American art

Majoris; *Cowbird*, Eta Ursae Majoris; *Pigeon*, Gamma Boötis; *Blue Jay*, Epsilon Boötis; *Owl*, Alpha Boötis (Arcturus); *Saw-whet Owl*, Eta Boötis

THE PAN: The little star Alcor

THE DEN: Mu and Delta Boötis and Corona Borealis' circle of stars

The Bear, represented here by the four stars of the Big Dipper's square, is being pursued by seven heavenly hunters. The first hunter was called Robin because this star has a red reflection; the second hunter was called Chickadee because his star was smaller than the others; the fifth was called Blue Jay because his star has blue reflections. The star Arcturus became the Owl because of its size; because of its reddish color, Eta Boötis became Saw-whet—a small owl whose head is covered with red feathers. Close to the second hunter is a very small star, Alcor, which represents the Pan in which the meat will be cooked. Above the hunters there is a group of stars, consisting mainly of the circle of the Corona Borealis, representing the Bear's Den.

When the Bear wakes up out of hibernation in late spring, she comes out of her Den and descends from the rocky hill in search of food. Chickadee sees her immediately but, since he is too small to hunt her down by himself, he calls the other hunters to his aid. Together the seven set out on the pursuit, and Chickadee, with his Pan, follows.

The hunters are famished and they diligently continue the pursuit but the Bear flees along the northern horizon all summer long. In the fall the hunters in the rear, one by one, begin to lose the tracks. The first to give up is Owl, who is the biggest and who does not fly as high as the others. He is followed by Blue Jay, Saw-whet, and Pigeon, so the only ones to remain are Robin, Chickadee, and Cowbird. These disappearances reflect the fact that these stars are not visible from October on. It is only halfway through the autumn that the remaining hunters finally succeed in catching their prey.

Attacked, the Bear rears up on her hind legs and prepares to defend herself. However, Robin hits her with an arrow and causes her to fall over onto her back (the stars of the Bear take up this position in the winter when they are upside-

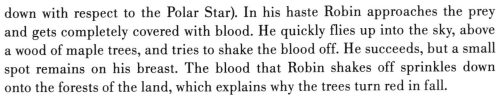

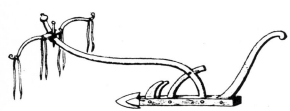

The Great Wagon with the charioteer represented by the little star Alcor

down with respect to the Polar Star). In his haste Robin approaches the prey and gets completely covered with blood. He quickly flies up into the sky, above a wood of maple trees, and tries to shake the blood off. He succeeds, but a small spot remains on his breast. The blood that Robin shakes off sprinkles down onto the forests of the land, which explains why the trees turn red in fall.

Chickadee reaches the prey, and he and Robin, together, cut up the Bear. They light the fire and cook the meat in the Pan. Finally the Cowbird arrives; he knew all along that the others would capture the Bear and cook the meat, and he arrives just in time to share it. For this reason, his nickname is He-Who-Arrives-at-the-Last-Moment.

Up in the sky, during the winter, lies the skeleton of the Bear on her back; but her spirit has entered into another Bear who is invisible inside her Den, where she is in hibernation. When spring returns, this Bear will come out of her Den to once again be pursued by the hunters so that the drama may repeat itself for all eternity.

The Wagon

A wagon or its wheel has always been associated with the seven stars of the Great Bear. The Sumerians called them the Long Wagon. In archaic Greece they were associated with the Wheel of Ixion, which symbolized the circular motion of the constellation around the Pole. This myth seems to have originated with the Sanskrit god Ashivan, whose name means Charioteer of the Axle. Axle, or *Axsha*, was the Sanskrit word for wagon, which for the Greeks became Ixion.

An ancient Celtic legend of King Arthur's Round Table associated the king with the Great Bear: his name in the Welsh language derives from *Arth*, or Bear, and *Uthyr*, or Luminous. This constellation, which visually describes a circle in the polar region of the sky, could represent the true origin of the famous Round Table of the son of Pendragon. For this reason the constellation has been called Arthur's Wain, or Arthur's Wagon, in Wales, Cornwall, and England; this title was still in use in the last century: "Arthur's slow wain his course doth roll,/In utter darkness, round the pole" *(Lay of the Last Minstrel).*

In Ireland the constellation was known by the name of King David's Chariot in honor of one of the ancient kings of the island.

The cabalists naturally chose the seventh trump card of the tarots, the Wagon, to represent this constellation.

The Plow

Ancient Greek plow

In many Euro-Asiatic countries the stars of the Bear were called Heavenly Plow Pulled by Oxen, while the Romans called the seven stars the Seven Oxen, or *Septem Triones*, from which our word septentrion (meaning north) derives.

The Coffin

In some cultures the slow and majestic movement of the seven main stars of Ursa around the pole has suggested the idea of a funeral, especially in communities with a distinctly profound cult of the dead.

The Arabs called the four stars that form the square the Coffin, while the three stars of the tail were three sorrowing people following the coffin. Among the Arabs of the Persian Gulf, there was a story about al-Naash (*naash* was a synonym for bier) and his children. Al-Naash had been assassinated by al-Jadi, the Polar Star, and his children, the three stars of the tail, followed the litter every night eager for revenge. The star Mizar represented al-Naash's daughter with her little son, represented by the small star Alcor, in her arms. The star Suhail (Canopus) comes slowly up from the south to their aid.

This is certainly a very dramatic conception of the circumpolar stars and it was very popular among the Arabs. Later the Christian-Arabic sects called the square of the Bear *Naash Laazar*, the Litter of Lazarus, while the funeral cortege consisted of Mary, Martha, and Ellemath or Magdalene.

The complete list of names assigned to these seven stars is too long to include here, but we can make the general observation that hunters saw a bear represented here, farmers a plow, and merchants and soldiers a wagon. In the south of France, a region famous for its food, the constellation even became a casserole. Other names were Butcher's Knife, and Brooding Hen Followed By Chicks. At the ancient court of China the constellation was the Government (the Polar Star was the emperor). In China's countryside, however, the peasants called it *Pih Tow*, the Bushel, and the poets and mystics called it *Ten Li*, or Heavenly Reason. The Hebrews saw here a woman sifting grain. In the eighteenth-century Christian revision of the stars it became Saint Peter's Boat. In North America of course, it is the Big Dipper.

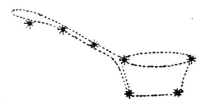

The stars of the Big Dipper

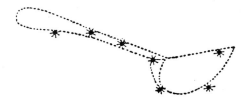

In the Coelum stellatum christianum *(1627) Ursa Major became the boat of Saint Peter*

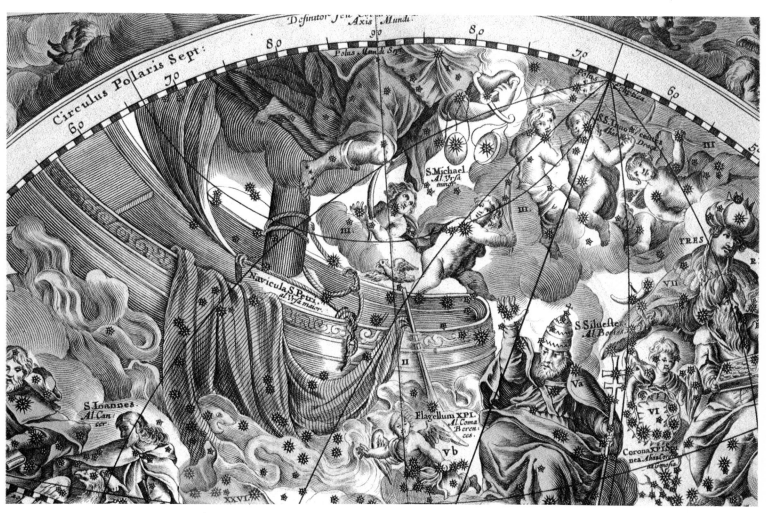

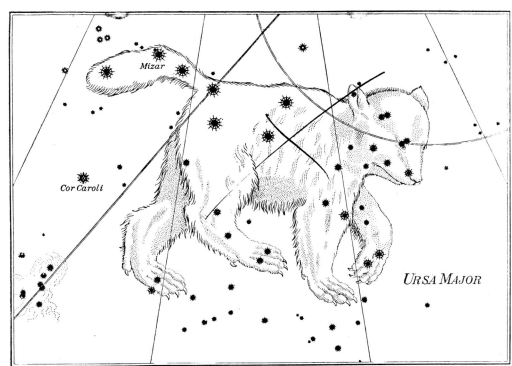

Ursa Major. From Petrus Apianus,
Cosmographia *(1545)*

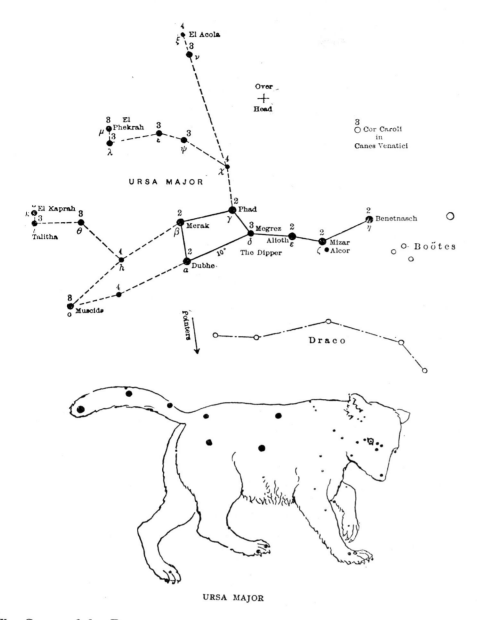

URSA MAJOR

The Stars of the Bear

Alpha Ursae Majoris carries the name *Dubhe*, or Bear, an abbreviation of the Arabic *Thahr al-Dubb al-Akbar*, the Back of the Great Bear, which is a literal translation from the list compiled by Ptolemy.

Beta Ursae Majoris is Merak or Mirak, from *al-Marakk*, meaning the Flank (of the Bear); Gamma Ursae Majoris is *Phekda*, the Thigh. Delta Ursae Majoris is Megrez, from *al-Maghrez*, the Root of the Tail. Eta Ursae Majoris is Alioth, a name derived from *Alyat*, the broad tail of the sheep in the Middle East.

Zeta Ursae Majoris is Mizar, or the Belt, which is a name that has been incorrectly given to it by Sealiger to replace the original Mirak. This star was also known as the Horse, and the small star Alcor, which is very close to it, was the Knight. Mizar, the first double discovered with the telescope, was recognized in Bologna in 1650 by the astronomer Riccioli. Alcor is a famous little star of astronomical folklore.

Alcor is often considered the Wagoneer who drives the Great Wagon. Eta Ursae Majoris is Benet Nash, from *Kaid Banat al-Naash*, or the Sorrowing Daughter of the Litter. In some catalogues this star is also called Alkaid; it is the last star in the tail of the Bear.

Ursa Major. From P. Carus, Chinese Astrology

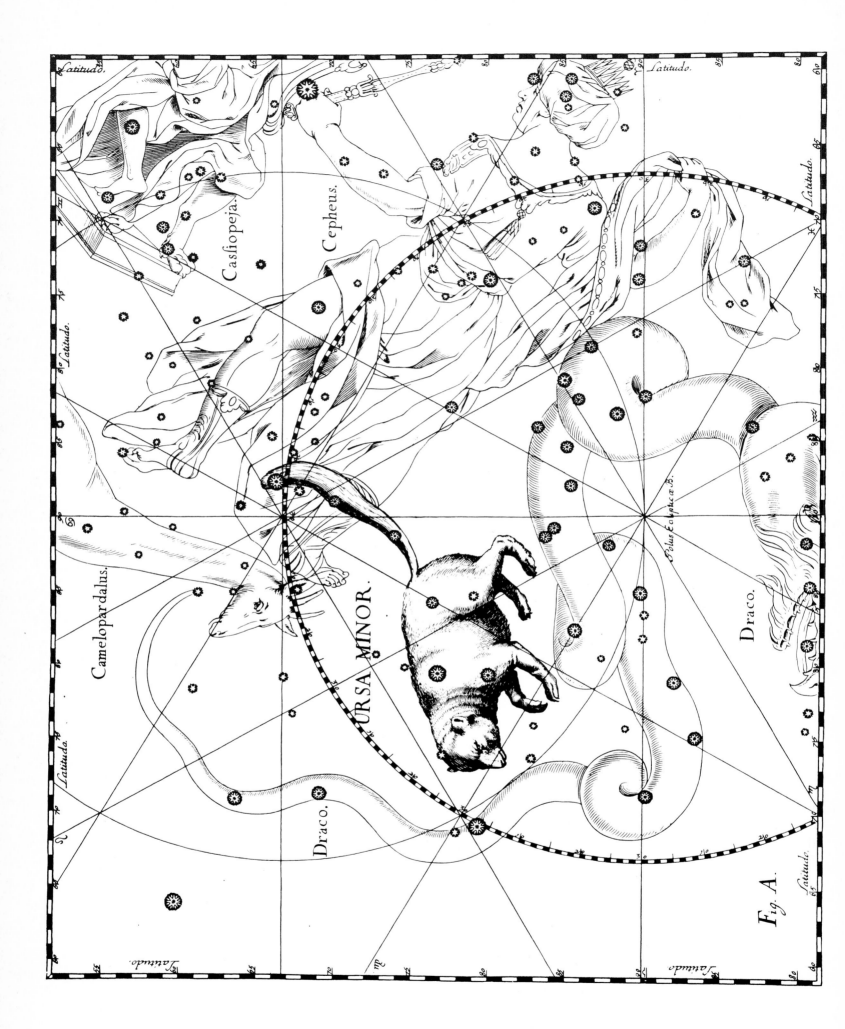

48
Ursa Minor

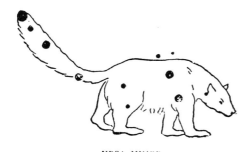

URSA MINOR

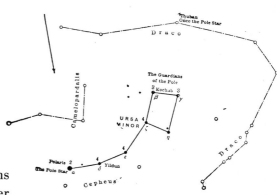

Although it does not appear on the list of the most ancient constellations and does not contain any first-magnitude stars, Ursa Minor, the Lesser Bear, is a very famous figure because it has been the closest star group to the North Pole for about three thousand years. This was not the case in very ancient times; from 5000 to 2000 B.C. the pole resided in Draco; in 2700 B.C. it was centered exactly on the star Alpha Draconis, or Thuban, toward which many temples and buildings were oriented.

At that time the figure of Draco looked more like that of a traditional dragon, that is, a large lizard like a Mesozoic dinosaur, with wings like those of the dragon slain by Saint George in the painting by Paolo Uccello. The wings were designed in the sky with the stars that today make up Ursa Minor, a constellation unknown to both Homer and Hesiod. It was Thales who introduced the new figure in Greece by depriving the dragon of its wings and creating the second bear.

The Phoenicians called these stars *Cynosura*, or the Tail of the Dog. We have no information about this name except for the elaborations of the historian Archibald Sayce and the astronomer Brown. Sayce had targeted a constellation in the Euphrates Valley called *An-ta-su-ra*, or the High Sphere, which Brown read as *An-nas-sur-ra*, or the High Spring, a name that is certainly appropriate for Ursa Minor. Brown continued the etymology, affirming that this name evolved into *Unosura* and *Kunosura*, thus giving rise to the Phoenician *Cynosura*.

Jensen identified Ursa Minor with the transposition into the stars of the Leopard of Babylon. Along the Nile the constellation was known as the Dog of Set who was the diabolical god of drought whose symbol was the Jackal. In fact, the Sacred Jackal appeared in the circular zodiac at Dendera in the place of the Bear. This animal is also present in the carvings along the walls of the Ramesseum.

In their myths the Greeks saw the form of young Arcas, son of the nymph Callisto and Zeus, in Ursa Minor. His story is told in the chapter on Ursa Major.

The nomads of the desert called the Polar Star Kid, or Star of the North; the more learned ones called it the Hole Where the Terrestrial Axis Was Born. It was widely accepted that fixed contemplation of this star cured itching eyes.

For Ursa Minor, the cabalists chose the twenty-first trump card of the tarots—the Universe.

Opposite: Ursa Minor. From Hevelius,
Uranographia totum coelum stellatum *(1690)*

The movement of the North Pole over a period of approximately five thousand years

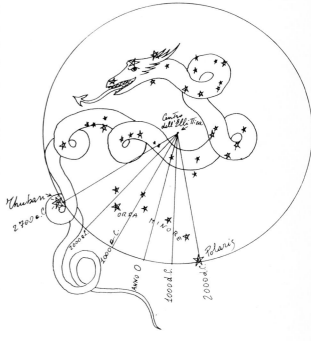

473

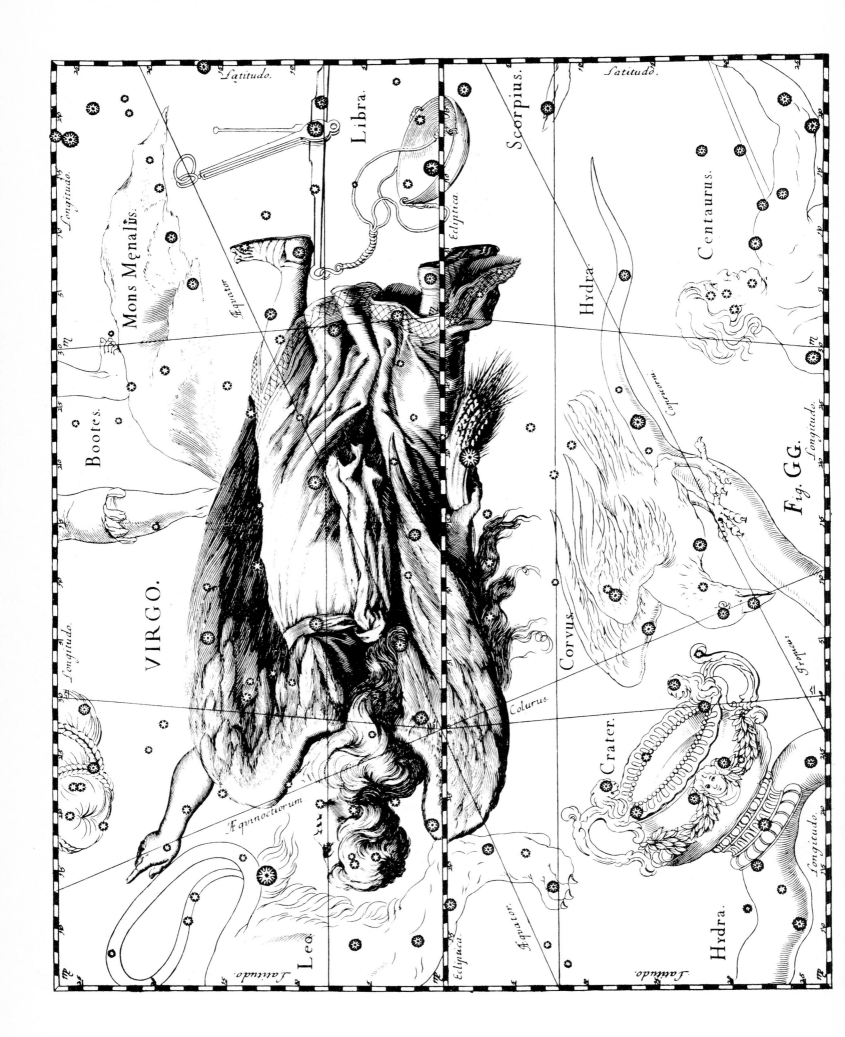

49
Virgo

When, on a beautiful, moonless summer night, we use our imagination to extend the curved line traced by the tail of Ursa Major toward the south, first we encounter the star Arcturus in the constellation of Boötes. Continuing along this imaginary arc, we then find a white star of first magnitude—the star Spica. This is the lucida of the constellation of Virgo, the Virgin. (Along with Arcturus and Denebola in Leo, Spica forms a large triangle that is useful in helping astronomers to orient themselves.) It appears in the east in March, rises in the southern region of the sky in April, May, and June, descends in July toward the west, and disappears in September among the evening mists.

In this region of the heavenly sphere the constellation-makers always saw a winged woman holding a stalk of grain in her left hand. This female figure, Spica, was seen as the goddess who ruled the harvest of barley and wheat by all grain-cultivating civilizations who worshiped her, at whatever latitude they lived. She even appears among the Aztecs who called her the Magical Mother or Mother Earth.

The universality of Virgo's qualification as goddess of the harvest of wheat and barley presents two parallel considerations that determine the parameters of this figure in history. The first consideration is anthropological and refers to the period of the birth of agriculture, of which the Virgin is the stellar celebration. The second is astronomical and requires calculating the position of these stars back when they coincided with the summer solstice—a time when the entrance of the sun into Virgo concurrently fixed the time for the solstice and the harvest.

Both these considerations take us to the two millennia from 6000 to 4000 B.C., when the summer solstice occurred in Virgo and the rudiments of agriculture were acquiring importance in human history. The contrast between a temporary camp in the Mesolithic period and a village of farmers in the Neolithic is so vivid that it justifies the use of the term Neolithic Revolution. Among its innovations were the cultivation of wheat and barley; the domestication of animals; the technique of grafting; and the concept of a city.

Women were entirely responsible for this revolution because, at least as far as the arts, sciences, and cults were concerned, society at that time was primarily matriarchal. Women's symbolic expression in terms of divinity was, at its highest level, the Great Mother—the ancient goddess about whom we know the least, despite the many references to her in the records. The reason for this is that she exhibited many contradictory aspects from culture to culture. As a result extensive and intricate myths developed about her.

Nana, Eve, Ishtar, Demeter, Hecate, Themis, Hera, Astraea, Diana of Ephesus, Cybele, Isis, Fortuna, Erigone, Sibylla, and the Virgin Mary are some of the metamorphoses of the Great Mother, the versatile goddess of many meanings. Before Zeus, before Poseidon and Apollo, before the concept of God the creator, masculine and primordial, she existed as the Great Mother, creator of all things, symbol of the power held by the prehistoric matriarchy.

Virgo. From Hyginus, Poetica astronomica *(1485 edition)*

Opposite: *Virgo. From Hevelius,* Uranographia totum coelum stellatum *(1690)*

Alignments to find the star Spica

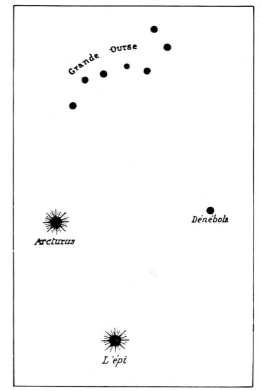

475

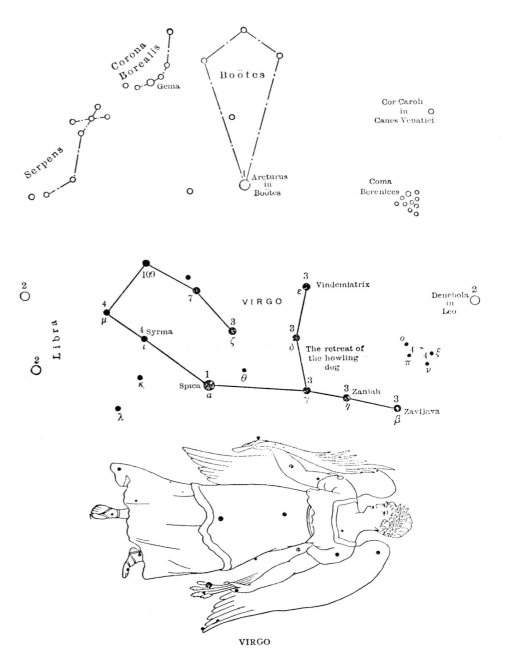

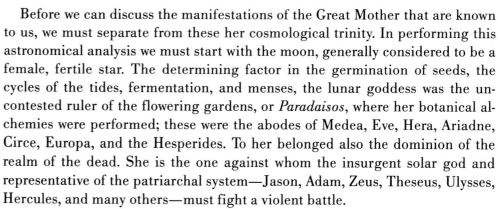

VIRGO

Hera

Before we can discuss the manifestations of the Great Mother that are known to us, we must separate from these her cosmological trinity. In performing this astronomical analysis we must start with the moon, generally considered to be a female, fertile star. The determining factor in the germination of seeds, the cycles of the tides, fermentation, and menses, the lunar goddess was the uncontested ruler of the flowering gardens, or *Paradaisos*, where her botanical alchemies were performed; these were the abodes of Medea, Eve, Hera, Ariadne, Circe, Europa, and the Hesperides. To her belonged also the dominion of the realm of the dead. She is the one against whom the insurgent solar god and representative of the patriarchal system—Jason, Adam, Zeus, Theseus, Ulysses, Hercules, and many others—must fight a violent battle.

In addition to her lunar manifestation, the Great Mother is also represented by the planet Venus separated into its two distinct aspects, that of the Evening Star (Hesperus) and therefore the love goddess, Aphrodite, and the Morning Star (Phosphorus) with the bellicose and ferocious qualities of Mars.

Lastly, there is her solar manifestation—the constellation of the Virgin—in which, during a period of twenty centuries, the sun reached its maximum declination at the summer solstice when the grain was ready to be cut.

Ishtar

The Sumerians, inventors of the first alphabet—cuneiform script—have recorded for us the most ancient written documents on the Middle Eastern manifestation of the Great Mother. She was first worshiped in the person of Nana (*Nanaia* to the Greeks), who was a Sumerian-Akkadian divinity and therefore not Semitic. Nana was the goddess of life and nature, of fertility and birth, and she was worshiped particularly in the very ancient city of Uruk in southern Mesopotamia. There she had her temple, the *Eanna,* or House of the Sky, which was founded by King Urbau around 3000 B.C. She was depicted in the nude, with an exaggerated physique, pressing her hands onto her breasts.

At some point, and for unknown reasons, Nana became Ishtar—the principal Assyro-Babylonian divinity—who, in the beginning, was invoked as "ruler of Eanna, ruler with the name of Nana" (Bassi, *Mitologia babilonese e assira*).

A distinction should be made between the Ishtar of popular tradition and the Ishtar of the official religious system and, at the same time, between the Babylonian and the Assyrian Ishtars, even though these last two later merged into one. Originally she was the goddess of vegetation who made things green again after the scorching heat of the dog days or the harsh winter cold. As such, she appears in a saga dating back to very remote times, which was called *Wandering Ishtar* or the *Pilgrimage of Ishtar*. The story tells how the goddess fell desperately in love with Tammuz, the Mesopotamian Adonis—the young man who was the incarnation of the ephemeral, passing beauty of youth and who was mortally wounded by a boar during the summer solstice.

Inconsolable over the premature loss of her lover, Ishtar descended into the realm of the dead to persuade Ereshkigal, the queen of the netherworld, to return Tammuz to her, but she was instead imprisoned in Avernus. The plant world ceased procreating while she was incarcerated, thus endangering the lives of animals and humans. In anguish the gods faced a squalid world devoid of love and fertility until the ruler of the gods, Ea (Capricornus), intervened by ordering Ereshkigal to liberate Ishtar and Tammuz.

The astronomical symbolism is quite evident: at the beginning of the spring the earth joins with the mild springtime sun (Tammuz) and is covered with green under his soft caresses; then the summer arrives with its ardent sun (the boar) who kills the sun of the months of spring, and the new seeds are interred (Ishtar and Tammuz in the world beyond the grave).

The underworld aspect of Ishtar is that of Ishtar as goddess of the earth, fertility, crops, and love, seen only as an indispensable component of plant life. Subsequently she was mainly considered to be the goddess of love and was identified both with the Evening Star, which precedes the appearance of the moon, and the Morning Star, which announces the coming of the sun.

The Evening Star was "the beautiful planet that inspires love," the goddess of love who pulls man to woman and binds them with sweet ties. Her priestesses were the Hierodules—beautiful young women who consecrated their bodies to the goddess and the devout by the practice of sacred prostitution. In fact, all women were required to go at least once in their life to the temple of Ishtar and there sell themselves for a silver coin to the first man who arrived.

As Morning Star she was imagined as a cold and cruel warrior who disdained pleasure and loved battle, a star announcing the sun of the new day with its toil and strife. In this aspect the goddess is the Assyrian Ishtar, "the reason why no one lives in rest and pleasure without her consent, the goddess of strife, the ruler of battles, the arbiter of the great divinities."

Opposing forces always converge in Ishtar. As the planet Venus she is at first

Ishtar, goddess of fertility and love

Priest worshiping Ishtar

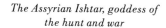

The Assyrian Ishtar, goddess of the hunt and war

the Evening Star, daughter of Anu, the sky, and goddess of love; then the Morning Star, daughter of Sin, the sun, and the Amazon of war. As goddess of nature she is the moon in its fertile and procreative aspect, while she is identified with the stars of the Virgin as godmother of the harvest and the crops.

Themis, the Hours, the Moerae, Tyche, Fortuna

In the period preceding Nana-Ishtar we find traces of the Great Mother only in images of stone and terra-cotta. Writing had not yet been invented, but oral tradition had handed down the very ancient archetype of a queen of the world. She had reigned uncontestedly since the dawn of our history until the invention of metals and the ascent of the male solar gods dethroned her, without ever being able to cancel her power completely.

We find her in the female Titan Themis, mother of the Seasons, the Hours, and the three Moerae. Originating from Greek Neolithic times, *Temi*, meaning Order, was the triple goddess who regulated the sequence of the thirteen months of the year in her manifestations as *Antea*, or Flowering—goddess of spring—*Iperea*, or She Who Stands Above—goddess of summer—and *Pittea*—goddess of the pine tree, who was worshiped in autumn.

As mother of the Moerae, Themis was known as the Powerful Moera, the great goddess of necessity with whom the gods did not dare contend. The Moerae, or Parche, represented the three aspects of the moon. They were called *Clotho*, the Spinner, *Lachesis*, the One Who Measures, and *Atropos*, She Who Cannot Be Avoided. The last was responsible for cutting the thread of life for all creatures.

The name *Moira*, which means phase, refers to the three phases of the moon. The first, that of the new moon, was the virgin goddess of spring or the first period of the year. The second, the full moon, was the goddess of summer or the second period of the year. The third, the waning moon, was the old goddess of autumn or the last period of the year. The mythical Hours, also daughters of Themis, were the three goddesses of civilization and peace. They were the guardians of the gates of heaven and Olympus. They were called Eunomia, or Legal Order; Dice, or Just Recompense; and Irene, or Peace.

Priestess of the Great Mother with lilies in her hand

Below: *The Hours and the horses of Hera. From Flaxman,* Iliad

O lady Aglaia! Euphrosyna, lover of song!
Daughters of the strongest god, hear me,
and hear me, Thalia, who delight in music:
look with favor now upon this chorus
stepping lightly.

Pindar, *Olympian 14*

The three Charities, Aglaia (ornament),
Euphrosine (joy), and Thalia (abundance) were
the triple manifestation of the Great Mother.
They were the source of amiability, eloquence,
and knowledge. In their honor the Charitesian
festivities were celebrated with poetry and
song contests. Their worship spread from the
Greeks to the Romans, who translated their
names to the Graces.

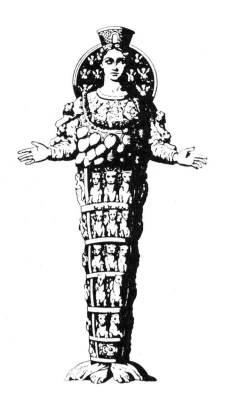

Ephesian Artemis

It was said of Dice that she had withdrawn to the mountains when men ceased to respect justice, and later she abandoned the earth altogether; from then on she was visible in the sky as the constellation of the Virgin.

Similarly, in the *Phaenomena*, the astronomical poem by Aratus, the Virgin is described as the daughter of Astraeus, the mythical inventor of the constellations and astronomy. During the Golden Age she lived freely among men and women under the name of Justice. At that time people lived free from war and had not yet invented navigation, but lived happily on the fruit of the land. The Golden Age was followed by the Age of Silver when people were less pure than their ancestors and more inclined to violence, deceit, and possessiveness. Justice did not live with humans at that time, but had withdrawn to the mountains from which she would periodically descend in order to try and dissuade men and women from their degenerate ways. At last the Bronze Age arrived, in which hatred, war, and violence spread uncontrollably. Swords were invented and, for the first time, people ate the meat of oxen. Saddened, Justice decided to abandon them and retired on high among the stars, where she became the constellation of Virgo.

The manifestations of the Great Mother are always linked to the calendar and the seasons, as in the case of Tyche whose wheel (the wheel of fortune) represented originally the solar year, as is indicated by her Latin name, Fortuna, derived from *Vortumna*, or She Who Turns (the year).

Isis, Osiris, and Horus

In Egypt, as in Mesopotamia, the cult of the moon preceded that of the sun. The cult of Isis, the lunar goddess, sister and spouse of Osiris the moon-god,

Isis nursing the infant Horus

and mother of Horus, the young moon, appears in the religious writings before the fifth dynasty (about 3000 B.C.). The cult of Ra, the god of the sun, appears only toward the end of the twelfth dynasty (about 1800 B.C.)

Even then, however, the cult of Ra did not supplant that of the moon. Rather, it was Osiris who was gradually assimilated by the solar god, still keeping his lunar character; he becomes the moon who, after his resurrection, is worshiped as the sun.

Originally Isis, like Nana, represented Mother Nature, or the Great Mother, and Osiris the moon. With the passing of the centuries, while Osiris became more and more closely identified with the sun, Isis became the quintessential lunar goddess. She represented the waxing moon and her nature was characterized by the double aspect of being mother-creator and nourisher of all beings, and being a destructive power.

She is often represented as a black goddess with a child in her arms (Horus); this image was so popular in the Greco-Roman world that many images of Isis

Isis

480   *The Glorious Constellations*

Isis and the little boy, in the planisphere at Dendera

and Horus were worshiped by the Christian communities that followed as the representation of the Virgin Mary and the baby Jesus. This would explain the special adoration that exists in Catholic and Orthodox churches for the Black Madonnas—who are direct descendants of the images of Isis with the little Horus—today considered to be particularly miraculous.

In a temple at Dendera in Egypt a ceiling has been found that is carved in a bas-relief representing the constellations. In the place where the Virgin would customarily be, there instead appear two female figures, one standing erect with a stalk of grain in her hand and the other sitting with a child in her arms.

Osiris, patron of agriculture and resurrection, symbolized the fertile power of the moon and the young sun, ruler of plant life. He was portrayed either with his face painted green or his body stretched out horizontally with twenty-eight new stalks of grain growing from it, which corresponded to a lunar month and to the growth of the dormant seeds that will rise again after the flooding of the Nile.

When Osiris (the fertility of the Nile Valley) was overcome by Set (the wind and the drought of the desert) and torn into fourteen parts, Isis, dressed in black, sailed in her boat until she succeeded in putting the body of her brother and spouse back together—with the one exception of the phallus. The missing part did reappear every year in a ceremony held during the winter solstice and in which Isis, in the guise of a golden cow covered by a black veil, was carried around the reliquary of Osiris seven times, representing her voyage. This was followed by chasing off Typhon (the destructive power of Set) and then resurrecting Osiris, symbol of the annual flooding of the Nile that guaranteed the fertility of the next year.

Demeter

The Mother of the Earth, *Demetra* in Greek, was ruler of the crops, vegetation, fertility, the harvest, and civilization. Before her existence humans were

Winged Isis

nomadic, living on tubers, plants, and fruit. With her, they became civilized, divided and cleared the land, founded cities, and organized armies. Perhaps this is the meaning of the biblical Eve, who ate the fruits of the tree of knowledge.

The center of her cult was at Eleusis, near Athens, where her mysteries were celebrated every year during the Thesmophoria, festivities whose name derives from her title of *Tesmofora*, She Who Brings Laws. These celebrations lasted five days, and only married women could participate.

She was generally represented with a sickle in one hand and a sheaf of stalks in the other; in addition, her head and clothes were sprinkled with poppies, flowers sacred to her because they grow with grain. The animal consecrated to her was the boar.

Demeter (Ceres to the Romans) had one daughter, the beautiful Core (Persephone or Proserpina), with whom the god of the underworld, Hades (Pluto), fell in love. Knowing that Core would never agree to marry him voluntarily, he decided one day to abduct her while the girl was gathering flowers in a field near Enna in Sicily, and so he took her with him to the realm of the dead.

After her daughter's disappearance Demeter roamed in despair from land to land searching for her in vain. One day Demeter arrived at the court of Celeus, father of Triptolemus, Eumolpus, and Eubuleus. Triptolemus told the goddess that Eubuleus, while taking the pigs to pasture, had heard a heavy thundering of hooves and seen a great crevice in the earth suddenly open up. A chariot had appeared, drawn by black horses and guided by a black rider whose face was invisible and who held in his arms a maiden crying for help. The rider had steered his chariot directly into the abyss, which closed up again after they had passed through. Demeter's sorrow was so great that the entire plant world grew pale and ceased producing leaves and generating fruit; grass even ceased to grow, with the result that humans and animals would soon have become extinct.

From Olympus Zeus tried to soothe her but Demeter would not yield. If Core was not returned to her, the world would become a desert. Thus Zeus was compelled to order his brother, Hades, to free Core, as long as she had not eaten any food in the realm of the dead. While Core was getting onto Hades' coach to be brought back to her mother, the gardener of the underworld, Ascalaphus, swore that he had seen her eat seven pomegranate seeds.

The meeting between Demeter and Core took place at Eleusis, under the protection of the goddess Hecate, whom Demeter had called to assist her. When Hades revealed the detail of the pomegranate seeds, a shadow came over the goddess' face and she threatened to continue the sterility of the earth. At that point Zeus decided that Core would remain in the company of Hades as

Pluto and Cerberus

queen of Tartarus for three months of the year, and she would spend the other nine months in the company of Demeter. The ancient Hecate was given the task of ensuring that the agreement was respected; she became Core's constant guardian.

In gratitude to Triptolemus, Demeter initiated him into her mysteries before returning to Olympus. She gave him seeds of grain, a wooden plow, and a chariot drawn by serpents. Thus equipped, she sent him throughout the world to teach the science of agriculture. This is why Triptolemus has gone down in history as the first farmer.

Here again the Great Mother is divided into three manifestations as she represents the goddess of the crops in her triple aspect of virgin nymph (Core), mature woman (Demeter), and old woman (Hecate). Core is the symbol of the green grain, Demeter of the mature grain, and Hecate of the harvested grain.

The pomegranate represented fertility and resurrection; as an ancient attribute of the Great Mother, it was also integrated into the cult of the child Dionysus when he was killed by the Titans and a pomegranate tree grew from

Hecate

Demeter, Triptolemus, and Persephone

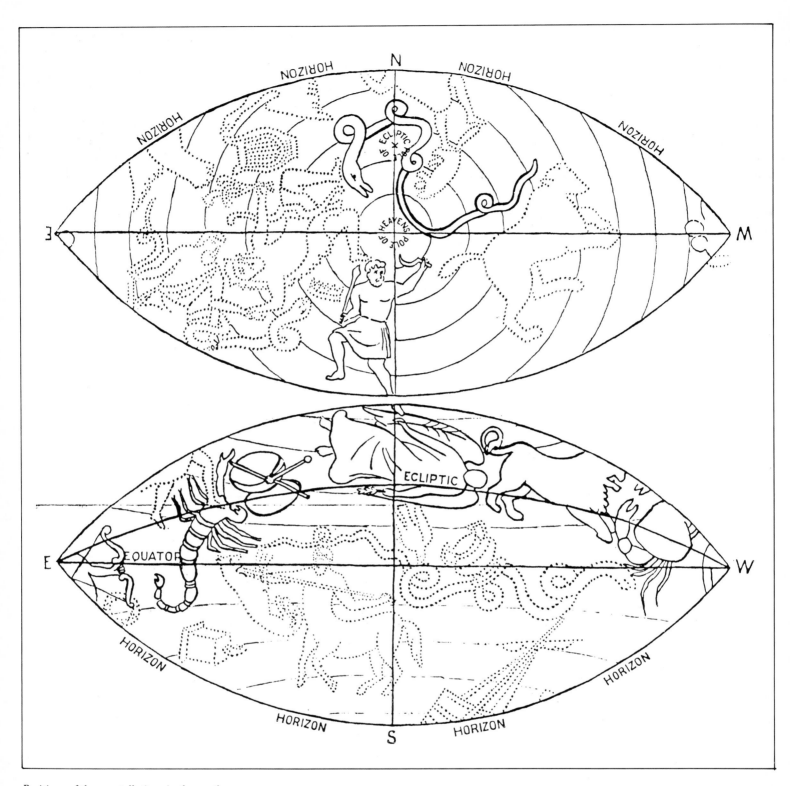

Positions of the constellations in the northern and southern hemispheres with respect to the meridian of the summer solstice in 5744 B.C.

his blood. The seven pomegranate seeds eaten by Core probably stand for the seven phases of the moon that constitute the interim period between the sowing of the grain and the sprouting of the plant (Graves, *The Greek Myths*).

In the chapter on Corona Borealis we encounter another manifestation of Demeter, the beautiful Ariadne. She was the ancient Cretan goddess of the moon and the crops who was originally called *Ar-ri-an-de*, or the Very Fertile Mother of Barley. She was also the Ruler of the Labyrinth or the goddess who dominated the world the labyrinth represented, namely Hades.

The Virgin and Boötes

The astronomers of the sixth and fifth millennia B.C. could observe that, during the equinoxes and solstices, the Virgin was always centered in the meridians with the constellation of the giant Boötes. Upright, with his head marked by the star Arcturus, and close to the ancient North Pole, he stood in a position very much like that of the Titan Atlas (see the chapter on Boötes).

This cohabitation of stars in points of such great astronomical importance seems to indicate that there existed an intimate link between these two figures. The original myth on this possible relationship belongs to oral tradition and is therefore not known, but it may be that a trace has remained with us in the story of Demeter's love affair with the Titan Iasion. It happened when the two met at a banquet given in celebration of the wedding of Cadmus and Harmonia, and, intoxicated with nectar, went off to couple on a plowed field.

From this Philomelus and Plutus were born. They never agreed with each other because Plutus, who was rich, never gave anything to his brother. Driven by need, Philomelus invented the wagon and used what little money he had to buy two oxen. So it happened that he maintained himself by plowing and cultivating the fields. In admiration of his invention Demeter immortalized him among the stars and called him Boötes, which means Wagoneer (Hyginus, *Poetica astronomica*, II.4).

Demeter's copulation with Iasion on the plowed field is a reference to the fertility rite during which the priestess of the grain would lie with the sacred king in a ritual ceremony during the autumnal plowing.

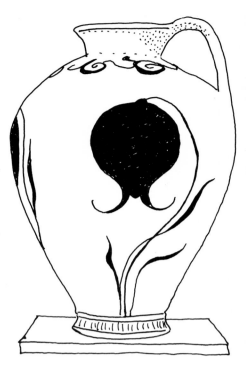

The pomegranate sacred to the Great Mother. Vase from Phylakopi (1500 B.C.)

Bayer's Virgo (1603)

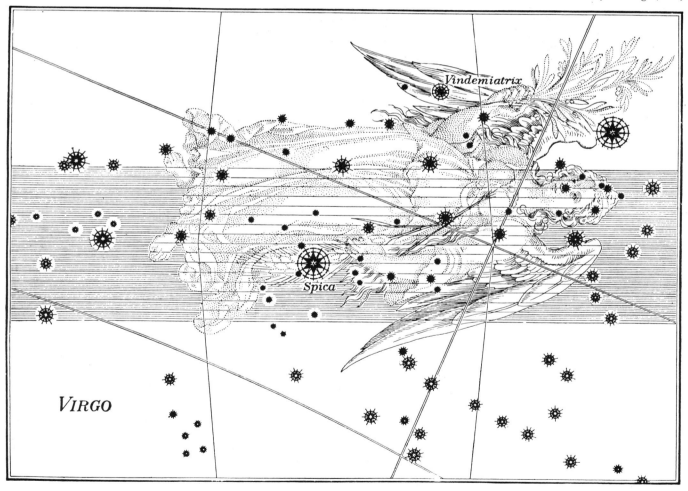

VIRGO

Ascendit
sicut Aurora
consurgens

Pulchra
ut Luna,
Electa ut Sol.

Another very ancient combination of the two constellations was recounted in the myth of the nymph Erigone, daughter of Icarius—who had been chosen by Dionysus to be the first man to plant and cultivate the vine in order to obtain wine. The myth presents him to us seated on a cart loaded with filled wineskins. He generously offers some shepherds a drink, and unfamiliar with the effects of the new beverage, they become drunk and fall asleep on the ground. Thinking that he has poisoned them, their companions kill Icarius and bury him under a pine tree. Returning home, Icarius' dog, Maera, barks at Erigone and convinces her to follow her to the place where her father lay buried. Upon discovering the body, the young girl is overcome by grief and commits suicide by hanging herself on the branches of the very same tree. Dionysus dedicated to Erigone the fertility rites of the vine and immortalized her among the stars of the Virgin. He placed Icarius among the stars of Boötes and he immortalized the dog, Maera, in the star Procyon (see the chapter on Boötes).

Eve and the Virgin Mary

In the section on the constellation of Draco, we were able to see the relationship of Eve to the figures of the Great Mother and Demeter in her role as the priestess of the flowering garden, the *Paradaisos* where she ate the forbidden fruit of knowledge and made man eat it. If this knowledge is taken to mean agriculture, the message implied by the parable of her first two sons becomes clear as well. Cain, which means stalk—he picked a stalk of grain for his mother as soon as he was born—is the representative of the new farmers. In order to be able to practice their new profession, they took possession of the lands and used force to chase away the nomadic shepherds (Abel) who did not recognize

Two representations of the Virgin Mary. From the Missale romanum, *Augusta Taurinorum (1893)*

anyone's right to own the land. The stalk of grain is the symbolic gift of agriculture to the great mother Demeter, the constellation of Virgo.

Later, with the birth of Jesus, there arises a new, powerful image of the eternal feminine principle with a marked tendency toward the protection of fertility and childbirth (the Virgin Mary). The new patriarchal and monastic religion of Christianity, with the Father, Son, and Holy Ghost of the resurrection as its pivot, lacked a female element in its cult. This was not provided even by Christ himself, who never worshiped his mother; therefore the first Christians chose the Mother of God, Mary, as a real-life model and attributed to her all those virtues that had belonged to the Great Mother in all her manifestations.

The image of the Virgin was used to counter that of Eve, toward whom the church's hostility against women was directed. Women were accused of being responsible for original sin and were seen as diabolical temptresses of the paradiselike state represented by the monastic orders.

As the daughter of Anna (the name of the ancient Sumerian goddess of the sky, wife of Anu), Mary is, in her appearance among the stars, the *Regina Coeli.* As such, she traditionally wears the azure-blue mantle, symbol of the sky that is often decorated with stars, while she stands with her naked feet on the serpent or the crescent moon—ancient symbol of chastity.

In the secular iconography of the Virgin Mary there are the following symbols: the Lily, purity; the Olive (of Minerva), peace (see, for example, the paintings of the schools of Siena and Florence); the Star (Ishtar), often painted on her mantle; the Stella Maris (Star of the Sea), which is the meaning of her Hebrew name, Miriam; the Apple, normally shown in the hand of the baby Jesus, the fruit of the tree of knowledge; the Grape Cluster, symbol of the blood

The Virgin of the Alfonsine Tables *(thirteenth century) and from a fifteenth-century woodcut*

Virgo. From Zodiaque chronologique et mythologique

of Christ, but also reminiscent of the ancient associations between Erigone and Icarius or Ariadne and Dionysus; the Stalk of Grain, considered to represent the body of Christ by the Christian tradition but whose message should be obvious in the light of the discussions in this book; the Pomegranate, the fruit of Hera and Proserpina, which had many meanings and which Christianity views as the symbol of resurrection; and finally, a small bird, an ancient symbol of the soul that abandons the body to rise again, generally held in the hand of the infant Jesus, almost always a goldfinch—the favorite bird of children because of the colors of its feathers and its joyous song.

Spica

The beautiful lucida of the constellation Virgo is Spica, Alpha Virginis, a first-magnitude star. It marks the stalk of grain that the Virgin holds in her hand. Due to its proximity to the ecliptic it has been frequently used by sailors for the coordinates of their routes. It culminates on May 27 at nine o'clock at night.

The Alexandrian astronomer Timocrates asserted that it was through observation of Spica and Regulus that Hipparchus discovered the precession of the equinoxes in the third century B.C., although there already existed a practical knowledge of this phenomenon at this time.

Nineteenth-century scholar Joseph Norman Lockyer maintained that there was a link between Spica and the prehistoric cult of the Egyptian god Min, an anthropomorphic being that served as a phallic symbol and had two tall fins on its head. It was subsequently integrated into the cult of Horus, whose temple at Thebes was oriented toward Spica in 3200 B.C. Also, the Temple of the Sun at Tell-al-Amarna was similarly oriented at around 2000 B.C.

Near Rhamnus, Greece, two temples have been found next to each other, both oriented toward Spica so that they could follow its slow precessional shifting; the first was erected in 1092 and the second in 747 B.C. Also in Greece, in the area of Tegea, two more temples were found with the same orientation. Temples dedicated to Hera and oriented toward Spica existed at Olympia, Argos, and Girgenti (an early name for Agrigento). The temple of Nike Apteros in Athens, dating from 1130 B.C., and that of Artemis of Ephesus dating from 715 B.C. had the same orientation.

The Astrology of the Virgin

"The stars of the head and those at the tip of the southern wing operate somewhat like Mercury and Mars; the other stars that sparkle in that same wing and those of the garland are similar to Mercury and, to some extent, Venus. . . . Those of the feet and the lower part of her robe are like Mercury, slightly influenced by Mars."

This is how Ptolemy analyzed the influence exerted by Virgo's stars, while he said that Spica is of the nature of Venus and Mars. Alvidas deemed it to belong to the spheres of Venus, Jupiter, and Mercury. Spica was the star of success, renewal, and science. However, these qualities had been superimposed on other, more ancient ones that were not at all positive, such as contempt, sterility, and injustice. These same qualities were valid for the entire sign as well.

In modern astrology Virgo is synonymous with discrimination, working relationships, formal perfection, health, hygiene, and diet. A sign of earth, changeable and feminine, Virgo is in the domain of Mercury. Its influence on the human body makes itself felt on the digestive system, lower dorsal nerves, nails, and spleen. In the tarots it is traditionally represented by the third trump card, the Empress, but nowadays some assign it the ninth, the Hermit.

As far as the Arab lunar stations, *manzil*, are concerned, there are two: *al-Awwa*, He Who Barks, which bestows benevolence, victory, travels, harvests, and freedom for prisoners; and *al-Simak*, the Defenseless, which bestows love of war, an interest in caring for the sick and in helping with navigation.

In India it is the twelfth *nakshatra, Citra*, or the Shiny, portrayed by a lamp or a pearl. Governed by Mars, it is favorable to friendship and love of war.

In China there are also two stations, or *sieu*: the twelfth, *Kio*, meaning the Horn or the Stinger, which is governed by Jupiter, and the thirteenth, *Kang*, meaning the Neck, which is governed by Venus.

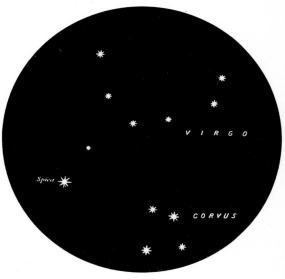

The stars of Virgo. From Easy Guide to the Constellations *(1916)*

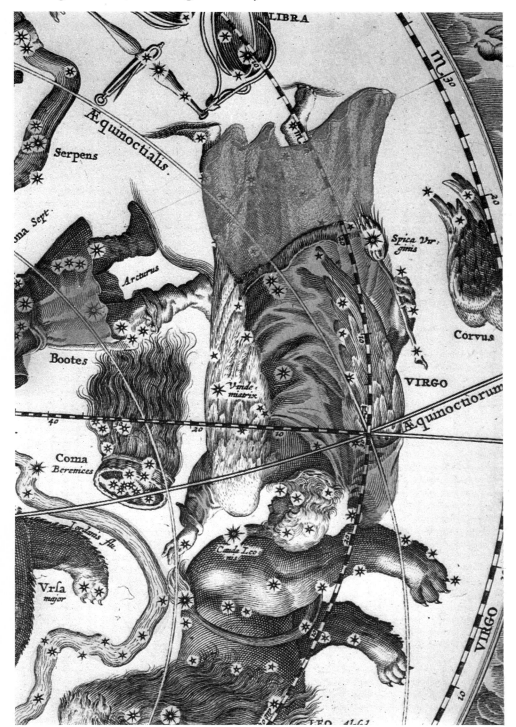

Virgo. From Cellarius, Harmonica macrocosmica *(1660)*

Virgo 489

Bibliography

BM = British Museum Library
RAS = Royal Astronomical Society Library

Agizza, Rosa. *Miti e leggende dell'antica Grecia*. Rome, 1985.
Allen, Richard Hinckley. *Star-names and Their Meanings*. London, 1899.
Apianus, Petrus. *Cosmographia*. 1545. (BM)
Apollonius of Rhodes. *Le Argonautiche*. Translated into Italian by G. Pompella. Naples, 1968.
———. *The Voyage of the Argo*. Translated by E. V. Rieu. London, 1959.
Aratus. *Phaenomena*. Translated by G. R. Mair. Loeb Classical Library. London, 1921.
Argelander, Friedrich. *Uranometria nova*. 1843. (RAS)
Armstrong, Edward. *The Folklore of Birds*. London, 1958.
Aurigemma, Luigi. *Il Segno zodiacale dello scorpione*. Turin, 1976.
Ball, Sir Robert Stawell. *Star-land*. London, 1889.
———. *The Story of the Heavens*. London, 1886.
Bassi, Domenico. *Mitologia Babilonese-Assira*. Milan, 1899.
Bayer, Johannes. *Rhainani uranometria*. 1640. (BM)
———. *Uranometria*. 1603. (BM)
Bernardini, Silvio. *Pievi toscane*. Turin, 1985.
Berry, Arthur. *A Short History of Astronomy*. 1898. Reprint, New York, 1961.
Bianchi, Ugo. *La Religione Greca*. Turin, 1975.
———. *Teogonie e cosmogonie*. Rome, 1960.
Bierhorst, John. *Miti pellerossa*. Translated into Italian by Franco Meli. Milan, 1984.
Bray and Trump. *Dictionary of Archeology*. London, 1970.
Brown, Robert. *The Celestial Equator of Aratus*. London, 1892. (RAS)
———. *Myth of Kirke*. London, 1883. (RAS)
Bulfinch, Thomas. *Bulfinch's Mythology*. London, 1963.
Bussagli, Mario, ed. *I Miti dell'oriente*. Rome, 1976.
Carus, Paul. *Chinese Astrology*. London, 1974.
Casanova, Angelo. *La Famiglia di Pandora*. Florence, 1979.
Chambers, G. F. *The Story of the Stars*. London, 1896.
Champeaux, G. de, and Sterckx, S. *Introduction au Monde des symboles*. St. Leger Vauban, 1972.
Chirassi, Ileana. *Elementi di culture precereali nei miti e riti Greci*. Rome, 1968.
Ciani, Maria Grazia. *Dionysos*. Padua, 1979.
Cirlot, J. E. *Diccionario de simbolos tradicionales*. 1958.
Clark, Ella E. *Indian Legends of the Pacific Northwest*. Los Angeles, 1953.
Clark, Rudle. *Myth and Symbol in Ancient Egypt*. London, 1959.
Colombo, Ileana Chirassi. *Le Religione in Grecia*. Bari, 1983.
Conio, Caterina. *Mito e filosofia nella tradizione Indiana*. Milan, 1974.
Covarrubias, Miguel. *Island of Bali*. New York, 1942.
Dante. *La Divina commedia*. Edited by Carlo Steiner.
Davidson, H. R. Ellis. *Gods and Myths of Northern Europe*.
Davidson, Martin. *The Stars and the Mind*. London, 1947.
Detienne, Marcel. *Dioniso e la pantera profumata*. Bari, 1981.
———. *I Giardini di Adone*. Turin, 1975.
———. *Il Mito, guida storica e critica*. Bari, 1982.
Doppelmayr, Johann Gabriel. *Atlas novus coelestis*. 1742. (BM)
———. *Hemispherum coelum australis*. 1730. (BM)
Drechsler, Adolph. *Der Arabische himmels globus*. 1873. (BM)
Dumezil, Georges. *Les Dieux des Germains*. Paris, 1959.
Dupuis, Charles François. *Memoire explicatif du zodiaque chronologique et mythologique*. Paris, 1806. (RAS)
Eliade, Mircea. *Gods, Goddesses, and Myths of Creation*. New York, 1967.
———. *Traite d'histoire des religions*. Paris, 1948.
Fix, William R. *Star Maps*. London, 1979.
Flammarion, Camille. *Atlas celeste*. 1877. (BM)

———. *Le Stelle*. Milan, 1904.
Flamsteed, John. *Atlas coelestis*. 1729. (BM)
Forman, Henry J. *Grecian Italy*. London, 1927.
Fox, Hugh. *Gods of the Cataclysm*. New York, 1976.
Frankfort, Henri and H. A.; Wilson, John A.; Jacobsen, Thorkild; and Irwin, William A. *The Intellectual Adventure of Ancient Man*. Chicago, 1946.
Frazer, Sir James George. *The Golden Bough*. London, 1922.
———. *La Paura dei morti nelle religioni primitive*. Milan, 1982.
Freeman, E. *Sicily: Phoenician, Greek, and Roman*. London, 1892.
Freeman and Grenville. *The Muslim and Christian Calendars*. London, 1963.
Fronzaroli, Pelio. *Leggenda di Aqhat*. Florence, 1955.
Furon, Raymond. *Manuel de prehistoire generale*. Parigi, 1958.
Galvano, Albino. *Artemis Efesia*. Milan, 1967.
Gaster, Theodor H. *Le Piu Antiche Storie del mondo*. Turin, 1979.
Gauquelin, Michel. *The Cosmic Clocks*. London, 1969.
Gernet, Louis. *Anthropologie de la Grece antique*. Parigi, 1968.
Gleadow, Rupert. *The Origin of the Zodiac*. London, 1968.
Gore, J. Ellard. *Astronomical Curiosities*. London, 1909.
Graves, Robert. *The Greek Myths*. London, 1955. Translated into Italian by Elisa Mopurgo as *I Miti Greci*. Milan, 1979.
———. *The White Goddess*. London, 1961.
——— and Patai, Raphael. *Hebrew Myths, The Book of Genesis*. 1963. Translated into Italian by M. V. Dazzi as *I Miti Ebraici*. Milan, 1980.
Gregory, Sir Richard. *The Vault of Heaven*. London, 1893.
Guerber, H. A. *The Myths of Greece and Rome*. London, 1907.
Guha, Belebasini, and Guha, Ahana. *Rig-Veda O Hakshatra or the Rig-Veda and the Constellations*. Calcutta, 1967. (RAS)
Haddad, Exarch John. *Astronomy and Astronomers*. 1924. (RAS)
Hall, James. *Dictionary of Subjects and Symbols in Art*. London, 1974.
Halleius. *Australis hemisphaerii tabulam*. 1680. (BM)
Harding. *Atlas novus*. 1856. (BM)
Harris. *Stellarum fixarum*. 1690. (BM)
Hawkins, Gerard S. *Stonehenge Decoded*. London, 1966.
Hearding, Ester. *Women's Mysteries: A Psychological Interpretation of the Feminine Principle as Portrayed in Myth, Story, and Dreams*. London, 1955.
Hermann, J. *Atlas zur astronomie*. 1973.
Hillman, James. *Saggio su Pan*. Milan, 1977.
Hire. *Planispheres celestes*. 1705. (BM)
Hommel, Fritz. *Storia di Babilonia e Assiria*. Milan, 1895.
Houseau. *Atlas de tous les etoiles visibles*. Paris, 1878. (RAS)
Hyginus. *The Myths of Hyginus*. Translated and edited by Mary Grant. University of Kansas Press, 1960.
Ionides, Stephen and Margaret. *One Day Telleth Another*. London, 1939.
Jahrbuch der Preussischen Kunstsammlungen. Berlin, 1943. (RAS)
Jamieson, Alexander. *Celestial Atlas*. 1822. (RAS) and (BM)
Jeanmaire, Henri. *Dioniso*. Turin, 1972.
Jeans, Sir James Hopwood. *The Stars in their Courses*. Cambridge, 1931.
Jung, Carl G. and Kerenyi, Karoly. *Prolegomeni allo studio scientifico della mitologia*. Turin, 1972.
Kawakib, Suwaru'l. *Uranometry*. 1373. 1974 edition. (RAS)
Kaye, George R. *Hindu Astronomy*. 1924. (RAS)
Kerenyi, Karoly. *Gli Dei e gli eroi della Grecia*. Milan, 1963.
———. *Miti e misteri*. Turin, 1979.
———. *Nel Labirinto*. Turin, 1983.
King, Henry C. *The Background of Astronomy*. London, 1957.
Kirk, G. S. *Myth, Its Meaning and Functions in Ancient and Other Cultures*. University of California Press, 1970.
———. *The Nature of Greek Myths*. London, 1954.
Klepesta, Josef, and Rukl, Antonin. *Constellations*. London, 1969.

Klibansky, Panofsky, and Saxl. *Satorno e la melancolia*. Turin, 1983.
Kravitz, David. *The Dictionary of Greek and Roman Mythology*. London, 1975.
Lamb. *Planispherium boreale*. 1679. (BM)
Lea. *North and South Celestial Hemisphere*. 1690. (BM)
Lewis, Sir George Cornewall. *Astronomy of the Ancients*. 1862. (RAS)
Lockyer, Joseph Norman. *Dawn of Astronomy*. London, 1894. (RAS)
————. *Stargazing: Past and Present*. London, 1878. (RAS)
Lubbock, Sir John William. *The Stars, in Six Maps*. London, 1883. (RAS)
Lucretius. *On the Nature of the Universe*. Translated by R. E. Latham. London, 1951.
Lumleyo. *North and South Hemysphere*. 1590. (BM)
Mackey, S. A. *Mythological Astronomy*. Norwich, 1824.
Mahaffy, J. Pentland. *Alexander's Empire*. London, 1887.
Manilius. *Astronomica*. Translated by G. P. Goold. Loeb Classical Library. London, 1971. (RAS)
Mann, A. T. *The Round Art*. London, 1979.
Masani, Alberto. *Storia della cosmologia*. Rome, 1980.
Mastrelli, C. A., trans. *L'Edda*. Florence, 1982.
Maunder, Walter. *The Astronomy of the Bible*. London, 1908.
McEvedy, Colin. *The Penguin Atlas of Ancient History*. London, 1967.
Merenduzzo, Antonio. *Le Cento novelle antiche*. Milan, 1924.
Middleton, J. *Celestial Atlas*. London, 1843.
Migliavacca, Renato. *Storia dell'astronomia*. Milan, 1976.
Mitchell, O. M. *Orbs of Heaven*. London, 1851.
Morretta, Angelo. *Miti Indiani*. Milan, 1982.
Muirden, James. *L'Astronomia col binocolo*. Milan, 1977.
Mukherji, Kalinath. *Atlas of Hindu Astronomy*. 1901. (RAS)
————. *Popular Hindu Astronomy*. Calcutta, 1905. (RAS)
Nasr, Seyyed Hossein. *Islamic Science*. London, 1976.
New Larousse Encyclopedia of Mythology. 1974.
Nonnus. *Dionysiaca*. Translated by W. H. D. Rouse. Loeb Classical Library. London, 1940.
Novacco, Domenico, ed. *Miti e leggende del medioevo*. Rome, 1976.
O'Flaherty, Wendy Doniger. *Hindu Myths*. London, 1975.
Olcott, W. T. *Star Lore*. New York, 1911.
Olmstead, Albert. *L'Impero Persiano*. Rome, 1982.
Ovid. *I Fasti*. Translated into Italian by Ferruccio Bernini. Bologna, 1979.
————. *Fasti*. Translated by Sir James George Frazer. London, 1931.
————. *Le Metamorfosi*. Translated into Italian by Ferruccio Bernini. Bologna, 1981.
————. *Metamorphoses*. Translated by Mary Innes. London, 1955.
Parker, Richard A., and Dubberstein, Waldo H. *Babylonian Chronology*. Brown University Press, 1969. (RAS)
Pater, Walter. *The Renaissance*. London, 1873.
Peck, W. *The Observer's Atlas of the Heavens*. London, 1898. (RAS)
Pestalozza, Uberto. *Eterno femminino Mediterraneo*. Venice, 1954.
Philippson, Paula. *Origini e forme del mito Greco*. Turin, 1983.
Pindar. *Odi e frammenti*. Translated into Italian by Leone Traverso. Florence, 1961.
————. *Olimpiche*. Translated into Italian by Luigi Lehnus. Milan, 1981.
Ponte, Renato del. *Dei e miti Italici*. Genoa, 1985.
Pouchet, F. A. *The Universe*. London, 1912.
Prince, C. Leeson. *A Literal Translation of the Astronomy and Meteorology of Aratus*. Lewes, 1895.
Proctor, Richard Anthony. *A Star Atlas*. 1870. (BM)
————. *Easy Star Lesson*. London, 1883.
————. *Myths and Marvels of Astronomy*. 1878.
Propp, Vladimir Jakolevic. *Le Radici storiche dei racconti di fate*. Turin, 1985.
Ptolemy. *Tetrabiblos*. Loeb Classical Library. London, 1940.
Quintus Smirneus. *The Fall of Troy*. Translated by Arthur Way. Loeb Classical Library. London, 1913.
Raschewiltz, Boris de. *I Miti egizi*. Milan, 1983.
Readingensen, J. B. *Astrolabium*. 1596. (BM)
Robson, Vivian E. *The Fixed Stars & Constellations in Astrology*. London, 1923.
Ronan, C. A. *Changing Views of the Universe*. London, 1961.
Roscoe, William. *Life of Lorenzo de' Medici*. London, 1796.
Sandars, N. K., ed. *L'Epopea di Gilgamesh*. Translated into Italian by A. Passi. Milan, 1986.
Santillana, Giorgio De. *Reflections on Men and Ideas*. The Massachusetts Institute of Technology, 1968.

———— and Dechend, Hertha von. *Il Molino d'Amleto*. Milan, 1983.
Saxl, Fritz. *La Fede negli astri*. Turin, 1985.
Sayce, A. H. *The Ancient Empires of the East*. London, 1884.
Schiapparelli, G. *Astronomy in the Old Testament*. Oxford, 1905.
Schneider, Marius. Articles that appeared in *Cognoscenti religiosa* 1970–1980. Translated into Italian by Elémire Zolla.
Seller, John. *Ascension and Declination of the Fixed Stars*. 1678. (BM)
————. *Atlas coelestis*. 1680. (BM)
Senes. *Zodiacus stellatus*. (BM)
Sidgwick and Jackson. *The Man in the Moon*. London, 1971. (RAS)
Sitchin, Z. *The Twelfth Planet*. London, 1977.
Smyth, Piazzi. *Our Inheritance in the Great Pyramid*. London, 1874.
Thiel, Rudolf. *And There Was Light*. New York, 1957.
Thorton, John. *Physiography*. London, 1897.
Uhlig, Helmut. *I Sumeri*. Milan, 1982.
Unger, Herman, et al. *Halley's Comet in History*. Edited by F. R. Stephenson and C. B. F. Walker. London, 1985.
Vernant, Jean-Pierre. *Mythe et société en Grèce ancienne, religion Grèque, religions antiques*. Paris, 1974–76.
Virgil. *Bucholiche*. Translated into Italian by M. Geymont. Milan, 1981.
————. *Georgiche*. Translated into Italian by Mario Ramous. Milan, 1982.
Volk-Schenk. *Hemisphei spherarum*. 1680. (BM)
————. *Planispherium Braheum*. 1680. (BM)
————. *Planispherium Copernicanum*. 1680. (BM)
Von Zach, F. *Neuester himmels atlas*. 1803. (BM)
Wesel, Uwe. *Il Mito del matriarcato*. Milan, 1985.
Wind, Edgar. *Misteri pagani nel rinascimento*. Milan, 1985.
Wo, Min Ming. *Fang Sing Tseunen T'oo*. 1711. (BM)
Wolkstein and Kramer. *Il Mito Sumero*. Milan, 1984.
Wollaston, Francis. *A Portraiture of the Heavens*. 1811. (RAS)
Woolsey. *The Celestial Companion*. 1802. (BM)
Zinner, E. *The Stars Above Us*. London, 1957.

ADDITIONAL ENGLISH-LANGUAGE BIBLIOGRAPHY

Apollonius of Rhodes. *The Argonautica*. Translated by R. C. Seaton. Cambridge, Mass.: Harvard University Press, 1961.
Carlyle, Thomas. *On Heroes and Hero Worship*. Everyman's Library. London: J. M. Dent & Sons, Ltd., 1967. First printed 1908.
Dante. *The Divine Comedy of Dante Alighieri*. Translated by Henry Wadsworth Longfellow. Boston: Ticknor and Fields, 1867.
Graves, Robert. *The Greek Myths*. London: Penguin Books, 1960. First printed 1955.
Hesiod. *Collected Works*. Translated by Rev. J. Banks. Loeb Classical Library. Cambridge, Mass.: Harvard University Press, 1977.
————. *The Homeric Hymns and Homerica*. Translated by H. G. Evelyn-White. Loeb Classical Library. Cambridge, Mass.: Harvard University Press, 1977. First printed 1914.
————. *The Remains of Hesiod the Ascraen*. Translated by Charles Abraham Eliot. London: Baldwin, Cradock, and Joy, 1815.
Kirk, G. S. *Myth: Its Meaning and Functions in Ancient and Other Cultures*. Cambridge: At the University Press, 1970.
Manilius. *Lucretius, His Six Books of Epicurean Philosophy, and Manilius, His Five Books Containing a System of the Ancient Astrology and Astronomy*. Edited and translated by Thomas Creech. London, 1700.
O'Flaherty, Wendy Doniger, ed. and trans. *The Rig-Veda: An Anthology*. New York and Harmondsworth: Penguin Books, 1981.
Ovid. *Fasti*. Edited and translated by Sir James George Frazer. London: MacMillan and Co., Ltd., 1929.
————. *Metamorphoses: Translated by Dryden, Congreve, and Other Eminent Persons*. London: Apollo Press, 1801; 1844.
Pindar. *Victory Songs*. Baltimore: The Johns Hopkins University Press, 1980.
Pound, Ezra. *The Cantos of Ezra Pound*. New York: New Directions Books, 1970.
Robson, Vivian E. *The Fixed Stars and Constellations in Astrology*. Cedar Hills, N.J.: Wehman Bros., 1969. First published 1923.
Sandars, N. K., trans. *The Epic of Gilgamesh*. New York and Harmondsworth: Penguin Books, 1977. First printing, 1960.
Virgil. *Eclogues, Georgics, Aeneid I–V* (vol. 1 of two volumes). Translated by H. Rushton Fairclough. Loeb Classical Library. Cambridge, Mass.: Harvard University Press, 1932. First printed 1916.

Index

Italian bank notes honoring Galileo Galilei

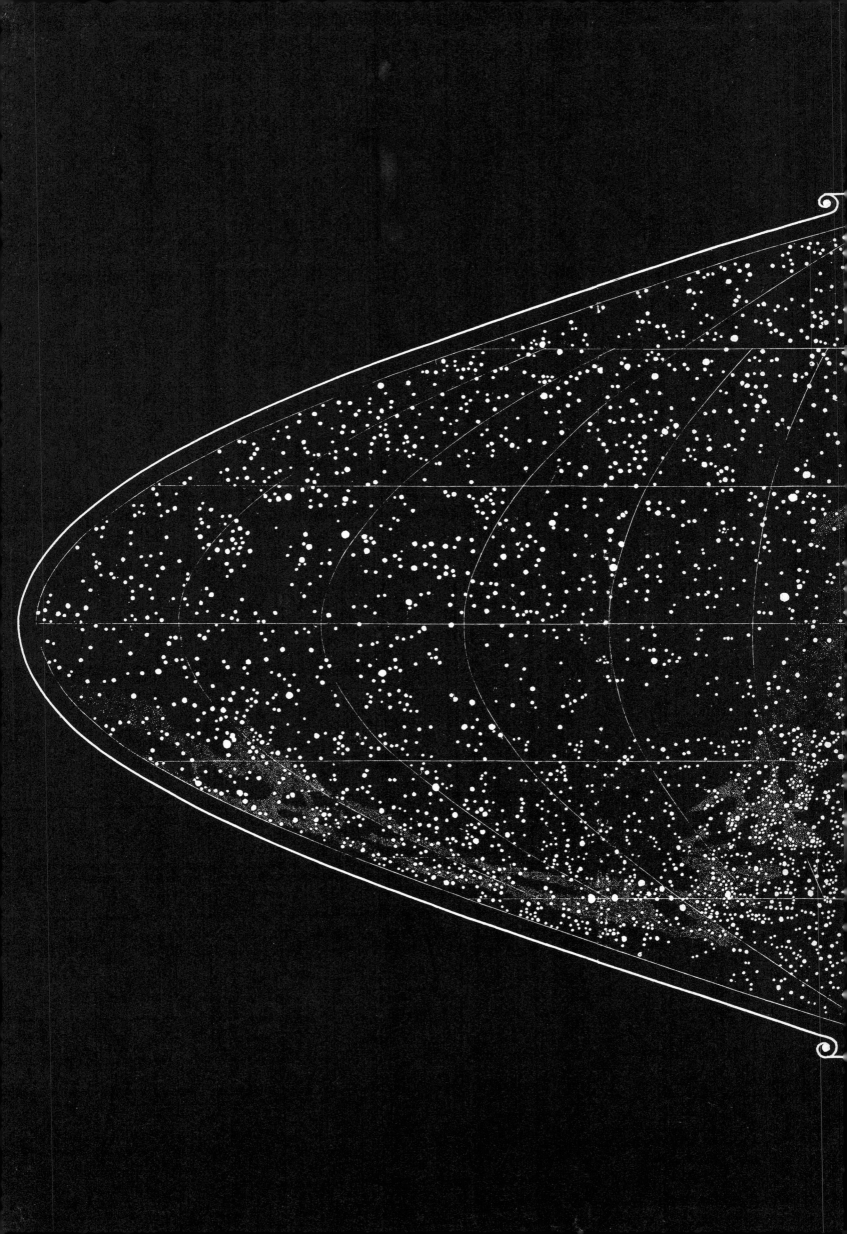